International Marketing

Expanding an organisation internationally presents both opportunities and challenges as marketing departments seek to understand different buying behaviours, power relations, preferences, loyalties and norms. *International Marketing* offers a uniquely adaptable strategy framework for firms of all sizes that are looking to internationalise their business, using Carl Arthur Solberg's tried and tested Nine Strategic Windows model.

This practical text offers the reader insights into:

- The globalisation phenomenon
- Partner relations and
- Strategic positioning in international markets.

Solberg has also created a brand new companion website for the text, replete with additional materials and instructor resources. This functional study is an ideal introduction to international marketing for advanced undergraduates and postgraduates in business and management. It also offers a pragmatic toolkit for managers and marketers who are seeking to expand their business into new territories.

Carl Arthur Solberg is Professor Emeritus of Marketing at BI Norwegian Business School, Norway. Before joining academia, he worked for ten years in industry, as a Consultant at the Export Council of Norway and as a Market Researcher and Strategic Planner in the petrochemical industry in Norway.

D1730054

International Marketing
Strategy Development and Implementation

Carl Arthur Solberg

Routledge
Taylor & Francis Group

LONDON AND NEW YORK

First published 2018
by Routledge
2 Park Square, Milton Park, Abingdon, Oxon OX14 4RN

and by Routledge
711 Third Avenue, New York, NY 10017

Routledge is an imprint of the Taylor & Francis Group, an informa business

© 2018 Carl Arthur Solberg

British Library Cataloguing in Publication Data
A catalogue record for this book is available from the British Library

Library of Congress Cataloging in Publication Data
Names: Solberg, Carl Arthur, author.
Title: International marketing: strategy development and implementation/ Carl Arthur Solberg.
Description: Abingdon, Oxon; New York, NY: Routledge, 2018. |
Includes bibliographical references and index.
Identifiers: LCCN 2017022757 (print) | LCCN 2017036296 (ebook) |
ISBN 9781315185026 (eBook) | ISBN 9781138737389 (hardback: alk. paper) |
ISBN 9781138738058 (pbk.: alk. paper)
Subjects: LCSH: Marketing–Cross-cultural studies. |
Marketing–Management.
Classification: LCC HF5415 (ebook) | LCC HF5415.S688 2018 (print) |
DDC 658.8/4–dc23
LC record available at https://lccn.loc.gov/2017022757

ISBN: 978-1-138-73738-9 (hbk)
ISBN: 978-1-138-73805-8 (pbk)
ISBN: 978-1-315-18502-6 (ebk)

Typeset in Times New Roman
by Sunrise Setting Ltd., Brixham, UK

Visit the companion website: www.routledge.com/cw/solberg

Contents

Figures

Tables

Preface

This book is the result of a long journey that started in the late 1970s when the Norwegian Export Council commissioned a text to be used in their export education programmes. At that time, I had experience both from the Export Council's Swedish representative office in Stockholm, giving me insight into the trade and export practices between Norway and Sweden, and from the nascent petrochemical industry in Norway in the then Saga Petrochemicals as&co, trying to build European market insight in that organisation. The text was perhaps more a handbook for exporters than an academic text in international marketing; but it was the first draft of the book you now hold in your hands. That book, *Eksportmarkedsføring* (in English: Export Marketing), was published by Universitetsforlaget, the largest academic publisher in Norway. With time, the book has gradually evolved into the present text. In 2014, it came out in its 9th edition, and the present version, the first edition in English, is an adapted text addressing an international audience.

I joined academia in 1982 at BI Norwegian School of Management (later to become BI Norwegian Business School – hereafter BI) and eventually earned my PhD at the University of Glasgow some ten years later. This was the time in which the "Single Market" in Europe was created, with the aim of achieving the free flow of goods, services, capital and people between EU members and associated states (Norway, Iceland and Liechtenstein). For many industries this situation constituted a great challenge. The drivers towards a more global market were already present, best epitomised by Ted Levitt's legendary article, "Globalization of markets", in *Harvard Business Review* in 1983. The psyche of globalisation was pervading both academia and business, and many conclusions and strategic decisions were based on the assumptions in Levitt's article. I joined the discussion through my thesis ("Strategy development in globalising markets"), defended in 1994, excerpts of which were later published in *Journal of International Marketing* in 1997. Here I postulated that strategic responses to globalisation depend on the degree to which globalisation affects the company, and the resources that it is able to muster in order to address its challenges; it is not for everyone to join the globalisation bandwagon. Therefore, I put some emphasis on the treatment of the internationalisation process of the firm. I deem it essential to understand this process in order to be able to identify critical aspects of the firm's room to manoeuvre in international markets.

The resultant "Nine Strategic Windows" model constitutes the backbone of the present book, in the sense that marketing strategies, and in particular, those that address international markets, to a great extent depend on the firm's position in this model. Over the years I have conducted several studies to empirically validate different aspects of the model through surveys of exporters in Norway, Britain, Singapore and Germany. It is an understatement to say that this research is challenging, particularly because of the complexity of the business environment that the model tries to capture. Still, in a first report ("Norwegian industries in globalising markets",

BI 1999) authored with Liv Karin Slåttebrekk and Birgitte Kristiansen, it was possible to identify patterns matching those of the original model. Also, together with Professor François Durrieu of Kedge Business School (Bordeaux, France) it has been possible to demonstrate significant associations suggested by the model. Not all the hypotheses that it is possible to derive from the model have been empirically explored. Yet I have ventured into discussing concrete inferences of the model to different parts of the international marketing effort – be it market selection, operation modes, partner relations, product, promotion, pricing, planning and organisation. This is possibly venturesome; on the other hand it will certainly give the practitioner food for thought, and instructors and students a starting point for strategy discussions.

Marketing as an academic discipline got its breakthrough in the 1950s. The first textbooks in *international* marketing appeared only some 20–30 years later. Today, many decades later, international marketing texts have proliferated – in different shapes and with the emphasis on different perspectives concerning scope (export marketing, international marketing, global marketing, global marketing strategy, etc.), geography (Asia, Europe, emerging markets) as well as approach (theoretical/practical/handbook). The present book offers two features that will distinguish it from other books. It takes a contingency approach, using the "Nine Strategic Windows" model, where the firm's international marketing strategy is discussed in view of its strategic position in international markets. As a consequence, it discusses the international marketing strategies of "all kinds" of firms – small and large, internationally experienced and inexperienced. The fate of small and medium-sized firms is therefore possibly treated in more detail in this book – both theoretically and through anecdotes – than in other texts on the topic. Furthermore, the "Nine Strategic Windows" model is partly based on Industrial Organisation; therefore, set against other texts in international marketing, the present text is putting more emphasis on the role of competition in strategy formulation.

Another distinguishing feature of this book is its emphasis on partner relations. This is in recognition of the overarching importance of the local member of the marketing organisation, be it the independent partner (agent, distributor, licensee, franchisee, etc.) or the firm's own subsidiary. The book discusses most facets of this relationship in Chapter 8, from identifying the partner, negotiating and contracting with him/her/them, monitoring and eventually ending the relations. But also in other chapters, particularly Chapter 3 on the internationalisation process, Chapter 5 on market information, Chapter 6 on market selection or Chapter 9 on standardisation/adaptation of the marketing mix, I highlight the importance of partner relationships.

The book is theory-based, but it also offers normative and practical advice to its readers. It is therefore a good starting point for both students and business practitioners alike. As a former colleague of the author, Professor Hans Matthias Thjömöe, used to say: "Nothing is as practical as a good theory!" Given the emphasis on strategy, I would recommend the text for graduate students, or for advanced undergraduates.

As a European, it is fair to say that I have given the book a European slant. This is possibly most conspicuous concerning the anecdotes I have chosen to include (although anecdotes from other continents are also reported). The issues and theories discussed in this book are, however, of a general character and will hopefully help the understanding of any reader and any student from whatever geographic context in which they might operate.

Some may claim that foreign distribution channels have been somewhat step-motherly treated in this book, and they are correct. My first excuse is that I have quite extensively discussed foreign operation modes with their many different alternatives. These may be viewed as the first member in the distribution channel in any country. Seen by headquarters, the fate of the international offering through the next members of the distribution channel (wholesalers, retailers, dealers) is then generally the responsibility of the local representative. The main task in the distribution chain for the exporter is therefore to motivate and support this first member in the channel, and this is comprehensively covered in Chapter 8. My second excuse is that this point has been, to some extent, covered in other parts of the book, particularly in Chapter 7 (Operation modes) and partly in other chapters.

I have struggled to find a title for this book; a title that reflects its uniqueness. Its features with emphasis on strategy, small and large firms, Europe, and relationships suggest that several angles could have been chosen. At one point in time I thought of letting the contingency nature of the Nine Strategic Windows model be reflected in the title, but it only covers part of the story. The final result, "International Marketing: Strategy Development and Implementation", embraces the essence of the book: an emphasis on strategy and implementation through partner relationships. In many ways the book can be regarded as a template for an international SWOT analysis, followed by strategic deliberations on how to conclude on this analysis.

The book itself does not include exercises with questions to be solved by students. For this I have – together with the publisher – developed a separate web page, including cases, questions for discussion and multiple choice exercises. The material is accessed by searching the Routledge website for *International Marketing* and clicking on the companion website link.

Acknowledgements

I am indebted to many people on my way to academic insight into international marketing and business, and in particular in writing this book. My good friend and former colleague, Odd Pettersen, has been a source of inspiration ever since we worked together at Norway Trade Centre in Stockholm in the first half of the 1970s. Then, Mr. Hans B. Thomsen, legal advisor at the Norwegian Export Council, and Mr. Bjarne Bakka, senior lecturer at the Norwegian School of Economics and Business Administration, serving on the board of directors of the Norwegian Export School invited me to edit and write the bulk of a first textbook on export marketing and shared their invaluable insight at this initial and defining time. Mr. Erik Juell of Universitetsforlaget also deserves mention. He has been my companion through the past five editions of the Norwegian text, and has generously allowed me to contract with Routledge. Professor Runar Framnes appointed me as an assistant professor at BI Norwegian School of Management back in 1982 and has been a steadfast and inspiring colleague throughout all the years we have spent together at the School.

Professor Lawrence Welch, now at Monash University (Australia), was the person who introduced me to the maze of academic research on internationalisation of the firm, followed up by professorial colleagues Geir Gripsrud and Gabriel Benito, with whom I have had the pleasure to publish. Professors Mika Gabrielsson, Vishnu Kirpalani and Pervez Ghauri gave me the opportunity to formalise my own interest on Born Globals in articles and handbooks (on Born Globals and SMEs). Special thanks go to Professor S. Tamer Cavusgil, who since the early 1990s has been the "grandfather" of international marketing through his generous support and encouraging attitude, as the founding editor of the *Journal of International Marketing*, but also through his initiation of and involvement in CIMaR, the Consortium of International Market Research, an informal group of researchers from around 40 countries across all continents.

For this particular edition of the book, I owe special thanks to my former student, Ms. Iuliia Diuba, whose analysis of the labyrinth of the standardisation/adaptation issues in international marketing excellently wraps up the discussion of this conundrum. Chapter 9, Section 3 of the book has extensively drawn upon her work. Also, Erik B. Nes, Professor Emeritus at BI, has directly contributed to the book with his knowledge in the area of country-of-origin – in Chapter 11, Section 5. Large parts of Chapter 8, Section 3.2 are based on Didier Rigault's book *International Business Agreements*, published by the Norwegian-based legal firm in which he was partner, Brækhus-Dege. Chapter 12, Section 6 is based on an article that I wrote together with Professors Barbara Stöttinger and Attila Yaprak. Furthermore, I had the pleasure of writing an article on Russian business relationships with Ms. Anzhelika Osmanova, parts of which are edited into the book – Chapter 8, Section 4.2. Professor Jon Bingen Sande has introduced me to contract economics, which I deem an appealing theory stream in buyer–supplier relationships, treated in the text in a step-motherly way, yet hopefully sufficient to trigger interest by those who want to pursue the study of contracts.

In my endeavour to adapt the text to an international audience, I have received vital support from good friends in academia in different parts of the world. They have helped me provide background material for anecdotes that help substantiate the theoretical issues raised in parts of the book. My thanks go to:

Joan Freixanet, GSOM – St. Petersburg State University
Henrik Jensen, BI Norwegian Business School
Tage Koed Madsen, University of Southern Denmark
Saeed Samiee, University of Tulsa
Carlos Sousa, University of Durham

I also have received advice from three reviewers of my initial proposal to the publisher. I have – at least to some extent – tried to follow their advice! Thank you.

In addition, I have throughout my years as a consultant and researcher had the privilege of meeting a great number of eminent practitioners of international marketing. Their experience – for the good and the bad – has greatly flavoured my approach to this field of research. Thanks to you, too.

Translating from Norwegian to English language is not straightforward. My daughter, Victoria Louise Solberg Hurley, who has been living in England for more than fifteen years, has helped me translate big parts of the text, and thus considerably speeded up the publication process. Finally, a big thanks goes to my wife, who has endured evenings and weekends over the past half year in the final writing spurt of this book. Without her encouragement and flexible tolerance, this book would not have seen the light of day.

May 2017
Høvik, Norway

1   Introduction

Although marketing – in principle – is the same in the domestic market as abroad, a number of differences exist, concerning both substance and practical tasks. Perhaps most conspicuously the external market environment is often dramatically different. Market conditions in the home market are normally fairly well understood by management; abroad everything is new and needs to be learned and comprehended. Distances are normally greater – both geographic and cultural. For most firms in small countries, both markets and market players – competitors, distribution channels and customers – are bigger. And, if they are not bigger than what is encountered in the home market, they are most likely different, concerning buyer behaviour, power relations, preferences, loyalties, norms, etc. For management, this implies greater information requirements and therefore higher risks than at home. For instance, it is normally more difficult to anticipate market demand, price development, competitive action, regulatory changes, etc. Of course, a firm well-entrenched in international markets has (or should have) a market intelligence system that would easily capture these aspects, both at home *and* abroad. However, not all firms are in that position – a fact that gives them a disadvantage when competing abroad.

These factors in themselves do not justify a text in international marketing. It suffices to describe the market conditions and let the firms involved draw their own conclusions. However, these market conditions have obvious consequences for strategy. The field of international marketing is therefore as much a study of strategy in international business environments as a study of this environment itself. Furthermore, some of the strategies carried out in international markets are often less relevant at home, even though they could theoretically be applied there. This is, for instance, true for entry modes such as licensing, management contracts and joint ventures that are more often used in an international setting than in the domestic market.

Such strategies are developed in the intersection between, on one hand, opportunities and threats in the international market place and, on the other hand, the resources and competencies inside the firm. The present text therefore gives an overview of the international business environment in view of the firm's international market involvement, before discussing how internal resources and competencies give management room for manoeuvre.

Since the late 1970s we have witnessed a gradually increasing trend towards a more interconnected world, where market demands in many sectors slowly converge and trade and transport barriers decrease. This led Levitt (1983) to claim that only those firms that take advantage of the subsequent increased market volumes by effectively exploiting economies of scale through standardisation will be the market winners. Markets will – according to Levitt – eventually be dominated by large, global firms that outcompete smaller ones; market players' actions will not only affect local market conditions but also indeed have ramifications beyond their own key markets (Hamel and Prahalad 1985). However, not all industries or all markets are equally affected by this development and, even though the main trend has been towards a more integrated business world, the development may also go in the other direction; de-globalisation is indeed a possible scenario in certain industries. Firms – small and large – therefore need to analyse potential consequences for their own development.

For this purpose, a great part of this book is structured around what we may term an international SWOT[1] analysis as shown in Figure 1.1. This figure shows a model where internal and external factors individually and in interaction impact on the development of the firm's international marketing strategy. The model is a 3×3 matrix, called the "Nine Strategic Windows" (Solberg 1997), because each cell in the matrix indicates a main strategic avenue for the firm in its pursuit of opportunities in international markets. The external (horizontal) axis is named "Industry globality" which denotes the extent to which firms in the industry operate on a global scale, or are more concentrated in their home markets. The internal (vertical) axis is called "Preparedness for internationalisation" and classifies the firm according to its resources and competencies.

One may say that on the left-hand side of the model, there are few signs of globalisation having any impact on the competition or the industry structure. On the right-hand side, globalisation drivers are strongly felt and constitute both threats and opportunities. In many ways, the model implies some kind of preparation for a more globalised industry, often with global market players that dominate the industry, the smaller firms adapting their strategies to their resources and competencies and usually occupying specialised segments in the market. As will be shown later, different industries are unevenly affected by this trend. The strategic response of firms that are less affected should therefore be quite different from that of those highly affected. The terms used to describe the individual "windows" indicate a main direction for the firm's strategic development. This will be further discussed in Chapter 4.

The model also suggests that firms should take into account their position in the matrix when developing and implementing strategies at the lower level – such as marketing strategies – and

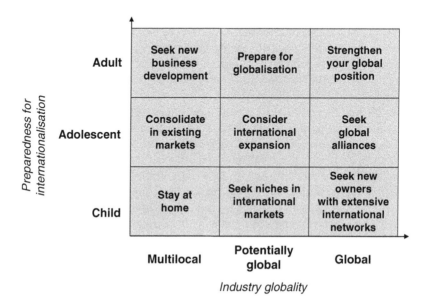

Figure 1.1 The Nine Strategic Windows.

Source: Solberg (1997)

accordingly adapt their organisation. When treating the different elements of the international marketing strategy, such as market selection, market portfolio and marketing mix (Part II of the book), and strategy implementation (Part III), we therefore bring up the model again – in a simplified version (2×2) – in order to discuss in somewhat more detail how the firm's position affects its strategic choices.

The book is divided into three parts, where Part I, Developing strategic thrust in a globalising world (Chapters 2–4), discusses the factors driving the development towards a more integrated and globalised business environment, and those that counteract this (Chapter 2). Chapter 3 explores the firm's internal resources and capabilities by way of describing the internationalisation process of firms – including that of Born Globals – and by way of analysing what distinguishes successful players in international markets from those that are less successful. Chapter 4 combines these two elements (the external business environment and internal resources and competencies) in the "Nine Strategic Windows" model to discuss strategic consequences for the firm.

Part II of the book (Chapters 5–12), Decisions in international marketing, starts with a discussion of the need for information and how to get hold of the necessary level of information to make the decisions (Chapter 5). Chapter 6 delves more substantially into the market selection/portfolio in international markets. The issues of entry modes are discussed in Chapter 7, whereas those of choosing and relating to business partners in different cultures are considered in Chapter 8. One of the main issues in international marketing is that of standardisation of the marketing mix. Chapter 9 is devoted to this discussion, before a look at each of the marketing mix elements – product, promotion and pricing (Chapters 10–12). The fourth marketing mix component, distribution, is indirectly treated in Chapter 7, Operation modes.

Part III is devoted to planning and controlling (Chapter 13) and organisation (Chapter 14) of the international marketing effort. Figure 1.2 portrays the structure of the book.

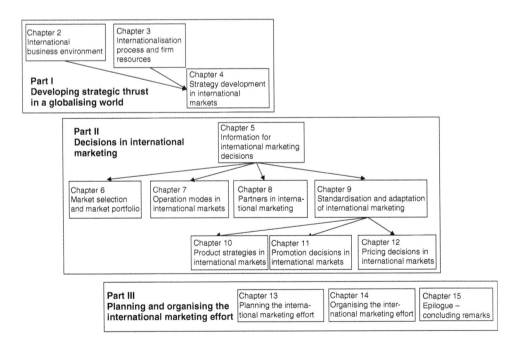

Figure 1.2 The plan of the book.

Note

1 SWOT – Strengths, Weaknesses, Opportunities and Threats – is ascribed to Albert Humphrey at Stanford Research Institute in the 1960s. The objective of this analysis is to identify strategic avenues and actions for the firm, given its strengths and weaknesses. SWOT analysis is described in most textbooks on strategy and marketing.

Part I

Developing strategic thrust in a globalising world

Globalisation has been the buzzword in the business community over the past 40 years. At the end of a volatile period in the 1970s – with the demise of the dollar exchange standard, the end of the Vietnam war, the dialogue between the US and China, the fall of President Richard Nixon, the first oil crisis with ensuing stagflation[1] across the world, labour unrest in Europe, and the Iranian revolution – the world was looking for new solutions. And indeed they came. Late in the 1970s and on into the 1980s, the British Prime Minister, Margaret Thatcher, had won the elections, and set out to liberalise the UK economy. President Ronald Reagan in the US had much the same agenda, and – in addition – initiated negotiations with the Soviet Union to downsize and control the devastating nuclear arsenal in both countries. The *glasnost* and *perestroika* initiated by the General Secretary of the communist party in the USSR, Mikhail Gorbachev, augured a new era in the relationship between the East and West. In China, Deng Xiaoping started what we may term the communist liberal capitalism that spurred the dormant giant to become the world's leading economy. Japan became the wonder-boy of manufacturing and logistics and its large *keiretsus* conquered the world automobile and electronics markets. The Uruguay round of trade liberalisation under the auspices of the General Agreements on Tariffs and Trade (GATT) was initiated and, concurrently, the European Economic Community (EEC) became the European Union (EU) with new members and resulted in the Single Market in 1992/1993. In South East Asia the new "economic tigers" (Singapore, Taiwan, Malaysia, South Korea) became the darlings of multinationals in quest of new economic opportunities.

Optimism was in the air, and large and small firms joined the bandwagon of a forceful internationalisation process that has yet to come to an end. After a euphoric 20 years – not without bumps and shocks – the dot.com bubble burst in 2002, and later – in 2008 – the financial crisis, with the downfall of Lehman Brothers, became a fact. Yet, multinational companies have thrived during all these decades, partly because of a fostering political framework and partly because of technological advances in virtually all sectors of the economy.

In this first part of the book, we shall delve more deeply into this process, both from a macro view, and from the perspective of the individual company. We shall explore different theoretical streams trying to explain what has happened, and possibly what will be happening in the future. Indeed, the political events of 2016 (with Brexit and the election of a nationalist US president, Donald Trump) and well into 2017 (with nationalist and anti-EU movements challenging the economic and political establishment) foreshadow a halt to the seemingly non-stop globalisation locomotive. We note with interest that Xi Jingping, China's current leader, has now taken the role of the new trade liberalist, and is the guarantor of the economic infrastructure meticulously built up since the Second World War.[2] At the same time, climate change has emerged as a "new" factor in the economic and political equation of the world, with yet many unresolved issues and with (not necessarily negative) consequences for the business community. Finally, the thawing between East and West experienced through the 25 years up to 2010 has now been replaced by new suspicions and jockeying for position in the world's political arena, adding new items into the equation.

The individual firm has to take a stance on these developments, comprehend their implications for its own development, and in this context assess its own position with regard to both its resources and its strategic alternatives. This is where the "Nine Strategic Windows" model, briefly presented in Chapter 1, comes in. We can say that this model is a kind of SWOT analysis with an assessment of how relevant issues in the external business environment give the premises for how the firm can exploit its (limited) resources in its quest for a position in world markets.

Notes

1 Stagflation was at the time a new term denoting the, until then, unlikely combination of economic stagnation and rising inflation.
2 In a speech at the World Economic Forum in Davos in February 2017, he reasserted China's interest in continuing to develop the world's economic system. Over the years China has gradually shifted from being a closed country to becoming one of the most ardent advocates of liberal foreign trade and investment regimes, well in tune with its own development as a net exporter and a considerable investor abroad.

2 International business environment

From local to global markets

2.1 Introduction

There are more than 200 countries in the world. The majority of these have their own language (many have several different languages), culture, laws and regulations, economic and political structures – all of which play a part in obstructing cross-border trade and other foreign economic activities. More specifically these factors include customs duties and tax for imported goods and services; cultural differences within trade and commerce, or how we use and consume our purchases; more dramatic conditions such as a boycott due to political conflicts; economic policies leading to uncertainty and currency fluctuations thereby disrupting price competitiveness; or it could be national business structures making it difficult for foreigners entering the market.

Yet ever since the dawn of time, international economic cooperation has played an important part of life. This is due to several contributing factors, of which the main one has traditionally been the uneven distribution of and access to resources throughout the world. Typical examples of this are fish and oil from Norway and Iceland being sold in "all corners of the world"; bauxite for the production of aluminium from Australia, China and Brazil (two-thirds of world production[1]); wool from Australia and New Zealand (with 70% of world exports[2]); or timber from Scandinavia, Russia and Canada. Trade can also be the result of uneven economic development leading to different cost structures between countries. It is fairly easy to understand that countries with low wages dominate the production of high labour intensity products (such as textiles from Asia).

Technological development has gradually contributed to increasing international trade. Advances that result in new products (such as sensors measuring pressures and temperatures in oil wells) or new processes for manufacturing products enable certain countries to develop a competitive edge, making them the preferred trade partner. This is where theories on industry clusters and economies of scale play a part. Economies of scale along with differences in wage levels have been the cornerstone of free trade ideology ever since Adam Smith (1792) and David Ricardo (1825) influenced the mainstream thinking in trade policy-making. The main principle has always been that resources are best used where production is most rational. Statistics back up the thinking behind this. Just in the past 30–35 years, the share of international trade of the world's gross national product has doubled from around 15% to closer to 30%.[3] This is, according to Chase-Dunn et al. (2000), a long-term trend, though not without its cyclical variations. An example of this is the strong downturn of world trade in the years between the First and the Second World War, mainly due to political measures to protect national industries. However, the main trend over the past 75 years remains a steady liberalisation of world trade.

In other words, the tendency has been to steadily increase economic integration between different countries, mainly through trade but also through direct investments abroad. This development is what we call economic globalisation. In this chapter, we will delve deeper into the various processes leading this globalisation and discuss the consequences these have for a company.

Globalisation has opened borders for foreign goods and services while also expanding each country's trade borders to encompass the majority of the world's trading nations. This development has also resulted in a restructuring of each country's trade and business, with great consequences for many. Over the past 20–30 years we have seen the results of this restructuring: a gradual shift of manufacturing capacity to Asia from the US and Western Europe.

The following points describe how the external environment has contributed to development:

- Technology is constantly making the world a smaller place through radically improving data and telecommunication. This in turn has improved the opportunities for information-gathering and exchange, money transfer across borders and also marketing and sales. An increasing number of companies use the internet as sole channel for their transactions.
- Despite dramatically increased oil prices it is cheaper both to travel and to transport goods over large distances.[4]
- Greater free trade cooperation through the World Trade Organisation (WTO) directly affects new sectors of business and industry, where agriculture in particular is especially exposed.
- The dynamics around the creation of the EU's single market in 1992/1993 and later the expansion of the EU has offered many exciting challenges for industry. Following the Single European Act of 1985 new optimism within the European economy reigned during the nineties, garnering new impulses with the EU expansions in 2004 and 2007. The establishment of a single market with nearly 500 million people has led many Western industry leaders to make strategic investments across borders to an extent hitherto unknown. In many ways, the EU is now at a crossroads where the discussion is between those who wish to deepen the institutional framework governing the union and those who would rather make the union less influential. First the euro crisis during the 2010s and then Brexit augured a new era of uncertainty around the future of the EU.
- The economic centre is gradually moving from Europe and the United States of America to eastern Asia and other emerging economies. This is the result of both an imbalance in the US economy following the dynamics of the (relatively) free trade between countries with great economic differences, and also because certain countries – perhaps particularly Russia – have for years been able to profit from high oil prices partly due to political instability. The so-called BRICS countries – Brazil, Russia, India, China and South Africa – experienced 10–20 years of ferocious growth until 2015, and some – in particular China and India – are predicted to overtake the global economic pole position within the next 20–30 years.

Russia's growth, however, came to a halt in the wake of the combined effect of a deep dive in oil prices (from 120 USD/barrel to less than 30 over a one year period in 2014/2015); and also Brazil has been ridden by stagnation – in spite of the optimism following the Olympic games in 2016. The consequences of Brexit (the UK's referendum in June 2016 on leaving the EU) are also difficult to fathom at this point in time (2017), particularly because no agreement on the conditions for exit has been negotiated. In addition, the talks of a closer economic cooperation across the Atlantic Ocean between the US and EU (the so-called TTIP: Transatlantic Trade and Investment Partnership – see later) seem to have been stalled, partly by political resistance in some of the participating countries and partly because of the uncertainties following Brexit.

In spite of some setbacks, we may still conclude that the general trend over the past 30–40 years has been towards a more integrated and globalised economy, where firms from "all corners of the world" compete in major markets, a process that is called "globalisation". Below is a theoretical background for the development of globalisation as a concept:

Globalisation – the definition of a word en vogue

Levitt (1983) ignited the debate on globalisation in the beginning of the eighties. He claimed that converging patterns of demand in Western countries lay the ground for companies to reap benefits from economies of scale within production, marketing, and research and development. This change is driven by consumers who, despite different cultural backgrounds, demand standardised products at a low price. Technology is too costly for companies to solely market their products in a single market. To benefit from economies of scale the company has to enter the global market. Standardisation of production and marketing is key, according to his analysis. A natural consequence of globalisation will therefore be fewer, but stronger, competitors in the market.

Keegan (1984) regards globalisation as a consequence of a management philosophy where companies cover needs within global segments by adjusting their strategies for the various markets. Increased standardisation of the marketing process (as opposed to the contents of the marketing – such as the products, the advertising, etc.) gives companies an organisational efficiency and, as a result, a competitive edge. Organisational efficiency enables the company to gain economies of scale within its marketing. Keegan's view, in contrast to Levitt's, is that the marketing has to be adapted to the various markets, but even so it is fully possible to gain economies of scale in marketing.

Porter (1986) emphasises the strategic aspects of globalisation. The most important goal for a company is competitive efficiency. The basis for competitive efficiency is comparative advantages, economies of scale, product differentiation, market information and technical know-how. Porter's starting point for globalisation is internal – it is the management's responsibility to develop global strategies – but implementation has to take into account the idiosyncrasies of the various markets. This view on globalisation has several parallels to Keegan's, with a nuanced view on the markets within which the companies operate. Increased globalisation can be explained by the sum of competitive development within the different industries.

In this book we will build on these definitions and define globalisation as a process where companies seek to gain large market shares in international markets, partly by establishing entry barriers (such as economies of scale or branding) and partly by benefiting from reduced trade barriers or surmounting such barriers, resulting in global oligopolies in the said industries.

This definition focuses on the consequences of globalisation for the development within business and industry around the world. Globalisation is of course a much broader phenomenon embodying political, environmental and cultural aspects. These all make up the conditions for

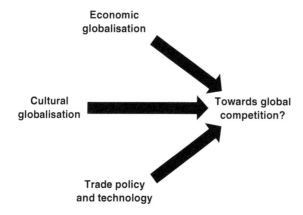

Figure 2.1 Chapter structure.

how companies reach their decisions, and therefore contribute, both directly and indirectly, to the global oligopolisation we are now witnessing.

Globalisation, according to our definition, places great demands on business leaders, and inevitably numerous businesses have had to go into liquidation or been taken over by others as the result of industry restructuring. On the other hand, some businesses have managed to fully exploit the new external environment and developed viable strategies for growth in international markets.

Critical voices claim that globalisation – or rather the consequences of globalisation – is not as dramatic as suggested by Levitt (1983). Ghemawat (2012), for instance, points out that the increased concentration predicted by Levitt has not happened. In some instances, it has actually dropped; the majority of the industries in his analysis have the same level of concentration as 30 years ago, and in some cases even lower. The accumulation of market power by dominant actors expected by Levitt (1983) is therefore not as prevalent. Nor is the cultural amalgamation as prominent as expected, despite companies such as H&M, Nike, Coca Cola, Starbucks, IKEA and Gant, to mention but a few, doing their utmost to make us believe otherwise. Local cultures and local consumer patterns are, in other words, fairly robust. Ghemawat also highlights other aspects making globalisation less prominent than previously believed: environmental effects, economic imbalances as the result of changes in competition between countries, economic vulnerability following financial crises, the continuing imbalance between rich and poor, or conflicts following political suppression. Ghemawat's conclusion is that what we see today is a so-called "semi-globalisation", where certain aspects clearly push for globalisation, whereas others are holding it back. This does not change our definition of globalisation but rather modifies both the fear of and exaltation for the phenomenon, as we will see later in this chapter.

In this chapter, we shall explore various factors impacting this process, whether facilitating stronger integration between countries or moving towards putting the brakes on integration. Figure 2.1 shows the links between the different sections of this chapter.

2.2 Economic globalisation

In the first part of this chapter we will explore how the world economy has gradually become more and more integrated, and how at times this has resulted in imbalance within the international economy, which in turn has led to trade conflicts. This has been a process of gradual liberalisation over the past 70 years that now, in 2017 – with Brexit and the increasingly challenging nationalism in the Western world (on both sides of the Atlantic) – seems to have come to a (temporary?) halt. We will discuss different theoretical explanations for the development and how new markets for growth are arising. We shall also look at the rise of multinational companies by analysing direct investments abroad. We will then give a short overview of the development of international financial markets and how this impacts trade and industry. Finally, we will discuss negative impacts of globalisation.

2.2.1 World trade – growth, barriers and conflicts

The increase in world trade has, ever since the Second World War, been one of the most important factors in the increasing globalisation of world markets. In the 1950s, world trade amounted to around 60 billion USD. In 2015 this figure reached 21 trillion USD (total exports at current prices) – a downturn since 2014 in the wake of a dramatically weaker oil price. In this chapter, we will look at the developments within world trade and give examples of how it – despite general liberalisation – is often bound by various agreements limiting free competition between the participants in international markets. We will also briefly discuss the developments in two quite particular market areas: Eastern Europe and developing countries. We begin, however, with theoretical explanations on why international trade arises in the first place.

Why do we engage in trade with other countries?

This question has been asked ever since Adam Smith's *On the Wealth of Nations* (1776). His theory on *absolute advantage* was based on the benefits of specialisation. Trade streams were explained by the fact that certain countries are particularly efficient at manufacturing specific products that they then want to export. At the start of the 19th century, David Ricardo introduced the theory of *comparative advantages*, where each country would benefit from specialising in the production of goods where it had the relatively lowest labour costs.

   The factor proportions model (Hecksher–Ohlin) is based on the fact that each country has different access to various production factors such as people, technology and natural resources. According to this theory, countries with good access to capital resources export capital-intensive goods, while countries low on capital but with good access to labour will export labour-intensive goods. This school of thought certainly holds in resource-rich countries such as Saudi Arabia, Russia, Canada, Norway, exporting energy (oil and gas) or energy-intensive products (aluminium) due to natural access and abundance. Without restrictions, trade will, according to the factor proportions model, be led by comparative advantages and economies of scale. The model is based on several restricting conditions not present in the real world. There have been numerous attempts at testing the model with modified conditions (such as Leontief 1953) with varying results. Central in the critique of the early theories on various advantages is that they predict a division of labour (specialisation) between countries, while in reality, trade exists to a great extent between homogenous countries and with similar products. Trade must therefore, partially or completely, be attributed to other reasons than factor proportions or comparative advantages.

   Linder (1961) addressed this critique and argued that the *structure of demand* is important for trade with processed goods. The extensive trade between countries with similar products, he explained, was due to local industry firstly producing for the home market. Should the companies start exporting, this will mainly be to countries with a demand structure similar to theirs.

A prediction of Linder's theory will therefore be that a group of countries will export variations of products similar to each other.

Several economists have maintained that industrialised countries will increase the export of technologically advanced goods, while at the same time increasing the import of goods with established technology. Vernon (1966) introduced the *international product life cycle* theory (IPLC). The different stages were defined as:

1   *Innovation stage.* Product development and production takes place in the country of innovation.
2   *Maturity stage.* Increasing demand beyond the country of innovation. This demand will be covered by export and possibly, later on, by own production and sales companies in the new country. New producers and increased competition follow as a result.
3   *Standardisation stage.* Increased standardisation results in increased price competition. This phase sees the original country of innovation importing the product and using its resources to develop new products for export.

This is how Vernon explains both the development of trade as well as development of investments, particularly between industrial and developing countries. We have seen this happen in, for instance, the automobile and information and communication industries.

Kotkin's (1992) book *Tribes* gives the basis for an unconventional explanation of specific parts of international trade, where he argues that *ethnicity* explains certain trade and investment streams. He describes how various ethnic groups have, by spreading to different parts of the world, laid the basis for new trade patterns. Jews, in particular, are renowned for creating fertile ground for the exchange of international trade throughout the years, where families such as the Rothschilds have for centuries played a central part in international trade. Another example is how, during the late medieval period, the German Hanseatic League established bridgeheads in large parts of Northern Europe and thus dominated trade in this region. We can similarly trace, according to Kotkin, the Anglo-American dominance of the world economy back to the glory days of the British Empire in the 18th and 19th centuries by the positioning of the military and bureaucrats along with businessmen in all corners of the world, the Empire cemented its trading culture – both legislation and a network of relations and corresponding preferences were established. More recent times have seen ethnic groups such as the Chinese, Indians and Pakistanis creating new trade patterns. In particular, the Chinese emigrants to the US have, according to Kotkin, contributed to the Chinese export surplus in their trade with the US. Since the new millennium, the Chinese have invested large sums in Africa and have also sent experts linked to development projects to several African countries. A long-term effect of this could be increased trade intercourse between these countries and China. From an insignificant amount in 1995, trade between Africa and China increased to around 130 billion USD 15 years later.[5] An underlying hypothesis is that the cultural closeness and the sense of loyalty that businesspeople with the same cultural background feel are natural incitements to developing trade relations. It also reduces the risk normally associated with trade between two countries.

Porter (1990) has taken this work further in explaining international trade by analysing how a nation develops its *international competitiveness*. He claims that natural resources could never be the backbone of a *modern* industrial nation. Rather, the company's own ability to build and further develop competitive advantages based on economies of scale and/or technological advantages creates competitive strength. By looking at the companies in detail, Porter poses questions on why and how they create unique skills and know-how in their chosen industries.

He maintains that a country's economic structure, values, institutions and history all amount to the determining factor for companies' progress in that country.

Porter argues that previous international trade theories have limited explanatory power. They have lacked important elements, such as globalisation of competition in certain industries and segments, as well as the ever-increasing importance of technology, both cost-wise and when it comes to people's opportunities and abilities to use it. Of course, conditions have changed drastically since these theories were first developed. The creation of business strategies or different trade- or industrial-political initiatives has had to make use of limited theories with the inevitable result of a one-dimensional perspective.

Michael Porter started the debate on the "old" definitions of competitiveness and turned the spotlight on the role of industry clusters when he published his book *The Competitive Advantage of Nations* in 1990. Porter claims that there are four elements in such clusters that affect a nation's various trades in a dynamic process.

1   *Factor conditions.* Production factors in developed economies are *created*, as opposed to inherited, as per the classic theory. The most important factor is the special expertise developed and enhanced within certain industries. This is in line with globalisation via international oligopolies, also often the result of specialisation and therefore the development of special expertise.
2   *Demand conditions.* Demand in the home market can provide an earlier and clearer picture of future demand. This may incite the company to innovate ahead of its foreign counterparts and thus create competitive advantages. This is also the case when countries have specific values influencing the product development in that country. These values can then be exported through products.
3   *Related and supporting industries.* An internationally competitive industry of subcontractors supports downstream industries in diverse ways. Most importantly here are perhaps short communication lines and a constant exchange of new ideas and innovation. There are numerous examples of how different countries develop such clusters of related industries. The Norwegian shipping industry has grown to become a sustainable industry. This is partly due to the number of competitive subcontractors closely connected to the downstream companies.
4   *Firm (or organisation) strategy, structure and rivalry.* National framework and conditions give strong pointers for the development, organisation and management of the company. Key here are competitive dynamics between companies on the home market. Porter (1990, p. 82) claims that firms tend to view foreign competitors more analytically and more distantly than close competitors, the relations with the latter becoming more personal. The success of foreign competitors is often explained by "unfair trading conditions", whereas there is no such excuse for being outcompeted by local players. The government more or less accommodates for the optimisation of industry clusters through research and development policies, investment in infrastructure, tax legislation, etc.

Porter's model has been criticised for explaining everything and nothing. It explains how Japan has become competitive in certain areas because it did not have the natural resources on which to base its industrial development. At the same time, it explains Sweden's industrial development precisely because of its access to natural resources – forest and iron ore (Leontiades 1990). What is more, in these global times, Porter is criticised for the term industry clusters, as a substantial number of companies are just as dependent on their network of partners, sources of finance, competence and subcontractors abroad as in their home markets.

Porter has introduced a framework that is more nuanced than traditional explanations of competitiveness – and therefore also of development of trade. He has particularly highlighted the importance of what he calls *created* competitive advantage rather than a nation's "natural" competitive advantage, and the importance of networks to be able to further develop these advantages in a company or trade. It is also interesting to note that, for many countries, the *natural* advantages of yesterday have gradually progressed into *created* advantages in today's competitive environment. Starting with natural competitive advantages such as fish or water-power, trades can advance into industry clusters where the most important driver would no longer be the natural resources, but the competence built based on these resources.

The above-mentioned theories have not attached great importance to the size of a country, and only indirectly (via cultural closeness for instance) have they included the distance between the trade partners. Empirical analyses of trade between countries using so-called gravity models of trade show that this plays a large part.[6] This research tradition started when Tinbergen (1962) – subsequently a Nobel Prize winner in economics – used Newton's law of universal gravitation in physics to describe the pattern of trade between two countries. The basic model predicts that trade between two countries is proportional with the countries' gross national product and inversely proportional to their geographical distance. Chaney (2013) refers to a so-called meta-analysis from 2008 examining 103 articles with calculations on various relationships between distance, GDP and export to different countries. According to the analysis, coefficients for both distance and GDP are around 1, implying that when the GDP of a country of import increases by 10% for instance, or the distance between the trade partners is reduced by 10%, exports will also increase by 10%. Regression analyses explain 80–90% of the variation in the dependent variable, i.e. export to different countries.

Solberg, Gripsrud and Hunneman (2014) analyse export patterns from Norway using an expanded gravity model, where GDP per inhabitant (measured in wealth), population (measured in size), a country's import share (measuring how easy or difficult it is to export to the country looking at both trade barriers and structure) and distance – both geographical and cultural (cost of transport and the ability to communicate) – all play a part. The analysis shows that prosperity, size and share of import are the most important factors, with coefficients of around 1, with distance also being significant, with coefficients of –0.56 (geographical) and –0.35 (cultural). The models[7] explain around 80–90% of Norway's export to the various countries. The analyses also show that Norway exports less than the model might indicate to countries such as France, Italy, Germany, the United States and Canada, while the country is over-represented in the Nordic countries, Poland, UK, Brazil, China and Japan. There is reason to believe that these deviations could be explained by trade structure in both Norway and the import country (such as fish to Japan, oil equipment to China and Brazil), and as such could be linked to Porter's industry clusters.

We have seen many different theories on why countries interact in trade. Gravity models go a long way by including various theoretical explanations, as mentioned above. Cultural conditions are mentioned by Linder (1961) amongst others, by looking at similarities in the pattern of demand, and by Kotkin (1992) by looking at diasporas. Industry structures (such as Ricardo's theory on comparative advantages, the Hekscher–Ohlin theory on factor proportion or Porter's industry clusters) all play an indirect part in connection with share of import – i.e. the need to complement own production to satisfy national demand. Adam Smith's absolute advantage, which explains specialisation, is also in evidence in various countries' trade structures. None of these theories explains all trade, but rather they give us a basic understanding of why countries engage in trade with each other. In the next sections, we will give a short overview of how world trade has developed and look at certain approaches to the problems arising due to this development.

International trade and economic conflicts

Ever since the Second World War world trade has had a much greater increase than the global GDP. Figure 2.2 shows how trade has increased in importance.

World trade is however very unevenly distributed. Ever since the 1970s the US has had a considerable trade deficit, and in 2006 this peaked at 760 billion USD (6.5% of the country's GDP) due to factors such as high import of oil and gas. The deficit has since then been gradually reduced, partly due to the financial crisis of 2008/2009 (reduced GNP = reduced imports) and partly due to the large finds of shale oil, which have reduced the import of oil and gas. In 2016, it stood at 502 billion USD. Countries such as China (347 billion USD in 2016), Japan (69 billion USD), Germany (65 billion USD) and Mexico (63 billion USD) can demonstrate large surplus in their trade with the US, but also with other countries. The 20 biggest surplus countries (mainly China, Japan, South Korea and those of Western Europe) can boast around 1,400 billion USD of combined trade surplus in 2015, almost 10% of world trade. When it comes to parts of the Far East (South Korea, China and Taiwan, for instance), these countries have a large trade surplus with the US and Western Europe. The Western European countries, with almost 500 million inhabitants, are each other's most important trading partners and also the biggest trading union overall. The Western European economy is, in other words, considerably integrated.

This development is due, amongst other factors, to the rebuilding of Western Europe after the Second World War that gradually enabled this region to compete in international markets. Later, in the 1970s and 1980s, other regions – particularly South East Asia and Japan as the most important drivers – have played an increasingly prominent role in international trade, with the result that the traditional great powers (the US, Germany, Great Britain and France) have seen their importance in the international economy diminish. Combined, these countries still

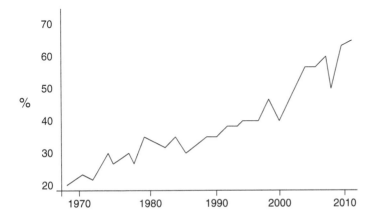

Figure 2.2 Total exports and imports as percentage of world GDP, 1970–2012.

Source: http://www.wto.org/res_e/statis_/its2013_/its2013_e.pdf.

Table 2.1 GNP in selected countries, 2016

	Billion USD	*% of world GNP*
USA	18,558	25.1
China	16,477	22.3
Japan	4,413	5.9
Germany	3,468	4.7
United Kingdom	2,761	3.8
France	2,465	3.3
India	2,289	3.1
Italy	1,849	2.5
Brazil	1,535	2.1
Canada	1,462	2.0
South Korea	1,321	1.8
Spain	1,242	1.7
Australia	1,201	1.6
Russia	1,133	1.5
World	73,994	100.0

Source: https://en.wikipedia.org/wiki/List_of_countries_by_GDP_(nominal).

dominate globally and together made up around 43% of the global GDP in 2016, a marked decline from eight years earlier (48%). We also note that the BRICS countries have increased their share of the global GDP since 2008 – from almost 15% to a solid 29% in 2016, China's share alone representing 22% in 2016 (it had passed the US already in 2015 in terms of Purchasing Power Parity – PPP). China is widely predicted to be the most dominant economic power as soon as 2018,[8] while India is already the seventh largest economy worldwide. It is also worth noting that the growth of another much talked about group of countries (MINT – Mexico, Indonesia, Nigeria, Turkey) is yet to fully take off – with an increase from 4.3% to only 4.5% of the global GDP over the five-year period ending in 2015.

This development is the root of the conflicting trade relations between the US and its trade partners – in particular Japan, China and Europe, but increasingly also Mexico. The conflicts bear the marks of domestic policy in the affected countries, with strong undertones of protectionism, nationalistic positioning and absence of acknowledgement of cultural attributes. The US, virtually self-sufficient in most areas (apart from oil), has not until recently had to compete with foreign suppliers in its domestic market, with the result that it greets foreign competition with distrust and cries for protection. Sentiments against imports have lately (2017) been exacerbated by President Donald Trump's rhetoric against his country's main trading partners, in particular Mexico and China.

Most countries are however guilty of such sentiments in some way or another. Japan is accused of being a very closed market, with distinctive laws that have resulted in a particularly fragmented pattern of distribution with restrictions of entry to the market in many different sectors. Furthermore, Japan has a unique structure in which families of companies belong to a more or less closed network of relations – the so-called *keiretsu*. European countries, for their part, have over the past 30–40 years slowed down the readjustment of their traditional industries through subsidies or other preferential treatments, and have thus contributed to reducing the competitiveness of industries such as steel, coal and agriculture. The Chinese, on the other hand, are accused of keeping their currency artificially low so that their industrial production reaps the cost benefits on Western markets. The US in particular has called for a change in the Chinese currency policy.

Antidumping

Every now and again various countries react to cheap imports by demanding inspections, either conducted by the WTO or themselves, where they seek to document that export countries accept unreasonably low prices to gain entry in the import country. Such prices can only be obtained unlawfully, by subsidies at home (Europe), by strong markets and distribution systems (Japan) or by state-regulated purchasing systems. If it is found that subsidies or other unfair anti-competitive measures have been taken, the government in the import country will evaluate and most likely implement penalties. Globally, the US has the most restrictive legislation for such cases. During the 1980s, 3,000 foreign companies were affected by such resolutions by the International Trade Commission (ITC). A case in point is Norsk Hydro's magnesium plant in Canada which was also strictly penalised in the 1990s as the result of subsidies from the Canadian government. It has been claimed that the US government and politicians willingly listen to industry lobbyists who feel their enterprise is being threatened by import competition, and that American demands for fair trade often fall within the category of protectionism. This is a discussion for another time but we will note that the United States' negative trade balance may be the result of antidumping measures. Other countries too, such as the EU members and Australia, are active users of these types of measures, and Norway has certainly felt the hard line taken by the EU on the interpretation of subsidies. Again it is mainly the Norwegian salmon export bearing the brunt of this.

The role of the US as the leading power of the global economy is consequently being challenged to such an extent that the stability of the trade regime, built since the Second World War, is threatened. A liberal trade system such as we have seen during the past 70 years can, according to Kindleberger (1973), only be established and maintained when there is a hegemonic leader willing to take control. A hegemony in this instance is defined by Keohane (1980) as a country that has both political and military strength as well as economic potential (raw materials, capital, markets and comparative advantages within production of high technology products).

The development of the US since 1960s has in this instance not contributed to sustaining the country's role as hegemonic. This is particularly evident looking at the economic area:

–   Control of raw materials (in particular energy, where the United States has been dependent on external sources of energy). Even so, this position is changing as a result of the discovery of oil and gas in the United States. In 2005 US oil imports represented almost 50% of consumption; in 2015 this share had fallen to around 38%.[9]
–   Capital (the weakening role of the dollar in international trade and capital transactions, and the American government's inability to adjust the imbalance of its internal economy).
–   Markets (the relative diminishing role of the United States in the global economy).
–   Comparative advantages within high technology production (for instance Japan's ability to exploit high technology industrially; nonetheless most Nobel Prize winners are American).

On the other hand, in terms of military strength, the United States still has an overwhelmingly leading role. US defence expenditure was around 580 billion USD in 2016, 3.7 times that of China. We need to add together the military budgets of the ten nations after the US to match the

Americans. This acknowledgement, along with the country's large trade deficit and the growth of BRICS – and China in particular – has contributed to reducing the United States' role as superpower compared with the 1990s. According to Kennedy (1988), the United States' military superiority will diminish in the long run because structurally (balance of payment and resource deployment) the country has so many military commitments outside its borders.

Intra-industry trade

Following the Second World War there has been a shift towards intra-industry trade, meaning export and import of products belonging to the same industry or business, supporting Linder's (1961) hypothesis that a country mainly exports to other countries that share the same demand structure.[10] Cars, furniture, machinery, food and wine produced in Germany are sold to France; at the same time, these same products are produced in France and sold to Germany.

The OECD found that intra-industry trade greatly varies from one country to other. While countries with a relatively broad industry base (like most Western European countries as well as the US) have an intra-industry trade of around 60–70% of total trade, countries with specific resource advantages have a considerably lower intra-industry trade – around 30–40%. Norway is amongst these, mainly because its oil and gas exports make up such a large share of the total and are not matched by corresponding imports. For Iceland (fish products) this share is only around 20%. While countries such as South Korea, Japan, the United States and Germany have experienced an increase of this trade since the nineties, most other industrial countries have shown signs of stagnation in intra-industry trade. We would claim that, with increased investments and growth in so-called "emerging markets", the importance of intra-industry trade will grow as more countries participate.

This development will result in increased mutual dependency between industrialised countries by strengthening the integration between them. Trade liberalisation through multilateral (GATT/WTO) and regional (EU/EFTA, NAFTA) frameworks increases the industrial specialisation because access to new markets allows economies of scale. This, in turn, leads to oligopolisation within the affected industries, because larger outputs then are produced by fewer players. In other words, oligopolisation confers on relatively few companies the competitive advantages of economies of scale within certain segments of the market.

Economies of scale vary from industry to industry – and even within industries. Industries with high fixed costs will experience significantly falling average costs when increasing production, which lays the foundations for increased specialisation and intra-industry trade. This becomes even more evident for costs such as R&D and marketing, in addition to traditional production costs. Examples here are pharmaceutical and car manufacturing industries, both of which experience high costs related to new and competitive products. This has created elevated barriers to entry for these types of businesses and therefore bolsters the incumbents' dominance.

When it comes to a completely new product, it is possible for newcomers to grow with the market. We have seen this for instance with certain PC producers (such as Apple from the United States and Acer from Taiwan[11]). The speed with which technology develops has given new players the opportunity to enter certain market segments, and grow with these. The companies have thus established small market niches where further down the road they can experience economies of scale within research and development through relatively high market shares.

Figure 2.3 sums up this discussion. The figure suggests that more liberal trade regimes influence technological innovation and economies of scale, and how the two together influence oligopolisation of markets, thus increasing intra-industry trade. It should be noted that technological development also influences in the other direction – towards an increased trade

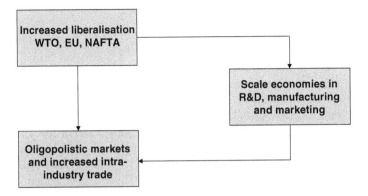

Figure 2.3 Globalisation through liberalisation and scale economies.

liberalisation. The active lobbying run by large multinational corporations (MNCs) to establish international standards is such an example. We have seen this in Western Europe, where Philips was the premier industry exponent for work towards the establishment of the Single Market (EU) in 1992. We will describe trade liberalisation and technological development in more detail in Section 2.3.

Eastern Europe's "new look"

Since the end of the 1980s, Eastern Europe has experienced more change than the previous 40 years since the Second World War. Revolutions in Eastern and Central Europe – where the various countries, with varying degrees of luck, have sought to transform their societies – have for many foreign companies offered market opportunities previously only available within Western industrialised countries. The biggest ground-breaker has in this instance been the Central European countries' memberships, first of NATO and later on of the EU in the 1990s and 2000s. These countries still have a way to go before they can match the living standards of their Western colleagues, but they now have access to an economic and political community that permits great optimism and economic growth.

The reality for the new EU members from Eastern and Central Europe (Estonia, Latvia, Lithuania, Poland, Hungary, the Czech Republic, Slovenia, Slovakia, Romania, Bulgaria and Croatia) is quickly changing. These countries are now establishing modern economic frameworks through liberalisation of the economy and membership of the EU as well as investments from the West.

The situation for companies exporting to these countries has changed dramatically. While they previously sold to central, state-owned foreign trade companies that took on the responsibility for further distribution to local affiliates towing the party line, as well as contracts giving a secure income, they now have to identify the end users and also new channels to reach them. The consequence of this is more complex marketing operations. At the same time this implies that the marketing towards these countries can be integrated into their general marketing activities.

The countries further east, the former members of the Soviet Union (with the exception of the Baltics), have a harder task at hand with regards to economic growth and improved prosperity.

The country that was divided into fifteen

The Soviet Union, the former superpower, is no more. From being built up around the autocratic communist party, the union collapsed in December 1991 and was split into 15 new republics, and 15 new sets of state institutions were established. Business contacts that were previously made via Moscow now have to be established in each and every republic. Market analysis seen as the norm in the West – with reliable information on competitors and customers – is difficult or costly to perform. The safest option is to go through official channels able to pass on the contact. This second-hand type of contact is not always reliable and can land you in places you weren't aiming for. Even if most of the new republics are rid of old dictatorships there are new rulers with dictatorial power and there are many hindrances before the area is politically stable. Internal ethnic conflict within the various republics – as well as between the republics – is probably the most critical factor. Further complicating matters is the feeling of alliance obligation some countries have towards ethnic groups in certain republics. This is particularly the case for Iran and Turkey, which both support the Muslims in Azerbaijan and their fight against the Armenians (Christians) in that country. The Baltic states face similar challenges; there are large minority groups of Polish, Belarusians and Russians in Latvia.

Another conflict that has been reignited is the one between the two most important previous members of the Soviet Union – Ukraine and Russia. These two have fought over atomic weapons on Ukrainian territory and the right to Crimea. Following attempts at independence from Ukraine in the 1990s, the people of Crimea chose in a disputed election to forge bonds with Russia in 2014. Ukraine is already split between a pro-Western and a pro-Russian part, making it even more problematic for the leaders to rule the country – no matter on which side of the conflict their loyalties lie.

The conflict in Chechnya was a horrifying example of how loaded the situation is in some of the previous states of the USSR. And Chechnya is just one of the 20 autonomous republics in the Russian Federation. The outcome of these conflicts is uncertain, but what is certain is that they will for a long time yet be the scourge of the economic development of the affected areas. In a situation lacking legal institutions coupled with not only weak economic growth but also economic crises for some parts of society, new situations of conflict could easily arise.

In addition to the political conflicts hanging over these countries, we observe the internal power structures already established, which in many ways can be seen as survivors of old positions of power from the Soviet era. People and milieus that previously enjoyed political power were, during the tumultuous times of the 1990s, in the perfect position to establish financial power through takeover of state-owned companies. The combination of financial and political power in these countries makes for a much more challenging marketing environment than traditionally seen in the West. This is particularly the case for strategic industries such as energy and telecommunications.

The main aim of highlighting the rather erratic development in this previously stable federal state is to point to the fact that there are numerous areas the world over where conflicts are just waiting to erupt. For companies, such a development involves great challenges. Customers can disappear overnight, contacts could be switched or simply "vanish", and payment methods could be somewhat unconventional – be it with plastic bags full of dollars or transfers from accounts in Guernsey or other tax havens.

We should not apply the same yardstick to all these new countries. Many of them experience abundant entrepreneurship with budding new industries. There are great opportunities to be had in this economic climate for the adventurer full of initiative. Russia enjoyed healthy growth in the economy until the collapse of the oil price in 2014. Foreign investments have started paying off, the currency is partly convertible. But at the same time, we are not short of stories of irregularities and corruption – well-nourished by tales of the building of the Olympic arenas in Sochi. Also, following the conflict with Ukraine, Western sanctions towards Russia have hit the country hard financially.

Developing countries or growing markets

Developing countries mainly consist of the countries in Africa, Asia and Latin America. We often associate them with poor standards of living, trade deficits, dependency on a single or few export goods, poorly developed industry and infrastructure, high unemployment, analphabetic population, uneven (and unfair) income distribution, etc. They represent a group of very dissimilar countries – anything from China, or rather parts of China, with its 1.4 billion inhabitants (GDP/capita 6,500 USD in 2015),[12] to the Central African Republic, with 5 million inhabitants, rated as the poorest country in the world (GDP/capita 639 USD in 2015, less than a tenth of that of China).[13] The simple numbers mentioned here highlight the developing countries' position in the world: they make up 80% of the total global population (7.4 billion), but only account for 21% of GDP and 28% of global trade. This is still an increase from 1990, mainly due to China's advance in the global economy. However, according to the OECD, developing countries will make up around 60% of global economic output by 2030 in terms of PPP.[14]

The growth of China

China has, ever since the beginning of the 1980s, been on an exhilarating journey whereby this enormous country with some 1.4 billion inhabitants has slowly but surely been integrated into the global economy. Its share of GDP in 2003 was 12%, and approached 20% only 13 years later. This development affects the West – both as sellers and buyers of goods and services, as investors in productive capacity in China and hosts for Chinese investments. Several Western companies have already established their own local production in China with the aim to cover the growing home market and also with a view to export. Still more companies have entered into contracts covering all or parts of their production – be it clothes, ship hulls or IT products. Low costs greatly aided by (artificially) low currency have played a part in this development. China's membership of the WTO also secures the country a seat at the table and access to export markets. However, it will take some time yet before China will be fully regarded as a secure country to invest in. This is particularly the case for industrial property rights, where Chinese authorities seldom carry out changes of rules and regulations safeguarding foreign investors against copycats. On the other hand, China is now a major investor in the world. In 2016, the country invested a record 145 billion USD abroad – surpassing Japan – with Italy being the main target with about 8 billion USD (the deal between ChemChina and Pirelli).[15]

Most developing countries share their ambition to improve their prosperity. More specifically they wish to increase the level of self-sufficiency of essential investment and consumer goods, as this would ease their payment situation with foreign countries and therefore boost their economic independence. Key issues here are industrialisation, upgrading of infrastructure, improvement of health services and the education system, and making agriculture more efficient. Industry in developed countries will play an increasingly active role in this development, partly by transferring technology and partly through financing.

While these characteristics may have common ground, what is more conspicuous are the differences, rather than the similarities, between the developing countries. Amongst them we find the so-called least developed countries, often poor and low on resources, while at the other end of the spectrum we can also include rich oil countries in the same group of developing countries. What they do have in common is their desire for economic and industrial progress. This goal is being realised with greatly varying means and within widely different economic, political and social systems.

The developing countries (excluding China) have a modest position within the current global trade. Digging somewhat deeper, we find conditions that are characteristic of trade concerning the developing countries. Three-quarters of their exports are raw materials, while a similar share of their imports is finished goods. In particular, the developing countries import investment goods, food and consumer goods. Considerable shares of this trade are dominated by large multinational companies which either negotiate directly with the national governments, and/or have their own processing plants in the developing countries.

We should also direct our attention to how some of the different ethnic minorities in the various countries dominate trade. While the Indians for instance are the dominant group driving international trade in several countries in the Middle East, the Chinese are the main drivers in East Asia. Table 2.2 shows the number of Chinese and their contribution to GDP in five Association of South East Asian Nations (ASEAN) countries.

The Chinese have always been regarded as petty traders in the countries where they have sought to establish themselves, despite the evident contribution they make to the economic development of their host nations. The most obvious example of this currently is in countries such as Malaysia and Indonesia, where the authorities have imposed restrictions on the Chinese and their economic and political activities, and where the ethnic majority groups take matters in their own hands. Following the fall of Indonesia's President Suharto in 1998, many Chinese tradespeople were persecuted, and some paid with their lives. This impacted on Western companies, as they were connected to Chinese companies directly affected by the riots.

Table 2.2 Chinese economic influence in selected ASEAN countries

	Share of local population %[a]	Number (mill.)[a]	% of local GDP[b]	GDP contribution/ population[b]
Malaysia	25	7.0	60	1.9
Indonesia	3	7.3	50	12.0
Philippines	2	1.5	40	40.0
Thailand	14	8.5	50	5.0
Vietnam	3	2.3	20	20.0

Sources: [a] http://www.newworldencyclopedia.org/entry/Overseas_Chinese#Statistics; [b] Lasserre and Schütte (1999).

Trade between developing countries only makes up around 20–30% of their total foreign transactions. This partly mirrors the above-mentioned conditions (influence of multinational companies), and is also partly linked to continued economic ties to their old colonial masters. These ties are strengthened by the establishment of the so-called Lomé Convention, later replaced by the Cotonou Agreement,[16] whereby the EU and most of the member countries' past colonies in Africa, the Caribbean and the Pacific Ocean have entered into agreements on economic cooperation. Such agreements constitute a hurdle for an exporter outside the EU wanting to access these established trade patterns. This is perhaps particularly evident in the relationships between France and its past colonies.

The developing countries have established their own free trade organisations and customs unions in an attempt to, amongst other things, increase intraregional trade to better exploit their resources. One must not exaggerate the significance of such organisations for companies from developing countries. This is partly due to the fact that member countries generally have their own production industry that rarely competes with Western products, and partly due to the difficulties organisations have experienced in trying to cooperate, often related to conflicting economic interests.

Another factor is political instability of the regimes in many developing countries. Internal conflicts may originate in ethnic and/or religious feuds – especially in Africa, where countries such as Sudan/South Sudan, the Central African Republic, Libya, Egypt and Tunisia have been particularly affected since 2010. But parts of Asia are also affected, such as Syria, Sri Lanka, Malaysia, Thailand and Indonesia. The conflicts sometimes bear the marks of "traditional" political disputes (along a right wing–left wing dimension), such as seen in Latin America. Naturally it is difficult to determine how decisive the threat of political insurgences could be for trade with the country in question. By studying the country's general economic situation, its loyalty to different alliances, the role of the military and so on, the level of risk can be reduced. Another way of minimising risk is by spreading it over several markets. Reduction of political risk is discussed in further detail in Chapter 12.

In line with changing political regimes with widely differing views on foreign trade, it is also worth mentioning general import regimes. Many developing countries have a negative trade balance with foreign countries and seek to protect their industry and currency by import bans, quota limits or high tariff barriers. More often than not, such restrictions on imports could push a company to consider other forms of market entry than exporting.

2.2.2 The growth of multinational corporations

Multinational corporations (MNCs) are companies that have established businesses in one or more foreign markets. MNCs have existed for several hundred years, often as a result of colonialism – particularly the British – and had a greater relative reach towards the end of the 19th century than what we see today, mainly due to liberal rules for direct foreign investment (Østerud 1999). It is only in the past 30–40 years that direct foreign investments have regained their influence to such an extent that politicians and society in general have again focused their attention on them. The reason for increased participation in international manufacturing is that the international markets for technology, information and management are more efficient than before, greatly helped by improved infrastructure, liberalised national finance markets and greater access to international markets. Even when there are barriers to international trade and financial transactions, we observe that companies will capitalise on intellectual property rights, capital and management resources through foreign direct investment (FDI).

FDI is one element of a package where control, management, technology and other resources are utilised from the parent company to develop competitive business units abroad. No matter what the motivation for the foreign investment, the consequence is that the companies will progress in a global direction. We will later discuss FDI seen from the individual company's point of view. In this section, we will look at the phenomenon from a bird's-eye perspective and discuss the spread and its consequences for world trade and economy.

Great increase in FDI

There are around 61,000 registered parent companies around the world with one or more affiliate companies in other countries, and there are about 900,000 such affiliate companies (UNCTAD 2013). Total stock of FDI is mounting to 25 trillion USD. Even though Western industrial countries dominate the statistics for registered MNCs, with 78% of global outward FDI stock, several developing countries and emerging economies also appear on the list. In 2015 these latter made up around 21% of the global outward FDI stock. One characteristic is that MNCs from developing countries are consistently smaller than those from the Western world.

Table 2.3 shows the share of FDI among different regions and countries in the period 2010–2015. Since the turn of the millennium, FDIs have experienced both highs (until the financial crisis of 2008) and lows. The table also shows that the main share of global investments is between industrialised nations.

The United States was for a long time the single most important country for both incoming and outgoing FDI. This has changed over recent years. In 2005, it experienced a negative balance in foreign investments, selling off (or closing down) more investments than were made.

Table 2.3 Average FDI inflows and outflows, 2010–2015 – selected countries

	FDI inflows		FDI outflows	
	2010	*2015*	*2010*	*2015*
Total[a]	1,388	1,762	1,392	1,474
Developed economies	700	962	983	1,065
– Western Europe	432	504	585	576
– Japan	−1	−3	56	129
– USA	198	379	278	300
– Canada	28	48	35	67
– Australia	36	22	20	−17
Newly industrialised countries	179	290	185	164
– Hong Kong	72	175	88	56
– Singapore	55	65	35	35
– South Korea	10	5	28	28
Developing/emerging economies[b]	625	765	358	377
– China	114	136	69	128
– India	27	44	16	8
– Brazil	84	65	22	3
Transition economies	64	35	50	31
– Russia	32	10	41	27

Source: *World Investment Report*, 2016, UNCTAD, Geneva.
Notes: [a] Figures in billions USD. Totals include other countries; [b] Including NICs.

It is also worth noting that many small countries are especially important as foreign investors; this is particularly the case for the Netherlands, Switzerland, Ireland, Hong Kong and Singapore, partly through foreign multinationals in those countries.

Furthermore, we note that the United States *receives* a relatively large share of the global direct investments. This reflects the fact that the United States is perceived to be a safe country in which to invest, and that European and Asian companies wish to enter the American market directly without risking being shut out due to various forms of protectionism. We also note that Western Europe is the biggest actor with regards to both outgoing investments and as a receiver of investments. The European desire to invest abroad also reflects an increased regional integration through intra European investments. Furthermore, we can see that the developing countries are, to a much greater extent than before, stronger participants of FDI as both investors and receivers.

Another distinguishing feature is that MNCs today account for a large share of international trade. Sales from subsidiaries of MNCs totalled 9,500 billion USD in 1997, thereby surpassing global trade of 6,400 billion USD in that year by almost 50%. This means that foreign subsidiaries of MNCs are more important when it comes to supplying foreign customers than is export directly from the home country. The majority of such sales occur internally in the host country, but also large parts are exported. Furthermore, a very large share of world trade is conducted by MNCs. Some commentators have estimated that multinationals – parents and subsidiaries combined – are responsible for 75% of the world's commodity trade (Dunning 1998).

MNCs with their head offices in the United States are regarded as more mature than those located in Japan or Europe. Mature MNCs will, to a large extent, supply the different markets through local production, while newer MNCs, more prevalent in Europe and particularly in Japan, tend to supply their markets from the home country. Another development is that, increasingly, a growing share of international trade is within MNCs, as intra-company trade – i.e. trade across borders but internally within MNCs. Figures from UNCTAD (1997) show that 27% of international trade happens within MNCs. Processed goods with a high degree of technological complexity seem to have a larger share of intra-company trade than other types of goods (UN 1988). When it comes to flow of internal capital and knowledge, this share rises to between 50% and 60%.

MNCs and their host country

It is safe to say that the largest global corporations play a dominant part in the world economy:[17] 1837 countries and 63 multinational corporations are amongst the 100 largest economies in the world.[18] Furthermore, the 100 largest MNCs account for one-third of foreign direct investment (Østerud 1999). Many have started questioning whether such a development is good for the global economy and for the economy in the various countries receiving the investments. In this case, the business leaders' task is to observe events and trends and to adjust within the framework of their company in that country. We will look at certain arguments to highlight important aspects of the discussion. This is not the place to look at all of the arguments but rather to look at some of them to stress a few dilemmas arising following FDI.

There is a fear in some circles that states' independence is threatened by multinational corporations. The MNCs dominate important parts of business in many countries, and through their strength they have attained a certain power to influence the authorities in the host countries. The threat of closure or cutbacks generally seems greater if the owner has no particular connection to the host country. The authorities in the host country will then be greatly tempted to give in to pressure and accept tax reductions, subsidies or other types of preferential treatments to attract or keep hold of investments and the ensuing competence.

Another topic in this debate – related to the fear of relocating – is the fear of losing national control over important sectors in the economy. That could include contributions to export income, GDP, technological advances, managerial competence or to national pride. It is on this basis that there are some grumblings in Norway regarding the cutbacks by the American multinational Kraft Industries carried out in Freia's Norwegian operations.[19] Similar discussions are found in other countries, perhaps particularly in France, where the saying "national pride" carries a special meaning (if possible, even more than in Norway). A string of foreign investors has large shares in a number of key companies, such as L'Oréal (cosmetics).

It has been documented that MNCs in certain cases "jump" from one country to another in their quest for low costs, but this is the exception rather than the rule. Moving investments to low-cost countries is however not without friction (Weiss 1997). Dunning (1998) observed four central features of foreign direct investments in the nineties:

1   The reduction of trade barriers has resulted in MNCs forming clusters in specialised areas of industry to mutually benefit from each other's competence, infrastructure and distribution network.
2   MNCs consistently seek areas where they can further develop their core competence, and this trend increases as their subsidiaries become more rooted in the host country (however this is not the case in developing countries).
3   MNCs now focus less on direct investments motivated by market size, low costs or resources, but rather look to areas that offer opportunities for increasing knowledge within their own core competence.
4   MNCs' direct investments in developing countries are still dominated by motivators such as markets, resources and low costs (for instance in China, India, Indonesia and Mexico), but even here there is increasing focus on conditions such as infrastructure, competence, etc.

According to Buckley and Casson (1998) one of the main challenges for business leaders today – particularly leaders of MNCs – is the vulnerability that follows globalisation (currency instabilities, regional economic crises, political unrest, immediate consequences – more on this later). This demands a strategic flexibility on behalf of the businesses enabling them to increasingly leave the value adding activities to the market (subcontracting, licensing), rather than internalise (invest, own and run themselves) large parts of the value chain. This is – according to Buckley and Casson – one of the reasons we are now witnessing downsizing and transfer of assignments to sub-contractors. The authors further claim that this vulnerability increases the risk, and that this explains the emergence of joint ventures towards the end of the 1900s and into the 2000s. The companies then enjoy a flexibility in which they can increase or reduce their share of ownership. They also envisage companies, to a greater extent than before, entering and pulling out of direct investments, depending on the prevalent conditions in the local markets at any point in time. With regional hubs, the companies can quickly adapt to different market conditions. Such hubs may have a corporate mandate for parts of the operation, while local spikes secure proximity to local markets, thereby reducing transport costs, and crucially enable better access to information than is gained by exporting from the home base. MNCs following the model of Buckley and Casson (1998) would then invest in such hubs with 100% share of ownership in so-called safe countries, meaning countries that offer what Dunning (1977) calls locational advantages, and rather exploit the market potential in other markets – in spikes (that carry more uncertainties and/or are more marginal) – either through joint ventures with processing and sales or through direct export. Buckley and Casson's (1998) description confirms the registration of production abroad, where MNCs from high-cost countries assign large parts or all of the production to countries offering great cost advantages – both to third parties and to units owned by themselves.

It has also been documented that MNCs seek to keep the decision-making process at their head offices, as we have seen in the Freia/Kraft case. But this picture is nuanced, too. Since the nineties, the strategic role of MNC subsidiaries has varied greatly, from completely self-sufficient units where the only tie to the parent company is financial ownership, and so where they solely operate in the local market, to what Poynter and Rugman (1982) call world man-dates, later called centres of excellence. This requires corporate mandate for certain strategic business units to be transferred to chosen second companies abroad that will assume responsibility for R&D and the marketing for their own product areas.[20]

The long-established Norwegian company Elkem (one of the world-leading manufac-turers of metallurgic silicone for use in several industries) was sold in 2011 for 2 billion USD to China National Bluestar – a part state-owned company within materials technology. Thus, the Chinese secured an important technological partner in silicone technology. This acquisition followed other acquisitions in Europe (France and Austria). Elkem's competence and position was the determining factor for the company gaining a world mandate within the Bluestar organisation.[21]

It is important to understand the mechanism behind the selection of such centres. It has been known in certain circumstances that the managers of the daughter companies in charge of such a mandate have possessed exceptional entrepreneurial skills and have created a position for themselves within the corporation – regardless of which strategic (or perhaps lack of strategic) decisions are taken by the head office. More objective criteria are the basis in other situations, where the management evaluate the strategic conditions surrounding the location of a centre of excellence. In any case, the competitiveness of different countries explains the establishment of a centre of excellence.[22] There are several examples of how some MNCs have received pref-erential treatment and contributions from the authorities in the host country so that they would invest there, only to move production at a later stage when the host country was unable to offer other and more substantial advantages – such as an industrial cluster or special competence.

2.2.3 *Globalisation of financial markets*

Bleeke and Bryan (1988) define globalisation of the financial markets as a process whereby the local financial markets are ever-closer bound together, so that the price for financial instruments and services in one market is significantly dependant on supply and demand in other markets. In this section we will briefly look at the most important development patterns in this market since the turn of the millennium. After the Second World War, international financial markets have gradually become more liberalised. Starting with a USD pegged to gold at a fixed price, passing through the build-up of international liquidity based on US balance of payment deficits in the 1960s, the process has gone through turbulent times with devaluations, floating currencies and different attempts to consolidate the international financial system. Well aided by international organisations (such as the OECD, IMF and the World Bank) the currency system has progressed from clearing balances via convertibility to close currency cooperation especially in Europe, but also within the G20 (see later) – though here on a looser basis. The future outlook is characterised by two distinct features: on the one hand the block formations and on the other hand the increasing mutual dependency.

> The trends towards globalisation have been more prominent in monetary, currency and bond markets than in the stock market. Every day, 24 hours a day, 200 different currencies are now traded in all the great financial centres. Both transaction volume and size shows how important currency is to the large financial markets; for instance, it is estimated that in October 2013 currency trade made up almost 3.9 trillion USD daily,[23] while the global trade for all of 2013 was around 18 trillion USD.[24]

While the USD has been the dominating currency since the Second World War, both the euro and yen have gradually contested this position. In 2015, the euro was the biggest currency in international trade with 37% of all transactions.[25] The USD was close behind, with 36%, while the British pound, the dominating currency in the early 1900s, and the Japanese yen are both trailing far behind with 8.5% and 2.4% respectively. Looking at the EU, this area – with the second biggest economy in the world – has aspired to become an economic superpower. However, following the problems in the wake of the Greek bailout in 2015–2017 and the frail economic position of key euro countries such as Greece, Portugal, Italy and Spain during the 2010s, this aspiration has been set back. The USD still dominates as reserve currency, but China, the EU and Japan have an economic foundation (such as currency reserves) that threatens the United States' position in the longer run.

Following the currency turmoil in Latin America towards the end of the 1990s it was suggested that all its currencies be bound to the USD as a step towards stabilising the economies of these countries. Such a link would strengthen the position of the dollar as a trading currency but would not alter the fundamental imbalances in the US economy. Japan has suffered from an internal structural crisis which weakened the position of the yen at the end of the 1990s. The euro still has a way to go before finding its true position: on the one hand, it is tied to several extremely varied economies with different outlooks, and on the other hand – partly as a result of this – certain key countries (France and Germany) have over a number of years broken the so-called stability pact that requires the deficit of the state budget not to exceed 3% and that the state debt does not exceed 60% of the state budget.

Since 2000, China has been a significant player on the global financial stage. With its enormous population, economic growth and not least the considerable size of its trade surplus (347 billion USD in 2016), the Chinese currency will sooner or later play an important part on the international financial markets. The stranglehold that the Chinese have on the economic development of Africa (both in terms of development aid and commercial investments) contributes, in our opinion, to the fact that the Chinese renminbi will first and foremost show its strength in this region. The Russian rouble is increasingly based on a solid surplus of foreign trade (149 billion USD in 2015)[26] and could in the long term – depending on developments in the Ukraine conflict and the oil price – be expected to play a role too. As of today, the rouble only makes up 0.7% of all trade transactions globally. During the summer of 2014, the BRICS countries entered into a deal to establish an international bank headquartered in Shanghai (New Development Bank) that will supplement (compete with?) institutions such as the IMF and the World Bank. The initiators are unhappy with their lack of influence in these existing financial

Table 2.4 The world's biggest banks, 2016 (in billion USD)

Bank	Total assets	Country
1) Industrial & Commercial Bank of China	3,545	China
2) China Construction Bank Corp	2,965	China
3) Agricultural Bank of China	2,852	China
4) Mitsubishi UFJ Financial Group	2,655	Japan
5) Bank of China	2,640	China
6) HSBC	2,596	Great Britain
7) JP Morgan Chase	2,424	USA
8) BNP Paribas	2,404	France
9) Bank of America	2,186	USA
10) Credit Agricole Groupe	2,007	France
11) Deutsche Bank	1,973	Germany
12) China Development Bank	1,906	China

Source: http://www.relbanks.com/worlds-top-banks/assets.

institutions – today dominated by the United States and partly Europe. We are yet to see what role this new institution will play.

The list of the world's 12 biggest banks in 2016 shows that Chinese banks enjoy a dominant position internationally with as many as five banks and occupying the four first places; four European and two American banks are among the 12, and only one Japanese. Looking at this list 20 years ago, during the mid-nineties, it would have been dominated by Japanese banks, but following severe problems in the Japanese economy throughout all of the nineties and up until today (2017) the banks went through rigorous cuts. A little further down the list we find several European, American and Japanese banks. We also note that the total assets of the world's biggest banks are about the same as the combined size of the GNP of the US and China (USD 29.9 trillion).

The liberalisation of the financial markets has led to an increased mutual dependency between different regions: a surge or decline in one market will easily affect other markets. This became apparent towards the end of the 1990s during the financial crisis in Asia, Russia and Brazil, and again during the financial crisis of 2008 when American banks led by the collapse of Lehman Brothers went bankrupt. A possible consequence of this development is that certain countries wish to halt the free flow of international short-term capital in a bid to avoid the depletion of the country's currency reserves. ATTAC (*Action pour la Taxation des Transactions financières pour l'Aide aux Citoyens*) proposes the introduction of the so-called Tobin tax.[27] On the other hand, regulating the international flows of capital will not solve the underlying problem for many of those countries affected during the crisis of the 1990s: growth financed by debt.

2.2.4 Globalisation, the environment and politics

Not everyone greets the global development enthusiastically, where goods cross borders with unnecessary energy consumption (long haul transport) and risks of contamination, where a few dominating multinational corporations are accused of dictating conditions (such as taxes) for their presence, and where MNCs can easily move their short-term, international receivables when the uncertainty in one country becomes too uncomfortable. In other words, globalisation has its downsides. Globalisation requires liberalisation of both trade and capital movements, without which it would be impossible to exploit economies of scale and resources in various parts of the world. Traditionally such resources have been raw materials, but now resources are increasingly considered to be industry clusters, competence and technological solutions. More and more countries now access these resources via trade, investments and technology transactions. Countries enabling these conditions therefore enjoy the economic growth that globalisation brings. Such a development raises several issues which we will briefly examine here:

–   Many countries are not yet ready to participate in the advancement of welfare that follows in the wake of globalisation. This makes for a skewed welfare distribution, which not only feels unfair but also reveals political opposites which can potentially lead to conflicts. Even in the developed world, we see that governments have not been able to cope with the negatives of globalisation, such as loss of jobs (transferred to low-wage countries) and unequal distribution of income.
–   Even if we were to succeed in bringing the poorest developing countries to the Western world's level of prosperity, the environmental strain this would cause our Earth would be beyond repair – at least with the technology of today. Many countries have entered international treaties (the most prominent one being the Paris agreement) for emission quotas for CO_2 or other gases to force more environmentally friendly technology exploitation in developing countries. This gives us breathing space in the short- and medium-term, but is nowhere near solving the formidable increase of environmental damage such growth would result in.
–   Another, perhaps underrated, consequence of globalisation is the increased danger of microorganisms being transmitted from one continent to another. In the leaflet *Nature's No: about the EU, free trade and organic chaos* Setreng (1998)[28] writes about the earthworm-eating worms from New Zealand that have arrived on European shores and destroy essential components in the soil; the insects "imported" from South America to Libya that eat the meat of live animals; and also the parasitical flatworms infesting the brains, livers or lungs of at least 40 million people – mainly in poor countries. These last are transmitted through foodstuffs, and there are fears that the international food trade is the main cause for this spread.
–   The fact that the accusations that globalisation entails the cynical exploitation of the cheapest resources – be they child labour or raw materials – as firms jump from one country to another are serious goes without saying. However, such claims are probably only relevant for a smaller share of the MNCs. The main trend is for the MNCs abroad to further develop their business where it's been established (Dunning 1998).

Some of the problems with this progress are in its very structure, where countries – rich as well as poor – seek to attract MNC investments to jump-start economic development. The glitch is that many of these countries don't have the backbone to make demands of the MNCs on issues such as environmental responsibilities. David Korten[29] claims in an interview in *Aftenposten* (28 October 1998) that: "We have numerous examples of businesses managing to get countries to undercut each other, so that a business will actually be paid to establish itself in a country." Furthermore, he states that many of these businesses are unaware of their environmental responsibilities. Korten's solution to such a development would be to limit FDI. With a multinational agreement on investments (MAI) there have been attempts at avoiding such undercutting with rules on FDI, first within the WTO and later within the OECD. These attempts have so far been unsuccessful, one reason being that many countries do not wish to limit their freedom to make their own demands of the MNCs (tacitly understood demands that are milder than those suggested). It is difficult to disagree with those who would like to see such international regulations introduced, where the nation state can make demands of the MNCs without being in danger of losing the investments they represent. Korten claims that the size of the MNCs is part of the problem. Both the United States and Europe have clear competition rules hindering domination of industries by a very few players. But while the rules are clear, their interpretation might be a bit looser. The ruling by the EU Commission against the Apple Corporation in Ireland illustrates this point. Apple was ordered to pay 13 billion euros to make up for unfair tax advantages in that country (0.005% against the normal rate of 12.5%).[30]

Of course, it is the responsibility of each and every politician to develop his or her nation into a better place to live. Democracy and prosperity are key words. We will not turn this into a debate on democracy, prosperity and development other than to point to the obvious gains economic growth can bring, as well as the equally obvious dangers that lack of democracy, growth and development can pose for the stability in a region or a country. Putting the brakes on globalisation by limiting international trade and investments would also result in suboptimal utilisation of resources, both material and immaterial. There is also the risk that such a slow-down would result in stronger frictions between the various trading nations than what we see today. Free trade and free flow of capital contribute to integrating the countries and making them increasingly mutually dependent, and will therefore also make them vulnerable for partisan measures that will enable gains in the short-term but that in the long run will damage the whole system. We have indeed seen signs of such policies during 2016–2017, with Brexit and Trump's repeated threats of renegotiating trade pacts.

We could then face a Catch-22, where on the one hand we are in danger of destroying our Earth by poisoning the environment, and on the other hand – if we don't continue with globalisation – we are in danger of contributing to economic stagnation, isolation and what is worse, the consequences this has for political development. One positive scenario of globalisation is that the economic growth that follows in its wake will give a foundation for increased technological development which in turn is a necessity to address the challenges we are facing. By putting the brakes on this development, the technological advances will become less prominent – and the solutions will be pushed further into the future.

2.2.5 *Summary*

This part of Chapter 2 has shown that there are several theories to seek an explanation to world trade. The best descriptions of the development of world trade during the past 30–40 years come from Linder (1961) with his theory on similar demand structure, Vernon (1966) with his international life cycle for products, Porter (1990) with his definition of competitiveness, and lastly the gravitation model of Kindleberger (1973) that encapsulates many of these different theories. We have also seen how this development has progressed and how the Western world has become increasingly integrated through intra-industry trade. We have looked at how multinational corporations (MNCs) have expanded their businesses in line with trade development. MNCs dominate large parts of the global trade: the fact that goods sold internally within MNCs make up between 30% and 40% of all international trade to several industrialised countries underscores their importance. MNCs have thus created a strong position of power that causes worry amongst certain groups. As a general rule, however, MNCs normally seek to further develop their business in a country once they have settled there. The MNCs' role in the international financial market is nevertheless a bigger worry. Starting out with a very nationalistic point of view, the MNCs have gradually become more and more liberalised so that short-term capital flows are easily moved across national borders. This makes countries with great debt burdens vulnerable as was seen during the Asia crisis of 1997–1998. The financial crisis affecting most parts of the world in 2008 made it clear how mutually dependent countries now are. At the same time, there has been a move towards three currency zones – focused on the USD, the euro and the yen. In the near future China's and Russia's strong positions amongst the global trading nations will create a platform for new currency zones focusing on the renminbi and possibly also the rouble. Finally, we have looked at the various negative sides to globalisation, with regards to both the environment and economic-political development. Unfortunately, there are no straightforward answers when it comes to these issues, but rather tough political dilemmas where either solution will have consequences impossible to foresee.

2.3 Culture and globalisation

It has been increasingly claimed over the past 20–30 years that we are heading towards a global culture, a global consumer culture where product preferences are the same in every country, enabling companies to transfer their marketing experiences from one country to another. Levitt (1983) made the globalisation discussion the order of the day, but his theory was built on premises that do not hold up in practice: that consumers in all markets are increasingly becoming more and more alike. This could be true in some cases, and examples from Coca-Cola, Marlboro and McDonald's *apparently* support this argument. Understanding culture and the creation of preferences and the behavioural patterns of our foreign business associates is essential for us in international marketing.

Culture is intrinsic for a human being to feel a sense of belonging – it is part of our identity. This is why culture is so important for human beings as consumers, but primarily as a member of society. Our cultural identity becomes evident in sporting events where loyalty to our own team is key to the tensions and atmosphere of, for example, a football match. This cultural identity is consciously taken advantage of in international trade with "buy Norwegian", "buy American" and "buy British" campaigns, etc. Such campaigns surface every now and again, whether as a result of politicians wishing to highlight the nation's industry or a company seeking its fellow countrymen's loyalty in the battle for market shares. An example of this latter is the marketing campaign that followed when Unilever-owned GB Glace in Sweden sought to enter the Norwegian market in the 1990s: the Norwegian market leader Diplom-Is made full use of nationalistic sentimentality and employed iconic poets like Bjørnstjerne Bjørnson to "warn" Norwegian consumers off the foreign intruders. Unilever's GB Glace is still not active in Norway.

Culture has been defined in many ways. Kroeber and Kluckhorn (1952) have identified more than 160 definitions. Some claim that culture can be defined as the sum of historical achievements or as transferrable knowledge from one generation to another. The definition most used in management literature comes from Hofstede (1980), who defines culture as "a collective programming of the human mind". In other words, we are programmed to think this way or that, to react in a particular manner, to solve problems in a certain way. The basis for the

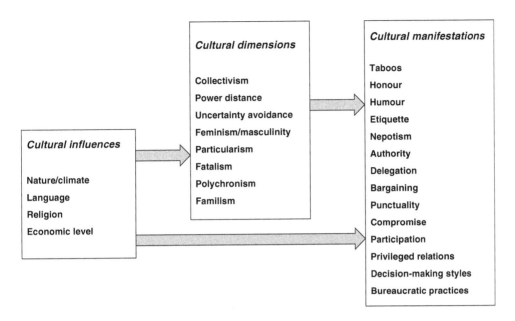

Figure 2.4 Three levels of culture.

programming is the collective experiences of society, which are transferred from one generation to the next.

Figure 2.4 shows different levels of cultural phenomena: cultural factors of influence, cultural dimensions and cultural manifestations. We will look at all these phenomena in this chapter.

Later in this book we will revisit the consequences culture may have for our strategy development. In this chapter, we will delve further into the concept of culture and discuss its various elements, albeit briefly as this is not a book on culture. By looking at certain examples we will be able to shine a light on how various phenomena, on the three above-mentioned levels, partly contribute to preserve our cultural individuality. This is particularly the case for level 3, cultural manifestations, as this includes countless variants and areas. In some cases, we shall see that national cultures converge.

2.3.1 Cultural influencers

Etymologically, the word culture comes from the Latin word *colonum*, which is related to the word to colonise – to lay claim to. Culture arises when humans seek to find solutions to various needs. How they do this is, of course, dependent on the circumstances at the time. Some circumstances depend on climate and nature, while others may have historical, political or religious explanations. The relationship between cause and effect is interesting. Take the influence technology has on our mind-set, for instance. Technological solutions originate from our natural surroundings – be it exploitation of wind or water, farming, utilising the ocean's resources, etc. At the same time though, the chosen technological solutions strongly influence our way of thinking and our way of organising ourselves.

The English historian Davies (1996, p.75) gives an interesting example of this, where he claims that European individualism has its origins in the cultivation of wheat. The method of cultivating enabled the farmer to free up his time to pursue other pastimes, to cultivate other types of grain, to acquire more land, to build, to fight and to do politics. This, according to Davies, is the basis for the individualism that now characterises European cultures. He compares this with East Asian cultures, where the growing of rice demands the full attention of the farmer all year round, as well as cooperation from several families. These countries have to a much greater extent what Hofstede (1980) calls collectivism (see later on). We will not delve deeper into such contemplations other than to state that cultural ways of expression – and in their wake rules for behaviours and mind-sets – are created over several hundred years, if not thousands, and that is the reason why it takes so long to alter them, no matter how much modern media, internet and travels to the farthest corners of the Earth affect us.

Language is perhaps the most obvious cultural manifestation. Through language we express how we think and how we argue. No one really knows how many languages there are. *Aschehoug og Gyldendals Store norske leksikon* (the main Norwegian encyclopaedia) mentions around 156 different languages but does not include the numerous Indian languages (around 20 languages and perhaps 1,000 dialects), the Indonesian varieties (250 dialects) or African languages. In Gambia alone, with its 1.5 million inhabitants, there are five large ethnic groups – each with its own language – and a number of smaller groups.

There are also many dialects in China, and the Chinese from different regions are incapable of understanding each other's spoken languages. The written language however is the same all over the country. The reason for this is that it is built not on letters but not on written images that each has its own complex meaning and is pronounced differently by each dialect. When two Chinese with different dialects meet they often draw the signs in their palm to clarify their communications.

Linguistic composition and manner of expression will vary too. We know how German verbs have a tendency to gather at the end of subordinate sentences, or how Latin languages put the object or indirect object before the verb, which is different again from Scandinavian languages for instance. Manners of expression and how these vary carry more importance for cultural differences. In the West – and perhaps particularly in Northern Europe and the United States – we have a very direct way of expressing ourselves, where we build our reasoning with objective and logical thought processes. In the Arabic language, on the other hand, direct speech is almost frowned upon. Arabs put great emphasis on rhetorical finesse and have an extravagant and profuse way of speech that enriches the language with nuances to such an extent that interpretation is often needed. Venturing further east, one will seldom experience any direct speech. Difficult subjects are often touched upon indirectly (Dahl and Habert 1986). Table 2.5 gives an overview of the most important languages and the approximate number of people with that language as their mother tongue.

Even if there are countless languages around the world, most people will regard the English language as a kind of *lingua franca*, that "everyone" understands, at least in the business world. Wikipedia's list of English-speaking people in different countries around the world shows that more than 1.1 billion people can make themselves understood in English.[31] More and more MNCs use English as their company language. We should however note Christian Tyler's statement in the *Financial Times*: "English is the easiest language to speak badly!"[32] The

Table 2.5 Languages and their distribution as mother tongue and as second
language (speakers in millions)

Language	Mother tongue	As second language
Chinese (Mandarin)	873	178
English	380	100
Spanish	358	600
Arabic	206	n/a
Hindi	181	948
Portuguese	178	20
Bengali	171	14
Russian	145	110
Japanese	122	2
German	101	70
Wu (Sino-Tibetan)	77	n/a
Javanese	76	n/a
Telugu (Andhra Pradesh in India)	70	10
Marathi (Western India, Mauritius)	68	3
Vietnamese	67	16
Korean	67	n/a
Tamil	66	10
French	65	250
Italian	62	n/a
Punjabi	60	n/a
Urdu	60	43
Cantonese	55	45

Source: Wikipedia 2007.

Table 2.6 Percentage of people able to follow a conversation in one or more foreign languages in
selected European countries

Country	Number of foreign languages in which a conversation can be followed			
	None	*One*	*Two*	*Three or more*
Belgium	28	72	50	27
Denmark	11	89	58	23
Germany	34	66	28	8
France	49	51	6	5
Italy	62	38	5	4
The Netherlands	6	94	77	37
Spain	54	46	5	5
Great Britain	61	39	14	5
Sweden	9	91	44	15

Source: http://ec.europa.eu/public_opinion/archives/ebs/ebs_386_sum_en.pdf.

knowledge of the English language varies greatly from country to country and certainly varies within the various markets. Even looking at Europe, it is not as fluently spoken and understood as one might suspect. Table 2.6 indicates that the knowledge of languages is incredibly varied in Europe (and the numbers only indicate the ability to *follow* a conversation): neither in Germany, France, Spain nor Italy could one necessarily make oneself understood in English. It is also interesting to note that the smaller countries have stronger knowledge of languages. We further note that even if English is the language most widely understood and spoken in the world today, around half of all English exporters experience language barriers in their business abroad. This is particularly interesting as around 60% of these companies sell to countries where English is not the mother tongue.[33]

Religion is, according to Dahl and Habert (1986, p. 80), "A system of beliefs that gives direction and content to an individual's way of thinking, evaluating and acting. Religion binds the present with what cannot be directly seen or experienced; it gives measures for interpretation that the human being uses to orientate him- or herself in life. Religion does not only say how things are, but also how they should be." Limited space does not allow for any informative discussion on the various religions, so we will have to be content with a few general observations on religion's significance for cultural ways of expression. Eliot (1948) claims that religion is the dominant factor in the creation of a common culture between different peoples (in Europe) – each with their own distinct culture. Table 2.7 shows how many belong to different dominant beliefs around the world (2012).

Religion lays the basis for the notions individuals hold on most issues in life: the relationship between a man and a woman, how we relate to the formation of values, moderation, authorities, behaviour, etc. In Northern Europe, for instance, it has been claimed that Protestantism has been key to the development of Western capitalism as we know it today: frugality and thrift honoured God, and it was acceptable to become rich if one followed those "rules". We clearly see the result of this, in particular in countries like Switzerland and Germany (with Reformers such as Calvin and Luther), but also in Scandinavia, the Netherlands, England and the United States. Catholicism on the other hand has had a more ambivalent relationship to earning money. Compared with Christianity – where secularisation of society has been permitted by living by the principle of "Give the emperor what belongs to the emperor, and give God what belongs to God" – Islam is altogether a more all-encompassing religion that regulates all areas of life. According to Leopold Weiss, Islam is not so much a religion as a way of life, not so much a theological system as a blueprint for social behaviour and interaction based on active consciousness of God (Waage 1989). Riches and prosperity are considered divine favours and therefore accepted and valued. Riches are however not considered the main goal, and the favoured is just a temporary guardian more than an owner.

This – coupled with fatalism, the conviction of an inevitable destiny, which some claim is part of Muslim faith – makes Muslims accept differences to a much greater extent (Ferraro 1990). Arabs often end their sentences with *inshallah* – "God willing" – something that signals a

Table 2.7 Dominating world religions, 2012

	Number of adherents in millions	*%*
Christianity	2,039	32
Islam	1,570	22
Hinduism	950	13
Chinese folk religions	390	6
Buddhism	360[a]	6
Sikhism	24	<1
Judaism	13	<1
Confucianism	6	<1
Shinto	3	<1

Source: www.religioustolerance.org/worldrel.htm.
Note: [a] There is no agreement on how many Buddhists there are globally. The figures vary from 350 million to 1.6 billion.

meaning in the direction of "The deal will be upheld, but I cannot vouch for conditions outside of my control." Dahl and Habert (1986, p.75, translated from Norwegian) write that, "Time is in Allah's power, not in the power of humans. Laying rigorous plans would be to undermine the will and power of Allah." Not everyone agrees that fatalism is typical of Islamic countries. Rodinson (1974) claims that the uncertainty of their surroundings is part of the reason Arabs don't make plans, and it has also been said that Islamic feats past and present (during the 800 years of Arab glory days, from around AD 650 to around 1450) demonstrate that not only do they see opportunities, but they also practise planning (Muna 1980).

Olson (1997) demonstrates how different dimensions of religion and world views can affect a society's consumer culture. Using fatalism versus belief in one's own freedom, and degrees of monotheism versus pantheism,[34] he finds four different types of consumers:

1   The active entrepreneur (monotheistic/freedom-orientated) can, through their consumption, influence their life situation, and has high demands for the supplier. Thus, they might frequently change supplier. This is a typical Western consumer, particularly in Protestant countries.
2   The pragmatic optimist (pantheistic/freedom-orientated) has a pluralistic perspective on their existence and sees several different solutions to any problem. They are eager to improve their life situation (for instance through consumption), but they would always consider society in their consumption and balances between change and continuity. Olson (1997) claims East Asian religions are typical in this category (Buddhism, Shintoism, Confucianism etc.).
3   The personal servant (monotheistic/fatalistic) is found in Muslim countries. In principle, the Muslim does not have any goal to increase their wealth (through consumption), but neither do they object to consumption, provided they remain an obedient servant of Allah. Loyalty to suppliers as long as they are honest and trustworthy is a typical trait. Therefore, it is particularly important to build strong relations and strong brands in Muslim countries.
4   The eternally reincarnated (pantheistic/fatalistic) is probably the most challenging category for the marketer. It is typically – though not exclusively – found in India (Hinduism). The eternally reincarnated accepts their situation and the belief in reincarnation gives hope of a better life next time. Thus, they have no reason to improve their own situation through consumption for instance.

This division into different consumer cultures is not empirically tested, but can contribute to discussions on how to angle the marketing of goods and services in different countries.

Economic development is generally strongly correlated to cultural dimensions and manifestations. Inglehart and Baker (2000) demonstrate how 65 countries are categorised along two dimensions of what they call broad cultural heritage: traditional values/religion versus rational/secular values on the one hand and survival values (that the attention is mainly focused on surviving until tomorrow) versus values of self-assertion on the other hand. As Figure 2.5 shows, Northern Europe (Protestant) scores high in both self-assertion and rational/secular values. The figure shows a strong correlation between economy and cultural values. It is interesting to note that the United States (North America) is below average for the traditional/rational axis, while China and Japan are correspondingly above average. Could this mean that the consumers in the two latter countries are more open to new products? Inglehart and Baker (2000) also show that these values change along with economic development. Since 1981 (when the recordings began), most Western countries have moved up to the right in the diagram (become more rational and self-assertive), while some countries have gone the other way. This is particularly the case for the previously communist countries in Europe, where liberalisation has

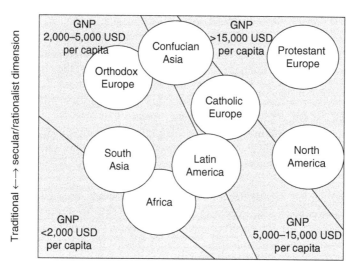

Figure 2.5 Tradition and survival versus rationality and self-realisation.

Source: Adapted from Inglehart and Baker (2000).

allowed the people to once again practise their religion, and which have during the transition period had their GDP greatly reduced. It is interesting to note that Americans have become increasingly more religious. Inglehart and Baker have also found that there is a certain correlation between people's level of income and their inclination to trust others. Norway (Protestant) has the highest score out of all when it comes to the latter factor (trust), while the scores of Catholics and Muslims are noticeably lower here. This could have an effect on how you relate to your partners abroad.

Inglehart and Baker (2000) discuss to what extent different cultures will converge as a result of society becoming more modernised. The theory of modernisation suggests that traditional values based on religion will change in line with economic prosperity. Even if there are differences between how various peoples experience the two sets of values researched by Inglehart and Baker, they also find distinct and lasting differences between, for instance, Protestants, Catholics, Orthodox and Muslims.

2.3.2 Cultural dimensions

Hofstede (1993) claims that culture is a *construct*, not immediately available for observation, but one that can be recognised from behaviour or assertions and that can assist in understanding other types of conduct. Hofstede is widely known for his cultural dimensions based on studies of IBM employees in more than 50 countries. His analysis identifies four cultural dimensions into which one can range various countries. Knowledge of these therefore enables the analyst to gain insight into his or her own culture compared with cultures in other countries. The four dimensions are:

1   *Individualism vs. collectivism.* Individualism represents a preference for a social framework more loosely composed where the individual is responsible for their own happiness

and in charge of his own and his closest family's development. On the other end of the scale we find collectivism, where group loyalty and mutual dependency are key. Typical individualistic countries are Anglo-Saxon countries like the United States, Great Britain, Australia and Canada, as well as – to a somewhat lesser extent – the Nordic countries, while Latin America and several Asian countries typically epitomise a more collectivistic culture.

2   *Power distance*. This dimension describes to what extent individuals of a society accept that power in institutions and organisations is unevenly distributed. Countries featuring great power distance hardly or never question the established hierarchical order, and automatically accept that everyone has their role to play. Typical examples of this are Latin American and Asian countries, while countries like South Korea and Japan are found halfway up on this scale. In countries where there is hardly any power distance, people normally strive for more equality between the members of an organisation and in society in general. Much of Europe is found in this part of the scale. France, however, is an exception. Power distance in France is much more prevalent than in Spain or Italy for instance. This has been attributed to the country's famously elitist educational system.

3   *Uncertainty avoidance*, which denotes the extent to which individuals in a society seek to set rules for their conduct and decisions. A high degree of uncertainty avoidance involves a society having strict rules for people's conduct and great intolerance of people diverging from the established pattern. Latin countries, both in Europe and in Latin America, belong to this group, along with certain Asian countries such as Japan. A low degree of uncertainty avoidance indicates that pragmatism is more important than principles for a society. Singapore is apparently the country with the most tolerant attitude to its people's conduct, followed by Denmark and Sweden, Great Britain and Ireland. Countries like Malaysia and India also apparently have a high degree of tolerance when it comes to deviation of conduct.

4   The final dimension is called *masculinity*, and describes to what extent society attaches importance to typical masculine values such as self-assertion, material success, hero worshipping, etc. More feminine societies typically highly rate human relationships, modesty, caring for the weak, etc. Latin countries all have high scores on the masculinity scale, though Japan, closely followed by Austria and other German-speaking countries, has the highest score here. Sweden, Norway, the Netherlands and Denmark top the list of the "soft" nations.

Hofstede has conducted these studies since the 1970s and the results have proved to be consistent over time. A fifth dimension – *long-term orientation* – was added at a later stage based on research together with Bond (Hofstede and Bond 1988), and this dimension became evident while they were studying a group of Chinese students along with students from 23 other countries. Figure 2.6 presents an example of his findings where we have highlighted two of his dimensions – power distance and uncertainty avoidance – and plotted the findings for 19 countries.

Figure 2.6 shows various nation clusters, where Norway is found in the same group of countries as the Netherlands, the United States and (perhaps surprisingly to some) to a smaller extent Great Britain, Sweden and Denmark. There is also a clear cluster with Spain, Italy and France. Japan is close here, while other Asian countries (such as Pakistan, Arab countries and Thailand) are found in the same quadrant, but still remain separate to Japan. It is worth noting that countries like Singapore and Hong Kong are closer to the Nordic cluster than the Latin cluster. Furthermore, we find a Germanic cluster (Germany, Austria and

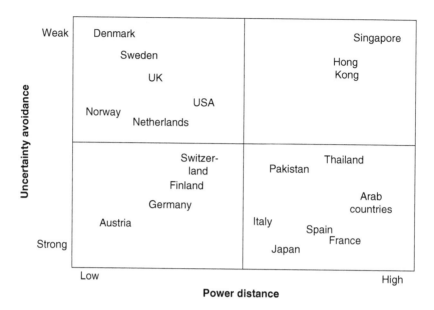

Figure 2.6 Uncertainty avoidance and power distance in 19 countries.

Source: Based on Hofstede (1980).

Switzerland), and interestingly Finland is found to be closer to these countries than to its Nordic neighbours.

Certain researchers have studied the connection between Hofstede's dimensions and different marketing strategies, for instance in relation to advertising messages and how to angle these (Roth 1995), or with regard to partners abroad (Nes et al. 2007), and the findings suggest that the dimensions provide a sound basis for specific strategy decisions. Still, perhaps inevitably, Hofstede's work has been criticised, partly because his research is only based on the employees in one multinational corporation (IBM), and partly because he himself represents one culture and therefore his whole analysis will be biased. For a critical analysis of cultural dimensions see Shenkar (2001).

Hofstede's cultural dimensions have been at the forefront of management literature for the past 25–30 years. Hampden-Turner and Trompenaars (1993, 2000) introduce a different set of cultural dimensions that partly overlap Hofstede's five dimensions. We will mention some of these here: universalism vs. particularism – which looks at the importance of rules compared with relations (for instance, who will win the contract – the best offer or the best friend?); emotionalism – to what extent we show emotions; specific vs. ambiguous – if we separate private life and business; sequential vs. synchronised – whether we can do one or several things at the same time (see Table 2.9 later – monochronic and polychronic cultures). Hall (1959) introduced the concept of high and low context cultures: in high context cultures, the message becomes apparent not only through the spoken word, but also through inferences of that culture. A typical example of a high context culture would be Japan, where family, friends, business relations and other groups involved in strong personal relations lay the foundations for communication where the message is implicit depending on the situation. Thus, day-to-day transactions will not require thorough background information; it will not be expected, rather it

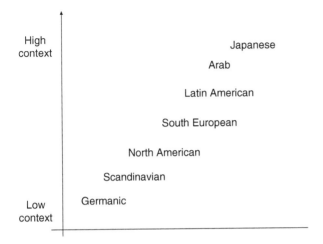

Figure 2.7 High and low context cultures.

Source: Based on Hall (1959).

would be frowned upon, to insist on repeating everything when communicating. Such relations are mainly observed in the East and in the areas surrounding the Mediterranean, while much less frequent in Northern Europe and the United States. Figure 2.7 shows the different nations and their place on a scale of low to high context cultures.

2.3.3 Cultural manifestations

The third level of culture is the tangible manifestation of cultural phenomena. This could be norms and traditions, preferences and attitudes towards different conditions in society. Most of these manifestations are specific to the various cultures, and the international marketer will experience this to varying degrees. Some might be considered simply curious or slightly difficult (such as the Chinese tradition of removing evil spirits from a building site before starting to dig), while others might create serious conflicts. In any case, they should be taken seriously by anyone wanting to create a business relationship, not only as it will clearly be beneficial but also as it is impossible to second-guess the reason behind someone's idiosyncrasy. Below, we will look at different types of cultural mani-festations – more as examples rather than a complete overview (as this would fill several books in itself).

Honour is credited to a person. Shame or "losing face" is the opposite of honour. In some Asian cultures, it will be far more dramatic to lose face than how it is experienced it in the West. This is seen in Islamic countries, where the families experience great shame if the women do not behave according to the set norms – by having a child outside of wedlock for instance or living with a non-Muslim. Generally speaking, people in the East will do anything to avoid losing face – and with it their self-respect. This is seen in how they discuss sensitive issues, where they will go to any lengths to avoid pointing out faults of others and rather seek harmonious relations. The bluntness of the West (to call a spade a spade) has generated many misunderstandings and broken relations with Eastern business partners.

Taboo is a prohibition ruled by norms, often as the result of religious traditions. For instance, it is taboo to show the sole of your shoe to an Arab – something that is easily done if you sit down opposite your Arabic counterpart and cross your legs. Another example is the taboo in Thailand of touching the head of a child as this is considered holy. Pork is taboo in Islamic countries as it is considered unclean. Alcohol is also taboo in Islamic countries, even if the enforcement of this prohibition greatly varies from one country to another – and some countries experience huge disparities internally.

Humour can in some instances cross national borders – and in some cases not at all. Humour in Southern Europe – and perhaps particularly in France – emphasises intellectual wit and play on words rather than the more slapstick humour found in Germanic cultures (including the Scandinavian countries). In Great Britain, humour is practically expected, where wit and practical jokes are an essential ingredient in a relationship. Danes are more known for their good temper rather than their good sense of humour (Mole 1992).

Nepotism means favouring your own family (the word has the same origins as nephew), and is disapproved of in all Western countries. It is important not to be seen to treat anyone unfairly (perhaps particularly in the egalitarian societies) but also as this might lead to suboptimal solutions (if, for instance, an underqualified person is hired just because he or she has a close relation to the employer). In other countries, the prioritising of family members is not frowned upon, but rather to the contrary: it is the duty of all to keep the best interests of every family member at heart. This is seen in Arabic countries, in China and to some extent in Southern Europe, where family plays an important role in society. In international relations with these countries, the principle of nepotism is likely to take centre stage.

In Scandinavia, it is customary to *delegate* responsibility throughout an organisation, something which is not as common in other cultures. More specifically, this can have a negative effect on how business leaders from other countries regard their negotiating partners. For instance, it is essential not to use juniors as envoys to negotiate important contracts with customers in the East. They will not be taken seriously and without direct access to the superiors, you will not gain the necessary trust of the customers. We can assume that a country's score on power distance gives a pointer to how acceptable it is to delegate responsibilities to juniors in international negotiations.

Legislation and rules provide another important area greatly affected by culture. The French and the German systems are influenced by the Roman law, where the law has the final say in legal matters. The *French* judicial system strongly protects the individual and the formal. This system is also found in Belgium, the Netherlands, Spain, Portugal, South America and the Southern states of the US. The *German* system, also found in Switzerland and Austria, has rules that, to a much greater degree than the French system, allow a judge to make a judgement call.

Anglo-American legislation is different. While laws do exist, they primarily practise case law. This is the case in the United States and in Great Britain, as well as in former British colonies. Semantics and systematics can vary greatly from continental law.

Islamic law, the *sharia*, is based on the *Quran* (The Holy Book) and on the *Hadith* (collections of records of the traditions or sayings of the Prophet Muhammad). Sharia gives rules on all matters in life – including commerce. The extraction of oil riches and increased foreign trade has forced the writing of new legislation, which is perhaps mainly characterised by the protection of national interests and a certain semantic reserve which is also found in French legislation.

The law and its logic is one matter, but quite different is how disputes are resolved in the various countries. The most extreme examples can generally be found in the United States, where disputes are resolved in court, with lengthy (and costly) use of lawyers, while in the East – and perhaps especially in Japan – they strive to reach an amicable resolution. It is furthermore no secret that certain countries have a court of law with a tendency to favour the domestic party in disputes concerning international participants. The notorious "brown envelopes" given to central members of a jury or judge are not unheard of in many countries. WJP Rule of Law Index shows the range of legal protection in different countries – see Table 2.8 (with a total of 99 countries). The scores are based on 44 different criteria, divided into 8 main factors (constraints on government powers, absence of corruption, open government, fundamental rights, order and security, regulatory enforcement, civil justice and criminal justice).[35]

We note that the Nordic countries are in the lead, while countries like France and the United States only come 18th and 19th. The table also clearly shows that resolving disputes in court can be risky, for instance in BRICS countries – and particularly in Russia and China. For small and medium-sized companies without the resources to sustain a lengthy and costly court procedure in countries with low levels of legal protection, the alternative is establishing and nourishing close relations with customers and partners which would: a) reduce the risk of conflict, and b) should conflict arise, minimise its effects and open up solutions via negotiations.

The ever-increasing international trade relations have resulted in a relatively homogenous Sale of Goods Act. There is still a great need for equal rules when it comes to international business law. UNCITRAL – the UN's commission that formulates and regulates international trade – does important work in this field. Following the Vienna Convention on international agreements on the sale of goods, UNCITRAL has composed rules and suggestions for a law on arbitration and been actively involved in numerous other areas. Another important organisation is the ICC – the International Chamber of Commerce – that cooperates with UNCITRAL. The ICC among others has created the often-applied definition of trade clauses: INCOTERMS (shipping clauses such as FOB, CIF, Ex works[36] and so on, regulating the costs and risk of transport of goods).

Table 2.8 Legal protection in selected countries

	Score	Ranking
Denmark	0.88	1
Norway	0.88	2
Sweden	0.85	3
Finland	0.84	4
Germany	0.80	9
Singapore	0.79	10
Japan	0.78	12
Great Britain	0.78	13
France	0.74	18
USA	0.71	19
Poland	0.67	21
South Africa	0.50	40
Brazil	0.54	42
India	0.48	66
Ukraine	0.47	68
China	0.46	76
Russia	0.45	80
Venezuela (last on the list)	0.43	99

Development of preferences is perhaps the area that will most concern the marketer. Matters such as aesthetics and design, choice of material and functional solutions, as well as the role various influencers have in the decision process, all play a part. What are the ultimately determining factors for the buyer and to what extent will these vary from one market to the next? Many business leaders have experienced difficulties in selling their ill-adapted concepts and products abroad. We will look at this in more detail later in this chapter. There are several conditions behind the reason such preferences may vary so strongly from one market to another:

–   Physical attributes such as colour, size and shape (design) all have different meanings in the different cultures. While black is the colour of mourning in the West, in certain countries in the Far East they use the colour white. Yellow has a particular significance in Buddhist countries (i.e. happiness), while, depending on where you are in the world, red can mean anything from death and love to power. Some have speculated whether the EU flag, with its blue background and yellow stars, reminded Norwegians of Sweden, and that this may have resulted in negative feelings for membership (which has been turned down in two referenda – 1972 and 1994). A bike will have a completely different function (mode of transport) in China, and partly also in the Netherlands and in Denmark, compared with a bike in the United States (leisure activity). Beer is mainly regarded as a thirst quencher in continental Europe, while in Scandinavia it is an alcoholic beverage. When it comes to consumption of alcohol there are clear differences. Figure 2.8 shows how the relationship of beer and wine consumption varies from one European country to another. Figure 2.8 shows that there are clear differences in the pattern of consumption that divides the North and the South. This is the case for numerous other products and in numerous other areas. Using different traditions and cultural influences as a starting point, physical attributes will carry greatly varied meanings in different countries.

Figure 2.8 Beer and wine consumption in selected European countries.

Source: Adapted from Williams (1991).

– There are also great differences from one country to another in traditional family roles. The traditional role of the woman in Northern Europe as being in charge of the purchase of household goods has changed dramatically during the past 50–60 years, while Southern and Eastern Europe have not experienced the same level of changes. Such differences can, to some extent, be deduced by looking at Hofstede's scale of masculinity. If we now take a look at the role distribution within organisations, the role as leader will in some cultures mean great power and authority, while in other cultures the role entails the task of coordinator. This again may be related to Hofstede's dimension on power distance. Such conditions matter to the marketer when it comes to whom it is important to influence, or whom to target with the marketing communication.

– It is often claimed that there are greater differences between different consumer segments within a country than there are between various countries. This is particularly the case when it comes to lifestyle. In a study on consumer behaviour and attitudes conducted in four countries (the United States, Brazil, Japan and France) Sheth and Eshghi (1985) state that national variables influence the consumer pattern more than lifestyle variables. In a study of the car market in five European countries, Kern et al. (1990) found that the composition of car buyers greatly varies from one country to another. While Italy is overrepresented in the so-called hedonistic (pleasure) segment, France is overrepresented in the traditionalist segment. Austria is heavily represented in the prestige segment. Several studies of advertising campaigns in international markets conclude that global campaigns – that is to say, campaigns aimed at appealing to the same needs and preferences across countries – do not have a significant effect in the various local markets (Vardar 1993).

Time and punctuality varies largely from one culture to another. Hall and Hall (1990) introduced the concept of poly- and monochronism, which looks at how time is considered. In monochronic societies, it is important to focus on one issue at a time and make sure that you don't waste time, therefore punctuality and meeting deadlines are essential. In the East, typical of polychronic cultures, there is a saying that "time comes" of course, one would like to meet one's obligations, but perhaps to a different schedule than was originally agreed. The view on existence is more holistic. People from polychronic cultures may have more than one thought at a time, and relate much more to human beings than to matters or institutions. Table 2.9 shows the different interpretations or perspectives monochronic and polychronic cultures have of the same phenomenon.

Table 2.9 Characteristics of polychronic and monochronic cultures

Polychronic cultures	Monochronic cultures
– Several things at the same time, easily distracted – Regard appointments as achievable – if possible – Lend and borrow money easily and often	– One thing at a time, concentrate on the job – Take schedules and deadlines seriously – Will seldom borrow/lend money (private property)
– Build lasting relations – Change plans easily and often – High context-oriented and have information	– Accept short-term relations – Stick to the plan, literally – Low context-oriented and need information

Source: Based on Hall and Hall (1990).

2.3.4 Converging consumer cultures

Even if cultural backgrounds, dimensions and cultural manifestations greatly vary from one country to another, there are still many signs of certain cultural manifestations converging or that elements of such manifestations are adopted, simply because it is seen as advantageous for the consumer. Increased international trade, increased travel and better communications, along with converging international subcultures in many areas, have all created both increased understanding for different cultures and a more homogenous demand pattern across national borders. We will now look at how certain forces influence this development, starting with consumer patterns.

Several studies have aimed to prove that globalisation of consumers takes place. One main conclusion to be drawn from these studies is that the globalisation process is driven more by supply than by demand. For example, a study of German businesses revealed that their marketing was generally standardised, despite the fact that the management acknowledged great differences between the various countries (Meffert and Althans 1986). Cultural differences in such instances are often ignored by the supplier, thereby risking a marketing "over-standardisation". MNCs are, according to Levitt (1983) and Ohmae (1985), important drivers in the homogenisation of the demand pattern. Demand for new product types usually originates in industrial countries and then spreads on to less developed countries in a relatively short space of time. The question here would be whether this is a result of cause or effect – is the marketing the catalyst for this, or is it a consequence of the economic development?

Dholakia and Firat (1988) maintain that MNCs gain advantages both in technology and management. Consumers in the various countries will prefer products with a superior technology that are marketed in a professional manner – with all the ensuing status for the consumer – over less developed, local products. The consequence of such a development is that consumers in less developed countries gradually adopt global products. To what extent such an adoption process happens and how long it takes is not empirically established.

One of Levitt's (1983) arguments for a more global market is that consumers across national borders will increasingly demand more technology-based products. It is thus natural to assume that industrial goods markets will be the primary market for a globally homogenous demand pattern. Nevertheless, studies of demand patterns in the United States and Europe indicate that there is little evidence of marketing of industrial products being more homogenous than that of consumer products (Boddewyn et al. 1986a).

The growth of multinational and international retailers and retail partnerships is another factor that seemingly influences the supplier towards developing more homogenous offers. Such concentration of the retail industry increases the negotiating strength, not just vis-à-vis MNCs, but also when it comes to smaller, domestic suppliers. The result could be that there will be more homogenous offers from a small number of pan-European and multinational brands, be it the retailers' own brands or the manufacturers' brands. Table 2.10 shows the biggest retailers in the world in 2015. It is interesting to note that Wal-Mart is more than three times the size of the next three on the list, British Tesco, American Costco and French Carrefour. Several of these retailers have grown via mergers and acquisitions. We also note that American retailers (with the exception of Wal-Mart) concentrate on the home market, as opposed to the European retailers where most have an international share of sales of between 35% and 75%.

One possible long-term scenario is that cultural differences between countries will gradually diminish, and that within certain dimensions this will create a more homogenous "world culture". A sign of this is that young people across borders have more in common with each other than with the older generation in their own country. This age group can be expected to

Table 2.10 Top retailers worldwide, 2015

Rank	Retailer	Head office	Type	Retail sales (USD billion)	Regions covered	International sales %
1	Wal-Mart Stores	USA	Discount store	476	Americas, Africa, Asia	29
2	Costco	USA	Cash & carry	105	North America	28
3	Carrefour	France	Hypermarket	99	Europe, Asia, Americas	53
4	Schwartz	Germany	Supermarket	99	Europe, Asia	58
5	Tesco plc	UK	Discount store	99	Europe, Asia	32
6	The Kroeger Co	USA	Supermarket	98	North America	0
7	Metro	Germany	Cash & carry	86	Europe	62
8	Aldi	Germany	Discount store	81	Europe, USA, Australia	59
9	Home Depot	USA	Ironmonger	79	North America	11
10	Target Corporation	USA	Warehouse	73	North America	2

Source: https://nrf.com/news/2015-top-250-global-powers-of-retailing.

hand on pan-cultural characteristics to the next generation. It is also reasonable to assume that "new" products, such as consumer electronics, cameras, mobile phones and expensive branded goods will be standardised across the borders to a greater degree than more culturally bound products such as building materials, food and "normal" clothes (Zaichowsky and Sood 1988). We can therefore expect a long-term trend where a segment of consumers can be called "global consumers" – at least when it comes to certain types of products through which they will share the same attitudes and preferences across borders.

All the same, national attributes are still prevalent, and we see that intrinsic cultural values still influence consumers' purchasing decisions. In a study of British, French and German consumers, Kantar Media[37] shows how German adult consumers are more methodical than their French and British counterparts. The French consumers are far more loyal to brands than the British and Germans, while the British display a lot more spontaneity in their purchasing decisions. The conclusion for the marketing executive could be that the use of market communication, both when it comes to content and channel, should vary from market to market.

In a survey of international brands in the United States, 11 European countries and Japan, it is claimed that there are only 19 brands worldwide that can be called global. Landor Associates (a brand consultancy affiliated with Leo Burnett) defines a global brand as one that offers the same advantages and is able to communicate these consistently to consumers across different regions and cultures. Furthermore, it needs to have a profile that ranges among the 50 best in Japan, the United States and Europe.

According to Alan Brew of Landor, "In 1985, only Coca-Cola achieved a global stature. Today we see a larger group of brands whose quality of product, branding and market positioning is recognised by consumers across the world." The brand consultancy group Interbrand carries out an annual evaluation of so-called global brands. Table 2.11 shows the list of the 20 most valuable brands worldwide (2016). It includes companies with international business ranging across at least three continents, exceeding 30% of sales and with a value of more than 1 billion USD. We note that 14 out of the 20 leading global brands are from the United States. If we look further down the list, we find several European and Asian (Japanese and South Korean) brands. The Swedes are represented in the top 100 list with H&M and IKEA

Table 2.11 Global brands, 2016

Rank	Company	Country
1	Apple	USA
2	Google	USA
3	Coca-Cola	USA
4	Microsoft	USA
5	Toyota	Japan
6	IBM	USA
7	Samsung	South Korea
8	Amazon	USA
9	Mercedes-Benz	Germany
10	General Electric	USA
11	BMW	Germany
12	McDonald's	USA
13	Disney	USA
14	Intel	USA
15	Facebook	USA
16	Cisco	USA
17	Oracle	USA
18	Nike	USA
19	Louis Vuitton	France
20	Hennes & Mauritz	Sweden

Source: http://interbrand.com/best-brands/best-global-brands/2016/ranking/.

at 20th and 26th places respectively Zara (Spain) is number 27. Nokia, which in 2006 occupied a respectable fifth place, has fallen out of 2016 list.

Landor carried out a large survey in the beginning of the 1990s that revealed a great degree of national orientation within the consumer structure. The results showed that all 15 top brands in Japan and the United States were from these respective countries, implying there could still be a long road ahead for global brands originating from outside these two countries. In Western Europe on the other hand, it seems as though the various countries have a more open attitude to and acceptance for foreign brands. Even if national allegiance still plays a vital part for consumer patterns and purchasing decisions in different parts of the world, there are signs of an emerging consumer culture where consumers from different countries have developed more or less the same preference. As a result, they are receptive to the same products. To the marketing executive, this means that it is important to analyse whether it is possible to use the same elements in the marketing mix in the various export markets. The younger generation plays a vital role here. They apparently have more in common with their "siblings" or peers across national borders than with the elders in their own country. Such a consumer culture will only reach a limited segment of the consumers in the various countries however and it is only within certain product areas that the natural conclusion would be product and marketing standardisation.

Nor should we ignore the fact that the advent of the "global consumers" may have been the deciding factor in the development of different companies' strategy for internationalisation, and thus has contributed to swifter globalisation than would have been the case otherwise. This development may have been one of the key factors behind a process where the consumer patterns within international markets have converged to a certain extent. It is still the case that the national prevails when it comes to both consumer patterns and marketing communications. We shall return to these issues when discussing standardisation and adaptation of the marketing effort in Chapter 9.

2.3.5 Summary

In this part, we have discussed the concept of culture from three levels: cultural influencers, cultural dimensions and cultural manifestations. While the first two levels essentially shape level three, it is difficult to immediately see the natural connection between them. It would still be advantageous for the international marketing executive to gain rudimentary knowledge of the first two levels, whether through literature, reading the history of the countries or through conversations with people with experience from the various places. There are also a number of books that describe business culture in several countries. These are a sound starting point for a learning process on the cultural contexts of various countries. Even so, there exist such copious amounts of cultural manifestations in every country that to truly understand them you need your own direct experience.

Even if each country has its own cultural characteristics, we see a gradual move towards what we call a "global consumer culture". This is happening for certain products and within certain parts of the population, where the younger generation distinguishes itself as particularly global. Many factors have contributed to this development but the role of the international retailers has perhaps so far been underrated. These contribute, via the power of the market, to a more homogenous product offering across national borders. We have also seen that there is an increasing number of brands that can be characterised as global. However, the local brands still dominate in most countries.

2.4 Trade policy and technology: two pillars of liberalisation

Earlier on, we pointed out that multinational corporations (MNCs) have had great opportunities to develop in a more global direction due to changing working conditions. We will here examine the most important contributing factors for these changing working conditions, focusing on the development of international trade policy and technological development.

2.4.1 Trade policy for global trade

This part of the chapter describes the most important trade organisations and institutions that have contributed to increased international exchange of goods. The WTO, the EU, the EEA and EFTA are particularly important for Europe's part.

World Trade Organisation (WTO)

The WTO was established in 1995, a trade organisation that as at July 2016 encompassed 164 countries. Its precursor, GATT (General Agreement on Tariffs and Trade), had since the Second World War gradually contributed to liberalising world trade, partly by reducing customs and partly by steadily expanding the agreement to include more and more countries. The WTO actively works to drive development of more all-encompassing and homogenous agreements for the regulation of world trade. The WTO agreement is the common denominator for these part agreements.

The main principle of the WTO – continued from GATT – is trade without discrimination, that no country can charge different customs duty rates from other member countries, the so-called principle of *most favoured nation* embedded in Article I of the agreement. Some deviations from the principle are allowed, the most famous being the EU, which seeks to increase the economic integration between the member countries by giving them preferential treatment in areas such as customs duty. The WTO also administers other agreements, three of which are particularly important: GATS, TRIPs and TRIMs. The GATS agreement (General Agreement on Trade in

Services) covers entry to market, openness and the removal of trade barriers for services. The TRIPs agreement (Agreement on Trade Related Aspects of Intellectual Property Rights) covers, among other things, patents, copyrights, brands, industrial design and moulding transferred from the parent company to a foreign division or representative. The TRIMs agreement (Agreement on Trade Related Investment Measures) concerns the regulation of trade. It is also the first agreement to address restrictions on a country's opportunities to protect its own industries. In short, the agreements prohibit any discrimination of national or international parties (GATT, article III), and they ban – with few exceptions – any form of quantitative trade quotas that would limit full access to the international market (GATT, article XIII).

Besides industrial products regulated by the GATT Agreement, services, intellectual property, environment and agriculture products as well as textiles and clothing are now included in the WTO Agreement. Areas such as maritime transport, telecommunication and financial services are still under negotiation.

WTO has more power than GATT. GATT resolutions were always unanimous as all the member countries could at the end of the day use their right of veto and block a suggestion. WTO is not an organisation making use of its power to force through unpopular issues against the will of the members, as most of the resolutions are dependent on consensus. Depending on the case at hand, it may be sufficient to have either simple or qualified (two-thirds or three-quarters) majority. The rule of decision making could be said to have been turned around, in that a decision will be made as long as there is no agreement *not* to make it.

The WTO's authority is at times sorely tested. This happened in 1998/1999 during the so-called "banana war" between the United States and the EU. The latter had settled on preferential measures with previous French and British colonies regarding the import of bananas, which were against the rules of the WTO. The EU therefore defied American interests, led by American fruit companies with vast banana plantations in Latin America. The Americans were not willing to wait for the WTO's deadline to implement anti-dumping duties, which would have impacted a range of European products. The United States decided therefore in the year 2000, under President George W. Bush, to introduce trade restrictions on steel, which led to strong reactions from not only the EU but also countries like Japan and Brazil. Using the legislation of the WTO, the EU threatened retaliation, where by selected goods from the United States would have special customs duties imposed. There are a range of cases that were brought to the WTO panel. In the recent years the number of complaints brought to the WTO has been between 10 and 20 annually.

Following the first rounds of negotiations in 1948, GATT has completed seven rounds of negotiations on mutual customs duty reductions. Table 2.12 gives an overview of these rounds. The Uruguay round opened in 1986. It took eight years for the negotiations to close and for the agreement to be ratified by the national assemblies of the member countries. Tough negotiations on agriculture were one of the main reasons it took such a long time.

In addition to rules on customs duties the WTO has also written rules on competition, which ban dumping (briefly defined as a lower price on products sold abroad, compared with equivalent products sold on the national market by the same manufacturer) and state subsidies (article VI). There are several exceptions to the rule. For instance, many countries actively subsidise their industries to maintain an industrial base or to soften the transition to international

Table 2.12 Negotiation rounds of GATT and the WTO

Negotiating round	Year	No. of member countries	Average customs duty (%) following negotiations
Geneva	1947	23	NA
Annecy	1949	13	NA
Torquay	1950	38	NA
Geneva	1956	26	NA
Dillon	1960–1961	26	NA
Kennedy	1962–1967	62	8.7
Tokyo	1973–1979	102	4.7
Uruguay	1986–1994	123	3.6
Doha	2001–2015[a]	164[b]	

Source: www.wto.org/english/thewto_e/whatis_e/tif_e/fact4_e.htm#rounds and www.wto.org/english/thewto_e/whatis_e/tif_e/org6_e.htm
Notes: NA = not available.
[a] The Doha round was eventually abandoned in 2015.
[b] Member countries as of 2017.

competition for their domestic companies. Even if the authorities in the affected countries were to protect employment in parts of the industry, such subsidies also make for a slower transition.

An important part of each of the agreements deals with conflict resolution. A dispute arises when a member government files a complaint over the conduct of another member government to the Dispute Settlement Body (DSB). Since 1995 over 500 complaints have been filed and around 350 cases have been settled. A brief review of the complaints reveals that the US (25%) and EU (16%) are the main "customers" of the DSB, both as complainants and respondents, with around 40% of the cases. The main respondents of US complaints are China (21) and the EU (19), whereas the EU has filed 33 complaints against the US.[38]

Car wars

Since the end of the 1960s and well into the 1990s the US and Japan were in conflict over an imbalance in trade of automobile products (vehicles and parts). A rising unrest in the US – among industry leaders, trade unions and policy makers – grew into frustration at what they alleged to be insurmountable trade barriers in Japan. Discussions between officials in both countries had been going on for decades – with various elements of trade restrictions such as voluntary export restraints (VER) and import reducing measures, for example Japanese assembly plants in the US – before they climaxed in July 1995. The backdrop of this conflict was the US' increasing trade deficit with Japan. The automobile industry represented a massive 60% of this deficit; American automobile manufacturers sold around 15,000 cars in Japan in 1994, while more than 3.5 million Japanese cars were sold in the US. The US demanded, with conditional support from the EU, that Japan had to open up its market for foreign automobile goods, and emphasised the gravity of the situation by threatening a 100% penalty customs duty on Japanese luxury cars on the American market, equalling a total value of import of almost 6 billion USD. EU support was dependent on whether the ensuing negotiated deal between the US and Japan clearly banned any form of preferential treatment of any nation's/trade bloc's competitive circumstance in a market. However, before the WTO had time to look at the case, the parties negotiated a compromise whereby the Japanese had to commit to increase production in the US by a quarter by 1998 and at the same time buy more components in the United States for the Japanese factories. Cars from Ford, GM and Chrysler were also to gain easier access to Japanese car dealerships via the customs and inspections authorities. The Japanese were very satisfied that they did not have to quantify how many American cars or car parts had to be exported to Japan for the deal to be said to be equal. Such a number would in the eyes of the Japanese be regarded as an unfavourable and unreasonable quota regulation.

The US car war did not stop there. China was admitted to the WTO in 2001. Not long after, the US administration filed a complaint against China accusing the government of misusing anti-dumping tariffs on American SUVs – of between 2% and 12.9%. The US claimed that car sales worth 5 billion USD were affected. The Chinese alleged that the cars were sold at a price below full cost, but for an anti-dumping tariff to be legal under the WTO agreements, the complainant needs to provide evidence of injury to their home industry. The Chinese did not provide such evidence and the complaint was ruled in favour of the US.[39]

The many conflicts between trading partners, and particularly those involving the United States, have escalated since President Donald Trump came to power. His concern for loss of jobs is genuine and his first act on day one of his presidency was to withdraw from negotiations of the Trans-Pacific Partnership (TPP). The TPP was to be a pact that aimed to deepen the economic cooperation between 12 nations bordering the Pacific Ocean. The US withdrawal was a major blow to the other participating nations. They are now discussing how to reorient the discussions without the US.

The schools of realists and independence: two views on the development of GATT/WTO

GATT and later the WTO have been the main pillars for the development of the global free trade regime since the Second World War. There are disagreements between various schools of thought about what the relative weakening of the United States (see earlier in this chapter) means for the future development of GATT/WTO. The followers of the school of realists claim that to maintain a regime of free trade, hegemony is necessary. The school of independence, represented by amongst others Keohane (1980), thinks that even if the establishment of a free trade regime needs active support and participation of a hegemon, it will be possible to safeguard the continuation with active, multinational cooperation where all parties are interested in maintaining and further developing the system. This view has been characterised as an ideological dream more than a logical development. The balance of power between the partners has been proved, in this instance, to determine the development. We have seen that the balance of power can be pushed to the disfavour of the United States – and that other nations can establish strong positions in the global economy. A prediction will therefore be that the free trade regime of today will eventually be replaced by something else.

The contours of a more regionalised trade cooperation are already visible, where the EU is one central power, NAFTA (US/Canada/Mexico) another, and where from 2003 AFTA (ASEAN Free Trade Area consisting of Indonesia, Malaysia, the Philippines, Thailand, Singapore, Brunei, Vietnam, Laos, Myanmar and Cambodia) supplements Japan and China in the development of a third power around the Pacific Rim. In this system, the various power blocs will seek what we may call a more pragmatic protectionism where trade borders will be opened or closed on an ad hoc basis, all depending on what best serves the interests of the region, without having to take into account what is best for everyone as a whole.

This scenario does not necessarily mean increased protectionism in a negative sense of the word. The cooperation on bloc creation may increase and new fora (or the further development of old ones, such as the G7 becoming G8, later G20) might emerge.

G8 and G20 – where important matters are discussed

G8 is a coalition of nations where the state leaders of eight important industrial nations (US, Japan, Germany, France, Great Britain, Italy, Canada and, since 1997 Russia – Group of 8) meet annually to discuss topical financial and political issues. A recurrent item on the agenda is trade disputes and the development of the WTO. Issues such as economic growth, technological development, debt problems and the development in areas of conflict around the world are also discussed. Its precursor, the G7 (= G8 minus Russia) was established in 1973 as a response to the oil embargo imposed by Arab countries after the US and UK intervened in the Yom Kippur war.

The significance that the G8 has for the development of the world economy is an open question. The most important contribution is perhaps that the leaders from the global financial superpowers get together and discuss common agendas, make contacts and not least get to know each other and the others' point of view. G8 has periodically been accused by smaller nations of being a rich boys' club with no regard for others. This criticism may be well-founded, but the members might not have acted much differently without G8. Russia has been temporarily excluded from the G8 meetings as the result of its role in the Ukraine conflict in 2014.

In 1999 the G8 was renamed G20 – including 12 new members in the coalition – in recognition of emerging markets playing an increasing role in the world economy. The member countries of G20 are Brazil, China, Saudi Arabia, Republic of Korea, France, Australia, China, Canada, Germany, Indonesia, Argentina, Turkey, India, Russia, South Africa, Mexico, Japan, United Kingdom, United States, as well as the European Union. It has been claimed that the inclusion of future economic powerhouses could potentially offer aid to fledging economies of the West.[40]

The significance of regional trading blocs

Since the Second World War several attempts have been made to establish various trade blocs with the aim of achieving regional economic integration. Besides the EU and EFTA, other blocs worth mentioning include Caricom, ASEAN and NAFTA. What these blocks share is the goal of attaining a favourable business environment in order for them to better exploit their absolute and comparative advantages. A country's aim and motive for a joining trade bloc might vary, but some main traits are recurring (Keohane 1980):

–   The members will achieve economic gains with a more efficient manufacturing structure and strengthened economic growth through FDI, experience-based knowledge, and research and development.

- The members may have non-economic goals, such as joint security (one of the main arguments for establishing the Coal and Steel Community in 1952, the precursor to the European Economic Community, subsequently the EU).
- Smaller countries may also seek greater security through easier market access.

As mentioned earlier, the various trade blocs seek to serve the interests of the region, though not necessarily at the expense – to some extent – of furthering global trade. The trade blocs are first and foremost built around the principle of most favoured nation, relatively liberal decisions on inclusion, profound integration and limits on anti-dumping measures.

The European Union (EU)

The EC (initially meaning The European Communities) is the common name for the three treaties signed by 12 European countries on cooperation in Europe: 1) the European Economic Community (EEC or the Common Market), 2) Euratom, with the aim of controlling and limiting the uses of nuclear power in Europe and 3) the European Coal and Steel Community. The treaties are all based on the Treaty of Rome (1957), originally signed by West Germany, France, Italy and the Benelux countries. The aim was primarily to create a larger market for the member countries and as such to stimulate the division of labour and better exploit the resources in the various countries.

The EC gradually evolved to become a dominant factor not only within trade in Europe, but also within areas such as industrial policy, agricultural policy, regional development and foreign policy.

In the Single European Act signed in 1986, the member countries focused on abolishing the remaining trade barriers between them. 'The Single Market' – the European Union (the EU) – came into being on 1 January 1993. Even if many trade barriers were reduced or completely abolished from that date, it would be many years until it could be called a market in line with the United States for instance – which incidentally is not a homogenous market, but a country with 50 states! Nevertheless, with the four freedoms (see below), the EU aims at establishing equal conditions for competition for all businesses within the member countries. Today (2017) the EU comprises 28 member countries (see Table 2.13), and the EU's increasing level of coordination, especially within trade policies, has contributed to increasing the influence of member countries at the expense of the United States and Japan.

Table 2.13 The evolution of the European Union

1957	1973	1981	1986	1994	2004	2007	2013	2019
Belgium	Denmark	Greece	Portugal	Finland	Estonia	Bulgaria	Croatia	Brexit?
France	Ireland		Spain	Sweden	Cyprus	Romania		
Italy	UK			Austria	Latvia			
Luxembourg					Lithuania			
Netherlands					Malta			
Germany					Poland			
					Slovakia			
					Slovenia			
					Czech Rep.			
					Hungary			

The four freedoms

The Single Market is based on the four freedoms and involves free movement of capital, goods, services and people between the EU members. The purpose is to develop an economic region where artificial barriers to economic growth (different technical standards, the regulation of capital and labour markets, etc.) and optimal exploitation of resources are removed.

At the meeting in Maastricht in December 1991, the then 12 member countries agreed to expand the cooperation to also include monetary, financial, defence and social policies . The aim was to create competitive conditions as equal as possible for all member countries. Not all countries have been uniformly enthusiastic over such a development. The Danish people voted against (50.7%) during the ratification process for the agreement in 1992. The French people voted for (52%) while the Irish were overwhelmingly in favour of this development with more than 70% voting yes. However, the EU did not have to wait too long: Denmark accepted the deal in May 1993, so that the Maastricht Treaty came into force on 1 November 1993. It is worth noting that the United Kingdom has never ratified the part of the treaty that deals with social conditions – namely the Social Chapter.

Three countries that were previously members of EFTA (see next section) – Austria, Finland and Sweden – all voted yes at their referenda in 1994 and became EU members from 1 January 1995. The Norwegian people voted no on 28 November 1994 for the second time (the first referendum on EC membership was in 1972) and as such Norway is – together with Iceland, Switzerland and Liechtenstein – one of the few EFTA nations not actively participating in the European integration process.

The EU expanded in 2004 with 10 new member countries, and again in 2007 with two more, Romania and Bulgaria, and finally (so far) with Croatia in 2013. Today the EU comprises 28 member countries, with a total of 500 million inhabitants (see Table 2.13).[41] Thus, the EU sets its position as an important force for the economic development of Central Europe. At the same time, an agreement was reached in 2005, following lengthy negotiations, to draft a constitution that would make the decision process easier and more democratic. This was however rejected by both France and the Netherlands and a watered-down version was agreed upon in 2008. Today, total agreement on the political measures taken by the EU is needed, and one single country could therefore in theory stop an otherwise healthy evolvement of the union.

Both projects – the expansion and the revised constitution – sorely tested the EU. In addition, European cooperation has proved to be much more complicated than expected, and the challenges have only been added to with the financial crisis of 2008. Greece, Spain, Portugal, Ireland and Italy have had major problems regarding business structure and state finances. They have all been forced by the European Central Bank and other creditors (led by Germany and the IMF) to introduce cuts in their economies, which in turn has led to unemployment and social unrest (unemployment in Greece and Spain in 2016 was around 25%). These conditions have caused great division in several European countries, and resulted in several so-called Eurosceptic parties in key European countries doing well at the elections for the European Parliament in the spring of 2014.

There is particular concern about the consequences of the Brexit vote in the UK in June 2016. The main arguments in Britain against the EU were that the British felt they had to pay too much to the EU, that they had little control of national matters, that immigration was out of control and that Brussels has too much power. The UK is however deeply entangled through thousands of regulations and legal acts in the EU system, both regarding internal issues to the EU, and trade deals and other agreements with third parties. However, the vote to leave was very close and divisive, making it difficult for the UK government to conduct effective negotiations for an exit that will satisfy the people and be accepted by the British Parliament. Speculation is high on how the Brits will be able to negotiate exit conditions and a new agreement with the EU that both parties can accept. Some suggest a deal along the lines of those that Norway and Iceland have with the EU (see later), whereas most seem to agree that an outcome along such lines would not address the British grievances raised against the EU. Another complicating factor is that the UK itself is a union of four countries/provinces, two of which (Scotland and Northern Ireland) threaten to break out of that union. Furthermore, the concerns of the British people are shared by an increasing number of other Europeans – particularly in the East but also in "hard core" EU members such as France and the Netherlands.

It is fair to say that the EU is facing a very challenging consolidation phase, both regarding the union as such and the European cooperation. New projects – be it expansion or stronger integration – are unlikely to be on the agenda in the near future. On the contrary, there is a fear that other countries will be inspired by the UK to hold referenda on membership status, with the risk of seeing other countries leave the EU. It will therefore take a while before the union will expand with new members. Talks have been entered into with Turkey but the view on possible Turkish membership is greatly divided. One of the reasons for this is that Turkey would be the only Muslim country in the EU and it also has various unsolved conflicts both internally and with the Greek part of Cyprus. With regard to Norway, Iceland, Switzerland and Liechtenstein, there is little probability that any of these countries will become members in the foreseeable future. Balkan states beyond Slovenia and Croatia are either in negotiations (Serbia and Montenegro) or have been given the status of candidate (Macedonia) or potential candidate (Bosnia-Herzegovina, Albania, Kosovo). However, the author of this book believes that membership for any of these countries is still a long way off. There has also been talk of the EU discussing membership for previous Soviet states like Ukraine, Moldova and Belarus. Such an expansion could lead to huge political conflict – as most recently seen in the Ukraine crisis – and is not likely to be happening any time soon. Nevertheless, during the spring of 2014, the EU and Ukraine entered an economic cooperation agreement where the aim is to strengthen the country's economic development and consequently its ties to Western Europe.

European Free Trade Area (EFTA)

EFTA was established (by the Stockholm Convention of 1959) as a response to the then EC. The member countries at the time were Great Britain, Switzerland, Austria, Sweden, Denmark, Portugal, Norway and Iceland. The main difference between EFTA and the EC is that, while the latter was a customs duty union where all members share one customs border, EFTA is a free trade agreement whereby there is free trade between the various member countries where each of these countries has its own customs agreements with non-members. Following the accession to membership of the EEC of Great Britain, Denmark, Portugal, Austria, Finland and Sweden, the remaining member countries of EFTA (Norway, Iceland, Switzerland and Liechtenstein) have forged links with the EU through bilateral trade agreements. In principle, these allow for mutual exemption from duty for all industrial goods.

While the trade agreement provides entry to the EU market for EFTA members' industry, it has also limited this freedom through the EU's anti-dumping rules: Should the EU Commission find proof of dumping, the offending party is given a minimum price that they must stick to. This means that it may not use low prices as a tool in its marketing, and therefore risk losing customers in the competition with local EU companies, for which there are no lower limits on price. Several Norwegian companies have experienced the consequences of the EU's anti-dumping rules, where industries such as salmon, timber and ferroalloys have repeatedly had to face accusations of dumping.

European Economic Area (EEA)

The EFTA countries – Iceland, Liechtenstein and Norway, but not Switzerland (which has opted for another solution) – have negotiated a deal on economic cooperation with the EU, called the EEA Agreement. This deal came into force on 1 January 1994 and gives firms in EFTA countries free access to Europe. This means that a market of 500 million people with considerable spending power is available with no major trade barriers. The EEA Agreement implies that several laws and regulations of the EFTA countries have had to change in order to comply with EU legislation, and that others will constantly need modifying as this legislation develops further: Technical standards that may seem to skew competition must be removed; anti-dumping measures should no longer be taken against EFTA products within the EU or vice versa (though fishing is still the exception here); public acquisitions are open for international competition within the whole of the EEA; the services market, such as banking and financial services, telecommunication and transport services, are open for European competition.

North American Free Trade Area (NAFTA)

On 1 January 1994 the NAFTA Agreement between the United States, Canada and Mexico came into force. The agreement is a free trade deal that regulates trade between the three and in principle this involves increased trade of goods between the countries. While the deal meets its purposes in many ways, there are sufficient exceptions and special measures in place to create difficulties. The rules on the country of origin of goods deviate from conventional trade definitions. For a Canadian garment to avoid duty in the United States, it must not only be knitted in Canada, but the wool must also originate from the NAFTA region. It has been claimed that with NAFTA the tendency to create trade blocs around the world will increase – in Europe, Northern Europe and the Pacific Rim. With this in mind, negotiations on the development of FTAA – Free Trade Area of the Americas – have been entered into with 34 participants from both continents (North and South America, including the Caribbean). Any agreement here however is still a long way off.

EU–USA

Economic interaction – both in terms of trade and investments – between the EU and the United States is extensive. Trade totals roughly 1 trillion euros with more than 100 billion imbalance in the EU's favour. Investment stocks amount to around 5 trillion euros (about half of which are European investments in the US and the other half are from the US into Europe).[42] It is claimed that the rewards of a transatlantic economic partnership (TTIP=Transatlantic Trade and Investment Partnership) could potentially be as much as 200 million USD for the two parties, and perhaps as much as 100 million USD for countries not included in the deal. Shared regulations and standards, and a framework that simplifies conflict resolution, are some of the benefits that could arise from such a partnership. The negotiations started in 2013. There are still major differences unresolved between the two parties. On one hand there is the Americans' more *laissez-faire* attitudes towards gene modified organisms, financial regulations and surveillance. On the other hand is their aggressive attitude in favour of sanctions against countries like Iran, Russia and until recently Cuba. Both make it difficult to have any sort of progress in the negotiations. In particularly with regard to the relationship with Russia, Europe and the United States have widely differing interests, as Europe is more financially dependent on Russia than is the United States. Furthermore, the Brexit vote constitutes a serious threat to the progress of the negotiations, and key people in countries such as France and Germany have voiced serious doubts about the whole venture. With Donald Trump as the US president the future of TTIP seems even more uncertain.

In October 2016, in the shadow of the TTIP negotiations, Canada and the EU signed a Comprehensive Economic and Trade Agreement (CETA) that aims at liberalising trade between the EU and Canada. It is claimed to boost trade between the two signatories by some 25% – both through lowering tariffs and liberalisation of regulations.[43] Both TTIP and CETA have been criticised for being too lenient on big business, not taking into consideration the concerns of consumers and the man in the street.

Other regional trade organisations

There are also other regional trade organisations. To name a few: LAIA (Latin American Integration Association), CACM (Central American Common Market), ASEAN (Association of South East Asian Nations), CARICOM (Caribbean Common Market), EACM (East African Common Market), ECOWAS (Economic Community of West African States) and Mercosur. In September 1995, Mercosur – which includes Argentina, Brazil, Uruguay, Paraguay and Venezuela (which is currently excluded) entered into negotiations with the EU for an agreement to establish the biggest free trade area worldwide. The negotiations are proving lengthy due to, amongst other things, opposing views on the role that trade plays for the economic relations between the two blocs.

Of the above-mentioned trade blocs it is primarily ASEAN – Brunei, the Philippines, Indonesia, Cambodia, Laos, Malaysia, Myanmar (Burma), Singapore, Thailand and Vietnam – that has experienced a certain progress. The organisation was established in 1967 but did not become operative until 1976. The aim is to integrate the economy of the member countries through programmes developing their industries, reducing customs duties and non-tariff trade barriers as well as synchronising their investment incentives. Even though ASEAN is still not a free trade area, the group has succeeded in quickly achieving economic growth, mainly through exports. This progress is due to high productivity in the related countries linked with the ability to develop a market network. The ASEAN countries have established the free trade agreement, AFTA, that came into force on 1 January 2003.

We should also mention one other trade organisation, APEC – Asia-Pacific Economic Cooperation. Ever since it was established in the late 1980s, this organisation has mainly existed as a discussion forum where the 17 member countries can meet and discuss trade and political matters. However, APEC has gradually focused more on entering binding trade deals.

2.4.2 Technology – a major globalisation driver

The world has seen dramatic technological developments since the Second World War. Below we will briefly look at the most important attributes of these developments, focusing particularly on the following:

– transport
– telecommunications

– development of data networks
– development of the media
– economies of scale.

Transport

The world increasingly becomes a "smaller" place through development in the opportunities for transport. Figure 2.9 attempts to illustrate how the globe has "shrunk" with the ever-increasing opportunities for transport.

On a weight basis, 75% of international transport of goods is via ships, while 16% is transported on land (road and rail). Airfreight only represents 0.03% of the total amount, but 10% of the value. The remaining 9% of goods are transported through oil and gas pipes.[44] Beyond the increase in speed, the progress in the development of transport has been staggering. Looking at aviation, it was estimated that we would undertake one billion journeys by plane by 1990, which represented a doubling from 1980. Twenty years later (in 2000) this figure was doubled again. IATA estimates that the figure for 2012 was 3.6 billion passengers – again a near-doubling in almost 12 years.[45] IATA has predicted that this figure may reach 7 billion in 2030, a forecast that hinges on smooth continuation of the development to date.

Major investments are made in Europe to develop modes of communication to rival air traffic. There are ambitious plans to improve the standard of roads to better link various countries. Train traffic will also have a revival in many areas: The new high-speed trains are incredibly competitive on medium to long journeys (50–500 km) and the stations are in the centre of towns. Trains are also more environmentally friendly, another reason for the major investment backing them.

Transport by sea has dominated world trade since the dawn of time. While it might not have become significantly speedier in the past 20–30 years it has become increasingly cheaper.

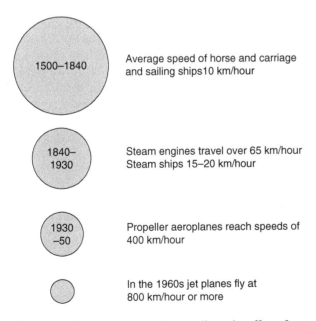

Figure 2.9 The globe is becoming smaller – the effect of new transport technology.

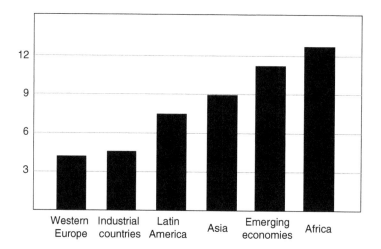

Figure 2.10 Transport cost averages as a percentage of import value.

Source: http://www.comcec.org/UserFiles/File/ulastirma/COMCEC-drwalid-present-final.pdf.

Figure 2.10 shows that the costs of transport varies greatly from one region to the next, a fact reflected by different standards of infrastructure (ports, roads, rail etc.).[46]

Technological development – tele- and data communications

Developments in communications enable global businesses to operate from anywhere in the world today in a cost-efficient manner. Data networks are the distribution systems of the future, and they will be able to efficiently internationalise operations. This is particularly the case for financial transactions, but also increasingly for order-handling and transport routines as well as internal communication between the various units of an MNC or between different business connections. The use of the internet is also increasing. Tables 2.14 and 2.15 show the use of internet and mobile phones in selected countries. There are significant differences between industrial nations and developing nations but even so the developing nations are closing in. Norway tops the list of internet users with 95 users per 100 inhabitants. Most developing nations are far behind. We note that in 2012, 42% of the population in China had access to the internet. The use of a mobile phone is much more widespread in developing nations and, in some cases, it even surpasses the mobile phone density of countries like the United States. This corresponds to the evolution of mobile phone subscriptions where the difference between industrial and developing nations only stands at 4 to 1. While there are nearly 160 mobile phones per 100 users in Luxembourg (people owning more than one phone) the equivalent figure for some African nations is at 4–5 (Chad, Burkina Faso).

Technological development – economies of scale

Since the industrial revolution, technological development has led to increasing production units through cost-efficient processes – a development that is yet to slow down. In an open market, this is crucial for business, and an improvement of cost-efficient competitiveness will in

Table 2.14 Internet users in selected countries, 2014

Country	No. of users (in millions)	Per 100 inhabitants
China	568.2	42.3
USA	254.3	81.0
India	151.6	12.6
Japan	100.7	79.1
Germany	68.3	84.0
Great Britain	54.9	87.0
France	54.5	83.0
Sweden	8.6	94.0
Denmark	5.2	93.0
Finland	4.8	91.0
Norway	4.5	95.0

Source: http://www.indexmundi.com/g/r.aspx?v=4010.

Table 2.15 Mobile phones in selected countries, 2014

Country	No. of mobile phones (in millions)	Per 100 inhabitants
China	1,227	74
India	904	64
USA	327	91
Brazil	273	119
Japan	121	95
Germany	107	128
Great Britain	76	132
France	72	100
Sweden	8.6	116
Denmark	5.2	127
Finland	8.4	160
Norway	6.1	119

Source: http://www.indexmundi.com/g/r.aspx?v=4010.

itself drive a more global industry structure. The advantages of economies of scale and specialisation therefore force businesses to enter several markets to look beyond their home market, which in turn demands an international network and international marketing competence.

Figure 2.11 shows how different industries can meet globalised competition through lower unit costs. This could happen through the standardisation of production, marketing of raw materials and semi-manufactured goods, or by establishing flexible manufacturing systems – FMS – for finished goods.

It has been documented that large-scale manufacturing reduces costs. Roughly estimated, capital expenditure increases by 0.6 for every additional unit resulting from increased manufacturing capacity (Moore 1959). This will naturally vary greatly from one industry to another. The greater the capital expenditure per manufactured unit, the greater the reward for large-scale manufacturing.

Regarding FMS, this technology has only really been in use in the past 25–30 years. Robots are key here. It is estimated that around 1.6 million robots are installed worldwide, or on average 69 robots per 10,000 employees. The industry is set to grow at a rate of 12% in the period 2016

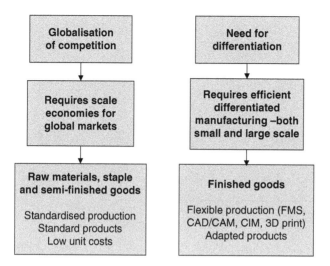

Figure 2.11 Economies of scale and the globalisation of different industrial sectors.

Table 2.16 Robot density in selected countries

Country	Robots per 10,000 employees in the manufacturing industries
South Korea	411
Japan	213
Germany	170
Sweden	159
Italy	126
Austria	95
USA	93
France[a]	55
UK	33
World average	69

Note: [a]Author's estimate.
Source: http://www.ifr.org/fileadmin/user_upload/downloads/World_Robotics/2016/
Executive_Summary_WR_Industrial_Robots_2016.pdf.

–2019 to some 2.6 million units. Table 2.16 shows the number of robots per 10,000 employees in selected countries.

The consequence of the breakthrough for FMS in several industries has been that with relatively modest costs it is possible for large business units with cost-effective manufacturing equipment to factor in different product variations in international markets. It is therefore to be expected that industries that so far have been dominated by small and locally-focused companies will be restructured towards fewer and larger units with more cost-efficient manufacturing. Nonetheless, Lyons (1980) shows that small companies could enjoy the same degree of efficiency in their manufacturing as larger companies: cost efficiency of scale all depends on the industry/product. This indicates that small and medium-size enterprises (SMEs) could be competitive within their product niche in a globalised industrial structure dominated by large units. With new technologies (FMS, 3D printing) becoming affordable for small firms, this opens up opportunities for small-scale operations adapted to local idiosyncrasies.

The opposite of economies of scale, diseconomies of scale, is not really considered in this instance. That means that the bigger the company, the more cost-inefficient it would be to run (it will be hard to fill the capacity, the technological risk becomes bigger, old-fashioned and rigid organisation). We have not seen any studies to demonstrate such connections. On the other hand, it has been shown that medium-sized companies may make greater progress in export markets than large companies. Solberg (1987, 1988) finds in a study of 114 Norwegian exporting companies that those considered successful had, on average, 400 employees, while those less successful were on average twice as big; the difference was statistically significant. This suggests that smaller organisations may have greater flexibility and ability to adapt to foreign markets than the larger ones. More recent studies in Norway show no statistical link between progress in export markets and size (Solberg et al. 2014).

2.5 Chapter summary – towards global competition?

We have seen that world trade – in the wake of trade and economic liberalisation – has gradually multiplied over recent decades. At the same time, certain sectors of the economy – for instance, services and agriculture – are hampered with protectionism. The emergence of multinational corporations has come along with the strong growth in trade, through foreign direct investments, in particular in the Triad of North America, West Europe and Japan (approximately 55% of FDI end up here). Alongside this development, the liberalisation of capital markets has triggered financial cross-border transactions. On the other hand, local consumption patterns seem to be more resilient. There are few signs of a convergence towards a pan-cultural consumption pattern – except for some famous global brands. Local consumption patterns still prevail in most countries.

Infrastructure such as telecommunications and transport have exploded both in terms of diffusion and cost efficiency. This has greatly reduced the role of physical distance as a barrier to trade. Development has also taken place in production technology where, on one hand, scale economies in the process and component industries have forced firms to extend their catchment area beyond their domestic markets, and on the other hand, flexible manufacturing systems in the finished goods industry have enabled firms to tailor their offerings and thereby enter new markets. This development is briefly summarised in Table 2.17.

Various industries are affected differently by this development. Figure 2.12 illustrates how some selected industries are located in this matrix of two dimensions: where there are structural barriers to entry characteristic of an industry, such as economies of scale or brand preferences; and the extent to which firms are affected by the globalisation trends as discussed above. Following this schema, we may classify industries into four categories: international and fragmented industries, national fragmented industries, global oligopolies and national oligopolies (or even monopolies). The last group of firms have the potential to become global if they are exposed to liberalisation forces. We have seen this in the telecoms business, where most countries had strict regulations leading to national monopolies or oligopolies. With the advent of mobile telephony in the early 1990s, these regulations were eased so as to allow foreign operators into many national markets. The position in the matrix of the telecoms industry then gradually moved towards the left-hand side of the model and the industry is possibly today – in spite of many local idiosyncrasies – one of the most global industries, with a handful of actors dominating the world scene. Transformation of industry

Table 2.17 Summary – main conclusions on globalisation factors

Factors	Globalisation drivers	Globalisation counter forces
New trade patterns	Development of BRICS (in particular China) and MINTS. Eastern Europe in EU.	Abandoned Doha round stalls the development of the global trading system.
FDI	25 trillion USD of FDI stock is increasingly benefiting emerging economies. Large MNCs build networks of subsidiaries in increasingly higher numbers of host countries.	In some cases, protectionism in host countries limits the diffusion of FDI.
Capital markets	Liberalisation of international capital markets creates opportunities – particularly for MNCs.	SMEs are not big enough to fully profit from this liberalisation. Tobin tax discussed – not yet implemented.
Consumption patterns	Emerging tendencies to pan-cultural consumers within certain product groups. International retailers prefer international brands. Internet is becoming a major force. Pan-European/international TV channels.	National culture and local consumption patterns still conspicuous. Few really global brands. Fragmented media picture in Europe and the world.
Trade treaties	Customs duties are insignificant (WTO, EU, NAFTA, etc.). New initiatives (i.e. CETA) potentially create a new dynamism in world trade. Regional free trade is on the increase.	Weak trade balance in the USA is a constant threat against trade liberalisation. Neo-nationalism and anti-globalisation sentiments (Brexit, USA, Netherlands, Hungary, Poland, France, etc). TTIP and TPP stalled. Regional free trade may lead to trading blocs that create barriers against other blocs.
Technology/ Environment	Scale economies in both process and down-stream encourage firms to internationalise. Transport and communications no longer represent obstacles in international trade.	Diseconomies of scale may give SMEs advantages in certain sectors → fragmented local industries.
Global oligopolies	FDI and strategic alliances by MNCs from both developed and emerging economies lead to global oligopolies.	Customer closeness and flexibility are increasingly important – offering opportunities for SMEs.

structure will follow different trajectories depending on how its underlying structure is affected by the globalisation trends. Some industries will most likely be more global as a result of technological developments and renewed efforts to further liberalise international exchange (in spite of Brexit and the American retreat from trade negotiations), whereas other industries will be less influenced, mainly because of fundamental structural factors such as tradition, climatic conditions that require special adaptations or few opportunities of scale economies.

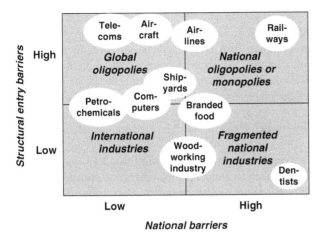

Figure 2.12 Industry classification – where do you belong?

Note: The location of the industries in the matrix is based on the author's assessments.

2.5.1 Global competition?

Globalisation is closely related to concentration of the competitive structure in international markets. Firms in small open economies such as the Nordic countries or in Benelux are active in this kind of market, some with considerable market shares. They are therefore exposed to this kind of competition (few market players and constant technological development) and depend on a dynamic development of their own competitive strengths. At the same time these firms should be able to achieve profits above those of their more locally-oriented counterparts, because they leverage their market position both nationally and internationally through better exploitation of resources in a more active network.

We may call the end result of this process a global industry structure or a global market, the most conspicuous features being the rise of internationally-oriented players that dominate large parts of central markets in the world. In some cases, this structure may be termed global oligopolies, but most often it resembles a more global monopolistic competitive structure – with fewer players, but where each individual firm has developed specific features in their offering differentiating them from their competitors. In such contexts, one will find market segments where even smaller firms with their special attributes will have a role to play. The rest of this chapter will discuss how this kind of market concentration has made an impact on the international economy.

2.5.2 Globalisation and global players

Concentration of economic power in the world's largest players has gradually increased over recent decades. The Fortune 500 (largest firms in the world) represent one-third of world GNP. This dominance is above all achieved through FDI, of which there are three groups: conglomerate, vertical and horizontal (or intra-industrial). Even if oligopolisation takes place in the two first groups (for example in the oil industry), it is particularly found in the horizontal FDIs (for instance the car industry, electronics industry, etc.).

BI Norwegian Business School has developed a globality index that measures the extent to which different industries can be termed global. The index consists of three factors: degree of concentration in the industry, degree of intra-industry trade, and trade barriers such as customs and quotas. This index is more complex than that of Ghemawat (2012), the latter only measuring industry concentration. Figure 2.13 shows this index for a number of selected industries. Least global on this list is dairy products and convenience food (16–17%), whereas aluminium, steel and pharmaceutical industries score far higher (between 30% and 41%). We may therefore conclude that there is a long way to go before most industries can be termed global; Ghemawat's concept of semi-globalisation may be more appropriate to describe the industry.

The pharmaceutical industry is a showcase in this context, see Table 2.18. Over the past two decades this industry in particular has been an arena for mega-mergers, such as the American firm Pfizer which has acquired or merged with a large number of other firms in the industry: in

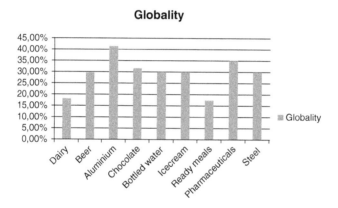

Figure 2.13 Globality index of selected industries.

Source: Burmo and Heedman (2014).

Table 2.18 World's ten largest pharmaceutical
companies, 2016

Company	USD bn
Johnson & Johnson, USA	70.0
Bayer, Germany	51.4
Novartis, Switzerland	49.4
Pfizer, USA	48.9
Roche, Switzerland	48.1
Merck, USA	39.5
Sanofi Genzyme, Switzerland	34.5
Gilead, USA	32.6
Astra Zeneca, UK/Sweden	24.7
GlaxoSmithKline, UK	23.9

Source: http://blog.proclinical.com/top-10-pharmaceutical-companies-2016.

1999, it merged with Warner Lambert (87 billion USD), in 2003 it bought the Swedish company Pharmacia (60 billion USD), and in 2009 it entered into a deal with the American firm Wyeth (59 billion USD). The last had been approached by a number of other contenders such as SmithKline in 1998. Number 3 on the list, Novartis, is the result of a merger between Ciba-Geigy and Sandoz, both based in Basel, Switzerland. Novartis also has big stakes in other pharmaceutical companies such as Roche (number 5 on the list). Smaller players have also been subject to acquisitions and mergers, such as the Norwegian company, Nycomed, in the course of the past 20 years, most recently by the Japanese pharmaceutical company, Takeda, number 13 on the list (not shown here).

Most of these mergers and acquisitions are entered into to secure technology or market power and access. Analysis of the industry globality should also include a more detailed investigation of each product area (anaesthetics, blood medicine, painkillers, cancer medicines, etc; there are hundreds of different product groups) as the competitive situation varies significantly between these.

In Norway, we find Weifa based in the small coastal town of Kragerø. The company is in the pink of health as a small player within the market for OTC (over the counter) medicines such as Paracetamol, Ibuprofen, etc. Their annual sales are around NOK 550 million – just around one per mille when compared with the largest pharmaceutical firms in the world. Weifa also exports precursors for the manufacture of medicines against diabetes. We find similar companies in most countries. In product areas that require heavy investments in R&D, the competitive situation leans towards global oligopoly.

Another example may be found in the petrochemical industry (plastics, man-made fibre, chemicals, etc.). Ineos is the world's third largest company within this sector. The company has grown gradually through mergers and the acquisition of a host of different units from a number of other firms across Europe, North America and Asia. Scandinavian companies have also been integrated into Ineos – Norsk Hydro (PVC) and Borealis (polyolefins). The venture started with management buying into BP's petrochemical complex in Antwerp in 1992. Through a bank mortgage, share offerings, equity companies and mergers, Ineos has evolved into a dominating factor in this industry worldwide, with 60 production units in 13 countries and a sales figure around 25 billion euros. The industry has gone through a dramatic reorganisation over the past two to three decades, partly as a response to increasing globalisation.

MNCs that operate in more locally-oriented (multi-local) markets do not represent the same level of threat to less internationalised SMEs. Industries such as furniture, construction, textiles/garments, parts of the food industry are examples of this. The industry structure is more fragmented and MNCs are not necessarily dominating in all markets, therefore reducing somewhat their oligopolistic gains. Smaller and local firms may in such cases control special market niches and maintain a high profitability through such control. Even so, we may conclude that MNCs throughout the 1980s, 1990s and 2000s could boast a markedly enlarged position in international markets.

2.5.3 Strategic alliances – oligopoly without FDI?

A strategic alliance (SA) is a partnership between two or more firms that wish to pursue one or several goals, but still want to remain independent. The participants share the value creation and contribute essential resources (market access/network, R&D, technology, capital, etc.) in order to reach the goals of the alliance (Yoshino and Rangan 1995). These alliances are not registered on a regular basis in the statistics, which therefore do not capture the whole picture. The last statistics available are from OECD (2000)[47] and show that in the period between 1989 and 1999 more than 60,000 strategic alliances had been registered across the world. Marketing alliances represented around 30% of all the contracts. The frequency of SAs varies dramatically over the years, 1995 seemingly being a top year with more than 9,000 SAs registered and 1989 a low year with only around 1,000 deals. We may assume that this development has continued into this century. The car industry is well known for engaging in SAs as shown below.

> Players in this industry have entered into numerous cooperative dealings with a range of different objectives. Mercedes and Mitsubishi have agreed to develop processes for recycling scrapped cars, as these represent an increasing challenge throughout the world. In Scandinavia, Volvo has represented Renault's sales, marketing and service organisation. These two companies also joined forces to cooperate in purchasing components and parts – for instance, using the same engines in several of their models. Honda has entered into a cooperation with the South Korean company Daewoo to produce Honda's top model, Legend. The two German rivals Daimler and BMW have decided to enter into a purchasing cooperation deal, allegedly achieving materials savings in the order of 4 billion euros.[48] In China, foreign automotive manufacturers are only allowed to produce cars if they enter into joint ventures with local Chinese firms, and indeed virtually all Western car manufacturers are present in China through strategic alliances. But investments now go also in the other direction; for instance the Swedish flagship, Volvo, was sold to Zhejiang Geely Holding Group of China in 2010 after a long courting period with different kinds of cooperation.[49]

2.5.4 Strategic orientation of MNCs

MNCs operating in many countries do not necessarily contribute to increased globalisation of industry, in the meaning we attribute to it in our context. Many MNCs have developed a market presence in individual *local* markets *without* resorting to central coordination of the individual units in the group, usually required to get a uniform identity and to leverage the diversity of resources represented in the group. Traditionally, European companies have been more oriented towards such local "self-rule" than American companies. Through acquisitions of

Table 2.19 Largest breweries in the world

Company	Share (%) of production
AB InBev	18.1
SAB/Miller	9.7
Heineken	8.8
Carlsberg	6.2
China Resource Snow	5.4

local firms, some MNCs choose to retain the original local brand and local market strategy in order to sustain the local market share of the acquired company, and without any regard to the international product portfolio of the MNC. This multi-local marketing strategy then contributes to reduce the global effects and to allow the entrance of smaller firms into the market.

One case in point is the beer industry, where the five largest groups control around 40% of world production.[50]

However, this production covers hundreds of different brands which were acquired over the past two decades. Even though this confers great power in their negotiations with the distribution channels, it also opens up a space for smaller breweries to cater to specific wants and needs in the market. Microbreweries pop up all around the world: in Berlin alone there are 19 such businesses;[51] in Ireland – once the home of 200 local breweries the number is now 16;[52] in Norway with two large groups dominating the market, there are at least 9 microbreweries.[53] Great Britain may be the world leader in microbreweries where around one thousand firms are registered.[54]

Nevertheless, more and more companies try to centralise their decision-making processes in order to leverage resources and capabilities in their network of subsidiaries and partners. The development in information and communication technologies makes such centralisation and coordination a more viable alternative for many companies. The result of this exercise is a more global orientation of MNCs.

3M underwent such great changes in the nineties. This is an American MNC that develops and markets a wide variety of products: data discs, post-it pads, road signs. Based on a wish to rationalise across borders and to enable the organisation to make faster and more effective decisions, the European arm of the company moved the strategic and operational responsibility from 19 local business centres to its head office in Paris. Activities such as logistics, IT, human resource development and finance have been moved from the smaller subsidiaries to ten regional centres. At the same time, national differences have been emphasised in the marketing of its products.[55] This is what Bartlett and Ghoshal term a "transnational" company – i.e. a company that is present "all over the world" with locally-adapted product propositions, but at the same time coordinating the activities between the different units of the company.

2.5.5 Flexibility and close to the customer

Increased globalisation implies new opportunities for the MNC. What then happens with the customer? Will the local adaptations vanish on the altar of economies of scale? Will marketing in all countries become more or less uniform? We do not believe that this will happen in the foreseeable future, partly because some activities necessarily need to be carried out locally in the country where the transaction takes place. Sales, service functions, design of selected marketing activities and R&D may be such activities. Porter (1986) mentions several industries that have gone a long way in their globalisation process, such as aircraft, electronic products and automobile manufacturers. Aircraft manufacturing is mentioned as one of the most globalised industries because companies – with a strong emphasis on coordination – concentrate their production activities and because their closeness to customers enables them to adapt (equipment, interior design, etc.) the planes to meet their demands. Also, the car industry is an example of companies with a global approach and at the same time maintaining a customer focus. They receive invaluable feedback from their dealer and service networks and translate this – enabled by robotics – into models that are more or less adapted to each market.

Even though there is a trend towards larger and fewer units in most industries, we also see that SMEs can survive in a global market. For example, in a small country like Norway (with around five million inhabitants), many SMEs are world leaders in their respective product areas. Contrary to the generally-received wisdom, it appears that many of these have better returns on sale than their much larger counterparts. The main reason for this is their ability to operate with slim organisations – implying both lower overhead costs and smoother decision processes, which again facilitates a flexible approach to customers. Furthermore, SMEs that operate internationally are generally driven into developing narrow market niches, catering to special needs and special solutions, which are out of reach for their bigger MNC "cousins" which seek economies of scale.

In Norway these companies are found in equipment manufacturing, supplying the oil and gas industry, but also in a number of other sectors such as snow ploughs for airports, ski wax, fishing gear/hooks, gas and chemical ship valves, electronic safes for hotels, just to mention a few. Each of these has carved out a market niche in which they are world leaders. Some of them have been subject to acquisition by larger MNCs but operate independently of their parent companies.

2.5.6 Summary

Globalisation affects in some way or another virtually all industries. It is therefore important for the individual firm to assess the implications of globalisation for its future strategy. One outcome of the globalisation trends is global oligopolies or monopolistic competition, represented by an increasing number of MNCs. These companies have over the years increased their influence through FDIs and strategic alliances, and thereby strengthened their market position. For instance, the 500 largest companies in the world represent around one-third of world GNP. Intracompany trade within MNCs represents some 30–40% of the foreign trade in countries such as the US, Japan and Great Britain.

The factors leading to such competitive structures are first and foremost:

1   The firm's ability to leverage technological advances and economies of scale;
2   A radically improved telecommunications infrastructure; and
3   Liberalisation of international trade and financial markets.

To a lesser extent – and only in some selected sectors – pan-cultural consumption patterns play a role in this context. With Brexit, the US under President Trump and emerging nationalism particularly in Europe, many ask themselves whether the world is heading towards de-globalisation.

A major issue in this respect is the shift of economic power in the world towards the East. We have seen how the rise of China is challenging the economic predominance of the US. China's accession to economic wealth also has given its government a more assertive stance in regional politics – claiming the rights to vast and contested areas in the Yellow Sea and South China Sea – and thereby bringing it in conflict with its neighbours, some of which are allies with the US. At the same time, the Chinese now seem to be the new champions of free trade, strongly advocating continued efforts to liberalise trade and investment regimes. Other major countries such as India and Indonesia also aspire to join the bandwagon of economic growth. A possible scenario for the next decade is that, as the US is withdrawing from or reducing its participation in international trade coalitions, the Chinese and other emerging nations will see their opportunity to take the lead. This will probably not happen without conflicts (Rachman 2016). This movement towards the East – termed *easternisation* (Rachman 2016) – also implies that market opportunities shift from the "traditional", developed markets to emerging markets in the East. The movement towards these markets started 25–30 years ago, but will most likely continue and be strengthened in the future. Furthermore, it follows that competition from this part of the world will become more conspicuous than before: 103 of the world's 500 largest companies are Chinese, 134 are American.

Firms of all sizes need to consider how they are affected by this development. We shall in the rest of Part I explore how a firm's resources and its position in the nine strategic windows affect its strategic choice.

Notes

1 http://www.mapsofworld.com/minerals/world-bauxite-producers.html
2 http://www.yarnsandfibers.com/preferredsupplier/reports_fullstory.php?id=560
3 http://web.a.ebscohost.com.ezproxy.library.bi.no/ehost/pdfviewer/pdfviewer?sid=6899ea9e-b1d9-417f-9d44-170a6d4f3088%40sessionmgr4003&vid=5&hid=4214
4 Crude oil was priced at around 1.2 USD/barrel in 1970 (price adjusted to 2017 it was around 20 USD). At its peak in 2012 it reached 155 USD/barrel (sources: http://www.macrotrends.net/1369/crude-oil-price-history-chart and https://www.statista.com/statistics/262858/change-in-opec-crude-oil-prices-since-1960/).
5 *The Economist:* http://www.economist.com/node/18586448
6 The sections on gravity models of trade are mainly based on Solberg et al. (2014).
7 Various models are used: for instance, with and without oil export, and with and without cultural distance.
8 http://www.economist.com/blogs/graphicdetail/2014/05/chinese-and-american-gdp-forecasts. Several other sources claim this position will be reached sooner. In 2010, the forecast was that China would not reach this position until 2030.
9 https://www.forbes.com/sites/rrapier/2016/04/11/where-america-gets-its-oil-the-top-10-suppliers-of-u-s-oil-imports/#9177884264c3
10 Grubel and Lloyd (1975) were the first to measure such trade. They defined it using the following formula: $IIT_i = [1 - |X_i - M_i|/(X_i + M_i)]$, where i is industry, X is export and M import. They found that the share of the intra-industrial trade increased from 36% in 1959 to 48% in 1967.
11 These are, of course, no longer considered newcomers. But they were when they were established towards the end of the 1970s and fighting large established companies such as IBM.
12 http://www.tradingeconomics.com/china/gdp-per-capita
13 http://www.businessinsider.com/the-25-poorest-countries-in-the-world-2016-4?r=UK&IR=T&IR=T/#25-tanzania–gdp-per-capita-2054-1430-1
14 http://www.oecd.org/dev/pgd/economydevelopingcountriessettoaccountfornearly60ofworldgdp-by2030accordingtonewestimates.htm
15 http://www.reuters.com/article/us-pirelli-chemchina-idUSKBN0MI0PQ20150323
16 Lomé and Cotonou are the capitals in Togo and Bénin respectively.
17 Parts of this section are based on C.A. Solberg: "Globalisering og Norges konkurranseevne." *Magma* nr. 3 1998.
18 http://www.corporationsandhealth.org/2015/08/27/the-100-largest-governments-and-corporations-by-revenue/

19 Norwegian market leader in chocolates and confectionaries, Freia, was acquired by Kraft Industries in 1993.
20 For those interested, see Birkinshaw and Hood (1998), which includes numerous article contributions from central researchers on this field.
21 http://www.china-bluestar.com/lanxingen/gywm/zzjg/webinfo/2012/01/1325312701595534.htm
22 This hypothesis has not been tested in a bigger setting, but research suggests that an ever-increasing share of MNC patents originate from the second companies abroad (see Cantwell and Harding 1997). This supports the idea that MNCs to a greater extent than before delegate central tasks to their foreign second companies.
23 *Wall Street Journal*, 28 January 2014.
24 WTO – http://www.wto.org/english/res_e/statis_e/quarterly_world_exp_e.htm
25 http://www.swift.com/about_swift/shownews?param_dcr=news.data/en/swift_com/2013/PR_RMB_september.xml
26 https://www.focus-economics.com/country-indicator/russia/trade-balance
27 Named after the Nobel Prize winner James Tobin. He suggested a uniform international tax to be placed on every currency transaction. Purely speculative transactions would therefore be taxed relatively heavily, because they occur very frequently – often several times a day.
28 In Norwegian: *Naturens Nei: om EU, frihandel og økologisk kaos.*
29 Author of the book *When Corporations Rule the World* (Korten 1995).
30 https://www.bloomberg.com/news/articles/2016-12-16/the-inside-story-of-apple-s-14-billion-tax-bill
31 http://en.wikipedia.org/wiki/EF_English_Proficiency_Index. Such numbers carry great ambiguity, and to what degree each person masters English varies greatly.
32 *Financial Times*, 5 April 1998.
33 Jane Martinson in the *Financial Times* supplement on export, October 1996.
34 Most Asian religions are pantheistic; they find the divine in all things, while Christianity, Judaism and Islam are all monotheistic, with a belief in a distinct God separate to the world.
35 http://worldjusticeproject.org/sites/default/files/files/wjp_rule_of_law_index_2014_report.pdf
36 FOB=Free on Board in port of shipping, CIF=Cost Insurance Freight to the port of unloading, Ex works=at the gate of the factory.
37 TGI Europa Study 2013.
38 https://www.wto.org/english/tratop_e/dispu_e/dispu_by_country_e.htm
39 https://crawford.anu.edu.au/pdf/pep/pep-310.pdf (Trade conflict between Japan and the United States over market access: the case of automobiles and automotive parts); David E. Sanger, "A deal on auto trade: the agreement US settles trade dispute, averting billion tariffs on Japanese luxury autos", *New York Times*, 29 June 1995; https://www.nytimes.com/2014/05/24/business/wto-ruling-on-chinese-tariffs-on-us-cars.html
40 http://www.differencebetween.net/miscellaneous/politics/differences-between-g8-and-g20/#ixzz4b-CH9ACs0
41 This is before the United Kingdom leaves the union – see below.
42 http://ec.europa.eu/trade/policy/countries-and-regions/countries/united-states/
43 http://www.lefigaro.fr/economie/le-scan-eco/explicateur/2017/01/21/29004-20170121ART-FIG00140-ceta-ce-qu-il-faut-savoir-sur-ce-traite-de-libre-echange-negocie-entre-l-ue-et-le-canada.php
44 http://www.imsf.info/Seabourne_Trade.html
45 http://www.iata.org/pressroom/pr/pages/2012-12-06-01.aspx
46 http://www.comcec.org/UserFiles/File/ulastirma/COMCEC-drwalid-present-final.pdf
47 Thomson Financial Securities Data: http://www.Olis.oecd.org/olis/2000doc.nsf/LinkTo/DSTI-DOC(2000)5
48 http://www.dw.com/en/cooperation-is-the-key-to-success-in-the-auto-sector/a-14779014
49 https://en.wikipedia.org/wiki/Geely
50 http://www.therichest.com/expensive-lifestyle/entertainment/top-five-largest-beer-brewing-companies-in-the-world/?view=all
51 http://www.visitberlin.de/en/keyword/brewerie
52 http://www.ireland.com/en-us/articles/ireland-microbreweries/
53 http://travelsquire.com/norways-mighty-microbreweries/
54 https://en.wikipedia.org/wiki/List_of_breweries_in_England#Breweries_in_England
55 *Financial Times*, 10 October 1993.

3 The internationalisation process and firm resources

3.1. Introduction

The paths businesses take to international markets have been subject to a great number of studies over the years. We may divide these contributions into two main schools: the economic school looks at internationalisation as a rational decision process based on objective economic estimations, such as market assessments, profitability and risks. The school of gradual internationalisation – also called the "Uppsala school of thought"[1] – propounds that internationalisation is a more or less conscious development of the firm, but also includes factors such as personal motives by managers or pure coincidences in the market during the initial phases of the export activity. As the firm gains experience, it will make conscious and rational decisions regarding its internationalisation.

This chapter will discuss different explanations of the internationalisation process of businesses. Insight into this process helps us understand how the firm is better able to exploit and develop its resources and competencies in international markets. In this context, we will also examine differences between what we may term successful and less successful exporters. The chapter focuses on mechanisms that lead the firm to seek international market opportunities and how information and experience form the bases for decisions; how the firm may (and should) tie up with partners to fill the gap of its deficiencies of its own resources; and not the least, how networks may contribute in this endeavour.

3.2. Stages of internationalisation

3.2.1 Internationalisation is a learning process

Internationalisation is learning: learning about strategies that work in different markets, about how to cooperate with partners in other countries, about how products and market activities should be adapted to local market conditions, about how to create preferences in different markets, how to secure managerial and financial resources to support the process, and so on. A firm will normally have insufficient access to information about market opportunities in the initial phases of this process, nor will it always have sufficient understanding of the risks associated with export initiatives. They will start export activities in their "blissful ignorance" and proceed through fearless spirit and a firm belief in their own products, until they meet difficulties that are more or less insurmountable. Examples of problems include agent behaviour that you do not understand because of cultural differences, leading to inevitable misinterpretations; currency fluctuations or unforeseen payment problems; costly product adaptations or other problems that the exporter is not prepared to meet. To illustrate the issue at hand we will take a closer look at three firms with largely the same point of departure. However, they seek widely different solutions to their entry in the German market:

A Norwegian supplier of traditional winter sportswear wants to start exporting. Management gets in touch with Innovation Norway (Norway's public industrial and export promotion agent) because they have heard rumours of an opportunity to participate in the Norwegian pavilion at the winter sport ISPO Messe (trade fair) in Munich in February. This is a major event in the sports gear and wear industry, gathering several hundred thousand businesspeople – mainly from Europe, but also from other parts of the world. The great advantage to participating at such a national pavilion – they are told – is that the firm is stronger (together with other exhibitors and with the national identity), sharing the costs, and in addition, one gets professional assistance before, during and after the event. The firm agrees to participate and starts preparations to identify products and develop display material, etc. They meet fifteen other exporters who will participate at the pavilion, exchange experience and get good advice. Well-established at ISPO, they meet the other Norwegian exporters and also German and other retailers who are interested in their products; Norway is after all a well-known winter sports nation, at least in the industry. The firm also gets in touch with a number of potential agents and expresses an interest in representing them in Germany – and other countries as well. Total costs: 165,000 NOK, of which 50,000 is covered by subsidies through Innovation Norway. Result: interesting contacts with potential agents and retailers that need to be followed up once they get home.

After a week, our friends get back home to the usual "jog trot" and to unattended business: pending meetings and appointments, Norwegian customers have to be followed up, concerns with unresolved personnel conflicts, suppliers that lag behind, bank relations to be nurtured, etc. Also, they have to make up lost time with their families. After two weeks, the marketing manager eventually finds time to follow up their new contacts in Germany and elsewhere. The problem is, however, that the present-mindedness of the ISPO Messe has now faded, and some of the persons that they met are not easy to remember. Even though they made good notes about the different wishes of the individual possible agents and buyers, details about their capabilities and potential are unclear. The marketing manager writes to some of them, makes appointments to meet with them and to further explore possible leads. Negotiation turns out to be difficult because the manager does not know the market conditions, and insists on contract clauses that the German partner finds difficult to satisfy. Perhaps they will end up with a contract, perhaps not; perhaps they will end up with a certain sale, perhaps not.

Compare this with their competitor. The manager of this firm decides to spend winter holidays in Garmisch Partenkirchen (a well-known winter sport resort in Germany) with his family. He too got in touch with Innovation Norway, but this time to get information on retailers worth visiting in the resort. He loads his Hi-Ace with the products he deems most interesting (after consultation with Innovation Norway), and heads with his family to southern Germany. They arrive late at night, but the following morning they go skiing and enjoy the sun and the German Alps. In the afternoon our marketing manager visits the retailers that were recommended to him, while the rest of the family still hangs around on the slopes. He gets in touch with the owner, asks him about suppliers, styles, fashion, customers, etc. and shows him the product range of the firm and asks whether he can leave behind some items for possible sale (at an agreed price). During a short week, he has established an agreeable relationship with two retailers that are willing to carry his products, as long as the products satisfy the quality requirements and the firm meets deadlines and the agreed quantities. Our friend promises to do his best, and returns to Norway with a happy family, and having made two new friends (Helga and Fritz). Total costs: 30,000 NOK. Result: a trial order of 20,000 NOK to two potential customers that he knows quite well (including their position in the local market, their competitors and ways of doing business), potential sales of 100,000 NOK in the first year and some knowledge about the local market in Garmisch Partenkirchen – and a family that comes home with a positive experience!

After a week, our friend gets back home to the usual "jog trot" and to unattended business: pending meetings and appointments, Norwegian customers have to be followed up, concerns with unresolved personnel conflicts, suppliers that lag behind, bank relations to be entertained, etc. After two weeks the marketing manager finds time to follow up his new German friends. The first trial orders can be dispatched. Both Fritz and Helga are happy with the supplies and place orders for more. The next year, our friend visits Garmisch Partenkirchen with his family and he reinforces the relations with his new friends. He asks advice about potential representatives in Germany, and after one more year the firm has an agent in Bavaria. He has managed to negotiate a good contract, because he has, with his own eyes and with assistance from Fritz and Helga, experienced what marketing is like in Germany. In this way, he has a good background to negotiate a better contract with the agent.

The third firm also participates at the ISPO trade fair. Ahead of the trade fair, the firm had been in contact with the large Intersport retail chain and during the week of the event they succeed in building good relationship with their purchasing manager. He reveals great interest in the firm's products and the enthusiasm in the export sales team is high towards the end of the week when Intersport places a trial order of 259,000 NOK, with an option of further orders if the products hold what they promise in the market place.

After a week, our friend gets back home to the usual "jog trot" and to unattended business: pending meetings and appointments, Norwegian customers have to be followed up, concerns with unresolved personnel conflicts, suppliers that lag behind, bank relations to be entertained, etc. Also, they have to make up lost time with their families. After two weeks, the marketing manager finds time to follow up their new German friends; the first shipment is dispatched.

The first trial shipment is well received by Intersport, and new orders are coming in. At the end of the year, sales reaches 3 million NOK and the year after the German market is more important than the home market. Goods worth 7 million NOK are now finding their way to Germany and Intersport's retailers. One problem however is that the margins on this business are rather low. Prices are under pressure and the organisation is devoting a disproportionate amount of time to satisfying its new foreign customer. Complaints of late deliveries from established Norwegian customers begin to come in. The firm does not get much information of what is happening out in the market place; it is more than busy filling orders from production and dispatching the goods in time. In the third year of contract negotiations, the managers find that competitors have entered the scene. Sales of 10 million NOK are possible but further discounts are expected as the competitors can offer not only far better prices, but also marketing support in the local German market. The firm is forced to accept new sales conditions or disrupt its ongoing business in Germany.

The account of the second firm is possibly somewhat glorified, and other outcomes of this approach are perceivable – such as the inability of the manager to get access to the local retailers, or that they did not manage to fulfil the orders to their satisfaction concerning quality or delivery time, or that the retailers were only marginal players in the market and that their advice about further operations in Germany therefore was inappropriate. The lesson we draw from the three cases is that a gradual approach to new markets secures a stepwise learning about local market conditions and a stepwise adaptation of a firm's resources to match the demands of the market and thereby increased control of both partners and resources.

A number of researchers have termed this learning process a stepwise process towards international markets. Penrose (1959) claims that firms will typically seek internally-generated growth as a result of pressures from different parts of the organisation. These pressures may stem from a desire to better exploit a firm's resources, or the testing of a new idea. Aharoni (1966) – studying foreign direct investments of American firms – maintains that firms consist of different individuals who work under hard and continuous pressure. Confronted with uncertainty and incomplete information, managers will not be able to make so-called rational decisions. He concludes that such decisions result from gradually increasing involvement by key managers in the organisation.

3.2.2 The Bakka model

Bakka (1973) was among the first to describe an internationalisation model in phases – from what he termed trial export, via extensive and intensive export to international marketing. His model describes factors that are assumed to affect the decision-making process in the different stages. For instance, the first export advances are thought to be a response to the initiative of others (such as request from abroad, existing local customers' own internationalisation, or an invitation to participate in government sponsored export initiatives) or to pressures from new competition at home. The main challenges for managers in this first trial export phase are:

–   Scant knowledge or expertise in the more technical aspects of exporting (international payments, currencies, freight, customs clearance, import regulations, standards, market research, etc). The first approach to export markets therefore is an onerous experience for most beginners, simply because too many technical mistakes are being made. For instance, a "straightforward" thing such as a credit line is one such pitfall; in Northern Europe the normal credit line is 30 days or less, whereas in Southern Europe, the credit often stretches over three months or more.
–   Insufficient knowledge about elementary conditions (structure in the distribution system, potential customers, competition) in the foreign market. Such ignorance increases the risk of engaging in business relations that may be detrimental to the beginner. For example it is not all that certain that an SME should have its first involvement in German trade with a large retailer such as Intersport; or that Norwegian strawberry exporters should sell through the large retailer Tesco in the UK. These firms play in a far different league from small first-time exporters. Even though big contracts may appear more than appealing to newcomers, this dimension (large customer) adds to the other challenges that they meet. The problem lies in that – because of limited market insight – these firms end up relating with the "wrong" customers or distribution channels. The exporter risks being trapped in an unwanted customer strategy over a certain period of time.
–   "All parts" of the firm should be involved in the export venture, and in particular, all top managers. This may possibly be the most important challenge, particularly in the initial phases of the export project. The saying "things take time" is of particular relevance in this context. The "thing" here is learning the rules of the game. Gripsrud et al. (2006) found a

demarcation line of five years: it often takes five years – sometimes longer – to develop the skills and insights necessary to reap the full benefits of the export sales and marketing investment. A small firm with limited financial resources will, in this setting, be confronted with demanding challenges. Confronted with such challenges – that often translate into poor financial results – members of top management often vacillate in their enthusiasm for the export venture. Also larger firms that start exporting will experience the same problem, not because of lack of financial resources, but because – with impatient accountants and financial managers – their time horizon is normally much shorter.

If the firm survives the trial export phase, the firm often enters into some sort of over-confidence – the *extensive export phase*. Here the exporter makes arrangements with a number of overseas agents and distributors – without really having the resources to follow up all the leads. Our friend in the first case above illustrates this point. Quite often the final objective is unclear, the general manager alone is carrying out the main activities such as visiting their partners in different markets, and the necessary export organisation is not being built up. The learning process about market conditions is limping because inadequate resources do not allow time or people to get deeply involved with local players (partners, customers and so on), and therefore customer loyalty is not being established. They discover that competition is different, using different marketing tools, often operating more aggressively than they are used to at home. Sales may have shown growth, but costs also have an awkward tendency to increase. Visiting all four corners of the world to entertain relationships with their new partners is particularly onerous. Profitability – if any – is therefore often dwindling in this phase of the export venture.

A manufacturer of high end PA (public address) products expressed this in another way: "I set the fishing net in many lakes; then I will see where the catch is good – and then I can concentrate my efforts on this lake." The consequence – however – is the same: spreading the resources on too many markets and – to continue to use the fishing metaphor – "hitting too many reefs on the way to haul the fishing nets in from too many lakes". The lesson for this firm was that before setting the net, they should have taken a closer look at the "sea map", and discussed with some "local fishermen" where to find the good catch.

The following example demonstrates how a firm reacted to this negative development.

A Scandinavian manufacturer of high quality sports gear with a solid position in its home market exported goods valued at 500,000 euros (about 20% of its total sales) to more than 30 markets, i.e. around 17,000 euros per market on average, but with some markets such as the US taking more than half of the exports, leaving the other markets with insignificant volumes and occasional sales. The managing director was directly responsible for export sales. A weakening dollar together with keener competition from low-cost suppliers both in the US and at home prompted a redefinition of the total marketing strategy of the firm:

- They deliberately set a goal to increase exports.
- They engaged an export manager to alleviate the burden of the managing director.
- They reduced the number of markets in order to concentrate on the few remaining areas.

After three years, the results of this shift in strategy showed that the firm achieved a stronger foothold and increased sales in a limited number of selected export markets. After some years, it acquired other sport gear manufacturers in order to better exploit their networks and sales organisation in those markets.

This firm then entered stage three in Bakka's model – *intensive exports*. The main product offering is still based on products developed for the domestic market, but with necessary adjustments; and it is still the sales people from headquarters at home who visit the export markets. However, the firm is slowly being coloured by the exporting activity and more people in the organisation are being involved in the venture. Exporting is now on the agenda in management and board meetings, and is a regular operation – including maintaining established relationships with local partners in overseas markets. As its experience grows richer, the firm is now in a position to make rational decisions based on reliable market insights. It will prune the product portfolio so as to achieve economies of scale on the products that yield the best rewards across markets, and it will withdraw from marginal and unprofitable markets and rather concentrate on primary markets.

The fourth stage, *international marketing*, requires management to make two important acknowledgements: first, the export activity is now seen as an active vehicle to attain the firm's goals, in line with home market activities. Secondly, it may now have reached more than 30– 40% of total sales and constitutes an integrated and inescapable part of the firm's strategy. Particularly for businesses from so-called SMOPECS (Small Open Economies such as for instance Nordic or Benelux countries) it is mainly from foreign markets that the most important growth impulses are generated, both in terms of sales, but possibly also in terms of product development. The home market is limited and a tougher competitive climate gives few opportunities to expand at home – except for diversification into different industries. The result is an increased dependence on international sales. Management must assess operation modes, possibly switching from independent partners in key markets to own sales subsidiaries.

On the other hand, its products or services must now be actively marketed by the firm itself. In other words, the firm must now collect detailed market information, set clear objectives for its operations overseas (market shares, brand image, etc.) and develop a strategy to reach its objectives. This includes market selection and segmentation; operation mode; product adaptation and development; active pricing, sales and distribution strategies; market communications and the export organisation.

Solberg (1986) later extended the model to include a fifth stage, *global marketing*, where standardisation of the marketing mix, control through foreign direct investments and a more uniform approach to the different markets are typical features. Figure 3.1 shows how the different phases in this model typically unfold with regard to a number of variables: from export motives, through different marketing mix elements to the export organisation. This is, of course, a very simplified model and the gradual process may not happen as distinctively and specifically as depicted here. On the other hand, it suggests a pattern that may well happen and helps managers avoid the many pitfalls in the course of this process. Figure 3.1 summarises the process described above.

3.2.3 The Uppsala school of thought

Johanson and Wiedersheim-Paul (1975) and, two years later, Johanson and Vahlne (1977) at the University of Uppsala (Sweden) drew our attention to the experience loop between the firm and its market, including the feedback to the business of information, market insight and operative

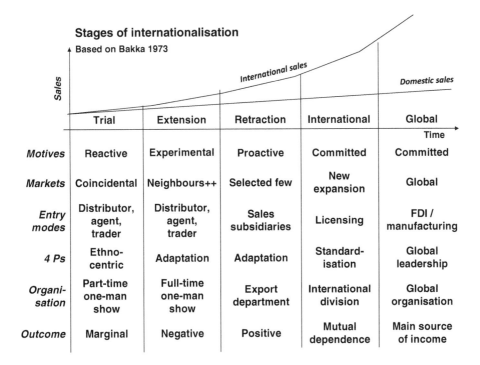

Figure 3.1 The internationalisation process.

experience. Based on this knowledge the firm, they claim, is in a position to take bolder steps abroad in line with Bakka's (1973) assumption. Johanson and Vahlne (1977) assume that firms in the introductory stages of their international venture tend to go for a cautious approach along two dimensions:

1   The nature of markets entered (neighbouring/similar to home market). Johanson and Vahlne (1977) term this as low psychic distance to the markets, reducing what they call "liability of foreignness". This implies that firms are less vulnerable to cultural and other differences between their home market and their first export markets.
2   The preferred entry mode is indirect, such as through local agents or distributors, implying lower risk compared with, for instance, creating a firm's own sales subsidiaries.

Only later, when they have acquired more knowledge and market insight, will exporters be prepared to take on more audacious steps to international markets further afield, and direct investments in sales subsidiaries. Johanson and Wiedersheim-Paul (1975) call the process an establishment chain defined in four stages, based on observations in four Swedish inter-nationalised firms: no regular export, independent representative (agent), sales subsidiary, production. The basic idea is that, as firms gain more experience and knowledge, they are prepared to make more commitments to the international venture.

Figure 3.2 shows how the interaction between the firm and its market gradually builds experience (the spirals indicating gradual accumulation of experience that goes on "forever"). We may therefore conclude that the internationalisation process in many ways is a *learning process*.

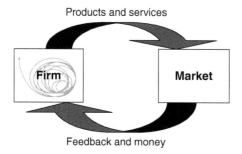

Products and services

Firm

Market

Feedback and money

Figure 3.2 Internationalisation is learning.

Around the same time, two American researchers, Bilkey and Tesar (1977), presented a internationalisation model in six stages:

–   Stage One. Management is not interested in exporting; would not even fulfil an unsolicited export order.
–   Stage Two. Management would fill an unsolicited export order, but makes no effort to explore the feasibility of exporting.
–   Stage Three (which can be skipped if unsolicited export orders are received). Management actively explores the feasibility of exporting.
–   Stage Four. The firm exports on an experimental basis to some psychologically close country.
–   Stage Five. The firm is an experienced exporter to that country and adjusts exports optimally to changing exchange rates, tariffs, etc.
–   Stage Six. Management explores the feasibility of exporting to additional countries that, psychologically, are further away.

Stompa Møbelfabrikk (a manufacturer of furniture for children), located near Trondheim in Norway, is one example of the unwilling exporter. They had participated at a trade fair at the Bella Centre in Copenhagen, Denmark, but they only got one genuine request – from a French mail order company. The firm was, until that day, unacquainted with this mode of distribution. At the time, in Norway, it was in fact viewed as a channel promoting low quality products. They were therefore sceptical when they got the request. They did not follow it up after the trade fair because France was not at all on their mind when they decided to participate at the trade fair. Management was however unaware that mail order was (and still is) a major channel in the furniture business in France, and that the interest from the French firm gave an exciting opportunity to start exporting. The French were nevertheless not willing to give up what they regarded as an interesting opportunity and travelled – after the rejection by the Stompa management – to Trondheim and insisted on buying from them. This appeared to be the start of a successful export venture: after a few years they had achieved sales of some 8 million NOK (about 1 million euros) to the French market. The firm developed sales to other European markets and underwent several of the stages in the Bilkey and Tesar model.

The stepwise internationalisation model of gradual learning and increased commitment has received support from many researchers (Cavusgil 1980, Luostarinen 1980a, Piercy 1981, Czinkota and Johnston 1983, Solberg 1987, 1988). The other hypotheses of the model – gradually stronger integration and expansion to more distant markets – have not to the same extent been supported by research. Nordström (1990) did not find evidence of Swedish firms starting in the Nordic countries, continuing in Europe and then later expanding overseas. He found that firms first establish sales subsidiaries in Germany, UK and US, before they enter the Nordic countries. In this way he got support for the economic-oriented theory of the role played by market attractiveness (i.e. market size), rather than low risk (i.e. cultural and financial). Also research from Norway reveals a different expansion pattern concerning foreign direct investments from the "rings-in-the-water" model (Benito and Gripsrud 1992). However, the selection of a country for FDI is a different matter, since FDIs are generally made at later stages of the process. In the service sector, other patterns exist. For instance, in the banking industry, international expansion is motivated by the appeal of international finance centres and by the attractiveness of being located close to financial sources rather than customers (Engwall and Wallenstål 1988, Grubel 1989). In the advertising industry, "follow-thy-customer", market size and competitive reaction ("if you enter my market, then I'll enter yours") have been important drivers of inter-national involvement of advertising agencies (Terpstra and Wu 1988). Also, the estab-lishment chain hypothesis (first independent entry mode, then switching to sales subsidiaries and then own production facility) has been questioned. Reid (1983), Turnbull (1987) and Rosson (1987) claim that this hypothesis is too deterministic and that other factors than market knowledge and experience affect entry mode and expansion patterns. They maintain that *internalisation* (as opposed to *internationalisation*) has far more impact on the choice of entry mode. We will return to this discussion in Chapter 7 (Operation modes).

Figure 3.3 suggests that, even though exporters need to partner with local firms (agents, distributors, licensees, franchisees, etc.), they risk seeing the partner "taking over the show", carrying out the marketing activities and as a result accruing most of the market knowledge, leaving only "crumbs" of learning for the exporter. The critical issue for the exporter, therefore, is to make sure in the contract – and to make allowances in the resource planning – that sales and marketing people from their organisation also get directly involved in the local marketing so as to secure the learning feedback loop.

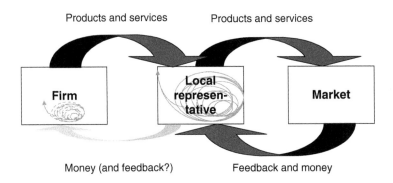

Figure 3.3 Who is learning here?

3.3. The role of networks

Johanson and Mattson (1986) suggest that theories of internationalisation must include the following elements:

–   The interaction between the business and its environment
–   Internal processes within the organisation
–   The firm's resources and activities
–   The various entry modes and expansion patterns, and their effects on interorganisational relations.

We have already discussed the three first bullet points; the fourth point needs further elaboration. Interorganisational relations in Johanson and Mattson's parlance implies networks as a critical factor in the internationalisation process. Later, in 2009, Johanson and Vahlne discuss this problem. They suggest the term "liability of outsidership" – that is, being disadvantaged as a result of not belonging to a particular network in international markets – as a more critical factor in the process than their original term "liability of foreignness". Without access to networks, the firm will not be able to expand in international markets. The role of such networks is first and foremost to reduce the uncertainty that any player experiences when seeking cooperation with new partners. Or rather, on a positive note: give the exporter a feeling of confidence.

> The relatively small horticultural firm that, in the wake of the liberalisation of international trade in agricultural produce, started looking for opportunities in Sweden eminently illustrates the role of networks. The owner had over the years been quite active in Nordic industry associations within horticulture and thereby established useful relations with key people and firms in Sweden, because at different meetings in the local Swedish association he had presented fresh ideas about his methods of cultivating tomato plants. In so doing, he had established a certain name and reputation in Sweden. When he decided to make his first attempt to enter the Swedish market, he therefore had a relatively easy time finding the right partners.

Networks provide what Coleman (1988) terms social capital, which has three functions:

1   It creates trust, obligations and expectations between the network partners. Trust fostered in networks constitutes a resource that enables the partners to more easily identify business opportunities and pitfalls, and thereby to devise appropriate strategies. Trust, furthermore, leads to commitment by the network partner (Morgan and Hunt 1994).
2   It promotes – through the trust embedded in the network – access to "privileged and difficult to price" information (Uzzi 1997, p. 43) that is fine-grained and directly relevant. There is a vast amount of information available in innumerable sources, and it is an insurmountable task for any organisation to uncover all relevant information for any specific decision. Networks alleviate this task by functioning as a screening device.
3   The relations formed in networks also create common norms and values among the partners, and therefore constitute an effective means of sanctions, preventing opportunism and shirking (Wathne and Heide 2000).

We claim that networks have more or less the same function as information: it reduces the uncertainty around decisions. The condition is, of course, that one can trust the information emanating from one's partners in the network. We are now moving into the heart of transaction cost theory (Williamson 1975) and agency theory (Eisenhardt 1989). The premise of these theories is that firms behave opportunistically. In our context, this implies that even though firms have a network, there is no promise that the information acquired therein is sufficient or even reliable to satisfy the needs of the decision to be taken. This depends on how close-knit and committed the network is, and how dependent the individual network member is upon the information provided by the other members. It also depends on the extent to which the information is relevant and useful, and whether it is reliable. Typical in such networks is that one day you may need some information from your network partners, and the next day they will need the same from you. If a network member fails to give correct information, or – worse – misleads the receiver of it, they have abused the trust conferred on them, and thereby also their position in the network and the possibility of taking advantage of the information and services embedded in the network in the future.

Family bonds (Italy, China), clans (Arab countries), diasporas (Jews, Armenians, Chinese, Indians, Pakistanis, etc.) and certain trades are examples of such bonds where – over years and even centuries – norms, mutual trust and understanding have been established (Kotkin 1992). We can see traits of this in the international trading of oil, finance and ship brokering, fish, diamonds and so on, where million-dollar deals are made over the telephone.

Information about market conditions in foreign markets is costly, partly because of the direct costs of not only accessing the data, but also integrating it into the organisation. It is also costly because exporters do not necessarily understand – or even recognise – the specifics of the market situation in a new setting. Different preferences and consumption patterns, different power plays between the actors in the market, different competitive behaviour, are all factors that make information-gathering difficult. It is not always straightforward to identify relevant factors to research. In this setting, trusted network partners play the role of a bridge to reliable and relevant data, at a minimal cost. This information (or most of it) will – with time and hands-on experience – eventually be embedded in the organisation.[2]

The Norwegian firm NorTre deals in styrofoam and building materials. Their experience in the Polish market may serve as an illustration of the role of networks in building a presence in foreign markets. The relations with their Polish partners started years before they identified the opportunities in Poland, when Polish workers came to Norway to pick strawberries in the short season between June and August. The relationships established during this period built a foundation for mutual trust and even friendship between Norwegian farmers and businesspeople and the Polish immigrant workers. When the Polish market opened for foreign investments in the early 1990s, the firm soon identified business opportunities in the construction industry and made considerable investments. After only two years they had reached profitable sales of around 40 million NOK. The most important key word here is – as in all other business – mutual trust. Trust over-rode the need for information, which in this case (after the opening of the Polish market after the Soviet era) would have been extremely difficult to obtain. The alternative – embarking on a detailed market research project – would most likely not have led to any rapid investment decision and the opportunity would then probably have vanished.

We observe here that establishing networks takes time, particularly because the necessary trust must be built. Breaking into new markets is indeed about breaking into existing bonds between existing partners in the market, and this may not happen quickly, depending on the strengths of these bonds. In Chapter 5 we shall return to the importance of networks in retrieving/substituting market information.

3.4 Born Globals and internationalisation process theory

The incremental internationalisation model was mainly developed at a time when firms operated in multi-domestic markets (Porter 1986) – implying that each country market was, if not an isolated island, at least functioning independently of other markets.[3] Firms, therefore, could slowly and confidently develop their international operations taking one step at a time. They could sneak, unobserved by competitors, into new markets (Solberg 1997) where management was most comfortable, without fearing retaliation or being copied on a global scale. For many firms this no longer seems to be the case. A new breed of businesses that went international right after inception was particularly conspicuous after the late 1980s, in great part spurred by globalisation drivers such as increasing international trade and investment flows in the wake of liberalisation of trade barriers and ease of communication across borders (Oviatt and McDougall 1994, Knight and Cavusgil 1996, Coviello and Munro 1997, Madsen and Servais 1997, Rialp et al. 2005, Aspelund et al. 2007, Gabrielsson et al. 2008). This group of companies is called Born Globals (BGs) – that is firms that start exporting shortly after their inception and to several countries around the world.[4] One new dimension of the economic environment is the interdependence between players in national markets, leading to a more complex competitive situation with firms from all corners of the world offering novel and competitive solutions to both new and old problems.

Thus, BGs are confronted with the challenges of scarcity of resources and they operate under extremely demanding circumstances. Often their products are introduced into markets where global incumbents have a firm market position, giving the latter leverage in the contest for market shares through their dominance of both distribution channels and industrial solutions. In spite of this, BGs elbow their way into markets, exploiting networks and using a range of different entry modes to capture customers. The advent of the internet has provided them with a powerful channel, although the use of this for marketing purposes does not always yield the expected results (Sinkovics and Pederzka 2010).

We have seen how early contributions on the internationalisation process of firms suggest that they start out with an agent or distributor, then – after some years of experience – replace the independent middleman with their own subsidiary, and eventually end up investing in a manufacturing unit to service the foreign market more efficiently (Johanson and Wiedersheim-Paul 1975). This gradual trajectory to international markets has been shown to yield better returns than the more direct route through international foreign direct investments in production capacity (Newbould et al. 1978). The trade-off between risk and growth in international markets is at the centre of this discussion (Andersen 1993). Market knowledge acquired through years of experience will reduce the risk of committing more resources than necessary to the international venture, at the expense of rapid international growth. All the same, the time it takes to accumulate the necessary insight into and understanding of local market conditions – thus reducing the investment risk – may jeopardise the development of the firm pursuing the cautious path to international markets, simply because competitors with more muscle are better placed to exploit the opportunities offered. Also, as the BG develops, it will need additional financing and new investors will be invited in, creating a new atmosphere inside the boardroom of these firms. This will possibly create different expectations and demands on management (Gabrielsson et al. 2008, Solberg and Bretteville 2012).

There is a question whether BG is a theory in its own right or rather a special case of the internationalisation theory. Certainly, there are differences: BGs start exporting at the very start or soon after inception, the pace of internationalisation is different, their resource base is generally limited and the two streams of literature – gradual internationalisation and Born Global – were developed in two very different contexts: multi-local vs. global markets. But this is a question of geography and context more than one of growth or business model. On the other hand both the traditional school of internationalisation process and BG contributions consider factors such as uncertainty and risk, experience, commitment, entry mode strategies, etc.

The Uppsala school model suggests that export activities are being triggered, the firm engages in export activities, experience is accumulated and the exporter is then committing more resources to the export venture based on that very experience – hence at lower risk (Johanson and Vahlne 1977). Gabrielsson et al. (2008) suggest that some of the mechanisms are the same, but that their details may vary and come in a different order. The detailed content of these drivers may vary: In the case of traditional exporters, the triggers are possibly limited to scale economies, competition and unsolicited orders; whereas for BGs, drivers such as the global vision of the founder(s) and access to markets (through internet, lower trade barriers, etc.) prevail. *Also the commitment of BGs comes before any export activity.* This however is a different kind of commitment. In the words of Gabrielsson et al. (2008, p. 398):

> we will term this *affective commitment* [emphasis added], which is triggered by identification with the goal of the BG venture (Meyer and Allen 1991). The essence in this context is that the initial commitment is created by the global perspectives of the entrepreneur and the opportunities represented by them. It is not created by market activities, experiential knowledge and specific investments. This kind of commitment of the BG entrepreneur will also permeate the staffing of the firm, which will in turn strengthen the affective commitment.

Figure 3.4 illustrates the two different trajectories to international markets – the traditional and Born Global route.

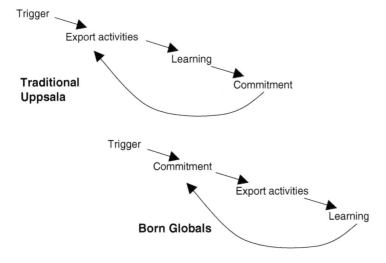

Figure 3.4 Different trajectories to internationalisation.

After the initial phases of the BG export life, the circular model presented by Johanson and Vahlne (1977) is being caught up by the BG, which then becomes a "normal company" (Gabrielsson et al. 2008).

ASK ASA, a projector manufacturer based in Norway, is a good example of a company that was internationally oriented from birth. Established in the middle of the 1980s, the firm got a head start in international markets through OEM arrangements (OEM = Original Equipment Manufacturer[5]) with a German and an American company. Having grown with these two companies, ASK developed its own marketing network with independent dealers – first in Germany, then in other European countries. It deliberately sought large markets in order to reach a certain threshold level in manufacturing. The distribution contracts had some key features: 1) they were non-exclusive – i.e. they had many dealers within the same region that competed against each other, and 2) they tied up the dealers with minimum purchase clauses. In this way they did not lock themselves into relations with individual dealers; rather they obtained a great deal of flexibility. At the same time, the company hired foreigners from the respective market areas to work in the central sales team at headquarters in Norway, thereby assuring ease of communication between HQ and local dealers, and thus more rapidly than otherwise developing a trusting relationship between the partners. It then established its own sales and distribution network in key markets such as the US, Great Britain and Singapore. In 1998 the company acquired one of its largest competitors, the American firm Proxima, and secured market access to the most important market in the world. Some years later, it merged with another large actor in the market, Infocus.

Even though most people think of BGs as hi-tech firms, this class of highly-internationalised firms is also found in other sectors. In Norway, examples abound of small non-hi-tech firms that operate in global markets soon after establishment.

SWIMS – a relatively young company, established in 2005 – is a showcase of impressive development since its start-up. Its first products were colourful galoshes, hardly a hi-tech product, but still very innovative because galoshes at that time were always black, conceived as dull and uninteresting to most people under 70! Today SWIMS has expanded its product range to include loafers, jackets, bags, umbrellas and so on, with modern, but still classic designs and bright colours, aiming at specific target groups: modern city-dwellers valuing leisure. The company's internationalisation started at a trade show in Florence, Italy, and has since rapidly been followed up through distribution agreements with dealers in more than 20 countries. It seeks exclusive distributors and products are sold in stores in more than 35 countries. The large retail chains are at this point in time too large for the company (or the other way around: SWIMS is too small for these chains). SWIMS is in the process of expanding its product range further to create a "lifestyle concept" in order to try and get an inroad into some larger retail chains. It has also entered into co-branding deals with luxury brands such as Hermes and Armani, aiming at becoming associated with the high-end market. The company's success hinges on the dialogue it enters into with its distributors. They meet twice-yearly to discuss the product portfolio and market activities – an interchange of experience and information indispensable for the firm to develop new products and refine its marketing techniques. These meetings also serve as a means of bonding between the distributors, creating a family feeling.

3.4.1 Born Globals and entry modes

The choice of entry mode[6] is one of the most important decisions made by international marketers (Hamill et al. 1989). This decision determines many other variables of the international marketing effort such as monitoring and control, use of financial and managerial resources and financial risk (Solberg 2006a). Entry mode decisions are therefore particularly critical for BGs since they lack resources – limiting entry mode options – and are confronted with the compounded risk of new (often fast-growing) markets and new products (Ansoff 1957).

The discussion around two competing theoretical explanations of operation modes – Transaction Cost Economics (TCE) and the Internationalisation Process model (IP) – is indeed relevant in this context. Given the resource constraints of BGs we may exclude some entry modes such as foreign direct investments in production capacity. On the other hand we may identify a number of less committing entry modes that Born Globals may realistically pursue. The list below, partly inspired by Gabrielsson and Kirpalani (2004), is organised according to increasing degrees of control over the firm's international operations:

- New owners taking over, funnelling the product/service through its own international distribution network.
- Alliance with a large, independent licensing or distribution partner.
- Gradual international involvement through agents/distributors in individual countries.
- Franchising to partners in individual markets.
- Setting up sales subsidiaries in individual markets.

Other strategies may certainly be conceivable, but the above list covers many of the most relevant approaches to international markets available to BGs.

New owners

This strategy may be seen as the "easy way out" for many founders of BGs. They realise that the task is too formidable or they simply want to capitalise on the values created in the firm. We may perceive that founders have a proclivity for pursuing their business idea to reap the fruits of their labour and to make sure that the firm is true to its original ideas. The stubbornness of founders to stick to their company is a well-known phenomenon in new ventures, so oftentimes when new owners come in, it is despite the will of the founders rather than by virtue of a deliberate strategy (Solberg 1997). In any event, this may be good for the firm if its new owners are prepared to and capable of following up on the business idea without the initial founders at the helm. Examples abound of both successful takeovers and more dubious takeovers where the whole venture is doomed (Solberg and Bretteville 2012).

Licensing/distribution partner

Licensing involves the transfer of production rights, know-how or patent (licensing object) to a partner that takes on the task of developing a market for the product (Welch et al. 2007). The advantage for the entrepreneur of pursuing this strategy is that (s)he does not need to build an organisation to drive the market introduction of the products. This part is taken over by the licensee. This entry mode into international markets is often seen in research parks or universities where top researchers have created an innovation with substantial commercial value, but do not have the resources or the willingness to bring it to the market (Macho-Stadler and Pérez-Castrillo 2010). But also new ventures (often emanating from these same places) may have to resort to a partnership with a large, often dominant partner that can take care of the commercial side of the venture. While the upside is evident (relatively few resources needed, royalties, rapid market deployment using the network and distribution channels of the licensee), the risks are equally clear: the licensor curtails its own development of the commercial potential of the invention and risks that the licensee could take over the whole product idea and become a competitor rather than a partner (Welch et al. 2007). In cases of a narrow window of opportunity, licensing may be the only conceivable strategy for the resource-poor BG, but it comes at a price: loss of control. Licensing rights may also be given to a *number of different* licensees in different countries. In this way the BG does not confer the rights to one sole partner, but disperses the risk of rights transfer to several licensees. Much of the same reasoning put forward for licensing to a large partner may also apply to a distribution relationship with a large OEM partner, the main difference being the firm (BG) is taking charge of the supply of the products or services, either by producing them itself or through contract manufacturing arrangements. In this way, it has some more control over greater parts of the value chain, though not branding or marketing.

Gradual internationalisation

According to the discussion in the previous section, this approach is generally seen as a safe way to enter international markets – but again may also be paved with challenges that make the BG vulnerable; market introduction risks going too slowly and competitors may enter the window of opportunity thus preventing the BG from taking advantage of its potential.

Franchising

Franchising entails the handover of the rights to exploit the commercial value of a business system and/or trademark (Welch et al. 2007). This strategy is being deployed at an increasing pace in international markets, often in service industries. The emergence of Zara (affordable fashion) and Starbucks (coffee shops) are cases in point. In both cases the firms have resorted to a strategy of franchising and have built up a system of control and monitoring of their franchising partners' activities in world markets. In the case of franchising the firm therefore has more control (than a licensor) of its operations through full ownership of its trademark. This control does not come without investments in monitoring systems so as to avoid opportunistic behaviour such as free-riding by the franchisee (Kidwell et al. 2007). Therefore this business solution is not necessarily for the unproven entrepreneur. On the other hand, BGs with the necessary resources to venture into international franchising may be well-rewarded.

Sales subsidiaries

In principle, sales subsidiaries give the BG full control of its foreign marketing operations. However, setting up sales subsidiaries is wrought with challenges such as manning the local unit with competent personnel, financing it, as well as monitoring and controlling its activities in the market. The lack of experience and local networks may therefore make investing in local sales subsidiaries an onerous endeavour for the BG. Examples abound of firms that wanted to "take control" early on and have encountered difficulties because they bit off more than they could chew. Even BGs with large financial resources and professional boards, that expand rapidly in international markets by the means of sales subsidiaries, may overstretch their limited managerial resources. They either may not have adequate experience in monitoring international marketing activities or have failed to get the routines and systems in place to deal with the task (Borsheim and Solberg 2002, Solberg and Bretteville 2012). Over-optimistic BGs have invested in sales offices in around ten markets in order to tap into a window of opportunity over a period of less than a year or two, only shortly thereafter to retract when problems piled up because of lack of understanding of local marketing conditions or because the firm did not have a satisfactory monitoring system in place. Evidently, this is the trade-off between control and risk inherent in the rapid growth of a firm.

> Voss of Norway (selling high-profile mineral water) is one such firm, which quickly established its own market and distribution subsidiary in New York and other metropolitan cities in the world, and has achieved a small niche in the "Michelin Guide" market. Its growth has, however, not been as spectacular as that of ASK (see above), partly due to its desire to control the marketing through its own subsidiaries. Limited resources – both financial and personnel – have constrained growth. Also, the costs involved in owning and monitoring its own sales and distribution network have proved particularly onerous for the company.

3.4.2 The Born Global dilemma

We may infer that the BG has to mould its strategy in the tension between control of its international expansion and its level of activity in order to grow and acquire new customers in international markets. BGs with the vision of servicing global markets need to first relinquish control of marketing and distribution in order to achieve the desired growth because they lack resources to wield the necessary clout to independently cover a broad range of markets. On the other hand, the need for rapid market introduction – which is inherent within BGs – is

Table 3.1 The trade-off between too much and too little

Issue	Effect on strategy	Possible outcomes
Too little control	Market control left to partner(s)	Loss of learning effects and control of own development
Too much control	Requires resources and market insight that the BG does not have	Stigmatises smooth and efficient development of international market expansion
Too passive	Too careful, invests too little in market development and positioning	Competitors will exploit the unique window of opportunity and the BG is left with insignificant customers in marginal markets
Too active	Too impatient and too eager to conquer world markets without the necessary financial or managerial clout	Risky path to retraction and potential bankruptcy

Too much control	The aggressive BG	The stigmatised BG
	The BG is overwhelmed by the need for resources (managerial and/or financial) and will relatively rapidly "hit the wall".	Gradual internationalisation gives control and learning, but the market will be lost to competition.
Too little control	The unruly BG	The lost case BG
	Rapid market introduction may lead to early foot hold in key markets, but the BG loses market control to its partner.	Neither control nor market penetration is achieved. The firm risks losing its momentum in international markets.
	Too active	**Too passive**

Figure 3.5 The Born Global dilemma.

Source: Solberg (2012).

time-sensitive for many firms because they are confronted with a window of opportunity that – if they do not exploit it and actively deploy market operations in key countries – would otherwise be exploited by competitors. But rapid international market expansion may lead the newcomer to make fatal decisions because of lack of local market understanding. Using a maritime metaphor we may say that they lack a proper chart to navigate and their navigation skills leave a lot to be desired. Table 3.1 sums up the discussion above.

Placing these two dimensions – control and level of activity – in a matrix we get the taxonomy illustrated in Figure 3.5.

Managers can draw important lessons from this discussion. The following factors are considered critical both for the short- and long-term success of the BG:

– Early access to key customers in the industry in several countries, to help the BG obtain references, setting the industry standard and getting the necessary cash-flow.
– Rapid deployment in the market to pre-empt competition to capture market shares.
– Control so that the long-term interests of the founders and BG shareholders are ascertained.

But how then to "have your cake and eat it"? The key word here is flexibility. For instance the BG needs to make sure that it is not getting stuck in contractual obligations with a dominant partner that it may not easily change. For newcomers to international markets it may be tempting to sign contracts that apparently secure sales growth and market coverage. However, the firm may risk ending up in the trap of getting too dependent on the partner without having had the opportunity to build necessary competence that would enable it to take control at a later stage (Solberg and Welch 1995). Furthermore, if the firm has a unique technology, design or product which is either patented or difficult to copy, the firm may have a great potential to draft an alliance package with a future partner that pays due attention to the above concerns. For instance it is conceivable to invite a licensing partner to set up a company (the licensee) financing the bulk of the investment, and where the licensor (the BG) has an option to gradually increase its share, for instance by gradually substituting part of the royalties due with new shares in the company. This point will be discussed in further detail in Chapter 7, Section 7.4.

Another issue is that of timing: when should the BG invite new investors to take a stake in the venture? If they are invited too early the BG and its founder(s) risk either ending up with a partner that takes over the firm or its technology without the original investors being able to reap the profits from its real potential, or receiving investments that are insufficient to finance the necessary expansion of the firm. If they are invited to invest in the company too late, the window of opportunity may be closed.

The control–growth dilemma is haunting management of many BGs in their strategic deliberations. Particularly firms with a narrow window of opportunity in world markets are vulnerable to the vagaries of the situation and, although the right answer to the dilemma may not be obvious, it will be decisive for the future development of the firm. This section has endeavoured to cast light on the dilemma, thereby elucidating likely outcomes and – hopefully – guiding management to viable solutions. This is an under-researched area of study and the proposed model may serve as a roadmap for further exploring the phenomenon.

3.5 The successful exporter

Attempts have been made to understand the mechanisms of export performance. This research is important in that it seeks to help our understanding of sustainable growth of firms in international markets. In one of the first reviews of the literature, Aaby and Slater (1989) found that one factor prevailed in explaining export performance: commitment by top management to the export venture. Another early contribution by Kamath et al. (1987) plainly concludes that "any strategy goes": shotgun or rifle; fast or slow; extensive or limited management experience; high or low R&D effort (except in high-tech industries); and excellent or poor financial strength – in other words, success hinges on numerous factors. This conclusion may still hold, but new research has completed the picture with a much richer variety of impacting factors being studied. Over the past 20 years more than 250 academic articles have been published on export performance. The impression is that, whereas it is difficult to find a general pattern of agreement on strategy variables leading to superior performance, other factors such as learning effectiveness and capabilities (Phromket and Ussahawanitchakit 2009), market orientation (Cadogan et al. 2009, Tantong et al. 2010), proactive attitudes (Okpara and Kabonga 2009), innovation (Lages et al. 2009) and proactive strategies (Solberg and Durrieu 2008) seem to prevail in explaining export performance. We may infer that softer and less perceptible variables impact on an exporter's financial and market performance, whereas superficial (but easily observable) indicators such as size, financial strength, R&D intensity and so on are much less consequential.

We conclude that the main lesson drawn from this string of research is that firms fare better in international markets where top management is actively involved in the export venture (Aaby and Slater 1989). Without such involvement, other parts of the firm will not get the necessary support to carry out tasks relating to the export activities. One critical factor is how the exporter is working with its network in foreign markets. This network is in one sense the company's extended arm in international markets and constitutes the cornerstone of the firm's export organisation. In the next section, we will report on research in Norway on export performance. One of the research projects (Solberg 1987, 1988) deals with what we may term the international organisational culture. The other one (Solberg et al. 2014) analyses different elements of strategy that firms can play with in their quest for international market shares.

3.5.1 Critical elements of international organisational culture

Above, we have briefly alluded to the role of top management in thriving export ventures. We have also seen how most researchers agree on the role of commitment in the internationalisation process of firms. We believe that such commitment stems from three factors: attitudes, competence, and the embodiment of them in the organisation. We will now look at each of these factors in some detail.

Attitudes

Solberg (1987, 1988) describes four groups of mindsets that affect the attitudes of members of the organisation: risk orientation, market orientation, cultural awareness and methods of approach to hurdles that firms will inevitably meet when entering foreign markets.

RISK ORIENTATION

Successful exporters appear to have a lower threshold of risk for entering foreign markets than those that are less prosperous in this. They often seek markets further out, and do so much earlier and at a faster pace than other firms (Gripsrud et al. 2015). According to Rauch et al. (2009, p. 763), risk-takers take "bold actions by venturing into the unknown, borrowing heavily, and/or committing significant resources to ventures in uncertain environments". Frishammar and Andersson (2009) link risk orientation or risk willingness to resource commitment. Hence, firms that are more risk-averse will devote fewer resources to a new venture than firms with the opposite position. However, risk also relates to development of new markets, products, processes and organizations. Risk-taking therefore relates to the willingness to think new when opportunities emerge and show courage to act.

This may be spurred by products that are better suited for international markets, or by critical network relations facilitating market access (Gripsrud et al. 2006, Johanson and Vahlne 2009). Risk takers may have a better financial position enabling them to do so. Also, connected with the next factor (competence), they may have better market knowledge, enabling them to judge the opportunities in the market more proactively. In any event, they are in a position to take bolder steps in international markets than others. Interestingly, research from Norway indicates that risk orientation is positively related to international orientation of the firm, which in turn positively and strongly affects international market performance. Also Solberg and Durrieu (2011) find that an aggressive stance to international markets is positively related to export performance.

Let us "pay a visit" to the board meeting of a small firm in the electronics industry. They have thrived over many years in Norway, exploiting their unique competence in data transfer technology. At the beginning of the 21st century, they gained access to the Norwegian oil sector, and prospects were that they could fare well by supplying to this customer base for years to come. Management had considered exporting as one alternative, but the main attitude in the boardroom was: "Why should we take the risk of going abroad?" They had at some point attempted to get an inroad into the Swedish market, but they did not manage to get involved with the "right" network and did not find what they considered the "right customers".[7] The follow-up was half-hearted because the firm had a more than sufficient workload in the domestic market. The discussions in the board meeting went back and forth with arguments concerning risk, lost opportunities, organisational strain, etc. Should they invest more determinedly in the Swedish market, follow up the local partners more actively and seriously? Or should they rather look for other markets or would they be better off concentrating on the Norwegian market? Entering export markets would entail investments in more people and in new partner relations. A committed entry into foreign markets would constitute a new dimension in the strategy of the firm and ruin the internal power balance of key managers, where those that do not wish to explore international markets are doomed to lose in the medium to long term. New competence would be required – not only technological competence but also competence in controlling and running relationships with foreign partners. In short, this firm was not ready to go international – not yet. A critical question is then: will they be prepared on the day they will be forced to do so?

Market orientation

More than half a century ago, Levitt (1960) showed in a legendary article in *Harvard Business Review* that management focus on customers and market development is imperative for a firm's long-term survival. Thirty years later, Narver and Slater (1990) claimed that market orientation is more than just understanding the underlying needs of customers; it also involves recognising how the firm's products are positioned in the market relative to those of its competitors. And it involves a strict attention to costs. This requires insight into customers and how their preferences are formed, competitors' strategic behaviour and that of distribution channels, and finally how laws and regulations affect demand patterns and product requirements. In short: market insight. This insight is much more challenging to acquire in international markets because everything there is new to the firm and it takes time for it to be anchored as an integral part of the strategic thinking of the firm. Developing this insight requires more than just market information; it constitutes an inseparable part of the company's *organisational culture* that is eventually translated into the strategic behaviour of the firm. This culture reflects basic values and norms that in turn affect "the ways things are done" within the organisation (Homburg and Pflesser 2000). The mainstream definition of market orientation therefore includes activities that firms carry out to that effect: market intelligence acquisition, dissemination of the intelligence in the organisation and responsiveness to the information (Kohli and Jaworski 1990). This culture is being nurtured by the activities of the firm through its relations with market players – customers, partners, dealers, government agencies and even competitors. Solberg et al. (2014) found that information attained through these sources is much more valuable than market research because the information embedded in these market players is directly relevant to the situation of the firm.

Most research on market orientation supports the hypothesis that it is in fact supporting business performance. In the *Journal of Marketing* in 2005, Kirca, Jayachandran and Bearden's meta-analysis on research to that date concluded that market orientation is indeed good for business. However, there are some caveats to this conclusion. Solberg and Olsson (2011) found in their research that in the ICT industry an important component of market orientation – customer orientation – relates negatively with firm export performance. They suggest that this has to do with firms that pay too much attention to satisfy customer needs, adapting to their specific requirements and incurring too high costs in that endeavour: customer orientation becomes *customer obsession*! In international markets this is particularly critical, since needs may differ from one country to another, and the adaptation to customer demand leads to ruining economies of scale. On the other hand, Solberg and Olsson (2011) found that technological orientation was strongly related to performance. They offer the explanation that in growth industries (such as the ICT industry) customers are not necessarily the ones that define the products; rather it is the engineers and product development teams that seize opportunities offered by new technologies, addressing needs in new ways that customers were not aware of. Market research or listening to customers and their preferences would therefore never provide information that would enable the technology firm to innovate. This is what Ghauri et al. (2016) call "market driving strategies".

Also the strategic orientation of the firm may moderate the effects of market orientation. Olson et al. (2005) found that the four elements of market orientation as defined by Narver and Slater (1990) – customer orientation, competitor orientation, innovation orientation and cost orientation – had significantly different effects depending on four strategic archetypes: prospectors, analysers, low-cost defenders and differentiated defenders.[8] For instance, customer orientation is positively associated with business performance in three of the four strategies; for low-cost defenders it was non-consequential (not significantly positive). Competitor orientation was *negatively* related to performance for prospectors. Innovation orientation is *positively* associated for prospectors, but *negatively* for analysers and low-cost defenders. Finally cost orientation is only positive for low-cost defenders.

We may still conclude that market orientation in general is not only positive, but in most cases necessary as a prerequisite for success. This is possibly more relevant for firms whose products are no longer in the innovation stage and where listening to customers is necessary to remain relevant or to position oneself against competitors. However, market orientation is more than collecting market information, disseminating it in the organisation and responding to it; it is a way of thinking that pervades the organisational culture and balances different concerns – for customers, the cost level of adapting to customer needs and competitors' activities.

Cultural awareness

A number of authors have described cultural distance (Hall 1959, Hofstede 1980, Hampden-Turner and Trompenaars 1993, 2000). Another matter is how managers of individual companies behave when confronted with people from different cultures. It is a truism that cultural awareness is critical when operating in international markets. Solberg (1987, 1988) finds that indeed there is something to that general claim: in his analysis, managers of successful exporters

Table 3.2 Cooperating with foreigners

	Successful exporters	Unsuccessful exporters
Swedes	2.1	2.1
British	2.2	2.5
North Americans	2.4	2.5
Danes	2.5	2.8
Finns	2.6	3.1
Germans	3.0	2.7
Japanese	3.0	3.6
French	3.4	3.4
South East Asians	3.2	3.4
Arabs	3.7	3.7
East Europeans[a]	3.8	3.9
Average	*2.9*	*3.1*

Note: Key: 1 = very easy to cooperate, 5 = very difficult to cooperate.
[a] The analysis was undertaken before the dissolution of the Soviet Union (and the Warsaw Pact).

generally respond more positively to questions of how easy it is to cooperate with people from different cultures. Table 3.2 shows the results. The general tendency is that successful exporters are more at ease when cooperating with foreigners. Only in a few instances are the differences significant (Finland and Japan). We may also add that the table tells the story of Norwegians as much as that of the foreigners included in the list!

PROBLEMS? NO PROBLEM!

Another attitude of successful exporters is the perspective they have when meeting obstacles and problems in foreign markets. In the literature, managers mention factors such as customs duties, transport costs, different cultures, lack of access to distribution channels, political risks and so on as major inhibitors to exporting or reasons to avoid certain markets. Instead of using such problems as a "good excuse" for poor performance or lack of market presence, successful exporters typically find ways of circumventing such impediments.

One case in point is Dynea ASA (producing adhesives for industrial use). This firm is involved in a large number of countries in South East Asia. Many of these countries have strict regulations regarding local capital as well as customs and import restrictions. For Dynea, these hurdles merely constituted "operating conditions" that they had to relate to in one way or another. Rather than giving up in these markets, Dynea has carried out projects with minority interests but still remains in control as it enters into management contracts with its partners. In this way, Dynea managers have their hands on the wheel, and – just as important – the learning effects are secured back to the Dynea organisation.

Another firm that took a very proactive stance to problems as stated above is Telenor, the Norwegian telecoms giant. There was a rush to invest in new opportunities when Russia liberalised its economy and opened up for foreign investors in the early 1990s. However, in the wake of the financial crisis in 1998, there was an equal exodus of foreign capital from Russia. Telenor went at that point against the tide and – when stock markets were at their lowest – made its most important and profitable investment abroad in what later became Vimpelcom, the second largest telecoms operator in Russia.

Competence

Concerning competence, we claim that most successful exporters are better able to "follow the textbook". In the following, we will discuss different elements of competence reported by Norwegian exporters.

MANAGEMENT SKILLS

Solberg (1987, 1988) found that successful and unsuccessful exporters seemingly do not differ regarding management skills in general. Successful exporters report better skills in only one of 12 areas: sales techniques. Concerning language, contract negotiations, cultural understanding, logistics, relations with distribution partners, market research and advertising there is no significant difference between the two groups. Interestingly and maybe thought-provokingly, when it comes to insight into government subsidies and export promotion programmes, the poor performers rank their skills higher than the successful exporters. The reason offered by Solberg (1987, 1988) is that these firms depend more on and make more use of such programmes, and therefore know them better.

A general conclusion is that skills in most of these areas are necessary but not sufficient to carry out successful export ventures. We therefore need to explore how exporters carry out their market activities in order to detect areas of expertise that distinguish the good performers from the poor ones.

MARKETING SKILLS

In fact, Solberg (1987, 1988) finds that the two groups of exporters place different emphasis on the traditional marketing mix elements – the four Ps.[9] For instance, based on Kotler and Keller's (2011) product concept – consisting of the core product, the generic product, the expected product, the augmented product and the potential product – he finds that in particular the augmented and potential products distinguish the winners from the losers in international markets. The augmented product comprises all the features that are added to the product in order to differentiate it from that of competitors; potential product is about future product development. Whereas all exporters claim to emphasise quality and design in their product offering, to excel in service, punctuality and so on, successful exporters seem to be more concerned with product development and with cooperation with customers. These two are often also related, since customer input in general is critical for product development to be successful.[10]

Regarding pricing, it appears that successful exporters are able to charge higher prices for their products. This may stem from the fact that these firms in general have higher market shares in their main markets abroad,[11] and accordingly are able to achieve higher prices (Buzzell and Gale 1987). In addition, it is likely that successful exporters – with better relations with their customers – are more able to develop products adapted to customer needs and thereby also charge a premium. In addition, Solberg (1987, 1988) found that good export performers have established better administrative routines for monitoring cost and profitability of their foreign activities.

Turning now to market communications we have already seen that sales people in successful firms have better competence: they travel more and they have a wider mandate from HQ regarding entering into contracts. Also good performers play with a broader spectrum of activities in their market communications such as trade fairs and advertisements.

The fourth P – place (distribution) – concerns the link between exporters and their partners and customers abroad. This element in the marketing mix is possibly the most important lever that exporters have in their strategic tool box (Solberg 2006c). In particular, social relations, flexibility (such as accepting changes in contracts when the situation warrants them, or willingness to try hard to fulfil rush orders, etc.), mutual trust and norms are more prevalent with successful exporters.

Embodiment

Even if these attitudes and competencies are present among certain co-workers of the firm, it will be to no avail if these do not permeate the whole organisation. This is in particular true concerning top management, which has a key role in signalling priorities of the firm. Doole and Lowe (2004) find that vacillating commitment by management is one of the most important reasons for export failure. When the local partner does not succeed in getting a break-through

Table 3.3 Priorities of the board of directors

	Successful exporters	*Unsuccessful exporters*
Next year's budget	1	1
Budget control	2	2
Overall strategy	2	5
Financial situation	4	3
New markets	5	8
Investments in production capacity	5	3
Product development	5	6
Organisational development	8	7

Note: Key: 1 = high priority, 8 = low priority.

with the exporter's product after a year or two, and the return on the export sales is negative, then it is not unusual that the board of directors start to groan and put into question the whole venture. Top management and the board of directors need to recognise the fact that "things take time", and that in exporting "things take a very long time" – new culture, new relations, new situations, new obstacles and a lot of learning that has to be done.

In Solberg's research (1988) it was revealed that the boards of directors of successful exporters focus more on overall strategy and investments in new markets. Table 3.3 gives interesting insights into the differences in priorities for the two groups of firms.

According to research from Norway in the woodworking industry, attention is seriously given to the export venture only when the export ratio is in the range of some 10–15%. At this stage, most parts of the organisation are involved in some manner. And at this stage it is not only the marketing and export managers who are engaged in exporting issues – the general manager, the finance manager, the accounting department, the production or technology manager are also all involved.

3.5.2 The beneficial export circle – the ACE model

Success in international markets depends on a wide range of factors. However it is first and foremost the commitment to and the support for the internationalisation process that eventually determines the outcome of this process. With commitment we surmise that insight and knowledge about international business will gradually develop, and that the organisation will commit resources – financial and human. The internationalisation process may therefore be described as a stepwise maturing of the organisational culture of the firm, through the development of **A**ttitudes, **C**ompetencies and a gradually deeper **E**mbodiment of both these within the organisation. We may call this the ACE model. Figure 3.6 illustrates this process.

The implication for newcomers to exporting is that they meet special challenges related to information and knowledge – not only about markets but also relating to factors of a more operative character, which essentially constrain their strategic options. Of course, the more advanced exporters have far better opportunities – mainly because their insights into international business and their attitudes towards internationalisation are better anchored in the organisation. The fully internationalised firms look at the entire world as their arena of operations and have only a fraction of their business in their home market. In this case the ACE triangle has quite a different context. For these firms, the cost level in high-cost countries such as most of Western Europe is of little relevance; rather they leverage advantages offered in local markets concerning resources and market potential.

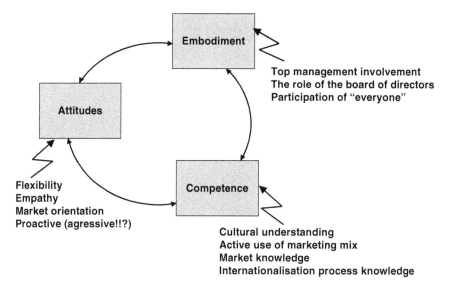

Figure 3.6 The beneficial export circle.

3.6 Chapter summary

This chapter has explored the question of why firms start to export, the process they go through in their search for international markets and what factors determine success in exporting. We have seen that learning is key to the process, and that establishment and development of net-works in the market is an essential ingredient of this. We claim that the most important form of learning is that which firms get from their own experience. We may therefore state that the more activities the exporter carries out in foreign markets, the more they will learn and the better foundation they will have with which to succeed in their export venture. We need to balance this point of view against the firm's resources – capital, people/management and technology – and also the business environment in which it operates. In this context Born Globals are particularly vulnerable: they are confronted with the risk of seeing large competitors exploiting oppor-tunities that the Born Globals had at the outset. Resource constraints and steep learning curves make this challenge particularly daunting.

The internationalisation process theory suggests that firms often start exporting because they get an unsolicited order, because their home market is too small or because competition forces them to find new arenas for their products and services. These are what we may term external or reactive motives for exporting. They do not stem from internal processes within the firm; rather they arise as a reaction to a situation. However, as firms gain experience, other motives prevail: they seek opportunities that exist in foreign markets more proactively, and this is based on knowledge – both about markets and the process itself. The internationalisation process theory also asserts that firms go international like ripples in the water: they start in neighbouring countries and spread gradually to more distant markets. However, this part of the theory has been criticised by many researchers. For instance, we have seen how Born Globals expand rapidly and that the mechanisms for this expansion perhaps first and foremost lie in the internal motivation and energy of the entrepreneurs. They are thereby able to "leapfrog" certain stages in the internationalisation process. Key features of these firms are that they above all have a team of managers/owners who are strongly committed and often have a state-of-the-art technology that gives them a head start in the market. They are also often confronted with a limited window of opportunity that they need to exploit quickly, before larger multinationals move in and secure the major market share for themselves.

Finally we have seen that successful exporters are engrossed in a "beneficial export circle" with proactive attitudes, enhanced competence and embodiment of these two in the whole organisation. The main point here is that successful internationalisation is nurtured by an organisational culture that is adopted by all parts of the firm: from the board of directors to the operators on the shop floor. The general manager has a particularly important role in this context; without his/her active involvement, the international venture risks becoming a marginal activity.

Notes

1 This school of thought got its name from researchers at Uppsala University in Sweden; they were among the earliest contributors to the gradual internationalisation school of thought.
2 We will elaborate more on these issues in Chapter 5.
3 This section is partly derived from my article, "The Born Global dilemma" (Solberg 2012).
4 There has been a big discussion about how to properly define the concept of Born Global. We will not dwell on this discussion other than referring to the most used definition which states that BGs are firms that reach an export ratio of 25% within three years of inception.
5 OEM is an arrangement whereby a subcontractor manufactures products under the name of a customer – i.e. some kind of private brand contract.
6 Entry modes – or more generally, operation modes – will be more thoroughly covered in Chapter 7.
7 In this industry, getting the right customers implies selling to firms that 1) challenge their competence, 2) give them input to new and better solutions and 3) are willing to pay the little extra for their competence.
8 These are inspired by Miles and Snow's (1978) original classification: prospectors, analysers, defenders and reactors.
9 The four Ps are: product, promotion, place and price. In the present paragraph we discuss the product.
10 This may be different for product innovations, i.e. products that are new to the market. As we have seen above, Solberg and Olsson (2011) show that customer orientation is negatively related with export performance in the ICT industry, an industry that still features high levels of technological development and innovation.
11 In Solberg's (1988) paper, market share is one of the measures of success.

4 Strategy development in international markets

4.1 Introduction

The two previous chapters have considered the external business environment in international markets and the internationalisation process of firms, including resources, and success factors of businesses operating in international markets. The present chapter endeavours to combine these two – external and internal factors – and discuss possible consequences of development of an international marketing strategy by the firm. It is based on the "Nine strategic windows" model as shown in Figure 1.1 in the introduction chapter. We will first discuss how to measure the firm's position on each of the two axes of the model (Industry globality and Preparedness for internationalisation) and then in some more detail explore the different strategic avenues open for businesses in each part of the matrix.

4.2 Industry globality

We have seen in Chapter 2 how markets and industries gradually become more globalised. We have seen how trade and investment flows have increased the interconnectedness of individual countries around the globe. We have seen how consumption patterns progressively tend to converge across borders and for certain sectors to create a global demand pattern. We have furthermore seen how both political and technological developments play in the same direction – facilitating the international exchange of goods and investments. However, political events after Brexit (Trumpism, nationalistic orientation in Europe) have put a (temporary) halt to the process of liberalisation of trade and investments. The extent to which these events also halt the development towards global competition remains to be seen.

In this section, we shall discuss ways of measuring industry globality. Most people have an idea of what markets are global and what are local. Intuitively, the market for haircuts – serviced by the hairdressing industry – is a typical local market, i.e. one that typically caters to local customers and is serviced by a large number of small shops, sometimes with some chain companies operating across the national market. At the other end of the scale, we find industries such as the aircraft industry, consisting of a very limited number of players, Boeing and Airbus, operating all across the globe. These two cases are rather clear-cut. However, between these two extremes there are hundreds – if not thousands – of industries that are difficult to classify, because of the large number of driving and counteracting forces that lead to different outcomes concerning the industry structure. Also the situation may differ from one country to another.

Consider, for example, the beer industry. In most countries, beer drinkers consume local beer, often with a substantial amount of pride. However, the local breweries are more often than not owned by large multinational firms such as Anheuser-Busch Inbev (US/Belgium), Carlsberg (Denmark), Heineken (Netherlands), Tsing Tao (China) and Kirin (Japan). Since the beginning of this millennium, the ten largest concerns have in fact increased their share of world beer consumption from around 20% to 60%. Global brands are normally produced by local subsidiaries of multinational firms or through licensing deals, in parallel with their production of local brands. At the same time, we still find a large range of smaller, local (and locally-owned) breweries that compete on different parameters to the large players – special taste, loyalty to the local brand, quality, etc. The development towards this structure has been prompted by different globalisation drivers, such as market power in the retail industry forcing beer manufacturers to merge in order to gain clout in the fight for shelf space, or the gradual emergence of global brands, in turn induced by homogenisation of demand and the market leaders' desire to gain economies of scale in marketing. Trade in the beer industry is on the other hand negligible (2% of total consumption) and does not constitute any driving force. So how should we classify the beer industry? Is it local, global, or rather something in between?

Solberg and Durrieu (2015a,b) suggest that both industry structure (in terms of concentration of competitors and customers) and globalisation drivers such as reduced tariffs, joint techno-logical standards and homogenisation of demand patterns impact on the outcome of different internationalisation strategies. These factors reflect the essence in the definition of our concept of industry globality (structural and international barriers to entry). The researchers find that these factors have an impact on the performance effects of a number of international marketing strategies. For instance, in markets with a large number of players, firms typically take advantage of a slow, step-by-step introduction to new markets. The line of reasoning is that, in crowded markets, it is easier to carve out a customer base without "disturbing" the local market leaders. In an oligopolistic setting, on the other hand, a new competitor would classically be met by counteractions in the form of price reductions or retaliation in other markets where the newcomer has a stronger position (Hamel and Prahalad 1985). Furthermore, standardisation of the mar-keting mix seems to be better suited to open and homogeneous markets and also to markets where competition is concentrated in a few players. This is much in line with Levitt's (1983) predictions.

Figure 2.12 in Chapter 2 shows a typology of industry structure based on two factors: structural barriers to entry and international barriers to entry. Figure 4.1 suggests strategic consequences of different industry constellations according to two related factors: number of players and globa-lisation drivers. This is the "cousin" of Figure 2.12 in Chapter 2. However, whereas Figure 2.12 is theoretically based, Figure 4.1 is possibly easier to use empirically, in that it is easier to assess the number of market players (and the extent to which some players are dominant) – and thereby the industry structure – than to assess the structural barriers to entry in an industry.

The figure indicates four different situations:

Multi-local (or multi-domestic) industries, suggesting that the market is primarily serviced by local firms. The likelihood of seeing competitors from other countries entering the market is rather slim, partly because the markets are protected either by regulations, traditions, or dis-tance, and partly because there is little to gain on economies of scale in these industries. Typical examples in this quadrant would be hairdressers, plumbers, carpenters, and electricians,

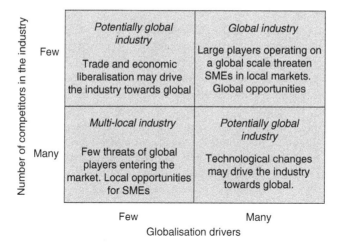

Figure 4.1 Classification of industries.

particularly those that cater for the consumer market, offering limited opportunities for scale economies. Domestic firms may encounter competition from foreign individuals entering the market offering low wages, sometimes operating in the black market. Over the past 20 years Central and Eastern Europeans have entered these trades in Western Europe, offering lower prices than domestic tradespeople. Many have also been hired by domestic firms – at minimum wages accepted by trade unions, thus curtailing the threat of competition.

Potentially global industries are found in two quadrants of the model. In the lower right section we find firms that operate in markets open to international competition, but where the number of industry players is quite high, essentially because of limited economies of scale. An example is the office furniture industry which is dominated by a large number of local players – particularly in large markets such as Germany, France, Italy, the UK and the US. In some markets and some segments however there are signs of concentration and thus also a slow movement towards a more global industry structure. This is driven by technological advances in manufacturing and the increasing importance of economies of scale.[1]

The upper left section of the matrix is also termed *Potentially global*, but this time because *globalisation drivers* potentially may push the industry towards a more global direction, i.e. more concentrated and internationally-oriented. The telecommunications business epitomises this situation, where since the 1980s the liberalisation of regulations in the telephone sector across countries opened the market for foreigners. This happened concurrently with the advent of new technologies such as mobile telephony (and also accelerated them). Companies such as Deutsche, Vodafone, Orange, Telia, Telekom Austria and Telenor are present in many markets across Europe, directly or indirectly through joint ventures. The industry is possibly not fully global in the present definition of the word, but has been driven in a global direction since the 1990s. New developments in the technology introduced by global leaders such as Google and Apple now (in 2016 and onwards) will challenge these players and possibly drive the industry to an even more global structure.

Global industries are those where few and large market players are in a position to exploit economies of scale and/or optimise operations by taking advantage of different countries' resources and competitive advantages. This gives them a competitive edge that makes smaller local firms less attractive in their home market, eventually outcompeting them – either by forcing them out of the market using lower prices, better quality or distribution, or simply by acquiring them. Rolls-Royce's development in the international maritime sector may epitomise this development. They have over recent decades acquired several market leaders in different niche segments of the maritime sector in Scandinavia (winches, diesel engines, propellers) and leverage these units' particular capabilities through their global marketing and servicing network.

4.2.1 Competitive structure

We now turn to measuring the two dimensions in this model, and begin with the number of players in the market. One factor complicating the task is that of properly defining competition. Caves and Porter (1977) discuss this in some depth and suggest that in all industries, mobility barriers (barriers that hinder entry *and* exit from an industry) create so-called strategic groups, which are firms that compete on similar terms (size, technology, business model, cost structure, marketing mix and so on), thus generating special market segments that cater to special customer groups. Firms in the same groups operate under roughly similar business conditions, and because they are more or less locked into their ways of operating – both through sunk costs and organisational culture – there is little mobility between the groups. Unambiguously discerning these segments and groups from one another is an overwhelming task. We have seen this in the beer industry. The airline industry is another case that illustrates this point. The low-cost airlines such as Ryanair, easyJet and Norwegian Air Shuttle have a very different cost structure and business model to those of the large major national carriers, and cater mostly to the tourist market. Lufthansa, British Airways, Air France, Singapore Airlines and Emirates – to mention just a few – have a different profile, traditionally attracting business passengers. Yet these latter compete head on in many markets with the low-cost airlines, considerably blurring the competitive picture. Also the national air carriers have tried to enter the low-cost market, but they have mostly failed.[2] The hotel industry is yet another case. In this industry there are several leagues of players that do not compete with each other – from the five-star Hiltons or Marriotts to the local hotels in and around the city centre, with no stars at all. Some compete on a global scale, whereas the great majority only cater to the local market.

The question therefore remains: how should we measure our competition? Traditionally, industry structure has been identified by tallying the number of competitors in the industry (as defined by industry nomenclatures, for instance SIC or NACE) and their respective market shares, and on this basis calculating a concentration index (see for instance Ghemawat 2012). The more concentrated the number of players in an industry, the fewer the number of global players, the more interdependent and intertwined the markets become. A concentration index therefore "translates" the concept of global oligopolies.

However, as we have seen, the competitive situation differs greatly *within* each industry, *within* market segments. Therefore, the concept of market share as measured by public statistics is at best equivocal. One way of circumventing this problem is to cognitively define the structure of the industry. Panagiotou (2006, 2007) claims in fact that cognitive conceptualisations of industry structures give a relevant picture of the competitive context in which firms operate. Based on their experience in the market place, firms normally have a notion of the players in their industry (number of competitors, their strengths and weaknesses, their market shares, their degree of international orientation, etc.). One possible approach to assess the globality of the industry is therefore to rate the degree of concentration of competitors in their respective industries, and to assess the extent to which players operate internationally.

4.2.2 Globalisation drivers

Assessing the effects of globalisation drivers – or their opposite number: barriers to trade – is also quite demanding. In this case it is essential to understand the most critical barriers in the market place that affect each individual industry and these may differ from one industry to the other. Globalisation drivers in general, such as cheaper transport and communications, or cultural convergence may be important indicators, but they are possibly too general to be of any value in each specific case. We deem the following indicators to be critical:[3]

- Technical or safety standards
- Cultural differences
- Trade barriers and purchasing practices.

Technical and safety standards often vary a lot between countries. Such standards have been developed as a response to public and consumer demands, in order to secure safe, environmentally-friendly and economical applications of products. One case in point is that of the building and construction industry, where national regulations and norms historically have been in place for many decades and are still prevailing. If we take the example of energy loss through walls, roofs, windows and doors (U-values), we can see different norms and recommendations across Europe. The requirements are quite strict in Northern Europe (0.18 W/m^{2}K in Sweden and Norway), decreasing to 0.70–0.80 in the Balkan countries.[4] It is conceivable that these different standards have implications for manufacturers: high standards in Northern Europe make it impossible for exporters from lower standard countries to enter these markets with their regular products; and lower standards in Southern Europe make manufacturers from high standard countries too expensive to be able to compete in those countries.

Another case is that of food products. Expanding trade has brought into sharper focus the divergence among different countries' food safety regulations and standards. These variations may reflect differences among their populations' tastes and preferences, ability to produce safe food, and willingness to pay for risk-reducing technology. As stated by the US Department of Agriculture:

> National tastes and preferences reflect a unique set of experiences and cultural traditions. Some countries may perceive a certain food safety risk as totally unacceptable, while others may place a low priority on addressing that same risk. Imports acceptable to one country may not be acceptable to another. For example, many European countries are willing to accept the risks of Listeria in cheese made from unpasteurized milk and select processing standards to minimize these risks. Other countries restrict such imports and even ban the sale of most of these cheeses.[5]

Culture in itself may represent an impediment to market entry. Different traditions that have developed over centuries and have shaped "ways of solving problems" may differ widely from one country to another. We have seen this in the food and building industry, but it is equally conspicuous in the garment, interior design and home-fitting industry. The international marketer may try to find niches of homogeneous demand (international fashion, modern design, ethnic food) where these differences matter less.

Customs duties represent the traditional hindrance to international trade. They vary greatly from one country to another and between products. Developing countries typically have a higher level of tariff protection for their industries (in general between 10 and 25%) than industrialised countries (anything from 0 to 15%, averaging 2–4%). As customs barriers have been reduced over the decades through WTO and regional trade arrangements (see Chapter 2), *protectionist purchasing* has taken over the role of reducing competition from foreign suppliers. This is particularly noticeable in the public sector, where local governments and community councils typically have a tendency to buy local in order to support local industry. This practice is sought to be dismantled in different international treaties, particularly in the EU and the EEA, in order to give players within the European market equal chances to win contracts. In many countries, the authorities include so-called "local content" clauses in order to secure activity in the home industries.

These practices (to favour local suppliers) may translate into nationalistic attitudes on the part of the buyer. In Japan, this is manifest through the strong relationships between members of the *keiretsus* (large industry groups including manufacturing, finance and insurance) where sub-contractors that are members of the "family" have long-term relationships with buyers, who are all members of the same group. What we see is, in principle, a search for reliable relationships between business partners – and perhaps a certain level of mistrust against outsiders, particularly foreign suppliers.

The next question is then how to measure the extent to which these three factors – standards, culture, and tariffs and purchasing practices – represent an impediment to market entry for the individual firm. We suggest a scale – say from 1 to 5 – whereby the analyst can rate the importance of each factor to her/his particular situation.

Putting these two factors together, we are now able to place the firm in the matrix in Figure 4.1, and to draw conclusions concerning the industry structure. We have to acknowledge that whatever method is used to measure industry structure (and therefore the nature of competition) and globalisation drivers, the result of the analysis is undoubtedly going to be woolly and will only reflect part of the picture. However, a business analyst once said: "It is better to be approximately correct, than to be accurately wrong." Therefore, the main idea is to simply understand the extent to which (global) competitors represent a threat to the firm's operations, and whether trade liberalisation opens up new opportunities in global markets – or, in the opposite case: whether trade protectionism hinders access by foreign players to our markets. On this basis, managers should be able to evaluate strategies to meet any potential situation.

4.3 Preparedness for internationalisation

The next question is: How prepared is each individual firm to cope with the competitive situation globally and to carve out a position in each individual market? And how do we measure this preparedness? Again, there is no fixed answer to these questions, but a number of indicators may help us assess the firm's resources in their broadest sense and their ability to handle the challenges of going international.

Many would claim that size should be included among such indicators. For instance Sui and Baum (2014) and Gripsrud et al. (2017) find that the larger the firm, the less the probability to *leave exporting* altogether, suggesting that larger firms are less vulnerable to the vacillations of international market involvement. On the other hand, others have found no relationship (Czinkota and Johnston 1983), or even a negative relationship (Solberg 1987, 1988), between firm size and *success in international markets*. These two (exit from exporting and export success) are not necessarily opposite numbers, rather they express different aspects of risks and opportunities in international market involvement. So while size helps firms to avoid failure, it is not absolutely necessary to secure growth in international markets. The reasons given for smaller firms being more successful in international markets may be summed up as follows (Solberg 1987, 1988):

– Smaller firms are more flexible and respond more swiftly to opportunities and changes in markets. Large firms are more bureaucratic and the lead time between the moment a new situation in the market place occurs and the firm's response is therefore generally longer.
– Smaller firms are often more innovative and entrepreneurial than their larger "cousins".

Therefore, size is *not* among the prime indicators of preparedness in this model. Three factors remain important in this context, some of which may correlate with firm size: the firm's international organisational culture, its market share in its reference markets (to be defined later), and its access to networks in international markets.

4.3.1 International organisational culture

International organisational culture may be defined as the set of attitudes, experiences and procedures that firms with extensive international involvement have developed over time. We have seen in Chapter 3 how the "beneficial export circle" – with attitudes, competencies and embodiment – gradually gains momentum. With increased international involvement, the firm's market insight and commitment (Johanson and Vahlne 1977, 1990), and its understanding of critical facets of the internationalisation process itself (Blomstermo and Deo Sharma 2003) will build up among key members of the organisation, thereby furthering its ability to carry out projects in international markets. Another factor that may contribute to an international mind-set of the organisation is recruitment of staff from different nations. One example is Opera Software of Norway, which over the years has built a team at its headquarters in Oslo consisting of some 50 different nationalities among its 1,000 or so employees. This is intended to infuse the organisation with an understanding of and respect for different cultures and also force employees to speak the *lingua franca*, which in most cases is English. Cultural understanding and proficiency in English do not necessarily make up for the international business skills developed over time, but it may help initiate the process.

A short-cut to this analysis is to use stages in the internationalisation process: the more advanced the stage, the better prepared the firm should be. Different researchers have developed different taxonomies of stages (Bakka 1973, Johanson and Vahlne 1977, Bilkey and Tesar 1977, Cavusgil 1980 – cf. Chapter 3). It is then a question of how to determine what taxonomy to use. We suggest two simple, yet reliable, measures: international sales ratio and mode of operation.

1   The former mirrors the firm's dependence on international markets and suggests that marginal sales abroad do not catch the attention of top management, and therefore will not be prioritised in the strategic thinking of the firm. For instance, research from Norway suggests that internationalisation starts to "take off" only when exports reach some 10–15% of total sales: before this threshold it is claimed that the board of directors and top management are not really directly concerned. Beyond this level, key members of the organisation will start to experience the effects of international sales and to give them more attention: finance, accounting, logistics, manufacturing, marketing will all in some way or another get directly in touch with issues regarding the foreign involvement of the firm. The more dependent the business is on international sales, the more attention top management will give to this part of its operations, the more committed the firm, and the more the

"beneficial export circle" will start to roll. A five-point scale – for instance <10%, 11–25%, 26–50%, 51–75% and >76% international sales ratio – may reflect different levels of competence built up in international marketing. It also suggests that, in an ascending order, an increasingly larger part of the organisation is directing its attention to international business operations, acquiring insights, attitudes and competencies beneficial to further develop the firm's international operations.

2   The other indicator is mode of operation.[6] This again signals degree of exposure to international operations and captures, in a more qualitative way, key members' experience of servicing foreign markets. Even though more committed operation modes normally follow increasing international sales ratios (Johanson and Vahlne 1977), many firms' export activities deviate from this pattern. For instance, a firm may operate only through distributors in international markets and still export more than 75% of their sales. Distributors and agents – as we shall see in Chapter 7 – are in relatively high control of local marketing activities and have an inherent interest in protecting their position vis-à-vis the exporter for fear of losing their representation; the more the exporter is involved in local marketing the more it will be able to develop local sales independently of its partner. Local partners are for this reason in many instances less willing to freely share critical market information, or let the exporter take an active part in marketing and sales, thus precluding the exporter from gaining necessary market insight or direct access to customers. We may therefore claim that the more committed the operation mode, offering more direct participation and control, the better equipped the organisation will be to tackle challenges in the market.

Anderson and Gatignon (1986) propose a hierarchy of operation modes in three levels – from offering high control (100% or dominant equity), through medium control (balanced equity) to low control (diffused equity). This taxonomy is based on ownership control and only partly reflects the effects of operation modes on organisational culture. Welch et al. (2007) distinguish between exporting (through distributors or agents), contractual forms (licensing and franchising, i.e. local production through third parties) and foreign direct investments (sales subsidiaries and/ or production). One aspect that may complicate either of these two classifications for our purpose (impact on international organisational culture of the firm) is that most firms with an active presence in international markets use a combination of operation modes, partly depending on the situation in each market. In order to get a reasonably reliable measure of the impact of operation mode on organisational culture, we therefore suggest the following classification.

INTERNATIONAL MARKETS ARE SERVICED THROUGH:

– Direct sales (for example, through the internet) giving only limited direct contact with customers.
– Independent representatives (such as agents or distributors) only. These give the exporter limited direct contact with and experience in international markets, but will still expose the firm to international business experiences through relationships with its foreign partner.
– Mainly through independent representatives/direct sales, but also in some selected markets through sales subsidiaries or contractual forms such as licensing or franchising. This sales and marketing structure denotes a situation whereby the marketing department is starting to get directly involved in foreign operations.
– Sales subsidiaries in all important markets, less important markets being serviced through contractual arrangements or by independent representatives. In this case the firm is getting

direct marketing and sales experience in all important markets and other departments at headquarters (i.e. finance) will be actively drawn into the operations.
–   Wholly- or partly-owned foreign production facilities in selected countries and sales subsidiaries in most markets, involving all parts of headquarters.

This classification scheme has one caveat: examples abound of firms that may for instance choose an operation mode far more demanding than their actual capability would suggest, thereby misleading the analyst to overrate the preparedness factor. Nonetheless, the experience firms gain through an overrated entry mode may in itself enhance their stock of knowledge of international operations, thus still giving some credence to the measure even in these cases.

4.3.2 Market share in reference market

Reference market is a concept that needs some deliberation. It is related to the concept of market share that has been long established as a critical factor in marketing (Buzzell and Gale 1987), but endeavours to give a more nuanced picture of the competitive situation within a market.

Let us first discuss market share. Research carried out by Boston Consulting Group suggests a strong correlation between market share and financial performance. The positive relationship between market share and financial performance has also been corroborated in research in international settings (Zou and Cavusgil 2002, Solberg and Durrieu 2015a,b). The logic behind this lies in three elements:

–   High market share implies that the firm can achieve scale advantages and hence supply products and services at lower cost than its competitors. Thereby it is able to offer lower prices and/or obtain higher margins than other market players.
–   High market share is also an indication of the general acceptance by the market of the firm's products and services – implying that they have good quality, often epitomised by a recognised brand. Customers generally trust the products and its seller, and they are willing to pay a premium for that, enhancing the margin even further.
–   In addition, a high market share suggests that the seller has a certain position in the market place, conferring power in two ways: in negotiations with customers (retailers/distributors/ wholesalers) that "need" to buy the product to have a full product range in their portfolio; and in confrontation with competitors, enabling the firm to challenge them by actively using the price in their defence of or quest for market share. Market leaders can do this through cross-subsidisation from other markets or other product lines (Hamel and Prahalad 1985).

The findings by Boston Consulting Group prompted them to develop the so-called BCG matrix, with the two dimensions being relative market share[7] and market growth. This is a generally accepted model, widely used (and misused) in strategic planning. The terminology Cash Cow, Star, Question Mark and Dog was subsequently developed to denote different strategic situations and their resulting conclusions. For instance a Dog situation is indicated by a low market share and low growth, suggesting that the firm should rid itself of the product line, principally because of low financial performance and limited future prospects. A Star situation indicates market leadership (= high performance) in a high growth market, recommending investments in the product line. Proceeds from the Cash Cow products (low growth/high market share) should be used to finance development of promising Question Mark products.

Market share is therefore a key element in developing marketing strategy. Determining market share is, however, not straightforward, mainly because the market is normally fragmented, and consists of many different – and often ill-defined – segments, making the definition of market (its boundaries and size) at best disputable. This has a direct relevance to our discussion on strategic groups in Section 4.2.1. The problem there was to establish the boundaries of an industry – and thereby also define competition. We have seen how small players in the beer market or in the hotel industry can thrive alongside large players. Referring to the total beer or hotel market and using the BCG logic, these small players should have been "wiped off the map", leaving the market to large multinational firms. Since this has not happened, we have to conclude that market share is a figure that needs qualification and a more detailed analysis.

Attempting to introduce logic into these apparent contradictions, we need to review the concept of market niches. A market niche is normally defined as a small segment of the market where small firms can prosper without fear of being outcompeted by larger firms. *The main reason for this is generally that there exist barriers to entry into the niche.* Examples of such barriers may be:

– Technological solutions that require access to know-how or patents that are not readily available.
– Special needs and preferences amongst customers in the niche that are too costly for others to adapt to. We may call this "strategic fit" between the niche player and its customers.
– Special relationships between the customers and the supplier that are difficult to "break into". Here we think about anything from trust, to friendship, to adapted routines between buyer and seller.
– The firm has developed a service level difficult to match by competitors.

The degree of protection within the niche provided by these barriers depends on technological developments both within manufacturing (new technologies allow cost-efficient small-scale production) and the product itself (i.e. developments within digital communications, creating new market constellations).

The analysis becomes even more complicated with the introduction of *international* markets. Let us consider three market situations – one where competition is limited to local suppliers only (multi-local), one where there is a certain exchange across national borders (potentially global) and one where competition is global. Figure 4.2 illustrates the nature of these three different industry (or competitive) situations: the more global, the more interconnected the

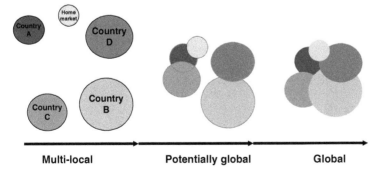

Figure 4.2 Globalisation implies gradually interwoven markets.

markets, and the more competitive moves in one country market will transfer across to other markets.

The reference market in this context therefore relates to the market where the firm can naturally define its competitors and customers. In a multi-local market situation, the reference market therefore is the firm's home market with a defined set of competitors and customers. In a potentially global market situation the market area is larger, and consists of those markets where the firm has a presence (and therefore also has other competitors). The competitors normally consist of a mix of those known from the domestic market and those met in export markets. Often both these groups of competitors are to some extent competing in each other's home markets, therefore expanding the reference market to all those markets in which the firm is operating. A fully global market exists when the firm's main competitors operate in all markets. The potentially global and, even more so, the global market situations create the basis for different scale economies as compared with multi-local markets. In order to tap into the three advantages of market share (scale, price premium and market power) mentioned above, the firm therefore needs to be present in all relevant markets. Leontiades (1984) cites the case of multinational companies operating in Great Britain, such as Ford, IBM and Texas Instruments, that have lower market shares than British companies in Great Britain, but who nevertheless display higher financial returns than their larger (in the British market) local competitors. In our context this implies that the reference market is not Great Britain, but rather a larger international (or maybe global?) market offering scale advantages not warranted by the much smaller British market.

Interestingly, if the market is classified as global, the reference market is global, even though the firm is only operating in the home market. Figure 4.3 illustrates this. In a multi-local market setting the size of the reference market equals that of the home market, and the firm has a comfortable market share (the dark segment). As globalisation proceeds and markets become more intertwined, the size of the reference market (open circles) increases. The relative market share in the home market, which in the multi-local market situation was a dominant one, dwindles when the industry globality increases (compare the small segments in the circles). The effects described here are dramatic, since the initial home market is a small country.

It is suggested that in order to measure a firm's share in its reference market, one should first determine whether the industry is multi-local, potentially global or global as suggested in Section 4.2 (see Figure 4.1). The next step is to make an assessment of ones own position in this reference market. Again, we would strongly advocate a judgemental analysis, since it is not possible to access accurate information on these issues (market share in a market that is difficult

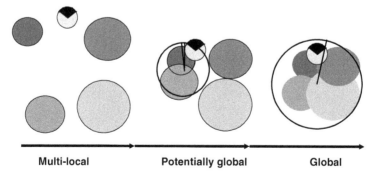

Multi-local   Potentially global   Global

Figure 4.3 What is your market share in your home market worth in a globalising industry?

to define). Research by Solberg and Durrieu (2006, 2008, 2015a) suggests a broad classification on a five point scale:

1 We are the largest player in our markets
2 We are number two or three
3 We are possibly number four or five
4 We are a small player
5 We are just a marginal player.

4.3.3 Access to customers through market networks

Access to customers is critical for any firm, but the more concentrated the customer structure (such as in the retail sector in many developed countries), the more imperative such access becomes, since firms are otherwise precluded from large parts of the market. The concentration rate in the retail industry differs among countries: for instance. the five largest retailers in the grocery sector control around or above 70% in smaller countries such as Hungary, Norway and Switzerland.[8] In larger countries, the retail structure is more dispersed, but still quite concentrated – Britain (62%), France (48%), Germany (55%).[9] On the other hand, the largest players are still dominating due to their sheer size, offering economies of scale to those that succeed in penetrating this part of the market. Therefore, the large players in the retail sector will typically prefer to buy from vendors who can offer low prices on a national (or even international) level, making market entry for smaller vendors a challenging and often futile exercise.

We have seen in Chapter 3 how market networks help exporters not only to link to potential customers, but also to provide reliable market information. We define market networks as interlinked relationships both at the individual and organisational level, and – in our context – more specifically linking the firm to its customers. Johanson and Vahlne (2009) have introduced the term "liability of outsidership", suggesting that not being integrated into the right kind of network in international markets implies a serious handicap in the firm's bid to enter new markets. In contrast, Solberg and Durrieu (2006) found that having access to key customers in international markets enhanced both the firm's commitment to and its control of the international marketing effort, eventually leading to better market performance. Measuring the role of network may be done by plainly ranking the firm's access to key customers in its main markets – for instance on a five point scale as suggested below:

1 No links to customers in foreign markets.
2 Indirect contacts to customers, through business associations, friends or government agencies in some selected markets.
3 Relations with customers in selected markets through independent representatives (agents, distributors).
4 Direct relations with key customers in selected markets.
5 Direct and close relations with key customers involving joint team work (marketing, R&D) in many markets.

Combining the scores from the three factors of organisational culture, market share and access to key customers will give a total score of preparedness for internationalisation.

1 The globally *immature company*. These have no or limited export activity and at the same time have no dominant position in their present markets. In international markets, this

company will be particularly vulnerable, in that it has limited experience and an unfavourable market share position.

2   The *adolescent company.* There are two types: those with virtually no foreign experience, but with a firm position in the home market (the home market adolescent); and those with a small to medium market share at home, and with extensive experience of international marketing (the international adolescent). Firms in the first category have the necessary economic strength to carry out an international marketing campaign, but lack the experience and organisational culture to do so and will probably make many mistakes in their first attempts to go abroad – following the incremental internationalisation model. Firms in the second category may have the required skills but not the strength to compete in global markets.

3   The internationally *mature company.* These companies have a dominant position in major markets and they are dependent on international sales – both exports and sales by foreign subsidiaries – with all that entails in terms of experience and organisational capacity. Companies with these features should be well-prepared to take on globalisation challenges. It is important to emphasise that this third category is not reserved only for large MNCs; many SMEs (or at least "MEs") have achieved considerable positions in key world markets within their narrow niche, making the traditional thinking regarding world players rather obsolete. It should also be stressed that preparedness for internationalisation should be considered relative to the market situation confronted by the firm. The requirements are much less demanding in a multi-local market situation than in a global market situation. This point is partly taken care of by the inclusion of market share in reference markets, the latter denoting the scope of the competitive challenges.

4.4 The Nine Strategic Windows

4.4.1 The model

We will now go back to the "Nine Strategic Windows" (see Figure 1.1) and discuss the strategic position of the individual firm.[10] Before doing so, it is important to consider the effect of the globalisation drivers on market shares in reference markets. A movement to the right in the grid entails a *larger reference market and a resulting weaker relative market share for the firm* of this market and vice versa. In a globalising industry, therefore, the passive firm will see its preparedness for internationalisation gradually deteriorate. This section describes the strategic posture of firms in each of the nine strategic windows of the matrix. It is important to note that the alternative strategies suggested in the nine windows delineate the *major international strategic focus* of top management. Many other tasks relating to technology, marketing, human resource management or financial subjects have not been captured by the matrix. Yet, the proposed focus will have ramifications for these areas, and the ways in which the company chooses to carry out these strategies will depend to a considerable extent on factors such as financial strength and its human resource base. These two factors have therefore been included in the discussion of the different approaches to help define relevant strategies.

Window 1: Stay at home

In this window, each country-market is isolated from the others by different kinds of entry barriers, and the threat of competitive entry from international or global players is limited and not likely in the near future. With limited international experience and a weak position in the home (reference) market there is little reason for the firm to engage in developing a position in international markets. The main focus of firms located in this part of the model should be on improving their performance and position in their home market. If the company has a weak financial position, it should consider strategies like cost reduction and/or market repositioning at home. With a better financial position and a management that takes a keen interest in international business development, it should consider initiatives outside its home market. One reason justifying such a step is the relation between success and export involvement (Solberg 1987, 1988). International sales will be a new dimension to the company and will force it to sharpen its competitive advantage. This in turn will also pay rewards in the home market. Firms in this window that embark on a cautious internationalisation process are normally "protected" by the multi-domestic nature of the individual national markets. They can then take a stepwise approach, whereby the company can move slowly and learn the "rules of the game" step by step without risking counterattacks in their home market.

Window 2: Consolidate your export markets

An environment with limited competitive threats is also true of firms in this window. Still, entrepreneurial companies have succeeded in entering foreign – most often neighbouring – markets. This is the case of, for instance, Scandinavian manufacturers of building products, furniture and sportswear which they sell in each other's markets and to some extent to the European continent. What, then, are the strategic options for a company in this situation? If the company has a weak financial position, management should review both the market and product mix and concentrate on the strategic business units (SBUs) that provide above-average returns. The remainder should be divested or harvested in a "traditional BCG manner". The cash generated from this operation should be used to reinforce the strategic position of the SBUs that are left. Given the relatively protected market climate (multi-domestic markets) the company may work its way out in what could be termed a "calm international setting". If the company has a strong financial base, it should also consider penetrating major existing markets and consider entering new ones. Due to the relatively closed markets, licensing and/or foreign direct investments are two possible entry modes for market expansion. Even though there are no signs of a globalising market environment, the company should capitalise on its international marketing know-how and competitive and financial strength. One day, the market factors may start to move in the global direction and the company should be positioned to play a new role.

Window 3: Develop new business

In this strategic window, the company has achieved a leadership position in its most important markets. The individual markets are nationally oriented, the competition is made up of nationals and the market accessibility is limited. The case of the financially weak company is similar to that in Window 2: consolidate, review your product/market mix. A company with sound finances, in contrast, should either seek to expand further into new international markets or enter new business areas in its home market. In this way, the company gradually builds its position in individual markets, thereby enhancing its ability to implement aggressive strategies when globalisation eventually occurs in the industry.

Window 4: Seek niches in international markets

In this window, the markets have been exposed to globalisation drivers to the extent that competition across borders is the rule, although it is not yet global. Firms in this position are often vulnerable because they lack both management and financial resources to confront the market situation. If the company's top management lacks interest/skills in international operations, the board of directors should initiate programmes to develop a more internationally proactive management team. With this in place, the company should identify niches in international markets. By developing niche strategies, the company erects entry barriers and redefines its role in the market (in fact, increasing its relative share in its reference market). The company will, therefore, be less vulnerable to global competitive forces. The question is, of course, to what extent a newcomer in international markets will be capable of identifying and developing niches in the market where the company can live "peacefully". The suggested strategies are in this case either to expand stepwise in neighbouring markets, following the traditional internationalisation process ladder (Johanson and Vahlne 1977), and/or − if the company has sound finances − to expand through acquisitions. This latter route to internationalisation, however, is a perilous one. Several studies (see for instance Kitching 1973) have found that only a small number of international acquisitions live up to expectations. If the company has no previous international experience, it will most likely lack the necessary organisational capacity to cope with foreign mergers and acquisitions. Of course, if the company has extensive experience of buy-outs in the home market, this may compensate for such shortcomings.

Window 5: Consider expansion in international markets

The middle of the grid denotes a situation full of potential both within the company and in the market. The company has "climbed" the internationalisation ladder and management is characterised by a proactive stance towards further international involvement. The challenge for management in this case is to carve out a position in the markets where their key competitors have a stronghold. This will increase the company's ability to react to competitive pressures in the event of a drive towards global markets. The expansion strategy that is selected will vary according to the specifics of the situation (for instance competitive structure, barriers to trade, demand pattern, etc.). Penetrating the home turf of key competitors, the company may wish to expand by inviting them to form strategic alliances, so as not to exacerbate the competitive situation. If the impeding factor is barriers to trade − for instance a closed distribution system (consumer goods with a handful of very powerful retail chains) − the company may again be advised to enter into some form of alliance with major players in the market, to buy a market share. Another way to get around the barriers is to enter into licensing agreements and joint ventures. The choice of one approach or the other will also vary according to the financial strength of the company. Exporting is still another possible entry approach, which may be feasible if the barriers and demand patterns do not constitute effective barriers to entry. In many ways, gradually increasing the company's market presence through what one could term "controlled" exports is preferable because the company slowly but surely builds the international experience necessary to take on even bigger tasks in the future (Newbould et al. 1978); in this way the international organisational culture is allowed time to become embedded in the company (Solberg 1987, 1988).

Window 6: Prepare for globalisation

The internationally mature company in a potentially global market is well-positioned to prepare itself for eventual shifts towards an even more global market. The analysis of the imminence and impact of the globalisation drivers is critical to companies in this window. To what extent, for instance, will the harmonisation of standards in the EU impact on industry structure? Will technological change alter the business model in the industry? Will our company's reactions to developments bring about changes in the industry structure?

A company with comfortable financial strength is in a position to adopt an aggressive stance to the possible changes in the industry through, for instance, acquisitions. A world leader in fertilisers, Yara, is an example of such behaviour. Since the middle of the 1970s they have stubbornly and consistently carved out a dominant position in the European fertiliser industry through acquisitions and joint ventures. The industry structure may still be classified as potentially global, with more than 500 players – some of which are dominant on several continents. However, Yara is well-placed to meet a more global market situation and influence this development through acquisitions.

A financially weaker company will have to play with other "instruments" to gain a market position. One alternative is to seek alliances with major actors in the individual markets.

Jordan of Norway, for example, is a market leader in toothbrush sales in Scandinavia and is active in a number of other European countries. With a sales volume of some 150 million USD, however, it is a dwarf against the big retail giants in Europe and against its main competitors such as Colgate, Sensodyne, and Procter and Gamble. In order to achieve leverage in this situation, Jordan seeks alliances through interactive participation with major local distributors of hygiene products, who have the necessary market power to deal with supermarket chains in each individual market.

One important distinction between the above types of alliances and "strategic alliances" lies in the scope of the latter. The competitive arena is more global and a failure is more consequential in strategic alliances than is the case with joint local ventures or acquisitions in individual markets (Hamill and El-Hajjar 1990). According to Perlmutter and Heenan (1986), "Not all efforts to mould international coalitions are either strategic or global; some are mere extensions of traditional joint ventures – localized partnership with a focus on a single national market." The above alliances seem to fall into this category. However, the aggregate effects of these local alliances may be to position the company to act more globally. Thus, the actions taken by the company may in themselves constitute a globalizing driving force; Yara may be a case in point.

Window 7: Seek new owners with an extensive international marketing network

In this strategic window, the company already finds itself in a global market and is a local dwarf among multinational giants. The company, most likely, has only a few possibilities to survive as an independent unit. It will have to develop a network of partners – financial, technological and marketing – in order to survive in a challenging global environment. It may divert into either of the following three windows:

–   Window 4, "Seek niches in international markets" through redefining the nature of the business, for instance, by entering more protected segments of the market (government contracts, fragmented or innovative distribution channels). Identifying and developing a niche, however, requires in-depth market insight, a competence not typical of this class of firms.

–   Window 8, "Seek global alliances" by inviting a third party with the necessary "prepared-ness for internationalisation" to enter into a licensing agreement or to take a (majority) stake in the firm. In this case the firm needs to develop relevant networks.
–   Window 5, "Consider expansion in international markets" through a combination of the two.

If this is not possible, the company should seek ways to increase its net worth so as to attract potential partners for a future buy-out bid. The essential criterion for partner selection should in this case be a marketing network, in order to secure sufficient sales volumes for large scale operations.

In this window, we find a number of Born Globals, typically hi-tech entrepreneurs with technological innovations targeting an international audience. In small countries such as Scandinavia, Benelux and Central European countries, there are a great many companies falling into this category, mainly emanating from the engineering-oriented *milieu* of technological universities. Their home markets are often too limited to warrant sufficient economies of scale and the orientation of management is towards the technology rather than the market. The challenge for these companies lies in the conflict between the lack of international organis-ational culture and of market or financial power on one hand, and the threat of larger inter-nationally-oriented competitors with a broad marketing coverage entering the arena on the other. This threat is exacerbated by the speed by which hi-tech innovations are diffused, copied or improved upon by competitors (Ohmae 1985).

Window 8: Seek global alliances

In this cell, the company is adolescent, and finds itself in a global market. With medium pre-paredness, the firm in this position may use strategic alliances in order to cope with larger and more powerful competitors, either through extensive joint venturing or through marketing, subcontracting or R&D arrangements. In this position the firm has acquired the necessary skills in international business operations (adolescent) and should be able to cope with the challenges posed by complex negotiations with potential partners without losing its independence. By means of an alliance, the firm may overcome its competitive disadvantages, whatever the field of activity (economies of scale, marketing network, technological development and so on; Porter 1986). The difference between the financially strong and weak company lies essentially in the leverage it will have in negotiations with its future partners, and in its capability to take the initiative. It seems, however, that companies in this position in the grid will not be able in the long run to defend their market position on their own, unless they are able to identify niches, or in other words change their position in the grid to the left (less globalised) and upward (through a larger market share in a smaller reference market).

Window 9: Strengthen your global position

Finally, the firm has reached a position where it operates in global markets, and where it is among the market leaders in key markets. Within its industry the company is among the major "chess players" in the global marketplace. Even if this seems to be the "end station" of a long voyage towards the "global village", the dynamism of international trade will force the players in this window to be alert and carry out both preventive and more proactive policies. Changes in demand patterns and customer preferences, the volatility of the reference market, changes in the cost position of both the different countries and the individual players in the market, new technologies, political events (Brexit, Trumpism) and so on will all contribute to a market being constantly on the move. A key element to becoming a global player seems to be the ability to secure access to large markets where competitors have a stronghold, be it the US, China, Japan or Europe. Without a firm foothold in such markets, the "global" firm is vulnerable to competitive attack. Citing Kverneland (1988, p. 225), "The success of Japanese firms in certain global industries could make counter-competitive actions in Japan an important component of their competitors' worldwide strategy." Companies in Window 9 should therefore identify the pivotal elements in this picture and develop an organisation capable of reacting rapidly to changes and events in the "global village". During the 1980s, different network-based organisational models were suggested (Hedlund 1986, Prahalad and Doz 1981, Bartlett and Ghoshal 1989) in a response to the challenges posed by a global industry structure. Bartlett and Ghoshal's model of transnational companies (think global – act local) may epitomise the organisational challenges of companies in this window.

4.4.2 Case company: ASK travelling through the matrix

ASK was a world leader in the projector industry (for PowerPoint presentations), located in Norway. This industry witnessed rapid technological development in its early years, from around 1985 until the early 1990s. A great number of firms sought to provide a technological solution for projecting images and information in large format and there was no established industry standard. Building on various core technologies, projectors were identified as a pre-ferred future standard in the early 1990s. Like the computer industry, initial customers in the projector market were professional users such as companies and universities, and later included home users, leading to the entry of a number of companies into the market that put intense pressure on margins. Today's projector industry includes large MNCs such as Sony, Toshiba and Compaq, and can be seen as a global industry (with approximately 40 brands and 10 manufacturers worldwide). However, despite convergence of product features, some segmentation exists, ranging from low-end to high-end, mostly sold through retailers and audio-visual reseller channels respectively. Markets tend to be served at a national level, especially in the sales and marketing function, to respond to local requirements.

Phase 1: Start-up

ASK, founded in 1984, originally conducted R&D within LCD technology for producing LCD screens but later turned its focus towards developing overhead panels for projecting images in larger formats. The Norwegian market was perceived as too small and the company had to act and think internationally. It defined its home market to be Europe but, as the firm suffered from unstable ownership and lack of financial support for marketing the innovations, it was unable to claim a position in the market. For example, the firm lost a contract for producing 10,000 LCD screens due to financial constraints, even though they had operational capacity. Facing this situation, it was difficult to fund R&D, and the firm initiated cooperation with Japanese devel-opers to ensure access to leading core technologies. Cooperative solutions were also sought with German and later American developers to try to ensure that ASK was prepared for whatever would become the industry standard. Through such vertical cooperation, the firm abandoned the difficulties of having a pure R&D focus, and could assemble a final, marketable product.

Phase 2: Born global – international networking

By 1991, Tandberg Data, a world leader in data storage products, assumed ownership of the firm, and, although not implying any operational synergies, this gave the necessary security for banks, lending institutions, customers and suppliers. ASK soon entered into an agreement with Polaroid, which marketed a line of overhead projectors in America under the label "For Polaroid – By ASK". With increasing competition, declining prices and a continuously increasing minimum efficient scale, the company undertook an aggressive marketing campaign, building a network of distributors in countries all over Europe and some in Asia. With a strong product, they could dictate to their distributors and through this capture market shares in Europe. Key individuals were recruited from technology-intensive industries from 12 different nations, providing both industry and market knowledge at HQ. In 1996, ASK was spun off from Tandberg Data. This facilitated a more realistic valuation of the firm and ASK was listed on the Oslo Stock Exchange later that year.

Initially with no established industry, it can be argued that the firms in the early years operated locally (i.e. in Window 1), but before long, as industry standards emerged, large MNCs were able to market the products globally. ASK lacked international experience, distribution channels and financial strength, and was then rapidly moved towards Window 7 in the framework. The firm relinquished the focus on R&D and sought to assemble a product by combining its own components with elements developed externally. Informal, personal relationships were developed into contracts and agreements in some cases. For example, the successful partnerships with Japanese developers were partly due to a somewhat accidental meeting with a Japanese-American individual, who introduced ASK representatives to the Japanese business community. Still, at this point, the firm's approach to Japan (and other external suppliers and distributors) was deliberate and planned, not an *ad hoc* process of further developing personal networks. Although complying with the overall network logic of Window 7, ASK was gradually moving towards Window 8, as evidenced by its strong negotiating power primarily thanks to its R&D competencies and product qualities. Tight links were established with suppliers, as the components were subject to a high degree of customisation. Further, the firm did not have the option of choosing from a wide range of entry modes due to limited financial resources. Through intense negotiations and providing leading products, the firm could enter the markets at the large scale required in the industry. By building on such external resources, it could compete head-on with larger MNCs within the various segments of the projection market, instead of being a niche provider.

Phase 3: Global consolidation

Investors appreciated the company's strong presence in Europe and Asia, and by 1998 the decision was taken to acquire its American competitor, Proxima Corporation, which was somewhat unstructured at the time. The new company, ASK Proxima ASA, sought scale economies while providing both brands through the large distribution networks in all key markets. In 1999 (and implemented from 2000), the company was restructured into three business units; Products and Manufacturing, Americas and Europe/Asia (which was split later in 2000), enabling a global and market-driven focus in product development, while retaining regional and local responsibility in the sales, marketing and service functions through regional business units and subsequently with local representative offices.

The company changed name to Proxima ASA in 2000, and as of 2005, the company was the second largest in the projector industry. A year later, the firm merged with the industry leader, InFocus, followed by further restructuring of global operations. This created an even stronger global foothold and allowed economies of scale to be exploited. This was increasingly important in the growing market with only ten manufacturers. Decision-making was centralised in the American HQ, whereas regional headquarters coordinated local sales offices. Production was outsourced to various low-cost Asian countries, and logistics was carried out by a global service firm. The former Norwegian HQ became an R&D unit with a global mandate, alongside a technological unit in Oregon, USA. The new and larger organisation could serve each market segment well; increasingly it sold through the PC reseller channel which replaced the traditional audio-visual channel, in addition to the growing number of units sold through the internet. Furthermore, the company assumed partial ownership in supplier firms, such as a lens manufacturer, still pursuing multiple technological standards, giving flexibility and reducing the risk from suppliers.

The extensive marketing network, together with the acquisition of Proxima, indicates a subsequent increase in preparedness, moving the firm from Window 8 towards Window 9. Here, the firm continuously increased and restructured its organisation, and combined the drives for global integration (especially in R&D and production), while retaining local responsiveness (in sales, marketing and service). The merger with InFocus further increased volumes, strengthened global presence and enabled a better approach to each market segment. Although the merger with InFocus can be seen as resulting in a loss of influence and decision power, it was a necessary consolidation to achieve the high volumes and global efficiency and coordination needed to face the intense competition. InFocus, traditionally servicing the professional market, has now lost some market share in a dramatically increased industry, yielding ground to firms like Sony and Toshiba. In our analysis, this may be due to a number of factors: ironically, loss of focus (sic.) due to too many brands in an industry where marketing skills and brand positioning would take over from engineering and R&D excellency as the technology matured.

4.5 Chapter summary

The "Nine Strategic Windows" framework demonstrates the effects of different international settings on business and marketing strategy. The approach taken differs from other frameworks in that it accounts for the combined effects of the degree of globality in the particular industry, the impact of globalisation drivers, and the degree of international preparedness of a company.

The general managerial implication of the model is that company management should carefully assess the outcome of a gradual concentration of competition. This concentration may take place in any industry depending on the underlying barriers to entry and the globalisation drivers affecting the industry.

Using the framework, the analyst should distinguish between the *state of the globality* and the *globalisation drivers*. In the former, the specific structure of the industry is the object of analysis. The analysis of industry structure does not entail the study of the process leading to the state. Rather, it is essential to define a measure of the extent to which the industry structure makes competitors in different local markets mutually interdependent in international markets.

An analysis of the globalisation drivers calls for a thorough understanding of the *forces* at work. These forces are: technological development (initiating changes in mobility barriers and thereby strategic groups); trade and capital market liberalisation (lowering international entry barriers); and internationalisation and concentration of customer structure (forcing suppliers to enter into strategic alliances or acquisitions).

Furthermore, caution needs to be taken in that the rather suggestive terminology in each window may mislead the analyst. For instance a company pursuing a global niche strategy may not necessarily find itself in Window 4: "Seek niches in international markets". It may well be located in Window 6 or even 9, simply because it is a leader in an industry with few specialised players operating on a global scale. Also, it is tempting to locate the firm in Window 8: "Seek global alliances" just because this is what typically characterises its strategy. In other words, the

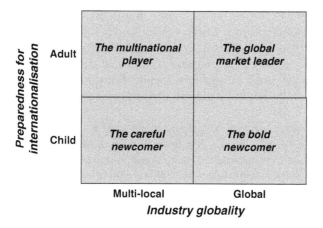

Figure 4.4 From Nine to Four Strategic Windows.

analysis should start with the two axes of the grid, and then conclude on the main thrust of the firm's strategy.

Another caveat is that of a misplaced company because of inaccurate analysis. This is particularly critical; take the example of a company that judged the market to be global, but where local idiosyncrasies in each market inhibited any large scale operations across markets, and therefore did not create the ground for large scale operations (and for MNCs to be interested). The firm, a newly established operation with limited resources and no international business experience, expanded into several markets with sales subsidiaries over a short period of time. Overstretching its resources, it filed for bankruptcy after five years.

One may ask whether it is possible to create an all-encompassing framework of analysis in which international newcomers and SMEs share space in the matrix with large multinational enterprises. The issues confronting these different categories of companies are undoubtedly widely different, and one may argue that they cannot be discussed in the same context. However, the framework does not deal with large MNCs as such, but rather with individual strategic business units within MNCs. In this perspective, many SBUs of large multinationals may embody certain common features with those of SMEs.

Whereas the "Nine Strategic Windows" model was originally developed to identify the main strategic thrust of companies, it is also well-suited for use as a guide when devising the different elements of an international marketing strategy. To this end we will apply a condensed model in the rest of the book, a 2×2 matrix, in order to simplify the analysis. Doing this we risk losing some nuances captured by the framework, but on the other hand, it may be difficult to clearly delineate the finely-tuned distinctions in a nine-cell model as compared with a four-cell model. Based on the terminology of the nine-cell model, we have given the collapsed model the taxonomy as shown in Figure 4.4, "The Four Strategic Windows".

Notes

1 Based on discussions with Mr. Lars Røyri, CEO of Scandinavian Business Seating.
2 Bjørn Kjos (CEO and main shareholder of Norwegian Air Shuttle), *Høyt og Lavt* (High and Low), Aschehoug, Oslo 2015.

3 These factors have also been discussed in Chapter 2. We bring them in here in order to highlight their relevance to the model in Figure 4.1.

4 Source: http://www.eurima.org/u-values-in-europe/. U-value expresses the heat loss in building materials and is defined as: W/m^2K. The lower the U-values, the stricter the regulation.

5 http://www.ers.usda.gov/amber-waves/2003-november/food-safety-and-trade-regulations,-risks,-and-reconciliation.aspx#.V68eFU1f1hg

6 Operation modes will be looked at in more detail in Chapter 7.

7 Relative market share means relative to the largest competitor.

8 Gabor Konig, 2009. *The Impact Of Investment And Concentration Among Food Suppliers And Retailers In Various OECD Countries*, Hungarian Ministry of Agriculture – Agricultural Economics Research Institute (AKI).

9 Brenda Cullen and Alan Whelan, 1997. "Concentration of the retail sector and trapped brands." *Long Range Planning*, 30(6): 906–916.

10 This section is adopted from the author's article, 1997. "A framework for analysis of strategy development in globalising markets." *Journal of International Marketing*, 5(1), 9–30.

Part II

Decisions in international marketing

Firms operating in international markets are exposed to a number of unknown situations that require decisions at all levels. Below is listed a number of such situations that describe only a fragment of possible dilemmas that management need to confront.[1]

1. It took three years of hard work by several members of top management and nearly 1.2 million euros of expenditure to finally get positive signals from their first Russian customer, a large firm in the oil exploration industry. Particularly time-consuming was establishing good relationships with their local partner. Identifying him, checking his credentials, understanding his way of thinking and negotiating an agency contract took much more time than anticipated. Now, they were comfortable with their choice and everything seemed to go smoothly. Indeed, their partner's ability to attract interest from this important customer was proof of the pudding. Then, as suddenly as a lightning bolt from a clear sky, the partner was under scrutiny by the police – allegedly because of tax fraud, but more likely, because he had at one point supported a political opponent of the regime. So there they were, without the crucial link to their potential customer and puzzled as to what to do next.

2. Another firm was exporting their toothbrushes to selected markets in Europe. They were typically number three of four among competitors, and in some smaller markets number two – except in their home market where they were market leaders. In Britain, representing around 9% of total sales and with a market share of some 15%, they were using marketing tools such as in-store activities and social media. Their most important customer was a big supermarket chain. This customer now demanded that they put money into TV advertising – a media hitherto not used by the firm – with budgets that they were not able to match. This was a major setback for the firm, since other customers only represented 30–35% of sales in Britain.

3. An exporter of agrochemicals had sent a shipload of their products to Mexico. The cargo was worth one million USD, and was to be transferred to the local distributor according to a CAD contract (Cash Against Documents – see Section 12.3.1). The firm nurtured good relations with this distributor through more than 10 years of business, and it had always paid without any delay. Yearly sales to Mexico had grown from zero to some 10 million USD over this period, and the firm had developed a marketing plan with the distributor, where the said shipload was the second out of five. As the ship was crossing the Atlantic, Mexico was declared insolvent and consequently put an embargo on all payments in foreign currency, including honouring letters of credit.

4. A firm, exporting groceries across Europe, is selling under private brand to a distributor in Germany, Europe's biggest market. This has been going on for several decades and the exporter is making good money on this deal. In fact, the firm's products have – through its

distributor's brand name – a dominant position in the German market. Now, the distributor has been acquired by one of the firm's major competitors in Europe, and the contract is therefore terminated by the new owners. In the meantime, the competitive climate in Germany (and in Europe generally) has considerably hardened and it will take both money and time to build anything near a similar market share – and with a very uncertain outcome.

5   A Scandinavian manufacturer of electronic devices for the car industry decided to present its products at the annual Geneva trade show. In reality, they already had some contacts with some of the large manufacturers in Italy, and aimed at firming up this relationship at the trade fair. In the meantime, the Italians appeared to be hesitant as to their original plans and withdrew from any further discussions. At the trade fair, the export manager was, however, approached by a representative of an Indian company that showed a keen interest in their technology; he proposed a licensing arrangement, potentially with a joint venture in India. Tempting as it appeared, India was still far from the actual mind-set of the firm and they had never before entered into licensing or joint venture deals with foreign (or any other) partners. Management, well-informed about the challenges of engaging in India (corruption, red tape, different culture in general), were hesitant to engage in serious discussions. After all, they had just made a board decision about entering Europe. India, then, did not really fit into this strategy.

6   A large fertiliser company with factories in Europe, Latin America, Canada and Australia had long operated through a distributor deal that had served them well in East Asia. In fact, their distributor had developed their business over the previous 15 years to become market leaders in this country. However, the distributor was adamant that the company should not get involved in local marketing activities; this was the realm of the distributor, without any interference from HQ. This was frustrating for the marketing department, which tried to get more hands-on experience and control in the market. The local market was essential for the operational efficiency of one of their plants, and management was therefore hesitant to terminate the contract with the distributor and set up their own operations there, potentially losing market shares. This situation would be exacerbated by the threat of the distributor to represent one of their major competitors.

7   The European leader in the office chair market was the result of a merger between four different brands from Nordic countries and the Netherlands, each with its own brand image and dealer network. In fact, the consolidated company was represented by some 1,500 dealers throughout Europe. Even though some dealers represented two of the brands, many of them had only one brand of the merged company in their portfolio. Also, the brand images overlapped somewhat. Some dealers were ardent supporters of "their" brand, buying into the brand idea and its image. However, the majority were more or less indifferent to the brand name as long as the product kept its promises. After the merger, the company had put a lot of effort into refining the "personalities" of the four brands, and they now appeared as distinct brands, with distinct qualities and images. However, they had highly different positions in the European market, and preferences and buying motives differed from one country to the other. Furthermore, competition in Europe was rather fragmented – the five largest players had a combined market share of less than 20%, and most of the competitors only operated within their national markets. So the company had several strategic options: should they create a new brand for the European market; should they refine the "House of Brands" hitherto pursued in the market; should they consolidate the dealership structure; should they use the same strategy throughout Europe even though the markets were rather different?

Seven cases, seven different strategic and operational situations, with very different potential solutions. It is about market selection, it is about entry mode (or more generally, operation mode), it is about positioning and branding, it is about standardisation, it is about economic and political risk, it is about structuring the organisation and it is about how to tackle cultural differences. They require different kinds of information, their solutions involve different kinds of resources, and their alternative solutions have radically different consequences for the firm's further development.

Part II of the book will delve into these kinds of situations, and provide a foundation for informed discussion, both in the classroom and the boardroom, about alternative avenues for the firm.

Note

1 Some of the anecdotes are fictitious, yet relevant, in order to protect sensitive information.

5 Information for international marketing decisions

5.1 Introduction

We have on different occasions underlined the importance of a good, basic understanding of local market conditions, and – in global markets – also general knowledge about the industry and international markets as a whole. Mostly, international market information is needed in order to make decisions concerning market entry (countries), operation modes and partner selection, positioning in the market, marketing activities and logistics. This is necessary not only to devise sales and marketing activities in foreign markets, but also to understand the overall strategic position of the firm. This chapter considers different aspects of market information. First, we will discuss what kind of information is collected – be it in the form of market research as it is described in textbooks on the subject or rather as information from network partners or through one's own experience in the market. Then different types of market research are looked at briefly, before we describe a market intelligence system.

5.2 Information through experience and networks or market research?

A company can get information in two major ways: from its network and own operational experience in the market or through dedicated market research projects. According to Diamantopoulos et al. (1990) and Schlegelmilch et al. (1993), only one in two exporters conduct any form of market research, and even fewer engage external consultants to do so. We have already suggested that information derived from operational experience in the market is better anchored in the organisation than information gained through research projects. It is also more frequently used to guide decision-making, partly because firms often have limited insights into the intricacies of international market research, but also because it is generally more expensive than market research at home. Managers therefore have a tendency to disbelieve foreign market research as a means of getting reliable and cheap information on issues about which they oftentimes already have a preconceived opinion. Sometimes they use it rather to confirm their own suspicions about market development or to justify a decision (Diamantopoulos and Souchon 1999).

The general manager of a medium-sized, Norwegian furniture manufacturer, Stompa, with a good performance in Germany and Britain once grumbled: "Market research – I don't believe in it!" He complained about the time and money spent on market research with uncertain value, resources which could be better spent on selling products and entertaining customers. At the same time he spoke warmly about how their sales people, together with their local agents, visited major customers and discussed with them preferences, opportunities and problems in the market.

It has been found that informal, person-to-person information gathering prevails as a means of getting reliable international market information (Keegan 1984, Benito et al. 1993, Gripsrud et al. 1999). This reflects the ownership managers take of information that they have collected themselves from sources that they trust. These sources can be partners, such as agents or distributors, customers or friends, and also acquaintances in different networks, such as members of rotary clubs, sport clubs, old school friends and so on. Granovetter (1985) discusses the reason for this:

- One trusts one's own information, which is gathered in a relevant business context.
- It is richer and more detailed (than information gained through market research projects).
- Firms and people in the network have an economic reason to give reliable information (if not they will be discarded as a network partner at the next crossroads).
- Network relations have a tendency to become more confidential, and opportunism will therefore be less relevant or conspicuous.

Local market partners are used much more than other sources, particularly in the initial phases of involvement in international markets, because alternative sources of information are not yet known. The longer the experience in the market, the more varied the sources, and the more value firms extract from its information capture (Gripsrud et al. 2006). Figure 5.1 shows a taxonomy of market information, based on two criteria: formal or informal market information, and ad hoc (i.e. market information for a concrete marketing decision) and continuous market information.

Reviewing the practice by Norwegian firms, Benito et al. (1993) found that both market investigation – which is defined as an informal way of getting information for decisions such as country selection, choice of entry mode or customer search – and market experience from operations by far prevail in this context. Market research is barely used by exporters, whereas market intelligence is even less used. Generally speaking, small firms are to a greater extent using informal information, whereas larger firms use markedly more consultants, statistics

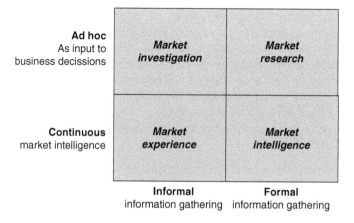

Figure 5.1 Different kinds of market information.

Source: Benito et al. (1993).

and databases (examples of formal information). Small firms on the other hand use government export promotion agencies. An interesting observation is that the more the firm has of market insight, the more it will look for market information and use formal information capture.

Based on the above discussion, we present a typology of exporters' information behaviour. Figure 5.2 gives a rough idea of the main characteristics of the different groups of firms, based on two kinds of information sources:

1   Information received through the exporter's marketing network and other networks in the market place. This information is, for the most part, informally collected and distributed in the organisation. It is generally received from trusted partners.
2   Information gained through more or less formalised data collection based on a pre-conceived need specification; we term this "objective market research". It is objective in the sense that the information is not transferred through a network of trusted informants.

There is reason to believe that most, if not all, firms combine these two information components in various proportions. They certainly offer different angles into marketing insight and they complement each other. It is also assumed that formal market research is more often used to make or justify decisions concerning specific marketing campaigns or activities. As such, it is more easily "forgotten" by the organisation, whereas market information and knowledge based on experience through operating in a network of market players is more "sticky". In the following, the four different groups in Figure 5.2 will be described.

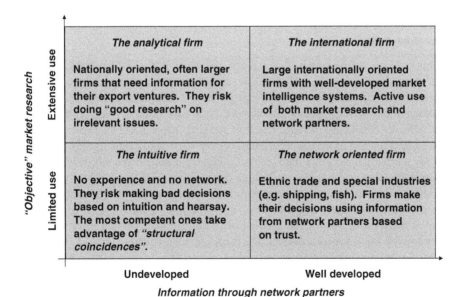

Figure 5.2 Model of information behaviour in international markets.

Source: Based on Solberg (2006b).

5.2.1 The intuitive firm

In this cell, we find firms with limited resources, which deters them from engaging in international market research with the aim to identify business opportunities abroad. Resources in this context must be understood broadly – as financial resources (or willingness to pay consultants for market research) and as the managerial ability within a firm to define and carry out market research in foreign markets. These companies also lack the necessary primary or secondary network relations to help them uncover foreign market opportunities. Unsolicited orders or participation in export promotion programmes normally constitute their first (hesitant) steps in international markets. Even though export assistance is often used by these firms, they will have problems in fathoming or contextualising the information provided, because they have neither the capacity, nor the competence, nor the experience to interpret this information. Export promotion agencies should therefore concentrate on leading these firms into relevant networks so as to give them a better foundation upon which to work. The term "structural coincidences" suggests that since all firms operate in networks in their home market, they will sometimes be indirectly linked to their network partners' international network, and as such they may be "dragged" into foreign markets.

> A case illustrating this point is the Swedish vendor of health care products that, through one of its local customers, was invited to bid for a large project in the United Arab Emirates. They did not have any intention of starting to export to this market, but since their customer happened to be linked to the Arab project, they decided to get involved. The trust between the partners was in a way a "substitute" for information about the future Arab customer and the context in which they operated (Axelsson and Johanson 1992).

5.2.2 The analytical firm

These firms have a good market position at home, and have for various reasons (globalisation, increased competition, technological advances, etc.) decided to expand internationally. Since their foreign network (limited foreign market activities) is inadequate, they need to make use of market research to uncover opportunities abroad. They have often decided on the country to export to (rather by default than through research, see next chapter), and their research is mainly concerned with identifying a local distributor. Given their leadership role in the domestic market, they normally have a qualified team of middle managers and analysts who engage in market research, either on their own or through commissioned research. However, their leadership position at home often makes these firms believe they are "invincible", and can transfer their successful domestic marketing practices to other countries. Rick's (1983) "Big Blunders in International Business" gives a good account of ill-defined international marketing projects carried out by well-known market leaders. The reason for many of these mistakes lies primarily in faulty market research, underestimating local idiosyncrasies in the problem definition phase. Information through network relations, although not the universal remedy to this situation, could potentially give direction to the research. Obviously, focus groups in the initial phases are one other way of achieving relevance to the research (Craig and Douglas 2009). Firms in this cell may have well-developed domestic networks, and may be skilful in monitoring and controlling their domestic marketing activities. However, on entering new markets, these attributes fall short of relevance.

A case in point is the Norwegian fast-moving consumer goods market leader Stabburet, whose attempt to enter the US crispbread market was a total failure. They believed the densely-populated states in the Midwest, with strong Scandinavian connections, would embrace a traditional bread – so-called "flatbread" – from the "old homeland". They positioned more or less in the same way as in Norway – same package and similar appearance, calling it "Grandma's flatbread",[1] playing on positive associations to traditions and the presumably good taste of homemade bread. They did some research on distribution channels, price levels, competitors and so on, but not on the issues that really counted: the marketability of the concept to its suggested target groups. Only after "going by the textbook" – using focus groups to develop an adapted concept – did the venture start to show results.[2]

5.2.3 The network firm

This group of firms can be found in a variety of trades, such as, for instance, diamond-mining, fishing, oil, etc. These are trades where million-dollar deals can be concluded over the telephone and where trust is the hallmark of relationships between business partners. The reliability of the information provided through this network is ascertained by the transparency of the network and the need for all members to maintain their good reputation (Granovetter 1985). Contrary to the assumption of neoclassic economists, Uzzi (1997) found that embedded relationships are indeed rational through positive effects like trust, fine-grained information transfer and joint problem-solving arrangements. Often these networks have been built over several generations of business partnerships. A special case of network relationships is represented by the diaspora of ethnic networks. Examples include Jewish tradespeople dispersed for centuries across the globe. Migrations of Indians, Pakistanis, Chinese and Turks since the Second World War have also opened new trading routes. For a Frenchperson, it is easier to develop a business relationship with a French expat in Egypt than with a local Egyptian.

The Norwegian fish trader who wanted to expand into Eastern Europe illustrates this point. Through friends in Norway he made contact with a Norwegian businessman who was married to a Romanian woman and settled in Bucharest. His local compatriot did some investigative work, and forged a link for him with Romanian importers. He visited the market and selected his local distributor in Romania, who eventually became a reliable and invaluable business partner (Gripsrud et al. 1999).

5.2.4 The international firm

These firms have a dense business network. They frequently carry out market research in international markets, both in order to get hold of information about new market opportunities and to control various parts of their strategic marketing decisions in established markets. Also these firms have generally set up a system for continuous market intelligence (see later in this chapter). These are usually large firms, with longstanding international marketing experience. Hewlett-Packard's Market Research and Information Centre, with more than 30 professionals making extensive use of external research suppliers, epitomises this group of firms (Kotler 1994).

The presented model gives useful signals as to how different types of firms should develop their information-gathering strategies in international markets. This is possibly more critical for the two former groups of firms (the intuitive and analytical) than for the two latter ones. The former are firms that, through a well-functioning export promotion support system, are led to relevant network partners in international markets. This is particularly vital for the intuitive firm, since it does not have sufficient expertise or resources to carry out in-depth market research. Given the lack of relevant information on local marketing conditions through networks, the analytical firm will also need cultural assistance in order to understand contextual idiosyncrasies in foreign markets and thus to be able to develop *relevant* market research projects. This is important in sectors such as food, a category where cultural expressions are particularly conspicuous (Askegaard and Madsen 1998).

A study of Norwegian exporters' information behaviour found that firms in the right-hand side of the matrix perform significantly better than firms on the left. This may suggest that information through networks provides a better foundation for decision-making in international markets. Unpublished data from the same study reveals that research in international markets in general is negatively correlated with export performance. Only firms with long relationships (more than five years) with their foreign partners seem to be capable of using international market research to their advantage.

We conclude this section by stating that both market research and obtaining market information through reliable network partners in the market are necessary to make viable international marketing decisions. Information through networks is crucial since it is embedded in the firm's concrete marketing context. In this way it helps guide the firm to ask relevant questions if or when it engages in specific market research projects.

The next two sections describe two types of data in international market research:

> *Secondary data* is information collected, structured and published for other purposes than for the relevant decision to be taken. Typical examples are public statistics and reports from government agencies (such as Census Bureaus), multi-client studies from consultants, databases, and articles in trade journals, newspapers, etc. Actually also internal data sources may be regarded as secondary data as long as they have been collected for other purposes than the decision at hand.

> *Primary data* is, on the other hand, information that is collected in order to elucidate critical factors relative to a concrete decision. Management must therefore initiate a specific market research project in order to obtain the required information. Primary data capture is generally more expensive since the project is tailored to fit the specific need.

5.3 Using secondary data

To get an understanding of what an international market analyst does, let us introduce Irene, a young market analyst who had been tasked with researching the structures of the global shipbuilding industry. Here's how she describes her search for data:

> After getting to know the general traits of the ship-building industry by, amongst other things, reading books such as *Maritime Economics* (Stopford 1997), I set out to identify relevant organisations and people within the industry. This had a snowballing effect where one contact knew a couple of others, who in turn had other contacts, and after a relatively short period of time I had an interesting network of insightful people who were able to give me relevant information on the various aspects of the ship-building industry.

The next phase involved searching for concrete data on the industry. I used the following sources:

Databases	*FTProfile* did not seem to have the main publications within ship-building. *Celex* provided me with specific information on EU regulations.
Publications	There are several publications on shipping and ship-building. Here are the ones I found the most interesting:
	– *Lloyd's Shipping Economist* – a brilliant source with updated information and interesting interviews – *Shipping Statistics*, Institute of Shipping and Economics, Bremen, quarterly – *Seatrade* – a weekly newsletter with detailed information on ship-building – *Financial Times* and *Wall Street Journal* cover much, but not specific enough, information
Reference books	*Lloyd's Maritime Directory* has information on shipyards, ship owners and various organisations within the ship-building industry.
Public and private organisations	In Japan there are several organisations where you can get useful information:

	– *Japan Ship Exporters' Association*
	– *The Cooperative of Japan Shipbuilders*
	– *The Ship Machinery Manufacturers' Association of Japan*
	– *Japan Ship Machinery External Trade Association*
	    In the US the *Shipbuilders' Council of America* keeps track of the global ship-building activity.
	    The *Federation of Norwegian Industries* and the *Federation of Norwegian Shipowners* have information on Norwegian industry. Ship brokers such as Platou, Fernleys, Bassøe, and Grieg will also have a great deal of information.
	    In other countries I have been in touch with the following organisations:
	– *The Korea Shipbuilders' Association, Seoul*
	– *Astelliros Espanoles SA, Madrid*
	– *German Shipbuilding and Ocean Industries Association, Hamburg*

Shipping conferences are held on a regular basis in various locations around the world, including in Norway every other year. These often turn out to be extremely useful and provide the perfect opportunity to meet key people to interview.

This was a project on shipbuilding and the sources mentioned are naturally specific to this particular industry. The analyst's observations were made 20 years ago, but despite the enormous increase in span and use of the internet since then, they would not have changed dramatically to this day. The main difference between then and now is probably the speed with which you can access the sources as well as the sheer amount of sources available. In this case, the most important issue is the awareness of how essential it is to home in on the right area early on so that the search process can focus on relevant sources.

For the first part of this section we will briefly describe general international secondary data sources, before looking at the following issues when obtaining and using international secondary data: data availability, reliability and comparability, and possible misinterpretations.

5.3.1 Secondary data sources

There are countless sources of data available for companies to use when gathering information on market conditions abroad. In this section we will describe some that we think are the most relevant to companies when assessing international business opportunities. The costs vary immensely depending on how great an interest there is in the information; the greater the interest, the larger the market for the information and the lower the per unit cost, and hence the cheaper the information. Generally, a market report could cost between 100 and 1,000 euros. More tailored information will increase the price accordingly: a single market report could cost tens of thousands of euros. It is worth noting that many market reports are based on the same data, but it is just given a new twist or angle and with a targeted customer-base in mind. The information agencies are, as a result, able to maximise their information costs by offering differentiated prices adjusted to the various customer-bases. Subscription services are also available, and some organisations offer handpicked, selective distribution of information that they deem of interest to the customer.

We have chosen to present the sources according to who publishes the various data. This will obviously be a general overview, focusing on some of the most important sources for the gathering of secondary data within international markets. Specific overviews on the various types of secondary data are publicly available.

International agencies

Numerous international agencies publish a range of publications of interest for companies. The Economist Group, Euromonitor and Predicasts Inc. are particularly useful. The Economist Group is a large British publishing concern incorporating The Economist Intelligence Unit and the weekly news magazine *The Economist*.

THE ECONOMIST INTELLIGENCE UNIT

http://www.eiu.com/home.aspx

This organisation is known to be particularly trustworthy. It contains a long list of general publications covering 205 countries. The subjects range from politics and macroeconomic factors to specialised product-related information. Overviews of The Economist Intelligence Unit's (EIU) publications are published in separate index publications. The most useful is therefore the *12-month Cumulative Index*, where one gets a complete and constantly updated overview of the relevant publications for the year in question.

Country Analysis consists of *Complete Country Coverage, Economic and Political Outlook, Business Environment* and *Country Risk*. Here, you will find monthly-updated coverage of the political and economic development in between 82 and 189 countries, depending on which report you are after.

Other publications are:

- *Industries and Commodities* – a quarterly analysis of the development of a range of industries in 60–70 countries (this varies depending on the industry analysed).
- *Data* – provides statistics for a number of economic and social variables (trade, stock market, demographics, market development, etc.).
- *Special Reports* – covers different areas such as broadband expansion, costs of living, and more in different countries.

EUROMONITOR

http://www.euromonitor.com/

Euromonitor publishes a range of publications of interest within international marketing. *Passport* is particularly worth a mention. It is a large database with information from 210 countries and covering 27 different industries with data since 1997. It also includes prognoses for five to six years in the future. Here you will find general, comparable, international statistics as well as smaller reports on market conditions and certain countries within specific product groups. It also contains surveys tracking consumer attitudes and behaviour. It has several thousand market reports covering areas as wide-ranging as nitrogen fertilisers in Saudi Arabia, cement in Indonesia, perfume in Spain or the DIY (do-it-yourself) market in England.

KOMPASS

http://Kompass.com

Kompass is also worth a mention. It is an organisation publishing information on more than 12 million companies in 66 countries. Using about 60 different search criteria, this reference directory can provide information about potential customers, competitors and representatives.

International organisations

A range of international organisations are useful for international marketers in their quest for information. We will briefly look at the most central ones: the OECD, World Bank, IMF, UN, EU and EFTA. For further information on possible sources, we advise taking a look at the *Yearbook of International Organizations*, which lists up to 10,000 different organisations.

OECD

http://www.oecd.org/

OECD publishes annually around 250 books and 40 statistical databases and a range of working papers, providing further information on economic and social conditions in the member countries as well as some other chosen countries.

– *OECD Economic Outlook* thoroughly analyses the economic development as well as making prognoses for further development for every OECD country. In addition, it regularly publishes various outlooks for a range of topics (migration, communications, the development of competence, etc.) and countries. It also covers non-member countries.
– The *OECD Factbook* is an annual publication with a summary of the most important macro-economic indicators for the OECD and BRICS countries.

THE WORLD BANK

http://data.worldbank.org/

The World Bank publishes a considerable number of reports, which have substantial value for the evaluation of developing countries. The Bank also publishes a range of country studies with detailed statistics as well as descriptions and evaluations of expected progress in each country. The *World Bank Publications Catalog* can be obtained by request from the World Bank, and this contains a complete overview of the Bank's publications.

IMF

https://www.imf.org

International Financial Statistics is a monthly publication with new key figures for most of the countries in the world. The data supplied is for the past eight years – quarterly for the past four years and monthly for the past two years.

THE UNITED NATIONS (UN)

https://unp.un.org/

Of all of the UN's publications, the following are of particular value: *The Statistical Yearbook, The Demographic Yearbook, The Yearbook of Industrial Statistics, The Yearbook of Labour Statistics, The Yearbook of National Accounts Statistics, Statistical Yearbook for Asia and the Pacific, Statistical Yearbook for Latin America* as well as the *World Trade Annual, Economic Survey of Europe* and the *World Economic and Social Survey.*

THE EU

http://publications.europa.eu/

There is an enormous amount of information to be obtained from the EU. An overview of it all can be found in *Publications of the European Communities*, which is published annually.

EUROSTAT is the EU's statistical body and is based in Luxemburg. The organisation publishes a range of statistics, including:

– *Eurostat Revue*, which gives information from the past 10 years for the member countries of the EU, plus Japan and the US, with statistics within a range of areas on a relatively cursory basis.
– *Eurostatistics. Data for Short-term Economic Analysis*, provides a brief overview of the main economic news, divided by topic and country.
– *Industry* provides an overview of industry in the EU compared with the US and Japan. Highlighted areas are structure and activities, employment, production, foreign trade with industrial goods, production indexes, and energy and raw material status.

National sources of information

Export promotion agencies generally have co-workers who keep track of the development within various professions and countries. They can provide assistance with tailored market information and related advice. For instance, in Norway, Innovation Norway also publishes a range of publications, where the *Export Hand Book* – http://www.innovasjonnorge.no/eksporthandboken/#. U8t5db44WtV – is worth a particular mention. This is a net-based databank which provides the reader with information on key conditions in 190 countries, such as restrictions on imports, contractual conditions, terms and conditions on delivery, transport requirements and more.

The largest commercial banks have generated various country profiles, which provide a more detailed description of the situations in countries that are central trading partners.

Databases

A great deal of the above-mentioned information is to be found on databases. In just under 5,000 different databases you will find several million articles, statistics and reports. You search by key words and accordingly gain easy access to information or knowledge of where the information is to be found. There are two different types of databases: reference bases and source bases. The former will only provide an overview of the information available via a short content summary. The researcher can then order the information online and will receive it in the post within a week. Source bases on the other hand allow you to obtain the information directly online.

Reference databases

Below is a brief list of key reference databases:

- PTS (Predicast's Terminal System) F6S Index. Contains articles and publications covering American and international companies, products and industry information.
- PTS Prompt (Predicast's Overview of Markets and Technology). Information on product launches, market shares, the management within certain companies and acquisitions.
- ABI/INFORM. A summary of articles from 1,400 English-speaking business and management publications.
- FIND/SVP Reports and Studies Index. A summary of industry and market analysis from American and international sources, as well as market, industry and company analysis.

Source databases

The following are worth noting:

- *Profile*, published by the *Financial Times*, is extensive. It contains full text databases for several newspapers and publications. *McCarthy Online* has business news from 60 English-speaking newspapers and magazines. *Euromonitor Market Direction* comprises market analysis for the consumer markets in Great Britain, the US, Germany, Italy and France.
- *D & B Dun's Market Identifiers*. Register of more than 1 million public and private companies with more than 10 employees, providing addresses, products, sales representatives, company structure, sister companies, trade information and predicted sales.
- *Comext* provides information on foreign trade statistics for all EU countries in six-digit Nimexe (a common customs tariff code that classifies products).
- *Celex* is the EU's database for legislation with an overview of sentences and decisions, directives, etc.
- *Cronos* – published by EUROSTAT – contains macro-economic factors influencing the business environment.
- *GlobalEdge*, established by the Michigan State University in the US, contains links to various databases.

Why don't you just look it up online?

We'd like to use an example from Finland to illustrate how to find relevant secondary data sources on the internet. A Finnish producer of instruments analysing gas discharges wanted to investigate the American market. The approach was as follows:

- Who buys these kind of instruments and what are their purchasing criteria?
- Who are the most important competitors?
- Which channels are used when selling these products?

The company used three different sources of research: newspapers and publications, homepages on the internet and existing market reports.

Newspapers/publications

To identify these, they searched various databases – mainly ProQuest – http://www. proquest.com/. By using key words such as air pollution, regulations, legislation, market and gas analysis instruments, and by limiting the search to the past three years, the analyst found some relevant articles. However, these were relatively unspecific. Several articles pointed to conditions for an increasing need for instruments analysing gas discharges – in publications as wide-ranging as *Chemical Market Report, Business Week* and *Scandinavian Journal of Management*. The conclusion here is that these types of sources provide good background information on the market conditions but that's about it.

Home pages

By going on to Alta Vista and using the same key words as above the analyst got several interesting hits. Two organisations were highlighted – EPA (Environmental Protection Agency) and Bay Area Air Quality Management District, which provide information on regulations, legislation and other databases covering environmental issues. Certain email addresses were also found here. These addresses were beneficial as they could be used for primary data collection at a later stage. The internet has the home pages to most relevant businesses and organisations within the field of analysing gas discharges; also found online were 9 competing and 14 different organisations able to provide information.

Existing market reports

Based on this internet search, the company found 18 different reports relating to the area of interest. These cost between 200 and 7,000 USD. By going on to the home pages of the publishers of these reports the analyst could search certain tables of contents of the reports and thus choose the report that was of greatest interest to them. They ended up with two reports – one from Frost and Sullivan and one from Strategic Directions International – at a total cost of 4,000 USD.

Our Finnish friends were able to obtain all of this information during the course of a few days (while also performing other tasks). It gave them a brilliant starting point from which they could make a decision about whether it was necessary to continue with further analysis while also giving them several contacts for future use.

Other sources

There are various other sources available, of which we will mention a few that could be of interest:

- *The Statesman's Yearbook* – http://www.statesmansyearbook.com/, published by Palgrave Macmillan.
- *Political Handbook of the World* – http://library.cqpress.com/phw/, published by Sage Publications.
- *The Europa World Year Book* – http://www.europaworld.com/pub/, published by Routledge.
- *World Almanac and Book of Facts*, published by Newspaper Enterprise Association, Inc.

The European Society for Opinion and Marketing Research (ESOMAR – https://www.esomar.org/) provides an overview of the institutes of market research in many countries.

5.3.2 Issues related to secondary data search

Data availability

While Western democracies publish statistics and reports on almost "any" social and economic phenomenon, this is a far cry from what other countries have in terms of publicly-accessible information. Public statistics in the Western world provide information on anything from the average price of timber and taxable income per tax group, through the number of deer in private forests, to production, investment and VAT per industry sector or county. Statistical information in many developing countries is incredibly sparse and often hopelessly out of date. There are of course exceptions. Take India for instance where they, following the period of British colonisation, inherited the British culture of statistics, and still have a relatively effective system of statistics. Another country, China, had – until the economic "revolution" starting in the 1980s – a rather underdeveloped statistical reporting system. This has improved dramatically over the years, but economic analysts are still suspicious about the reliability of Chinese public statistics.

Of all the public statistical information available, statistics on foreign trade from Western countries can be particularly useful to exporters – partly because they are updated monthly, and partly because they are relatively detailed. Such statistics can also be used to obtain information on imports in countries with a less well-developed statistical system. One possible course of action is to look at Western countries' export statistics to the countries in question, for instance Uganda. This way it is at least possible to establish their trade with Western countries.

However, the levels of detail are more often than not insufficient to cover the specific information needs of a company. We will include a few examples of this, based on the Norwegian version of Harmonised System (HS) for the classification of products (see Tables 5.1 and 5.2 below).

These statistics do not reveal anything regarding fashion or style, factors of much greater importance to the company than what the shirt is made of. Fashion might be deduced by looking at the exporting country, but considering the amount of outsourcing within this industry this is a method with a great risk of arriving at the wrong conclusions.

While this provides valuable information for a company, there is no information on the variety of quality of the various polyolefines – 30–40 each – ending up in the various end-user segments. Should you need such specific information, you would have to pay around 10,000–20,000 USD for a report from one of the consulting agencies within the petrochemical industry.

Table 5.1 Harmonised system and national number of shirts (men)

Shirts (men)		
HS number		National number
61.05	in cotton	1,000
	in synthetic fibres	2,000
	in other textile fibres	9,000

Table 5.2 Harmonised system and national number of polyolefines

Polyolefines (plastic raw material)		
HS number		*National number*
39.02	Polypropylene	1,001
	– containing	
	chlorofluorocarbons	1,009
	– Or	
	Polyisobutylene	2,000
	Copolymers of propylene	3,000
	Others	9,000

Data reliability and misinterpretations

A general rule of thumb is that data reliability follows the same pattern as data availability: the more Western and industrialised a country, the more you can trust its data. According to Norwegian exporters, information from the Nordic countries and Germany is the most reliable, while statistics from countries such as France are considerably less reliable, and from Eastern countries even less so (Solberg and Andersen 1991). We are of the opinion that such evaluations are often based on (lack of) language skills and a less accessible culture than actual differences in reliability. In evaluating data reliability, the market analyst should ask the following questions:

- Who published the data?
- To what purpose?
- How is the data collected?

In Peru, there not is a great discrepancy in information on numbers of fishing vessels, depending of types of vessel, type of fishing and source. Some sources say there are fewer than 9,000 fishing vessels operating along the 3,000 km long coast, while others claim there are only 90. Some say there are around 700–800 commercial vessels operating in Peru. The most accurate figures are possibly given by the UN Food and Agriculture Organisation (FAO) which divides the number of vessels into four categories: purse seiners, trawlers, and others. Yet, the discrepancies are high: for instance, 586 purse seiners in one overview vs. "around" 1,200 of them in another. All the while there might only be around 100 of these that could be possible customers for a foreign manufacturer of technologically-advanced fishing equipment.[3]

It is often in the publisher's best interest to paint a rosy picture of the country being analysed, rather than relaying the bare facts, which leads to the concealing of or avoiding presenting uncomfortable information. This is particularly the case where the publisher wishes to attract foreign investors. There are also cases of otherwise reliable information being incorrectly registered during the trade classification stage. Multi-client studies and statistical reports should obviously serve the consulting agency's clients in the best possible way, but they must also be profitable. Methodical mistakes during data collection and "jumping to conclusions" happen. It is therefore essential to not blindly trust all data and perhaps seek out at least two different sources with information on the same phenomenon.

However, it is also important to note that easily accessible low-cost multi-client statistics and market reports often provide a good first insight into the market structure in the various countries, and that this should not be disregarded just because there might be some mis-information at times.

One other risk with secondary data is that the market analyst could misinterpret correctly-registered data, because he or she lacks the necessary background on certain conditions in the markets.

The classic example of selling shoes to Africa is worth a mention. Two shoe salespeople went to Africa to sell shoes. One returned with a report that there wasn't a market for selling shoes: "No one wears shoes here, so there is no point in us being here." The other one came back and enthusiastically exclaimed: "No one wears shoes here; we have an enormous opportunity!"

A different – and perhaps more relevant – example is the internal trade happening between multinational companies across national borders, which of course is registered as export and import in each country respectively. This trade can be found particularly within the electronics industry, the textile and garment industries (outsourcing) and the petrochemical industry. It represents a trend that will only multiply with the increasing globalisation within many industries today.

In the trade statistics between Belgium and Germany, petrochemical raw materials are traded back and forth in large volumes, which to the untrained eye could indicate that this is an interesting market worth taking a slice of. Taking a closer look however, one will find that the main bulk of this trade is internal deliveries between BASF in Ludwigshaven (Germany) and its sister company in Antwerp (Belgium). The opportunities to enter this market therefore are rather miniscule.

Other elements that could easily derail an analyst are inflation of several hundred percent in some counties; or currency exchange often in the shape of several devaluations per year; and purchasing power parities – where comparisons of the purchasing power of different countries are easily meaningless due to completely different consumer structures and relative price levels in the respective countries. This takes us on to the next topic.

Data comparability

In this section, we will briefly look at data comparability between countries, limiting our-selves to a few examples of how this could pose a problem for the market analyst. It is worth emphasising that comparison of international market data is not always relevant to business managers. In some cases, the national markets have a life of their own, quite special, and should be analysed as such. Furthermore, relatively few businesses sell to more than a handful of markets, which in itself reduces the need for comparisons. Continued globali-sation will however constantly increase the need for more and more businesses to cast a wider net for their market analysis as well as considering the increasing volume of data to be compared. We will look at two different circumstances for decisions that could demand comparable data:

1   Choice of market for introduction/marketing campaign.

-   Supermarkets are classified differently in various countries. If a supermarket is important for the choice of market, the analyst must ensure that the data used employs the same definition in all of the countries to be evaluated.
-   Different countries employ different terminology (classifications) in their statistical publications. We have already mentioned HS, which employs a uniform terminology in Western Europe concerning the first four numbers in their goods (for instance 61.01 – shirts, men; 39.02 – polyolefines). The last four digits, however, have a different terminology in various European countries, both with regards to the numbers and the actual information hiding behind the numbers. The UN statistics and American statistics use the somewhat rougher Standard International Trade Classification (SITC), which deviates from the HS classification. This sometimes makes it tricky when comparing trade statistics.
-   Issues can also present themselves when comparing data within the shipping industry. Figures are in gross tonnage and deadweight tonnage. Lloyd's mainly employs figures in gross tonnage; however when analysing the global fleet, the figures are mentioned as deadweight tonnage. Furthermore, there are different weight limits employed in the statistics. Some statistics do not include ships below 500 gross tons while the limit in other countries is 2,000 gross tons. Another issue is the registering with convenience flags (Liberia, Panama, the Bahamas, etc.) which will considerably skew the "truth".
-   Finally, we will mention an example of a statistical mess, which sometimes makes it impossible to compare between the countries. In the building industry, the market analyst will at times truly have to compare apples with oranges, and will most likely end up with a rather inedible fruit salad. In Table 5.3 is the "menu" – *Bon appétit!*

2   Development of an international advertising campaign to be rolled out in several countries:

-   We have previously seen that it is important that the consumers in different countries have the same view of a standardised advertising message. Conversely a campaign for bicycles will have to be adjusted to the various markets. In the US, the campaign may show a young athlete for instance, as cycling in this country is mainly viewed as a leisure activity. In the Netherlands or Denmark on the other hand, the bicycle is used

Table 5.3 Statistical classification differences in the building industry

	Great Britain	Denmark	Netherlands	Finland
1	Private Housing	Housing	Housing	Housing
2	Public Housing	–	–	–
3	Public Construction	Public Construction	Schools, Hospitals	Schools, Hospitals
4	Industrial Construction	Industrial Construction	Industrial Construction	Industrial Construction
	Commercial	Commercial	–	–
	–	–	–	Offices
	–	–	–	Theatres/cinemas
5	Maintenance	–	–	–
6	–	–	Miscellaneous	Miscellaneous

by most people as a means of transport to and from work and so a different image will naturally be employed to get their message across.

- In continental Europe, beer is almost regarded as a kind of mineral water, while in Norway and Sweden it is seen as an alcoholic drink and is therefore off limits for advertising.

Data comparability is viewed as a relatively big issue by Norwegian companies. On a scale from 1 (no problem at all) to 3 (a big problem) Norwegian companies claim that data comparability ranks between 1.6 and 1.9, depending on which country or region the data stems from (Solberg and Andersen 1991).

5.3.3 Summary

There are numerous opportunities to collect secondary data in international markets. Amongst the more reliable sources, we find – in addition to the international organisations (the UN, the IMF, the OECD, the EU, etc.) and national statistical agencies – serious consultants such as SRI International, the Economist Intelligence Unit and Euromonitor. The extent to which the different sources can be of use varies from situation to situation. Some industries are better served with secondary sources than others – the automobile and the petrochemical industries being good examples of this.

However, the accessibility, reliability and comparability of international market data is an area where the market analyst must tread carefully. There may well be huge variations in data from one area to another. An example of this is a story of what a young businessman experienced on his first visit to Somalia, where he encountered more problems than just the gathering of the data:

> Well, these are certainly different conditions. Quite impossible to gather data and absolutely no structure in the market. I stopped by the Ministry of Planning, and they were impressed I had data from three years ago! This was data I had obtained from the Institute of Foreign Policy amongst others. I went for a walk today to take some photos. By the 13th photo I was stopped by the police and asked for my permission to take photos. I had not received any information from the consulate that this was necessary. I was brought to the office for censorship, where both film and camera were confiscated. I am to pick it up tomorrow. God only knows how much I will have to pay in fines to retrieve it. As this is my first visit to Somalia they let me off without having to spend a night in jail. It's interesting to experience different cultures, but I'm quite happy knowing I'm going home on Thursday.

Table 5.4 sums up how these factors operate in different countries.

Table 5.4 Quality of secondary data in different countries

	Democracy	*Single party rule*
Industrial countries	Good access and often reliable, however not always detailed enough to develop a marketing mix. Both private and public sources.	Some data is available, often skewed. Rough figures are available for certain countries. Private sources from Western agencies are often more reliable.
Developing countries	Limited access and varied reliability. A good start for choice of country. Public sources may be skewed to benefit the country.	Severely limited access to data and questionable reliability. Private Western agencies are preferable.

5.4 Primary data

When the market analyst has looked at what exists amongst secondary data he or she will most likely realise that the business will need more information in order to come to a conclusion. This is particularly the case for the operative decisions on a marketing mix. There are two main categories of primary data and both involve the market analyst conducting interviews with an interviewee (or a respondent):

– Qualitative data, often gathered in connection with exploratory market studies, often as a precursor to a questionnaire.
– Quantitative data, normally gathered on the basis of a questionnaire where the firm wishes to analyse the extent of a phenomenon (descriptive research) or to understand the relationship between, for instance, the effort put into marketing activities and the results (causal research).

5.4.1 Qualitative research techniques

We have already highlighted the need for exploratory research within international markets and the usual methods employed are qualitative. Qualitative methods can also be used in descriptive and, in some cases, causal studies. One example is from Japanese businesses that don't particularly rely on questionnaires to paint a picture of the market situation on which they base their decisions.

> When Sony researched the market for portable, lightweight cassette players during the 1980s, the results from the market analysis showed that the consumer would not buy a cassette player if it did not record. The chairman of the board, Akio Morita, decided to introduce the Walkman nonetheless, and the rest, as they say, is history. The cassette player was in its time one of Sony's most successful products.
>
> (Johanson and Nonaka 1987)

Another example is given by Gillian Tett in the *Financial Times*:

> A number of years ago, Coca-Cola, the mighty US beverage group, decided to sell bottled tea products in China. It set about marketing its fruit-flavoured, sugary teas, which were already popular in the US. The venture was an unexpected flop. In desperation, the company then asked social scientists to conduct so-called "ethnographic" research (on-the-ground cultural analysis) into what had gone wrong. This produced a fascinating explanation: in America the word "tea" is associated with indulgence and pleasure, so adding fruit flavours makes cultural sense; in China, by contrast, "tea" has different associations and significance. "Tea – like meditation – is a tool in Chinese culture for revealing the true self," writes Christian Madsbjerg, a consultant with knowledge of the Coca-Cola project, in a new book, *Sensemaking*. "The experience should take away irritants and distractions like noise, pollution and stress." So, Coca-Cola removed the sugar and flavours from its Chinese products – to great success. As Madsbjerg explains: "It wasn't until Coke incorporated this fundamentally different understanding of the 'tea experience' that their bottled products gained significant market share." On one level, this is just a trivial tale. On another, it is highly revealing. It is often tempting to think that the 21st-century world is so closely integrated and digitised that the issue of culture is becoming irrelevant. But behind the scenes, a growing number of companies appear to be quietly

realising that the reverse is true: as the world becomes more globalised, there is actually more – not less – need to understand cultural difference."[4]

The reason that qualitative methods are often preferable in the introductory stages of gathering market information lies in their great superior ability to dig deeper into the response levels of the interviewees face to face compared with analysing answers to questionnaires. Cooper and Branthwaite (1977) use Figure 5.3 to illustrate this point.

In this section, we will describe two different types of qualitative methods: observation and in-depth interviews.

Observation

Observations can be made in numerous different ways, ranging from the more "exotic" way of analysing fingerprints on newspapers in order to uncover what adverts are being read, via studying the contents of a garbage bin to see whether the consumer buys private brands or branded goods(!), the use of experiments where stimuli are planted in the purchasing situation in order to evaluate the consumer's reaction (Craig and Douglas 2009), to the somewhat more down-to-earth methods where one observes the purchasing behaviour in store, or working habits (i.e. the sales visit by a representative or the level of service the sales personnel provide in the showroom), or by studying the functionality of the infrastructure (ports, railways, telecommunications, advertising displays, etc.) in a specific country. The former methods belong more in scientific research and can also be of use for in-depth analysis of consumer behaviour.

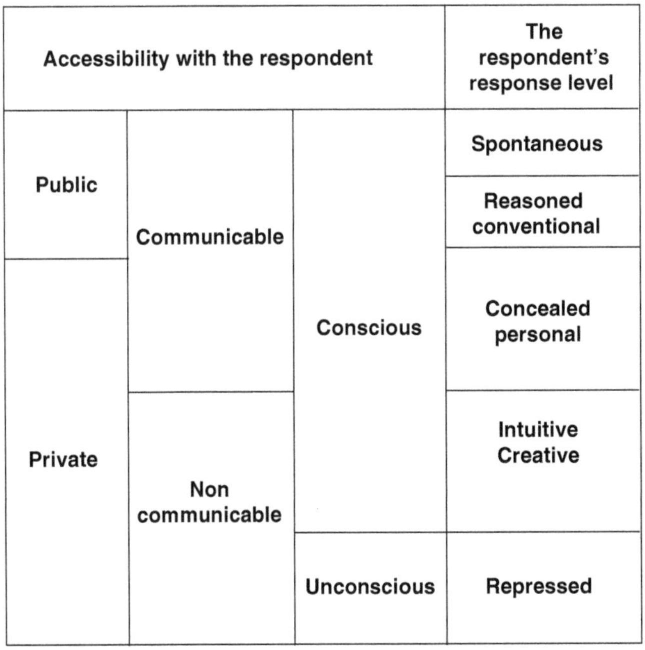

Accessibility with the respondent			The respondent's response level
Public	Communicable		Spontaneous
			Reasoned conventional
		Conscious	Concealed personal
Private	Non communicable		Intuitive Creative
		Unconscious	Repressed

Figure 5.3 Response levels of interviewees.

Source: Adapted from Cooper and Branthwaite (1977).

One deciding question is: Who will make the observations and interpret the data? Should management leave this to a local consultant, or should they send one of their own representatives or even a consultant from their home country? In the latter case, there is of course a risk that the data could be misinterpreted – what in one culture could be regarded as an "amicable discussion" on price, could be experienced by a foreigner as a tough argument. On the other hand, a representative from the company might be more likely to observe the relevant cultural differences than the local observer.

There is also the question of how scientific the observation method needs to be for the decision-maker. The more "scientific and waterproof" a method, the costlier the project, as well as more time-consuming. As a result, fewer variables will be researched. There are numerous examples of sensible and practical ways of carrying out observations where the local representative or the export manager could be actively involved.

A Norwegian bakery wanted to introduce their buns to the Swedish market. The manager went across the border to visit a few key towns and their cafés and bakeries, where he asked the owners to display the buns. He then took a seat and observed how the customers reacted to his goods; first at the point of purchase, then when they were sampled. He also took the opportunity to discuss purchasing routines, price levels, etc. with the owners. After just three days he had gathered quality first-hand information.

When Mustad & Søn AS, the leading global supplier of fish hooks, realised that sales in the US were stagnating, they sent sales representatives to the ironmongers and sports retailers in various locations around the country to investigate. The sales representatives simulated three different consumer categories (the beginners, the "I know best" customer and the professional buyer) and went shopping. In this way, they were able to evaluate how the sales personnel of the retailers/shops treated the various categories. They could soon conclude that this type of low interest item (costing between $1–2 per pack) held almost zero interest – and therefore little product knowledge – among the retailers' sales personnel. As a result of this, Mustad developed more colourful and appealing packaging with a self-explanatory text. This way they could ease the work for the sales personnel who were neither interested nor knowledgeable, as well as attracting the attention of the customers. Such conclusions could not have been made based on a questionnaire, no matter what size or amount of money spent on it.

When Canon (cameras) wanted to re-evaluate their distribution strategy in the US in 1972, Tatehiro Tsuruta, the Managing Director, went on a six-week round-trip, visiting camera shops and retailers around the country. Upon entering each shop, he looked around pretending to be a customer, enabling him to observe how the cameras were displayed and how the sales personnel served the customers. After each "shopping expedition" he asked the owner out to lunch. Through these lunch conversations Tsuruta quickly understood that the retailers did not actively sell Canon as their sales forces were too small. He was also able to uncover the kind of sales support that would make the biggest difference in the shops (Johanson and Nonaka 1987).

Table 5.5 Advantages and disadvantages of in-depth interviews

Advantages	Disadvantages
– The ability to penetrate different levels of responses – The possibility of directing the discussion towards particular areas of interest for the interviewee	– Expertise necessary – Locations normally needed to carry out interviews – The ability to get under the skin of people is often overrated

The scientist may say that this approach lacks rigour and takes a somewhat casual approach to the issue at hand. However, seen through the eyes of a businessperson, these methods provided sufficient grounds on which to base the decisions taken in the various situations. The methods are less costly (even taking into consideration the cost of the manager's time), the company can use their own personnel and finally the information is immediately absorbed (available, interpreted, understood) within the organisation (as opposed to just being read by the management). There is, of course, always a risk of misinterpreting the situation. However this is reduced by using locally-employed personnel, as seen in the Mustad example.

In-depth interviews

In-depth interviews can take many shapes and sizes. We are going to look at individual interviews and group interviews (focus groups), both with advantages and disadvantages; see Table 5.5.

Let us remind ourselves of the concept of high-context and low-context cultures (Hall 1959 – see also pages 40–41). Japan and the Arab nations are regarded as high-context cultures, while Germany, Scandinavia and, to a certain degree, the US are low-context cultures. The British and Latin Europeans are somewhere in between. In a cross-cultural market analysis, the phenomenon will limit the opportunities to use local personnel from low-context cultures to carry out in-depth interviews. Let us have a look at what a Scandinavian sales engineer experienced in England:

> "Very interesting", was the short answer the Englishman gave after hearing the salesman's offer. Little did our friend understand when he was later told that the company was not at all interested. He did not have any experience with the English, their manners and innate politeness, and their inability to refuse an offer or idea in person. "Very interesting" was the Englishman's way of politely saying: "You are a nice chap, but I don't like your products!"

Another cultural condition is the willingness of respondents in various countries to give information. In Japan, it would be extremely difficult to acquire any information on the company policy without the agreement of the entire management. In the US, it can be tricky getting any data on a company's sales and profits.

Focus groups are small and often demographically-diverse groups of people. The analyst studies their reactions to different proposals, for example, about a new product or an advertising campaign, to determine the reactions that can be expected from a larger population. The attention of the participants in focus groups brings a sort of synergy that stimulates the discussion. A comment from one participant, for instance, could trigger an answer or a line of thought or ideas with the other participants. Furthermore, the open ways of expressing themselves will bring an element of social feeling to the group, thus accentuating the situation and enabling the more cautious participants to voice their own opinions (Craig and Douglas 2009).

When is the right time to use in-depth interviews, and when is it best to employ focus groups? If the goal is to uncover attitudes, reasons, motivations and understandings of the customer/buyer that are difficult to access – in other words to get a deeper understanding of the response levels of the interviewees – using focus groups could be the more sensible approach. Two or more group discussions to fully understand the issues at hand are normally necessary. The group should always be led by a professionally-trained consultant; expertise is necessary in order to stimulate the right group atmosphere and to extract the information required. In some instances, a representative from the company could join as a participant. Note however that this is not advisable when the aim is to discuss negative aspects of the company's conduct.

In-depth interviews are preferable when the market analyst wishes to map the market situation in general or to obtain general market knowledge and views from the interviewee. This will often happen as an unstructured interview with key representatives in organisations, with importers, banks, potential customers, etc. A typical course of action is as follows:

An exporter of building materials wished to explore various market opportunities in Germany. The Export Promotion Agency in Stuttgart had already sent over some background information and had also organised meetings with potential representatives, potential customers and public agencies of immediate importance. Via the interviews, which were more like discussions on how best to approach the market, the exporter was able to get a good picture of the market structure, the most important players in the market, special demands to be met, and the best way to tackle the market. Total cost for all of this information? One week of hard work and 4,000 euros of direct expenses.

Export promotion agencies will often organise fact-finding missions, where they invite various companies to visit the more distant markets, where the official backing of the agency provides an entry to normally-closed doors. During these visits the group will be introduced to a number of important business people and public figures in the host country, often on the back of a seminar, and the representatives of the group will then have the chance to meet potential business partners.

Such missions can be very rewarding. However, there are also many examples of businesses that have participated in such visits but where management did not have a clear idea of what they wanted to achieve. In one case – after a visit to Malaysia – a company ended up investing in the country without having researched whether there existed a market for its products. As it turned out, there was not, and the company ended up exporting to the US from Malaysia – not quite the business opportunity the management had in mind originally.

5.4.2 Questionnaires

All textbooks on market analysis include extensive descriptions of the analysis process and the use of different questionnaire techniques. We will therefore not cover that here in great detail. Our aim is rather to look at particular aspects of questionnaire surveys in certain countries. Before going into detail, we will look at Kellogg Europe, which wanted to analyse 12 countries in Europe (Crossman and Jarret 1984).

One of Kellogg's aims is to be a low-cost producer of the best possible food goods in order to meet an increasingly competitive market. As such they wished to develop a more effective marketing and production organisation in Europe. Treating Europe as one area is an almost impossible task: 12 countries with a different view of what breakfast should generally consist of, and specifically what cereals are, with different spends per capita – from 1 to 100! – with cultures as different as Finland and Portugal, along with all the various possible consequences for the measuring scales on attitude questions. In addition, you have the national sales organisations from 12 countries all wanting their own views promoted in such a questionnaire. However, there are rewards to reap from using such a format:

- Design of questionnaire, pilot testing, specifications, data analysis and interpretation is done once instead of 12 times, with a cost saving of an estimated 20%.
- The results are processed with the same specifications, with the same tables and formats, which naturally facilitates data comparability.

The first step was to establish an understanding of the project in the local sales organisations in each of the 12 countries. Without this step, the local "kings" could potentially regard the whole project as a threat and an intrusion into their domain, and therefore there would be a risk of them ignoring the results or at least regarding them with strong scepticism. The next steps were as follows:

- discussions between Kellogg and their market analysis consultant on possible undertakings
- offer from consultant, negotiations and the signing of a contract
- a pilot study with interviews done in person with the target group of one country (Great Britain) to establish critical variables
- local translation of questionnaire
- pilot testing of questionnaire in each country
- debriefing in each country with a representative from the consulting agency
- end discussions following the debriefing to finalise the definitive questionnaire for each country
- fieldwork in all 12 countries.

The results of this study were to be presented during the national planning meetings in each market at the beginning of the year. The survey revealed that there were greater similarities between the markets and the products than originally thought. Kellogg Europe gained invaluable contributions for the development of their marketing mix strategy and therefore also their total marketing concept for Western Europe. However, the similarities were not great enough for them to combine all of Europe as one marketing mix.

The critical factors of the project included:

- local binding commitment from every national representative
- the use of the same questionnaire in all countries, reducing the cost – in this instance by 20%
- the possibility of comparing the results.

We would maintain that the first factor in particular (local commitment) is of key importance for such a project to be a success. This is the case for all stages of the project:

1   The definition of the problem (what are we researching?)
2   Specifying the information requirement (which questions should we ask?)
3   Developing the questionnaire (how are we going to pose the questions?)
4   The selection of respondents (to whom should we ask the questions?)
5   Data collection (how should we gather the data?)
6   The analysis of the data (what does the research tell us?)
7   The conclusions (how do we proceed based on our new knowledge?)

The first five questions on the list above will be looked at in this section; you are advised to refer to general literature for further reading on market analysis. Marketing conclusions are discussed in Part III of this book.

Problem definitions and specifications of the need for information

The problem definition phase is the most critical phase as it determines what it is you are researching, or rather the information a company needs in order to make a particular decision. "The problem" could be as simple as the company wishing to export and the need to investigate where to begin and then how to proceed. However, the problem could naturally be of a more complicated nature.

Customers in France have significantly reduced their purchases, while the purchasing level remains steady in other countries. What are the possible reasons for this?

–   Are they buying from someone else?
–   Are the representatives doing a poor job?
–   Are their needs covered in other ways?
–   Is the country experiencing a recession?

The analysis could take completely different directions, depending on the answer to these four questions.

An engineering company had pitched several times for different projects (the building of power plants, ports, etc.) in developing nations. While they were not more expensive or had dramatically different bids to their competitors, their pitch would hardly ever win. They were also known for their high standards. They wished to look into this issue, suspecting that one reason could be the possible misunderstanding of purchasing behaviour in these particular markets, which for projects of that size are known to be complicated. The final decision is influenced by many factors and participants. The engineering company therefore decided to investigate what typically happens in the various phases of the decision-making process for this type of project. Specifically, they sought answers to the following questions:

- What are the various phases of the decision-making process in these countries?
- Which of these are the most critical?
- Who participates in these phases, and what is their role?
- What kind of relations do the participants have with each other and with other possible suppliers in these phases?

Each issue demands its own particular questions to be able to dig deeper for an answer. And each of these questions will in turn uncover new questions, and so on. It is therefore necessary for the problem definition phase to acknowledge the issue at hand and to perform some sort of preliminary analysis or an exploratory analysis. Such a preliminary analysis could be discussions amongst the management or with the local representative, possibly linked with examining internal reports or statistics. Contacting certain customers – for instance those with whom they enjoy good relations – could also give a pointer as to possible connections and issues. We have seen how Stabburet carried out focus group interviews in order to uncover the actual purchasing situation for potential consumers of "Grandma's Flatbread" (page 129). More complicated cases would call for an examining of literature in order to obtain a more theoretical, yet practical, definition of the problem. Issues could include customer loyalty to different manufacturers, the effects of an advertising campaign, problems regarding cooperating with distributors, etc. One will often find complicated relationships and so assistance from specialists within the field will be hugely beneficial (advertising agencies, research agencies, management schools and the like). Certain cases will call for the testing of different hypotheses on various relationships (for instance, between marketing activities and sales) – a large topic within marketing research which is not covered in this book.

Developing the questionnaire

The next phase is whittling the general questions down to the specific questions to be formulated in the questionnaire. This could be full of pitfalls and it is essential for the questions to reflect the topic to be investigated. We will not delve deeply into material which is already well-covered by others, but rather briefly look at certain important aspects. The following issues are important in this context:

- Does the respondent have the information asked for in the questionnaire/does he or she have the ability to easily get an answer?
- Is the respondent willing to answer the question?
- Is the question formulated in such a way that he or she understands it?

These questions become even more crucial in international market analysis as respondents from different cultures will have different attitudes to what one can and is willing to answer. This is also important to factor in when looking at the response rate which tends to vary greatly from one country to another. In some countries, they are more reticent about giving information than in others.

> We have already commented on the Americans' reservation when answering questions about a company's finances. This is firmly embedded in the American culture as their right to individual freedom. In such cases Americans will often not answer questions that in other cultures (such as the Nordic culture) would not be considered problematic.
>
> In Sweden, the attitude is quite different. When a researcher approached the respondents to discuss a sensitive issue, he was met with the following comment: "Well – you will find out anyway, so it is better you get the information from me!"

In other cultures, people may be guarded against questions regarding topics such as religion, sex or personal income, but also general topics. The Chinese for instance (compared with others such as Malays or Indians) are known to answer "no" or "don't know" to a much greater extent than others and have a tendency to give fewer answers to open questions (Mitchell 1965). Another example is the British and Irish hesitancy in answering income-related questions compared with respondents from other EU countries (Douglas and Schoemacher 1981).

The issue becomes further complicated when factoring in how questions may be differently understood in the various countries. Let us remind ourselves of some examples that we have already discussed: While Norwegians and Swedes regard beer as an alcoholic beverage, further south in Europe it will be considered more of a thirst quencher. Bicycles have a completely different function in Denmark and the Netherlands (transport) compared with a bicycle in the US (leisure activity). Assorted social events such as engagements, weddings and birthdays will be marked in completely different ways in various countries. In conclusion: the wording of the question may give different answers depending on the culture rather than on the consumer preferences or buyer behaviour

There are generally two types of questions in a questionnaire:

1   Open-ended questions, where the respondent is free to formulate his or her own answers. The advantage lies in the freedom this represents, while the disadvantage is the difficulties the market analyst will most likely face when interpreting the answers and being able to sensibly classify the data.
2   Closed questions. There are three ways to formulate these:

    –   yes/no
    –   multiple-choice answers
    –   scales.

These methods are thoroughly covered in most reference books and will not be further discussed here.[5]

Cultural differences play a big part when it comes to formulating the questions. Craig and Douglas (2009) mention two conditions the market analyst must ascertain, namely whether the questions cover:

–   *Calibration equivalence* – whether the scale shows comparable values in the countries studied
–   *Conceptual equivalence* – whether the concepts used in the questionnaire measure the same item in the countries studied.

The simplest example of *calibration equivalence* is the use of local currency when asking for price or value of an item. It becomes somewhat more complicated when asking for units of measurement such as pressure: Pressure can be measured in pounds per square inch (lbs/inch^2) or in kilos per square centimetre (kg/cm^2). These measurements are still relatively easy to "translate" into the countries of relevance. It becomes more challenging when having to use two types of scales: the scale of semantic differentials (such as reliable – unreliable; small – big; low price – high price) and the Likert scale (completely agree – completely disagree). These are frequently used when looking at attitudes to or notions of various conditions. Two questions need to be asked here: First, what is the range of the scale, i.e. 1–5 or 1–7 or 1–10? Second, whether the scale should consist of even numbers (1–4) or odd numbers (1–5)?

Another point is that various cultures systematically respond differently to scales. In some cultures, the respondents tend to cluster around certain parts of the scale. A case in point here is the previously-mentioned Kellogg study where it could be seen that French and Italians are more impulsive and therefore had a stronger tendency to be found in the extremes of the scale compared with the somewhat more reserved Nordic respondents (Crossman and Jarret 1984). This tendency is also found in other studies. Williams (1991) also mentions how the Italians' answers constantly tend to be in the extremities while the Germans are more often found in the middle. However, in this study the French proved to have a more prudent attitude to the subject analysed (the benefits of information of an advertising campaign). Williams suggests solving the issue of different respondent cultures by measuring the scores of each question against an average for all relevant questions for each country. This enables you to measure the relative emphasis given to each factor reflected by the question. Table 5.6 shows an example of how this could be the case.

The table indicates that the Germans value the information content highest of all, relatively speaking, even though they respond with the second-lowest value on this variable. This could be completely misinterpreted if one takes the answers at face value without looking at the whole picture.

When it comes to *conceptual equivalence*, we are talking about the direct translation of a single word, the translation of what something signifies, and transferability of a concept used in the various questions. Williams (1991) shows how a statement (in the Likert scale) in English becomes somewhat milder than the French version:

"There are times when it is right to disobey the law."

This was translated into French as:

"Il y a des fois où désobéir aux lois est une bonne chose."

Table 5.6 Calibrating "cultural" answers on the Likert scale

	Average all questions	Average level of the specific question	Level of information, index vs. average
Italy	6.95	6.77	97
Great Britain	6.59	6.52	99
Spain	5.90	5.86	99
Denmark	5.81	6.15	106
France	5.75	5.59	97
Germany	5.25	5.84	111

Source: Williams (1991). *Marketing Research: New Tasks, New Methods,* New Scenarios. Ljubljana, February 1991, pp. 159–177.

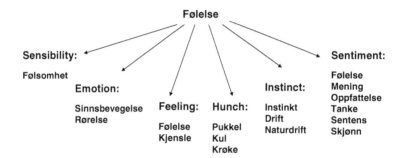

Figure 5.4 Translation and back-translation in a questionnaire.

The French expression *une bonne chose* (a good thing) is somewhat less strict than the English *right*. The answers from the studies in the two countries duly reflected this and showed great differences: In such situations, there should be a basic requirement to translate the statement or question back into the original language to see to what extent you have captured the right expression in the language it has been translated into. Figure 5.4 demonstrates how difficult this could prove to be. The Norwegian word for feeling ("følelse") can be translated into six different English words, which, when translated back into Norwegian, can have 17 different, more or less comparable meanings.

Looking at this further, questions and statements that could give clear answers in one context could in another be completely without meaning or worse still, have a totally different meaning. Statements such as:

> *"We drink more wine these days."*

This can be relevant in Northern Europe, where by agreeing to this you acknowledge that you live more of a Continental lifestyle than before. In the Mediterranean countries, where wine is frequently drunk both at lunch and dinner, agreeing to this statement would most likely signify something completely different. To measure how religious people are, two statements were used:

> *"Religion plays an important role in my life."*

> *"I regularly attend church."*

In Great Britain, 75% responded positively to the first question, while only 10% responded that they regularly attended church. In Italy on the other hand, 55% said they went to church, while only 30% said they were religious. A church visit in Italy signifies much more than going to confession or hearing God's word. Here they will meet friends and neighbours and get the latest news, which gives the church a completely different function altogether (Williams 1991).

Sampling methods

Most market analyses will be based on only a small selection – a sample – of those you really wish to study, since polling the whole population is prohibitively onerous. There is therefore always the risk that the decision-maker draws conclusions based on insufficient grounds.

Table 5.7 Sampling procedures

Probability sampling	Non-probability sampling
Single random sampling	Snowball sampling
Structurally random sampling	Convenience sampling
Stratified sampling	Evaluation sampling
Cluster sampling	Quota sampling

However, this is a risk he or she must take as usually the population will be too large, whether measuring the common consumer (1.3 million in Estonia or 326 million in the US) or a number of businesses in a particular industry. In some singular cases, the population will only consist of a few people or businesses – for example, if you want to look at project managers working in engineering firms suppling oil companies in the North Sea. In such a case there might be only around 50 project managers spread across a few large engineering companies.

There are two main sampling methods: probability sampling (where the selection is random) and non-probability sampling (the sampling selection follows set criteria). The terms indicate that the former case enables the possibility to measure the probability for skewed distribution compared with the population as a whole, while this is not possible in the latter case. Probability sampling implies that all the members of the sample stand an equal chance of being selected. We will not describe these further other than to include some examples of sampling methods within each category; see Table 5.7.

Whether the management chooses one method or another depends on their need for information, which probability margins they require in order to make decisions, the existing sampling frames and how the data is going to be used. Does the management only need an indication on certain conditions or is there a requirement for 99% certainty? If the goal is to establish and explain concepts (for instance concerning an advertising campaign) it might be more advantageous to ask a group of experts rather than a random sample. If you need to map the consumer pattern for a product or a service on the other hand, a probability sampling might be required.

An issue within this context is the selection of the *sampling frame*. A sampling frame is a list of people from whom you can make your selection for the sample. They are relatively well-developed in Western countries, be it the phone book, the Yellow Pages, member lists of professional organisations (engineers, doctors, economists), or more specialised publications such as Kompass or Dun & Bradstreet (which usually only mentions the name of the CEO). In other countries, the types of companies or people listed in such publications might be more arbitrarily selected, thereby risking the reliability of the analysis.

The international market researcher should notice the problems of *sampling equivalence*. Craig and Douglas (2009) highlight two conditions:

1   In some countries, it is often difficult to identify both the sampling frame and the respondent/interviewee. The availability of sampling frames varies from country to country, based on various sources or different definitions for the samples (such as household or home).

The phone book and industry directories (for instance Kompass or the Yellow Pages) are often used as a sampling frame in market analysis. This is a simple and inexpensive way of selecting your samples. Phone density will vary greatly from country to country, however, and more often than not professional catalogues are not always complete or correct.

Household shopping is more or less equally shared between the spouses in Scandinavia, while in Latin countries this is still a task mainly performed by women. This will naturally have an effect on who to ask when researching shopping habits in different countries.

Table 5.8 Data collection methods

Aspect	Telephone	Face-to-face	Postal	On-line
– Cost	Medium	Very high	Relatively low	Very low
– Time	Fast	Time-consuming	Time-consuming	Relatively fast
– Respondents	Relatively many	Few	Many	Many
– Response rate	High	High	Low	Low
– Selection availability	Depends on phone company	Relatively high	Depends on the postal system	Depends on internet access
– Interviewer's influence	Little or some	Very high	None	None
– Interviewer's adaptability	Some	Complete	None	None
– In-depth questions	Limited	Yes	None	None
– Statistical analysis	Varies	Varies	Yes	Yes

Equally, we see that the task distribution within companies varies from culture to culture. We have already seen that decision-makers in Finland rank higher in the hierarchy within the company compared with those in Denmark. It could also be that a decision is generally taken by groups of managers, while in other cultures the decisions are made by one senior manager.

2   Sampling methods that systematically over- or underestimate a group within the population will naturally give a different outcome in countries where these groups are unevenly represented within the total population. In such cases the market analyst should consider whether to use different sampling methods, such as stratified sampling.

Data collection methods

Traditionally there are four methods by which you collect data with regards to questionnaires: over the telephone, face-to-face interview, postal questionnaires and on-line questionnaires. Table 5.8 shows the consequences of employing the various methods.

One issue that continues to be raised is the response rate of postal questionnaires, which can vary greatly from country to country and even within a country in certain cases. In Scandinavia and Germany, for example, the response rate could be anything from 20% to 50–60% or even higher in some cases (see below). In other countries, such as the US, Latin countries and developing countries, the response rate will often be below 5%.

When Saga Petrochemicals (now Ineos) wanted to study European refinery managers' opinions on the addition of methanol to petrol as a replacement for lead (as an octane booster), they had a surprisingly high response rate (66%) even though the questionnaire was in English for all countries involved. There are several reasons behind this: At the time, this was a very current and much-discussed topic within the industry which concerned many involved; and the respondents were therefore promised a short summary of the report. They carried out one follow-up round which resulted in 40% more answers than the first round. Furthermore, the "oil language" is English, so most of the respondents, whether French, German or Swedish, spoke the language well. Even so there were clear differences between the countries: [6]

France	45%
Germany	67%
Great Britain	71%
Norway	81%
Denmark	86%
Sweden	88%

There are several ways in which one can increase the response rate:

- One should always carry out a follow-up round (postal or web). This resulted in a clear gain in Saga's case.
- Offer a short summary of the main conclusions. This was done in Saga's research, without having to reveal information that was sensitive to the company.
- One should always take into account the effect of the sender. In many cases the company will be a completely unknown entity in international markets, and so the respondents will not have any interest or feelings of obligation to answer. On the other hand, there is a reasoning behind not revealing the name of the company so that you avoid the respondent taking this into consideration when responding. In both cases it could be advisable to link up with a known or respected sender in the local market. The commercial attaché at an embassy or a local marketing agency could be good options in this case.
- Answering the questions should be straightforward, and the questions must be relevant to the respondent. While this last point is an absolute must, many questionnaires give the impression of a complete lack of understanding of the issues facing the respondent. Solid groundwork is therefore essential, using exploratory research through secondary data and face-to-face interviews in order to personalise the questionnaire as much as possible.

Zimmerman and Szenberg (1996) have analysed how American multinationals evaluate the availability of market research agencies, combined with the quality and costs related to the various data collection methods, across 17 countries. The availability in Europe is rated relatively good across all types of studies (telephone, postal and face-to-face), while this varies greatly in developing countries and partly also newly-industrialised countries. In such markets, it is wiser to employ face-to-face interviews. Nonetheless, the main impression is that telephone interviews usually offer good results in certain Asian countries like Malaysia, Indonesia, China and South Korea (even though there are few research agencies offering this service). Interviews in the street, in public meeting spaces (such as a shopping centre) or at home with the respondents do not, on the other hand, seem to be particularly effective in these countries. Japan comes out on top for all types of data collection with regards to cost, though market research services are relatively cheap in Asia. Figure 5.5 illustrates the situation for telephone interviews and face-to-face interviews (focus groups).

5.5 International market intelligence

At the start of this chapter we identified four types of market information: investigation, analysis, experience and intelligence. This closing section focuses on the latter.

Using a market intelligence system enables the company to appropriately learn from and to keep track of the market development. The aim of market intelligence is to organise this

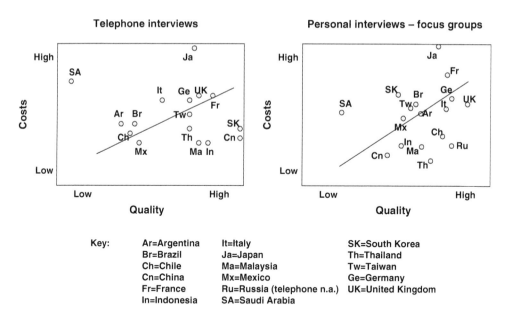

Figure 5.5 Quality and cost of telephone and face-to-face interviews in 17 countries.

Source: Zimmerman and Szenberg (1996).

information for the company to make use of it when making decisions. One might say that *market intelligence is an organised capture and treatment of market data via an external network of information channels and an internal system for the evaluation and use of this*. The definition encompasses important parts of the concept of market orientation, such as the information collection and its distribution (Kohli and Jaworski 1990), but also includes the analysis and handling of it (Solberg et al. 2013). Earlier on in this chapter we saw how these three – collection, analysis and distribution – are crucial when establishing market insight.

Benito et al. (1993) found that mainly large companies and/or highly internationalised companies have developed such systems. Both sense the need to keep track of developments in the market and they have the necessary resources to do so. Most small companies seek to obtain such information through informal conversations with other people in the industry, their representatives and customers as well as through reading industry-related business publications. The information can be found by chance, however, without the management having thoroughly considered the kind of information they need, or from where to obtain it. There is then a risk that critical information will be inaccessible or that the costs related to the flow of information are too high. Figure 5.6 illustrates the wealth of information sources available to management; the question is what sources to use?

Market intelligence involves three areas:

1   To spot and observe trends and changes in the international business environment.
2   To control and follow up on the results in the various markets.
3   To identify new market opportunities and projects.

We will now look at each of these three areas and examine how they should be tackled. The *observation of trends* can happen on one of two levels: macro level, which includes economic

Figure 5.6 Relevant information sources for international market intelligence.

Table 5.9 Observation of trends

	Personal channels	*Public channels*
Macro level		
– Growth	Representatives, customers,	OECD, UN, WTO statistics,
– Balance of payment	banks, export promotion agencies,	national statistics, financial
– Political development	embassies, etc.	publications
Micro level		
– Market volume	Representatives, distributors,	Industry organisations, exchange
– Market share	customers, analysis agencies,	of data between market participants,
– Competition	consultants, advertising agencies,	industry publications, subscription
– Pattern of distribution	fairs, etc.	to news alerts, Nielsen store
– Customer structure		indexes, annual reports, databases
– New regulations		such as FTProfile and Celex,
		legal databases, multi-client studies

and political development, and micro level, that is the company's product markets. The information channels can also be divided between personal and public channels. Table 5.9 shows how certain elements of information play a part in the trend observations.

What to include in such overviews is always up for discussion and Table 5.9 is one example. We will not examine in detail every suggestion included here, only limit ourselves to a short commentary. Industry publications and organisations will sufficiently cover the continuous need for information for some product and market areas, while for other areas it will be very difficult to obtain secondary data. In such cases, tailor-made solutions are required in order to get the desired data. One option is to go through all markets during the annual meetings with local sales offices, representatives, distributors, etc. In certain European industries, senior market analysts from various participants meet and exchange information. This provides insight into how the different participants *officially* view their future development. Such meetings can however feel a bit like the massaging of egos, and within the EU they have been dismissed as there is a fear of collusion amongst competitors. As a result, certain data exchanges have either been limited or banned.

Controlling performance should also happen regularly, depending on whether strategic control or more operational control is in focus. Sales and financial performance should normally be examined monthly, while information on market share may not necessarily require such frequent observation – perhaps rather every six months or even annually. We have previously discussed the difficulties in measuring the market shares. The crucial element here is to define which market is relevant for the company. For example: Should the market encompass all of Germany, is it only our shares with a certain type of businesses, or should it be limited to Bavaria? This depends on several factors, such as competitive structure and the existence of niches and market segments. With regards to customer attitudes or customer knowledge of the company's products, a six-monthly or even annual review could be sufficient, perhaps in connection with various initiatives such as an advertising campaign. Table 5.10 shows a suggestion for different subject areas to control, and how to gather data for these. The information channels have been divided between internal and external.

Let us look at some of these aspects. *Accounting reports* for instance do not always provide essential information to the marketing department. It is important to highlight contributions to various products and market levels to enable marketing management to follow up on considerable deviations from plans and budgets. Therefore, it is key to involve the marketing department when establishing the accounting system. As soon as such a system is established it

Table 5.10 Controlling performance

Area of analysis	Country				Internal sources	External sources
	Sweden	Denmark	Germany	UK		
Sales growth – Product A – Product B – Product C – Product ...					Sales figures and sales reports Relevant accounting reports	–
Market shares – Product A – Product B – Product C – Product ...					Internal customer research, conversations with competitors and distributors	Industry statistics, import statistics, Nielsen store indexes
Sales margins – Product A – Product B – Product C – Product ...					Relevant accounting reports	–
Representatives' results					Reports, sales figures (as above)	Conversations with other industry participants
Customer attitudes					Close customer relations	Omnibus surveys

will be difficult to change it, even though it might not provide the desired information – both due to time and resources needed, but perhaps most of all, because of general organisational inertia. *Omnibus surveys* are a service some market research agencies offer their customers to keep an eye on various market aspects, such as customer attitudes. The agency will gather questions from their employers and pose these to a pre-selected, agreed sample. This gives good access to a range of issues while being relatively inexpensive. One may ask questions on knowledge of, attitudes to and experiences with a company's products within given market segments.

Finally, we will look at the importance of ensuring the organisation access to *impulses and ideas for future development* – whether new markets or new technology, such as:

– Product development
– New market segments
– New markets
– New marketing methods
– Technological development
– Development of business and manufacturing processes.

Relevant channels could be symposiums, conferences and seminars – all interesting networking arenas. The social part of such events often enables you to meet like-minded people you can then get in touch with for concrete specific facts and general information. Getting actively involved in an industry organisation is also a good option. One example here is the manager of a Norwegian manufacturer of food additives supplied to bakeries. He became the chairman of the European industry organisation which gave him valuable insight and networks. There are, of course, pros and cons with such an arrangement. Clear cons include the frustrating, apparent waste of time often associated with dull, organisational politics, which is "bound to happen" in such organisations. On the other hand, you occupy a central position in the industry and will automatically gain a broad range of contacts you can draw on in different situations. Figure 5.7 sums up most of this discussion. Crucially, each individual company must find a system that provides them with sufficient, cost-efficient and reliable information. Another important aspect is that this information becomes part of the various areas of the organisation, so it can be used by all and not just the market analyst.

A survey of the information behaviour of Norwegian exporters showed that informal reporting to management was the most widespread method, while written reports are also relatively commonly used – see Table 5.11 (Benito et al. 1993). The table further shows that making use of data tools in order to analyse the data is *not* common practice. We also note that representatives apparently play an important part in data collection and market planning.

There is however a tendency towards large companies being more formal in their way of reporting and their more widespread use of data tools for analysis. They will also include their local representatives in data collection and market planning to a much greater extent than smaller companies. Quite often though, expensive market reports remain virtually unread, and there are cases where the market researcher sits in his or her office gathering information that captures limited interest from operations managers who are generally more concerned with short-term challenges than long-term visions. That is why the whole management should participate in setting up such an intelligence system, and also why they should only include the subjects the management has decided for the system.

Data comparability is another issue. The question is then: comparable in what way? It can be misleading to use the same format when comparing the results from each individual country. When evaluating market shares for instance, local conditions should be taken into account, such

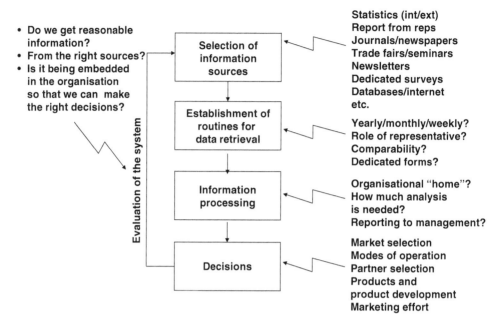

Figure 5.7 Establishing a market intelligence system.

Table 5.11 Analysis and communication of market intelligence to management

	Average	*Number of responses*
Verbal reporting to top management	1.7	195
Verbal reporting to the marketing management	1.7	183
Written reports	2.0	195
Other forms of reporting	3.2	43
Analysis/planning using data tools	3.7	172
Participation from local representatives within:		
– information gathering	1.7	194
– market planning	1.8	193

Source: Benito et al. (1993).
Note: $N = 221$; 1 = always, 5 = never.

as different competitor structures, distribution channels and structures of segments and customer groups. Or when evaluating contributions from the various markets, it is important to note that even though, for example, Britain's contribution may be lower than that of other countries, it might still be worth continuing a certain level of activity in that market. This could either be because our biggest competitors have this as their main market, or because that particular market is key with regards to impulses for product development. By not actively participating in this market, such signals might be missed.

Another important aspect is to what extent one should involve the local representative and seek to standardise data collection. This last point could be necessary in order to obtain comparable data. There are many instances where the headquarters will give their local representatives an overload of forms to fill out every month, with numerous details on market shares, competitors, trends, etc. It is important to find the right balance between the actual need for information from the HQ's point of view, the opportunities the representatives actually have to gather this information without incurring too high costs, and the representatives' own experience of seeing the results of their input included in the strategic decisions taken by the centre. Too much bureaucracy can easily alienate the representatives, while too little might lead to suboptimal solutions to the information issue. Data systems connected with accounting, sales and marketing help companies to keep track of easily retrievable data (total sales, sales per salesperson, sales per product, liquidity, etc.).

5.6 Chapter summary

In this chapter, we have discussed various methods of gathering and organising market information. Textbooks will often emphasise the importance of market analysis, with which we wholeheartedly agree. It is important to bear in mind that market analysis is not always the be all and end all with regards to accessing information. Informal conversations with market participants have proved to be good sources of information for the majority of smaller companies in order for them to make a sound decision. What is important is to adapt the resources of the company to the worth of the market research. We have pointed to the fact that an active network can in fact be the basis of information in many instances but also that this will be slightly different for companies with considerable business activities in many countries, where there are different and complex market and competitor situations. In such cases it is necessary to occasionally have a thorough look at the situation in a more structured and systematic way. This will often be done in connection with the planning of an advertising campaign, where the aim of the analysis will be to get input for the message or the testing of it. We have discussed various data sources – secondary data and primary data – and shown possible pitfalls. Finally, we have discussed the creation of a market intelligence system, where the choice of information sources, the establishment of routines, the treatment of data as well as evaluating the usefulness of it are all key issues. For the remainder of Part II we will take a closer look at the decision-making areas where the market intelligence will be put to use.

Notes

1 Instead of its Norwegian name, Mors Flatbrød – which means "Mother's Flatbread".
2 Communication with the marketing manager of Stabburet.
3 http://www.fao.org/fishery/facp/PER/en#CountrySector-Statistics; www.fao.org/fileadmin/user_upload/fisheries/docs/Peru_-_28_April.doc; https://www.researchgate.net/figure/222517632_fig1_Fig-5-Number-of-vessels-fishing-off-the-coast-of-Peru-July-December-1999-Actual
4 Gillian Tett, "An anthropologist in the boardroom", *Financial Times*, 17 April 2017. https://www.ft.com/content/38e276a2-2487-11e7-a34a-538b4cb30025?accessToken=zwAAAVucSeRgkc844naiJIcR59OjSlOLTLMAJQ.MEUCIGlFkWqd_sSOilWUvbJ33Px1Z31QVKpK7INO_JTIQVZzAiEAxfoAPPgOJh73FjK0RtfOKU4YWq2g5k8x_1qzwadf88w&sharetype=gift
5 See for instance, Malhotra (2010).
6 Personal experience of the author.

6 Market selection and market portfolio

6.1 Introduction

What should be the destination(s) of our international marketing activities? What countries, how many, which segments and even more specifically: which customers? These decisions are – for the international marketer – not only important; they are decisive. They will determine the use of resources, the orientation of the firm's capabilities, and will influence its organisational culture. Yet, many firms take an unconscious stance on this critical issue when they take their first steps into international markets. Also in the further expansion, market entry decisions often seem to follow a heuristic approach, more governed by intuition, hearsay and mimicry than by rational analysis. Clearly, there is a difference between the market entry behaviour of the newcomer to international markets and the well-seasoned multinational enterprise. We would also claim that the behaviour of these two classes of firms varies greatly depending on their position in the Nine Strategic Windows framework.

In this chapter, we will first discuss different approaches to international market selection, and explore how different strategic positions influence the thinking of management. We will furthermore examine how different positions in the Strategic Windows framework influence the market selection process. Finally, we will explore the various roles that different markets play in the portfolios of firms.

6.2 A systematic approach to international market selection

The majority of first entries into international markets go into neighbouring countries and nations that are culturally close, such as Canada for the US – and vice versa, Norway to Sweden or Denmark – and vice versa (Gripsrud et al. 2015, Sui and Baum 2014). It is almost default decision behaviour because first-time exporters deem it less risky, more familiar, less cumbersome and less costly to engage in neighbouring countries. In Finland it has been found that as many as 95% of exporters seek their first export markets in neighbouring/close countries (Luostarinen 1980a). Research from Australia supports this pattern (Dow 2000). We may also add that the physical distance from, for example, Aachen in Germany to Brussels in Belgium is just a fifth of that to Frankfurt (am Main); from Toronto (Canada) to Detroit (USA) is just a tenth of that to Vancouver; or from Uddevalla (Sweden) to Fredrikstad (Norway) is only a sixth of that to Luluå in Northern Sweden. Firms in those regions may well be tempted to go to the closest markets, and even claim that these markets in principle should be considered their "home market".

Not only short *physical*, but also short *psychic* distance is important in country selection. The Portuguese toy manufacturer, Science4you, started their operations in 2008, and they started exporting the year after. Their first export market was neighbouring Spain, entered in 2009. The Spanish and Portuguese, although speaking different languages, tend to understand each other quite well. The following year they entered Angola and Brazil, both Portuguese-speaking countries and former colonies, but quite a physical distance from Portugal. Then, three years later, they established a representation in the US, and the next year they entered the UK. It seems as though they had completed their apprenticeship years in markets close to their own – both physically and psychically – and then, feeling more confident, they could enter different markets.[1]

Acting like this, firms may miss interesting opportunities in other, more lucrative markets. The fear of distant markets may, of course, be well-justified: logistical costs, customs tariffs or other trade barriers, in addition to unfamiliar cultures may be decisive factors limiting the exporters' willingness to invest in otherwise exciting opportunities. However, it does not take much work to explore the main components in the market situation in order to get a general picture of its potential.

The market selection process has been the object of a number of scientific articles over the past three decades. For instance, it has been found that systematic market selection – involving the scanning of trade journals, visits to potential markets, doing local market research and using public statistics – pays off in terms of higher export performance (Brouthers and Nakos 2005). Many suggest models that require input from a number of different sources (Marchi et al. 2014). For the large multinational that considers investing in a new country, this may be a relevant approach; for the small newcomer to international markets, however, such information input may well sway the decision-maker into "less rational" market selection procedures. In the following, we will discuss a systematic approach to market selection that does not involve massive efforts from the manager.

The information jungle is huge and complex, so a good starting point would be to consider key criteria – such as culture, distance and language proficiency – to determine market entry. Generally, such criteria are already, in principle, considered during the decision process when entering neighbouring markets and the decision is taken without further examination. However, in a study of Norwegian exporters Solberg (1987, 1988) found that *market growth and demand volume* were the two most important factors, whereas transport costs and culture did not really matter much (see Table 6.1). This finding is in apparent conflict with the fact that most firms enter neighbouring markets first. However, most of the respondents in the survey were experienced exporters that had "climbed the internationalisation ladder" and therefore did not consider psychic or geographic distance as insurmountable obstacles; so, for their next market entry they valued criteria that revealed opportunities (such as growth and volume) over criteria representing obstacles (such as psychic distance).

We have now indirectly stated that this ranking varies with the situation of each firm. For instance, a company with a strained balance sheet and low profitability may value country solvency, political stability and access to distribution channels (for rapid introduction to customers) higher than other firms, simply because it needs to secure fast and smooth payback. A more established firm, with healthy finances, may be willing to discard these criteria if market growth and volume are promising. A European firm in the ICT industry may rate technological levels (represented by industry clusters or research centres) much higher than cultural closeness and therefore enter Japan or Taiwan before looking at their

Table 6.1 Factors determining country selection

Market volume	2.0
Market growth	2.1
Competition	2.5
Country solvency	2.5
Political stability	2.7
Access to distribution channels	2.8
Few or no technical barriers	2.8
Nationalistic purchasing practices	3.1
Technological level	3.2
Low customs barrier	3.3
Language	3.4
Transport costs	3.6
Similar consumption patterns	3.6
Similar culture	3.9
Relations to Norway	3.9

Note: 1= very important, 5 = not important at all.

European neighbours. A firm in the construction or electro-mechanical industry may be more concerned about easy technical approval of their products in the country than market size or growth. For example:

A Norwegian manufacturer of sewage pipes in ABS plastics applied for approval for their products in Sweden. The standard in Sweden was, however, PVC plastics for this kind of pipe and no regulation for ABS was established. In spite of the fact that ABS is superior to PVC for the purpose, it took five years of testing and analysis by the Swedish technical agency before their products were approved.[2]

The lesson learnt from this brief discussion is that management needs to define a limited number of key criteria for market selection. In this way, the work of identifying potential markets for entry is reduced to a minimum. Any firm may easily adopt the following practice:

1   Identify a set of criteria for market selection. This exercise should be carried out by a group of relevant managers. The list should take into account the concrete strategic situation of the firm (finance, competitive threats, long-term objectives, etc.).
2   Invite top management to weigh the criteria by voting for what they consider most impor-tant. It may well be that one criterion obtains a high score (import volume, market growth, access to distribution channels or country solvency) – and that may take priority over most of the other criteria in the list.
3   Fact-finding to satisfy the information need pertaining to each criterion. Based on the information obtained, rate each criterion on a scale (for example 1–5).
4   Multiply the weight with the score for each criterion, and then add the final scores. The country with the highest score is then a candidate for entry. A hypothetical evaluation for market selection is given in Table 6.2.

The evaluation in Table 6.2 went in favour of the Czech Republic, by a small margin, implying that different scores or values attributed to each criterion may alter the outcome of the

Table 6.2 Country evaluation for German exporter to selected European countries

Factor	Weight	Switzerland		Czech Republic		Austria	
		Score	Total	Score	Total	Score	Total
Import volume	0.20	4	0.80	2	0.40	3	0.60
Import growth	0.15	2	0.30	4	0.60	3	0.45
Exchange rate changes	0.15	4	0.60	3	0.45	5	0.75
Competition	0.15	1	0.15	5	0.75	2	0.30
Access to distribution channels	0.10	2	0.20	3	0.30	4	0.40
Nationalistic purchase	0.10	3	0.30	4	0.40	2	0.20
Technical regulations	0.10	2	0.20	4	0.40	3	0.30
Language	0.05	4	0.20	2	0.10	5	0.25
Total evaluation	1.00		2.75		3.40		3.35

calculation. For instance, what is the basis for the scores? Are we confident that our assessment of the competition is reflecting the real situation in each market? And, what about our judgement of nationalistic purchasing practices or access to distribution channels? Are there any factors that have been left out in this examination? One conclusion from the table, however, is that Switzerland may be put on hold at this moment in time. Management should therefore discuss the total scores for the two other countries, just to make sure that they are confident of the result.

This approach differs from the popular PESTEL[3] analysis, in that *only issues that matter* for the firm and for the markets under study are brought up. Since the countries being considered are closely-tied to or members of the EU for instance, there is little need to include legal or political factors in the set. This might have been different if countries such as Ukraine or Moldova were examined. Nor is geographic distance (transport costs) a major concern since only neighbouring countries are analysed. In this way, one ascertains that only information that matters to the concrete decision at hand will be collected.

This exercise has also shown that it is important to choose criteria that can straightforwardly be "translated" into concrete and easily accessible information (such as public statistics and reports). In this way, the cost of information may be considerably reduced. For example, we have used imports instead of total demand, because it is easier to get hold of detailed import statistics than those of total consumption. Import statistics are also "fresher", as they – in most developed countries – are published just a couple of months after they are reported. Also, import statistics may reflect the potential for a new *foreign vendor* to the country. For the same reasons, import growth information will be more readily available, and may – in many instances – be a good substitute for market growth data.

Import statistics may however conceal the real market potential. In cases where there are insurmountable import barriers, imports will be virtually nil, but the market may still be very promising. In such cases, other criteria should be examined such as the general business climate, combined with the firm's preparedness and ability to seek entry modes other than exporting (licensing or foreign direct investments) to overcome the import restrictions.

In a similar vein, price levels may be a representative measure of competitive climate (higher prices → less competition). Again, import statistics may help the analyst to get a first insight (dividing value by number of units). And again, there are caveats: even though import statistics are quite detailed, they do not capture quality differences or specific variants of products. Means and averages in this context then become meaningless. A better way to assess the nature of competition is possibly to engage in discussions with insightful persons with experience of the market, in order to get a qualified opinion. Relevant questions to ask would be: Are the main competitors local firms or multinationals? What are their market shares? Do they service any specific segments of the market? – and so on. The same is true with access to distribution channels and nationalistic purchase practices. A search in Google may supplement the information thus obtained.

Currency stability is a critical factor in international trade and should always be counted in the country selection process. In addition, currency fluctuations may alter the relative price of imported goods to a country – and thereby the price competitiveness – more or less overnight. For instance, in the wake of the Brexit vote, the pound weakened by an average of around 15% over a four-month period, making British exports less expensive and imports into Britain more expensive. In the above exercise the Swiss franc has strengthened considerably over a nine-year period (2008–2016), from 1.7 to 1.1 to the euro, thus improving Germany's price competitiveness in Switzerland by around a third; the Czech koruna has, during the same period, weakened by some 10%, having the opposite effect for German exports.[4] However, both the Swiss franc and the koruna have fluctuated during this period of time, rendering any scoring unreliable. Selling to Austria does not imply any currency risk at all, since both Germany and Austria use the euro. Then, how to give correct scores on this factor is a question of judgement.

The extent to which technical standards constitute a deterrent to enter the markets should first be tackled by visiting the home page of the relevant regulatory agency in the country. In principle, EU regulations have substantially facilitated this task in Europe, so if the German seller uses the same standards in the EU as in Germany, it should be rather confident. However, in some instances national regulations prevail and there are cases where local courts have ruled in favour of national regulations and been supported by the European Court of Justice.[5]

Finally, rating the importance of language will depend on at least two factors: the language proficiency of key staff within the firm and that of the business community in the importing country. In the exercise above it is assumed that this is not a major concern for the firm, but the scores still suggest that differences may sway the balance.

Table 6.2 does not include political risk. When exporting to politically-safe countries (such as OECD members), such considerations may not be part of the exercise at all, although in the years after 2010, signs of weakening economies and the ensuing rise of populistic governments in Europe may alter this simplified analysis. The world has witnessed time and again how regimes have been overthrown, where coup d'états have been attempted (and quashed, such as Turkey in 2016), or where the death of the ruler creates a political vacuum and an uncertain business environment. The death in 1980 of the Yugoslav leader marshal Josip Tito and the fall of communism was followed by a bitter civil war between the different nations that once constituted the country (today seven countries). More recently, in 2016, the deaths of King Bhumibol of Thailand and President Karimov in Uzbekistan have left both countries in a state of uncertainty, suggesting that firms should be vigilant before committing resources in those markets.

Political risk is, however, much more than these abrupt events: for instance, it is a common practice in many countries for local governments to rule in favour of local firms at the expense of foreign firms; or where previously powerful partners are being deposed by an authoritarian and unpredictable regime; or where corruption is largely accepted as a way to "solve the situation". The rule of law is not applied or even considered – see also Table 2.8 (page 43). Many factors need consideration:

- Does the country have a well-developed and entrenched democratic rule?
- What is the political role of the military forces/police?
- Does the country have legislation in place to protect intellectual or real estate property rights?

-   Are there conflicts between ethnic or religious groups or different clans?
-   Are the relations between employers and employees characterised by conflict or cooperation?

In the worst case, the risk is that firms may lose their total investment (confiscation); or that decisions on purchases or licences take much longer than planned; or that "extraordinary commissions" (or in plain English: corrupt payments) need to be paid in order to get things done; or that payments for unknown reasons are held back.

> The ban by Western countries on exports of sensitive products and technology to Iran during the first decades of the 21st century was the object of a controversial interpretation by the Norwegian security agency. In 2013, the Norwegian shipyard, Båtservice AS, had entered into a contract with the Iranian coastguard to deliver 19 rescue vessels. However, the Norwegian security agency deemed this contract to fall into the category of products affected by the ban.[6] In this case, the determining factor was not the target country's financial position or internal tensions; rather it was the Norwegian authorities' *interpretation* of rules and regulations.

Most of the information needed to make a decision at this level (in order to identify a relevant country to approach for investment/entry) is available in public statistics – both national and international (UN, EU, IMF, World Bank, WTO, etc.), from forwarding agents, business journals, multi-client studies, country reports published by law firms or government white papers. The trained analyst may need a day or two to collate the relevant information to fill in a table like Table 6.2. When candidates for market entry have been selected, management should visit the country(/ies), in order to get a more detailed understanding of the market situation – to meet potential partners, visit public agencies, spot promising targets and visit relevant trade fairs, etc.

The great majority of first-time exporters do not normally follow this kind of procedure when they start exporting, the reason being that they operate in a reality where unsolicited enquiries flow in from more or less serious would-be partners, where coincidences "destroy" established plans, where "bait" laid out in one market is unexpectedly taken by a customer in another market. The extent to which discrete decisions are taken by the manager is more based on general considerations than on information purposely collected to cast light on opportunities. In many instances, firms "follow the crowd" or participate in trade missions organised by export promotion agencies.

Furthermore, in some industries it is more relevant to talk about selection of distributor than market selection:

> A supplier of airport control systems is a case in point. This industry consists of various players such as equipment providers, consultants and engineering firms, installation firms, distributors and agents. Often, several of these functions are assembled in one firm. Construction of major infrastructure projects such as airports is not carried out every year in the same country; rather such projects are implemented at infrequent periods of time, implying that vendors in this industry have to seek representation in different markets at different times. The said firm therefore chose to export, offering total project packages (engineering, components from different vendors and installation) through a distributor located in Belgium, operating worldwide. Hence, the market selection was done by the

distributor, rather than by the exporter itself. The firm is in this way "automatically" represented in a host of different markets around the world. For a small firm, this may have the secondary effect of obliging them, at short notice, to send technical teams to carry out repair and maintenance work in "all corners of the world". With lots of requests from different markets, this may involve disproportionate resources for a small player. On the other hand, the firm will be present – indirectly through its partner – in numerous markets that would otherwise be inaccessible.

We have seen that firms in general select markets using very rough criteria, such as psychic or geographic distance, and end up in neighbouring markets – more or less by default. The above system is a low-cost process that may function as a "safety valve" for top management. When the market selection is intuitive, disagreements in parts of management may surface – particularly if market performance in the selected country is below expectations. Uncertainties may stem from different opinions concerning required product adaptations, currency risks, terms of payment, etc. A methodology such as described above may then serve as a soothing mechanism, whereby the weighting of criteria used to select markets and the scores given will be subject to scrutiny and deliberation. The process is – in other words – an exercise in enhanced attention and insight into a range of critical strategic issues, and the end result will likely be a top management team more confident with the country selection.

6.3 Market selection strategy in different strategic positions

We have seen that there are two main approaches to market selection:

1   Systematic, based on analysis and evaluation of market attractiveness.
2   Unsystematic, based on evaluation of psychic distance or random queries from foreign buyers.

International market selection is not made in a vacuum; the context is that of the firm, and of the specific decision-makers inside the firm. It is their judgement of the situation, of the need for information, and of risks and opportunities involved that determines what market(s) the firm will eventually enter. Figure 6.1 sums up the situation of four different groups of firms according to the "Four Strategic Windows".

6.3.1 Unmethodical or random market selection

In this cell, the preparedness for internationalisation is limited and the firm is operating in a multi-local market. This implies inadequate managerial resources and scant information about business opportunities abroad. Such information can be bought (as suggested in Chapter 5), but their ability to translate that type of information into concrete business proposals is limited. Furthermore, firms in this cell are not threatened by globalisation forces (i.e. large MNCs entering their home market) and opportunities derived from such are not eye-catching. Therefore, firms may choose to enter one or a few markets, as discussed in Chapter 3, whereby they can "sneak in" unobserved by larger (local) competitors and therefore operate without fear of counterattack in their own home markets. Market entry in this instance often comes as a result of unsolicited or unexpected orders, in which case it is the buyer that chooses the seller, and the term market "selection" becomes rather illusory. Responding to a single order from another country may not involve anything more than selling to a customer in the domestic market. This is particularly true within the Eurozone, where

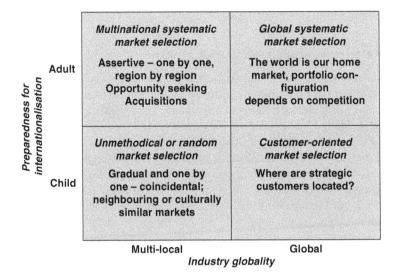

Figure 6.1 Market selection approaches in different strategic positions.

both trade friction and currency issues are reduced to a minimum. If the firm wants to go beyond just one sale to a foreign customer, it needs to assess the contacts obtained in this way by securing references, and evaluate future prospects in the said market before getting too heavily involved.

Sometimes the firms participate in trade fairs, but again it is rather random as to which prospective buyers may come to visit the exhibition booth (see Stompa, Chapter 5.2 – page 126). The exporter may also have concrete plans for market entry into specific countries, either because they have purchased goods from these countries and therefore have some networks and knowledge of potential customers (Korhonen et al. 1996), or because they have some other links to a country (holidays, family). In principle, it is all about exploiting a business opportunity at the lowest possible cost. If the firm – as an alternative – decides to carry out in-depth market research, the bill will rapidly exceed tens of thousands of euros, and it is far from certain that the analysis will give the necessary – or even correct – answers for management to take an informed decision on market entry (see The analytical firm in Chapter 5).

6.3.2 Customer-oriented market selection

In this case firms are not endowed with a lot of resources, but they operate in a global market context, full of opportunities and challenges. Through networks in the industry, this type of firm is often well-informed about most markets – and also about the most important global players in the trade. They may have even met some of them at international conferences and trade fairs.

> Opera Software develops and markets web browsers to large customers such as Apple, Huawai and Samsung. These vendors build Opera Software's solutions into their own products. Opera is therefore indirectly represented in most countries throughout the world, without being directly involved in the marketing to the final customer. Another example is the firm that sells equipment through engineering firms in the airport market (see Section 6.1).

These firms do not regard countries as their markets; rather they choose strategic partners that lead them to global markets.

6.3.3 Multinational or regional systematic market selection

In this cell, firms have both the resources and the capacity to collect concrete and detailed market information about customers, buyer behaviour, competitors, rules and regulations. They have a completely different starting point from which to make market selection, based on knowledge and rational consideration of alternatives. At the same time, there is no imminent threat of competitive retaliation (for example, in the firm's own home market) from local or multinational competitors. Each market can be considered in its own right, allowing the firm to use objective and country-specific criteria for market selection without considering the greater "global" picture. Research should be used because the firm's competence to carry it out is deemed part of its high-preparedness for internationalisation, and because market entry can be implemented based on the firm's own strategic consider-ations rather than as a response to initiatives by unknown distributors or agents, from a country that was not in the exporter's mind-set at the outset (as is often the case for the unmethodical/random firm). The market information that is acquired through the request in an unmethodical/random situation will, in this case, need to be substituted by concrete information.

When Orkla Foods, Norway's largest company within the FMCG (fast moving consumer goods) sector, with sales of 3.5 billion euros, entered the Baltic market (Estonia, Latvia and Lithuania) in the late 1990s, they did not consider market size as a critical criterion. With a total Baltic population of 7 million, many other markets would stand out as much more promising. On the other hand, these were markets with little competition and potentially high long-term growth. Therefore, Orkla Foods were in a position to mould the markets which were on the brink of taking off. Germany – with their 80 million inhabitants and with a language and a culture that are much closer to Norway's – would perhaps constitute a more interesting prospective market for other firms. However, competition, close – and sometimes impenetrable – relations between vendors and buyers, and lower growth compounded with the fact that an introduction to this large market would entail prohibitive disbursements, played an important part in Orkla's decision to do otherwise. Instead, the firm decided to invest in the Baltics. Since they mostly operate in a multi-local industry, the potential threat of competitive retaliation was not overwhelming.

6.3.4 Global, systematic market selection

Firms in this cell have the resources, the knowledge and the strategic position to be able to shape the international industry structure through acquisitions and mergers and through brand posi-tioning in world markets. In this case, market selection is really not the issue, since firms in this position by definition are present in most important international markets – be it where the largest customers are located or where the most powerful competitors have their strongholds. In the opposite case, they risk being outmanoeuvred by their keener peers in the market: competitors with a solid share in large home markets – such as the US, Japan, Germany, China – may use this position to exercise price pressures without risking retaliation. As we have seen in Chapter 4, such a home market constitutes the basis for scale economies both in production, R&D and marketing, covering the bulk of the fixed costs of the operation. Attacks on other – and smaller – markets can be carried out with heavily-subsidised price levels or with a massive marketing campaign.

Rather than selecting markets for entry, the critical issue here is to determine what role each market will play in their total portfolio. Rather than *where*, it is a question of *how*. This will be the main topic in the next section.

6.4 Market portfolio – primary and secondary markets

Different markets play different roles in the development of the firm. Prioritising between market investments and developing a market portfolio are the topics of this section.

6.4.1 Objectives and priorities

Many firms are present in several foreign markets without really having a well-founded foothold. With a negligible share in export markets, these firms risk becoming victims of marginalisation during economic downturns or when the industry is restructured. We have seen this in many industries (see Chapter 2). The marginal player will in most cases be the first to be excluded by the customer, mainly because either the player is not sufficiently important in a restructured industry – and therefore lacks clout in negotiations – or because it has not yet developed a satisfactory relationship with the purchaser. The main reason for this is often a lack of a conscious strategy for each market. The international marketer needs to address a number of questions in this context:

- What are my objectives in each market?
- What are my sales goals?
- On what market segment should I concentrate?
- How will the market selection and objectives influence my organisation?

It boils down to the overarching question: *what role do I want to play in the market?* The answer to this question will vary with the situation of each firm. In principle, two main strategies are relevant:

1. *Concentrated market portfolio*. In this case, the firm focuses their marketing activities on a limited number of markets (two or three) where they achieve a firm footing – both in the distribution channels and in their relationship with individual customers, covering a broad range of customer groups. They have developed a market presence that is sufficiently strong to withstand competitive attack or occasional downturns in the market.
2. *International niches*. In this case, the exporter sells to many markets, but in doing so, concentrates on specialised niches, in which they have developed entry barriers in the form of close relationships, catering to specific technological or logistical needs of the customer-base, making entry by any competitor onerous. They too reduce their vulnerability to changes in the market but only in the narrow segment that they dominate.

Many firms combine these two strategies: they achieve market leadership or challenger roles (Kotler and Keller 2011) in one or two export markets and then export to a number of other markets, where the aim is much less ambitious. We term the first category primary markets, whereas the other markets are called secondary markets.

> SB Seating is a European company producing office chairs, with manufacturing in the Netherlands, Norway and Sweden. They are clearly number 1 in the swivel-chair segment in Scandinavia, and number 2 in the Netherlands. They are also present in many other European countries (particularly Germany, Austria, Switzerland and the UK) and have started to approach Asia. Currently, 70% of sales are concentrated in four markets whereas the rest are dispersed between 15 to 20 markets. In Europe – with more than perhaps 50 vendors – they are among the four or five biggest players. In that endeavour SB Seating service their major markets through their own sales subsidiaries which in turn sell through an exclusive dealer network – "exclusive" in the sense that not everyone in the market is eligible to carry their products. Then again, the exclusivity is not geographic, so two or more dealers could compete to get the same job with the same products.[7]

The main difference between primary and secondary markets is the role that the exporter plays in these, and – consequently – the marketing tools and resources deployed to achieve or maintain this role.

> The ski wax market is a relatively narrow segment of sports and leisure.[8] Swix is one of the world leaders in this niche. The main customers are in Europe and partly North America, but countries such as Japan, China (PRC) and Argentina are also represented in their 25–30 country portfolio. Originating in Sweden, the company was taken over by Norwegian investors in the 1960s. The firm is particularly strong in Sweden and Norway – where the brand is iconic among skiers – but they have also a leadership or challenger position in other leading winter sports nations such as Russia, the US, Finland, France, Switzerland and Germany. Local market leaders on the European continent and in Finland make these markets especially challenging. On the other hand, in markets such as the US and Japan, they are market leaders. Other markets are regarded as more secondary.[9]

In the case of Swix we can split the markets into a number of subcategories of primary and secondary markets.

6.4.2 *Primary markets*

"*Established markets*" are those where the firm has a good footing (they are among the leading firms in the market) and where the share of total sales has reached a considerable volume. For Swix, these would typically be Sweden and Norway; management is compelled to devote particular attention to these two markets in order to safeguard their business. The main strategic task will be to maintain, defend and further develop their market shares through constant refinement of their marketing activities, both through marketing communication and product development/new products. This will require a great deal of monitoring and control, and will as such impact on the organisation of the international marketing effort. We may liken established markets to the "Cash cow" in the BCG matrix (see Chapter 4.3.2, page 112).

Management should typically concentrate on the following marketing activities in this position:

–   Create barriers to competition. The firm is in a leadership position in parts of the market and competitors are constantly challenging this position either through product improvements, new media, better customer service or channel innovations. The firm should therefore pre-emptively introduce countermeasures. In order to do so, management needs a well-functioning market intelligence system (see Chapter 5.4)
–   Assess future growth prospects. These are markets that until now have constituted the "bread and butter" of the business, and are therefore strategically critical for the firm. This may well change in the future, for various reasons: local, economic and political changes; hardening competition; maturing demand. If the future is bleak, these markets may be degraded into secondary markets. Several actions are relevant here: product repositioning, new products, new channels of distribution and communication, broadening the market, new target groups.
–   Reassert the operation mode to ascertain marketing control. A firm with distributors or agents in this kind of market may want to switch into more committed operation modes such as wholly-owned sales subsidiary.

"Investment markets" (for Swix this is the US, Canada and Japan) will play a different role in the firm's strategy. Here the firm has a long-term objective to establish a leadership position in parts of the market and to make these markets a main contributor to its earnings in the future. We may equate this category with the "Star" position in the BCG matrix. This requires a long-term perspective – in some countries which are difficult for foreigners to understand, such as Japan, possibly more than ten years – with targeted and relatively large investments both in terms of direct expenditures and people. It is therefore critical for management to get a comprehensive understanding of the market – either through market research, through experience or both – so as to be able to define clear strategies before embarking on this kind of investment. The role that these markets will play in the firm's future portfolio is a key element in the development of this strategy. Often, the future role will be a new "established market" as described above. Also other roles may be considered, such as *"retaliation market"*. Here the firm will not necessarily be a future market leader (that position is most likely already staunchly taken by a local vendor), but they will nevertheless be big enough to retaliate if their main competitors in these markets become provokingly aggressive in the firm's own established market (Hamel and Prahalad 1985). As we have seen in Chapter 4, this element is becoming increasingly relevant. For Swix, countries such as Germany and Finland may be termed retaliation markets because their most important competitors are located there.

In this position, the marketing strategy will have a slightly different emphasis:

–   Gaining market share. In a highly competitive market, where the market leaders defend their position with "all means", the firm should consider avoiding head-on competition, and rather seek peripheral segments and specialised customer groups, where the leader has less interest. Doing so it should differentiate its offering in order to "stand out", either by adding features to the product, offering better customer service or a lower price.
–   If the firm has not yet established a local sales office, it should consider doing so in order to gain better control with the market investments to be made.

6.4.3 Secondary markets

Normally the company has a lower market share in secondary markets, and the share of the firm's total sales is also less significant. Therefore it is of lesser strategic interest to hold on to this type of market. Consequently, both the dedication of management and the resources given to these markets will normally be more moderate. This does not necessarily imply that the return on sales is lower than in other markets. For instance, seasonal variations in primary markets may call for capacity utilisation to be dispensed in less important markets at reduced prices. These markets may be termed "*Accordion markets*" (because sales vary greatly from one year to the other – expanding and contracting like an accordion), where the firm has a network of distributors that can unload surplus capacity without too much effort from management, and where the price contagion between markets is less conspicuous. This network is often typically composed of trading houses (see later). Typical features of accordion market strategies are:

- Exploiting market opportunities by using the price mechanism (marginal pricing – see Chapter 12) in order to fill capacity.
- Selling standard products that do not require any extra adaptation costs.
- Using indirect operation modes such as trading houses or export management companies.

"*Exploration markets*" are those where the firm wants to evaluate future roles: should the firm aim for a leadership position sometime in the future or should it rather content itself with a challenger role? Or should the market only constitute a marginal element in the strategy? The evaluation process may best be carried out through a concrete presence in the market, where the firm builds up experience and market insight without investing too much. In the case of Swix, China and South Korea epitomise this class of markets, and may best be compared with "Question marks" in BCG parlance. Here the exporter might consider the following strategic moves:

- In order not to invest too much in this exploratory phase the exporter should primarily use independent representation in these markets.
- They should sell standard products or products with minimal adaptations in the beginning. Then later on, when they have acquired market insight they can adapt their products to the market requirements.

"*Peripheral markets*" are another type of market in this classification. These are where the firm typically only responds to requests, but where it does not have an active involvement other than perhaps having a local agent or distributor.

In addition, we may also use the term "*Pull-out markets*" – somewhat similar to the "Dog" position of the BCG matrix – which are markets that the firm, for various reasons, wants to withdraw from. These are markets where the firm has been active but where conditions have changed for the worse. They are no longer of any strategic importance for the firm (low/negative growth, poor performance, limited role in the portfolio), and they cost more than they yield (in terms of, for instance, payment problems, transport costs, marginal customers, price level, etc.). Another reason to pull out of a market may be internal political and economic uncertainties. Certain countries in the Middle East (Syria, Yemen) or South America (Venezuela) may be candidates for withdrawal in the year 2017. For the more gregarious firm, such circumstances may be a good argument to get involved in the market, precisely because – in the wake of such uncertainties – interesting business opportunities may arise and be lost to others if one is not there to capitalise on the situation. Whether the firm then opts to be present depends on its access to information and its network/trustworthy cooperation with a partner.

6.4.4 The international market portfolio

We have made allusion to the BCG model throughout this section. The difference between the original BCG matrix and our model lies chiefly in the unit of analysis. In the original model that is the firm's products, whereas in our model the different markets are in focus. Figure 6.2 illustrates where these different market categories are potentially located in the matrix.[10]

This market classification gives management a more finely-tuned foundation to make market decisions. One may say that primary markets are located on the left in the model whereas secondary markets are on the right-hand side. One exception may be investment markets, which often start where the firm has low market shares. Nothing in this world is static, and this is certainly true also in this context. Established markets may, for diverse reasons, be demoted to accordion markets. Exploration markets may become investment or established markets. Management needs to be constantly on its toes to be able to judge the status of each market in its portfolio, in order to allocate the right "medicine" in each instance.

As a summary the two categories may be characterised as shown in Table 6.3.

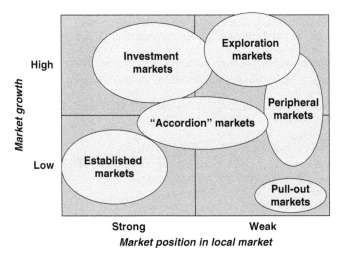

Figure 6.2 International market portfolio.

Source: Inspired by Boston Consulting Group.

Table 6.3 Features of primary and secondary markets

Primary markets	Secondary markets
High market shares	Generally low and/or varying market share
Relatively high return on sales	Varying profitability
Large and loyal customer groups where the firm is one of the main suppliers.	Few customers and/or customers where the firm is a marginal vendor
Efficient use of marketing tools	Vulnerable to price competition
Extensive monitoring and control through own sales subsidiaries	Monitoring and control are constrained by indirect operation mode (distributors, agents, licensees)

6.5 Chapter summary

In this chapter we have seen that market selection is often carried out in a rather heuristic way, almost by default to neighbouring countries. There are, however, gains to be made by intro-ducing a more rational approach to market selection, through a low-cost process that involves top management. This process involves establishing a set of selection criteria – critical for the firm – weighing the criteria and seeking data to cover the information need. Such a process may serve the purpose of a "security valve" for an otherwise erroneous market choice.

The approach to market selection may vary from one strategic position to the next. By way of using the Strategic Windows model, we identify four different types of market selection approaches: Unsystematic or random, Systematic multinational, Customer-oriented and Global systematic market selection.

Finally, market selection also involves prioritising between primary and secondary markets. These two categories can be subdivided into different classes of markets, enabling management to devise appropriate strategies for each individual market.

Notes

1　Based on information given on the company home page: https://www.science4youtoys.com/
2　This incident took place before EU regulations on standardisation were in place.
3　PESTEL: Political, Economic, Social, Technological, Environmental, Legal factors.
4　Based on figures retrieved from Wikipedia.
5　There is a plethora of articles and presentations on this issue. Here are some examples:

  – http://www.uniassignment.com/essay-samples/law/the-relationship-between-eu-and-national-law-law-european-essay.php
  – http://www.era-comm.eu/oldoku/SNLLaw/01_Overview/2012_11_Brkan_EN.pdf
  – https://en.wikipedia.org/wiki/European_Union_law#Goods

6　*Dagens Næringsliv*, 17 July 2014.
7　Communication with company managers.
8　For non-skiers: Skiing conditions vary considerably depending on the quality of the snow. There are many different grades of wax. Ski wax is applied under the ski in order to optimise the gliding surface between the ski and the snow.
9　Communications with company managers.
10　It is acknowledged that the model – as stated in Chapter 4 – is sometimes difficult to use, since the two dimensions are extremely difficult to measure. What is high growth in one industry may not be in another industry; and as we have seen, market share is a measure that varies with how one defines the market. The location of the different market categories in Figure 6.1 gives a pointer to potential strategic conclusions.

7 Operation modes in international markets

7.1 Introduction

Operation mode may be defined as the way firms want to organise their presence in the market.[1] The decision on operation mode is one of the most critical ones in international marketing (Hamill et al. 1989; Welch et al. 2007), because it determines how resources and control of marketing activities are distributed between the marketing partners. A plethora of different operation modes exist, from market-based, low-commitment and low-control modes such as using local independent distributors, to hierarchically-governed and wholly-owned direct engagements with 100% control, using sales subsidiaries or local manufacturing. Between these two we find a number of hybrid forms – between market and hierarchies – such as licensing, franchising and joint ventures. Anderson and Gatignon (1986) claim that independent agents or distributors are the default entry mode, since the cost of setting up a subsidiary is both onerous and involves operational risks when the firm enters into unchartered waters.

Table 7.1 gives an overview of different operation modes that are relevant in international marketing. It is based on Luostarinen's (1980a) taxonomy, dividing between operation modes with or without investments, and with or without local production of goods and services.

This chapter shall discuss these modes in some detail. It is worth noting that strategic alliances (SAs) are not in this list. This is because SAs manifest themselves in many different shades and forms, and can in principle appear anywhere in the table. SAs will therefore be the object of a separate discussion. Before doing so, however, we shall discuss factors that determine the choice of operation mode, both from a practical business viewpoint and from a more theoretical viewpoint.

7.2 Key factors in the choice of operation mode

7.2.1 The business viewpoint

The businessperson would typically state that there are two main factors that determine operation mode strategy: 1) *internal* strategic goals and resources, and 2) the *external* business environment. This section discusses some of the most relevant ones in this context.

Internal factors

Section 3.3.1 describes the internationalisation process of firms, and how they develop their international business culture in stages through experience and gradually increase their

Table 7.1 Operation modes in international markets

	Without investments	With investments
Without local production	Trading houses Distributors/importers Agents Directly to final customer	Sales subsidiary Storage facility Service unit
With local production	Licensing and franchising Contract manufacturing Management contracts	Production unit

Source: Based on Luostarinen (1980a).

commitment to international markets. The following example illustrates how these factors affect the operation mode decision.

A small firm has recently developed an innovative product primarily for use in the nascent electric automobile industry. It is based on state of the art technology and at present there is no similar technology available on the market. However, once the product is introduced to the market, the solutions built into the product will be understood and copied by larger competitors. This may take some time, but after a couple of years, larger competitors will most likely offer similar products to the markets. The firm has insufficient resources and insight to develop international sales on their own during the two-year window of opportunity.

We have already touched upon this situation in Chapter 3.2 (the Born Global dilemma). The said firm has several options to engage in international markets. The most relevant are:

1   The firm may license out its newly-acquired technology and cash in yearly royalty payments from the licensee, in which case it should choose a partner with an extensive marketing network. If licensing gives the firm a profitable and "easy" entry into the market, without investments in market development other than identifying and negotiating with the licensing partner, it also entails loss of control. The firm risks being prevented from developing its own marketing organisation and building international marketing experience, both of which are critical to develop the firm further.

2   Through fear of overstretching its limited resources, the firm may choose to seek a firm foothold in just a few markets . This will typically imply that the firm will perhaps have to secure financial backing over a three to five year period before any payback, because this is the time it takes to gain entry and then acceptance by customers (product testing, engineering and design with the car manufacturer, etc.) and eventually reap a positive cash-flow from operations. In this way, the firm will control its own sales and marketing effort, and thereby its own development. But the risk is that established competitors that already have an active network in the industry will pick up the idea and outmanoeuvre the firm in the course of a couple of years because they have more financial and marketing clout.

3   Another option is to actively develop relations with independent agents or distributors in several countries. This might then be a good foundation to capture a wider market. Experience suggests, however, that establishing relations with agents and distributors is a long-term process, and that more than one attempt is often needed before the firm is satisfied with its marketing network. Identifying partners and negotiating contracts with them will take time, even though the firm may get assistance from consultants and export promotion agencies. At least one or two years will elapse before the firm has an

operative market network – and even longer before it can hope to make any inroads into potential key customer relationships. Again, the risk of competitors entering the arena is high.

4   A fourth option is to be taken over by and integrated into a larger multinational firm which has the right resources and market access to get rapid acceptance of the innovation by key customers. The control is minimal, but so are the risks, and the short-term financial returns are perhaps more interesting.

A key element in this analysis is the relationship between control over the firm's own market development and available resources, particularly in the form of commitment to invest in market activities. Generalising on the above discussion, we may claim that three internal factors determine the choice of operation mode by exporters:

1   Their *objectives* in the market – such as market shares, sales volumes and growth, and not least, control of the marketing effort and thereby the feedback loop (of experience) from the market.
2   The resources available to be devoted to the export venture – both financial and managerial.
3   The basis for the whole venture, viz. a competitive advantage, be it based on superior technology, design, and some cost or resource advantage.

External market factors

Four important external factors are relevant in this context:

CUSTOMER AND DISTRIBUTION STRUCTURE

How easily accessible are the final customers and the middlemen that connect the exporter to these customers? In some markets there are just a few relevant customers – perhaps only one,[2] and there is a question whether one needs a middleman at all. However, this depends on factors such as the purchasing behaviour of the potential customer: Who is the real decision-maker in the buying centre? Who has influencing power in this context? Do we have access to key personnel without going through local agents?

> An example of impenetrable access to decision-makers is found in Arab countries. In these countries, top leaders may have a commercial interest in a specific contract, either directly through ownership of a subcontractor or agent, or indirectly through family or clan members who might have a "finger in the pie". Without in-depth knowledge of such structures the foreign vendor has no chance to get involved with key members of the buying centre, not to mention securing the contract (Solberg 2002a).

In some markets, established relations between vendors and buyers are dense and long-term, making any introduction of a newcomer, if not insurmountable, at least difficult and costly.

Figure 7.1 illustrates this situation with four key managers in the selling (incumbent and new) and the buying firms, the weight of the lines denoting the strength of the ties between the players. It demonstrates that breaking into existing ties is not straightforward.

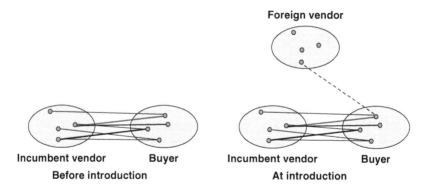

Figure 7.1 Ties between vendors and buyers before and at introduction.

Such relationships are partly culturally bound. We have already alluded to the deep relation-ships in the *keiretsu* system in Japan. Making inroads into this market is challenging. We have seen the role of the family and clan in Arab countries. Also, Olson (1997) suggests that Muslim countries are more loyal to their suppliers than, for instance, protestant countries. However, Germany has also been said to have such close relationships between business partners.

> When the US petrochemical giant Dow Chemical tried to enter the German market they found the local incumbents, such as Bayer and BASF, incredibly strong. At the time, the market was very much cemented into stable relationships between the major players. However, Dow Chemical persisted and spent ten years before they managed to "break the code". As the then chairman of the board explained: "Our vision is that we will persist in the German market for the next hundred years, so we should manage to overcome a ten-year investment period."[3]

So the question boils down to the following: How (direct or through intermediary) and with what resources can the firm get access to key customers?

DISTRIBUTION CHANNELS

Although chains have taken over most of the retail trade in Western economies and have streamlined the transactions from the manufacturer down to the consumer, the structure of the distribution system is sometimes complex and seemingly quite "irrational", as is shown below.

Japan's channels of distribution of seafood in transition[4]

The biggest fish markets in Japan are found in Tokyo, Osaka and Fukuoka, and they make up the majority of total sales. The Tsjukiji market in Tokyo is the biggest of the three – it is actually the biggest in the world. It was established as early as the end of the 15th century and has continued to grow due to a rich culture for fish and also because they have enjoyed certain privileges from the government. Around 2,400 tonnes of fish of all kinds worth 20 million USD are traded here every day, which makes up around 15%

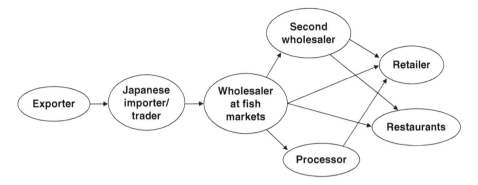

Figure 7.2 Distribution system in the seafood sector in Japan.

of all fish in Japan; 14,000 people work at this market and more than 35,000 buyers make their daily purchases here. Seven wholesale dealers and auction firms operate in this market, with licences from the Department of Agriculture and Fisheries in Tokyo. This is where it has been decided, amongst other things, that the sales commission is set at 5.5%.

In addition to the three largest markets, you have around 40 medium-sized markets. All in all there are nearly 800 fish markets spread across Japan, divided into 54 central and more than 700 regional markets, so it's safe to say it is a very fragmented trade. There are no definite numbers, but according to some estimates 80–90% of the total turnover for the salmon trade comes from these markets.

Tradition in this industry is crucial, and you rarely see written contracts. Most of the trade is based on trust and experience that has been established through long-standing relations between the traders. The price is set at the spot market, but is also established during the weekly sales. The volumes usually remain stable over time, and a typical order is 2–3 tonnes. One of the importers said the following: "We will usually know the volume we're able to sell when we place an order. The order made on a Tuesday will arrive on the following Sunday, and will be sold during the next three days. On Fridays we place our orders for delivery on Thursday–Saturday. This way we are certain of a constant flow of fish."

The Japanese eat a lot of varied seafood, and this is one reason why there is a system with numerous market participants and levels in the distribution chains. A Japanese meal of sushi typically consists of several types of seafood, which is why the consumers expect a broad range in both restaurants and the local shops. The restaurants and shops therefore wish to have a large number of suppliers who can secure access to different raw materials. Another reason for the fragmented market is that there used to be a set of rules that hindered the establishment of large stores and so the smaller shops still prevail.

The purchasing patterns of the Japanese consumer follow the tradition of preferring to make frequent visits to the local corner shop. The majority of Japanese live in small apartments and they use the local shop almost as their refrigerator. Interestingly, the five biggest supermarket chains in Japan only make up 20% of the retail sales, compared with 60–80% in Europe.

Over the past few years, however, changes have occurred in the distribution pattern due to, amongst other things, difficult financial times in Japan in the 1990s. During these years many fish importers had to declare bankruptcy or leave the market. What is left now is a smaller number of stable or larger importers who generally have five to six suppliers of various types of fish. These changes have been initiated by the larger retailers and restaurant chains. As expected, the reason for this is the ever-present pressure on profit margins.

In the revised direct-supply system, the main point of contact for the exporter is still the importer, but the importer will be in direct contact with the large retailers and will thus skip at least two, if not three, links in the chain. These importers have taken full control of the process (filleting, packing, types of dishes, etc.) either contractually or through their own means.

This new way of operating is still in its infancy, but it is expected that the new form of distribution will be much more important in the years to come. For an exporter who has been selling through the traditional system, the question is: What are the risks of switching to the new system?

The distribution system structure is often based on traditions, where different players have specific roles – be it as traders, financiers, insurers or marketers; and the exporter needs to adapt its own marketing – hence its operation mode – to this structure. For example, agents just brokering transactions are frequently used in the industrial goods trade, where the final buying company often has its own import routines (so competence in customs clearance handling and local logistics are taken care of). The more technical the product, the more the exporter needs to actively participate in the sales process; the role of the agent becomes more that of a "path finder". Exporting to a large number of buyers in the market requires possibly a local distributor with its own local dealer network. The distributor normally has responsibility for after-sales, service, storage, etc.

COMPETITION

Also the structure of the competition may influence the choice of operation mode. Hamel and Prahalad (1985) argue that, in a concentrated industry setting, firms hold each other hostage to their respective positions in international markets. In order to be able to respond to competitive pressures in such contexts, firms need to control their foreign operations, and this is better done through hierarchical integration (i.e. sales subsidiaries) than through independent solutions (distributors or agents). Solberg and Durrieu (2015b) found that integrated marketing channels give better results in concentrated industry settings. For a newcomer without the strength or experience to invest in the next level of the chain, this setting is particularly challenging since some competitors will have power and ability to outsmart newcomers to the market.

One possible solution for the newcomer is to study the buyer structure, the potential bonds between buyers and the dominant competitors, preferences and purchasing decision patterns, in the hope of identifying "holes" in the market, where the dominant players have less influence. One possible strategy would be to "slip in through the backdoor" by working on meticulously-chosen customers, either directly or through specialised middlemen. Later, when the firm has achieved a certain foothold with these customers, it is time to consider new customer groups and establish itself in the strongholds of its competitors. A question, then, remains whether the agent who was originally chosen for the venture is the one to lead the firm into a broader market. A switch of operation mode may become necessary.

In some cases it may be appropriate to enter into an alliance with a competitor in order to achieve this – either through some form of joint venture or licensing arrangement.

The Norwegian company Simrad, which supplies electronic equipment to the maritime and defence industries, entered into an alliance with the largest French supplier of defence electronics, Thompson, with a view to getting contracts in France. Thompson acquired a 15% ownership stake in Simrad and developed a joint marketing programme directed at the French Navy.

Such alliances imply that the firm will have to relinquish strategic control in the said market. Management, therefore, needs to consider what is most important: long-term control or rapid market introduction.

To illustrate this point we will travel to Denmark and pay a visit to Pandora, the third-largest jewellery company in the world after Cartier and Tiffany & Co. Starting modestly in 1982, in 2016 they had total sales of about 1.8 billion euros (20 billion DKK), with sales in six continents.

Through franchising, international expansion started for real in 2003 in North America. In Europe, the firm entered into a distribution agreement with the Kasi Group. In fact, this firm had been extremely successful introducing Pandora's jewellery – first to the German, Austrian and Swiss markets, and later also to Eastern Europe – and this was one of the main contributing factors to Pandora's international success. However, Pandora, experiencing loss of control in these markets, invited the Kasi Group to renegotiate the distribution contract. The Kasi Group, feeling threatened by Pandora's intention to set up its own distribution system in Kasi's markets, agreed to transfer the distribution to a joint venture, Pandora CWE, with Pandora holding 51% and the Kasi Group 49%. Through an Initial Public Offering (IPO) in 2010 at the Copenhagen Stock Exchange, Pandora was able to to offer Jesper Lautrup Nielsen, the Kasi Group's main shareholder, an earn-out deal, based on Pandora's performance in Kasi Group's former markets.[5]

Alternatives are much more plentiful in a fragmented competitive structure. There is no dominant player, and entering a broader spectrum of the market is therefore possible. Choosing the appropriate operation mode will depend more on other factors, for instance the firm's own objectives and resources.

OTHER EXTERNAL FACTORS

Legal regulations vary considerably from one country to the other. Some countries do not allow ownership by foreigners of more than 49% of a company, forcing foreign vendors into joint ventures with local firms. In other markets, such as in many Middle Eastern countries, foreign firms are not allowed to sell directly to local customers, so lining up with an agent or distributor is mandatory.

Saudi Arabia epitomises this point where restrictions are in abundance. However, the regulations vary between industry sectors. For example, foreigners may own up to 75% of a professional services (e.g. engineering or legal services) operation, whereas the rest must be owned by local Saudis. Similarly, Saudi Arabia issues foreign investors with a business licence to engage in wholesale or retail distribution activities with a maximum ownership of 75% when the foreign capital contribution is at least SR 20 million (around 5 million euros).[6]

Political risk is another factor to be considered, particularly regarding foreign direct investments. In politically-unstable countries, the risk of a shift in the regime may wipe out all foreigners from the market. The most dramatic example of this is possibly the volte-face after the Russian revolution in 1917, when foreign-owned factories were confiscated by the Lenin regime and large fortunes were lost.

Many countries – particularly in the developing world – require local content in the bids to get orders. The nascent petroleum sector in Brazil is one such example. In order to be considered, foreign firms therefore subcontract part of the job to local industry – either through some form of joint venture or licensing arrangement, or merely as a simple subcontracting deal.

Owens Corning, makers of pipes and tanks in reinforced polyester, established a joint venture with local interests in Dubai in order to exploit their know-how in a fast-growing market (the Emirates and Middle East in general). In addition to the local production, Owens Corning exported considerable amounts of fixtures and smaller pipes to complete the local product range.[7]

In addition to making market access possible, local production may also help to establish good relationships with local authorities, who may then be more willing to accept direct exports from the country of origin. The point here is that, when business opportunities have been spotted, the exporter often needs to find approaches other than mere exports to tap into the market.

7.2.2 Theoretical perspectives on operation modes

This section will delve more deeply into theoretical explanations of different modes of operation in foreign markets. Transaction cost economics (TCE) – or internalisation theory – is the dominant theoretical string in this context (along with its "cousin" – theories on foreign direct investments), although the Uppsala school of gradual internationalisation has also contributed greatly to our understanding of foreign operation modes. This is partly described in Chapter 3. The main issue here is whether the local marketing operations should be carried out by the firm itself (if the firm should integrate and exercise ownership control – hierarchy) or whether they should let an independent player carry out the local marketing.

The basic assumption in TCE is that firms behave opportunistically, implying that they have a tendency to seek their own interests – with guile (Williamson 1975). That partners can behave opportunistically is more apparent in international marketing than in the domestic arena, information asymmetry being more likely to occur in such settings (see also Chapter 5). The local middleman may more easily get away with shirking (for example, not giving the agreed level of service to customers and thereby saving costs) or with faulty or imperfect information (to cover up their own deficiencies in the marketing) because the exporter is generally less-informed about local market conditions than local partners.

The more the exporter has invested in its foreign partner – for example local storage facilities, training, product adaptations, logistics: in other words, transaction specific investments that become worthless outside the relationship – the more vulnerable it is to any opportunistic behaviour of the middleman. Therefore the firm must seek ways to control its partner in foreign markets. There are in principle three ways of exerting such control:

1   Integration – i.e. ownership of the members in the value chain
2   Partner selection
3   Partner relations.

We shall concentrate on the first of these three control modes; the other two are based on agency theory and social exchange theory respectively and will be considered later (see Chapter 8).

TCE predicts that high specific investments in the relationshop incite the firm to integrate in order to protect these investments. In our case this means seeking ownership of the next members in the value chain (for instance, the distributor), and in this way exerting *hier-archical control* of its operations. The higher the specific investment, the higher the incentive to control through integration. This discussion is at the heart of the theory of the multinational enterprise (MNE), which assumes that firms – under certain circumstances – want to control their competitive advantages (such as patent, know-how, brand) rather than let an inde-pendent player carry out marketing (through an agency, distributor or franchising contract) and production (through a licensing contract) on their behalf. It is difficult to evaluate the case of immaterial competitive advantages (Buckley and Casson 1976). What is the value of, for instance, a new and unproved patent in the market? The buyer would typically offer a low price, whereas the seller would want to charge a high price, but no one really knows the "correct price" in the market. Rather than letting a third party exploit the patent at a too-low price, the patent owner would prefer to internalise the exploitation – i.e. exploit the patent him- or herself. The theory predicts that direct investments will then be preferred over licensing when costs related to controlling the external exploitation of the competitive advantage are high.

Companies involved with the international marketing of services – and professional services in particular – have a tendency to prefer integrated modes of operation. For example, business consulting across borders is normally carried out through local permanent staff employed by a subsidiary. The main reason for this lies in the desire to control internally-developed com-petence, without which the exporting firm risks misuse of its systems and know-how, which in the end will tarnish its image.

TCE also predicts that frequency and the value of transactions between the partners will influence the decision to integrate: more frequent transactions and higher values suggest that the firm might prefer to exploit the scale economies therein on its own. This is why an exporter that starts to sell through an independent middleman would want to take over the operation after a while – when sales have reached a certain threshold value. This is about control, but also about reaping the benefits of economies of scale.

We have shown in Chapter 3 that the Uppsala school explains direct investments rather as a sequence in what is called the "establishment chain" (Andersen 1993). The increasing com-mitment – from independent sales representatives to wholly-owned manufacturing – is the hallmark of the internationalisation process and comes as a result of the gradual learning of the game. Experience and market knowledge accrue to the firm and its managers, and thus pave the way to bolder steps (such as direct investments) and more control. This is in line with Solberg and Askeland (2006) who claim that firms in the introductory phases of their internationalisation will seldom have the necessary resources – neither financial nor managerial – to engage in direct investments to achieve such control. They also do not have the necessary information to make *rational* decisions on independent vs. hierarchical local representation. They will therefore have to content themselves with cooperating with external partners to carry out their nascent internationalisation, and then run the risk of being trapped in a flawed relationship. Direct investments are for the more seasoned firms.

Solberg and Nes (2002) found that control was best exercised through sales subsidiaries, and the worst through distributors, agents being somewhere in between, thus lending support to the TCE hypothesis. However, they did not find that sales subsidiaries necessarily lead to better financial performance. Concerning commitment, the main divide lies between dependent (sales subsidiary) and independent (agent *and* distributor) forms of representation. However, even though TCE predicts better control through wholly-owned subsidiaries, this is not always straightforward in practice; even within a hierarchy, ownership control does not necessarily solve the governance problem. Daughter companies have a "depressing" tendency to develop their own ways and strategies – independent of the directions given by headquarters (Prahalad and Doz 1981, Ghauri 1990). Again, this mostly stems from information asymmetry, where key managers of the local subsidiary have not only learnt the local "rules of the game" but have also built a network of local market players. They have what French and Raven (1959) term "expert power" and are therefore also in a position to convince the centre of local solutions being the "best".

Our discussion has so far centred on integration or not between the exporter and the next member of the chain in the market; on hierarchy (100% ownership) or market (independent partner). Over the past 30–40 years, a hybrid form of operation mode has become increasingly important: strategic alliances. These may take a number of different forms, but try in different ways to bridge the gap between independent and dependent intermediaries in international markets – something between governance through hierarchy and the market. A strategic alliance seeks to combine different concerns present in TCE theory: getting control in order to curb opportunism on the part of the partner; reaping the gains of economies of scale and frequency of transactions; through mutual specific investments achieving commitment from both partners, and balancing the stakes of the partners.

There are many kinds of strategic alliances:

- Vertical (for example: subcontracting – assembly; production – marketing: R&D – production) vs. horizontal (cooperation in R&D, production, marketing).
- Project-based (once the project is finalised, the SA is dissolved) vs. long-term relationships.
- Equity vs. non-equity alliances.

Some of these are strategic considerations (i.e. what is the role of the venture in the firms' strategy: vertical/horizontal; project/long term; countering competition; access to customers?). Others relate to legal issues (host country regulations or tax issues). Yet others have to do with resource constraints (project is too big for the firm to go it alone). We shall later discuss strategic alliances in some detail – see Chapter 7, Section 7.4.5.

Having treated both business considerations and theoretical aspects of different entry modes, we will now treat a number of specific operation modes, starting with export modes (production at home) and then proceeding to discuss operation modes entailing foreign production.

7.3 Export operation modes

Operation modes available to the exporter are first and foremost the following:

- Trading company/trading house
- Distributor/importer
- Agent
- Sales subsidiary
- Direct exports without middleman.

All of these different operation modes have the same objective: to reduce the effects of distance (both geographic and cultural) and other obstacles that otherwise hinder a smooth relationship between the exporter and its customers in the export market. However, they do this in different ways, partly depending on the structure in the local distribution system, and partly depending on the tasks that the exporter itself can carry out on its own.

The exporter may still determine the extent to which different tasks required to successfully operate in the market should be executed by themselves, rather than by a local middleman and their network of business partners. Whereas the newcomer to the market needs assistance for most of its activities, the more-seasoned exporter can possibly carry out these activities through wholly-owned local companies (these issues are also discussed in Chapter 14, Organisation). Before the exporter determines its role in the distribution of tasks, it should examine the role of others:

- The forwarding agent can perform the freight, customs clearance, settlements, VAT functions and represent the exporter in the local market in many ways.
- Factoring firms can take over the invoicing of customers, thus freeing the exporters from time spent following up customer debts. Furthermore, the exporter's financial position will not be burdened with outstanding dues.
- Other members of the distribution chain may ensure several tasks – for example, a whole-salers' storage function is key.
- The advent of the internet as a marketing channel for sales has simplified many functions in the chain, through safe payment systems over the net and the dispatch of goods.

We shall now proceed to describe the different export modes of operation. The presentation starts with the simplest form of exports – using a trading house – in which most activities relating to the export process are taken care of by the middleman. It ends with exports handled without any middleman, where all the tasks are taken over by the exporter.

7.3.1 Export through trading house – indirect exports

A trading house – also called an export house – is generally associated with a firm that buys and resells products, or just brokers the goods on a commission basis to clients outside the home market of the manufacturer/service provider. This kind of company has existed for thousands of years.[8] Today trading houses exist in a variety of forms, anything from traditional trading companies trading in raw materials (paper, timber, metals, fish, agricultural commodities, oil and gas) or specific geographic areas; to export management companies that carry a variety of non-competing goods (more common in the US) and piggybacking. This latter is an arrangement whereby the manufacturer or service firm sells their product/service through another exporter already active in international markets, normally complementing the exporter's product line. Table 7.2 presents a list of leading trading houses.

Table 7.2 Leading trading houses

Company	Domicile	Net revenue (2013, billion USD)	Commodity
Vitol	Swiss	307	Oil and gas
Glencore	Swiss	233	Energy, metals
Cargill	US	137	Grains
Trafigura	Dutch	133	Oil
Koch	US	115	Oil, man-made fibres
Mercuria	Swiss	112	Oil
Noble	Hong Kong	98	Metals
Gunvor	Swiss	91	Oil
ADM	US	90	Oilseeds
Louis Dreyfus	French/Swiss	64	Cotton, grains

Source: Gibbon (2014).

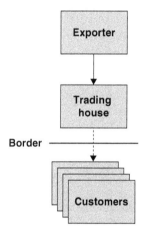

Figure 7.3 Exporting through trading houses.

These companies trade in mostly high-volume raw materials. They have, however, a large number of "smaller cousins" that operate as general traders (all kinds of products) or deal in specific commodities. In the Far East these kinds of firms are dominating certain trades, and operate both as exporters and importers – and also between third countries. Great *sogo shoshas* (trading houses) such as Itochu, Marubeni, Toyo Cotton Mitsui, Mitsubishi and Nichimen have worldwide marketing and purchasing networks. It has been claimed that Japanese traders represent almost half of the US exports to Japan, and that at one point Mitsui was the sixth-largest US exporter (Dziubla 1982). In South Korea, a related kind of trading house – the so-called *chaebols* – have emerged, with the best-known being Hyundai, Samsung, Hanwha and Hanjin. In countries such as Azerbaijan, Saudi Arabia, Russia, China, Thailand and Oman the governments have established import traders in order to bypass traditional trading houses (Blas 2015).

In this mode, the firm is, in reality, not an exporter – it merely sells its products to a middleman that handles the exporting on behalf of the firm. The middleman buys the goods "exworks" or "FOB",[9] and resells the product(s) through their own network abroad in their name. This relationship is shown in Figure 7.3.

The figure illustrates that the "exporter" in fact is not an exporter; it sells to another firm that is located in the home country (and sometimes in a third country). In its purest form, this mode does not give the exporter direct contact with the market and therefore also reduces control over the marketing to a minimum. All contact goes through the middleman. The learning opportunities are confined to reports on the market situation given by the middleman. The greatest advantage of this form of representation is that the firm has to spend few resources to get its products sold abroad. The trading house finances the operation and incurs the currency risk. Through its network abroad it will carry out marketing activities – including a credit line to the next member in the chain.

This mode of exporting does not involve the firm in the daily chores of the export activities, and therefore it is suitable for small, resource-poor firms or firms that are beginners. In the agricultural sector it is seen in the form of cooperatives that handle exporting on behalf of the farmers. It is also seen in the fishing sector with wholesalers located in the home country operating as the international arm of local fishermen or fish farmers. And it is seen in specialist trades to emerging markets, where specific knowledge, not only about the market, but also insight into local mind-sets, is critical to land a contract. Yet another case is the exportation of so-called complete packages, fully-equipped vessels, plants and so on. The lead contractor subcontracts to a number of suppliers and assembles the product into a complete delivery, the subcontractors then indirectly becoming exporters.

Even if we assert that indirect exports are the small exporters' mode of operation, we hasten to add that large firms may also take advantage of selling profitably through this class of middlemen. The raw materials industry illustrates this point, in spite of the fact that most firms in this sector are large, with extensive networks of local sales subsidiaries. However, two arguments speak in favour of also using trading houses for these firms:

1 They may serve as a low-cost buffer in times when demand is low in other markets.
2 Trading houses are a flexible solution in markets where permanent representation is otherwise too onerous – because of erratic demand or because they are too difficult for the firm to operate in with its own salesforce.

Trading houses also broker sales to international markets on an agency basis. In this case their remuneration comes in the form of a commission. The trading house offers its expertise and marketing network, but the exporters have to find other solutions to the financing and logistics of the transactions. One may say that the firm comes one step closer to the market and gets in direct touch with the next member of the distribution chain – as can be seen from the arrows in Figure 7.4. In this case the firm becomes the *real exporter*, and the learning back to its organisation stands better chances of having a lasting effect than in the case of the distributor model discussed above.

7.3.2 *Exporting through local distributors*

Whereas the trading house is often located in the home country of the exporter, or in a third country, the distributor generally operates in the relevant export market. The main structural difference between the two is that the distributor handles the product only after border crossing, while the trading house takes over full responsibility of the goods before they cross the border, often at the gate of the factory. The distributor operates in its own name, takes title to the goods and therefore is fully responsible for the local marketing and for the financing of the transactions in the local market. In this, there are both advantages and

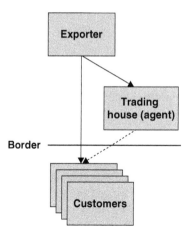

Figure 7.4 Exporting through trading house (agent).

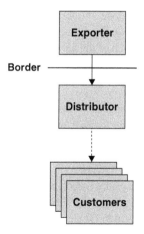

Figure 7.5 Exporting through distributors.

disadvantages: the financial risk for the exporter is alleviated in the same manner as with the trading house; at the same time – the risk is concentrated on one customer in the case of exclusive distribution rights. In other words, the exporter depends on just one customer in the relevant market, the latter being the one who is in touch with customers. Figure 7.5 illustrates this.

Even though the market contact is considerably better than in the previous mode (by the mere fact of actually *exporting*), the exporter has no formal contact with the next level in the distribution chain. This makes the exporter particularly vulnerable to changes in the relationship with the distributor, for instance, if the distributor files for bankruptcy or if for some reason the contract is cancelled. This latter situation is exacerbated when the distributor also has a Private Brand contract.

Jordan (toothbrushes) experienced this situation in Germany. They had, for many years, sold their products through a Private Brand arrangement with Blendax, Germany's largest player in this market. Their products were actually market leaders in Germany – but their name was totally unknown since it was the Blendax brand that was positioned in the market. By the mere size of the German market, this deal was an important part of Jordan's international strategy – until the day Blendax was taken over by the US giant, Procter and Gamble, and the contract with Blendax ceased. Jordan was at this point cast out from the German market, without any name, any contact with the retail level, or any marketing organisation that could take over the marketing effort – except for a country manager at HQ. What had been a flourishing business turned into a collapse from almost one day to the next.[10]

The above situation emerged because the exporter did not have the necessary organisational clout to enter the German market on its own. The operation mode served the company well for many years and secured a cash-flow that allowed them to enter other markets. They could however have prevented this situation by building a parallel distribution channel in Germany, thereby gradually developing market knowledge and a market position of their own. The problem, however, is that it is normally the distributor who is the stronger partner in exporter–distributor relationships, both concerning the local marketing expertise and the size of the partnership (Leonidou 1989), and the stronger partner is in a position to dictate terms of the contract – such as an exclusive right to the market.

The case above suggests that exporters selling through distributors need to build a close relationship with the local partner in order to develop market insight and thereby become a relevant interlocutor in discussions concerning marketing strategy. This is particularly true when it comes to pricing policy in the local market, which is the realm of the distributor. Giving the distributor instructions on pricing may in some markets – for example, the EU – be sanctioned with fines that can amount to prohibitive numbers.

For many exporters the time comes when it is pertinent to change the distribution in a market (taking over the functions/finding a new partner), either because they outgrow the distributors, want more control, are dissatisfied with the partnership, or because the partners themselves decide to end the relationship. On such occasions a "friendly divorce" is desirable, both to secure a smooth takeover and to prevent legal pursuits.

When Nilfisk (suppliers of professional cleaning equipment) wanted to take over the operations of their Spanish distributor, they were met by hefty opposition. The owner did not want to sell and he organised a campaign involving distributors in other countries to work against the company. This was of course detrimental to Nilfisk, not only in Spain, and they had to put off the whole project (Petersen et al. 2000).

This presentation has hitherto had a slightly negative slant towards the distributor solution. On the other hand, being aware of the caveats of this operation mode, the exporter may take appropriate counter-measures when negotiating contracts with distributors. And indeed, the downbeat description is "unfair" to an operation mode which is called the "default mode" (Anderson and Gatignon 1986), and used by most small exporters around the world. The distributor fulfils a wide range of functions in the distribution system: financing, storage, promotion, sales and distribution to the next level, service and complaint handling, and maintenance of the customer base. Most exporters are not in a position to carry out all these functions in all markets. Even the larger and more experienced exporters find distributors to be an appropriate solution in secondary markets.

7.3.3 Exporting through agents

Agents operate in a fundamentally different way from distributors. They do not take title to the products and therefore bring the exporter one step closer to its customer base; they only broker the transaction between the exporter and its foreign customer, and charge a commission for the job. In this way, the exporter gets in direct contact with its final customer-base in the market, through contract negotiations, the dispatch of the products to and the payment from the customers, and through servicing the customer with maintenance, repairs, etc.

Nordox is selling cuprous oxide to the paint industry across the world for some 50 million euros per year (2016). They service the market through an extensive network of agents who mediate the contact with paint factories in 23 countries throughout the world. The customer structure varies from one country to another, but generally speaking, the paint industry is rather concentrated – with only a few customers in each country. The agent's job is first and foremost to nurture the contact with the customers in each country, and organise visits from the exporter when necessary. In many markets – particularly the more "exotic" ones (seen with European eyes) – where language and cultural barriers make the contact more challenging, the use of agents has traditionally been vital. The commission of some 2–3% is well worth the money. However, buyer – seller relations have been made easier with increasing globalisation and the ensuing concentration of industries (including the paint industry) – involving fewer and larger customers and where language poses less of a problem ("everyone" speaks English). In later years, Nordox has ceased a number of the agency relationships they previously had and taken over the marketing directly from HQ. Even though a sales commission of 2–3% is worth the money in some markets, it still makes itself felt in times when margins are constantly under pressure. Also, the fact that some of its customers are themselves multinational firms – with subsidiaries in many countries, and sometimes coordinating the purchasing function across borders, speaks in favour of concentrating the sales effort.[11]

Figure 7.6 shows how the exporter is getting closer to the customer through agents. Some claim that in many ways agents may be regarded as part of one's own organisation, because this operation mode offers the possibility of getting in closer contact with the buyers (Bello and Lohtia 1995). Figure 7.6 shows how the exporter has direct contact with its customer base.

Selling through agents therefore gives the exporter a better basis (than selling through a distributor) to make judgements for the future development of the market, including inputs to the product development process in the firm, pricing, competition, customer structure, etc. Also – if the agency contract is terminated – the exporter still keeps its customer base (as opposed to selling through distributors – see above). This is one of the reasons law-makers in many countries have introduced a paragraph in their commercial laws that protects the agent from opportunistic behaviour by the exporter. In Europe, for instance, agents are eligible to receive an after-commission of at least three months of the last couple of years' commission disbursements. This kind of regulation sometimes deters the exporter from entering into agency contracts with their foreign partners. We perceive such apprehension to be quite counter-productive. First, selling through agents may be the norm in the market, and it is difficult to perceive of any other realistic alternative. Second, the advantages following the agent solution

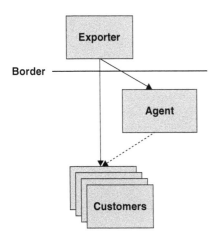

Figure 7.6 Exporting through agents.

(direct customer contact) should in the longer-term by far outweigh the risk of paying the equivalent of three months' commission.

Exporting through agents still has its caveats. For instance, the commission system may incite the agent to chase as many customers as possible in the short-term, rather than recruiting customers that bear long-term potential. Also – short of clauses in the contract protecting the exporter from such sales – the agent may, for the sake of pursuit of volume, sell to customers who have a bad payment record. This kind of agent behaviour is a source of conflict and eventually leads to contract termination. Then, of course, the after-commission clause may pose a problem for the exporter.

Sometimes, specifics in the local market make it necessary to have more than just one agent:

In Arab countries the contact with the final customer often goes through several players. Partners operate as traders and agents, carrying out marketing operations in an "ordinary" way. Others only lend their names and their network power – called *wasta*,[12] whereas the principal must organise other partners to execute the necessary activities in the market. It is essential for the agents' work to develop and maintain relations with what may be referred to as a sponsor or partner, i.e. persons with close relations with the Arab part of the buying centre. Even in the case of a good agent, it is possible for other people (for example, the sponsor) to derive economic benefits from their role in the buying process. If this is done, one is advised to demand services in return such as customs exemptions for parts of the delivery or less red tape at border crossings. These persons are often highly-placed and they are generally capable of influencing these processes. Again, we see the effects of *wasta* power. It is appropriate at this point to acknowledge that both the giving and taking of bribes are regarded as a crime by the Qur'an. On the other hand, if one receives something in return for the "special commissions" paid, then it is considered a business transaction (Solberg 2002a).

7.3.4 Exporting through sales subsidiaries

The weaknesses of exporting through the above types of middlemen are alleviated by setting up one's own sales subsidiaries. This operation mode offers the best possibilities for contact with

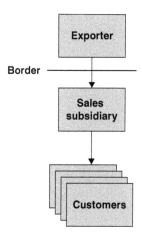

Figure 7.7 Exporting through sales subsidiaries.

customers. According to the Uppsala tradition, it secures better feedback to headquarters and greater insight of local market conditions, and hence gives management a strong foundation on which the local marketing strategy can be developed. Furthermore, in TCE parlance, sales subsidiaries offer better control of local marketing and therefore reduce the risks of oppor-tunism by the middleman (i.e. the subsidiary).

The observant reader will have discovered the structural similarities with the distributor sol-ution (see Figure 7.7). We have already warned against a situation where the sales subsidiary develops its own strategies, in spite of the directions given by HQ (see page 186). In the present context we remind ourselves of the fact that also units within the boundaries of the firm may act opportunistically; however, the hierarchical control exercised by HQ gives the exporter the upper hand in the relationship – both in the selection of managers of the sales unit, and in its monitoring.

Håg AS – one of Europe's five leading manufacturers of swivel chairs – had for more than 20 years sold through a distributor in the UK, but never really managed to penetrate the market, their market share lurking around 1%. They had, however, during these years developed a close working relationship with their distributor, and as a result acquired a pretty good knowledge of local market conditions. They were therefore in a better position to invest in a local sales subsidiary, and decided to go it alone. As a leading player in Europe they considered a firmer presence in the UK to be a necessary move.

This is a classic example of investing in a sales subsidiary because of dissatisfaction with the performance of the distributor. As we have already discussed, some types of products and services require more attention and a deeper representation in the local market than others (see page 184).

Guard Systems ASA markets GPS- and radio-based systems for the tracking of objects (mainly stolen cars), and GPS-based car fleet management systems. In order to operate in this market they need to get in place a lot of elements of the package to be sold to their customers: approval from the national telecommunications authorities in order to establish a system for radio tracking, border crossing alert stations, search from aeroplanes, arrangements with insurance companies and the police, and establish relations with a network of dealers (particularly car dealers) and leasing companies. Such an infrastructure of contracts, approvals, distribution and set-ups of tracking systems represents very heavy investments in both time and money before financial returns can be realised. Such investments deter any independent player from getting involved in the venture, and at the same time they require considerable specific investments – in time, money and competence. Own sales subsidiaries were therefore the natural operation mode for this company.

Setting up a sales subsidiary involves a much wider range of organisational and administrative consequences for the firm: legal forms, tax consequences, personnel policies (local or home country managers), establishing administrative routines, local legislation and local norms.

Even though sending an expatriate to head the local sales subsidiary in many instances yields good rewards for the exporter, it is not a straightforward exercise for anyone. A US healthcare and personal hygiene company set up a sales subsidiary in Japan, and appointed one of its promising young managers (37 years old) from headquarters to lead the job. Having settled in Japan, the young manager started to build up a marketing and sales staff, but encountered difficulties finding personnel who fitted all the requirements (experienced sales/marketing, knowledge of products and mastering English language). He found a Japanese sales manager – a 47 year old well-experienced man in the trade – but did not find a local marketing manager, so he asked HQ to send a person who could shoulder the marketing post.

For their first product launch the manager and his American marketing man insisted that they carried out test marketing in Nagoya, in order to build experience for the broader launch on the entire Japanese market, and thereby make sure that the product could succeed. The Japanese sales manager warned against this on several grounds: "The trade will doubt our commitment and competition will pick up our ideas and hit back before we can launch the product in the whole market." But the Americans were persistent, saying, "That's the way we do it in the US, and it's costly to launch a campaign in the whole market before we know for sure." They tested the campaign in Nagoya. Unnecessary to rub it in: the campaign was a failure. The company also met problems in its advertising campaign, since it was not allowed to advertise two benefits for healthcare products in Japan. Then the distribution was a problem: they were happy making a major deal with a large wholesaler, but the sales did not take off. They were soon told that it is not the wholesaler's job to market the product at the retail level in Japan – that is the supplier's role. All these experiences led to strains within the company's organisation and things did not get better when the sales manager had to report to his much younger marketing manager – unheard of in Japan where respect for seniority is a key cultural feature. Reporting back to HQ the local general manager was not met with much sympathy (Willoughby 1983).

7.3.5 *Direct exporting – without the middleman*

Many firms sell directly to their customers abroad, particularly in neighbouring markets and with certain industrial goods. This operation mode gives the exporter direct access to its

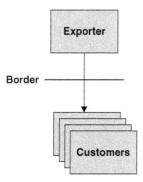

Figure 7.8 Direct exporting.

customers – without any middleman. This places more demands on the organisation at head-quarters. Figure 7.8 shows the relationships between the exporter and its clients in the market, using the same template as above.

   Advantages abound: lower direct costs, closer relations to the final customer, direct feedback to HQ and thereby improved learning, better control of the whole process – particularly in complex projects. This operation mode is chiefly used in the following situations:

–   Neighbouring markets
–   Few customers in the market
–   The customers have good administrative import routines to handle the transaction
–   No realistic alternative (no relevant distribution channel as competitors block them)
–   Exports through the internet
–   Direct exports as an entry mode to get to know the market before wider involvement.

We have already seen this last approach in our presentation of the three exporters of winter sports gear to Germany (Chapter 3, Section 3.2.1). Getting to know the market through limited direct sales in an introductory phase – and in this way learning the "rules of the game" without too much commitment – is feasible in sectors where the distribution channel consists of many independent players. With a concentrated channel structure, this entry strategy may be more difficult, simply because there are fewer options available.

7.3.6 Costs of export operation modes

We have seen that different operation modes are being compensated for in different ways or incur different kinds of costs:

–   Distributor → mark-up
–   Agent → commission
–   Sales subsidiary → office rent, wages, operational costs.

The distributor is not directly compensated by the exporter; rather they retain a profit margin on the mark-up, based on the export price level of the transaction.

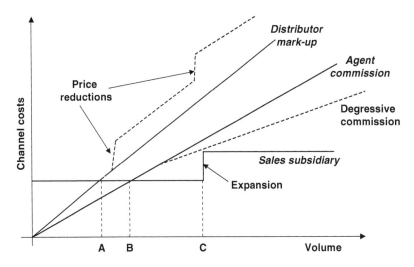

Figure 7.9 Cost levels of different operation modes.

Figure 7.9 exhibits relative cost consequences of these three. The parameters are set arbitrarily. Nevertheless, we notice that the compensation level of the distributor is higher than that of the agent. The reason for this difference lies primarily in the financial risk taken by the distributor (who finances the whole operation and stores the products), and that it usually has wider functions than those of the agent. We also notice that at a certain level (A), a sales office becomes more economical than exporting through a distributor, and this occurs at a larger volume (B) with the agent solution.

The compensation to the agent depends generally on sales volume. The commission rate may vary – anything between 0.5% and as much as 15% – depending on industry norms, market and the agent's responsibilities (i.e. *del credere*). Sometimes the agent may be willing to accept a decreasing commission rate. They know that at a certain sales volume, the exporter will most likely take over the operations and establish its own sales subsidiary – or export directly from home. Ideally this should be the intersection between the commission curve and the cost level of establishing a sales subsidiary (point B in the figure), and the agent – rather than losing the agency – may be interested in lowering the commission rate (as illustrated by the dotted line in the figure). On the other hand, the distributor may suggest price reductions – in the form of bonuses or volume-based rebates (again the dotted line) – on increasing sales volumes, in order to tap into scale economies gained by the exporter. We also notice that at point C, the sales subsidiary needs to expand (more personnel and office space). Sometimes a firm can operate with both operation modes in parallel:

Relats in Barcelona, Spain (making insulating fibreglass hoses for electrical wiring in electro appliances, engines, transformers and vehicles), started internationalisation in the 1980s. They had just invested in new technology to replace their old copper/cotton hoses and now had excess production capacity that had to be sold outside their home market.

Europe was initially their prime export market, concentrating on Germany, the UK, France, Italy and Portugal. They used two distinct entry modes in these markets:

1   To the electrical appliance market, they sold mainly through distributors who served small clients such as engine repair shops, and with margins of 30% or more.
2   This margin was too onerous to be competitive in the car industry, with big multinational customers such as Ford, Volkswagen, Audi, BMW, PSA, Saab and Volvo. This market was therefore serviced through agents who also represented other brands. For each European country they had one agent specialising in the car industry. This also led them into direct contact with the main decision centres of car manufacturers.
3   In countries outside Europe, they cooperated with only one company in each country with exclusivity contracts, both on a distribution basis (taking title to the goods) and on an agency basis, the function depending on the type of product and client.[13]

The cost of operations is however just one aspect when evaluating different exporting modes. More important than costs is the long-term strategic role of the market in the firm's portfolio and how it chooses to build its organisation. This is the subject for a later chapter (Chapter 14).

7.4 Operation modes with production abroad

The operation modes treated above do not involve local production in target markets. We have shown in Chapter 3 that local production normally comes at later stages in the internationalisation process. The arguments for setting out production in the target market are many and diverse:

–   "Jumping over" trade barriers has traditionally been one of the main reasons for establishing production abroad. With hard-pressed profit margins, overcoming the cost disadvantage of 5–10% or even more in customs duties is certainly a reason to invest in local production. Local manufacturing confers protection against other foreign players that export to this market, and gives the firm a level playing field compared with local vendors. There are even anecdotes of firms that succeed in convincing local governments to *raise* customs tariffs as a favour in exchange for establishing a manufacturing unit in the country. Of course, over the past 40 years, with the advent of international trade deals (EU, WTO, NAFTA, etc.), customs tariffs have been gradually reduced – in many cases to zero, reducing the weight of this argument. But in several countries tariff levels are well above 10% for certain goods and the outlook for further liberalisation does at the time of writing not look promising.
–   Reducing transport and manufacturing costs is another argument for local manufacturing, either by transferring the whole production to the country in question or just parts of it – for instance, the assembly of parts that are produced elsewhere. Cost levels in manufacturing vary greatly from one country to the other and from the exporter's viewpoint this justifies the transfer of production capacity to the target market – or to third countries. This has been seen in a wide range of industries, most prominently in the fashion and clothing industry and particularly in Asia. Also other industries have experienced an exodus from high-cost countries – electronics, construction materials, shipyards, etc. We will not delve into this well-known issue more than presenting Table 7.3 showing manufacturing labour cost differences in a number of countries.

Table 7.3 Labour cost levels of selected countries, 2015 (USA=100)

Switzerland	175	Italy	83	Portugal	29
Norway	132	United Kingdom	82	Estonia	29
Belgium	123	Canada	82	Czech Republic	27
Denmark	118	Singapore	67	Taiwan	25
Germany	112	Spain	63	Poland	23
Sweden	111	Japan	63	Hungary	22
Austria	104	South Korea	60	Brazil	21
Australia	103	Israel	58	Mexico	16
France	100	Argentina	55	Turkey	15
Netherlands	97	Greece	41	Philippines	6
Ireland	96	Slovakia	30		

Source: https://www.conference-board.org/ilcprogram/index.cfm?id=38269.

- Seeking other factor advantages (than labour costs) is a key argument for many players, the most evident one being access to raw materials (oil, bauxite, iron, farmland). This factor is possibly the original reason for firms investing in other countries. Increasingly, tapping into industrial clusters has dominated the search for competitive advantage by multinational firms, be it in Silicon Valley (ICT), Basel or Uppsala (pharmacy), Milan (fashion), London or Luxembourg (finance), or Houston or Stavanger (oil and gas technology). Even smaller firms now set up satellites in such centres to gain inspiration, take advantage of local expertise and build networks.
- The – until recently – growing liberalisation and business-friendly investment regimes, such as subsidies and low taxes, have attracted investments from foreign investors – large as well as small.[14] Actually, most countries have established so-called investment promotion agencies (IPAs) that, with different levers, try to attract foreign direct investments to their region.[15] They offer subsidised rent and loans, tax credits and other benefits in order to attract foreign investors, particularly to promote specific industrial development in hi-tech, green investments, etc. Ireland has been a "favourite scapegoat" in this regard, with its incentives to firms such as Google, Apple, Microsoft and others. However, many firms, even though such bait appeals to them, should consider the potential drawbacks of such incentives:

Norsk Hydro was at one time one of the leaders in the world magnesium (light metal) market. Electricity is one of the main inputs to magnesium production, and the province of Quebec in Canada offered reasonably-priced (subsidised?) electricity to Norsk Hydro to supply a new magnesium plant. The plant was originally built to service the US market, but as it was completed and ready to run, the firm was accused by a small US manufacturer of dumping, based on subsidised energy prices. After some years, Norsk Hydro was forced to give up the plant, and scrapped it all together.

- From a marketing viewpoint, perhaps one of the most compelling arguments to move production nearer to the target market is the potential for closer relations with key customers. The latter seek secure and stable deliveries from trusted partners, and will therefore readily enter into long-term supplier relationships with firms that are willing to invest in local manufacturing facilities. This is particularly the case in subcontracting relationships, such as car parts. Short communication lines mean rapid feedback if any delivery problems occur, and joint product development projects are much easier to initiate with physical closeness.

Let us revisit Relats. During the 1980s they observed that the car industry was increasingly affected by nascent globalisation, with several new trends: consolidation in the industry, more demanding quality standards necessitating closer collaboration between customers and suppliers, tougher global competition, and the entry of Japanese car manufacturers into Europe by setting up manufacturing units in the UK. The British market was quite special, being their third most important one after Spain and Germany, but they also learned that the British tended to establish more intense relationships with suppliers from the Commonwealth than those from continental Europe. They had already operated through their local partner, Kelrocy Ltd, for some years, and had experienced the hurdles of getting entrenched with British buyers. For all these reasons management at Relats considered it imperative to nurture closer ties with Britain. Coincidentally, an opportunity arose to acquire a local player in the industry, Suflex Sleeving Ltd, the second largest in Britain.[16]

–   Increasingly, positioning against competitors plays a role in foreign investments and production planning. This is first and foremost relevant for firms in the upper-right corner in the "Nine Strategic Windows" framework. They have the strength, but above all the strategic argument to enter foreign manufacturing. Manufacturing in key markets makes the firm a credible threat to main competitors in those same markets, and may deter other firms from investing, and thus get an upper hand in the contest for market shares.

We will now describe five different operation modes that are most relevant for the international marketer:

1   Contract manufacturing
2   Licensing and franchising
3   Management contracts
4   Investment in own production
5   Strategic alliances.

7.4.1 Contract manufacturing

This is the "easiest" way of manufacturing abroad. The contractor enters into an agreement with one or several companies to manufacture products for sale through the contractor's own network, based on products developed and/or designed by the latter. The products are specified in detail, and the contract involves items such as controls, safeguarding of property rights, confidence clauses, restrictions on further exploitation of production technology, etc.

The main motives for this operation mode are the following:

–   Lack of managerial or financial capacity to carry out its own investments abroad. This is particularly relevant for small firms where the prime competence lies in design or technology, and where they do not want to spend resources on manufacturing. Rather, resources should be spent on building a marketing network abroad.
–   A wish to exploit local technological competence or low manufacturing cost. This latter is seen across the textile/garment industry.
–   A wish to exploit an established market organisation in order to market products that complete the existing product range, or that rationalise one's own production lines.

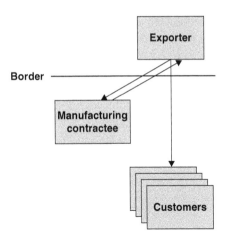

Figure 7.10 Contract manufacturing.

Contract manufacturing may be described as shown in Figure 7.10. A key feature of this figure is the emphasis on the exporter being responsible for the marketing activities. This can be done in ways already described in Section 7.2 (export modes). Selection of the partner – the contractee – should therefore first and foremost be dictated by their technical competence and/or production cost.

Odlo (a sportswear company) abandoned their own manufacturing and outsourced their production to Norwegian subcontractors in 1981. In this way they could instead concentrate on marketing activities. After having achieved a foothold in the US sportswear market, they started contract manufacturing there as well. In this way they "jumped" all kinds of barriers to the US market: transport, customs and other barriers, and at the same time avoided the uncertainty surrounding the vacillations of the dollar against other currencies. Later they moved a large part of the production to their own plants in Portugal and Romania, and subcontracted a growing amount of their output to contractees in Asia. The firm is marketing their products throughout the world through 4,500 retailers. They claim to have a 20–50% market share for their products in their different markets, the main emphasis being in Europe (Germany, Switzerland, France, Austria, Benelux and Norway).[17]

Odlo has "wandered" around, both geographically and in terms of entry mode. This has given them flexibility to leverage local advantages, and with increased resources they have taken back parts of the manufacturing (today around 80% of the output), and thereby also increased control.

Another type of contract manufacturing is so-called co-production arrangements, in which two competing firms agree to swap products in each other's markets. This happens quite frequently in the process industries, such as plastics, for example. The product range is determined by the specific process of the plant.[18] Such processes may sometimes become a straightjacket, where the manufacturer is locked into customers demanding the narrow product range of the selected process. Therefore, in order to widen their market coverage, and gain scale economies in their marketing, they may enter into co-production deals with a competitor. Practically, supplier A delivers a product it can easily produce to the foreign competitor B in A's home market, and vice versa. In one way, this practice creates or strengthens the competitor in their own home market. On the other hand, there is a limit to how big a market share can become in a company's home market, and through this arrangement both firms can increase their share in each other's market – *at the expense of other suppliers*. The advantage of this kind of arrangement is that the producer may then avoid investing in a plant (with the alternative process), and can exploit economies of scale both in terms of rational operation (fewer qualities) and capacity utilisation. The contracting partners should however be aware that such co-production arrangements may be subject to scrutiny by competition agencies (e.g. article 85 of the Treaty of Rome).

7.4.2 Licensing and franchising

Licensing and franchising are more far-reaching than contract manufacturing. They may be described as a right conferred on the partner to economically exploit a patent, a brand or know-how. These two operation modes have similarities, but also distinct differences as shown in Table 7.4.

Licensing and franchising involve more than the core object (the know-how, patent or brand). Successful licensing and franchising depend on long-term, trusting relationships between the partners, with information exchange, mutual exploitation of product development, assistance related to installation and service, etc. One may call it a "package" with many elements other than the patent or brand – see Figure 7.11.

Licensing

Here, the licensor confers to the licensee the right to produce and/or market a patent, know-how, a product or process. Figure 7.12, showing the relationship between the licensor, the licensee and the end customer, illustrates that the licensee is responsible not only for the production (as with the contract manufacturer), but also for the marketing and sales of the products. The dotted lines indicate that the licensor has only limited (if any) contact with the end customer. Therefore, when selecting a licensing partner the most critical criterion is the partner's marketing network and competence.

Normally the consequence of this structure is that the licensor has virtually no control of the marketing – and that the licensee is empowered through his market contact and insight.

Table 7.4 Licensing and franchising

	Licensing	*Franchising*
Emphasis	Research and development	Marketing
Partners	Licensor	Franchisor
	Licensee	Franchisee
Object	Patent	Brand
	Product	Product
	Know-how	System
	Technology	
Marketing control	Limited	High (depends on contract)

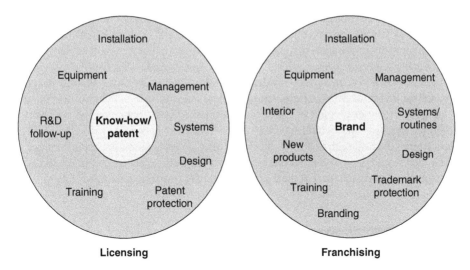

Figure 7.11 Licensing and franchising.

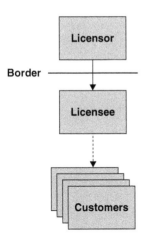

Figure 7.12 Licensing.

The licensor is indeed compensated through the payment of a royalty, but is totally alienated from contact with the market covered by the licensee. The structure is akin to that of the distributor (Figure 7.5), but with the important difference of the latter normally using the exporter's brand and therefore cooperating with the exporter on the general guidelines for marketing strategy.

In many cases licensing is for firms that have limited resources – financial, managerial and marketing – to exploit their technology in a wider international market. We have already in Sections 3.2 and 7.1 shown how firms risk becoming vulnerable in licensing. Licensing is also used as an alternative to a company's own production in secondary markets, or in markets where there are restrictions for foreigners to operate.

Nycomed (pharmaceuticals) experienced this situation when they licensed the patent and know-how of their flagship product, contrast liquid for use in medical diagnostics, to a large international pharmaceutical company, Schering. According to the contract, Schering was to cover the "German-speaking world" (Germany, Austria and Switzerland). This was done at a time when Nycomed had relatively scarce resources to undertake the necessary marketing investments to tap the potential of these markets on their own. As the firm grew stronger – partly as a result of the successful marketing by Schering and with that the ensuing royalties – they would have wanted to remain in control of the marketing, but were locked into the deal with Schering. It is, of course, possible to terminate the contract; but then they would need to build a marketing network from scratch – and in the meantime relinquish an important part of their earnings (royalty from the licensee).[19]

Some maintain that licensing carries the risk of the licensee gradually turning into a competitor in the longer run as it absorbs the licensor's know-how. This is indeed a potential danger, but there are several ways to curb this kind of risk. Patenting gives the licensor legal protection over a certain period of time – varying from country to country, generally 15 to 20 years. For smaller firms, patenting may be costly if one wants to cover several markets. Patenting also implies that the technology is published, and competitors may find ways (such as scrutinising the details of the patent application) to circumvent the patent. For others, still, patenting is more or less vain, since the technology development is so fast that new solutions find their way on to the market long before the patent-holder reaps the economic benefit of the patent. The best protection in this case is intensified R&D, pre-empting any such new competitive developments.

Intellectual property rights (IPR)

International commercial contracts – and in particular licensing and franchising contracts – involve IPR, know-how and confidentiality. Most countries have sanctioned international conventions concerning patents. The rules and the enforceability may differ from one country to the other, but the main objective is to protect the innovator. A level of innovation and a degree of novelty are necessary to obtain a patent. Therefore, the innovation should not be described in any way (for instance in an article or at a trade fair) before the patent application. Patent engineers are possibly the best people to handle this kind of issue. They also can handle trademark registrations.

Know-how is, in its simplest form, something one knows and that another party is willing to pay for. As opposed to patents and trademarks, know-how is not possible to register. Therefore it has a dynamic and flexible character, whereas registrable property rights are "frozen" at registration. Therefore – and because of the novelty requirement for patents – secrecy is of the utmost importance, and confidentiality clauses are critical at an early stage of the discussions.

Another way to protect against undue competition from licensees is to meticulously specify the licensing object in such a way that the core technology resides with the licensor. The licensee can appropriate the right to assemble the product, but not the right to produce the core technology. Coca-Cola is possibly the best-known example of this strategy, whereby they produce the syrup according to a secret recipe, but license out the right to mix the syrup with water, to bottle and to market it. Another way to cover the risk is to invest considerable resources in developing deep relations with the licensee. Often a significant part of the contract is the exchange of research and development information. This gives the licensor an important lever to sanction licensees who breach the contract – to exclude them from this essential information exchange. Also the technology transfer may go in the other direction; where the licensee is licensing its own technology to the licensor this is called cross licensing.

Some firms build a network of licensees in different countries. In this case the licensor develops a "family" of licensees who not only take part in the technological development, but also help to improve the products or processes through their own contributions based on their own experience. In this way the licensor builds a network of mutual obligations to develop the products/processes of the firm and also the market position of the whole family.

Licensing is a *relatively* rapid and inexpensive way to reach out to international markets (as opposed to investing in the firm's own manufacturing and marketing units). However, the costs and the time it takes to identify, negotiate, train and follow-up the licensee should not be underestimated. An issue during negotiations is often the need to present and explain the technology to the licensee, and the question of protection arises. The potential partner needs enough information to be able to evaluate the proposed contract. At the same time, the licensor risks that this partner says "No, thank you" and then uses the information to start up production on their own. One can safeguard against this risk by ensuring the potential partner signs a confidentiality agreement, whereby they agree not to exploit or divulge the material under inspection. Breach of the agreement would result in a substantial fine.[20]

The licensing contract is relatively complex, although standard contracts are available on the net. Apart from protecting the technology, one of the most important issues in the contract is that of royalties, which can take many different forms (Luostarinen and Welch 1990):

- A lump sum, which is transferred at contract signing and covers the technology transfer once and for all.
- A preliminary payment, which is disbursed at contract signing and is paid to cover costs relating to feasibility studies and documentation for the technology.
- A so-called "down payment" to cover the technology transfer as such, and the right to exploit the technology.
- Yearly royalties, which cover the right to use the technology.

A combination of these elements is not unusual (except, of course, in the case of the lump sum).

Two areas of concern are taxes and competition laws. Concerning the first ones, the licensor needs to take into account that taxes at the source apply in some countries, sometimes at 40–50%. This may come as an unpleasant surprise if not taken into account when royalty rates are discussed. Also EU competitive regulations may apply and conferring exclusive rights to a licensee may violate these rules. Legal advice is essential to avoid pitfalls.

Franchising

International franchising is becoming increasingly widespread, particularly in fast food (McDonald's, Burger King, Kentucky Fried Chicken, Pizza Hut, Prêt à Manger), coffee bars (Starbucks, Lavazza, Wayne's Coffee), mineral water (Coca-Cola, Pepsi Cola, Schweppes, Perrier), fashion (Benetton, Hennes & Mauritz, Zara), petrol (Exxon, Shell, BP, Total), sports products (Intersport), fast-moving consumer goods (Tesco, Carrefour, Aldi) and more . . .

There are two main motives for engaging in international franchising as an operation mode:

1   The firm may have a brand and marketing knowledge that it perceives as having a potential in markets other than its home market.
2   It is a relatively fast and economic way to reach out to foreign markets with this brand, compared with doing it alone. The franchisee builds the local marketing organisation and therefore also carries the risk. If the franchising system is well-established, the franchisor may cover many markets in a short period of time.

The advantages do not come without risks: even if the firm can apply for trademark registration in all countries, it is not so easy to protect all parts of the franchising package, such as interior design, purchasing procedures or quality controls. So the franchisor risks training a competitor. Another issue is that of free-riding, i.e. the franchisee does not live up to the standards set by the franchisor. In order to prevent this happening, franchisors need to set up a control system, and also develop close relationships with their franchisees (Kidwell et al. 2007) – see also Chapter 8, Section 8.4. The main difference from licensing is that the franchisee has worked to establish the trademark, and that other potential partners may be lining up to take over. But even if one registers the trademark, problems may arise.

Helly Hansen's (HH) introduction to the Japanese market is a case in point. At an early stage of their presence in Japan, HH used an agent who targeted the yachting market. This was a "one-man-show" kind of operation and HH decided after some years to broaden their market coverage using a larger firm with more marketing muscle. When they terminated the contract with the agent, they discovered to their surprise that this latter had registered the HH trademark in both the sporting sector and all other areas (altogether 15 sectors), for which HH had to buy him out.

At present, HH has contracts with partners in China, South Korea and Japan that are at the crossroad between franchising and licensing. Their partners have the right and obligations to use HH's marketing template in their respective markets, and they are also allowed to make local adaptations. The problem arises when those adaptations deviate too much from the template and HH's image is not sufficiently respected. They experienced this in China, and after several unsuccessful attempts to align their partner, they decided to change to a partner that they could monitor.[21]

7.4.3 Own production

This section started by listing arguments for transferring the production abroad. Why and how, then, should the firm invest in their *own* overseas production facilities? There are basically two motives for this: control and economic rent. Dunning (1977, 1988) sums this discussion up in what he terms the eclectic paradigm based on three pillars: ownership specific advantages, internalisation advantages and localisation advantages. We will briefly discuss these three below:

1   Ownership specific advantages are those that stem from a patent, know-how or a brand, as we have discussed under licensing and franchising above. But also advantages derived from experience of operations in the home market, or from specific knowledge of factors in

international markets (leveraging factor costs or market insight), may prompt the firm to invest in their own production facilities abroad. These advantages are most conspicuous in industries such as high technology, services or where a brand plays an important role (Caves 1982). One may say that ownership-specific advantages explain why *a certain firm* should make the investment in a foreign production plant. In other words: *who* is likely to invest in production abroad?

2   Internalisation advantages are advantages that come from internalising the transaction within the firm. We have already discussed this in Chapter 3, and will briefly return to the discussion into the present context. This is the realm of TCE and – applied to international business – it is about reducing the risks and uncertainties of uncontrolled dissemination of one's core know-how. But it is also about distribution between the partners of the economic gains of the operation, either because there are clear scale economies that the firm wants to internalise or because of uncertainty about the worth of the know-how (Buckley and Casson 1976). Internalisation advantages explain why the firm wants to take over the production itself, or in other words: *how* the advantage is going to be exploited.

3   Localisation advantages are those pertaining to some of the arguments discussed in the introduction to this section: "jumping" trade barriers, reducing transport costs, seeking (low-cost) production factors or industrial clusters, taking advantage of local incentives. Whereas the two former advantages explain who and why, the localisation advantages explain *where*.

So far the eclectic paradigm. We have seen in Chapter 3 that investing in own production is the last stage in a firm's internationalisation process (Johanson and Vahlne 1977). It starts with exporting through a distributor or agent, passes over to its own sales subsidiary, then transfers production to local subcontracting and/or assembly and ends up with a wholly-owned production unit abroad. In spite of the experience and insight gained through this process, there are risks involved in foreign direct investments. In fact, deviations between budgets and real costs and income vary dramatically – and may go both ways, positive and negative, as shown in Table 7.5

This is an area fraught with innumerable risk factors – political, financial, cultural – described in other texts (Hill and Hult 2017, Cavusgil et al. 2017). Foreign direct investments imply a dramatic change in the firm's operations that involves the operative staff as well as external parties, from authorities (both local and at home), to lenders and owners. We will not delve into these matters in this marketing text, other than to assert that FDI also has organisational consequences that may affect the marketing function. For example, the local sales subsidiary that was previously under the global marketing function at HQ may now be transferred to the local

Table 7.5 Estimate deviations in international projects (%)

	From	To
Capital costs	− 10	+ 25
Sales volume	− 50	+ 150
Sales price	− 50	+ 20
Raw material prices	− 25	+ 50
Inflation	− 10	+ 100
Interest level	− 5	+ 50
Scrap value	− 100	+ 10

Source: Kharbanda and Stallworthy (1983).

head of operations. This has to do with the function of the foreign unit. Poynter and White (1984/1985) suggest five different functions:

1   A *marketing satellite* is simply a sales subsidiary, ranging from just an importing unit (for instance replacing an agent) to a fully-fledged marketing operation with market research, advertising, distribution and customer support services. This unit is typically under the wing of the parent company, implementing its marketing strategies in the local market.

2   The *miniature replica* is a small-scale local copy of the firm's operations in its home market, with production, distribution and marketing. It is particularly relevant when economies of scale are less pronounced. Some need tailoring to local needs – others not (depending on local market conditions). It basically services the host market, but may also engage in exporting to neighbouring markets.

3   *Rationalised manufacturers* are established with a mandate from HQ to produce a set of specialised components or products for an international market. This subsidiary is generally set up to tap into some factor advantages of the host country (skilled labour, raw material, cluster strength, geographic location and tax reliefs/subsidies). Products are normally sold through the mother company's marketing satellites.

4   A *product specialist* develops, produces and markets a limited product line for global markets. The subsidiary has strategic control over its established product range, but not over major strategic shifts. Products may be sold through the subsidiary's own marketing channel.

5   A *strategic independent unit* operates freely without any strategic constraints from the parent, and services markets according to their own strategic plan – be they global, regional or just national/local. Administrative and financial links are the only connections with HQ.

The last two groups of subsidiaries have been termed "world product mandates", where the local unit is given extensive freedom to develop their own strategic platform. This is quite different from the first three groups of subsidiaries which play an integrated role in the value chain of the parent, providing anything from marketing to subcontracting and local "caretaker" services (Birkinshaw 1996).

7.4.4 Management contracts

A management contract is a deal where one firm – acting on behalf of another company – takes over management responsibilities of the total or part of an operation, in exchange for some kind of remuneration. Such an arrangement can last over a short period of time (for instance over the introductory stage of running a factory) or for several years. The simplest form of the management contract is schematically shown in Figure 7.13.

This operation mode is relevant when there are ownership restrictions in a country, where local interests invest in the operations or the political risks are high. In the last case the managing company can withdraw without risking the loss of high sunk costs in physical equipment. Another case is when the managing company has extensive operational know-how, but lacks capital to invest in a plant or unit. Management contracts are frequently found in the hotel, oil and gas extraction, and shipping industries. This kind of contract is often used together with other operation modes, for instance joint ventures, franchising or licensing, but can also be seen as stand-alone contracts.

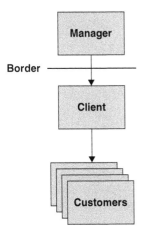

Figure 7.13 Management contract.

The main advantage seen by the managing company is that, through its operations in the local market, it gains experience and insight into local conditions. It has direct contact with the end customers and may – if the contract is terminated and if conditions otherwise allow it – start a competitive operation. Even though it is less resource-demanding than investing in a fully-fledged operation (plant, hotel, ship, etc.), it is resource-demanding in terms of management expertise. The extent to which the company really has managers and operational personnel available to spend on this kind of operations is another question.

7.4.5 Strategic alliances

The borderline between a strategic alliance (SA) and a "traditional" business relationship as we have discussed above is sometimes difficult to determine. For instance, a sole distributorship contract between an exporter and distributor covering the whole of the EU is definitely strategic for both partners; but what about a contract that covers only the Netherlands or the Benelux? We tend to agree with Hamill and El Hajjar (1990) who suggest that an alliance becomes strategic when the potential failure of a partnership has negative consequences for the competitiveness of the partners. Conversely, an alliance that concerns only one market or one product/service, then, is most likely not a strategic alliance. In any event, SAs seek to reduce the risks of the partners through joint investments (time and money), or to tap into market or technological potential that might otherwise be unattainable.

SAs may address a number of different strategic objectives such as product standard setting, research and product development, manufacturing for a specific product or service and/or for a specific market, but also marketing and distribution in one or several markets. Often they involve direct investments, but without 100% control. Financial performance generally being the ultimate objective of an SA, such collaborative arrangements normally have other under-lying motivations such as: capitalising on different resources and capabilities of the particip-ating firms, countering competition by lining up with a major player in the market, accessing new markets or enhancing learning (Nielsen 2007).

Strategic alliances are relevant for both small and large companies. For instance, the American chemical giant DuPont formed a strategic alliance with ChemChina, giving the former access to the Chinese market and at the same time improving its position in global markets.

DuPont Fluoropolymer Solutions and China National Chemical Corp (ChemChina) have agreed a 50:50 joint venture for the production and marketing of fluoroelastomer gums and pre-compounds in China. The joint venture with Zhonghao Chenguang Chemical Research Institute Co. Ltd, a subsidiary of ChemChina, has been created to meet the "rapidly expanding" fluoroelastomer market in China. The venture, named DuPont Haohua Chenguang Fluoromaterials (Shanghai) Co. Ltd, will sell fluoroelastomers under the Chenguang and Viton brands. It will also build a new pre-compound manufacturing facility in Shanghai. "This joint venture is ideally positioned to support China's growing market for fluoroelastomers, particularly for high-performance applications in China's expanding automotive, aerospace, energy, electronics and telecommunications markets," said Thierry Vanlancker, president of DuPont Chemicals & Fluoroproducts. "This strategic alliance will combine the complementary strengths of Chenguang and DuPont, and also add strategic investments in new capacity," said Robert Lu, vice-president of ChemChina. "This also will create a new entity that can more effectively serve customers in China and globally through new technologies and speciality fluoroelastomers."[22]

The advantages of SAs are numerous, depending on the specifics of the alliance:

– Shared costs and risks
– Exchange of knowledge
– Access to markets and resources
– Scale and scope economies
– Reduced competition.

The literature suggests, however, mixed performance outcomes of strategic alliances (Lunnan and Haugland 2008). Depending on the performance measure used, between 30% and 70% of strategic alliances fail. Reasons for failure have been studied by many but may be summed up as follows:

– Internal competition between the partners
– Unfair exchange of resources and distribution of benefits
– The governance structure of the alliance
– Lack of shared vision by the partners
– Lack of trust – which has a tendency to be lower with increased cultural distance.

On the other hand, success is related to both the attention given to the SA by partners, the complementarity of the input from the partners and the specific investments in the venture (Lunnan and Haugland 2008). Often a successful SA also springs out of previous relationships that gradually become strategic as the partners discover the benefits of cooperation.

SAs are – as we have seen – a multifaceted group of operation modes. Figure 7.14 describes one kind of SA, which combines different operation modes and therefore tries to combine different concerns of the involved parties.

This partnership is quite complex and focuses on production and marketing using Partner A's technological know-how, and both partners' marketing networks. Furthermore, both partners contribute with equity capital and management knowledge. Partner A has possibly more control of the operation through four levers: capital, management contract, licensing contract and

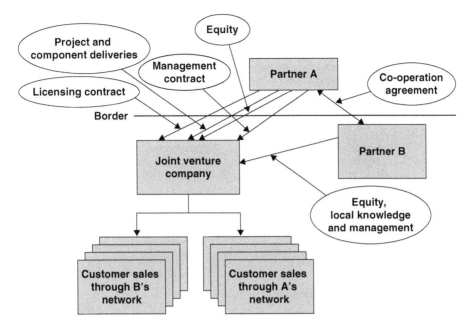

Figure 7.14 Example of a strategic alliance involving combinations of operation modes.

deliveries of components to both set up the manufacturing unit and for the daily operations of the joint venture. A cornerstone contract is the cooperation agreement – often in the form of a shareholder agreement – between the partners where the whole arrangement is described: anything from the purpose of the venture, to the distribution of shares, voting rights and the management responsibilities (for instance, defining market areas), to the affiliated contracts (licensing, management and deliveries).

The above structure also offers to Partner A different ways of recouping capital investments in the form of dividends, royalties, sales income of components, management fees. The mix of different revenues will depend on both real factors underlying the individual transactions, but also tax regimes in the countries involved. This is not the object of the present text, but marketers should be aware of both the risks involved – including penalties for tax evasion – and the potential gains to be reaped.

One may also build into the contract provisions concerning potential future changes of the contractual rights and obligations (such as equity shares and management). In the present schema each partner is responsible for their specific markets. This provision may come under the scrutiny of antitrust regulators in the EU and US, particularly if it is described as exclusive distribution rights for each of the partners, and it involves dominant partners.

The structure of the partnership in Figure 7.14 may be challenged by several factors. First of all is the common vision that partners originally hold of the SA, which after some time may not be that common after all.

7.5 Operation modes and the firm's strategic position

The "Nine Strategic Windows" model proposes different strategic responses to globalisation drivers depending on their resources – see Chapter 4. In this section we will resume this

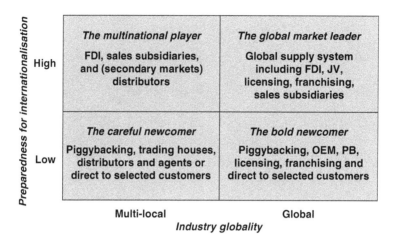

Figure 7.15 Operation modes in different strategic positions.

discussion with a view to exploring the consequences of a firm's position concerning operation modes. Figure 7.15 shows the simplified model with four cells with suggested operation modes.

Below, we will look at each of the four cells.

7.5.1 *The careful newcomer*

We have already claimed that firms in the lower left part of the matrix should take a cautious stance regarding their international involvement. Whereas their market selection strategy is characterised by "one market at a time", their operation mode should feature the small step philosophy in order to learn and avoid incurring risks beyond their resources and capabilities. The corresponding repertoire of operation modes for these firms is therefore restrained to indirect exporting or exporting through independent middlemen abroad. We have already seen that many newcomers to international markets start to sell through trading houses or through piggybacking arrangements. These are low-risk, low-cost, but also low-learn operation modes that nevertheless give the exporter some contact with international markets, and may represent a cautious start to "climb the internationalisation ladder".

What about the eclectic paradigm as described above of licensing vs. FDI? First, the constrained resources inhibit any bold step towards investment in production facilities abroad (Solberg and Askeland 2006). If leveraging any factor advantages in foreign countries is relevant – such as labour costs or tapping into industry clusters – then the firm should first subcontract to an independent manufacturer in the country in question, then supply its home market to gain experience with the operation mode, and then eventually consider entering new markets through traditional sales channels (distributors, agents). Setting up a sales unit to prevent opportunistic behaviour and control the quality of the delivery of the local marketing is possibly as far as the firm should go, but then it risks overstretching its resources and capabilities. It may be preferable to first select one or two clients in a neighbouring market, and service these with resources from home before making any major move through direct investments locally in the market.

Second, the globalisation forces are less prevalent and therefore do not pose a threat to the firm's position in any market, so any major retaliatory move is in principle irrelevant.

7.5.2 *The multinational player*

In this cell, the firm has a much stronger position both at home and in selected foreign markets. The firm has already been exporting for a number of years and is in a position to make rational business decisions based on market insight and financial and managerial resources. It is now possibly only a question of time before the firm decides to set up local sales subsidiaries to cement and/or further develop its position abroad. In this way it will not only secure hierarchical control and acquire market insight through direct handling of local market activities, but also take over potential economic gains of scale in the operation.

Some firms – with a strong position at home but no extensive international operations – expand by acquisitions. Acquisitions secure firms an instant market position and reduce the uncertainty surrounding market development, including establishing a brand.

Norway's largest player in the fast moving consumer goods sector, Orkla, initiated an acquisition campaign in the 1990s which lasted well into the 2010s. In the nineties they bought into the Swedish and Finnish mineral water and beer markets. Their acqusitions, Pripps and Hartwall, were both market leaders in their respective countries. Based on their Finnish acquisition in the beer market, they entered a very profitable operation in Russia, acquiring Baltic Breweries, and thus became a major player in the Northern European beer market. Attracted by Orkla's success, Carlsberg (among the five largest breweries in the world) then came to the fore and the two entered into a strategic alliance in the beverage sector in 1998. It appeared after some years that the two joint venture partners did not share the same philosophies, and Carlsberg ended up buying out Orkla's stake in their joint venture in 2004. Orkla lost its position in the Northern European beer market (quitting the sector altogether), but on the other hand sold out with a healthy profit. Some would claim that the junior partner was outmanoeuvred by the much larger Carlsberg in this situation.

During this period of time, Orkla has strengthened its position in branded foods, through an acquisition spree involving a number of companies in Scandinavia and elsewhere: canned food (Abba and Kalles), condiments (Felix) and Paulúns (muesli) in Sweden; Pastella (pasta) and Beauvais (canned food and condiments) in Denmark; Spilva (condiments) in Latvia – also covering other Baltic markets. In 2007, they acquired a leading branded foods company in India, MTR, with sales in a number of countries outside India (South East Asia, Australia, Germany and the UK). Through the acquisition of the Norwegian market leader in soups (Toro), they also gained control of the Czech company Vitana, which also bought Hamé in the Czech Republic and Slovakia. In this way, Orkla has now the leadership or number two position with different brand names in many markets.

A critical marketing issue in acquisitions is that of branding. As we have seen above, Orkla has over a 20-year period bought a large number of branded food companies – mostly in Northern Europe. They have chosen to keep the acquired companies' brands in their respective markets. This is in principle not a problem for companies in a multi-local position. On the other hand, Orkla is not benefiting from potential gains in scale economies, and will not be able to position its brands globally (should this be of interest).

7.5.3 *The bold newcomer*

The lower right cell of the matrix is named "Seek new owners with extensive international networks" in the original nine-cell version (page 115).[23] Whereas this is a tempting proposition for some, others find this strategy completely unacceptable and would prefer to struggle with globalisation forces and try to carve out a position in a global competitive climate and reap the benefits in a longer perspective.

> Logitech – founded in 1981 – epitomises the successful development of a bold newcomer. They started as a software company, developing desktop publishing software for Ricoh (Japan), a large multinational in the photo/publishing industry. A year later they established their first subsidiary in the US, in order to get closer to Ricoh's development centre. Meanwhile, a little-known (at the time) device called a "computer mouse" was coming on to the market and caught the interest of the Logitech team. It was a perfect navigation aid for its graphic interface, which soon developed into a global niche. With their mouse, Logitech then entered into OEM deals (OEM=Original Equipment Manufacturers) with a number of large players – HP, IBM, Apple and Compaq. These contracts gave them the financial muscle to develop their own retail operations in parallel. In 1986, they opened a manufacturing unit in Taiwan and two years later they went public on the SWX Exchange in Switzerland. Today, Logitech is a world leader in computer peripherals. The entry mode chosen by Logitech, first through direct sales to a large customer, secured critical income during the first years of operation. Then, through OEM contracts, Logitech secured further growth, developed skills and built market coverage with their own name through retailers, before investing in their own subsidiaries (Anonymous 2006).

The main challenge for this class of firm is to embark on a rapid growth track in order to pre-emptively position themselves in the market, so as to gain first-entry advantages on a global scale and thereby making any potential entry less appealing for larger companies with a global market presence. A lack of resources and competencies may force these firms to adopt strategies that involve some kind of alliances, which at the same time curtail their independence. On one hand, the firm needs to secure access to resources, competencies and marketing networks, and on the other hand, they desire to maintain control over the long-term strategic development of the firm. This has been discussed as the "Born Global dilemma" in Chapter 3, Section 3.

Table 7.6 shows a repertoire of different strategies with buy-out (new owners), licensing and strategic alliances in one form or another possibly being the most relevant ones.

7.5.4 *Global market leader*

Firms in this quadrant are basically strong and they operate in a world market which is very much interlinked; strategic moves in one market are rapidly reciprocated or copied by competitors in other markets. In this case, the firm needs to consider a wide range of different operation modes. By definition, the firm is represented in key markets in some way or another. We therefore fall back on the role that each country market should play in the firm's portfolio. First, the largest markets and those where the main competitors are strong should be serviced through some kind of direct investments. If possible, they should aim for 100% ownership (although some countries demand local ownership through JVs). This gives the company the necessary leverage, through threats of retaliation in the competition's territory, to withstand

Table 7.6 Rapid and risky? Entry modes for resource-poor firms

Strategic approach	Strategic consequences
1 New owners	Founders risk losing control, but the firm remains independent. Make sure they have a marketing network to rapidly reach out to key markets, and capital to sustain the demands of growth.
2 Licensing with international partners	Solves the marketing problem (network) and partly also the capital problem as there is no need for own production capacity. The risks of licensing are of course present, including the risk of not being connected to and learning from the market.
3 Sole distribution arrangement with international partner	Solves the marketing problem (network). The firm remains in control over production and technological development, but control of marketing is partly left to the distributor. A variant of this arrangement is an OEM contract (Original Equipment Manufacturer) involving subcontracting to an assembly contractor who resells the product under their private brand. Piggybacking is another variant.
4 Franchising in key international markets	Secures rapid market coverage through external partners. Requires rapid establishment of control mechanisms to monitor franchisees in each market. Gives control of the brand. Requires market insight (which a newcomer does not necessarily have).
5 Gradual internationalisation	This means lower sales growth, but also gradual (and safer) development of resources, hence easier to control. Risk of being outcompeted by larger firms with existing marketing networks.

competitive moves on the firm's home turf (Hamel and Prahalad 1985). Second, the firm has enough resources to take advantage of differential resource bases and relative cost positions in different markets, so as to optimise its operations. For this purpose it has an array of options: licensing, joint ventures, contract manufacturing, own plants, assembly centres and R&D centres. Again, Poynter and White's (1984/1985) categories of subsidiary mandates (see page 207) are relevant for this discussion. In particular, the three groups of subsidiaries that play an integrating/rationalising role (marketing satellite, miniature replica and rationalised manufacturer) are relevant for companies in this cell. The extent to which the firm opts to resort to foreign direct investments rather than independent partners through licensing or subcontracting will depend on local idiosyncrasies (tax, regulations, etc.) and TCE considerations (internalisation gains – Williamson 1975). This is what Doole and Lowe (2004) call a "global supply system".

Buckley and Casson (1998) suggest a structure of units consisting of hubs (regional headquarters) and spikes (local sales subsidiaries, independent middlemen, sourcing units), which is flexible in the sense that the hubs are long-term investments, whereas the operation modes in the spike network may vary according to changing conditions in each market. In this way, the firm will secure a stable presence in the region and at the same time operate optimally on the fringes.

In the process of building and reasserting its position in global markets, the firm will often fall back on acquisitions instead of "green field" investments.[24] Again the issue of multi-brand becomes relevant and in this case, more acutely than in the case of the multinational player. Global competitors may ride on scale and the advantages of brandishing more or less the same image across the world. Therefore the acquiring firm needs to consider ways of rebranding the acquired firm's products.

7.6 Chapter summary

Operation mode decisions are among the most critical ones in international marketing. It is first and foremost about balancing resources (financial and management) and operational and marketing control, and thereby also acquiring market insight. In this endeavour, the firm has a wide range of alternatives giving different combinations of resource spending and control, from indirect exporting with virtually no control of marketing and no resources spent, to own local production with 100% control over all functions and substantial investments.

Figure 7.16 suggests a distribution of the balance between control and resources spent. The figure indicates a commensurate balance between these two elements, except for management contracts and strategic alliances. Apparently, the latter require fewer resources and give more control relative to the other operation modes in the figure. On the other hand, they are not always relevant alternatives (such as management contracts) or they involve complex relationships which make them more vulnerable to failure (for example, strategic alliances). In Chapter 8 we shall see that partner selection and relationship building may alleviate some of the shortcomings of the different operation modes.

The choice of operation mode is also about positioning in international markets. The firm should weigh the above balance against its location in the Strategic Windows framework. Firms in the lower part of this model have resource constraints that limit their options. Some firms make bolder steps than warranted by their position (for instance, creating a sales subsidiary instead of engaging an agent or distributor), and therefore risk overstretching their resources – both financially, but possibly more importantly their managerial capabilities. They need therefore to opt for a mode that is lower down in the figure. In this balancing act the firm should make sure that it is not interlocked into contractual arrangements that foreclose direct contact with the market – both in the short- and long-term, and thereby building experience and market insight. In the upper part of the model – and in particular the upper right – firms need to seek modes that give them the flexibility to act and to swiftly change tack, depending on local market conditions (Buckley and Casson 1998).

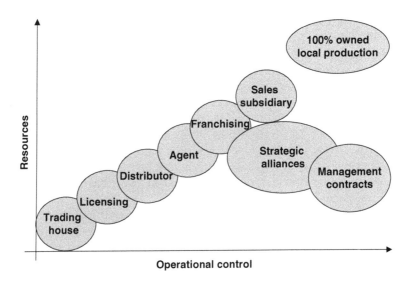

Figure 7.16 Operation modes – balancing between control and resources.

Notes

1 Operation mode is also often called entry mode. There is however a difference: entry mode is the method by which one *enters* the market *for the first time*, whereas operation mode is the general term, i.e. also after the firm has switched mode from, for example, agent to sales subsidiary.

2 We have seen that in the retail sector in some countries there are only three or four dominant players; in public procurement in the defence sector there is normally only one; in Nordic countries the sale of alcohol is organised in state monopolies; in some sectors such as in the car, shipping or heavy machinery industries, or in the metal or chemical industries, there are seldom more than just a few players in each industry; MNCs have sometimes coordinated their purchases across countries, and concentrated the purchase function in one centre – see later in Chapter 14.

3 Paraphrased by the author, based on a private conversation with the chairman of Dow Chemical in 1987.

4 Morten Abrahamsen, BI Norwegian Business School, 2014.

5 This section is based on conversations with post doc Henrik Jensen at BI Norwegian Business School, Pandora's Annual Report 2016, and newspaper clippings from *Børsen* (Denmark's main financial newspaper). It later appeared that the earn-out deal was riven with unclear passages, so the whole transaction ended up in court.

6 http://www.oxfordbusinessgroup.com/analysis/open-investment-regulations-relating-foreign-investors.

7 Former R&D manager of Owens Corning Norway.

8 In Europe, the Hanseatic companies in the Middle Ages were archetypal of the trading companies of the time. Later, in the era of geographic European conquests of Asia, Africa and South America, such companies grew up as a consequence of exploitation by Europe of colonial resources and the need for industrial products in the colonies. Today, trading houses are a diversified group of companies.

9 Ex-works and FOB are two Incoterm clauses that define responsibilities of the exporter and the freighter relating to the transport and insurance of goods. They are treated in some more detail in Chapter 12, Section 12.3.1.

10 Conversation with former managing director.

11 Lars Tomasgård, President of Nordox.

12 *Wasta* may be likened to an "old boys network", but it is much more than that, more like the Chinese *guangxi*. According to Cunningham and Sarayrah (1993), *wasta* refers to both the act of compromising and finding solutions, *and* the person who performs this act. The *wasta* "seeks to achieve what is assumed otherwise unattainable by the supplicant" (p. 1), such as access to decision-makers or mediation in conflicts.

13 Information for this anecdote is provided by Professor Joan Freixanet, University of St. Petersburg.

14 For a review of corporate tax levels across the world, see: https://home.kpmg.com/xx/en/home/services/tax/tax-tools-and-resources/tax-rates-online/corporate-tax-rates-table.html

15 See for instance the report by UNCTAD: http://unctad.org/en/Docs/poiteipcd3.en.pdf

16 Information for this anecdote is provided by Professor Joan Freixanet, University of St. Petersburg.

17 Conversation with previous management and http://www.odlo.com/en/our-world/about-us/facts-and-figures.html

18 In the petrochemical industry there are numerous different processes to make, for example, polyethylene. These processes end up with variations of this raw plastic material that are suited for different kinds of end uses (bags, bottles, plastic tanks, dinghies, lining for milk cartons, corrugated building material, etc.).

19 Nycomed has since been subject to mergers and takeovers. Today it is owned by Japanese Takeda, number 13 among world pharmaceutical companies.

20 This problem is at the heart of the theory of the multinational firm as it has been described by Buckley and Casson (1976) and Dunning (1977) – see Section 7.1.

21 Communication with company managers.

22 http://www.european-rubber-journal.com/2015/01/28/dupont-chemchina-form-fluoroelastomers-jv/.

23 In the first version of the model (Solberg 1997), this cell was termed "Prepare for a buy-out".

24 Green field investments involve investments from scratch, where the firm has to build all of the infrastructure surrounding a manufacturing plant – often having to "dig into" a field with vegetation (i.e. green field).

8 Partners in international marketing

8.1 Introduction

Operation modes set out the structural boundaries of the export venture, and as such confer different levels of power and possibilities to govern the relationship between the partners. This in itself is an important factor in setting up a successful marketing organisation abroad. In this chapter, we shall discuss other levers available to the exporter to govern the relationship with its partner/subsidiaries. First, we shall describe ways to select partners. In fact, partner selection is possibly more consequential than the operation mode, since the specific partner – with its organisation, resources, networks, culture and skills – will be the exporter's actual link between itself and the market. The partner is the one who will carry out the bulk of the local marketing activities, give the exporter feedback on the market situation and information that helps the exporter adapt its marketing to local requirements. Partner selection, therefore, is about how two organisations can work together in the best possible way to reach the marketing goals of the exporter.

Furthermore, we shall look into some critical aspects of contracting with the partner, and the subsequent collaboration between the two. We claim that this is the most critical part of the international marketing effort. Partner selection may be important, but relations with him or her need to be nurtured and progressed so that both parties can extract the best from the contract. Some would even claim that in flourishing partnerships, when the contract is signed, and the partners start to work together, the contract is placed in a drawer and never looked at again. Partnerships are about finding a platform for cooperation between two (or more) organisational cultures, so as to reduce scope for opportunism, build mutual trust, and create an atmosphere of inspiration and support.

Finally, we shall describe ways to part from each other. Most business relationships have an end, mainly because the partners develop different goals or because market conditions pull the carpet out from under the platform on which the collaboration was founded. This should already be present in the minds of the partners at contract signing.

8.2 Selecting the partner

Selecting export partners is about choosing the platform for expansion in international markets. In this endeavour, the exporter invests in training, in joint marketing activities, in setting up routines for a smooth operation. These investments are specific to the relationship and will be worthless if the partnership breaks apart. Still – even if the sunk costs in the relationship are high – breaking out of it is sometimes the best solution. In some markets, this is utterly problematic because of local norms or regulations. For instance, in some Arab countries, an agency contract is likened to a "catholic marriage", which is – if not impossible – at least costly to get out of. Sometimes the local customer loyalty is more towards the partner than the exporter and its product/services. In some markets, such as Belgium, entering into a distributor relationship is seen as a life-long commitment (as opposed to an agency contract). Furthermore, one may be fascinated by the person who may appear knowledgeable and energetic, but who later on may reveal his or her ideas that contradict one's own, and therefore make any further cooperation difficult.

> Exporters to some Arab countries often encounter a phenomenon called the "dual roles" of the agent. This is best illustrated by the following scenario: A power plant is being planned by the Electricity Board of X-city. During the design phase the chief engineer specifies equipment for which he in his free time seeks agencies. "Surprise, surprise": it was exactly those suppliers who won the contract. Civil servants work for the public agency in the morning and run their own business in the evening. This practice of "dual role" gives them ample opportunity to open markets for principals of their choice. Some allege that this is not a big problem, either because it does not really represent a conflict of roles (different businesses) or maybe because they represent another kind of ethics. Others are very suspicious of the practice of dual roles. As one government official bluntly puts it: "Of course there is conflict of interest, but people don't pay attention to conflict of interest, do they?" An Arab businessman made the following comment: "The dual role system is very common, and the lower you go in the hierarchy, the more it is likely to occur. Civil servants take advantage as far as information is concerned and some of them are shameless! Most often it is too late to bid at the tender publication." In some cases, projects are split into smaller pieces, enabling different people to take advantage of the dual role system.[1]

Agency theory[2] has introduced the concept of pre-contractual opportunism, which is the propensity to conceal information or intentions before the partners enter into the cooperation contract. For instance, the potential partner may already cooperate with a competing firm, and wants to protect the competitor by entering into agency relationships with other suppliers in the market in order to control existing suppliers' potential competitors. Alternatively, the partner may cover a much smaller part of the market than would be of interest for the exporter and does not have the ambition to expand. Or, he/she does not have the necessary competence or organisation to realistically carry out the local marketing of one's products or services. Ideally, the exporter, therefore, should screen a number of partners before committing itself; and when the final choice is made, should enter into a trial period of, say, one year, before signing a more permanent contract.

Studies of partnering suggest that exporters seldom make a *conscious selection* of partners, in the sense that one should identify three or four potential candidates, meticulously analyse their capabilities, and then eventually make the final, rational decision. More often, firms "slide into" partnerships through their existing networks without actively doing any research (Håkansson and Snehota 1995, Gripsrud et al. 1999). Alternatively, it is the potential partner who emerges and airs an interest in cooperation. We have seen this in Chapter 3 (the role of networks and the fortuitous export order) and above (Arab civil servants). Whether sliding into a partnership or systematically selecting a partner, the firm should examine the candidate's seriousness, intentions, position in the market and capabilities before entering into a contract.

When first entering a new market, the selection of a partner is particularly challenging. Even though the exporter may have done its "homework", analysed the market and studied different candidates, it will seldom have the necessary background to rationally evaluate the different alternatives at hand. We have seen that small-scale direct exporting in an introductory phase may be a precursor to a more permanent relationship. We have also seen that basic market research, followed up with visits to the market, can give the exporter a good starting point for selection of local partner.

Simrad Yachting, a world leader in electronic navigation devices and echo-sounders for pleasure craft and fishing vessels, used an interesting approach to field research in order to identify candidates for future partnerships in their early days as exporters. Their export manager visited important fishing ports in the market, boarded a number of vessels while they were moored to the quay and offered to discuss with the skipper different issues concerning electronic equipment on board the vessels. Touching upon competitors, dealers, the needs and preferences of the different kinds of fishing vessels, he was able to draw pretty solid conclusions concerning potential candidates for partnership. His approach was not very scientific; on the other hand, he got in-depth and critical viewpoints from the target group not only about specific candidates but also about the market itself – invaluable information to prepare him for concrete negotiations with his future partner.

An alternative method was used by the Swedish consulting firm Lars Weibull AB, on behalf of clients. After identification of a number of potential candidates, the firm wrote to them, airing the possibility of representing their client. They sent a form to the candidates with general questions concerning their organisation, the products and brands they carry, their market, the competitive situation and so forth. The number of responses and their quality gave an indication not only of the appropriateness of the different candidates, but also general information about the market situation.

Many firms recruit their future partners at Trade Fairs. This is an interesting meeting place and should be considered by the exporter. There is, nevertheless, one caveat to this method: exhibiting products at Trade Fairs without having established a dealer network or any other permanent representation in the market may frustrate potential customers who have no local representative to go to after the Trade Fair closes its doors.

The next step is to check the credit rating of the candidates. Such ratings are not complete, but will still give the exporter a clue as to the financial status of the firm. In addition, one may ask other firms selling through the candidate in order to get a second opinion.

It is fair to say that "the impeccable and perfect partner" – whatever that is – does not really exist; and, if it does exist, it is most likely to already be lined up with a competitor! Therefore, one has to content oneself with a partner who has the potential to grow with the exporter. The selection criteria depend on two factors: the marketing objectives of the firm, and the desired allocation of roles between the partners. The first consideration, therefore, is what type of partner does one really want? Is it a large company, offering exclusive distribution, with a full range of products that covers the whole market? We would claim that, for a small exporter, this is definitely not a dream partner. The exporter and its products risk being "lost" among all the other products and brands in their partner's portfolio, lacking the power to push them through the labyrinth of budgeting and prioritising mechanisms inside the partner firm. The opposite alternative, a small firm, perhaps a "one-man-show" – an "eager beaver" with market insight and an appetite for new business, but with limited potential to grow with the exporter in the market – may be tempting but also risky.

Below is an "almost complete list" of criteria that can be used for selection:

– Geographical coverage
– Industry coverage
– Customer contact – which customers and what kind of contact?
– Marketing organisation/sales force
– Product range – competing or complementing?
– Logistics network
– Service network
– Financial strength
– Reputation
– General market and product knowledge.

Time is now ripe to visit the most relevant among the candidates, to make a thorough presentation of the firm, its products, its organisation, its ideas and objectives in the market; and not the least, to learn about the future partner. During the interviews and negotiations, the exporter should check two more criteria:

1   To what extent do key personnel in the partner's organisation identify themselves with the products, the brand and the basic ideas of the exporter? Buying into the exporter's business philosophy will inevitably ease the cooperation between the partners.
2   To what extent do key personnel get along? Matching "chemistries" between these partners will facilitate collaboration.

We will end this section by citing a Western businessperson in Abu Dhabi, who gave the following advice to a newcomer in the market: "Have a long courtship before you get engaged; once engaged, you should have a long engagement period; then you can marry."

8.3 The contract between the partners

Selecting the preferred partner is one thing; negotiating the contract with him or her is another matter. Even if the exporter has found the "ideal partner", it is necessary to delineate their respective responsibilities and roles. This is normally done through negotiations that eventually end up in some form of contract. The role of the contract is then first to specify each partner's commitments and obligations. Since the contracting partners have different cultural and business backgrounds, they normally have different perspectives of the goals of the relationship, and how to reach them – i.e. what obligations are to be undertaken by each partner. In addition, entering into relationships with a foreign partner involves a certain level of risk. Therefore, the contract should serve as a risk-reducing device, through mechanisms that curtail opportunism and encourage goal alignment. These concerns should be addressed during the negotiations on the final content of the contract. Three strings of theory are relevant in this regard. *Agency theory* is studying the contract itself, with an emphasis on how to unite the goals of each partner and how to reduce risks (Eisenhardt 1989). *Transaction Cost Economics (TCE)* – with its emphasis on the transaction proper – discusses how to reduce the costs of the cooperation, and distribute the gains (Williamson 1975, 1985). *Social exchange theory* seeks to explain mechanisms of relationships between partners such as trust-building processes.

This section shall discuss three distinct aspects of contracting: 1) formal contracting vs. relational contracting, 2) the concrete content of formal contracts, and 3) negotiations.

8.3.1 Formal vs. relational contracts

Whereas formal contracts are usually written and legally enforceable, relational contracts are based on implicit expectations, credible commitments and trust. Normally, both coexist in a business relationship. One may say that they are two extremes on a continuum, where the formal contract – with strict and detailed regulations on all perceivable contingencies – is at one end. At the other end, we find business transactions without any formalisation except for agreed price, quantities, delivery conditions and so on, leading to a relationship between the partners with expectations based on experience and trust. Between these two extremes, we find a vast area of different kinds of contracts that are more or less loosely defined, and where the partners find solutions to issues as they arise. Generally, formal contracts are difficult to negotiate *ex ante*, because it is difficult to anticipate all the contingencies that could occur in the relationship; and even if they were identified, the solutions suggested in the contract may not always be optimal. Open contracts may be more onerous to renegotiate because of lack of clarity.

Table 8.1 suggests advantages and disadvantages of both types of contracts (based on Mooi and Ghosh 2010).

Mooi and Ghosh (2010) suggest that the complexity and size of the transaction involving, for example, both physical products, software and services, requiring extensive coordination between the partners, warrant more detailed contract clauses. Such coordination is needed in order to reduce uncertainty in the design and implementation phase of the delivery. Formalising the responsibilities of the partners will, in this case, reduce the costs of renegotiation. Furthermore, in contracts with high-asset specificity – for instance, where the exporter has invested in training, joint marketing activities and physical assets such as storage – the different aspects of the relationship will typically be more specified; we might call it a quasi-hierarchical relationship with checks and balances throughout the transactions. In the same vein, the more dependent the exporter is on the intermediary, the more they tend to formalise the relationship with their partner (Aulakh and Genctürk 2008).

Table 8.1 Detailed and open contracts

Detailed contract terms	*Open contracts*

Enables managers to
  – Set goals
  – Clarify expectations
  – Reduce misunderstandings
  – Reduce counterparty opportunism
	Enables parties to make value-enhancing adjustments.
	Is likely to foster trust between the parties, because they do not hold each other to precise terms of the contract.

Requires expenditures in
  – Searching for information
  – Projecting scenarios/contingencies
  – Negotiating acceptable solutions
	May lead to opportunism, because the counterparty can exploit unspecified loopholes that lead to wasteful renegotiations and hold-ups.

Source: Based on Mooi and Ghosh (2010).

Deligonul and Cavusgil (2006) find export experiences tend to lead to legal (formal) contracting, possibly because experienced partners are more aware of the critical contingencies in a business relationship and are therefore more capable of formalising them and suggesting reasonable solutions. This has also been found by Aulakh and Genctürk (2008). They suggest that firms seek to formalise contracts when markets are volatile, because of the perceived risks in such environments and the subsequent need to safeguard.

What, then, is an optimal specification level of a contract? Finding the right balance between, on one hand, open and relational contracts and, on the other hand, specified and detailed ones is not straightforward. If the contract is "over-specified", the negotiation costs ahead of the contract signing will be disproportionately onerous, and also likely to embitter the climate between the partners. Conversely, if the contract is underspecified, the partners will spend too much time (and money) trying to renegotiate acceptable solutions to their problems, and again risk stalling an otherwise good relationship. Aulakh and Genctürk (2008) found in their research that flexibility (relational contracts) is particularly favourable in situations of economic uncertainty such as volatile exchange rates, uncertain demand conditions and high inflation.

Culture may also play a role in this balancing exercise. It has been found that Asians are inclined to be relationally-oriented: the main purpose for the negotiations is not the contract as such; rather it is about creating trust and a long-lasting relationship. Perhaps therefore, they prefer general principles rather than specific clauses regulating different situations that might occur in a transaction. For Americans, and to some extent also the British, this seems to be the other way around (Salacuse 2004). A Norwegian lawyer living in Shanghai expressed the following (cited from Gottschalk Sveaas and Thorstensen 2013): "The Chinese often view the contract as a letter of intent and as a framework where the road is laid as you go. If something changes along the way in a contractual relationship, we talk about how to solve the problems, while a Westerner is used to everything being pre-regulated in the contract."[3] We speculate that this may be ascribed to Hofstede's (1980) cultural dimensions such as collectivism and uncertainty avoidance, as both generally scored higher in Asia than in the West. A relatively weak judicial system may also play a part in this. With weak legal protection, partners develop other mechanisms to protect their interests such as relationships characterised by deep trust (see also Section 2.3.3).

8.3.2 Exporter–intermediary contracts

A legal contract is enforceable, implying that it can be tried in a court, which in turn means that it gives the parties to the agreement the opportunity to invoke dispute resolution mechanisms, and coercive power to enforce contract obligations. This is also the reason why it is important to state the jurisdiction of the contract – i.e. the law under which the contract is regulated. In some countries, not only the legal process but also the enforcement of the outcome of a case are both doubtful and risky – particularly for foreigners. Taking a quick look at the legal protection index in Chapter 2 (Table 2.8), we get an idea of countries where exporters are most exposed to these kinds of uncertainties.

When Telenor (a leading mobile phone operator) renegotiated their joint venture deal with their Russian partner, Altimo, concerning their joint interests in Vimpelcom (the second-largest mobile operator in Russia) and Kyivstar (a market leader in Ukraine), they eventually got acceptance for using New York state jurisdiction for conflict resolutions. This came after years of conflict, not only with their JV partner but also with the Russian tax authorities. As a senior vice-president of Telenor said: "Altimo's CEO thrives in 'friendly' litigations, and is a master of exploiting his close relations with the Russian authorities, using Russian courts to intimidate their foreign partners." Altimo eventually conceded in the negotiations because their international operations were dependent on goodwill from international markets.

A small Norwegian exporter of proprietary IT insisted on Norwegian jurisdiction in their negotiations with a large American partner. They were inexperienced in international law in general and the US judicial system in particular, and did not want to take any unnecessary legal risks. The Americans, for their part, insisted on US jurisdiction, but the Norwegian company was adamant about their requirement. The Americans withdrew from the discussions, only to get back to the negotiation table after a couple of months. Evidently, the strength of the Norwegian party's technology was too tempting, and the Americans decided to abandon their initial demand. One may not always be in a position to put forward such an ultimate claim; this little anecdote shows that even when confronted with a strong partner, it is possible to prevail.

This section will deal with exporter–intermediary contracts. A number of other kinds of contracts are relevant in international business. These will not be described in this book.[4]

We have already described the structural differences between an agent and a distributor. Also, the legal differences are significant.

> *The agent* represents the principal (in our case the exporter), may conclude contracts on behalf of the principal, or may only broker the contact between the exporter and the customer. He may receive orders, but not necessarily confirm them. He receives instructions from the principal and gets paid in the form of a commission – normally a percentage of the sales.

> *The distributor* buys the goods from the exporter, and is – in this capacity – a customer of the exporter. The distributor's income is in the form of a mark-up, implying that they themselves carry out the local marketing, *on their behalf* and with *their strategies*, including pricing.

According to the Treaty of Rome, article 85, a vendor has no right to dictate the local price or set other sales conditions in a distributor relationship. In the agency mode, this is not only possible, but it is a consequence given the structure of the mode (see Figures 7.3 and 7.5). Regulations for termination of the contract are also different. Even seasoned exporters often use the two terms – agent and distributor – interchangeably, but the terminology in itself is not of any importance for the legal interpretation of the contract; it is the concrete clauses in the agreement that determine whether, in legal terms, one talks about an agency or distributor contract.

The term agent expresses slightly different things in different languages. "Handelsvertreter" in Germany and Austria, "Agent" in Switzerland, "handelsagent" in the Netherlands, "agent commercial" in France, and "représentant de commerce" in Belgium. An "agente" in Italy is one that brokers the sale, whereas a "representante" is one that has the power to conclude the sale. In the Nordic countries the term "agent" is normally used for both situations. In the UK the term is "manufacturer's agent", normally with wide powers to conclude sales on behalf of the principal.

In the case of an agency contract, there are always two distinct agreements with *different parties*: one involving the exporter and the agent (the *representation contract*), and the other one being the *sales contract* between the exporter and the final customer (see Figures 7.3 and 7.5). The relationship with the distributor should also be regulated in two separate kinds of contracts, but this time both of them will be between the *same parties*: the exporter and the distributor:

1 A *representation contract* that describes the obligations and rights of each partner concerning the operations in the market; and
2 A *sales contract for each purchase*, describing the concrete terms of the transaction (price, volume, terms of payment, etc.).

The latter may vary from one transaction to the other, whereas the representation contract should be a long-term cooperation agreement. It has been said that the best contracts are those that are never read again after the signing. The negotiations to get there, determining the obligations and the rights, and the boundaries of power yielded to the partner, will resolve potential disagreements from the outset. Then, as the partners get to learn about each other, the relationships will be shaped, based on experience, and sometimes also deviate from the initial intentions set out in the contract. Bello and Gilliland (1997, p. 31) find that the best relationships are those where – when some unexpected situation arises – "Both parties would rather work out a new deal than hold each other to the original terms."

Contract clauses in the representation contract

The most important clauses in the contract are those defining the partners, their rights and obligations, exclusivity, sales volume, termination and choice of law.[5] The headline should indicate the kind of contract (distributor, agency, franchising, licensing or joint venture). Then the parties to the contract should be defined. If the exporter is a large firm with different units and products/services, it is relevant to specify both the unit and the products/services that are the object of the contract. The same is true of the definition of the territory. This is a thorny question, particularly in Europe, because one risks breaching EU regulations. A clause forbidding the sale of the product to another country is in conflict with article 85 in the Treaty of Rome, and heavy fines have been given to firms that strictly regulate territories in their contracts with distributors. The background for this article lies in the whole idea of the EU: one market and low price levels. If the exporter were given the right to partition its market by country, it may also differentiate the pricing in each market in order to take advantage of different general price levels within the EU. Banning a partner from selling to EU countries other than the one covered by the contract will constitute a breach of article 85.

In 2002, the European Commission imposed a total fine of 167.8 million euros on Japanese video games maker Nintendo and seven of its official distributors in Europe for colluding to prevent exports to high-priced from low-priced countries. The fine on Nintendo alone was calculated at 149 million euros to reflect its size in the market concerned, the fact that it was the driving force behind the illicit behaviour and also because it continued with the infringement even after it knew the investigation was going on. Prices for play consoles and games differed widely from one European Union country to another during the period investigated by the Commission, with the United Kingdom up to 65% cheaper than Germany and the Netherlands. "Every year, millions of European families spend large amounts of money on video games. They have the right to buy the games and consoles at the lowest price the market can possibly offer and we will not tolerate collusive behaviour intended to keep prices artificially high," European Competition Commissioner Mario Monti said.

The Commission collected evidence showing that Nintendo and its distributors colluded to maintain artificially high price differences in the EU between January 1991 and 1998. According to the arrangements, *each distributor was under the obligation to prevent parallel trade from its territory*, i.e. exports from one country to another via unofficial distribution channels. Under the leadership of Nintendo, the companies intensively colla-borated to find the source of any parallel trade. Traders that allowed parallel exports to occur were punished by being given smaller shipments or by being boycotted altogether.[6]

The obligations of the distributor/agent

The partner's obligations are first and foremost to sell the exporter's product. Normally this is specified in the form of minimum sales volumes. The stipulation of minimum sales should be realistic, and take into account that it takes time to build a market.

In some cases it is relevant to include a clause on the handling of extremely large orders. A Scandinavian manufacturer of log cabins experienced this with the contract they had entered into with their American agent in Vermont. In the first year there was slightly over the minimum sales requirement of orders for cabins. The next two years, however, the agent got orders for cabins in a large project involving the delivery of far more than the minimum sales requirement. The exporter was happy to expand its plant to fulfil the orders, only to find that the following year – after the completion of the project – the order level sank to the minimum sales, creating problems for the manufacturer. This situation could have been avoided with a clause on financial commitment by the agent in cases of sales exceeding a certain level.

A clause on loyalty – i.e. not representing competitors – may be relevant. This is particularly appropriate in the case of agents, whereas distributors more often carry a range of products and brands that at least partly compete with each other. This clause should also include a passage on quarantine beyond the end of the agreement of, for instance, one year. If the prohibition to sell competitors' products after contract termination is too severe, courts may put this clause aside.

It should be specified in the contract that the partner has an obligation to inform the exporter about developments in the market, new customers, competition, trends, etc. This may be seen as obvious, but it is still advisable to include such a clause, particularly because sales people are more prone to sell than to analyse.

The obligations of the principal

If the agent's duty is to secure minimum sales, the reciprocal duty of the principal is to supply the goods. In this regard, they should keep the agent informed about changes in production, prices, models, etc. The exporter should also pay agent commission, pending payment from the final customer, a so-called *del credere* clause.[7] Costs incurred in developing marketing materials and setting up after-sales service facilities may be shared. A simple formula such as "marketing costs corresponding to 5% (or any other percentage) of total sales will be covered by the principal" may be a good solution. In that case, the exporter should also have a say in the development of the marketing strategy of the distributor. The exporter should also register the brand – and not leave this to the intermediary.

Ahead of the signature on a sales contract, attention needs to be drawn to the interest that tax and customs duty authorities may have in the deal. For instance, if the price is set far below the going market price for similar products, the customs duty office may intervene and require an uplift of the price, on which basis the customs tariff and VAT will be calculated.

Contract termination

The background for contract termination will vary (see also later in this chapter, Section 8.6). Sometimes the contract is restricted to a certain period (for instance one year, or until completion of a large project), and there is no need for a specific termination clause. Normally, the representation contract does not have a date, rather it is renewed automatically each year until one of the parties announces termination. Alternatively, the parties need to announce say three months ahead of expiration that they want to renew the contract.

Some countries have mandatory regulations concerning contract cessation. In German agency law, the agent cannot relinquish their right to get after-commission. In Italy, Austria and Switzerland, the law is even more challenging (for the exporter), where the after-commission has the character of a pension, unless the termination is based on agent misbehaviour. Benelux countries have adapted regulations that are based on German legislation, and Sweden and Norway have agency laws that are essentially similar. Concerning distributors, only Belgium (in the EU) has mandatory regulations protecting distributors from being dismissed without compensation. There is a tendency to let agency laws also pertain to distributorship relations in this regard. It is furthermore worth noting that distributors – after a long-term relationship – may gain the right to use the brand, even after contract cessation.

Conflict resolution

It is highly advisable to regulate how potential conflicts will be resolved. Normally, contracts have a provision that states that conflicts should be settled through amicable mediation. If this does not lead to agreement between the partners, most contracts suggest arbitration. The advantage of arbitration is that its decisions are irrevocable and that it is normally less costly than litigation in public courts. A decision in the lower courts can be appealed to a higher court, and then re-appealed, resulting in endless and costly court dealings. The court proceedings may therefore stretch out over time, and stall any operative action in the market.

Force majeure

Force majeure is a situation where one party to a contract is prevented from honouring his/her obligations according to the terms of the contract. For example, a buyer of industrial equipment has invested in preparations to install a machine. Just a few days before the delivery the seller's factory has been completely destroyed by an earthquake, and the seller has no alternative means to manufacture the machinery in the foreseeable future. The contract is frustrated. Other incidents may be relevant: strikes, fire, political embargo, war, revolution, etc. In short, *force majeure* is a clause to protect the parties when incidents that they could not have predicted happen. Therefore, tornados, earthquakes and avalanches are not always accepted as *force majeure* in areas where one can expect such incidents. The contract should contain a clause defining *force majeure*.

8.3.3 Negotiating the contract

Hundreds of books and articles have been written on negotiations, and we shall try to condense these texts into a few pages. In their book *Getting to Yes*, Fisher et al. (2011) warn that negotiating parties should first and foremost try to understand each other's underlying motivations for the collaboration, rather than posting a concrete position on specific issues. The latter approach often ends up in stalled discussions and sometimes inconclusive negotiations. A position is normally adopted *as a result of underlying motivations*, and is based on pre-conceived ideas of *how to solve a problem* or defend one's interests.

When buying one item on the weekly market in Inca (Mallorca) the buyer is confronted with one single price for the one item. The price may or may not be negotiated down, and the whole deal is about how to distribute the salesperson's purchase and rental costs, and his/her mark-up, with subsequent loss or gain for the trading parties. However, as most negotiations are about more than just one issue (for instance, price), there are normally different ways to satisfy both partners' fundamental interests. For instance, in a joint venture both partners want to achieve control of the operations. The straightforward way of securing control is to ask for a majority shareholding, or a majority of voting shares in the venture. But only one party to the deal can have the majority (unless it is a 50–50 deal). There are, however, many ways of achieving control: one may ask to appoint the chairman of the board, managing director or other key managers; one may request a qualified majority (for instance 60% in a 55–45 JV) for certain critical decisions; one may deliver critical components (see Section 7.4.5); one may require frequent information, etc.

Another issue could be different attitudes to risk and preferences. For example: a distributor normally takes a risk (to sit back with unsold products) when buying a product that is new to the market for resale, and may therefore want to minimise this risk by proposing to buy a limited amount during the first year. The exporter may achieve significant economies of scale if the distributor agrees to buy considerably beyond this limited amount. In order to stimulate the distributor to buy more, the exporter can offer a rebate (the distributor then taking part in the gains of scale) or offer to contribute to cover marketing costs, or part-financing storage.

A third issue might be that of the level of royalties in a licensing contract. If the licensee is only willing to pay a 10% royalty for a licence instead of the 13% demanded by the licensor, the latter may consider sweetening the pill by giving access to new developments, or to participate directly in projects with their R&D team. The extent to which the potential licensee responds positively to such proposals depends on their preference (for long-term relationships and technology development). In addition, the licensor may (as the exporter above) chip in an offer to cover parts of the marketing costs. This in turn raises the issue of giving the licensor some say and some control of the licensee's marketing plan, use of brand name, etc. In other words, as new issues are brought to the negotiation table, new items to be negotiated are generated.

The essence of these examples is that different risk attitudes and preferences of the negotiating parties may be open for solutions that cater to their real interests, rather than stalling the negotiations because of some preconceived positions. This brings us to the issue of the popular win–win concept. There are two basic negotiation strategies (Lewicki et al. 2015):

1   *Distributive strategies* (competitive, value claiming) implying that the partners should divide the pie into pieces, the sizes of which are to be negotiated. A larger piece of the pie to one party means a correspondingly smaller piece to the other party – a null sum game. This is a single-issue negotiation involving limited information exchange and problem-solving behaviour, and more use of pressure tactics. Power may determine the outcome of the negotiation. Still, we observe with Kuhri (1968, p. 704) that:

> Bargaining, an attribute of free market systems of economic exchange, serves an economic purpose, that is to regulate prices in societies where suspicion and uncertainty of the value of commodities dominate. In the Middle East, bargaining is not for fun, nor merely for the sake of bargaining. Through the manipulation of cultural norms and symbols, a bargainer, whether seller or buyer, aims to eliminate suspicion of commodity and price and establish instead an atmosphere of trust often leading to client-relationships and occasionally friendship.

2   *Integrative strategies* imply more issues to be brought to the table and, hence, that there is potential for both parties to gain. Also, in integrative negotiation strategies people ideally are separate from the issues. The aim is to identify the important issues for both parties, so as to find the optimal trade-offs of different preferences and end goals. This means that rather than using pressure tactics, the parties exchange information and seek to solve problems. The goals of the parties in integrative negotiation are not necessarily mutually exclusive, thus one party's gain is not always at the other party's expense. Whereas the pie is constant in distributive negotiations, it is possible to increase it in integrative negotiations, because several issues – with different preferences by the parties – are generated. This in itself is an incentive to use integrative strategies.

According to Fisher et al. (2011), negotiators taking a distributive stance confronting negotiators with an integrative approach will often "win" the negotiation – at least in the short-term. In the longer-term, such a "victory" may be detrimental to the relationship between the partners, because the "loser" feels he/she has been treated unfairly. The best outcome is obtained when all negotiating partners take an integrative approach; the pie is widened and each partner is interested in different parts.

Salacuse (2004) found that the Japanese in general take a win–win – integrative – approach to negotiations; in Spain, he found this is much less customary. More generally, we may infer that Asians are more inclined to apply an integrative approach to negotiations, and that perhaps the opposite is the case for Westerners. Having said this, we should also be prepared to face a lose–lose situation, in the sense that on some issues of less priority, the negotiator may accept to lose, as long as he/she will win on other issues (where the other party loses).

Salacuse (2004) reports that time is perceived differently in different cultures. For instance rushing through negotiations in order to sign a contract may be counterproductive in Asia, since negotiators there need time to build trust and relationships (see above – 8.3.2 Contracts); in Europe and North America time is money. The maxim "in the East, time is coming – in the West time is flying" is possibly more than just a maxim; it is a reality. Salacuse (2004, p. 4) refers to negotiations between Enron and Maharashtra State Government in India:

> a long-term electricity supply contract between an ENRON subsidiary, the Dabhol Power Company, and the Maharashtra state government in India, was subject to significant challenge and was ultimately cancelled on the grounds that it was concluded in "unseemly haste" and had been subject to "fast track procedures" that circumvented established practice for developing such projects in the past. Important segments of the Indian public automatically assumed that the government had failed to protect the public interest because the negotiations were so quick. In the company's defense, Rebecca Mark, chairman and CEO of Enron International, pointed out to the press: "We were extremely concerned with time, because time is money for us."

Fisher et al. (2011) suggest a stepwise process in four steps to successful integrative negotiations. The first three steps are creating the value, and the last or fourth step is claiming the value, which is the Best Alternative To Negotiated Agreement (BATNA).

1   Identify and define the problem. This first step is the most difficult step, since several parties are involved, with different problems and goals.
2   Surface interests and needs. This step is considered the key to successful negotiations, since it enables the parties to understand each other's interests and priorities.
3   Generate alternative solutions aimed at creating a variety of options or solutions to the problem. This step is about trading off several issues with different priorities to satisfy every party. It is worth noting that the different parties may have the same intentions and objectives, but perhaps very different understandings and approaches on how to achieve them.
4   Evaluate and select alternatives. The last step aims at evaluating the alternatives in order to reach BATNA.

The BATNA is, in principle, the yardstick against which the negotiated agreement should be measured. For the negotiator to be able to assess his or her BATNA, he/she needs not only to collect relevant information about the alternatives, but also to develop a deep understanding of them. We have seen in Chapter 3 how exporters "gradually slide into relationships" or unintentionally line up with partners that lock the firm into a strategic position that may in the longer-term be in conflict with their market objectives. When at a later stage the exporter wants to break out of or change the conditions of the relationship, it needs first to establish relevant alternatives in order to get more control over operations: set up a sales subsidiary; buy out the partner; enter into a joint venture with the partner. These alternative actions have different consequences concerning both resource requirements (finance/management) and acceptance in the market. Before entering negotiations the exporter should have a clear opinion about how each of these alternatives affects the long-term position of the firm in the market (is it easy to maintain the market position with the alternative?), and also their costs. We shall later discuss switching partners in Section 8.6.

8.4 Partner relationships

The contract gives the parties a legal foundation for their cooperation. However, it is the nitty gritty of the daily business operations that forms the factual collaboration between the partners. Whatever operation mode, whatever partner selected and whatever contract, it is when "business as usual" starts that the relationship is put to the test. In a relationship there are at least two parties and therefore normally two different opinions on how to carry out the business operations. Occasionally these opinions are in conflict with each other, other times the parties may have an interest to find alternative solutions to the ones proposed by the exporter, or even conceal facts in order to promote their own interests. A classical exporter–middleman disagreement concerns the extent to which the marketing mix needs to be adapted to the local market situation. This is about the conflict between economies of scale (with a standardised marketing mix) at the centre and the need to adapt the marketing at the local level. In order to curb the middleman's penchant for becoming "too independent", the exporter therefore needs to put in place control and monitoring systems. The more subsidiaries and the more independent middlemen in different countries, the more challenging the task of monitoring and coordinating the marketing effort will be. The goal must be to find models that align the interests of the partners.

There are also other sources of conflict that stem from more operational elements: late deliveries, delays in payments, damage to or malfunction of goods, failure to inform, etc. These kinds of episodes should be rectified by procedures other than monitoring of the partner's operations. Prompt and frank information about such situations and a flexible and empathetic stance towards the partner are – we would claim – in themselves conducive to create a supportive and positive atmosphere between the partners. We will in this section not delve into these operative aspects of the relationships between the exporter and its middleman; rather we shall outline different monitoring mechanisms to control the partner's activities and to develop a cooperative relationship. The mechanisms to create a mutually beneficial relationship, then, rest on the partners' ability to evaluate the performance of their business relations.

This section approaches this issue from three different angles, trying to answer three questions:

1 Should the firm centralise its international marketing decisions or rather leave the responsibility to its local partners?
2 What levers might the exporter have at hand for the monitoring of the intermediary in international markets?
3 How does the strategic position of the firm affect the monitoring of the intermediary?

8.4.1 Local self-governed barons, or a federation of partners?

Who should make the local marketing decisions: the local intermediary or the exporter? This is a source of an ever-returning argument between the centre and the periphery. The standardisation–adaptation conflict is at the core of this discussion. The worst-case scenario for the exporter is a patchwork of different local solutions concerning product and promotion strategies, where he/she sees scope for substantial gains from a standardised approach. The emphasis in this discussion has been almost exclusively on the trade-off between local market conditions and economies of scale. One exception is Mårtenson (1987), who addresses external (demand homogeneity, role of advertising agency) and internal forces (locus of decision power, corporate culture), thereby introducing other important determinants of the standardisation–adaptation issue. The locus of decision power is appropriately described by Chase et al. (2000, p. 27a) in an interview with Procter & Gamble's international vice-president, Edwin Artz, who stated that: "There is no way the company can impose a direction on them (local managers) . . . We can challenge them, but it is their ideas that make or break these brands." In contrast, Procter & Gamble's worldwide marketing campaigns of brands such as Pampers or Pantene are good examples of maintaining loyalty to the major theme on the mission, proposition and concept levels while fine-tuning the

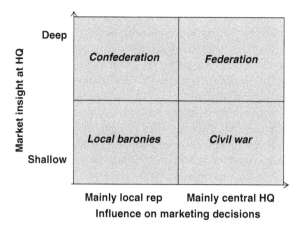

Figure 8.1 Who is in charge here?

Source: Solberg (2000).

execution to take into consideration different local cultures and regulations (van Raaij 1997). Later, we shall discuss the standardisation/adaptation issue when looking at the individual marketing mix elements.

We believe that the locus of the decision power largely depends on the organisational culture at HQ, or in other words: what is the creed of top management at HQ – local adaptation or central standardisation? Solberg (2000, 2002) addresses this issue in an international marketing governance model; see Figure 8.1.

Local barons

A company with limited market knowledge and local representatives with a high degree of autonomy tends to adapt its communications more than other companies. The limited market knowledge at the exporter HQ level makes the company the victim of representatives who gradually increase their leverage towards the HQ in discussions on marketing strategies and activities in each local market. Also, the local representatives' use of local advertising agents, which is a natural consequence of this situation, aggravates the distance between HQ and the local marketing activities. In these circumstances, each representative usually develops his or her own marketing strategies independently of HQ. The HQ's role is then reduced to responding to the requirements put forward by each representative – the ultimate consequence being a product-market portfolio that may be likened to a patchwork. The HQ's limited understanding of local market conditions reduces its potential to be a well-informed discussion partner with its representatives regarding the positioning of the company's product in the local market. Alternatively, the company may have too few people employed in marketing at HQ to monitor the international marketing, or both situations may exist. Therefore, the local representative – whether independent or company-owned – has the upper hand in most of the marketing decisions in their area.

Civil war

Companies can thrive with the local barony strategy as long as the markets live their lives independently from one another, and globalisation forces have not conspicuously influenced the industry. The challenges arise when globalising competitors start to coordinate their marketing strategies and activities worldwide. With limited market insight and the local marketing expertise mainly bestowed in the local middleman, the HQ has limited opportunities to initiate the necessary learning and maturing processes internally and therefore has little legitimate authority to mandate strategic changes. These companies – to a greater extent than others – tend to be confronted with the not-invented-here syndrome and an unwillingness to cooperate.

Confederation

A confederation is an alliance of independent, sovereign states in a union of common norms and rules in which the operations are defined and carried out by each state. Transferred to the marketing context, a confederation may be considered an extension of the barony situation described above, but the barons' authority and independence are somewhat curtailed. With a high level of market knowledge but low influence and a degree of coordination by the HQ, the company may consciously adopt a local adaptation strategy, being well aware of the consequences of its choice. This strategy is typically adopted by companies operating in markets with considerable cultural differences, and where adaptation is not simply desirable but necessary to achieve satisfactory market shares. European MNEs, such as Nestlé and Unilever, seem to fit into this definition, whereas US-based Procter & Gamble is probably located somewhere towards the borderline between the federation and confederation. The role of the HQ in this case will be one of coordinator more than conductor. However, research from Norway (Solberg 2002b) suggests that intermediaries in this quadrant tend to accept standardised approaches to their local marketing. A possible reason for this is that headquarters – with its deep insights into the different local market situations – is in a position to identify the least common denominators of major markets, and thereby also capable of devising marketing strategies that are accepted by all intermediaries.

In the long run, the development of this kind of MNE may be based on internal networks, in which the company leaves specific functional HQ tasks to units in other countries or particular products or brands are handled by foreign selected subsidiaries, much in line with the world product mandate described by Poynter and White (1984/1985). The individual foreign unit may then draw on certain competencies of other parts of the firm in another country, without necessarily going through HQ. At the same time, this may imply that knowledge about the whole company should be embedded in all parts of the MNE (Hedlund and Rolander 1990).

Federation

In contrast to the confederation, the federation has a strong central power and the individual states have much less authority. This description fits companies such as Coca-Cola, McDonald's and IBM. A paramount feature of their strategy is to operate with a single profile in international markets. The desire to control the development of their brand images and control costs is a stronger driving force for companies in this category than are factors such as local cultural idiosyncrasies (Isdell-Carpenter 1986). The difference between civil war companies and federated companies lies primarily in the ability of the HQ to capture the essence of local market know-how and service its network of sales offices and independent representatives.

Helly Hansen travelling through the matrix

Helly Hansen sells outdoor and casual apparel and had sales in 2014 of around 1.6 billion NOK (160 million euros) (Solberg 2000). The company has three primary groups of products: outdoor sportswear and work wear, and to an increasing extent fashion/streetwear. Sales are divided as follows: Nordic countries 30%, rest of Europe 25%, United States 30% and 15% rest of the world (mostly Asia). In Scandinavia, Helly Hansen has a market leader position, whereas in the rest of Europe it operates with a market share below 5%. However, all the markets are well acquainted with Helly Hansen products. In Germany, for example, brand recognition is around 60% (2013).

Helly Hansen was established already in the 19th century, but did not start to internationalise until after the Second World War. They chose local distributors that typically had a local market in mind, without regard to any potential common story to tell. In fact, the products sold in different countries varied from kids' raingear, to warm clothing for winter sports, to work clothes and yacht gear. Each market developed a network according to the product focus of each distributor, and consequently the brand image differed from one country to the other. During this first phase, the company would typically be placed in the local barons' cell.

In the 1980s and into the 1990s, the high end of the casual wear market had become increasingly more uniform. Two forces in particular were at work in this process: first, a gradually increasing iconolatry of sports idols who represent brand-name labels, and second, active standardised marketing by large brand-name suppliers of sportswear, particularly manufacturers of sports shoes, such as Nike, Adidas and Reebok. This has also occurred in other product areas, such as skis (e.g. Rossignol, Fisher, Head, K2). Such a standardised approach contributed to creating a common market consciousness at the upper levels of the consumer pyramid and thereby a global profile for these products. Other forces of globalisation, such as the internationalisation of media, the concentration of the top tier of the industry and the establishment of international retailer chains, have also played a role. The result of this standardisation has been the establishment of a world sector at the top levels of the sportswear and casual wear market that, mostly, thinks and consumes alike and thereby respond to more or less the same marketing stimuli worldwide.

Helly Hansen reacted relatively late to these trends. It has had, during all this time, a broad collection that has made it possible for the individual sales companies and distributors to market quite different clothes from one market to the next. In other words, Helly Hansen had a collection that was developed on the basis of signals from each market. This led to very different profiles in the various markets. Helly Hansen previously had developed a design manual for the use of logos and letterhead, and the company also had a common set of photographs to be used in its local marketing activities. Nonetheless, the HQ in Norway noted that each local sales company used the logo in its own way, developed its own advertising and point-of-sales material in cooperation with local advertising agencies, and had defined on its own target groups based on the collection it had chosen. Early in the 1990s, Helly Hansen took the initiative to take control of this situation, but management believed, after several years in the red (due to, among other things, an unfortunate investment in a new but ill-defined logistics system), that the company was too vulnerable to oppose the local barons' requests on marketing issues.

Throughout this period, Helly Hansen headquarters in Norway developed relatively good contact with the market and thereby built up a good market understanding of its particular niche. All the same, the company was not able to gain greater centralised control and tighter standardisation of the marketing strategy when it saw the need. Management did not put enough muscle behind its new argument for standardisation when this issue was brought up. Therefore, in 1995, when still in the red, new owners and a new management with a different view on the business logic sought to cut the collection and the cost level, with dramatic consequences for the organisation. Key people were either dismissed, or they left the company, leading to a loss of parts of its market knowledge and understanding. This happened at the same time that the company was seeking to centralise marketing decisions in order to control costs. The result became what can be referred to as a minor civil war, in which top management responded by establishing routines for the participation of local sales forces in the company's strategy development. In 1997, the HQ was in the process of rebuilding market understanding while reasserting control of marketing activities: one advertising agency for the whole world, one common collection for Europe and one for the United States, and a clear vision of a future integrated collection. The company was, in other words, in the process of becoming an actor with a vision of a global market, led by an organisation that thinks and acts, if not yet globally, then at least regionally (United States and Europe).

A change of ownership at Helly Hansen occurred again in the spring of 1997. The Arab investment company Invest Corp entered as a majority shareholder with a clearly defined goal to develop further the value of the Helly Hansen brand. Following up on the initiatives that had already been taken to establish control over the marketing activities was of key importance in this process. It could now claim to have a European and an American collection, and product development responsibility was subsequently given to the marketing directors for the United States and Europe. An important element in this process was to terminate the relations with local advertising agencies that the local subsidiaries had established. The company hired a Swedish advertising agency that had experience with international campaigns for other fashion brands, such as Hennes & Mauritz and Gant. This was a difficult process, because management in the individual sales offices was deprived of a considerable part of its independence. From being managing directors in the local markets, they now became local sales managers, with responsibility for the implementation of strategy. The establishment of a Product Market Council, in which management of the individual sales companies met with marketing management at HQ, was of key importance in this context. The primary role of the PMC is to provide feedback about the marketing strategy, which thereby enabled the individual sales companies to take part in setting the guidelines for their own operations. Nonetheless, it is the HQ that now decides the product collection and the marketing communication and directs the marketing companies to apply the strategy.

The company still struggled to get back into the black. Years of ill-defined marketing strategies and shifting owners with different emphasis on different parts of the value chain (logistics one day, cost-cutting the next and global branding the third) had taken their toll on the organisation. It would take another ten years and new owners to turn the company around. Today Helly Hansen is a well-recognised global brand and enjoys a good reputation for its products.

8.4.2 Control and monitoring levers in international marketing

The locus of decision power, and the authority in the network of partners that the HQ has gained through its market insight, give pointers to the relationships between the exporter and its foreign partners. The latter should however be followed up, controlled and monitored in order to successfully carry out the marketing activities in each local market. To this end, we will discuss two types of control: unilateral and bilateral (Bello and Gilliland 1997).

Unilateral and bilateral controls

Again, we will borrow from agency theory and introduce terms such as post-contractual opportunism, information asymmetry, control and governance. Opportunism in agency theory is defined as a behaviour sought by one of the parties to take advantage of the situation, the other party being unaware of the alternatives. But also another theory string is relevant – relationship governance – with writers representing the IMP[8] school of thought and relational contracting with scholars such as Håkansson and Snehota (1995), and Heide (1994). Bello and Gilliland (1997) claim that there are two ways of curbing opportunism: unilateral control and bilateral control. **Unilateral control** is based on agency theory, where the principal – through different control mechanisms – seeks to align the agent's behaviour with the objectives of the principal.[9] The exporter has two ways of exercising such control:

> *Outcome control* is where the exporter controls the performance of the activity of the agent, such as sales volume, market share, sales growth, financial performance (in the case of a sales subsidiary). This can be done in the form of commission or bonuses that reward the agent according to a set of performance criteria. In this way, the agent, attracted by the rewards, can be enticed to work towards objectives that are common with those of the principal.

> *Behaviour control* is about controlling the concrete activities undertaken by the agent. For instance, through the marketing plan, the agent gets instructions to visit a particular group of customers, to participate at certain trade fairs, to advertise in certain media, etc. Then, these activities are followed up by the principal. The agent gets his/her reward based on the work that is done, independent of the result of the work. In both cases of unilateral controls, one depends on the measurability of the elements that are controlled. This may be challenging in international marketing – and perhaps particularly so regarding behaviour control, where cultural differences can distort information about activities, leading to misinterpretations.

Bilateral control suggests that both parties are involved in the control mechanism. In this case we see elements of trust, loyalty and solidarity in the relationship. This helps to tone down any over-zealous control of outcome or behaviour. The agent's interests are aligned with those of the principal simply because they share the same basic beliefs (in the product or services, the business model, the brand) and they genuinely work to pursue these, regardless of how the rewards are being calculated. Scholars have given this kind of "control" different names: clan control (Ouchi 1977, Solberg 2006b), relational norms (Heide 1994), social control (Aulakh et al. 1996), relational control (de Mortanges and Vossen 1999) or relationalism (Bello et al. 2003). In the following, we will use the term clan control because it denotes some kind of kinship.[10] It is all about establishing an organisational culture that goes beyond the confines of the firm itself, reaching to the agents and dealers, where the exporter – through socialising, and establishment of a set of values and norms – achieves adherence to their goals and, thereby, develops reciprocal trust that in turn will reduce proclivity to opportunistic behaviour.

Solberg (2006d) shows that clan control, taken alone, yields the highest rewards, ahead of outcome control, behaviour control being least effective. However most – if not all –exporters apply a combination of control mechanisms to govern the relations with their partners. The optimal mix will depend on a number of different factors, such as resources, the organisational culture, the role of the market (primary or secondary) and the power balance between the partners. Also, the effects of different control modes vary greatly with the operation mode. For instance, it is obviously easier to build clan control within a hierarchy in a fully-owned sales subsidiary; and it definitely pays off (Solberg 2006d). On the other hand, agents and particularly distributors are better governed through outcome control, whereas behaviour control has negative effects on exporter–distributor relationships. This latter finding is not surprising since the distributor operates more independently of the exporter than the other two, and therefore has no culture of being given instructions. Furthermore, in an introductory phase of the relationship, the clan feel has yet to be established, and outcome control (which is also less demanding of resources) yields the best result. It is only when the relationship is well-established that clan control is rewarding.

Trust – the backbone of relationships.

Trust is generally understood as the willingness to rely on a partner and to have confidence in a partner's integrity. A trusting relationship between partners is, according to Morgan and Hunt (1994), beneficial since it leads to enhanced commitment and cooperation, and alleviates uncertainties (of not having adequate information or about inferior capabilities to make the right decision). Zucker (1986) identifies three bases of trust: process-based trust, emerging from relations and recurring transactions; characteristic-based trust that rests on social similarity; and institution-based trust based on social structures such as referrals, contracts or a legal frameworks. Most of the literature on partner relationships agrees that shared values facilitate trust, and that communication helps to build and secure a trusting relationship (Morgan and Hunt 1994). Hence, trust is also evolving over time – from semi-strong to hard core (Barney and Hansen 1994), from calculative to affective (McAlister 1995), from business relations to friendship (Heide and Wathne 2006).

In principle, trust between two potential partners initially unknown to each other does not exist; indeed mistrust may even exist between them, based on lack of knowledge or prejudices of characteristics, such as nationality. For two or more parties to engage in a relationship, therefore, some trust-initiating mechanisms need to be "activated". This may be referrals from a trusted third party (institution-based), or information obtained through a partner search process, or the trust may be calculative in the sense that the allure of economic benefit may moderate any lack of initial trust between the parties.

The need for such mechanisms is greater in relationship developments between partners from different cultures. For instance, Solberg and Osmanova (2017) find that Russians appear to nurture suspicion and secrecy particularly in the initiating phases of a relationship. These traits are suggested to be an outcome of Russian history (both tsarist and soviet legacies). The boundary-spanning abilities of the parties may compensate for the lack of initial trust, driving the parties towards a decision to commit to the relationship. Then, the experience with this initial relationship will determine the extent to which it will develop into a fruitful one. And, it is indeed at this stage that cultural misunderstandings may impair an otherwise promising business partnership. This is why it is utterly important to prepare oneself for a "bumpy road" to a committed relationship, characterised by economic gains, but also by different kinds of surprises and incidences and interpretations of such incidences, reflecting reactions to cultural differences.

For instance, the Russians' apparent proclivity to nurture suspicion, secrecy and pride may be misinterpreted as opportunistic behaviour by an unknowing Western European partner. Here is the reaction of a Western businessman when asked about these issues: "It is not so easy to create relationships of trust even in the long term. Everything needs to be negotiated. Everything needs to be checked. Otherwise any opportunity the Russians see where they can be opportunistic they will take it." Such a statement is possibly as much an indication of lack of understanding by the non-Russian partner as opportunism by the Russian counterpart. However, this is not necessarily a sign of opportunism the way it has been defined in the literature; it may rather be a part of a negotiation game (Solberg and Osmanova 2017).

Developing a trusting relationship takes time. It is about understanding the partner's business logic, their motivations and strategic goals, and recognising and respecting their ways of doing business.

A foreign businessman recalled from his experience in the Arab world: "In order to land this contract (a large contract in Kuwait) I had to drink tea with my counterpart in the Arab organization several times a week during nine months! We did not necessarily talk about the terms of the contract, rather it was what I would call a courtesy visit in order to forge the relationship and to enhance the trust of the partner". In this way the firm instilled trust in the relationship, the basic foundation for any large contract award. The same businessman had experienced exactly the same in the UAE. Alluding to the importance of relationships, he quoted a Saudi counterpart as saying: "Can you hear the chains? You know from now on you are linked to us with chains!!" (Solberg 2002b).

Accepting the "ways of doing business" should not be interpreted too literally. Even though corruption or what we may term "dubious business practices" may prevail as the "normal way of doing business" in some countries, we would strongly advise against falling for the temptation of giving in to those kinds of practices. Yet, examples abound of firms falling victim to the wrong choices in this way.

One of the most recent examples is the Norwegian telecommunications giant Telenor, which was said to have paid nearly 20 million euros in bribes to obtain licences in Uzbekistan through Vimpelcom, Telenor's partially-owned subsidiary. Similarly, Swedish firm TeliaSonera, which had also been working in the Central Asian region since 2007, was accused of paying about 300 million USD to a company supposedly associated with the Uzbek president's daughter to enter the country's market.[11] According to Transparency International, Uzbekistan's corruption score is 18 out of 100, which puts Uzbekistan in line with the most corrupt countries in the world. Taking into account the relatively low corruption levels of Norway and Sweden (scores 86 and 87 respectively), one might logically assume that the cultural sensitivity of Scandinavians and their willingness to adapt to the host market's conditions despite their home country's societal norms did have a role to play in these scandals.[12]

In essence developing trust is about acknowledging cultural manifestations such as have been discussed in Section 2.3. Understanding the underlying reasons for the observed behaviour helps the partners accept the situation and perhaps accommodate their counterparts, without tainting the relationship. For example, both Arab and Russian managers have been reproached for their lack of planning (Saprykin 2005, Ferraro 1990) and authoritarian leadership styles (Gilbert 2001, Khadra 1990), which may be a frustrating experience for the non-informed foreign business partner. Without an understanding of the background for such potential behaviours (such as history or vicissitudes of nature), it may be difficult to muster resources to entertain a committed relationship. Therefore, the clear advice to all who venture into unchartered waters is preparation: reading history and literature from the country is possibly as important as reading market reports.

The ability to observe, decipher and make sense of cultural differences, and to adapt the behaviour to the partner's expectations, has been termed cultural sensitivity (Shapiro et al. 2008). In a sense it is a learning process, whereby the individual (for example the export manager) accommodates new "orientations to action" (Eckstein 1988) and even internalises the foreign culture's norms and the values of the partner's culture. Studies on cultural sensitivity have been found to be positively associated with performance. It enhances the distributors' commitment (Skarmeas et al. 2002), information exchange and prevents conflict situations (LaBahn and Harich 1997, Pedersen and Rokkan 2006).

The rewards of trust are – as we have seen – commitment and enhanced cooperation. It may lead to friendship and hospitality, and it may confer advantages such as being part of privileged networks. Being part of such networks gives access to what is known in China as *guangxi*. *Guangxi* involves more than trust and develops into what the Chinese call *xinren* – deep trust – through levers such as *bao* (give and take) and *ren quin* (human feelings) (Matthyssens and Faes 2006). This is quite different from the way in which trust has been defined in traditional Western literature by authors such as Morgan and Hunt (1994). In Russia this special relationship is called *blat*. It is by nature reciprocal – *"Ty mne, ya tebe"* ("I will do something for you and you will then do something for me"). From this point of view, *blat* is different from bribery, which usually has a discrete money-based nature. In Arab countries it is called *wasta* (see also page 193 and note 16 on page 217). These practices are embedded in the society and confer on the beholder great advantages, such as access to critical information, access to decision-makers, etc. Foreign businesspeople may indirectly take part in these prerogatives, but not as players actively wielding such power.

Summarising this discussion we believe that initial (low) trust is alleviated by different mechanisms such as referrals, boundary spanners and economic allure, leading to some commitment which – with (positive) experiences – enhances trust, which in turn – through reward mechanisms – reinforces the commitment. The challenge is then to be able to interpret the cultural experiences in a manner that does not damage the relationship and the emerging trust between the partners. Cultural sensitivity helps to speed up the learning process!

Culture and product complexity – two critical contingency factors

Managing relationships with one's partners is about creating a trusting atmosphere. We have seen that different control modes have different effects depending on the operation mode and stage in the export venture. What then does it take to create trust and cooperative attitudes among partners from different cultures? The trust creation process takes different pathways in different cultures. For instance, there is reason to believe that managers in countries scoring high on uncertainty avoidance and power distance are more willing to accept instructions from the exporter, reducing their uncertainty. Similarly, individualism might be related to a need to operate independently of centrally-established policies (Usunier 1996, p. 80). Also, the *role distribution* between the partners may differ, contingent on cultural background: for instance high uncertainty avoidance may speak in favour of the local partner playing a bigger role, since the end customer may feel uneasy if confronted with a sales representative from a different culture. Or – as has been seen in the Middle East – the end customer needs to meet, not only personnel from the exporter, but sometimes the top manager or even the chairman, in order to get reassurance of the sincerity of their involvement (Solberg 2002b).

Also, the nature of the products or services sold affects the partner relations and the effectiveness of control modes. It is easy to accept that a simple product (such as a toothbrush, vegetables or cutlery or any fast moving consumer good) does not need lots of interaction with

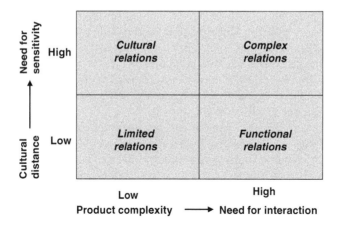

Figure 8.2 Partner relations in international marketing.

Source: Solberg (2007).

the exporter – training, assistance in the sales process, after-sales service, etc. – to be sold successfully in a foreign country. On the other hand, a large-scale project – for instance setting up a petrochemical plant – needs lots of interaction and therefore also quite a different kind of relationship in order to effectively carry out the sales and marketing through the partner. The more complex the product/service, the more interaction is required and the more complex the monitoring of the local partner.

Putting these two dimensions – cultural distance and product complexity – together gives us the matrix in Figure 8.2. The following discussion is based on Solberg (2007).

Generally speaking, clan control pervades the picture, although in varying degrees. For instance, it seems to be less straightforward to establish a clan culture with partners from distant cultures. Exercising outcome control also has a positive effect on relationship quality, but much less so in functional and cultural relations. Behaviour control has virtually no effect across the board when other control modes are used. Including other levers – in particular social bonding, flexibility and information exchange – contributes greatly to enhance the quality of relationships between partners We will now briefly discuss the situation in each of the four cells.

Limited relations

In this quadrant, given the uncomplicated nature of the trading relations, it has been found that social relations with the intermediary yield better returns (higher relationship quality) relative to other mechanisms. Any heavy investments in understanding each other are unwarranted (easy product and close culture), and social bonding is a relatively straightforward way of linking the partners. Also, even though clan control is important, developing social relations significantly reduces its importance. In this quadrant, the role distribution seems to be critical: the partner or subsidiary does not appreciate interference or assistance in carrying out its local marketing activities. These are indeed best carried out locally. Also, worth noticing is the finding that the agent should primarily play a role in the introductory phase of the entry to the market. In later stages the exporter may well consider taking over the bulk of the marketing itself. It is then worthwhile pondering how this may be reflected in the long-term relationship and potential consequences in concrete contract clauses.

Functional relations

Here – with complex products offered through partners in countries with similar cultural backgrounds – the emphasis should be on ascertaining that the partner has a thorough understanding of the products. Therefore, information exchange plays an essential role in relations, and the partners need to take a flexible and problem-solving stance to the dealings. For the same reason, clan control emerges as the most effective monitoring vehicle. An embedded clan culture ensures that the partner does the "right thing" in selling and carrying out the transaction. In this kind of delivery (complicated products) most of the communications between the exporter and the final customer take place between specialists in each firm, sometimes leaving the middleman on the side-line. Therefore, what enhances the partner relations is active participation in the local marketing by the exporter.

Cultural relations

Time and again cultural distance has been shown to be a serious impediment to partner relationships in international business (Ruedi and Lawrence 1970, Hofstede 1980, Zhang et al. 2003, Ivens 2006, Nes et al. 2007). Building a trusting relationship is therefore primarily assured through *personal* understanding – mostly through socialising activities, but also showing a flexible stand to potential misunderstandings that might occur. Clan control is in this context less effective, since building a common clan feel between two distant cultures is difficult. (The following case illustrates this point: for US employees it was quite an eccentric experience to be invited to sing the company song before work started when the Japanese owners tried transferring this ritual to their newly-acquired US subsidiary in order to build a corporate culture.) Furthermore, as opposed to limited relations, the local partner will typically play a long-term role in the relationship.

Complex relationships

The challenges of cultural relations are in this case compounded by the complexity of the delivery (large projects, technologically-advanced products). In this setting, clan control emerges yet again as the most important control mode, more because of the complexity of the product than because of cultural distance. The need for personal relationships through social activity is now superseded by the trust embedded in the clan mechanism. Given the combined challenges of cultural distance and complexity of the delivery, flexibility yet again is a critical factor in the relationship.

In summary, firms often develop their own "theories" on how to treat their partners, based on experience from a limited number of relationships, and transfer this "conviction" across countries without any conscious adaptation to each country. However, as we have seen, managers should be aware of the potential gains in differentiating their handling of relations with their foreign trading partners. Simply put: different situations warrant different treatments. We shall later, in Part III of the book, discuss monitoring and control, relating to the marketing plan and budget in more detail.

Developing a clan culture

Since clan control – or relational norms – appears as critical in most settings, we should discuss how to develop the clan relationship between the partners. We have already considered the importance of partner selection in this context. However, building a close relationship with common values and mutual trust takes time. Solberg (2006b) finds that resources spent on this, in terms of time and money utilised on socialising with the partner – in other words: "wining and dining" in its broadest meaning – are particularly effective. But also, power – to influence the middleman to act according to the interests of the exporter – seems to enhance the effects of clan control. According to French and Raven (1959) there are a number of power sources. We believe that the most critical ones in our context are: identification power (buying into the concept: brand, know-how, patent), expert power (your sales depend on our competence), reward power (bonuses, commissions, royalties) and legal (coercive) power (hierarchy, contracts, laws). Furthermore, an accommodating attitude to solve unexpected problems, flexibility – even if it deviates from the initial terms of the contract – contributes positively to establish good relationships (as opposed to zealously interpreting the contract).

Joint meetings between the exporter and its local representatives in different countries are an important means to build relationships and ensure adherence to the firm's business philosophy. The anecdote below illustrates the lengths the Norwegian firm Håg (swivel chairs) went to in order to create enthusiasm within a group of dealers from Sweden. The firm had developed a passion for their products among many of their dealers, and called themselves "Hågians":[13]

> This Hågian "movement" and culture was being nurtured by the main owner and managing director, Mr. Grimsrud's eccentric impulses. For example, he invited all the Swedish dealers to come to their main plant in Røros, Norway, in the middle of February, the coldest month in this region with temperatures well into the minus 30s (Centigrade). Half-way from the Stockholm Airport he had made sure that the pilot on the chartered plane made a 360 degrees turn – announcing over the PA system that Røros Airport was closed due to fog and that they were diverted to some obscure airport in the middle of nowhere at the Kola peninsula. Landing then (on schedule) at Røros (alias Kola) airport all the dealers came shuddering out of the plane, convinced that they were close to "Siberia", a conviction that was reinforced by the fact that the airport had banners in the Russian language and scores of Russian cars in the parking lot (Mr. Grimsrud had in fact managed to get virtually all the Ladas in the community to join in this extraordinary practical joke). Then entering the arrival hall, they were met with a booth where vodka and snacks were served in abundance ... To the (positive) surprise of the dealers, they finally realised that they were actually at Røros Airport.

We should warn that this kind of practical joke will probably not go down well with all kinds of cultures.

Joint meetings are often held in conjunction with a major event, for instance a trade fair or a conference. Here, the industry in general meets its peers, exhibits its innovations and exchanges views on trends. Spending one or two days extra – before or after the event – with dealers, agents and sales subsidiaries can enhance the whole atmosphere within the exporter's network. Others organise within-firm study programmes or sales meetings with participants from across the world, in order to instil members with the philosophies of the firm. Some may claim that such meetings are onerous and too general to be helpful to the individual participant. Against this argument, we claim that such "plenary" meetings facilitate the transfer of new impulses, best practices and give a family feel to the whole group of middlemen. Still, this kind of general meeting is quite costly and may not be for the small exporter.

8.5 Monitoring and control in different strategic situations

Different strategic situations may influence the way in which the exporter treats their network of middlemen, be they sales subsidiaries, agents or distributors. Figure 8.3 gives a rough idea of the different approaches.

Let your local partners do the job

In this cell, the exporter has little experience and limited market knowledge, and operates in an environment where there are few threats of global competitors entering their market. The markets are *not* interlinked and the main competitors are most likely local. The local distributor is probably larger and more powerful than the exporter. Here the advice is clear: do not try to coordinate the marketing effort between markets (they are not interlinked); do not try to standardise your marketing programmes (the markets are very dissimilar); and do not give detailed instructions to your local partner (you do not have credible insight). In other words: let the local middleman operate relatively freely without too much interference (no behaviour control). However, the exporter should also monitor the partners, mostly through outcome control (more straightforward and less costly), and through socialising activities in order to build personal relationships, and later – when the exporter has gained legitimate power in the relations – create the foundations of an emerging clan culture.

Confer and monitor – but allow local implementation

Here the exporter still operates in a multi-local setting, but has a very different starting point, with a comfortable position in some markets and also good experience from international marketing. Coordination is not really warranted, given the "multi-locality" of the industry. On the other hand, the experience gained from several markets may help the exporter to enter into fruitful strategic discussions with the local middleman. The firm is in a position to start developing a clan culture, and may in this way be able to bridge differing local viewpoints that initially make any standardised approach to marketing difficult. The market position, the market insight, and possibly also the strengths of the brand confer power on the exporter in his

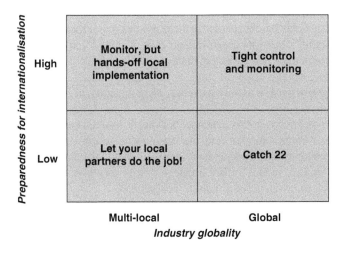

Figure 8.3 Monitoring and control in four strategic situations.

Table 8.2 The perennial dispute between centre and periphery

Headquarters concerns	Subsidiary concerns
Our subsidiaries are bad marketers; they cannot sell what we develop	Our HQ develops products that nobody needs
Unless we constantly control our subsidiaries, we run risks, synergies are not exploited and things get out of hand	We get 200 visits a year and we have to fill out dozens of forms; I don't have time to get my job done!
Very often our strategies are not executed at the local level	HQ strategies are unrealistic; they completely disregard the local realities
Our HQ is getting bigger and bigger and we get less and less done!	I have enough bosses to do what I think is best

or her dealings with the local partner. Monitoring through clan and outcome control seems to be advisable.

Catch 22

In this position, the exporter is small and internationally inexperienced, and vulnerable to globalisation forces. Normally they need to be associated with one or perhaps a few strong partners with networks covering several markets. Whatever the need in terms of coordination between the markets, partners are in a much better position to carry it out. With limited resources, the firm will struggle to embark on a necessary learning process – at least in an introductory phase. Outcome control is considered the only control mode possible for this strategic position. Nevertheless, the exporter should evaluate the strength of their products, services, technology and/or business model in order to create some kind of power base. In addition, socialising with the partner may provide some additional strength in this context.

Tight control and monitoring

In this cell, the firm is among global market leaders with extensive coverage in major markets. Also, it is operating in a global market setting, often involving global customers as well as global competitors. These firms play "global chess" in the sense that major markets are seen as pawns on a large "checkerboard", their role depending on each other and that of competitors. Coordination and control in each market are essential in this context, giving vital market insight to headquarters in order to leverage scale advantages and opportunities across markets. However, this is not straightforward, and the sequence of complaints in Table 8.2 is, if caricatured, not uncommon.

Developing a clan culture is critical in this instance, because it reduces the costs of introducing meticulous, unilateral control modes, and the subsequent grumbling by important partners – be they owned subsidiaries or independent intermediaries. Still, the firm needs to apply a broad repertoire of control modes – also unilateral – with an emphasis on outcome control, in order to keep track of developments in each local market.

8.6 Switching partners and operation modes

The internationalisation process as described in Chapter 3 depicts a trajectory towards more committed and integrated operation modes as firms gain experience in international markets.

Following the considerations in the Strategic Windows discussed earlier, the firm needs to evaluate not only its operation modes, but also how it relates to its partners. Several motives may prompt such a switch:[14]

1   The firm is dissatisfied with the existing mode or partner, and wants to secure direct control in the individual local market and to carry out their marketing activities on their own. This is particularly the case in what we may term intra-mode switches (for example agent to agent, distributor to distributor).
2   The exporter decides that the intermediary is too big, and has too much power in the relationship. The exporter considers that its products are neglected by the intermediary. Also in such cases the switch is mostly intra-modal.
3   The exporter needs to assert its role in the market as the market becomes more important in the firm's portfolio – from secondary to primary market – and invests in its own sales subsidiary.
4   The firm wants to gain hands-on experience in its international operations, in preparation for further steps in its internationalisation process.
5   The market is growing, rendering direct control more attractive and economically feasible. Conversely, an economic downturn in the market may force the firm to close down or reduce its activities – including a less committed operation mode.
6   The host country changes tack in its policies towards foreign investments, offering opportunities to achieve better control through ownership in local operations.

Studies from Denmark (Petersen et al. 2006) and Norway (Solberg 2010) suggest that the most frequent mode changes involve replacement of one independent intermediary with another one (shifting partner, or shifting from distributor to agent), and from an intermediary to own sales subsidiary. Terminating a relationship is, however, not straightforward and may lead to undesirable situations.

First, contractual restrictions – including clauses on severance payments – may deter the exporter from terminating the contract, and lead to an unfavourable maintenance of the relationship. We have already discussed this in the previous section (customer loyalty follows the intermediary not the exporter, indemnities, and the need to rebuild market network). Pedersen et al. (1997) have shown that this is one of the most important deterrents to termination of intermediary relationships.

Second, in a rebuild phase, the firm may lose sales to competitors (sometimes taking over the rejected middleman). As a preparation to forestall such development, the exporter should first and foremost build market insight by regular visits to and follow up of local customers. Also, it should make a concrete plan on how to (re)conquer customers through alternative channels (new dealers, e-marketing, direct sales). Gripsrud et al. (1999) found that it generally takes two years before the exporter is "back to normal" after a contract termination.

Third, the specific investments, both in the relationship with the partner and in physical assets (i.e. storage facilities) or administrative routines, will dissuade the exporter's preparedness to change partner/operation mode. Such investments are made by both partners – the exporter *and* the middleman. The middleman's specific investments will, in principle, lead to a cooperative stance towards the exporter (for fear of losing the agency) – and will therefore also contribute to resistance to end the relationship. A contractual clause indemnifying the middleman in case of termination will then restore a balance.

Petersen et al. (2006) call this situation the termination dilemma; a dilemma for both partners:

–   For the middleman, it is about how much he or she should invest in local marketing activities on behalf of the principal, and how successful should those marketing activities become before he or she becomes a hostage to threats of termination by the exporter. If they are performing too well, they will be replaced by the exporter's own sales subsidiary, the latter seeking to accrue the gains of economies of scale; if underperforming, they will be replaced by another middleman.
–   For the exporter, the dilemma is somewhat different: if they invest too much in training, storage facilities and relationship activities in general, they risk becoming too dependent on the middleman, and thus a victim of potential opportunistic behaviour of the partner. Given the problems relating to contract termination, they are inclined to delay ending the relationship. If they do not invest in the relationship, the middleman will prioritise other principals and their products.

Petersen et al. (2000) suggest a model of four different strategies to meet the situations described above. An important issue in this context is whether the exporter should reveal or conceal their strategic intentions vis-à-vis the middleman: integrate (i.e. acquire the middleman) or terminate the relationship – see Figure 8.4.

While the exporter in the cell "Open relations" clearly announces already at contract entry that the relationship is not expected to last "for ever" and that they will at some stage invest in their own local subsidiary, they equally clearly declare in a "Letter of intent" that their objective is to take over the middleman's activities at one point in time – for example in five to six years, pending the development of the relations. A risk in this latter case is that a critical or even cantankerous partner may force the exporter to a hostile buy-out, key personnel may quit and eventually establish a competing business; not a good starting point for carrying on the operations.

Another risk of revealing one's intentions is that the local partner will not wholeheartedly invest as much in the relationship – for instance in training, sales and marketing activities. In this case, the exporter may offer participation in the form of cost-sharing or indemnities at the end of the relationship.

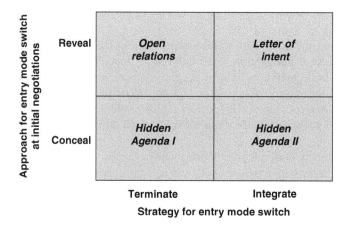

Figure 8.4 Approaches to partner and operation mode switch.

Source: Based on Petersen et al. (2000).

Concealing one's strategic intentions (Hidden agenda I and II) is possibly relevant in cases where the exporter has not a clear opinion on future developments in the market, or where the transfer of technology is critical. However, the exporter may be forced to flag their intentions because the counterpart raises the issue during negotiations. Playing with open cards, then, may endanger an otherwise fruitful negotiation climate, where the potential partner will re-evaluate the whole business concept. In some cultures (Arab countries, for instance), airing the conditions for termination of the relationship according to the above schema before even entering into it is generally unheard of and may ruin the atmosphere. However, revealing its intention to integrate is in many instances a natural strategy because "it is on the cards" – based on the exporter's record in other markets.

> The Danish toymaker Lego has used both conceal and reveal approaches in its negotiations with partners in South East Asia. They operated a number of fully-owned sales subsidiaries (in Hong Kong and Singapore), but the distribution was taken care of by local, independent distributors. In Taiwan, Indonesia and the Philippines, they adopted a Hidden agenda II strategy (concealing intentions to integrate), whereas in Thailand, Malaysia and China opted for an openness about their intentions to take over the local sales (mainly by taking over key sales people). Sometimes they have taken over both marketing and sales, leaving the logistics function to their former marketing partner (Petersen et al. 2000).

Whatever the termination strategy, the exporter should make every effort to nurture fruitful and proactive relations with their foreign partner. The day will eventually come when – for different reasons – the relationship is going to end; better then to do it amicably and with as little hassle as possible.

8.7 Chapter summary

This chapter has emphasised the importance of relationships with one's foreign marketing partners, first by selecting the right partners, then by developing the contractual foundations for the relationships, and, eventually, by nurturing and furthering these relationships. The essence of relationship building is to develop trust between the partners. Innumerable articles and anecdotes tell us about mechanisms that foster trust: honesty, flexibility, communications and shared values, but also control (not necessarily because of mistrust, but in order to be able to follow up). A key term is here "clan control" – which is essentially a common set of values, norms and worldviews that help guide the decisions of the individual partner. Instilling a clan culture throughout the organisation is both rewarding and challenging: rewarding, in that strategy is more straightforwardly developed and implemented in local markets; challenging, because the international parts of the firm, including a diversity of countries, have different management cultures and practices – and because independent partners have their own agenda. We have discussed some models that may help managers prescribe the correct "medicine" given different market situations. Finally, we have described critical issues in ending partner relationships. The essence is here to prepare for the eventuality already in the contract, and reduce the negative consequences of a mode switch.

Notes

1 This paragraph is an excerpt from a report by the author in 1998, "Arabian Nights: Buyer behavior in Arab countries", Research Report, Norsk Institutt for Markedsforskning NiM.

2 Agency theory is a popular string of economic science that endeavours to explain economic behaviour of partners. In its origin, it studied the relationship between owners of a firm and its managers (Jensen and Meckling 1976), but has now expanded into virtually every kind of governance relationship (boss–employee, seller–dealer, alliance partners, etc.). In the present context we apply the theory to the exporter–local middleman relationship. In spite of its name (agency theory), it deals with any kind of relationship between economic actors, including distributors, dealers, trading houses, etc. – and of course, agents as they have been described in the present text. The theory has also been termed principal–agent theory, in our context the exporter being the principal.

3 Cited from Sveaas and Thorstensen (2013).

4 International Chamber of Commerce publishes a number of so-called "model contracts" that can be used as a starting point for most commercial relationships: International sales of goods, licensing, franchising, acquisition, etc. ICC's homepage: https://iccwbo.org/. Also Rigault (2011), gives examples of different contracts relating to international commercial relations.

5 This section is based on Rigault (2011).

6 http://europa.eu/rapid/press-release_IP-02-1584_en.htm?locale=en

7 This provision is important. There are cases of exporters who pay commission to the agent before the payment from the final customer has been effectuated, and where no such payment is made. This is called a *del credere* provision, implying that no commission is disbursed to the agent before payment from the customer is received, thus ascertaining that the agent is pursuing orders from solvent customers.

8 IMP=International (or industrial) marketing and purchasing.

9 Just a reminder: agency theory talks about the principal in several different guises, be it owners, employers, exporters, licensors or the head of the organisation, the agent occurring in the form of any subordinate, and in the case of exporting/international marketing: agent, distributor, sales manager of a subsidiary, licensee and so on.

10 According to Wikipedia a clan is "a group of people united by actual or perceived kinship and descent . . . clan members may be organized around a founding member . . . The kinship-based bonds may be symbolic, whereby the clan shares a 'stipulated' common ancestor that is a symbol of the clan's unity."

11 Richard Milne, "Telia to cop $1.4 bn fine over corruption in Uzbekistan", *Financial Times*, 15 September 2016.

12 Sources:

   1. http://www.vg.no/nyheter/meninger/mobil-og-tele/telenor-og-usbekistan/a/23338555/
   2. https://www.nrk.no/norge/slik-havnet-telenor-i-klisteret-i-usbekistan-1.12635559
   3. http://e24.no/boers-og-finans/telia/usbekistan-oppgjoer-svir-for-telia/23826181

13 Hågians (in Norwegian Hågianere) – with a clear connotation of the dedicated religious sect called Haugianere (Haugians) after its leader Hans Nielsen Hauge, the charismatic Norwegian protestant lay preacher and entrepreneur who lived at the turn of the 18th century.

14 See: Calof and Beamish (1995), Pedersen et al. (1997), Benito et al. (1999), Petersen et al. (2006), Solberg (2010).

9   Standardisation and adaptation of international marketing

9.1 Introduction

The discussion on global standardisation or local market adaptation is one of the key issues in international marketing. Intuitively, it is easy to understand that the firm should adapt to local tastes and requirements and that these are in immediate conflict with the central demands of rationalisation and scale economies leading to standardised solutions – both in marketing and manufacturing. In this chapter, we shall discuss this conflict and its causes, and give examples of how it has been solved in different firms. In subsequent chapters, on the marketing mix elements, we shall return to the discussion and explore how each of them is affected by the conflict.

9.2   A perennial dilemma

Examples are the bounty of firms that do not take this discussion seriously. Based on what we may call ethnocentric myopia, many firms use their domestic market experience as a pointer in their international market expansion. Below is an account of a Norwegian brewery, Mack's, and their efforts to enter the US market.[1]

> Throughout the 1980s, the US market for imported beer witnessed a phenomenal growth – some 10% per year, whereas the total beer market grew by less than 3%. After repeated requests from a local agent, Mack's eventually decided to try to take part in this development. However, things were not straightforward. After some time of slow sales, they decided to reassess their "American adventure". They received the following report (abridged):
>
>   First, the question of "agent selection" was raised. There are pros and cons of "jumping on a floating board" and we shall not delve into this issue more than referring to Section 8.2 in this text, where we discuss partner selection in more detail. Next, the report pointed towards the undifferentiated approach to the "American market" as if it were just one market. In reality, the US consists of a vast amount of markets, each representing greater volumes than Mack's home market. Individual states such as Wisconsin, Minnesota and Washington (with large populations of Norwegian ancestry) and cities in those states (Madison, Minneapolis and Seattle) may have a positive attitude towards Norwegian (and Scandinavian) products. Furthermore, beer consumption varies quite a lot from one state to the other – especially concerning imported beer. This class of beer is typically premium priced as compared with "domestic beer", and has a greater appeal to high-income groups of consumers.

The beer was initially introduced as Norwegian. This may be a good sales argument for the most "Norwegianised" parts of the US (there are more than 4 million people of Norwegian ancestry there), but will probably be without any value for other areas. On the other hand, the concept of "Scandinavia" has strong, positive connotations in the general American population and is also used as the country of origin for many Norwegian products.

Then, the bottle: in order not to interrupt the daily production process of the brewery, management decided to use the ordinary, small and brown bottles used in Norway. Tests in the local American market showed that this was way off the target! Brown beer bottles epitomise local beer, whereas imported (premium) beer is typically found in green bottles with a high neck. On the neck, a label indicating "Imported beer" should show that the person can not only afford the imported beer, but also is a sophisticated beer drinker who knows "What real beer drinkers want." Interestingly though, taste-testing reveals that even those with clear preferences for imported beer had difficulty discerning imported from local American beer. The brewery strongly advocated the brown bottle as it is apparently better able to keep the quality of the beer much longer than green bottles, and therefore would sustain a longer shelf life – which might well be needed with a high priced beer that most would believe to be local. The brewery missed yet another problem: American consumers no longer use a bottle opener and so were quite surprised and irritated when they were not able to twist off the cap.

The next question concerned the name on the label, "Mack's Polar Bear Beer". The brewery did not realise that Mack is the dominant truck brand in the US, and that a beer with this name would risk being called a truck driver's beer; not necessarily a disadvantage in general (as many truck drivers supposedly drink beer). But for a premium imported brand the question may be different.

The name was later changed to "Arctic beer" with a large polar bear as the eye-catching label.

This anecdote reveals at least two matters of importance: first, it shows how managers gradually gain market insight through experience: what works, what does not work. Second, it demonstrates how consumers with basically the same need can develop widely different preferences based on marginal differences, such as the colour of the bottle, or the length of the bottleneck. Yet, such differences are critical and may determine success or failure in a new market. For other kinds of products, such differences may be far less consequential. Between these two product categories, there are innumerable products that in the main are similar from one country to the other, but which still have different functional solutions.

Tommy Hilfiger's struggle and ensuing volte-face in Europe is an interesting account of the market adaptation of a brand that epitomises global branding.

From their website in 2017 we can read that "Tommy Hilfiger is a [US-based] global apparel and retail company with more than 17,000 associates worldwide. With the support of strong global consumer recognition, Tommy Hilfiger has built an extensive distribution network in over 115 countries and more than 1,600 retail stores throughout North America, Europe, Latin America and the Asia Pacific region. Global retail sales of the *Tommy Hilfiger* brand were US $6.5 billion in 2015."

Back in 1999 Tommy Hilfiger's management realised that something had to happen to its product line in Europe. Hilfiger began its push into Europe in 1997, and took some hard knocks. Mr. Hilfiger, then at the height of his popularity in America, stormed into London in 1999 with a new store on Bond Street and a gala featuring celebrities such as the model Kate Moss and actress Goldie Hawn.

The road to global markets has however not been free of bumps and adjustments. The company was founded in 1985 and grew rapidly to become one of the favourite fashion brands in the US with sales peaking at 1.9 billion USD in 2000. Sales growth in its US home market had however dwindled, and further growth prospects in this market were bleak. Department stores were consolidating and introducing their own brands. In addition, the company faced competition from upstarts such as urban-wear labels Sean John and Rocawear and the racy Abercrombie & Fitch. Fashion editors, believing Hilfiger's fashion moment had passed, largely ignored the brand.

Recognising that further growth had to take place in other markets, they launched the brand in Europe with a fanfare, "storming" into London in 1999. The Hilfiger organisation "gave in to the demands" from retailers eager to stock the hot products. They flooded stores with too much merchandise but sales did not take off.

It was not enough to enter department stores (the pillar of their US distribution strategy) such as Galleries Lafayette in France or Cortés Inglés in Spain. They also wooed small independent accounts – some 4,500 of them in 15 European countries. "The fragmentation of dealing with all these little mom-and-pop stores is so alien to American businesses," Mr. Gehring, the European vice-president at the time, recalls in an interview with the *Wall Street Journal*. "Yet these stores are the backbone of every major brand." Consequently, and in contrast to other US fashion houses that centralised distribution in Europe, they built showrooms in 21 locations across Europe, increasing operating costs but also attracting the "grass-root" retailers and meeting competitors on their own terms. For instance, their largest German players had showrooms in all six major towns in Germany. The extra costs were offset by higher prices in Europe.

They also acknowledged that the products had to be adapted to the more sophisticated European audience. They used high quality cotton in their shirts – realising that Europeans were willing to pay for quality; they switched their cotton knit sweater sold in the US to lamb's wool knit jerseys in Europe; they gave the European jeans a slimmer silhouette than those sold in the US ("Baggy jeans didn't sell in Europe"); and reduced the oversized flag (their logo). They also adjusted their brand strategy to target an older customer group – 25–40 years, as opposed to teens in the US.[2]

It is a popular assertion that industrial products and services are more standardised across the world as compared with consumer goods. This is not necessarily true, partly because of technical and/or political requirements (which are increasingly being internationalised – but not fully), be it pharmaceutical products (different strength of active compounds), climatic factors (offshore oil drilling equipment in the North Sea as compared with the Gulf of Mexico), or traditions (electrical devices such as sockets and plugs).

One might believe that a plough is a plough whether it is sold in Sweden or in Portugal. That is however not the case. One of the world's leading plough manufacturers, the

Japanese-owned Kverneland, supplies ploughs to a wide range of countries. For every new country, they have to develop new variants with regard to:

- Traditions (How deep will it plough? How is the soil thrown out of the ground?)
- The quality of the earth (sandy, pebbles/stones, clay, etc.)
- Climate (rain, drought, seasons).

The standardisation–adaptation issue is not only related to the apparent conflict between cultural and economic (cost/scale) prerequisites, but is also directly associated to internal organisational problems within the firm. The case described below illustrates how firms may address the challenges, how their perception of the problem evolves over time, and how their own decisions constrain their freedom of action through the structures (partners, acquisitions) built around their international marketing.

Export Products Ltd[3] in the UK has grown rapidly in foreign markets over the past few years, with the aid of an active network of partners. The partners have focused on different kinds of customer groups in different markets and given feedback to the exporter that the products are being well-received, but that sales volumes will increase markedly if the firm adapts the products and the marketing to local market conditions in order to match competitors and a slightly different local taste. The exporter responds positively and, as a consequence, sales increase. First in Ireland, then in the Netherlands, and then further on in Europe and overseas. The problem is that as the firm responds positively to the partners' requests to adapt, it also slowly and surely develops different profiles in each market. In an attempt to control the development, the firm eventually takes over the marketing in some key markets and establishes sales subsidiaries, whereas in other markets it buys out the local distributor.

To their astonishment, top management discover that local managers of the wholly-owned subsidiaries are not as loyal to the ideas developed at the centre as expected. These managers are after all the ones that keep a constant eye on the local market, and therefore are the best ones to develop the local marketing strategies and activities. They sometimes operate more as petty kings (or local barons as suggested in Figure 8.1), and they are prone to secure their own independence from any involvement from the centre.

And if this was not enough, the firm has, in the process, acquired two competitors – one in France and another one in Belgium, both countries being regarded as difficult markets. Therefore it is considered more advantageous to expand in these markets by acquiring established firms, rather than trying to force oneself on to the market with own brands. But how should the firm tackle the diversity of profiles that has developed in their different markets? It is after all rather irrational to operate with several brands in their different markets, particularly because they are pretty close to each other in usage, target group and positioning. In addition, they find that their main competitors have started to coordinate their international marketing activities. The answer was so obvious that it hit the CEO between his eyes: the firm had to centralise development of their international marketing strategies, including product development and brand positioning, so as to get control over their operations. At one point, the marketing manager had, in her frustration, exclaimed: "Look at all these product pamphlets and brochures; they look more like a bunch of weekly magazines on display in a well-stocked airport news stand!"

How could this happen? If we go back some years, we will find that initially, exporting was seen as a marginal part of the firm's operations. An export manager was employed and she would soon become responsible for Ireland, the Netherlands and Scandinavia. After some very prosperous years, sales reached some 30 million pounds, half of which was made abroad. Later, a new export co-worker joined the firm, responsible for the rest of Europe; and then yet another one, to take care of other overseas markets. Today the firm's total sales reach some 60 million pounds, most of which is in Europe, but also more than 15 million overseas. The domestic market makes up some 12 million pounds.

The ill-fated problem for this firm was that during its gradual growth into international markets it had not developed sufficient capacity or ability to perceive, receive and interpret the information from all its markets, or to translate this information into marketing decisions and activities that took the whole firm into consideration. This was left to the local market networks, and it was the local partners that in reality developed the marketing strategy of the firm. However, these partners have a different perspective from that of the exporter. Their main emphasis is on *sales volume in the local market* more than what happens in other markets. So, what initially was a scarce resource – management competence in international markets – became a strategic dilemma, since their strategy developed into one that spread out in all directions.

Even though this description is somewhat caricatured, we believe that many exporters recognise the pattern. Other scenarios are possible. For instance, Prahalad and Doz (1981), Forsgren and Holm (1990) and Ghauri (1990) observe how power gradually transfers to the periphery in large multinationals. As the subsidiary develops its own local market network and deepens its relations with its network partners, it also develops an urge to build local strategies – in defiance of directions from the centre. Once again, we get an illustration of the importance of monitoring and control in international marketing.

A study of 53 medium-sized Norwegian exporters of branded goods shows that the local representatives in fact have a greater say in many export decisions – in particular the selection of media and advertising agency and local adaptation (Jensson and Lintho 1994). The exporter was mostly in charge of general strategy and communication budgets. We also notice that cooperation between the exporter and its subsidiary/partner is not prevalent in this sample, except for one item: communications platform. Table 9.1 shows the detailed results, and illustrates a very telling story about how different firms address their international marketing strategies.

This chapter deals primarily with product (product, brand, positioning) and market communications (message, creative solutions, media, sales force, sales promotions) in general. We will deal with these in more detail in other chapters. Figure 9.1 indicates four main strategic approaches to this issue. First, dual adaptation, suggesting that both the product *and* the market communications are adapted to the local market situation. This strategy is the most onerous one in terms of costs and management attention. Diagonally opposite is the straight extension or dual standardisation – implying no adaptation of either marketing mix element. Virtually no firm will adopt this theoretical and extreme case. In most cases, firms need to do some adaptation of both product (to comply with local regulations) and/or communications (language), but strive to keep this at a minimum in order to attain scale economies offered by standardised solutions.

Table 9.1 Who is in charge here?

Main influence on decision	Decision						
	Selection of advertising agency	Local market research	Marketing budget	Media selection	Local adaptation	Communication platform	Market strategy
Headquarters	40	43	50	21	26	37	57
Cooperation	16	26	18	26	24	38	19
Subsidiary/ partner	44	31	32	53	50	25	24

Source: Jensson and Lintho (1994).

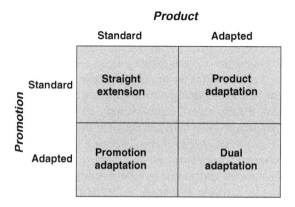

Figure 9.1 Four adaptation/standardisation strategies in international marketing.

Two other strategies are: product adaptation and promotion adaptation. Local customisation is a variant of local adaptation, the difference being that the exporter does not use the domestic product and marketing programme as a starting point for the adapted product. Rather, the product is created for the specific export market, and the marketing programme is tailored to the new product. It is all about taking the local consumers seriously, and requires in-depth insight in order to create a new product with a new positioning in the market. Adaptation on the other hand is less consequential; it is rather about making changes to the existing domestic product and exporting a variant that holds more or less the same benefits, usages, target groups and positioning.

On the other hand, examples abound of firms that seek standardisation, and which succeed in doing so – be they McDonald's, Coca-Cola, H&M, Gant or Yves Saint Laurent and many other well-known brands. Common to these firms is their dominant position in their respective markets.

In the next section we will discuss different theoretical and empirical contributions to this area of study.

9.3 Standardisation or adaptation: a never-ending debate

The debate over the standardisation versus adaptation of international marketing strategy has been going on for more than 50 years, addressing the issue from different perspectives and applying various approaches to test the feasibility and effectiveness of either strategy alternative.[4] Nevertheless, the results and conclusions still seem unsettled and often contradictory.

The existence of between-country differences, be it in legal, economic or cultural terms, is bound to influence firms' operations worldwide. Still, many researchers and practitioners believe that the forces of globalisation make such distinctions less and less significant. One of the most cited proponents of the globalisation of markets, Levitt (1983), sees technological development and globalisation as the drivers of demand homogenisation and opportunities for operating on a worldwide scale. Supporters of this logic view standardisation of a firm's international strategy as a natural step, which is made possible and economically effective by the growing similarity in world markets and therefore possibilities of economies of scale. They argue that standardisation is facilitated through availability of international communication channels, transportation and global media, trade liberalisation and growing international travel (Theodosiou and Leonidou 2003). Often such benefits of the standardised approach such as economies of scale, uniformity of the corporate/brand image, learning effects and less complex management processes are mentioned.

Opposing this line of thought are the proponents of adaptation, arguing that national differences across countries have not diminished with the advancement of globalisation, but continue to thrive.[5] They stress the fact that a firm's goal is not only to provide a lower price, but to satisfy its customers in the long run, thus implying a thorough understanding of and catering to the varying needs and requirements of consumers across countries. They stress that tailoring a firm's proposition to local idiosyncrasies will allow it to gain a larger market share and increase growth potential.

To bridge these polar views on international marketing strategy a new perspective, often termed contingency perspective, has emerged. It generally addresses the issues of standardisation and adaptations as extreme cases on a single continuum, where the optimal decision lies somewhere in the middle, and a firm's task is to achieve a fit between the company's strategy, internal characteristics and the specific environment in which it operates. This usually implies "breaking down" the overall international strategy into specific elements. The feasibility of applying standardisation or adaptation can then be considered. The contingency perspective, broadly speaking, seems to have become the dominating view for most researchers of the topic of standardisation vs. adaptation, since most recognise the impossibility of applying any one of them in the "pure form". It has been noted that studies inclined towards contingency view constitute a majority of all literature – their relative share growing consistently over the years (Waheeduzzaman and Dube 2004).[6]

We will apply the approach used by Theodosiou and Leonidou (2003), first addressing the forces that influence the firm's decisions to standardise or adapt its international marketing strategy, then viewing the possible strategic choices and the impact of such decisions on firm performance.

9.3.1 *Influencing factors*

Various researchers have tried to identify and classify factors that affect a firm's choice to standardise its marketing activities. For instance, Ozsomer et al. (1991) classify such factors into three broad categories: *host country environment* (evaluating the differences between the home and host country in terms of infrastructure and legal practice), *product-related marketing factors* (marketing mix, local vs. international branding, product life-cycle stage, target consumers) and *subsidiary-related factors* (centralisation vs. decentralisation of decision-making, industry, ownership structure, sales volume). Their study of MNCs in Turkey allowed them to conclude that there are different levels of standardisation for various elements of the marketing mix (product-related elements seemed to be the most standardised, while distribution and retail pricing were more susceptible to adaptation). They found that similarities between the operating environments in the home and host countries (competitive, legal environments, distribution infrastructure), target consumer segments, product life-cycle stage and headquarters' control (strength in making marketing decisions) generally led to higher levels of standardisation across the marketing mix elements. These findings are supported by other studies (Douglas and Wind 1987, Walters 1986, Cavusgil and Zou 1994). Research generally promotes a view that certain *types of products* such as industrial goods or luxury items present more opportunities for standardisation (Douglas and Wind 1987). Rosen et al. (1989) found that – over a 15-year period – American exporters of industrial products to Europe increasingly standardised their offerings, whereas the picture was a bit more nuanced concerning B2C (Business to Consumer) products, supporting this view. For grocery products the trend was towards more adaptation, while at the same time the development for consumer capital goods was a higher degree of standardisation. Solberg (2014) suggests two product categories relating to this discussion:

1   Products that have been developed in a certain cultural context and satisfy basic needs, such as food, clothes, shelter and rituals (weddings, birthdays, holidays, etc.). These are products that are local, idiosyncratic solutions to generic needs that have found their shape and function over generations, based on local resources and traditions. One example is given in Table 9.2, showing how breakfast is composed in different countries.These "solutions" to the "breakfast problem" may eventually be influenced by globalisation trends, but still seem quite resilient to external factors.

2   Products that have been developed over the past 50–60 years, typically after the Second World War. These are the same whether they are sold in Paris or in Tashkent. The PC and the mobile phone are archetypal, where no previous consumption pattern has been allowed to develop independently in each country or region, and where the standards of local manufacturers have not therefore had the chance to set a norm. These products have been created in a period when scale economies have not only been possible, but also vital for the competitiveness of their manufacturers, forcing them to go beyond their domestic markets. A more open trading regime has made sales of such innovations possible to all corners of the world. Even though the products are used differently in various countries, this is of little consequence for their manufacturers.[7]

While proponents of standardisation name the increasing homogenisation of demand worldwide and opportunities for cost reduction through economies of scale as important antecedents to standardisation, critics claim that these are not so straightforward (Douglas and Wind 1987). First, they argue that there is no proof of a *universal* trend towards demand homogenisation. Although such tendencies may exist in some industries/product categories,

Table 9.2 Breakfast in different countries

Country	Food	Drinks
England	Egg and bacon	Tea or coffee
France	Baguette and jam, croissant	Expresso or café au lait
Italy	Croissant	Espresso or café latte
China	Rice pudding	Green tea
Scandinavia	Open sandwich or muesli	Coffee
USA	Cornflakes or pancakes	Coffee

substantial regional and country differences have been found to thrive. For example, Walters (1986) states that, even if identification of international market segments displaying similarities in lifestyles and attitudes were possible, it would not imply that consumer behaviour in these segments is uniform, since it is largely affected by the context in which consumers operate.[8] Furthermore, these authors argue that the emphasis placed on the importance of a low product price for consumers is overrated, for there is no evidence that a majority of consumers are willing to substitute additional features, functions, design, etc. in favour of lower prices. Economic differences across countries (especially between developed and developing countries) can also undermine low price positioning of products in those markets.

When it comes to economies of scale, the obvious benefits are questioned. Technological development has enabled such economies to be achieved at lower levels of output, which allows more adaptation at the same low cost. Even more, the cost of production (which is usually implied under economies of scale) is not necessarily the main component of the total product cost and price (Douglas and Wind 1987, Walters 1986). No hard data is available as to the actual costs of customisation, making comparison of the trade-offs between standardising and adapting impossible.[9] Mandatory adaptation,[10] which is the result of government-imposed laws and regulations (quality standards, taxes, use of local components, etc.), not only makes complete standardisation practically impossible, but may even offset the benefits of economies of scale (Walters 1986).

Other studies have addressed the influence of cultural factors on management's propensity to standardise or adapt its international marketing strategy. For example, Evans and Bridson's (2005) research pointed out that retailers tend to favour adaptation strategies with the increase of psychic distance between the home and host countries.[11] Another study identified culture-based characteristics of consumers, which allowed them to be grouped into several clusters, with a specific marketing mix selected for each cluster (Kale 1995). Based on Hofstede's (1980) four dimensions (uncertainty avoidance, masculinity, individualism and power distance – see pages 37–39), Kale (1995) identified three cultural clusters in Europe.[12]

Latin cluster. Comprising France, Spain, Portugal, Belgium, Greece and Turkey – representing some 180 million inhabitants. These countries are typically characterised by medium to high power distance and uncertainty avoidance, and medium masculinity. For marketing, this implies emphasis on status (power distance); functionality and risk reducing messages (uncertainty avoidance).

Anglo-Germanic cluster. Austria, Germany, Switzerland, the UK and Ireland, but also Italy are in this group, with around 200 million people. Masculinity and individualism are typically high in these countries suggesting high performance products, desire for novelty and variety. Advertising themes would typically be "successful achievers".

Nordic-Dutch cluster. Denmark, Finland, the Netherlands, Norway and Sweden. This is the smallest group in terms of population with around 40 million inhabitants. These countries rank low on power distance, masculinity and uncertainty avoidance and high on individualism, with the following inferences for marketing: low resistance to new products and variety seeking (low uncertainty avoidance) and therefore perhaps a fertile ground for testing new products; environmentally friendly and socially conscious (low masculinity).

This general picture fits well with our intuitive classification of countries. Some may however question lumping countries like Italy, Germany and the UK together in the same group; or splitting two of the Benelux countries (Belgium and the Netherlands). The reason is the scores on Hofstede's cultural dimensions, suggesting that in our marketing decisions we may be misled by our preconceived perceptions.

Another factor is the firms' market knowledge which is closely related to the organisational aspect of management and the learning process as illustrated above (see Mack's Brewery in Section 9.2). This dimension of the issue has received little attention. One of the few to tackle this topic was Solberg (2000, 2002). He addressed the role of the local subsidiaries/representatives (and local advertising agencies) in influencing a firm's strategic choice between standardisation and adaptation of the international marketing mix. The author showed how sufficient market knowledge and influence on marketing decisions determines the extent to which a firm's HQ coordinates its activities on a global basis ("cooperative centralisation") as opposed to a "patchwork" situation, with little consistency across different markets and limited learning potential (Solberg 2000). We have seen this in Section 8.4.1, where we discussed monitoring and control of the local partner (Local barons, Civil war, Confederation and Federation).

The intensity of competition is also deemed an important factor in determining strategy choice. On the whole, it seems that researchers agree that more intensive competition stimulates marketing strategy adaptation, in order to outperform competitors and gain a larger market share (Solberg 1989, Solberg and Durrieu 2015a,b). Furthermore, the presence of global competitors forces a firm to compete on a global level (not just in separate local markets), thus leading to a more standardised (global) marketing strategy (Solberg and Durrieu 2015a). According to Porter (1986), a global industry is an industry "in which a firm's competitive position in one country is significantly affected by its position in other countries and vice versa". Thus, as an industry globalises, pressures to standardise the overall strategy would also increase. This issue was addressed by Solberg et al. (2013), showing that a firm's ability to advertise internationally (based on its available resources and market knowledge, which constitute its "internal environment") and the globality of the industry in which it operates ("external environment") both influence the firm's ability (propensity) to apply either standardisation or adaptation approaches to its advertising strategy. We shall later – in Chapter 11 – return to this discussion.

Few researchers have viewed standardisation decisions in a dynamic perspective. One exception is a study by Cavusgil and Zou (1994), where correlates of product adaptation are viewed at the time of market entry ("upon entry") and after entry. They found that the relative influence of different factors on adaptation decisions varied upon and after entry: cultural specificity of the product and technological orientation are significant factors affecting product adaptation in both cases; the initial adaptation decision is influenced by the legal environment, while subsequent adaptation takes into account the management's international experience, the competitive intensity of the export market and the export customers' familiarity with the product (Cavusgil and Zou 1994).

9.3.2 *Strategic responses*

Many studies have addressed standardisation–adaptation choices at "lower levels" of analysis, considering specific elements of the marketing mix, sometimes focusing on various aspects of those elements. Research has shown that different elements/aspects of the marketing programme can enjoy different levels of standardisation, which allows companies to tailor the general marketing strategy to adjust to particular conditions (Zou et al. 1997).[13] This result was supported by Kotler (1986) in his survey of 46 product-categories, which suggested varying degrees of standardisation across marketing activities. Since the emphasis in this respect was given to *promotion standardisation*, some consistent findings can be listed. Generally, it was discovered that rather than adapting the actual products, firms are more inclined to adapt their *positioning, packaging/labelling and promotional approach* (Cavusgil and Zou 1994). Also, firms tend to fix (standardise) their basic advertising mission and message (often at the HQ level), leaving the actual execution of their communication to local adaptation (Solberg 2014, Sorenson and Wiechmann 1975). Following the same logic, van Raaij (1997) identifies four levels of marketing communication: mission, proposition, creative concept and execution – with the message being similar at each of the levels or modified at several or all levels (global, adaptation, differentiation and local communications strategies). Other elements of the marketing mix are predominantly adapted when it is either economically or legally mandatory and/ or when the costs of adaptation are not significant. For *product*, a high degree of standardisation was noted in brand names, physical characteristics of products and packaging (Sorenson and Wiechmann 1975). Brands and packaging standardisation are necessary to provide global brand recognition and consistency of the corporate image, as well as to protect the company's own trademark. Price and distribution seem to be harder to standardise, since they tend to be influenced the most by differences across countries: income levels, varying exchange rates, distribution infrastructure, etc.[14] Despite the evident difficulties in establishing a uniform retail price (different taxes, transport, income levels and distribution systems), standardised positioning can be achieved by setting the relative price level – for example, a premium price, compared with other products in the market (Sorenson and Wiechmann 1975).

Takeuchi and Porter (1986) suggest – based on Sorenson and Wiechmann (1975) – that different elements of the marketing mix lend themselves to standardisation in various degrees; see Table 9.3.

Practice shows that using standardised marketing programmes on a worldwide basis may not be possible while it is often more feasible and sensible to apply *process* standardisation. Ozsomer et al. (1991) give a distinction between programme standardisation and process standardisation, where the former refers to the uniformity of the marketing mix elements, while the latter deals with the overall marketing philosophy, principles and systems for planning and implementing marketing decisions. Process standardisation was indirectly addressed by those researchers who have studied organisational issues relating to international marketing standardisation (Solberg 2000), and issues of configuring and coordinating international marketing activities as part of the overall company strategy (Porter 1986).[15] Walters (1986) concludes in his article that standardisation is most apparent with regard to marketing planning and control processes.

The diversity of factors influencing a firm's strategic choice has led many researchers to advocate a combination of both approaches, resulting in some kind of a *"hybrid strategy"*, when some of the targeted market segments are global, while others are regional, some products are global, while others are regional or local, etc. (Douglas and Wind 1987).

Table 9.3 Adaptation and standardisation in international markets

Easy to standardise ⟵ ———————— ⟶ *Necessary to adapt*		
Brand	Entry mode	Media
Product	Communication message	Distribution channel
Positioning	Creative solution	Pricing
		Service
		Sales promotion
		Sales
		Packaging

Source: Based on Porter and Takeuch (1986).

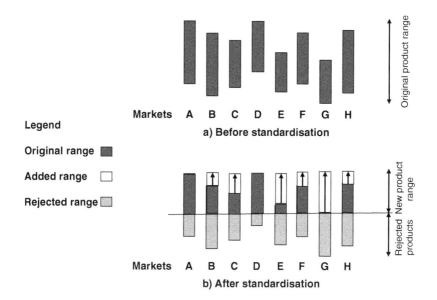

Figure 9.2 International rationalisation of product range.

Source: Based on Porter and Takeuch (1986).

A proactive approach to offering standardised products ("universal products") worldwide was proposed by Porter (1986). He argues that a firm can "create demand" for a universal or inexpensively modified product. This is made possible through substantial marketing investments.

Despite obvious differences in market conditions, research has shown that many MNCs still choose to standardise their marketing activities (Sorenson and Wiechmann 1975, Walters 1986, Solberg and Durrieu 2015a,b). We believe that this has to do with the increasing desire among managers to cut costs and control developments in each individual foreign market (Isdell-Carpenter 1986) as they expand internationally.

Takeuchi and Porter (1986) suggest a model to rationalise the marketing mix across countries, see Figure 9.2. We notice that both countries A and D maintain most of their products, whereas country G needs to introduce a completely new product range. All the markets have relinquished some products in their portfolio, but most have – in return – increased the range in the other end, in order to comply with the new product strategy of the company. The arrows in the white columns indicate the increase in product range of countries B, C, E, F, G and H.

9.3.3 *Effects on performance*

Whereas the standardisation/adaptation issue in general has been studied in more than 220 articles,[16] only a few have been aimed at testing the relationship between the strategy (standardisation or adaptation) and performance. Early contributions include Samiee and Roth (1992) who found, contrary to expectations, that global standardisation does not lead to superior profitability. Cavusgil and Zou (1994) found that reaching a fit between context (internal and external factors) and strategy (through product adaptation) had a positive impact on measures of performance, whereas promotion adaptation had a moderately negative impact on export venture performance. Furthermore, Szymanski et al. (1993) tested a model, representing a relationship between strategic levers, industry drivers and business performance (relative market share and profit) across Western markets (the US, the UK, Canada and Western Europe). The results suggested a positive relationship between product line breadths, the quality of products sold, high levels of customer service and market share. Also between the high quality of products, vertical integration, focus on new products, increasing market share, sharing customers among business units, competing in high-growth markets and superior profits (Szymanski et al. 1993).

Later, into the 2000s, Zou and Cavusgil (2002) found that global market strategies (standardisation of the four Ps, integration and coordination) are positively related to strategic and financial performance in a sample of US *global* firms. Xu et al. (2006) found that the fit between strategy, organisational structure and process is positively associated with performance. Schilke et al. (2009) found that the standardisation–performance link is significantly stronger in larger firms with a homogeneous product offering, higher market penetration, and cost leadership and coordination advantages. Solberg and Durrieu (2015a) show that performance effects of product standardisation increase with globalisation drivers, such as trade liberalisation, converging regulatory standards and consumer patterns. They also find that product standardisation yields better results in terms of *market position* in concentrated industries (Solberg and Durrieu 2015b). Its effect on *financial performance* however is lower (but still positive) in concentrated compared with fragmented industries. They speculate that in concentrated industries (with larger players in international markets) the gains in terms of a standard image across markets giving better market position are not directly matched by financial performance because players in this industry are larger, hence they have more complex structures and higher coordination costs.

The general impression from these studies is that *product* standardisation yields better returns than standardisation of *promotion*. This is particularly true for larger firms. Especially, global market conditions seem to favour standardisation of product, but not necessarily promotion, thus partly supporting Levitt's (1983) premise of globalisation. On the other hand, product adaptation is good for performance in fragmented (multi-local) markets. So the conclusion on the performance effects is that there is no clear-cut answer, and that "it depends": on the market context, on the industry structure, on the firm and product category.

9.4 Chapter summary

Figure 9.3 sums up this discussion. It shows on one hand what factors or drivers influence the decision on standardisation/adaptation in international markets, and on the other hand the extent to which the firm itself has the ability to influence the factor in question. The positioning of the different factors is the author's subjective judgement and is his best assessment based on the above discussion.

The figure suggests three groups of factors:

Group 1: Actionable factors

These are factors the firm can influence, and which at the same time appear to have a great impact on strategy development:

-   Product strategy (including target groups, positioning and branding) is possibly the one factor that provides the basis for the rest of the strategy. We saw it in the case of imported

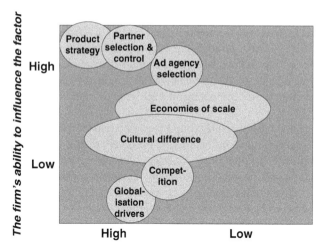

The impact of the factor on firm strategy

Figure 9.3 Influencing and "influenceable" factors.

beer to the US, and we have seen it in other cases (crispbread – "Grandma's flatbread", page 129; loafers – Swims, page 84; mineral water – Voss, page 88). Product strategy is often a given, an embedded part of the culture of the company – *la raison d'être* of the company. Still the company can and, as we have seen, sometimes should adapt the product to local conditions.

– Partner selection, and the ability of the exporter to monitor and control its partner(s), is also deemed important in this context. The partner is the exporter's extended arm in foreign markets and – as shown both throughout Chapter 8 and in the case described above (Export Products Ltd) – that choice of partner is critical. The partner's ability and willingness to adopt the strategies defined by the exporter, its propensity to cooperate with the exporter (share information, discuss strategies) will determine the positioning of the brand in the market.

– In the same vein, the selection of an advertising agency will have some impact on the direction of the strategy. Typically a local agency in the export market (for example, the local partner's advertising agency) will tend to tailor the message, whereas an international agency with subsidiaries and associates across different markets may be more likely to take a more global view.

Group 2: Attention factors

These factors must indeed be taken into consideration, but their impact on strategy can vary widely between industries and product categories.

– Economies of scale are critical in some industries (such as software, process industries), whereas technological advances (such as robotics) in other industries have rendered more tailored solutions possible. In yet other industries, it is of limited consequence for our discussion (hairdressers, plumbers). On the other hand, the firm usually has

limited influence on the technology itself but can, in most cases, choose between technologies that give more or less flexibility in this regard – hence the location in the middle of the matrix.
– Cultural distance – the favourite factor of the "adaptationists" – is indeed influential in determining the need for adaptation, yet the importance of this factor varies largely between different industry sectors and even within industries. Firms have limited influence on cultural distance, of course, but can enter markets that are more or less similar, and thereby – in reality – to some extent "choose" the importance of this factor.

Group 3: Given factors

Firms can do little to influence these factors. In some extreme cases – where firms dominate world markets (for example: Google, Microsoft or Apple) – the actions of leading industry players may influence the impact these factors have on strategy development. On the other hand, they do have a significant impact on strategy formulation. Therefore, firms need to take them into account when formulating their strategies.

– Globalisation drivers (trade liberalisation, homogenisation of demand and regulations) have been shown to impact on the effectiveness of standardisation: firms operating in global markets may do well to standardise their product offerings, and their marketing in general.
– Also, industry structure and the nature of competition play a role in this context. We have seen that standardisation is preferable in concentrated industries where there are few global competitors and vice versa.

The next chapters will deal in more detail with the marketing mix elements: Product, Promotion and Price. Place – as the fourth P in the original marketing mix construct – was partly covered in the discussion of operation modes (Chapter 7).

Notes

1 This anecdote has been provided by Mr. Runar Framnes, senior lecturer at BI Norwegian Business School.
2 This story is based on an article by Teri Agins that appeared in the *Wall Street Journal*, 2 February 2007.
3 This is a fictitious case, based on a great number of anecdotes and case histories seen or experienced by the author.
4 This section is adopted from Iuliia Diuba's work, "Standardisation and adaptation in international marketing and management – A bibliometric study", BI Norwegian Business School, Oslo, Norway, 2011.
5 Some even suggest that those differences have become more pronounced (Douglas and Wind 1987).
6 Share of the articles inclined towards standardisation (23%), towards adaptation (33%), towards contingency (40%), no specific inclination (4%) – out of 130 articles analysed in 2004 (Waheeduzzaman and Dube 2004).
7 This hypothesis is supported by Cavusgil and Zou (1994) who found that technological orientation of the industry strongly and negatively correlated with product and promotion adaptation.
8 This encompasses economic environment, cultural background and institutional infrastructure (Walters 1986).
9 For example, Kotler (1986) supplies the following argument: a modified product that better satisfies local consumers would lead to increased sales, and the additional revenue may outweigh the costs incurred in customisation.

10 *Mandatory* (or according to Sorenson and Wiechmann (1975) – *obligatory custom-tailoring*) as opposed to *discretionary custom-tailoring*, when the management does have to make adaptations, but rather chooses to do so.

11 Results showed that the perception of the market structure, business practices and language differences has a significant positive relationship to adaptation of the retail offer (Evans and Bridson's 2005).

12 Adapted from Kale (1995).

13 It should be noted that specific elements of the international marketing strategy which would have a higher degree of adaptation (standardisation) would vary for certain industries and companies. Research on firms from developing countries shows that these would differ from their counterparts in more developed countries. According to Zou et al. (1997), Colombian firms tended to place more emphasis on standardising the peripherals of their products as well as the promotional budget. These results suggested that firms from LDCs may perceive a need to adapt to more demanding, developed markets. Thus, they may be less inclined to simply follow their domestic marketing strategy (as opposed to, for example, American companies, which tend to use a more standardised approach across foreign markets).

14 Nevertheless, in the study by Sorenson and Wiechmann (1975), distribution modes seemed to be highly standardised, although the authors explained this as being "more accidental than intentional".

15 Porter (1986) stresses the importance of a specific industry context and puts an emphasis on the ability of a firm to coordinate its global activities (rather than simply choose to standardise or modify its marketing strategy worldwide).

16 As registered in Business Source Complete.

10 Product strategies in international markets

10.1 Introduction

For most people a product is something tangible, something you can touch, use for various purposes, eat, drive with, sit in, play and work with, etc. A product normally consists of a range of components that before being assembled into the "product" were products in their own right. Take a Toyota car: it consists of around 30,000 parts that need to be assembled into the car, each of these being itself a product and made up by a number of parts.[1]

The price and quality of a product are generally closely-related. How then to define quality, and who decides that certain products are of a certain quality? We will not discuss this in detail but briefly ascertain that these are relative concepts. Quality could indeed mean that a product tastes good, or has a beautiful design, but what tastes good or looks beautiful to one person does not necessarily mean the same to another person. It could also mean that the product does not rust, or that it can withstand strains such as extreme temperatures or knocks, without falling apart. The buyer does not always need such a product, however, and therefore the quality of the product must be seen in conjunction with the expectations of the buyer.

Consequently, a product is not manufactured for the sake of the product itself, but to satisfy the need of the consumer. The product and its role for the consumer are therefore interlinked. In other words: we do not sell products, but solutions; or rather, the seller of a drill is not selling a drill but the possibility to make holes! But it doesn't end there, as the next question is why do you need a hole? If it is because you wish to join two components with a screw, you also need screws and a screwdriver. However, there are other ways to join two components, such as gluing them together or constructing them so they can be put together in certain ways (such as Lego). Bearing all this in mind, the manufacturer of the drill is in this scenario covering a need that competes with suppliers of several other solutions.

The method chosen in order to join the two components depends on a range of factors, where the area for usage (for instance, requirements for durability or aesthetics), traditions or rules and regulations are all crucial. For instance, the Norwegian firm, OSO Hotwater, met problems by convincing German plumbers to use their stainless steel hot water tanks, as people in Germany normally use enamelled tanks. We have also seen how breakfast habits vary across countries. The point here is to show that the product should be placed in a context, and this context may vary from one country to another, implying that the physical product may also vary – although it basically covers the same needs.

Throughout this chapter we shall examine the different aspects of a company's product offering in international markets. We will start by looking at what constitutes a product – what elements it consists of – as seen through the eyes of a marketer. More specifically we shall discuss elements of the product concept such as tangibility, packaging and logistics. Then we shall examine the different aspects of standardisation and adaptation of the product, before discussing how the company's position in the Strategic Windows framework impacts upon product decisions.

10.2 A product is more than a product!

The product concept in marketing literature has been divided into several levels – from core benefit (such as the joining qualities discussed above) through to physical product, augmented product and symbolic product.[2] The core product reflects the purpose for which the product is intended (such as the assembling of components); the actual physical product is what we call the object to be sold; the augmented product includes the additional features and benefits required for the object to fulfil the expectations and needs of the buyer; and the symbolic product includes the branding, colours, packaging, etc. Table 10.1 gives some examples of how to describe various products within the four levels.

Let us discuss some of the issues raised in this table. For the *retail trade* in Germany it will probably not be sufficient to offer tinned sardines at 55 cents per tin. The buyer whose role it is to present the product to the management of the department stores will have to argue the product be taken on board at the expense of another product. That is why it is essential to offer a complete marketing plan for those parts of the German market that one wishes to export to. This plan should include – the sardine itself notwithstanding – the different taste varieties and the contents of the tin required by the market, as well as the price, and the promotional activities necessary to reach a certain sales volume during a specified period of time in a selected area. The packaging must also be adapted to the customers' taste and the German authorities' requirements for detailed contents. These requirements met, the offer may be accepted, even if it means the price of the tins will increase by 10 cents. The product offering as it is now presented shows the company has a thorough knowledge of the market and that they know how to best market sardines in Germany. This is a great reassurance for the German buyer and his or her faith that the product is well-deserving of a good spot in the display shelves.

If we look at selling *furniture* in the Netherlands, a crucial element of the product offering would be the training and motivation of the sales personnel. Having Dutch-speaking representatives is key to ensure local integration. While most Dutch people speak English, this is not always the case and not necessarily to a level that boosts motivation with the sales personnel at the dealer level (and there is also the chance that the Swedish exporter will be lacking in English knowledge). Furthermore, building a story around the creation of the product itself, the way it is manufactured, or around the designer – creating a sort of myth around it – could be a good idea as it adds to the feeling that the customer is getting something extra or buying something unique.

Similarly, selling *packaging machinery* to Switzerland requires more than just the machine and its price. Installation, the training of staff, access to spare parts and a speedy repair service and guarantees are all just as important parts of the offer as the price and machine itself. If the sale is in connection with a bigger project, financing will play an important role in the total offer.

When it comes to selling in bulk, such as for *plastic raw materials*, there are not as many variables to take into account. Quality and price will be the main determinants for the offer. Nevertheless, factors such as the ability to maintain a stable quality, delivery time, delivery flexibility and loyalty when times are tough will all play a part when the customer decides whether or not to establish a relationship with the supplier. Access to knowledge within research and product development could prove to be crucial in this instance.

Table 10.1 Content in product levels for four products

Level	Plastic raw material	Packaging machinery for drinks	Sofa group	Tinned sardines
Core product	The raw material must satisfy the customer's demand for guaranteed delivery, for the plant to run without interruption and stable quality.	The machinery must satisfy the customer's need for quick and reliable filling of drinks in order for costs to be kept at a minimum.	The sofa group must satisfy both the dealer's need for a profit and the final buyer's need for status and well-being.	The sardines must satisfy trade partners' demand for profit as well as the final buyer's taste expectations and ease of use.
Physical product	The raw material must be adapted to match the quality of the customer's machinery and requirements from their own customers with regards to quality.	The machinery must have certain specifications with regards to capacity, size, flexibility and quality of packaging.	The sofa group must be expandable with modules to modify it for different homes. The design should be elegant and give the impression of solidity.	The sardines will be offered in various sauces (mustard, tomato, olive, oriental, curry) in two different packaging sizes.
Augmented product	Joint research and development services to develop improved plastic qualities. Logistic systems for efficient delivery.	Installation and training. 24-hour service to ensure steady running. Access to spare parts. Finance solutions.	Training of dealers' sales staff, assembly assistance, sales support. Pamphlet with interior design tips for customers.	Panel for tasting and advertising support for the retail chain. Recipe suggestions on the packaging.
Symbolic product	Plastics from Norway may symbolise independence (small, "non-threatening" country) or integrated raw materials situation (North Sea).	The trademark offers security for the buyer. The colour of the machinery indicates different atmospheres.	The trademark symbolises status. A brochure with the product's history, the designer of the sofa, etc. may offer the customer perceived value.	The trademark and design signal quality and an enhanced taste experience. A story of the brand's origin gives consumers a feel of authenticity.

10.2.1 *From tangible products to intangible services*

It is common to separate the tangible product and the intangible service in marketing literature. However, there is no clear divide between the two categories. A few examples: shipping transport is classified as a service, but this service would not be possible were it not for one or more products, most importantly the ship itself and all its capacity, loading facilities and seaworthiness, but also the port facilities such as the cranes and the supply systems – over the quality of which the ship owner will have no control. Another feature of a service is that its consumption will often require involvement from the buyer. Some have called the consumer of services a *prosumer* (producer and consumer). Teaching services will, for instance, require some sort of participation from the student, and the more active the student, the more he or she will get out of the class and experience it as useful. Equally, one could say that a doctor's services naturally require the patient to be available for observation and treatment, or that a hotel stay requires the guest to be present. Not all services need this participation however. If we take another look at shipping transport, there is a minimal contribution required from the buyer of the service; or legal services, where perhaps one will only require a clarification on a legal subject (such as double taxation or patent rights for instance). And so the list continues with varying levels of customer participation in the creation of value.

By entering the two – participation and level of tangible product – in a matrix, you get Figure 10.1 (inspired by Engelhardt et al. 1993).

The figure shows different examples that could be relevant in the market. None of the placements of the examples is 100% definite, as it is often up to the supplier to decide how much the customer should participate in the process, and to what extent the supplier should extend the actual physical product within the service. One example could be that the manufacturer of furniture would like to present the furniture in their own store, perhaps in combination with interior design tips and tricks. Habitat (interior design concept store) is one such example of a designer and restaurateur that went down that route and found themselves somewhere between cells 6 and 10 in Figure 10.1. We could say that IKEA has gone one step further from cell 6 with their "knock down"/DIY concept, where the customer has to assemble the furniture themselves. When it comes to cell 7, we have suggested the so-called "turn-key" deliveries, meaning deliveries of installations (factories, power plants, ports, airports, etc.) from one contractor. For instance, the supplier of the packaging machinery for drinks would in this case also take on the responsibility of building the whole plant, including the machinery itself, but also offices, storage facilities, etc. These require a high level of customer input, from the design phase through to specific requirements and during the actual construction and installation period with regards to the training of the staff.

Take one step to the right, to cell 11, and you will find engineering, which includes designing the production structures for instance, but where the actual delivery will be made by a third party. In cell 8, we have what we suggest calling Build–Operate–Transfer-deliveries (B-O-T), which would entail the supplier assuming responsibility for running the plant during the first

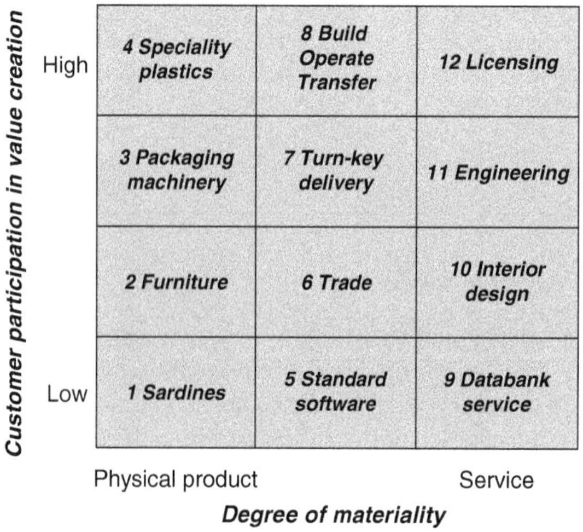

		Physical product		Service
High	4 Speciality plastics	8 Build Operate Transfer	12 Licensing
	3 Packaging machinery	7 Turn-key delivery	11 Engineering
	2 Furniture	6 Trade	10 Interior design
Low	1 Sardines	5 Standard software	9 Databank service

Figure 10.1 Participation and materiality of the value creation.

Source: Inspired by Engelhardt et al. (1993).

phase of installation, before handing the management over to the owners at a later stage. There are many variants of such agreements, such as part-ownerships in different forms of joint ventures. By moving one more step to the right in the figure we find licensing in cell 12, where ownership of the product for sale involves the right to manufacture the product, but where this right will be meaningless without the participation of the customer (licensee).

Key for the supplier here is to define the company's role in the value creation process. Should we participate with ownership, should we limit ourselves to selling a licence, should we only focus on the engineering, or should we also take responsibility for the delivery of the machinery (the packaging machinery in Figure 10.1) or the product (advanced plastic raw material)? All of these product categories can in many ways use the same technological base as their starting points, even if the supplier decides to take on different roles in their market participation. This definition of a role will depend on a range of factors, such as availability and cost levels of the following: labour, raw material, engineering competence, the company's – as well as the industry's – traditions in general, quality control of the end product, competence and the control of the use of management resources. The latter will determine whether to go for licensing or B-O-T, in other words whether one should leave more or less of the added value creation with the customer.

Boddewyn et al.'s (1986b) division of services into three categories provides a useful contribution in this connection:

1   Services that can be separated from the manufacturing process, such as a software program. Such services are easily exported.
2   Location-bound services, which necessitate the local presence of the supplier. This could include anything from running a hotel or a cleaning service to the repair service for machinery, where the customer will to varying degrees participate in the execution.
3   A combination of the two, where you can replace the local presence with other solutions. Other solutions could include an express service with a base at the exporter's headquarters or consulting services with a temporary base on the customer's site.

The Spanish firm, Portbooker.com, represents an interesting case of the use of the internet in the development of their business model. Since 2008, this company has shaken up the nautical world which is traditionally reluctant to introduce new information and communications technologies. A group of Majorcan entrepreneurs with a wide knowledge of the nautical world – including the manager of a marina, a former Olympic yachtsman and a computer expert – cracked the idea of an internet service offered to marinas around the world. This booming sector, with more than one million leisure craft in Europe alone, had grown by more than 30% over the past decade. The idea was to make berth reservations for yachtsmen possible by a simple key stroke, and to offer advantages to marina owners such as advance payments, simplification of bookings, a powerful promotion tool, and the advantage of being in an up-to-date online marina guide. Using Google Earth technology they designed a program that enabled an interface between the website and the subscribing marinas. The business model involves a commission for the online reservation service, and the advertisements of websites offered by Portbooker – one for each port loaded on the website. This site is particularly interesting, given the high growth in digital adverts and indeed also the high-income target group. In addition, it provided cross-interactive sales of complementary and relevant services: hotels, rental cars, restaurants, tourist information and boat rentals. The site receives more than 5,300 unique daily visits in the high season, averaging 2,500 daily visits yearly, accredited by Google Analytics. These figures establish Portbooker.com as the web leader for berth and charter bookings and its online marina guide.[3]

The less the supplier participates in the physical value creation, and the more intangible the delivery (such as a franchisor's trademark/systems or a licensor's know-how), the more important it becomes to ensure the quality of the end product or that the customer does not abuse the competence. We have already discussed parts of this issue during operation modes (see Chapter 7), but will revisit the issue here as this is closely related to product strategies. Using transaction cost theory as a starting point, some researchers endeavour to explain why service companies have a much greater tendency to integrate their business further down the value chain compared with manufacturing companies (Enderwick 1989). This is clearly seen in hotel management, where the large international chains seek to control all areas with strict franchising contracts, and preferably through part-ownership and management contracts. Likewise, most machinery suppliers will want to control the quality. This can be quite challenging in countries with a completely different cultural background and understanding of what is understood as good quality by the exporter.

10.2.2 Packaging

The product's packaging needs to cover two main purposes:

1   protection during transport (the augmented product)
2   goods exposure (the symbolic product).

The extensive internationalisation of trade has, for many products, resulted in a uniform *transport packaging*. This includes containers, sacks and bags, Euro pallets, barrels (for chemicals) and tanks. It is important not to assume that the customer will have the same receiving facilities whether they are in Germany, France, South Africa, Peru or Singapore for instance. That is why it is crucial to pay attention to these issues before committing with prices and delivery conditions. Who are my potential customers, how do they prefer their goods transported, what are the relevant rules regarding the transport of hazardous goods, and so on are all essential questions to be answered.

While the main task of the transport packaging is to protect the product and its packaging and to ease the transport itself, the *product packaging* has two functions: to protect and to display. The latter is particularly important when adapting to various markets. The following factors are of importance:

–   *Trademark and brand name* do not only bear consequence for consumer goods, but also for industrial goods. It is crucial in international markets to have a trademark/name that works in all or most countries. There are stories where companies have chosen a trademark/name that in other languages will have a particular meaning – and not one that necessarily bears positive connotations – which will then affect sales.

The classic story is that of Chevrolet's Nova brand, which they attempted to market in Mexico. Little did they realise the meaning of Nova in Spanish: "Does not go". No need to say that sales did not really take off . . .[4]

Western companies need to be particularly careful when transliterating their names in Asia. First, names have a deep significance and for that reason alone need to be chosen with care. Second, finding the right characters in written languages such as Chinese, Japanese or Korean is not straight forward, as experienced by Coca-Cola. When they first entered China in 1927, they identified some 200 characters that might give the same sound "Coca-Cola" when pronounced in different dialects in China. They discovered too late that the first attempt to write Coca-Cola in Chinese would translate as "Bite the wax tadpole" or "Female horse fastened with wax"! So researching the matter further, Coca-Cola could not ignore the meaning of the characters. They ended up with "K'o K'ou K'o Lê" (可口可乐), the closest phonetic equivalent to Coca-Cola in Mandarin dialects (spoken by some two-thirds of all Chinese) which means something like "Happiness in the mouth".[5]

In 1988, the General Electric Company (GEC) and Plessey combined to create a new telecommunications giant. A brand name was desired that evoked technology and innovation. The winning proposal was GPT for *GEC-Plessey Telecommunications*. Not a very innovative name, not suggestive of technology and a total disaster for European branding. GPT is pronounced in French as "J'ai pété" or in its English translation: "I've farted".[6]

There are many pitfalls, and there are examples where partners have been able to take over the property rights (such as a trademark) because the company, for reasons of lack of capacity, allowed the partner to carry out the registration (see for example page 205–206: Helly Hansen's experience in Japan).

- *The language* is also central when considering the packaging text. If you export to several markets with different languages, it is customary to let the packaging include all languages in question. Today, most products carry at least major Western European languages, Russian, Chinese and Japanese. In certain markets (perhaps particularly in Eastern Europe and developing countries) and for certain products, having a foreign text can be to your advantage. The product will gain higher status, and the manufacturer will reap the ensuing benefits (higher price).
- *The size* of the packaging can vary from market to market depending on how the product is being purchased. This is often seen in the fast moving consumer goods market, and especially relevant when considering the various customs and habits in the different markets. Having a freezer at home, for instance, is now standard in most homes in the developed world. This has resulted in food being bought in greater quantities, which in turn has an impact on the shape and size of the packaging. This is however not the case for all markets. Marketing to the bottom of the pyramid in African or Asian countries is very different and where, for example, cigarettes are sold by the piece.
- We should also pay attention to *the colour* of the packaging. Colours carry specific meanings in different contexts and cultures. Red is the most popular colour, but carries different connotations in different countries and contexts (communism, royalty, love, spicy, danger) and so on (de Bortoli and Maroto 2001). In the Far East white and blue are colours of sorrow, while these are the colours of the national flag in Greece and therefore carry positive

associations in this country. Muslims have a preference for green, and particularly for Shiite Muslims this colour is sacred. Yellow apparently is disliked in Pakistan, Israel and Venezuela, while in China yellow is regarded as positive. As an example, Red Bull uses gold (symbol of wealth and happiness) and red (good luck) on their tins in China, as opposed to blue (youth spirituality and peace), red (action and courage) and silver (maturity) in North America.[7]

- *Sustainability.* As people become more environmentally conscious, and managers with them, the issue of recycling and reusing packaging is becoming more relevant. One thing is recycling, for which many countries have elaborate systems, mostly beverages (plastic, tins and glass bottles) but also for other packaging material. Another matter is that of reuse: in certain countries, perhaps particularly in developing countries, it might be worth researching whether the receiver/customer can reuse the packaging.
- Finally we should mention that governments in certain markets demand that the declarations of contents are detailed and precise. Most countries have particular requirements for the display of additives and preservatives in food. It is worth having a thorough declaration of contents as this could have a positive impact on sales regardless of official requirements.

10.2.3 Logistics – a part of the product

The customer's requirements for a delivery period, frequency and delivery guarantees can all be regarded as part of the product on offer, and have direct consequences for how the retailer will develop their logistics systems. Different solutions will also have different cost consequences. We will briefly touch upon certain central points of relevance for the final chosen logistical solution. The case below describes how an actual situation could unfold for a Norwegian manufacturer of mooring winches.

Shipping equipment to Japan

Jensen Maritime Equipment (JME)[8] have long been a manufacturer of deck equipment for ships – mainly loading and anchor winches – as a subcontractor to Norwegian and other Scandinavian shipyards and repair workshops. As the shipyard crisis in the Nordic countries worsened in the 1990s, the company's position became increasingly difficult.

To combat this negative trend, JME wanted to focus on their international competitiveness in the manufacturing of deck machinery. They had managed to land a trial order of 48 winches from a shipyard in Japan – with a view to continuing to deliver the same amount of winches every 6 months. It takes 72 days to produce 48 winches. Whether the total order should be ready and shipped within 72 days, or whether it should be divided into part deliveries with a few days in between, is a typical logistics issue facing JME.

It is a CIF contract,[9] which means that JME can control transport and insurance, and is required to cover costs related to this within the price agreed upon for the winches.

JME has however limited knowledge of international transport, or international logistics. Due to their rather fragile financial position and the small margins between production costs and price, it was simply decided to go for the cheapest transport solution, and JME contacted a well-known haulier and an experienced shipping company. This resulted in an offer from the shipping company of either 960 USD per skip containing six winches, a total of 7,680 USD for the whole lot, or around 180 USD per winch, transported separately.

The haulier had a more interesting offer – by transporting the whole lot they could reduce the cost by around 40% – almost 3,000 USD. This was immediately regarded as the best choice.

However, the Japanese buyer made it clear that receiving only 48 winches per transport was insufficient and not a viable solution for future business.

The choice of logistic system will in this case be a matter of judgement based on the selling price, cost of transport (which in this case was marginal compared with the selling price), considering the buyer's wishes (be it frequency, need for speedy delivery, regular delivery, secure transport, storage capacity, etc.), the desire for good relations in the future and not least the capital costs involved for the winches should the whole period of production happen before payment.

To a foreign customer it is essential that the transaction with the exporter is as smooth and inexpensive as possible. This can be quite challenging at times, as border crossings are generally a magnet for hindrances such as demands for documentation and customs clearance. Even if there are certain areas where these processes have been simplified – internal border crossings within the EU and the EEA is one of the more straightforward examples – crossing the border in most other areas is generally characterised by extensive formalities, with ensuing costs and loss of time.

In some circumstances such procedures have been introduced as a hindrance or, at least, to limit the exports from one country to another. In the 1980s, for instance, France introduced a peculiar rule whereby all consumer electronics had to clear customs in one place only – Poitiers in Poitou in the middle of France. However, there was a glitch in this system: They did not have enough customs officers to be able to process and deal with the amount of goods, which in due course filled their storage facility to the brim. A complaint was made to GATT and France had to change its rule.

The conditions can also vary greatly from one country to the next. The following is the account of a Maltese shipper's nightmare in the port of Conakry in Guinea on the west coast of Africa:

It should have been a simple delivery of sacks of rice, but it was anything but. Local dockers pilfered from the load, the ship was attacked by armed criminals and the customs clearance was hindered by hostile and corrupt customs officers. After two months, the bunker was running on empty. The captain took the dramatic decision to leave Conakry even though all the certificates were with the local port authorities. The ship would later get a new name and new documents from Malta (Timlen 2000).

Even though international logistics are complex and companies are met with many obstacles on the way, technological advances have helped to simplify matters, especially regarding documents, through EDI (electronic data interchange), which guarantees uniform documentation throughout. Global logistics systems are becoming more and more reliable and it is now possible for the exporter to check the location of their goods at any given time. This is highly

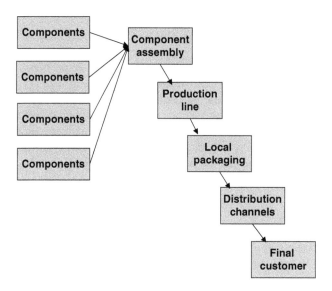

Figure 10.2 Links in a global logistics system.

necessary as the complexity of logistics continually increases with the outsourcing of production to low-cost countries; with the components assembly happening locally in the market; and the packaging being done by a third-party logistics partner, etc. This is not something we will look at in detail here, other than to point out that these challenges exist.

10.3 Standardisation and adaptation of the product mix

We have already discussed the issues of whether to standardise or to adapt (see Chapter 9), and concluded that a company's ability to capture market information and translate this to concrete decisions on product development and market communications has been underestimated. A range of researchers have discussed various issues regarding this (Takeuchi and Porter 1986, Usunier 1996, Douglas and Wind 1987, to mention a few). We will now look at different aspects of product strategies with this as a starting point. Amongst the many factors at play here, we will highlight the following: cultural conditions, technical restrictions, the product's life-cycle as well as a company's product offering, goals and profitability.

10.3.1 The role of culture

Cultural conditions have to do with how the market defines its solutions to the needs that the company is seeking to meet with their products. We have already looked at some examples of this (OSO Hotwater, the conjoining of components). The company has three options to deal with such conditions:

1 It can seek to adjust the products to the market's demands.
2 It can run a marketing campaign to influence ("teach") the market to demand their product.
3 It can choose to focus on a small segment of the market that is not sensitive to any cultural content the product may contain.

The first solution immediately catches the eye. There are however several examples where this would not apply:

> IKEA offers the same product range across the world – some 8,000–10,000 different products depending on store size. However, store layout and the presentation of the goods, home solutions and price levels differ from one market to the other. In China, IKEA has had to make several adaptations to their Western retail strategy. IKEA had to abandon their standard retail outlets in suburban areas of main cities. Most consumers use public transport and their 18 stores have therefore been set up in the outskirts of the big cities connected with rail or metro services. The usual "Do-it-yourself" concept with flat-pack products has been replaced by a home delivery and assembly service.

> It is possible to adapt the design and still maintain the ethnical feel that is emblematic to the product. Dale of Norway, manufacturers of the characteristic Norwegian cardigans and jumpers known as *lusekofte*, succeeded in this and agreed on four contracts worth a total of NOK 185 million in the US. In connection with the Olympic Games in Salt Lake City in 2002 Dale of Norway provided 15,000 Olympic volunteers with the Norwegian knitted jumper. In addition, the company manufactured the Olympic Games collection for the American participants between 1998 and 2002, as well as producing other licensed products on the American market. They also entered into an agreement with the American ski association, the US Ski Team, as well as the organisations for skiing instructors and rescue teams. These contracts increased the annual turnover by around NOK 150 million, enabling the company to build a profile and identity.[10] Such contracts provided Dale with a new lease of life and the opportunity to access other markets (with the same products) in a completely different way from before.

Sunshine stories such as this with beneficial consequences for the company are few and far between. There are, on the other hand, numerous examples of companies which, to a greater or lesser extent, have had to adapt their products to the various expectations of the market.

> One example of a product adaptation can be taken from Bergans (backpacks and sports equipment). Their introduction of backpacks for mountain climbers and mountaineers in Switzerland and France made no impact on the market. The main reason was that the mountaineers were not familiar with the traditional backpacks sold in Norway with their back frame, which is Bergan's own carrying system and their unique selling point. Instead of running an advertising campaign for Bergans and their backpacks with the back frames, management decided to develop a backpack without this structure, while still ensuring it was adjusted to perfectly fit the back. By adjusting the product and the sales argument (back-adjusted backpack), Bergans were able to introduce a product that differentiated them from their competitors. During the product development, it was of great importance that the backpack should not be more expensive than those of their competitors. To ensure they had the necessary design input the head of product

development interviewed, along with the export manager, a range of specialist retailers in Switzerland (both Swiss and French mountaineers have parallel demands on the functioning of a backpack).[11]

Food is an example of a product area that is often adapted when sold internationally. Chinese food in the US and Europe is rarely the same as in China. And examples abound of McDonald's hamburgers that have to fit local tastes, in spite of the fact that standardised menus are the hallmark of the fast food chain. But how standardised are these menus? In a review of McDonald's menus in five countries, it was found that these differed greatly from one country to the other: only 2 of 18 products of the US menu are offered in India, and their presentation is different. In other countries, such as Canada, South Africa, Australia and the UK, only between 7 and 8 products were the same as in the US (Loukakou Maria and Membe 2012).

Not all products should be adapted to the local market. French wine is possibly one such example. The wine would not be French (Bordeaux, Bourgogne or any other region) if one tried to adapt the taste to local preferences. It is precisely the taste of Bordeaux and Bourgogne that the consumers go for. Most nations have their very specific food traditions, and altering the taste will also change the whole product. A less-known example comes from Norway:

The Norwegian brown goat's cheese has a specific, sweetish taste, and is a household foodstuff in most Norwegian homes. Its particular taste is kept in export markets (primarily the US), as it is the characteristic taste that sells this product in the first place. On the other hand, the market has most likely been restricted to aficionados of Norway. In order to attract a larger market segment, it would have been necessary to adjust these products to suit the local demand, implying that it is no longer the "real" goat's cheese that you are selling. That would completely alter the product, its positioning, and potentially increase sales. Whereas the product itself is the same, the brand name is different, "Ski Queen" in the US – "Gudbrandsdal" in Norway (the name of a valley in Norway, denoting some kind of origin of the cheese).

10.3.2 Technical restrictions

Design and taste aside, a product must satisfy two factors:

1   The customers' technical specifications
2   Norms, legislation and regulations.

Different aspects of these factors have also been treated above (see Chapter 2). Products in focus include food, building materials, electrical goods, vehicles, vessels, or components for these. This is a situation you will find in any market. Getting a product approved by various authorities, or breaking through to conservative potential customers used to "their way of solving problems", is often time-consuming work, which requires a great deal of patience and staying power.

One possible limitation for a manufacturing company is its existing product range, which might be irrelevant to new markets (in terms of design, colours, quality). Products that are widely accepted on the domestic market might not necessarily be a great hit when exported. Equipment and manufacturing machinery may be unsuitable for producing the required quality demanded by export markets and therefore constitute a critical impediment to freely choosing their marketing strategy. One solution would be to focus the production on certain (main) qualities and supplement the product range by use of subcontractors.

Despite rules on non-discrimination embedded into international agreements, the number of *technical and non-tariff trade barriers* have steadily increased. This is perhaps particularly the case in times of economic decline, when governments in different countries will be accused by some of exercising unseemly zeal when products are crossing borders. There is no shortage of examples of countries trying to create hindrances for "bothersome" competitors from other countries. We have already seen this in Chapter 2, where local manufacturers often spend a lot of time wooing the authorities to get hindrances in place. With regards to the manufacturing of the product itself, it could be a case of local standards being agreed upon in a completely different context but which are being frequently employed to hinder foreign competition. Ed Conway in *The Times* gives an example of this from the drinks industry:

> Unless you are a connoisseur, you might easily mistake an Indian whisky for its Scottish cousin. The drinks taste pretty similar (the Indian variety is perhaps a bit sweeter), are distilled in much the same way and deliver comparable hangovers. Yet according to the powers that be, technically speaking only one of these drinks is a whisky; the other is an imposter.

> Somewhere in its code of product regulations, the European Union has determined that a drink cannot be "whisky" unless it is distilled from cereals and matured for three years. Indian whiskies are mostly made from molasses rather than the grain that goes into Scotch, so cannot be marketed as such in Europe.

> This arcane rule has contributed to one of the world's longest-running trade battles. In retaliation for what it sees as an unfair trade barrier, India has slapped eye-watering tariffs on imported whiskies, constraining British access to the world's biggest market for the drink (Conway 2017).

Korneliussen and Øwre (1998) carried out a survey on Norwegian industry and found that, in particular, demands made concerning the shape and content of a product, along with specific requirements for quality and certification, create issues for Norwegian industry, especially felt by the fishing industry. Their conclusion is that product requirements play a big part in most industries. Quality requirements are hugely important in the fishing and fish-farming industries. For instance, in Russia, a number of companies in these industries have been excluded due to claims of poor health and safety measures, claims that are contested by Norwegian suppliers. Requirements for certification on the other hand create challenges for the technology industry as well as the furniture and interior decorating industry. Five out of six technical export barriers are of great importance within the building industry, while the lack of recognition of Norwegian tests and certificates, additional national requirements and lengthy procedures present further challenges to this industry.

International agreements such as the EU/EEA and the WTO/GATT seek to hinder such practices, but there are claims that there will always be inventive local forces looking for loopholes covering them for such discriminating measures. There have been countless disputes over the years between various trading partners on the legality of the import barrier measures practised by certain countries. This is particularly the case between the US on the one hand (which has a liberal attitude concerning GMO within the food industry, for instance) and Japan and the EU on the other hand, where stricter rules are practised, where the result has been disputes brought to the WTO court. We will not look at these disputes in detail, but rather note that technical trade barriers can efficiently prevent exporters, and that it is crucial to research the various norms and rules to be observed for each case in order to be able to export successfully to a different country.

We will also briefly mention the importance of the *rules of origin* to be able to enjoy duty-free border passing. In order to avoid customs duty on components from third-party countries outside free trade areas, the company's product must change the number in the so-called HS code.[12] Failure to do this means the product will be regarded as imported directly from the third-party country and therefore subject to customs duty. There is thus the risk of double duty, first when importing to, for instance, a non-EU country, and later on when further exporting to the EU. Duty credits are offered when purchasing raw material and components in EU countries. This may pop up again in the UK in the wake of Brexit, where manufacturers who have sourced components from third countries risk having to pay customs duty on those parts, since the UK will no longer be an EU member.

Concerning norms and regulations, companies may potentially get directly involved in efforts to standardise international product definitions so as to secure their own interests when such norms and requirements are developed. Many companies are active to the extent that they have succeeded in getting their own product specifications recognised as the European norms within for instance CEN (Comité Européen de Normalisation) in Brussels.

Finally, we mention the increasing *ethical and environmental awareness* amongst various customer groups abroad. The consequence is that they have certain demands as to how the product is manufactured, which raw materials have been employed, where it is being manufactured, and to what extent the product can be recycled at the end of its life cycle. Such requirements vary from one country to the next, with Western countries possibly being more alert on these issues.

10.3.3 Product life cycle

Most products go through a sales trajectory called PLC (Product Life Cycle) as schematically shown in Table 10.2 and Figure 10.3. Asserting the products' location on this curve is not straightforward, but some characteristics can be identified as suggested in Table 10.2.[13]

This presentation is a general pattern identified in a great many products. An interesting feature is that of *refinements* to the product. As competition increases and the marketer

Table 10.2 Features of the product life cycle

Characteristics	Stage				
	Introduction	Growth	Maturity	Stagnation	Decline
Investments	Very high	High	Low	Low	Low/disinvestments
Sales	Low	Increasing	High	High	Declining
Competition	None/Varies	Increases	High	High	High
Refinements	None	Few	Increasing	No further	No further
Profits	Negative	Zero	High	High	Declining → negative

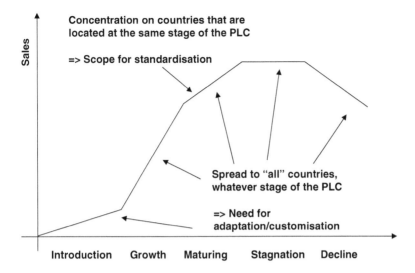

Figure 10.3 Adaptation or standardisation of products along the PLC.

identifies new customer groups and nuances in the demand pattern, refinements in the form of product improvements will be introduced to the market. As the product progresses through its life-cycle, the firm is learning about each market and how to position its products, including its refinements and presentation through media and distribution channels. Another feature is that of profits, which are almost invariably negative in the introductory stage, mainly due to high initial investments.

Particularly for newcomers to international markets – with new and unknown user groups, buyer behaviour, distribution and promotion channels, and price structure – chances are that the introductory stage will stretch out longer than in the domestic market. For the veteran exporter, having operated in international markets for many years, the issue becomes one of capitalising on learning from one market to the other, stretching the life cycle of the product across and into new markets. Given the need for refinements along the PLC, it is reasonable to assume that adaptation to markets positioned at different stages of the cycle will be necessary in order to yield positive returns. Alternatively, the firm may choose to concentrate on markets that have reached the same stage on the PLC. This invites businesses to standardise their products as far as possible. Companies with great scale economies and little flexibility in the manufacturing process may adopt this approach. The two strategies are illustrated in Figure 10.3.

10.3.4 International product portfolio

In Chapter 6, we discussed different market categories, basically primary and secondary markets, where the firm has adopted different objectives with regard to customer service, market share, use of marketing mix, etc. In primary markets, the firm needs to actively monitor its competitors' product development and seek to introduce new products in order to maintain its market share (established markets) or to increase its shares (investment markets). In secondary markets, the firm needs to comply with legal and technical standards; adaptation beyond this – for example cultural adaptation – depends on their character (accordion markets → limited adaptation/exploration markets → more adaptation).

Normally, a few products will represent the bulk of the earnings. We can assume that the firm is active in the following product/market segments as indicated in Table 10.3. The figures show the net contribution in 100,000 of euros.

Assessing the product net contribution, we notice that Alpha 2 and Beta 1 represent almost 60% of the total. However, we will not detect that Beta 3 in segment 2 in France contributes negatively (100,000 euros). The questions then remain: for how long can the firm sustain a negative contribution in Beta 2/segment 2 in France? Does the product play a role in the total portfolio? In Section 12.4, we shall explore these issues in more detail. In the present context, we content ourselves with pointing at the importance of a review of the PM matrix in detail in order to obtain a financially-optimal product mix.

In addition to this analysis, management also should consider analysing the product portfolio by use of the BCG matrix (see also page 107), or any variants thereof, in order to assess the position of the product in these markets. We will then be able to identify weak and strong market positions relative to the market attractiveness, and get a foundation for a product mix decision. Let us assume that the firm sells three product groups in six countries. Figure 10.4

Table 10.3 Financial analysis of product-market portfolio

Market		Product						Market contribution
		Alpha product range			Beta product range			
		Alpha 1	Alpha 2	Alpha 3	Beta 1	Beta 2	Beta 3	
UK	Segment 1	2						2
	Segment 2		3			1	2	6
	Segment 3							
France	Segment 1				1		1	2
	Segment 2		5		3	2	(1)	9
	Segment 3						2	2
Product contribution		2	8		4	3	4	21

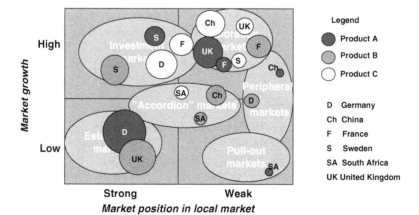

Figure 10.4 International market and product portfolio.

exhibits a hypothetical image of the market position of these three products in the said markets (the size of the circles indicates the sales volume of each product/market).

The figure gives rise to a wide range of questions that should be raised in management meetings. We shall not delve into any detailed deliberation, but rather suggest some general issues to be discussed. We note that the figure corresponds to that presented in Section 6.4.4. The reader may therefore relate to the discussion in that chapter.

First we observe that products A (dark grey) and B (grey) are in a leadership position in three countries (UK, Germany and Sweden), although product B has really not had any breakthrough in Germany. We further notice that the UK and Germany provide the financial backbone of the firm, with products in the Established market (Cash Cow) position. Sweden is a growth market and despite its relatively small size (10 million inhabitants) represents an interesting future Cash Cow (today: investment and exploration market). France is in an uncertain position given its relatively low sales in all product groups, but in a stage of the PLC that holds promises for the future. South Africa has yet to find an entrenched position in the portfolio with products located in Pull-out markets and Accordion markets.

There is a pattern of a relatively fragmented positioning of products A and B, and management should consider how to reposition these two products in the three main markets – Germany, the UK and Sweden. The only product that shows a consistent pattern is C, for which a concerted (global?) marketing approach seems possible. There is a question as to whether the firm should continue its operations in South Africa.

10.4 Product strategies in different strategic positions

The Strategic Windows model suggests that firms in different locations in the matrix should develop different strategies. This is also true for product strategy. Figure 10.5 proposes a terminology for international product strategy. In this section, we shall analyse how the issues discussed in Section 10.2 may find different answers depending on the position of the firm in each cell of the matrix. As a point of departure we shall use the four product levels (core product, physical product, augmented product and symbolic product) to discuss the issues of

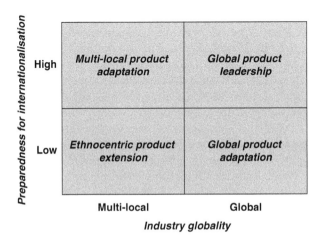

Figure 10.5 Product strategies in different strategic positions.

Table 10.4 Product strategies and product levels – standardisation or adaptation?

	Ethnocentric product extension	Multi-local product adaptation	Global product adaptation	Global product leadership
Core product	Standardisation	Adaptation	Standardisation	Standardisation
Physical product	Standardisation	Adaptation	Standardisation	Standardisation
Augmented product	Standardisation/ Adaptation	Adaptation	Standardisation	Adaptation
Symbolic product	Standardisation	Adaptation	Standardisation	Standardisation/ Adaptation

standardisation and adaptation. Table 10.4 – inspired by van Raaij (1997)[14] – displays a suggested strategy for each of the cells in the matrix.

10.4.1 Ethnocentric product extension

Firms in this cell of the matrix are newcomers to international markets and these markets are typically nationally-oriented – usually local brands holding a dominant position. These brands are often setting the national "norms" for products in their category, not only for the consumption pattern, but also for technical standards in the market. It could be Fray Bentos in Britain (steak and kidney pie), Gruyère in Switzerland (cheese) or Abba in Sweden (canned herring). Some imports may occur, and for some product categories they may be dominant (such as food products by Kraft Foods, Nestlé and Unilever) in virtually all markets.

A newcomer in this market context will normally take its product range from its domestic market. The motivation may be the desire to exploit scale economies, or to offset shares lost to "invading" foreign competitors. The most "international" of their products are then candidates for export. Scale economies may help their cost calculations to make them price competitive. Therefore, they would prefer a standardised product in order to achieve scale economies. In addition, their lack of knowledge of foreign market conditions limits their capability to tailor the product to the chosen market(s). The mind-set of management is almost inevitably ethnocentric, i.e. their starting point is the domestic product when different levels of the product concept are to be defined. Local requirements concerning technical standards (physical product) naturally need to be satisfied, but other than that the basis for the product is laid in the home market. We have seen how Mack's (beer) entered into a cultural minefield during their campaign in the US (see Section 9.2). Beer is not only beer; it is patriotism, it is local attachment, and it is status (imported beer) – and the product has to be positioned accordingly. Mack's did not take this factor seriously when they first entered the American market.

Concerning the extended product – such as packaging, labels, manuals, credit terms, service level, etc. – the firm should be prepared to adapt to the local market conditions. On the other hand, offering the product as it stands in the domestic market may help the firm to "stand out from the crowd". "Grandma's flatbread" (see Section 5.3.2) is a case in point, selling the same product as in Norway and using the same packaging (adapting the name only). It was not a success. The symbolic product is closely connected to the communications mix adopted by the firm (see Chapter 11). The firm is also dependent on how its local partner works with the brand. Since the independent partner is precisely that – independent – it will tend to apply its own definitions/frame of mind to position the product in the market.

The main problem with product extensions based on the domestic market experience is that firm preconceived ideas of what the product should be – "everyone in every country should like it!" One example could be chocolate, the taste of which differs from one country to the other. Finnish chocolate is the best in the world in Finland, but not necessarily in other parts of the world, where Swiss or Belgian chocolates are the favourites. Another challenge is that a product that functions well in the home market would in principle also function well in other countries. However, different technical requirements, either because of different traditions or because detailed technical standards differ (such as different climatic conditions), mean that it will not function as well in a particular foreign market. Offshore technology (for petroleum exploration) exemplifies this point, where rough waters in the North Sea set standards for products, but these should not necessarily apply to other areas with milder conditions. Suppliers to the North Sea explorers and operators should therefore consider adapting their quality standards when offering solutions to other regions.

10.4.2 Multi-local product adaptation

Firms in this cell are confronted with more or less the same competitive constellations as in the previous cell, but they have a much better point of departure for their international market involvement – both managerially and financially. They therefore have a wider repertoire of strategic alternatives concerning product portfolio and positioning. In multi-local markets, the consumers' need – expressed through the physical product – may have a totally different manifestation than in the firm's domestic market. In order to become relevant, management needs to understand how to position the core product relative to market leaders in each market.

The augmented product may best be adapted through a modular system, where the individual elements can be used in different combinations depending on the need in each market. Obvious examples are ski racks and winter tyres in European countries and North America. Another example may be the information for and training of farmers on how to use fertilisers; in North America the farming industry is well-developed and consists of large units with modern equipment. In some developing economies, farmers may need more education in order to make use of the fertilisers. We have also seen how IKEA in China needed to augment the product with assembly services, much less in demand in other countries. The symbolic product, being an integral part of the total product concept, then needs to be adapted accordingly.

New product launches may – in this position – be carried out in a stepwise manner, one market at a time. In this way, management can get concrete feedback on its new products, acquire experience from the use of the marketing mix before introducing it into other markets, without unnecessarily pushing the marketing organisation.

Alternatively, firms in this cell may seek a more standardised approach, which we may term "adapted ethnocentrism", in well-defined niches where the customers have more or less the same attitudes, experiences, points of reference and so on across national borders. The firm may, for instance, actively play on the specific national and cultural (and – for foreigners – exotic) features from the country of origin. R.E. Meyer, former chairman of the board of Grey Advertising, claimed that products that are bearers of national cultural traits lend themselves to standardised solutions.[15] Examples are Coca-Cola and McDonald's from the US, L'Oréal and Louis Vuitton from France, cheese fondue from Switzerland, feta cheese from Greece.

10.4.3 Global product adaptation

Here we find firms with limited resources and positions in international markets, but who have products that address a uniformly-expressed need across countries, where few large competitors offer alternative solutions to address the same need. Small hi-tech firms or "hi-design" firms are located in this cell. This position is in many ways the opposite of multi-local adaptation, and it is desirable to introduce standardised solutions – both because of scale economies, and because of a uniform demand pattern. The extended product, such as user manuals or packaging, may initially be written in the English language, but as the market grows, the firm should rapidly develop a multilingual user manual. Critical in this cell is to gain acceptance of the product in a small niche, but as globally as possible, short of which the firm runs the risk of "inviting" globally-oriented competitors to take over the market before the potential has been recognised.

> Little did management of the Danish robot manufacturer, Universal Robots, know that their products would conquer the world in ten years, when they developed their lightweight robot in 2005. With funding from regional and state investment funds they sold their first robots through distributors in Denmark and Germany in 2009. Eight years later, sales are approaching 10,000 units in 55 countries worldwide. The success of the robot, called "Cobot" (collaboration robot), comes from two factors: easy installation and programming, and safety of operation. The product itself is extremely advanced, but it can be operated by virtually anyone: the German engineer with advanced technological knowledge, and the Chinese shop-floor operator who just started to use the technology. Universal Robots' first product was the UR5, a six-jointed articulated arm robot that revolutionised the market for industrial robots. The UR5 weighs 18 kg, has a lifting capacity of up to 5 kg and a working radius of 85 cm. One important feature was the standard product that could be sold to all countries. The customisation – with localised tools and features – takes place at the customers' workshop sites. In this way, the manufacture of the Cobot can be simplified. Since the introduction of the UR5, the firm has launched two other products, UR10 and UR 3, to broaden its catchment area (10 and 3 kg lifting capacity respectively). The company was sold to a US firm, Teradyne, for 285 million USD in 2015.[16]

> Kahoot!, a Norwegian web-based supplier of educational quiz games, is another case in point. They decided early on – because of limited resources – that they should limit the language of the main program to English, letting the users determine the language of the specific quiz games developed individually. We may say that the "physical" product (the game system) is standardised, whereas the augmented product (the quiz content) is customised. Today they are market leaders in the educational quiz game market, with more than 40 million users per month in around 180 countries. Obviously, translating the basic program to possibly more than 100 languages would be too onerous for this small start-up company.[17]

10.4.4 Global product leadership

This strategy is the best fit for firms with high market shares in central markets in a globalised industry. Indeed, Solberg and Durrieu (2015a) show that standardised product strategies affect the firm's market performance significantly more positively in globalised markets than in multi-local markets. In a purely global market it is possible to offer 100% standardised products to all customers across the world. This is however a theoretical and extreme position. Even if the competitive situation can be described as global – as it has been presented in Chapters 2 and 4 (perhaps also with a few customers who also operate globally) – the products still need to be adapted to different local conditions. However, there is scope for standardisation of the main part of the core and physical product (except technical standards). In order to arrive at a minimum common denominator for such standardisation the firm should enter into a close dialogue with user groups in key countries.

10.5 Chapter summary

In this chapter we have discussed key issues regarding product offering in international markets. We have seen that a product is much more than a physical object to be manufactured or a service to be created and sold in the market. These products and services cover specific needs, and the ways in which these needs are expressed vary from one country to the next. One may define the product at four different levels: the core product, the physical product, the augmented product and the symbolic product. The challenge of product strategy is to then offer the different levels in a financially sound way – usually implying economies of scale – and at the same time satisfy local demands for adaptation in the various countries. On the other hand, the physical manufacture of products is increasingly outsourced to low-cost countries, and the manufacturing cost is often only a fraction of the retail price in the market.

We have also seen that the product strategy varies with the strategic position of the firm. We have identified four main strategies: 1) ethnocentric product extension, 2) multi-local product adaptation, 3) global product adaptation and 4) global product leadership. Figure 10.6 gives a hypothetical example of the product portfolios of firms in each cell, using the BCG matrix as it has been discussed in this chapter.

In strategies 1 and 3 the firm will generally sell the same product in all markets; however the market portfolio is much more diverse in strategy 3. Concerning strategies 2 and 4 we note that

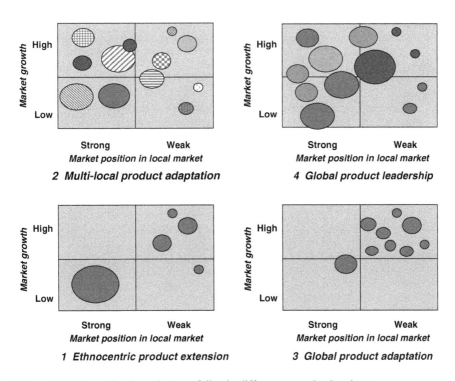

Figure 10.6 International product portfolios in different strategic situations.

the market portfolios are quite diversified (they have leadership positions in their markets), but that the product portfolio and brands are very different from one market to the other in case 2 (marked by the diversity of patterns in the products). In case 4 the products have similarities across markets (marked by different shades of grey) – implying just minor adaptations to local markets.

Notes

1 https://www.toyota.co.jp/en/kids/faq/d/01/04/
2 This concept has been transformed over the years, and over the editions of Philip T. Kotler's *Marketing Management* textbook (15th edition, Pearson 2016), now co-authored with Kevin Lane Keller. In their latest version they present the product in five levels: core product, generic product, expected product, augmented product and potential product. We shall not get embroiled in an academic discussion of these different definitions. Our definition is from an earlier edition and fits the purpose for our discussion in the present text.
3 Information for this anecdote is provided by Professor Joan Freixanet, University of St. Petersburg.
4 Allegedly – this appears to be an urban legend that cannot be verified.
5 http://www.coca-colacompany.com/stories/bite-the-wax-ta
6 For more fun, we suggest the following website by Islam Ezzeldin Mostafa: https://www.linkedin.com/pulse/20141011224311-99993053-top-63-international-marketing-mistakes-pitfalls or Ricks (2006).
7 http://www.nerdynaut.com/business/product-standardization-vs-product-adaptation
8 This case is written by Petter Omholdt, senior lecturer at BI Norwegian Business School. Company names, cities and goods in the description are fictitious. The description does however use realistic events and approaches.
9 CIF, Cost Insurance Freight, is one of many terms of delivery, so-called Incoterms.
10 *Dagens Næringsliv.*
11 Interview with former export manager of Bergans, Jo Kobro.
12 HS – Harmonised System – is a system for goods classification and is used within the EU and EFTA for customs duty and statistical registrations.
13 These are described in most marketing textbooks, and will not be elaborated on here.
14 Van Raaij's article discussed different levels in the communications mix of international advertisers. We shall return to his classification in the next chapter.
15 Cited by Fannin (1984).
16 Sources:

    1. https://www.universal-robots.com/about-universal-robots/our-history/
    2. https://roboticsandautomationnews.com/2016/05/24/a-history-of-collaborative-robots-by-universal-robots/4684/
    3. *Børsen*, 25 February 2016; *Fyens Stifstidende*, 25 February 2016, p. 12.

17 Interview with Johan Brand, co-founder of Kahoot!

11 Promotion decisions in international markets

11.1 Introduction

Promotion – or market communications – involves the strategies that the firm carries out to develop the demand for its products. We may say that already decisions on product, market segment, price and distribution channel represent such strategies, and constitute in principle an integrated part of the more specific communication – be it advertising, personal sales, participation at trade fairs, communications through social media, etc. All these help to position the firm in each market, and to give the business and its products what has been termed brand personality, i.e. the (human) traits that different consumer groups or buyers emotionally associate with the product and brand. This implies that the products and the firm develop an identity that goes beyond the functional need satisfaction (drinking imported beer covers more needs than just quenching the thirst). The task of the communications strategy is therefore to create the specific personality of the brand as perceived by customers. This task is increasingly challenging as the firm enters international markets. An interesting case may be found in the chocolate market.

A chocolate is not just a chocolate! KitKat (wafers covered with milk chocolate in bars) is known in the UK and elsewhere as the chocolate you eat when you have a break – when you go to the movies, in the office, at home, on an outing – everywhere really. It is eaten in any situation, with friends, family or colleagues. Their slogan, "Have a break, have a KitKat," has been running for decades and leaves us with a positive impression of a tasty companion that makes us forget other things. In Norway, practically the same chocolate, Kvikk Lunsj (in English: Quick Lunch – it looks and tastes the same as KitKat), has a very distinct usage; it has for generations been advertised as an easy meal to bring with you, primarily when you are skiing (cross country), but also in other sport contexts. Particularly around Easter holidays, its manufacturer, Freia (a subsidiary of Kraft), runs advertising campaigns to remind Norwegians that they should not forget to bring their Kvikk Lunsj on their excursions in the snowy mountains.[1]

Usually, brand personality has been divided into five different types: excitement, sincerity, ruggedness, competence and sophistication (Aaker 1997). Therefore, although the wafer chocolate bar has a very general usage in the UK and other countries where it is sold, and has a personality linked with sincerity (kindness, family values), it has a very different personality in Norway. There it is a rugged, outdoorsy and easy meal when you really need to renew your energies, particularly when you are out skiing. It goes without saying that this concept is not easily exported to many countries. On the other hand the personality (ruggedness) may apply in other sports contexts; but then it has a formidable competitor in KitKat.

Brand personality develops in a complex interaction between the different aspects of the firm's marketing mix elements and the consumers of the product, including who they are and how they use the product. The market communications play a specific role in this context. This chapter will not deal with all aspects of market communication, but rather focus on those parts that play a specific role as seen by the international marketer. In marketing literature, advertising normally receives most of the attention. However, for the exporter – or more generally the international marketer – it is a question of how to orchestrate, through its partner network, the implementation of all the elements of the communications mix: advertising, sales promotion, PR, personal sales. For instance, in the allocation of the sales and marketing budget of medium-sized Norwegian exporters of branded goods, the emphasis is on the relationship-building activities of the export manager or regional sales manager. The next items in the list are trade fair participation, sales promotion activities and sponsoring. International advertisements consti-tute only a small amount (between 10% and 20%) of the total international marketing budget of these firms:[2] the local advertising is left to the local partner or subsidiary. Some companies contribute a certain percentage of total sales to support the local partner's marketing budget – perhaps some 4–6% of sales through the partner.

The general conclusion is that the local partner/subsidiary plays a critical role in the implementation of the marketing strategy in each individual market. In a start-up phase, the exporter will typically leave most of the local marketing activities to the local representative – both because of lack of resources and because of limited market insight by the exporter. As local sales grow, the exporter will take a more active interest and participate in what is going on in the local market. We have already discussed the challenges relating to this transition ("Local barons" and "Civil war") in Section 8.4 and Chapter 9. It is mostly about developing a common understanding of the local vs. the central perspectives of the international marketing effort.

Having re-emphasised the (inter)organisational challenges of the international communi-cations effort, we shall now elaborate on the international aspects of the traditional marketing communications model – sender → message → communication channel → receiver – described in general marketing textbooks (see Figure 11.1).

The model illustrates that as the message is developed by the sender, based on the sender's references, it is transferred to the receiver through communication channels that "hit" the receiver. The circles (or rather ellipses) illustrate an overlap between the sender's and receiver's

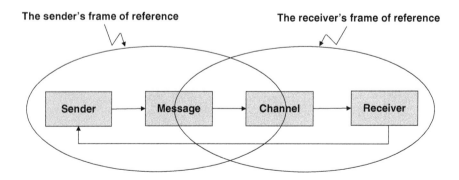

Figure 11.1 International marketing communication model.

frames of reference – i.e. cultural backgrounds, and other relevant contexts (competition, economic environment, etc.). This overlap may be greater or smaller depending on the understanding of each player in the model. The following sections will elaborate on this model, starting with an analysis of the receiver.

11.2 Analysis of the receiver

Market communications should start with the receiver, who is the one who deciphers the message as it is expressed by the sender. The receiver may be the purchasing manager of a retail chain – Lidl in Germany, Carrefour in France or Tesco in Britain; it may be the members of the design team in Volvo (Sweden) or Fiat (Italy); it may be the department manager in a government agency in the council of Birmingham, Barcelona or Brisbane; it may be the individual dealers in a car dealer network; or it may be "the man in the street", the general consumer. Often the receiver is not a decision-maker/buyer of the product; he or she may be the expert who influences the final buyer; it may be the spouse who "sanctions" the purchase of the outfit.

When introducing a product into a new market one of the greatest challenges is usually that potential customers do not know the product/brand or the firm. They start at the bottom of what Colley (1961) called the effect hierarchy, describing the effect that an advertisement has on the consumer – from total ignorance to the concrete purchase action; see Figure 11.2.

This model describes the assumed process that a buyer goes through on his/her way from unawareness to actual purchase. The model is helpful in that it informs the seller about how best to argue and use appropriate channels to persuade the potential buyer. In an introductory phase, the task is to inform the market about the mere existence of the firm and the brand. As the market is "educated", and understands the product and its advantages, the communication may take for granted that the product is recognised, and may therefore harp on other aspects (sentiments or just recognition). Therefore, the firm needs to understand the location of the potential customer in this effect hierarchy in order to optimise its market communications; and that location often differs from one market to another.[3]

This way of considering the effect of market communications is generally used in advertising, but may in principle be used in other contexts such as personal sales or at a trade fair. However, creating preference does not always go through this "rational" model; it is possible to create preference with only simple messages, and persuade the customer to buy directly as a consequence of communication, without necessarily going through all the stages of the model (Thjømøe 1996). This varies with product category. For instance, low-involvement products (low-cost, routine purchases – such as toothpaste or pastilles) will, to a greater extent than high involvement products (cars, yachts), lend themselves to this kind of direct preference formation (buy-like-learn). A model that has been developed in a collaboration between the American advertising agency Foote, Cone and Belding, and Professor Ratchford at New York State University – the

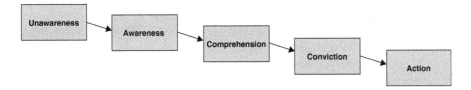

Figure 11.2 The effect hierarchy in advertising (UACCA).

Source: Adapted from Colley (1961).

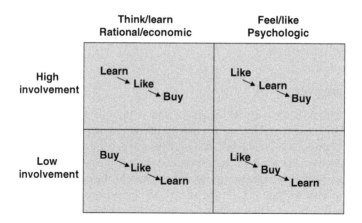

Figure 11.3 The FCB matrix.

Source: Adapted from Berger (1986).

so-called FCB matrix (Berger 1986) – takes as a starting point high–low involvement products and degree of rationality in the purchase decision (the degree of consideration ahead of the decision). The four quadrants in the matrix in Figure 11.3 illustrate that the purchase decision often is a far cry from the rational path suggested by the above models (UACCA or AIDA).

The basic thought behind the FCB model (and other similar models from other advertising agencies)[4] is typically directed towards the consumer market. Industrial products will in the main be located in the high involvement – "think first" quadrant of the matrix, even though routine or replacement purchases may be located in its lower parts. Vardar (1993) maintains that this model is particularly relevant for multinational companies, because the same types of products will be located in the same place in the matrix across countries. In other words, consumers in different countries go more or less through the same process when purchasing products and services. We will return to this in Section 11.4.

Introduction to new markets involves not only promoting products to new customers who at the outset do not know them, but also breaking into existing relationships – and loyalties – between players in the market. This aspect has been discussed in Section 7.2, but deserves to be repeated in the present context. Even though we have stated above that B2B relations are characterised by rational behaviour, we also assert that one of the most defining criteria for this class of purchase is trust: trust gained over years of relationships and therefore a very rational factor. It should be noted that also in the B2C sector, there is a considerable B2B component: the wholesaler, dealer and retailer. These players do not buy the product for their need satisfaction; they buy it for the profit they can generate in their business! Hence, the same aspects need to be considered in this sector of the economy, where the role of the local partner is to provide the amount of trust towards the customer (retailer, dealer) in order to sway him or her to buy our products.

The strengths of such relational bounds may vary from one country to the other. It has been claimed that in countries such as Japan or Germany such bonds are particularly strong and resilient. In Arab countries, these relationships are entrenched in the tribal system. Understanding the role of the tribe and the different members of the tribe then becomes a key to analysing Arab organisations and buyer behaviour: they live in a reality and their freedom of action is curtailed by their *sharaf*, their family honour (Brøgger 1993, p. 210). Therefore, Arabs will never give precedence to long-term business relationships that they have developed with (foreign) sellers and business partners over their commitment to close family ties. Tribal traditions may therefore explain cultural manifestations such as nepotism. We infer that organisational structure and role distribution (for instance, who has purchase decision power) not only vary among organisations, but also have some country specific traits.

In a survey of purchase behaviour of robotics in Nordic countries it was found that Danish firms leave the purchase decisions to the purchasing or technical manager for investments of up to 30,000 euros, whereas in Finland this decision is taken by the managing director. For investments of more than 70,000 euros, it is the board of directors that make the decision in Finland, whereas in Denmark this decision is taken at the managing director level. In Sweden, it is somewhere in between.

This has consequences for sales promotion. In Denmark, the sales person may approach the purchasing/technical manager (or the managing director) of the potential customer directly; in Finland, the decision-makers are much less accessible (directors). The technical/purchasing managers now enter the role of consultants, preparing the investment case for the board, and as such, they remain important. However, the board will often be presented with at least two alternative propositions, and may be tempted to use the one of which they have best knowledge and trust. For a newcomer to the Finnish market, therefore, it may be important to advertise in professional/business (local) magazines in order to reach the final decision-makers, in addition to working on the operative management of the firm.

Considering the buyer behaviour of foreign customers, the international marketer should ask a number of questions:

– How well do the buyers know my company?
– What media do they read/listen to? What trade fairs do they visit?
– What are their motives; how should they be persuaded?
– To what extent is the purchase decision affected by the opinions of experts or other influencers?

Knowing the answers to these questions helps the exporter to concentrate the promotion on target groups that already know the firm and its products (but are not yet customers). In a setting with limited resources and limited recognition in the market (often the case for new entrants), it is therefore relevant to divide the market into the following groups:

– Active users of the firm's product.
– Potential users showing an interest in the firm's product.
– Users of competitors' products that know neither the firm nor its products.
– Users of competitors' products that are not interested.

These may be represented in different segments or user groups (primary, secondary and peripheral segments). Using digitally-generated databases, combining different criteria, it is possible to narrow down the communications to specific target groups, concerning both message and channel – see also later. In B2B markets, where customers are generally more easily traceable than in a B2C setting, this analysis is also more straight-forward. Figure 11.4 illustrates this and gives an example of the ranking of target groups (from A1 to C2).

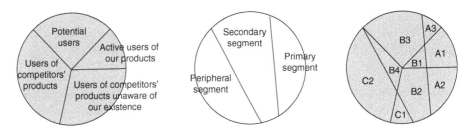

Figure 11.4 "Micro-segmentation" of international market communications.

Table 11.1 Distribution of advertising expenditure per country, 2015

Country	TV	Newspaper	Magazines	Radio	Cinema	Outdoor	Digital
Denmark	21.4	25.7	7.7	1.9	1.3	5.3	36.8
Sweden	25.8	24.3	6.6	2.6	0.7	4.9	35.1
Finland	23.2	38.3	8.9	4.4	0.3	3.6	21.3
Norway	23.8	27.4	5.7	3.7	0.9	3.4	32.2
Netherlands	22.5	19.7	10.0	6.2	0.2	3.9	37.5
Belgium	40.7	22.6	7.0	13.7	1.1	8.8	6.1
Germany	39.6	20.4	16.8	6.8	0.6	4.5	11.3
Great Britain	28.8	17.7	6.7	2.7	1.1	6.1	36.8
France	33.7	11.6	13.1	7.9	1.0	11.4	21.4
Poland	55.5	3.4	6.2	8.6	2.3	6.1	17.9
Italy	53.2	8.9	6.4	5.5	0.3	4.6	21.1
USA	39.1	13.3	11.3	9.4	0.6	3.9	22.4
China	57.2	9.0	1.3	2.7	na*	12.9	16.9
Japan	31.9	10.2	4.1	2.0	na*	8.5	27.4
Thailand	53.6	18.7	5.0	5.8	6.6	9.3	1.1
Brazil	72.5	9.8	5.3	4.1	0.3	3.5	4.5

Source: Dentsu Aegis Network: Global Advertising Expenditure Report, May 2015 / Carat Norge.
Note: *na=not available. Numerical values in per cent.

11.3 Communication channels in international marketing

Communication channels are the media through which the message is transferred to the target group (receiver). The media availability in foreign markets is generally different from that in the domestic market. A closer look at TV media reveals that Sweden and Norway, countries where TV advertising was banned until the beginning of the 1990s, have now passed Finland where this channel has been active since the birth of TV. In Italy (with more than 350 commercial TV channels) and Poland, it makes up more than 50%, and in some emerging markets even more than that. Whereas advertising expenditure in newspapers and weekly magazines constituted around 70–80% of the total in the year 2000 in many North European countries, the figure today is around 30–40%, mostly "eaten up" by digital media. Table 11.1 gives examples of the distribution of advertising expenditures in selected countries.

We observe that digital media are used far less in countries such as Belgium and Germany, and in emerging economies. Nevertheless, in most European countries, digital advertisements make up some 25–35% of total advertising expenditure. The nature of the web potentially gives exporters access to all countries of the world – both through advertising, but also through their own home page.

Many claim that the advent of the internet has democratised marketing in the sense that access to potential customers has become cheaper and more targeted. Every time we enter the net, we leave behind traces (cookies) that are registered in the database of the host. These, in turn, are sold to media firms around the world, which pass it on to their customers. Not many years ago, the advertiser had to pay for a great number of irrelevant readers/listeners/viewers in order to reach out to their target group. Through advertisements on YouTube, Instagram, Twitter, Google, Facebook, Wikipedia, Yahoo, etc. it is possible to tailor the message to very specific target groups.

This may be an engineer between 35 and 50, living in the greater Houston area (Texas, USA), working in the oil and gas industry, interested in classical music; or women of 20–30 years, with higher education, interested in sailing, and living in London. The media agencies can tailor a media package that is more targeted than traditional media, thereby rendering the price per (relevant) reader/viewer much more affordable. Also, the exporter can itself tailor the message to the individual receiver depending on his or her stage in the effect hierarchy (see Figure 11.2). By attracting the unaware potential customer – using relevant key words – in their search for information, they can provide relevant links for his/her further research, which will eventually result in direct requests to the company, so-called "inbound marketing".

The internet has also revolutionised what is called "word of mouth" in marketing. Through social media, firms now foster relations with their constituencies and, in this way, strengthen their brand image and bonds with their customers. This is even more effective if independent bloggers write about the products.

Swims

Swims (loafers/leisure clothes) increasingly uses the internet in its international marketing. The firm is a small "mosquito" in a global market (see also Section 3.4) and has a relatively small marketing budget. Originally, they concentrated their marketing efforts on distributors and dealers, whereas they have recently employed a person who is working full-time on developing market communications on the net. She is active, posting her own contributions; but even more important they have engaged three bloggers (in France, Great Britain and Canada). They write about "all" topics, but also about Swims – which pays them in the form of products. For instance, the blogger in Great Britain has some 50,000 followers – and each time he writes about Swims (perhaps once or twice a week) they receive 40–50 enquiries.

Swims encounters many challenges in their marketing. One is access to high-end dealers around the world. This is important because they hope, in this way, to appear as the "*Original Product*", and dismiss competitors as copyists. For instance, once introduced into Nordstrom stores with their 123 outlets in the US and Canada,[5] the task is to get their sales staff to talk warmly about the products. These are reached in different ways, both in blogs and/or through advertisements on the net.

Kahoot!

Kahoot!'s (see also Section 10.3.3) exponential growth in number of users (40 million per month in 2017) is because the firm has ardently embraced social media in their international marketing communication. They concentrated on Twitter because 20–30% of their target audience in the US are active there. Every tweet posted has given rise to a great number of responses. That in turn has led to new responses and so on, just like a snow-balling effect. They were also active in the EdTech circles (http://www.edtechmagazine.com), making them "thought leaders", building an image of a brand that "actually is caring" for the users. They established a support system that all co-workers should (and wanted to) use from day one. This is their most important contact point with customers – not only because the customers get support, but it converts them into ambassadors of the product.

Furthermore, YouTube has been particularly effective in promoting their quiz games, although this was initiated by enthusiasts among their users. In fact, the users – being content developers on the Kahoot! platform – have been encouraged by Kahoot! to post videos sharing their experience with their social network and on YouTube, building a hype around their brand. The result has been exposure through perhaps a million blogs, Facebook pages and even some TV programmes targeted at teachers. In a way, we may say that not only the market communications have been actively built up around social media and word of mouth dissemination, but the product itself and the brand are designed around it. The effect has been dramatic: since its launch in 2013 (to 2017), one billion players have used their quiz game![6] Kahoot!'s experience with digital media is possibly better than most firms could dream of. Most importantly however, it reflects a mind-set and a determination that – we would claim – are prerequisite to succeed with this communication channel. And of course: the bottom line is that they have a good product!

The development in electronic media has been substantial over the past couple of decades. Most conspicuously, the technological developments of satellite and cable TV, and the internet have revolutionised both information retrieval and the way in which people communicate and search for information.

A critical review of the firm's use of different channels of communication is therefore relevant for many firms. Generally, most advertisers only make superficial assessments ahead of channel decisions (Helgesen 1992), and therefore risk wasting time and money on redundant channels. International trade fairs may be one such example. Participation at professional trade fairs is often the first step in international markets, but this is not always the right channel. Such trade fairs are visited by perhaps as many as 100,000–150,000 businesspeople in search of new partners and products, or who wish to reinforce existing ties with their partners. Many small firms participate at such events on a yearly basis, and spend time and money on potential customers that they do not have time to follow up.

A well-prepared presentation at a trade fair, with clear objectives, is still worth consideration. Participation may easily cost some 25,000–50,000 euros or more (depending on the event and the stand), and in addition preparations, stand decoration, transport of products, travel, advertisements, etc. can easily bring the costs up to more than 100,000 euros.

Export promotion agencies are often helpful in planning participation in trade fairs. They may sometimes also organise a joint presentation at the national level, where exporters are invited to take part. For the small- and medium-sized exporter, this may be an interesting opportunity to be more visible, and possibly have more impact, therefore attracting more visitors.

The Portuguese firm Science4you (toys) participates actively in trade fairs around the world. They use them in their networking development and attribute their international success largely to participation at such events. For instance, in 2015 they attended toys trade fairs in London, Nüremberg and Hong Kong, partly supported by Portuguese export promotion funding. After a modest start in 2008 with sales of 50,000 euros in Portugal, they grew slowly until they started to attend international trade fairs in 2012. The breakthrough year came in 2013 when sales amounted to 3.2 million euros. In 2016, sales reached 15 million euros.[7]

This was also the case for Dynaplast (plastic containers), when they – in search of new markets – got a great order for crates for beer and mineral water bottles, at the Interpack Trade Fair in Düsseldorf, Germany. Interpack was chosen based on an evaluation of the number and kind of visitors; the event was visited by key purchasers from all around Europe, particularly Germany, Great Britain, Benelux and Scandinavia. Representatives from Schweppes visited their stand, and after a year of deliberations they ended up with a contract of 1.7 million crates over three years. In addition to the contract itself, the order gave them an invaluable reference, new impulses and experience.[8]

Visiting trade fairs is also an interesting opportunity to collect market information and to get a grasp of the competition.

Table 11.2 presents a number of alternative scenarios concerning the use of communication channels in international markets by a company producing equipment for radio stations. We notice that market share, marketing and communications objectives, as well as operation mode, play a role in the selection of communications channel (local and international trade fairs, professional magazines, personal sales – alone or together with the local partner, seminars, electronic media). We also observe how an international trade fair may play a role as a channel in local markets. The firm is seemingly a latecomer in the use of social media. Their homepage is primarily in English and steps will be taken to "localise" their homepage to the German and French markets, and at the same time to establish a chat line (in English only, since no one on the technical staff speaks other languages). The German distributor has agreed to release news in the German language on their German homepage. Finally, we observe that TV and radio as well as sponsoring are absent in this firm's media mix.

This case is fictitious, yet realistic, and illustrates how a medium-sized player in an industry needs to factor in different elements in the total media mix (market shares, sales objectives, operation mode, competitive position, language proficiency, resources). A more resourceful company may have a very different situation and adopt a more aggressive communications strategy.

The globalisation of the media industry, with the "traditional" media players such as AOL-Time Warner, Bertelsmann, News Corp, Vivendi and Viacom, etc. alongside the new media (Google, Twitter, YouTube, Instagram, etc.), is indeed an important part of the total picture. On the other hand, diversification and specialisation find their place through a plethora of small, specialised magazines and channels. In many countries, there are special interest periodicals for most hobbies: sports, leisure, auto, fashion, garden, wine, food, fungus (mushrooms), travel, animals, bridge, games – the list is endless. For instance, concerning animals, there are

Table 11.2 Communication channels in international markets: case study of exports of equipment to radio stations

	France	Germany	Netherlands	Great Britain
Market share	2%	5%	15%	30%
Sales (euros)	95,000	0.8 million	0.6 million	4.5 million
Sales goal next year (euros)	160,000	1.4 million	1.2 million	5 million
Competitive position	Competitors don't see you	Competitors have spotted you	You are getting quite annoying to the market leader	You are the market leader
Operation mode	Direct to customers	Distributor	Agent	Sales subsidiary
Communications objectives	Awareness by new customers in the private sector. New orders from established customers	New orders from established customers. Establish new customer relations	New orders from established customers. Motivate the agent	Maintain customer loyalty (and market share)
National communication channels	Personal visits to existing customers. Seek new customers assisted by export promo agency (seminar reception)	Distributor participates at a local trade fair/conference and places adverts in local business periodicals (supported by the exporter)	Advertise in local business periodicals. Visit established and new customers together with the agent	Frequent adverts in business/technical periodicals. Sales office follow up personal sales, and participate at local trade fair
International communication channels	Invite selected existing and potential customers to CEBIT	Participation at CEBIT in co-operation with the German distributor. Other European partners are invited to come	Invite selected existing and potential customers to CEBIT	Adverts in international periodical (related to CEBIT). Invite selected customers to CEBIT
Social media	Develop a French language version of the home page	Develop a German language version of the home page. News releases in German	Chat service	Develop a chat service in English. News releases on line

Note: CEBIT (Centrum für Büroautomation, Informationstechnologie und Telekommunikation), which translates as "Center for Office Automation, Information Technology and Telecommunication", is a yearly trade fair and Festival for innovation and digitalisation, organised by Deutche Messe in Hannover. It is said to be the world's most important event in the computer industry.

specialist periodicals on cats, dogs, horses, birds – right down to pigeons. In addition, there are numerous periodicals addressing special industries – many of which are international (for example, the *Oil and Gas Journal* or *European Chemical News*). These are all candidates for targeted adverts by the exporter.

11.4 Development of the message

The message is possibly the one element of the "communications package" that contributes most to the process of developing a brand personality. The message is targeted to trigger a response from specific customer groups, and as such, the wording, the atmosphere, the setting of the message and the imagery used will all set the tone for how the audience perceives the message. The question then arises as to whether it is possible or desirable to create the same personality across countries, and if yes, whether one should use the same adverts or the same catchphrases. A message that is not adapted may paralyse the marketing campaign, well-illustrated by the following case, drawn from David Ricks' wonderful book, *Big Blunders in International Business* (1983).

> When Pepsodent, in their marketing campaign in South East Asia, stressed the advantage of the whitening qualities of their toothpaste, they totally ignored the status associated with dark teeth in some local societies of this part of the world. Here the people have for centuries chewed betel nuts, which has a side effect; to discolour the teeth. In addition, they used a slogan, "Wonder where the yellow went?", possibly not the best slogan in South East Asia.

The basic slogans used to develop or emphasise the brand's qualities and personality are one thing. Whether the underlying nature of the qualities used in the communication will affect its outcome in terms of awareness, sympathy or market share for the brand is another. Roth's (1995) study is relevant in this context. He analysed the effects of different brand image strategies in international advertising:[9]

- Functional brand image (i.e. problem solving and problem prevention).
- Social brand image (i.e. social approval, status, accreditation).
- Sensory brand image (i.e. stimulation, gratification, variety seeking).

Across all countries, he did not find any significant effect of using one or another strategy. However, when studying the moderating effects of Hofstede's (1980) cultural dimensions, and of the income level in different cities, a certain pattern emerged. He found that both power distance and individualism (but not uncertainty avoidance[10]) modify the effects of an advertising message on market share.

- Functional brand image works well in countries scoring high on individualism.
- Social brand image works well in countries scoring high on power distance (where wealth, status and prestige are highly valued), and low on individualism.
- Sensory brand image works well in countries scoring high on both power distance and individualism.

Studying the effects of GDP per capita, he also concludes that messages stressing functional qualities of the brand are more successful in low-income countries, and that sensory and social brand images are effective in high-income countries.

Roth's (1995) study is interesting in that it suggests using a different brand image emphasis in advertising depending on both cultural and socioeconomic factors. If his results are to be taken seriously, managers should diversify their advertisements and establish groups of countries that score more or less the same on individualism and power distance. For instance, using Kale's (1995) euro-clusters (see Section 9.3), in the Nordic-Dutch and Anglo-Germanic clusters, with high individualism, low power distance and high income levels, advertisements should typically stress functional and sensory brand images, whereas in the Latin cluster (medium power distance, varying individualism and medium income levels) sensory and social brand images would be more appropriate. Since sensory brand image seems to be a common denominator of both clusters, it would be worthwhile exploring adverts with that emphasis.

Still, the basic expression in the advert may vary. An interesting example is given by the following adverts by Audi in Germany and the UK.

> The advert was adapted to each country, yet had the same basic communication platform and idea. In Germany the car was presented as a high tech vehicle with high status, showing a glossy picture of the car. This was in many ways also the main theme of the British advert, which basically adopted the same idea and the same text (translated). However, the picture was quite different: the car was transformed into a carrot with four wheels! The advert, in an archetypal British way, poked fun at the perfectionist Germans, while at the same time it expressed an admiration for their technical competencies (Purdy and Carl-Zepp 1988).

A number of comparisons between advertising styles in different countries have been carried out over the years. Most of them corroborate that our intuitive idea of the values and norms of each country are to some extent expressed in the ways advertising is performed. For instance – as shown above – British adverts typically play on humour and understatements and to a lesser degree on information about the product. British advertising agencies display more than most others a capacity to relate the message to their local audience (de Mooij 2013). French advertisers play more on symbols and implicit messages and seldom on product (Zandpour et al. 1992). Adverts in Japan are also indirect, but – in spite of Japan's high score on collectivism on Hofstede's (1980) scale – they often feature individualistic messages. This may be a sign of a gradual development away from the traditional group orientation that one typically finds in Asian countries (Mueller 1992). Also, status is conspicuous in Japanese advertisements. German adverts are much more oriented towards seriousness and functional product information. In the US, on the other hand, adverts are often direct and "hard sell".

Even though it is possible to develop standardised messages, it is often desirable to adapt the creative expression to local market conditions, as shown in the Audi case above. De Mooij (2013) suggests that the implementation can be divided into three steps:

1   Analyse the most important aspects of the message so as not to end up in embarrassing situations (see Pepsodent in Asia, above).
2   Analyse what approaches can and cannot be used across borders.
3   Make sure that the creative solution is not dramatically different or it will lead to extra costs when adapted to other countries.

The most successful global advertisers have managed to build a culture around their brand by developing a personality, thereby identifying a common platform across countries, be it Marlborough, Levi, McDonald's or Coca-Cola. Van Raaij (1997) suggests a communications strategy on four levels:

1   The *role* that the firm and its brand want to play in the market, its personality. This is about the long-term goal the company has in its relations with its target groups, and its position in the market. What should we be for our customers? What personality should our brand(s) have?
2   The *communications platform* used in the advert – or more generally in the market communications. The platform is part of the long-term strategy of the firm and is critical – particularly if the objective is to enhance knowledge of and attitude towards a brand, to change consumer behaviour.
3   The *creative idea* in the market communications. How should the personality be "translated" into a language that is relevant for the target group? The language – not only the English, Dutch, French or German, Japanese, Hindi or Chinese language, but the cultural language that also contains metaphors and associations that make the product interesting for potential buyers.

> Van Raaij (1997) mentions the case of a VW advert where the car owner was presented as an independent and self-conscious person. In Italy, this concept was staged as a large herd of sheep, one of which was black – in that country a symbol of independence. In other countries, a black sheep has quite different connotations and would scarcely be used as a sign of independence.

4   The *execution* of the creative idea is about style, typography, visual presentation and the person presenting the message (the person in the street or a well-known artist/person).

So, the question then becomes: which of these levels of communication can be standardised? Van Raaij (1997) suggests the classification system in Table 11.3 (see below) based on this hierarchy of communication strategies.

De Mooij (2013) brings up the same theme from a practitioner standpoint and offers three levels of standardisation/adaptation:

1   *Export advertisements*, implying full standardisation and centralisation regarding development of the message. In this context she gives the example of French cosmetics. This

Table 11.3 Standardisation or adaptation of message in international communications

Communication level	Global	Adapted	Differentiated	Local
Role, objective, personality	Standardisation	Standardisation	Standardisation	Standardisation/ Adaptation
Communications platform	Standardisation	Standardisation	Standardisation	Adaptation
Creative idea/concept	Standardisation	Standardisation	Customisation	Adaptation
Execution	Standardisation	Adaptation	Adaptation	Adaptation

Source: Adapted from van Raaij (1997).

message may well be written in French, since it will emphasise the origin of the product and, in this way, create a personality around the brand.

2   In *prototype advertisements*, the exporter gives instructions for the basic expression of the adverts, such as use of logo, positioning, use of advertising themes and "no-themes", etc. This gives the exporter some more control, but compliance with the instructions depends on the local subsidiary/partner and the ability of the exporter to follow up and control.

3   *Guideline advertisements*, where the advertiser gives general instructions for the development of the concept, but where the individual local sales subsidiary/partner oversees the creative idea and its execution. We have previously seen how too much freedom will give the local advertising agency too much leeway to come up with their own ideas; the risk here is that the original concept may be distorted and be quite different from what was originally intended by the exporter.

We shall return to these approaches in Section 11.6.

11.5 The sender – the role of country of origin

The position of the sender of a message – the brand owner – has consequences for both media channel and content decisions.[11] This is particularly the case for large global brands, with both positive consequences – in that "everyone" knows what they are and what they stand for – and negative consequences – in the sense that their reputation is much more vulnerable to negative PR. Cases such as Shell in Nigeria (oil spills), Apple in Ireland (tax evasion) and Union Carbide in India (poisonous gas in Bhopal) illustrate the harmful effects of incidents that, with a heightened attention to social responsibility, could have been avoided.[12] Smaller exporters are in quite a different position, unknown to most and with limited resources to wield any clout in international markets. One possible way to achieve attention, and recognition, for these firms and their brands is to play on country-of-origin effects. The rest of this section will therefore discuss different aspects of such effects.

Country-of-origin is one of the most researched issues in international marketing. Country-of-origin effects are what happens to purchasing behaviour in relation to the image of the country that is associated with the product. It has been called "*the made in ... effect*", but the association of a product to a country may be communicated by many means other than a "made in" label. In fact, the home of the brand may be more important than where it is made. Country-of-origin effects are documented for consumer products and for products that are distributed on the business-to-business market. Countries give both strong and weak impressions and consumers use these to form opinions about products that they associate with the country. For instance, Germany has an image of excellent workmanship and technology, and this has contributed to its reputation for making excellent cars and machines. Germany's image for creativity, design and artistic expression is lower. Therefore, German manufacturers of personal toiletries, modern textiles and shoes benefit less from being associated with Germany. Italy, on the other hand, is known for excellence in design and fashion products. The Italian fashion industry dates back several centuries, and its excellence in design and arts is also expressed through famous painters and architecture. Italian luxury goods are known all over the world for high quality and perfect elegance and refinement. The label "Made in Italy" for fashion products expresses excellence in creativity, quality of materials and craftsmanship. Italy is, in this sense, a brand. From Italy come famous brands like Gucci,

Prada, Armani and many others. If each of the brands mentioned above is worth millions of euros – then what is the worth of "Made in Italy"?

The tremendous worth of the "Made in Italy" label in the textile and fashion industry is illustrated by the development of Chinese "sweatshops" in Prato, the historic capital of Italy's textile business. Prato has attracted the largest concentration of small-scale Chinese industry in Europe. As many as 50,000 Chinese live and work in the area, making clothes bearing the prized "Made in Italy" label. "Made in Italy" differentiates their products from garments produced in China itself.

Country-of-origin may affect buying behaviour through three routes: cognitive effects, affective effects and normative effects (Verlegh and Steenkamp 1999). The routes are not fixed, but rather constantly interacting.

The most important *cognitive effects* are those of the country-of-origin on perceived product quality. There is a positive relationship between this and the degree of economic development. Highly-developed countries often have good standards of education, technology, quality control, innovativeness and other factors that are important in high-quality products. Products from rich, highly-industrialized countries are therefore often perceived to be of higher quality than products from developing countries. This is an important liability for producers in developing countries. Many countries develop reputations for excellence in specific product groups. Such reputations may be grounded in historic factors, culture, climate and nature and others. For example, Belgian chocolate, Swiss watches and French wine. Recognition of excellence in specific product groups – such as Colombian coffee, Indian cotton, Chinese silk, Cuban cigars and Nigerian cocoa – is also widespread in developing and emerging nations.

The *affective impact* of country-of-origin is how consumption of a product from a country may affect how you feel about yourself (psychological impact) and how it may influence how other people feel about you (social impact). People often have strong feelings and opinions about foreign countries. We call negative feelings *country animosity*. These may be due to a history of war, economic exploitation of other countries, hostile and unfair politics and unfriendly people (Nes et al 2012). People often avoid buying products from countries that they really dislike because they do not want to be associated with or support the country in any way. Some people are aware of this and some are not. For example, an eager socialist may refrain from buying a Chevrolet, because this may negatively influence how she looks upon herself and how other people would evaluate her. Interestingly, perceived quality does not compensate for animosity against the country-of-origin. Our socialist may be of the impression that Chevrolets are good cars, but would never buy one.

Some foreign countries we really, really like. We call love for a foreign country "*country affinity*" (Nes et al. 2014). Research shows that the main reasons we love foreign countries are for their culture and arts, nature, language and entertainment. The same underlying factors may be operational for both animosity and affinity. A feeling that the *people* are hostile and unfriendly is negative. But more prevalent are positive feelings for friendly people with attractive lifestyles, which stimulate affinity. *Politics* may also be either a positive or a negative, but tends to be a stronger animosity driver than affinity driver. We observe a positive relationship between country affinity and buying behaviour. As an example, a person who loves France may feel good about expressing her/his affinity by driving a French car, wearing French clothes, enjoying French wine and French artists.

The *normative effect* is the third route of influence of country-of-origin on buying behaviour. Normative impact is about how people *ought* to act. People all over the world evaluate products made in their home country higher than foreigners do. This is explained by "consumer ethnocentrism" which is the tendency to support domestic producers to save jobs and express patriotism (Shimp and Sharma 1987). Consumer ethnocentrism is especially important for agricultural products. It is less important for raw materials where it is difficult to identify the country-of-origin in the final product, e.g. oil. Consumer boycotts of products from countries with politics they perceive as unacceptable are another expression of the normative impact of country-of-origin.

The country-of-origin is not a straightforward issue. A company in one country may market a brand which has its origin in another country, which is designed in a third country, and produced in a fourth country with parts from all over the world. So, what is the country-of-origin? In fact, marketers have much freedom in choosing the country, if any, they want associate with the product.

One example is Volkswagen, which is built all over the world. For VW, it is important to be associated with the German reputation for excellence in cars. Often, they include the term "Das Auto" in their international advertising to remind the consumer of their German origin. IKEA ties into Scandinavian culture by emphasising functional product attributes. IKEA sources its products from low-cost countries. However, its colours (blue and yellow) are the same as in the Swedish flag, and the international names for the various products are Scandinavian.

Another case from the car industry: Sweden is the perceived country-of-origin and the actual country-of-brand of Volvo. However, the Volvo XC60 is designed in a design centre in the US which is headed by a British designer with a background in the German car industry. The company is owned by Geely Automobil, a Chinese company, and built in Belgium. But it is headquartered in Sweden.

For both IKEA, Volvo and VW, the home of the brand is more important than the country of production. The important question is which country the consumer associates with the brand, and "country-of-brand" is often a better expression than "country-of-origin". The country-of-origin that consumers associate with the product is usually what we would call the country-of-brand but not the country of production. For example, iPhones and Nike athletic shoes are made in Asia, but perceived as American.

Marketers may communicate the country-of-origin directly or indirectly, such as the use of language (VW and "Das Auto"), the use of colours (Lego uses the colours on the Danish flag, red and white), typical or famous models and spokespersons (e.g. traditional Colombian coffee farmers, Marlborough man), famous national landmarks (L'Oréal and the Eiffel tower), "designed in ..." (Nike uses Designed in US), and other ways that innovative marketers apply to provide links between the product and a country that supports the brand image. Marketers have a lot of freedom, but must always communicate a believable brand story, which enhances brand equity.

A study on Helly Hansen's brand image (with its HH logo) in Germany shows that such associations to the country of origin are important also for well known brands which initially are promoted without a country of origin link (the national origin of HH was generally unknown in international markets). The study demonstrated that Norway (HH's brand origin) is associated with rough weather which poses high demands on the quality of outdoor garments. It also suggested that when HH was linked to Norway, the brand image and the consumers' belief in HH's brand promise was heightened.

(Nes and Gripsrud 2014)

11.6 International promotion and the firm's strategic position

We have seen in this chapter how different factors affect the firm's international market communications.[13] Critical issues in this context are:

– How should the communication package be sewn together?
– Who should be responsible for the development of this package?
– How should one bridge the gap between the natural divergences between the centre and periphery?
– To what extent should one use an advertising agency, and how?

There is no universal recipe to answer these questions. The Strategic Windows model suggests that firms take different approaches to international market communications depending on their position in this model. More specifically, we anticipate that firms in the four cells will adopt different control and monitoring structures, information behaviour, and market communication strategies; see Figure 11.5. The following sections give a brief outline of some of the archetypal features expected in each cell of the model.

11.6.1 The local brander – guideline advertising

The *local brander* typically epitomises the newcomer to international markets, with limited resources, experience or marketing insight, and with local representatives, who generally work closely with *their own* local advertising agencies, making most of the marketing decisions on their

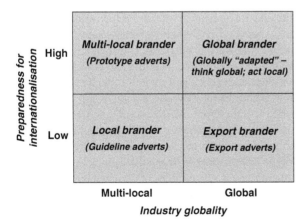

Figure 11.5 International branding in different strategic positions.

Source: Solberg (2014).

behalf. The local brander, with limited capability to gather control information, simply has to trust that its representatives (distributor, agent, sales subsidiary, etc.) will make the best out of each individual marketing situation. The more seasoned among the firms in this category may address the situation by developing common guidelines that place some restrictions on the local representatives and their advertising agencies. However, since more often than not the guidelines are developed by the exporter – with help from an advertising agency in the firm's home country – and the exporter operates in a multi-domestic market setting, the concept may not easily transfer to other markets. Therefore, the local partner and advertising agencies would prefer to do things in their own way, rather than complying with the suggested guidelines. The result is local adaptations – and potentially quite different brand personalities in each market (de Mooij 2013).

Tine – the leading Norwegian dairy group (sales of 22 billion NOK/2.5 billion euros) – belongs in this cell. They export only 5% of their output, and even though their Jarlsberg cheese has attained a certain status in some markets (particularly in the US), it is difficult for the company to get any major impact by using a centrally-developed advertising campaign. In cooperation with a Norwegian advertising agency, they created a campaign to be run internationally, where the main theme was Norwegian nature, with fjords and mountains, underlining the cleanliness of the product. However, the distributors had different views on what to emphasise in the ads for their cheese and did not "buy into" the campaign, which soon was aborted.

The communication channels available for the local branders are local trade fairs and advertising in local media. The local representative, normally a distributor or an agent, should be the one to initiate and carry out these kinds of activities, often with some support from the exporter.

11.6.2 The multi-domestic brander – prototype advertising

The multi-domestic branders generally have a higher market share in their main export markets. Firms in this position also have more experience in international markets, and therefore tend to acquire more detailed market information (Benito et al. 1993). Consequently, they are better equipped to evaluate local requirements in each market, including suggestions made by their local marketing partners – be it their own sales subsidiary or an independent representative – and their advertising agencies. On the other hand, they also acknowledge that local market conditions warrant local solutions, and will therefore tend to accept that brand image and the communication mix may differ from one country to another, possibly with different degrees of adaptation at different levels in the communication mix (mission, proposition, creative idea, execution – van Raaij 1997). Prototype advertising (de Mooij 2013) may be one solution for firms in this position: "definite instructions are given, usually covering numerous aspects of the execution. Prototype advertising provides better control than guideline advertising" (de Mooij 2013, p. 234).

Firms in this cell normally have more clout in their relations with their local partners than those in the previous cell, and will therefore also be in a better position to "dictate" the use of content, the photos, the themes and the brand.

Jordan (who make oral hygiene products) are located here. They monitor their local distributors in their local market activities keenly, but allow deviations to the instructions given centrally. Rather than unilaterally monitoring their distributors' local marketing activities, Jordan nurtures close cooperation with their distributors, thus indirectly influencing them on Jordan's ideas. There are however exceptions: when Jordan launched their international campaign for dental floss, they discovered that their Finnish distributor had already developed their own ideas based on idiosyncrasies in the local market and made investments on their own. This draft campaign deviated considerably from Jordan's own centrally-developed marketing plans, and led to a great deal of discussion. Eventually, the local Finnish proposals were sanctioned since the tests carried out by the distributor appeared to be unambiguously positive.

11.6.3 Export branders – export adverts

Export branders are firms that rate low on the preparedness axis, with limited resources to develop advanced marketing campaigns. They operate in a global industry setting, sometimes with a blurred and undefined competitive picture since their products and services are often the result of innovations, the positioning of their products/services is therefore not straightforward. These firms risk meeting large competitors that can rapidly pick up their ideas and launch them internationally through their network.

In this situation, the firm should address an international audience from the start, actively using digital marketing tools, be it Facebook, Twitter, YouTube, Instagram, etc. or engaging in blogs. We have seen how Kahoot! – a dwarf against giants such as Microsoft or Amazon – managed to develop brand recognition and usage among one billion users over a period of only three years. Another channel may be international trade fairs, addressing a global audience, in order to seek rapid recognition among its core target group. Many firms seek their distributor(s) at such trade fairs. We have already discussed the caveats of premature trade fair participation (Section 11.3), and would advise exporters in this position to secure cooperation with a large (global) partner – or a few select partners in key markets – that is able to follow up the "rush of queries" that (hopefully) will ensue. This will also give the international marketing campaign a more grounded foundation, the partner giving advice on the development of the advertising material.

With limited resources, firms in this position should typically develop standardised solutions that transfer more or less easily to other regions. However, even in global markets, the execution needs sometimes to be localised (Walliser and Usunier, 1998, de Mooij 2013). As they do not have sufficient resources to adapt to the local flavour, they are nevertheless expected to run the same campaign across all markets, with the same mission, campaign theme and creative idea, and often also the same execution. "Export advertising is imposed upon the world unadapted, or simply with the copy translated. This is the ultimate form of centralization" (de Mooij 2013, p. 234). Export branders have limited market shares and they will therefore spend comparatively less time and money on advertising than on other marketing tasks, such as, for example, product development or securing appropriate distribution partners in international markets. On the other hand, the strategy may as well be, if not "dictated", at least heavily influenced by the latter, given their information leverage in their respective markets. Therefore, even though the external conditions for standardisation are present, export branders may be compelled to accept local branding carried out through their more powerful trading partners.

11.6.4 Global branders – "Think global – act local"

Finally, *global branders* – market leaders in global markets – spend considerable resources to sew together a branding strategy and a communication package that addresses both the need for customised solutions, the advantages of scale economies and a global brand image. Most firms in this cell have their own subsidiaries in local markets and would therefore be more prone to decree the content and the execution of the marketing communications. On the other hand, even global brands need to make some local adjustments in their marketing.

> Coca-Cola is one of the world's most global brands.[14] They are present in about 200 countries and are the world leader in the soft drinks market. Their iconographic identity (the name and the red colour) is known across the world and suggests a truly standardised, global brand. This trademark is nevertheless translated into different languages (for example into Chinese – see Section 10.3.2). Also, the company has tailored taste, packaging, price and advertising to deal with specific preferences in different market. Local managers are assigned responsibility for sales and distribution programmes. They use different advertising agencies – at present there are four: Mercado-McCann, Santo, Sra. Rushmore and Ogilvy & Mather – and give strict instructions on how the commercials are to use the logo, positioning and themes. Their slogan is: *"Think global, act global, but leverage local"*.[15]

However, examples abound of firms in this position that enforce centralised solutions on their local partners and subsidiaries, and that later experience the harsh realities of internal conflicts and opposition (Quelch and Hoff 1986). Examples are multinationals such as Parker Pens, which failed to globalise its marketing communications in the early 1990s (Lipman 1988), or smaller firms such as the Norwegian leisure and sports gear supplier Helly Hansen/ HH in China (see Section 8.4.1).

> On their road to becoming a global brand, HH had to go through many rounds over more than a decade. Because they did not adequately monitor their partners, each one of them incorporated their own preferences into the brand, and therefore developed different meanings in their different markets: in Denmark they were seen as rain gear, in Japan as yachting wear, in US as hip-hop, in Canada as ski/snowboard outfits, and in Norway they were just about all of these. This made the transformation process troublesome and led to several changes in both personnel and organisational structure.

The road to a global brand image is bumpy and takes time. It is about developing a uniform brand personality. It is about monitoring the partners and sales subsidiaries and finding a common theme across markets. Firms in the global brander position need to put considerable work into developing a common "world view" inside the organisation: their role in the market, the personality of the products, the associations created in their target groups by the market communications. This is important because the international media typically used (be it CNN or Eurosport; the *Financial Times* or *Yachting World*; the *New York Times* or *Vogue*) have a reach far beyond their countries of publication. Global branders generally have their own sales subsidiaries in key markets, and it should therefore be easier to develop a common platform for their marketing communications (see also Section 8.4.2). We have seen how local managers of sales subsidiaries have a "bad habit", developing their own ideas of local marketing campaigns (Section 8.6) based on local market characteristics, and their own urge to "freely" define local approaches to marketing. The perspective of headquarters is naturally different: inconsistent brand identities and differing priorities risk jeopardising the development towards a global brand image.

Quelch and Hoff (1986) describe a process whereby the main objective is to develop an organisational culture that focuses on a common purpose (identification power) rather than carrying out strict monitoring and control (legal or coercive power). Global firms using this process may avoid the main pitfalls of centralised global advertising campaigns. The process consists of five steps:

1 *Information exchange* (to establish a common understanding of challenges, objectives and visions)
2 *Persuasion* (where HQ, through the above information exchange, persuades their local partners)
3 *Coordination* (use of one advertising agency for all markets)
4 *Local acceptance* (what parts should be globalised and what parts can remain local?)
5 *Supervision* (using both carrots and sticks, the latter still being necessary – even if some kind of clan feel is established).

The process suggested by Quelch and Hoff is one of many. Whatever process is used to arrive at a more or less uniform communication in international markets, it will most likely meet natural resistance in the subsidiary and partner network. We believe that the most important component in this process is the involvement of local managers in some way or another.

11.7 Chapter summary

We have seen that establishing a brand personality is critical to developing effective international marketing promotion strategies. The tension between local adaptation and central standardisation is particularly present in this regard. Sometimes, it is better just to let the brands develop in their own way in each individual market, but in most cases, there is scope for some standardisation. The great challenge here is to bridge the gap between cultural expressions in different countries. Also, the different media realities in different countries make this job more demanding. The use of the communication model (sender–message–channel–receiver) helps us analyse the communication task in more detail. Particularly the country-of-origin effects are interesting in this context, and may be used more actively by exporters. Finally, the identification of the strategic position of firms, as defined by their location in the Strategic Windows model, may help the firm to understand their choices concerning their approach to standardisation/adaptation of their marketing communications and hence, the positioning of their brands in international markets. A critical factor in any attempt to standardise the marketing communications is the relationships between centre and periphery – and clan culture is a key consideration here.

Notes

1 As the reader may know, Norwegians are ardent skiers. At Easter, virtually "half of the Norwegian population" leave town in order to get the last spots of snow in the mountains before summer sets in.

2 Jensson and Lintho (1994).

3 Other models were introduced later, such as for instance AIDA – Awareness, Interest, Desire and Action. This acronym is possibly easier to remember given the well-known opera of the same name (Giuseppe Verdi's *Aida* from 1871).

4 For example, CAPP (Continuous Advertising Planning Programme developed by Leo Burnett) or 4C (Cross Cultural Consumer Characterization by Young and Rubicam).

5 Nordstrom is one of the US's largest up-scale department stores, with annual sales approaching 14.5 billion USD (2015). Source Wikipedia.

6 Johan Brand, co-founder.

7 http://www.science4youtoys.com/pages/about-us

8 Conversation with former export manager. Dynaplast has since been taken over by RPC Group, UK.

9 His sample was for brand strategies: 209 cases of brand strategy in 11 firms in the apparel (jeans)/athletic shoe industry; for socioeconomic data: 60 cities in 10 countries (South America, Europe and Japan).

10 He did not investigate the effects of masculinity.

11 This section is an adapted version of a PM written in 2017 by Professor Emeritus Erik Nes, BI Norwegian Business School.

12 Such issues are well described in the general marketing literature, and will not be dealt with here.

13 This section is an adapted version of the author's article, "International branding: A framework for classification and analysis," published in *Journal of Euromarketing* (Solberg, 2014).

14 Coca-Cola is number 3 on Interbrand's 2016 ranking.

15 Based on Coca-Cola's website: http://www.coca-colacompany.com/stories/taste-the-feeling-launch, and presentation by Coca-Cola Europe, Brussels, 1994.

12 Pricing decisions in international markets

12.1 Introduction

Pricing is an integral part of the marketing mix. It is an expression of the positioning of the brand, and at the same time the foundation for the profitability and competitiveness of the firm. It is closely linked to the other elements of the marketing mix in that price adaptation to each individual market generally follows product, promotion and distribution adaptation (Sousa and Bradley 2008). It is the also the easiest element of the marketing mix to alter, up or down, just by the stroke of a pen! The pricing strategy of a firm is established in the tension between different parts of the firm: accounting wants as high a price as possible in order to increase profits; sales and marketing want a low price in order to facilitate sales; production/operations are somewhere in between and would normally see price pressures as a challenge to bring costs down. In the end, a competitive price depends on the cost level in the firm. Solberg et al. (2014) found that cost level (defined as cost leadership) is indeed among the most important factors that determine performance in international markets. For firms in high-cost countries, typically in parts of the Western world, this represents a challenge which can be met by developing a business model involving different alternatives, such as outsourcing to low-cost countries, rationalisation of manufacturing processes, targeting high quality (and therefore high price) segments of the market that expect higher costs to be reflected in the price. This is not the prime subject of this text, but will still be part of pricing strategies.

International pricing has been said to be a field that causes trouble for exporters (Kublin 1990, Myers 1997). A general assertion by American exporters was reported to be that they did not have any control over the pricing through the distribution channels (Kublin 1990). Exporters therefore seemingly acquiesced with that situation, and calculated their export price based on their domestic experience.

This chapter explores special factors relating to international pricing. The following topics are covered:

- Establishing the base price
- Pricing and profitability
- Pricing in practice
- International pricing and the firm's strategic position.

12.2 Establishing the base price

Base price may be defined as the price that the customer pays in the market. This customer may be a distributor, dealer or an end-user, in an organisation, or an individual consumer. The calculation will then appear as follows:

Base price
- Variablemanufacturing/operationscosts
- Internationalmarketingcosts
- Freight,customs,etc.
= Contributionofinternationalsales

The contribution of international sales is then supposed to cover fixed costs of the operations, in addition to a profit. This way of regarding pricing – *the contribution or market-based method* – is clearly market-oriented in that it considers the potential in the market rather than the costs that need to be covered in order to achieve acceptable returns – *the cost plus method*. The point of departure for this latter method is a stipulated volume across which the fixed costs are distributed using a calculated key. The price in this case will, in principle, be the same to all countries at the gate of the factory (Ex-works – see later). The differences from one market to the next will then depend on customs tariffs, freight costs, the dealer mark-up structure, and will not take into account different competitive situations or a willingness to pay by the customer, both of which may differ from one market to the other. The cost plus method, therefore, makes it somewhat more difficult to use the price as a tool to proactively reach specific objectives locally in individual markets. Yet, this method is used by a majority of exporters (Solberg 1987, 1988, Kublin 1990), in spite of the fact that they forsake the possibility to charge higher prices. The blunt statement of a sales engineer in a large engineering firm eloquently illustrates this point: "I think that it is now high time to lose a contract because of too high a price!"

Jordan (toothbrushes/oral hygiene) is active in many countries, mainly in Europe, but also overseas. Their approach to pricing is as follows:

1   The first step is to position the brand in the market. The positioning varies from one market to the other, depending on the number of competitors, who they are, and their market shares. In markets with oligopoly – i.e. three to five players of more or less equal size – it will be difficult to break into the market (retail chains, supermarkets) because the potential customers have enough potential suppliers to be able to play one against the other to get a good deal. If there is one or perhaps two dominant competitors, the interest in finding new suppliers is greater, giving a different opportunity to position the brand concerning price. In a more atomistic or fragmented market with many small suppliers, there are more entry opportunities, but they usually also come with prices that are more depressed.

2   The point of departure for their calculations is what Jordan terms a "value fraction". The advantages of the brand are in the numerator, whereas the price is in the denominator. The product advantages that go into the fraction are a) functional (physical quality), b) emotional (trustworthiness/brand image) and 3) sensorial (colour, shape, packaging etc.). The firm measures how consumers perceive these three quality factors in each market and gets a good foundation from which to discuss pricing with their local distributor. In this way they get substantial insights into each market where they are active.

3   Most markets have a prohibition on dictating prices through distributors to the retail level. Therefore, it is at the discretion of the trade partners to determine the final price to the consumer. Jordan is still able to negotiate the price up or down according to their guidelines and strategic objectives.[1]

Objectives
- Market share/positioning
- Return on investments
- Time perspective
- Primary/secondary markets

Approaches to pricing
- Cost plus
- Market-based
- Marginal pricing
- Combined/flexible

International pricing policy

Cost factors
- Variable/fixed
- Adaptation
- Export costs
- Customs, transport, etc.
- Risk/terms of payment
- Currency risks

Market factors
- Consumption patterns
- Preferences
- Competition
- Distribution structure
- Product life cycle
- Taxes, legal aspects, etc.

Figure 12.1 Factors in international pricing.

Depending on the operation mode (and thereby the channel structure), different kinds of costs will be included in the base price calculus. If the firm exports through distributors (who take title to the products), then direct control with further marketing activities including pricing ends at the entry gate of its partner. Even though the firm might desire to price the products all the way to the final consumer, it will in principle not be able to do this through the distributor. Attempts to achieve such control are illegal in most countries and may be heavily fined. Another matter is, of course, that exporters may cooperate with their distributors and dealers all the way down to the final buyer of the product/service. Selling through an agent (who brokers the transaction – on behalf of the exporter) and through a sales subsidiary is different. In such cases, the exporter controls pricing further down the chain.

Figure 12.1 exhibits the main factors affecting international pricing. The following section explores these in some more detail.

12.2.1 Objectives

Return on investment is the most important factor here, both short-term and long-term. This will vary with the marketing objectives of the firm. In primary markets, the firm may be willing to accept low profitability (low introductory prices or high entry costs) in an introductory phase in order to retrieve, at a later stage, those losses when they have achieved a secure market position. We have already reported the effects of market share on profitability (PIMS (profit impact on market strategy) – see the Boston Consulting Group – see Section 4.3.2). In a secondary market, the contributions from sales need to at least cover the costs of export operations – also in the short-term they should cover part of the fixed costs. Therefore, prevailing market conditions will determine the base price. The extent to which the firm should engage in the market will depend, in this instance, on marginal cost considerations more than long-term objectives in the market.

The causal relationship between market share and return on sales strongly suggests that market share is an objective in itself. There are two main explanations for such relationships:

1   Economies of scale (which vary greatly from one sector to another), both in production, marketing and export operations.
2   Brand awareness in the market (people tend to pay more for a well-known brand).

Getting there is another matter. It is all about developing an effective marketing strategy, not only pricing but all the critical elements of the marketing mix. When the firm and its products/ brands are generally recognised in the market, the customers tend to trust the supplier and make purchases without fear of running great risks.

> Nordox is market leader in many countries within cuprous oxide (used to combat fungal and bacterial infections on crops as a result of unfavourable weather conditions – such as tropical rain storms). For the farmer it is critical to trust the fungicide has the desired effect. Nordox's products have a stable quality and efficiency, better than many of their competitors' cuprous chemicals. Cuprous oxide from Nordox is red as opposed to those of their competitors that are green or blue, a fact that they use in their marketing with the slogan: "Stick to the red". This slogan is accompanied by solid documentation of the bonding properties offered by red cuprous oxide and has led to a market leadership position in many countries. Customers are therefore willing to pay more for Nordox's products than for those of their competitors – a fact that is more conspicuous in markets where they are dominant.[2]

Table 12.1 sums up this discussion.

12.2.2 Approaches to pricing

These have – in part – already been discussed in the introduction to this section. Cost plus and contribution – or market-based methods are the two main approaches to pricing in general. In

Table 12.1 International pricing in different market situations

Market category	Objectives	Pricing strategy
Primary markets		
Long-term	– Among the leaders in the market – High return	High price
Short-term	– Building market share	Introductory (low) pricing or "normal" market price accompanied by (heavy) marketing campaign
Secondary markets		
Long-term	– Service the market reasonably (without too much cost). The market may be a future primary market. – Capacity utilisation	Should give reasonable contributions
Short-term	– Exploit a concrete business opportunity	Marginal pricing, should cover at least extra export costs (get as high a price as possible, as warranted by the market situation)

addition, we introduce two other approaches which in principle are variants of the two main methods: flexible and marginal pricing. In this section we will briefly summarise the main points in the discussion.

Cost plus method

This approach has also been termed rigid cost plus, which implies in principle that the same price calculation is applied across all markets. Its main advantage is that it is easy to apply: the firm does not need to research foreign market conditions, thereby saving costs on information and management time; it only needs information about internal costs and to evenly distribute overhead costs between markets according to the budgeted sales volume. This gives management full cost control over pricing. Another advantage of the cost plus method is that it conveys a uniform message to foreign customers: there is no room for price negotiations! For firms selling globally through the internet this is more than an advantage; it easily becomes a necessity.

The disadvantages may possibly outweigh the advantages. First of all – as we have seen above – cost plus is inflexible and not adapted to the market. This implies that in one market with low price levels, the exporter will be outcompeted on price; in another high price level market it will leave the customer with what has been called "consumer surplus" (Myers and Harvey 2001, p. 278). In other words: cost plus does not take into account the local market situation, and may therefore eventually lead the firm to have quite different brand images across countries. Another weakness of cost plus pricing is that it totally alienates the local marketing partner in the pricing decision. The active and embedded involvement of the partner in all facets of the local marketing effort – including pricing – is an integral part of the motivation and monitoring of the partner as described in Chapter 8. Giving partners a say in the local price setting will also make them partly responsible for their results in the market.

Market-based pricing – contribution method

The advantages and disadvantages of this method are in a way the mirror of the cost plus situation. Advantages: the price is adapted to the local market situation, and the firm may reap the potential of high price level markets. It should also include the local representatives in the process to define the "optimal" local base price, and thereby get their involvement as committed partners. There are also caveats to market pricing. It gives the exporter a blurred image among customers. For instance, at international trade fairs, the exporter meets with potential customers from all parts of the world: it is then quite difficult to argue that the Brazilian customer should be charged a lower price than the Japanese customer.

The contribution method has also a tendency to lead to lower margins – at least in an export setting (Solberg 1987, 1988). One possible explanation for this is that when using this method at the introductory stage to a market, the exporter risks being stuck in a low price trap, where it is difficult at a later stage to raise the price. Another risk is that the local distributor or sales subsidiary may be in a position to "talk the price down", since they are better informed about local market conditions and may overrule less knowledgeable regional managers at HQ in their arguments. Market-based pricing actually requires detailed market information in each market, so as to enable management to optimally calibrate the price level accordingly. Export managers may have such market insight, but most often, they are confronted with local partners that are more knowledgeable and therefore are in the position to "dictate" – or perhaps a kinder word – persuade the exporter to charge lower prices than originally anticipated. Information asymmetry is a major factor in principal–agent theory (Eisenhardt 1989), and in the exporter–local partner relationships that have yet to be forged, the exporter runs the risk of being "talked into" lower price levels. The case above, describing Jordan's market-oriented pricing methodology (the value fraction), is an example of how to avoid getting into this trap.

Another risk of market-based pricing is the spill-over effect from one market to another, so-called grey markets. Particularly if pricing policies differ dramatically from one market to the next, the exporter risks seeing a parallel market emerge, outside of its control. This has been seen in the pharmaceutical industry where partners in low price countries re-export products to high price countries and reap the resultant profit. It should also be noted that price equalisation is one of the objectives of the EU Commission, in an attempt to achieve low price level across all EU members. The Treaty of Rome article 85 in fact gives the EU Commission an effective weapon in its endeavour to fight price discrimination.

Other methods

If the contribution method enables the firm to adapt to local market conditions, the firm should still not discard the cost plus method as a monitoring vehicle. A possible approach is to calculate a general base price using the cost plus method. This allows the firm to get an overall picture of the cost situation of the firm. Next, management should engage in discussions with their local partners in order to map the local market situation, and identify potential for higher prices, or the necessity to charge lower prices. Risks of spill-over or EU sanctions should then be considered.

12.2.3 Market factors

Markets differ from one country to the other, and even within countries. Competition, demand, purchase behaviour, government regulations, distribution structure and product life cycle are factors that occur with different strength in different settings. Therefore one should not expect a firm that is actively involved in several markets to keep the same price level in all.

The two extreme *competition* models – atomistic markets and monopoly – seldom occur in their purest forms in international markets. Normally, the market will be dominated by some large suppliers (market leaders and challengers), while others (market followers) adapt their bids to these leading players. Most firms belong to this latter "adapted" category. However, as we have discussed in Chapter 4, the market is, for most products, quite differentiated and divided into segments, where even the smallest player may carve out a market leadership position (market nichers).

A European engineering service company has built its business over several decades, specialising in site characterisation. They are technology leaders as well as a market leader in key markets with a dominant position in some of their market segments. Competition is mostly local or regional, and consists of smaller engineering firms. Their services are needed in the early phases of large projects in order to ascertain the ground characteristics of the soil. Often the total amount of a contract constitutes not more than a small percentage of the total plant.

Based on the company's advice, firms make decisions on foundations for large plants, oilrigs or major construction work. An error in the analysis of the earth conditions may have fatal consequences for the customer. Being technology leaders, the company is the preferred partner for the majority of customers. Buying from local competitors in fact involves an element of risk for the purchaser ("if you buy from us you know what you get"). It also implies some hassle, because most of them cannot offer the whole range of services needed to do the job, so customers have to interact with several suppliers of related services. This gives the company an advantage in the bidding process, where they can maintain a relatively high price level in spite of local competitors undercutting their price. They are willing to pay the extra amount of money – which is just a minuscule part of the total budget – to be on the safe side.[3]

Competitive structure is one thing; competitive intensity is quite another – disregarding its structure. A study of French exporters (Obadia 2013) reveals that competition in export markets indeed incites firms to give discounts, extend credit and cushion currency fluctuation for the foreign customer. This is particularly true in situations of high market ambiguity – i.e. in situations where the exporter has problems in interpreting critical factors in the market. However, such downward price manipulations in general do not appear to have any impact on export performance – up or down. Interestingly, only in fertile exporter–partner relationships – where the partner does not hide market information (low information asymmetry) – do such adaptations seem to pay off.

The role of government – or their agencies – is also decisive for price strategies. In some countries, a price freeze is frequently used to try to fight inflation. Financial policies often have a direct impact on currency exchange rates. The most conspicuous example over the past decade has been Chinese policies designed – according to critics, particularly American business-people and politicians – to keep their currency, the Renminbi, artificially low, thereby rendering Chinese products more price competitive than their competitors (which in turn influences the latter's pricing). Also, competition regulations in different countries – inspired by American antitrust legislation from 1890 – will impact on pricing. This is particularly relevant for large firms with dominant market positions. In the EU, such regulation is introduced in order to impede division of the market, opening up opportunities for discriminatory pricing.

Another encumbrance that exporters sometimes meet is antidumping duties that are applied when government agencies suspect the exporter of charging prices below cost. Particularly zealous in this respect are countries such as the US, Australia, Canada, Mexico and Argentina, and the EU. These made up three-quarters of all anti-dumping cases reported to GATT in the period 1987–1997 (Miranda et al. 1998). For example, in the US and EU the total value of imports affected by anti-dumping during this ten-year period were 818 and 739 billion USD respectively. In the wake of such accusations, the firm can expect an audit of its accounts in order to verify the cost structure of the products under scrutiny, and potentially be given a fine. The effect of these actions is that the pricing instrument becomes less attractive to use actively (the exporter will be forced to charge a minimum price).

In 2011, the EU imposed anti-dumping penalties on three American chemical firms (Celanese, LyondellBasell Acetyls and Dow Chemical), amounting to 12.1%, 13% and 13.8% respectively of total sales in Europe over a six-month period on the chemical compound, vinyl acetate. The purpose was to "re-establish fair competition" inside the EU, based on a complaint in 2010 from two of the EU's largest manufacturers, Ineos in the UK and Wacker in Germany. These two represent more than 25% of the European market. EU agents had to carry out relatively thorough inspections and obtain documentation from the concerned parties, so as not to operate arbitrarily. Such actions may easily be interpreted by the accused party as protectionist measures. In such cases, the WTO is the court of appeal.[4]

Distribution structure is another field that plays a role in pricing and it varies greatly from one market to another. We have already seen how complex the distribution of fish is in Japan, with importers, national wholesalers, second/regional wholesalers and retailers (Section 7.2.1).

Types of product – and thereby different market mechanisms – influence the amount of leeway firms have on pricing. The market price of raw materials (such as oil, iron ore, coal, wheat, etc.) is dictated by supply and demand in the global market, and is for most players a given – a barrel of oil has the same price in New Orleans as in Osaka or Amsterdam (given the same quality). For differentiated products and services catering to specific needs and segments in the market, firms have much more leverage to determine the pricing of their products, and thereby differentiate their price between countries.

Also, the stage of the *product life cycle* may play a part in international pricing. Markets that are in the introductory stages may be treated differently to those having reached mature stages.

Jordan (toothbrushes, oral hygiene) is an interesting case in this respect. The firm exports to some 80 markets, 25 with active marketing operations. Since both competition and consumer preferences vary widely from one market to the other, price formation is, as a result, different in each individual market. In addition, Jordan's marketing objectives have to be substantiated for each market. Only then can they determine the profile and establish the price level accordingly. Generally, Jordan endeavours to price their products just above the average in the market, though below the most expensive ones. As a result of these guiding principles, their price levels vary – in Europe alone – from 12 NOK (Denmark) to 25 NOK (Norway).[5]

12.2.4 Cost factors

International marketing and exporting in particular involve higher marketing costs than selling only in the domestic market – costs that need to be factored into the firm's pricing calculation. We may divide these costs into three groups: 1) marketing/sales costs; 2) variable production/manufacturing costs; and 3) fixed production and capital costs. In this section, we will focus on marketing/selling costs. Variable production costs are covered in Chapter 10 (product decisions). The role of fixed costs is discussed in Section 12.2.1 in the current chapter.

International marketing and sales costs are those incurred as a direct result of exporting. It may be anything from market research, product development and adaptation, foreign marketing activities, risk, credits/discounts, or agent commissions. Credit risks are discussed in Section 12.3.2. In addition, different terms of delivery may also involve extra costs (in particular C- and D-clauses[6]).

Market research and product development/adaptation may be divided into two main groups: those that can be considered as investments to be depreciated over a number of years, and those that can be deducted from earnings the year they are incurred. Depreciation periods depend mainly upon two factors: internal accounting considerations and tax legislation in the country. In principle, sound accounting practice suggests that the period be as short as possible, whereas tax legislation often dictates that at least part of these expenditures should be capitalised, since the net earnings (and the basis for tax calculation) then will be higher at an early stage. Newly established firms (for instance Born Globals) may be tempted to capitalise these expenditures before sales really take off, in order to "reduce" (in terms of accounting) an otherwise extraordinary high loss figure. In particular, product development costs may reach excessive levels, not only the development/adaptation itself, but also *testing, certification, approval, and documentation.* For example, in the pharmaceutical industry – one of the most R&D intensive industries in the world – it takes on average some 12 years to develop a new drug, and the average cost is 802 million USD! (see Adams and Brantner 2016). This is an extreme case, but R&D in general bites substantially into the product costs. In a study of product development costs in the valve industry, the authors found that product development costs make up some 20% of total product costs (Chwastyk and Kołosowski 2014). The costs of adapting the products to each individual market vary considerably. We have already explored this in Chapter 10.

Sales and marketing costs include all additional costs, of staff allocated to international sales and all marketing materials and activities dedicated to international markets. We will return to the marketing planning in Chapter 13, but will briefly review some of the main items here.

– Actively operating in international markets involves personnel resources such as regional sales managers, support staff and independent agents (on commission).
– Marketing and sales material must be translated/adapted.
– Adverts and participation at trade fairs.
– Travel costs will weigh heavily on the budget – finding, nurturing relations with, controlling and switching agents and distributors, customer visits and after-sales service. These costs are often underestimated, particularly in early phases of the internationalisation of the firm, but are supposedly the most important part of the budget, except for personnel.

The *risk* of operating in different markets is a cost element that is easy to measure because one can cover this risk with insurance through banks or insurance companies. Most countries have government agencies that offer partly-subsidised financial and insurance arrangements. In this context, we notice that terms of payment differ from one country to another – see also the next section. A survey by NCM Credit Insurance (UK) of European credit terms suggests that these vary from 24 days to 84 in different EU members. "Best in class" are the Nordic countries with the Finns at the top (between 24 and 37 days), whereas Southern Europe notoriously is in the lower range (64–84 days). Great Britain, Ireland, Benelux and Germany are somewhere in between (38–50 days).[7]

Another risk factor is *currency fluctuation*. We have already seen how the pound has fallen against the euro after the Brexit vote (Section 6.2). Other currencies are far more volatile; *Market Insights* named the ten most volatile currencies in 2014 against the USD:[8] 1) Russian Rouble, 2) Argentinian Peso, 3) Coloumbian Peso, 4) Norwegian Krone, 5) Hungarian Forint, 6) Polish złoty, 7) Japanese Yen, 8) Brazilian Real, 9) Mexican Peso and 10) Euro. It is possible to hedge against such fluctuations, by buying the local currency forward. This again has a cost – which varies from one currency to the other – that needs to be included in the total calculation of the base price in each market. We will in the next section look at risks in more detail.

Freight costs may amount to 10% or more of the exporter's ex-works[9] price. However, the importance of this cost element is not necessarily a handicap, since most players in many industries are off-shoring their production to roughly the same geographic regions and thereby incur essentially the same transport costs to their respective markets.

Customs tariffs have gradually been lowered over the past sixty years (see GATT, WTO). Whereas within some regions, such as the European Union (and for most products: the European Economic Area – EEA), the tariffs are brought down to zero, non-EEA exporters to those regions are confronted with tariffs. In industrial countries, these are on average quite low, between 2% and 4%. In many emerging markets, tariffs amount to some 7–10%. However, for some products – in particular agricultural and food products – tariffs may amount to more than 100%, prohibitive levels for any would-be exporter.[10]

Also *local sales taxes*, such as value added tax (VAT), goods and services tax (GST) or sales tax, vary from one country to another. In Europe, the VAT level is between 17% (Luxemburg) and 27% (Hungary); in China the general VAT level is 17%, in Russia 18%, and in India 13.5%; in the US, sales tax varies between the states – from 0% to 7.5%; in Australia, New Zealand and Canada the tax is called GST and varies between 5% and 15%. In addition to different kinds of general sales taxes, most countries collect luxury taxes (for instance on perfume, cars and jewellery) or taxes on tobacco or alcohol. Whereas customs duties distort the price competition between local and imported goods, these taxes are normally collected without discrimination.[11]

A sensitive area in international pricing is that of *internal or transfer pricing* – i.e. charging different prices between subsidiaries in multinational firms. In the previous section, we discussed price differentiation based on the competition and market potential offered in each individual market. Transfer pricing has another focus: to optimise the tax and customs burdens in different countries. This practice is increasingly common within MNCs that transfer parts and components between units (Stevenson and Cabell 2002). Briefly, the MNC sells goods at a low price from countries with high tax rates (in order to reduce the taxable net income) to its own sales subsidiaries in low tax countries, so-called tax havens. These sales subsidiaries then re-export the products to other countries and the company reaps an extraordinary tax benefit. This practice, if common, is also questionable in that companies unduly seek tax evasion.

Apple's operations in Ireland have been subject to scrutiny by European and American tax authorities. The company's European headquarters in Ireland has been buying cheap products from its manufacturing unit in China, and reselling them expensively to other countries in Europe, sitting back with a substantial profit in Ireland, benefiting not only from a low corporate tax regime in this country, but also from a special deal with Irish tax authorities. Apple claims that its Irish unit has the economic rights to its intellectual property and therefore can require a surcharge billing from that unit. This viewpoint has been contested by American tax authorities, who maintain that the brainwork was done in the US. Also the OECD and the European Union have been investigating Apple and Ireland for illegal tax reliefs over a 20-year period. Apple has been accused of using a "double Irish sandwich with Dutch associations" structure that allows it to route profits through Ireland and significantly reduce tax.[12]

Transfer pricing and tax evasion are extremely complex issues involving tax legislation in numerous different countries. They may also have ramifications for the customs authorities (who would prefer high transfer prices for imports). These are topics more relevant for lawyers and accountants than for marketers. However, the marketer should indeed be aware of the issue and be prepared to discuss the marketing viewpoint when setting the international price level.

Exporting involves extra costs, but it does not necessarily entail higher total costs than in the domestic market, simply because economies of scale bring down the general cost level of the operation, thereby reducing the per unit cost.

12.3 Risk in international trade

Marketing abroad involves factors of uncertainty not encountered in the domestic market, and therefore also means higher risks for the exporter. These risks are mostly connected to the transport of products and credit terms given by the exporter. They involve costs that need to be taken into account in the price calculation of the products. In this section we will briefly discuss the main factors that come into play in this context: terms of delivery, terms of payment and risk coverage.

12.3.1 Terms of delivery – Incoterms

The International Chamber of Commerce (ICC) has developed standard terms for sales of goods – Incoterms (International Commercial Terms) – that are widely used across the world. These terms determine the responsibility of the transport of goods between the seller and buyer such as who is paying for what part of the transport, and who runs the risk for the transport and pays the insurance to cover potential damage or loss. These terms have been amended over the years, the first version being published in 1936, and the latest in 2010. There are 13 such terms:[13]

– **E-clause** – the buyer pays the whole transport costs.

  EXW – Ex-works: the goods are made available at the gate of the seller's premises. The buyer has full responsibility from that point, both to contract with a carrier and to insure the transport.

– **F-clauses** – main carriage not paid by the seller.

  FCA – Free carrier: the goods are delivered at a named place, to be taken over by the carrier contracted by the buyer. The buyer clears the goods for export.

  FAS – Free alongside ship: the seller bears the cost of transport and insurance to the ship, and clears the goods for export.

  FOB – Free on board: seller delivers the goods past the rail of the ship, and the buyer bears all costs and risks after that point.

– **C-clauses** – main carriage paid by the seller.

  CFR – Cost and freight: the transport to the destination is paid by the seller. The title, risk and insurance pass to the buyer when the cargo is delivered on board the ship.

  CIF – Cost, insurance, freight: same as CFR, but the title of goods pass to the buyer at the destination port. Used for maritime transport.

  CPT – Carriage paid to: basically the same as CFR, but is general for any mode of transportation.

  CIP – Carriage and insurance paid: the same as CIF, but used for any mode of transportation.

- **D-clauses** – seller bears the risks and the costs to a named destination (in country of import).

  DAF – Delivered at frontier: the seller is responsible for the transport to the border point, but not cleared for import.

  DES – Delivered ex-ship: the seller bears all costs to the destination, but not to discharge the cargo or clear it for imports.

  DEQ – Delivered ex-quay: in this clause, the seller is, in addition, responsible for import clearance.

  DDU – Delivered duty unpaid: the buyer takes over the goods unloaded and not yet cleared for import.

  DDP – Delivered duty paid: the same as DDU, but now the import clearance is paid.

Even though these terms are very precise, the interpretation of them may vary from one country to another. The Incoterm agreed in the contract has consequences for both parties. Large and seasoned exporters have an organisation that can take care of the transport; others leave it to forwarding agents; still others leave it to the importer.

12.3.2 Terms of payment in international sales

Settlement of international sales is in principle not different from settlements in general. However, different currencies, laws and regulations, traditions and cultures justify special mention of payments across borders. There are four main groups of settlements:

1 Advance payment
2 Payment against documents
3 Credit
4 Countertrade.

Advance payment is traditionally used in exports of capital goods (machinery, ships, trains, aeroplanes, etc.) and normally constitutes some 10–30% of the total amount. One may say that advance payment serves two purposes: first, it is a means to share the risk of the transaction between the buyer and seller – particularly when engaging in large projects; second, it is a means for the seller to finance the start-up of the work. To cover the risk, the buyer requires that the seller takes out insurance, often called a performance bond – which may cost 0.5–2% of the total contract price – to reduce the buyer's risk of non-performance by the seller (see also later under risk coverage).

Payment against documents can be divided into two groups:

1 *Cash against documents* (CAD) implies that the importer pays for the products before receiving them. The products are released to the importer against presentation of a "document", for instance a Bill of Lading or any other transferrable freight document, obtained from a third party (for instance a bank) at payment of the invoice. The exporter runs a risk that the goods are dispatched to the point of destination and that the importer does not pay. This risk is alleviated when using a Letter of Credit.

2   *Letter of Credit* (L/C) is a more secure form of settlement than CAD. Its purpose is to give the seller the guarantee of a settlement, and the buyer a guarantee that the products are dispatched according to the specifications in the contract. Even if the buyer refuses delivery (and to pay), the seller receives the settlement. The process is as follows: The buyer opens an L/C at their bank, which in turn guarantees payment of the amount due to the seller's bank. A *confirmed and irrevocable* L/C gives the best security for the seller. If it is not confirmed, the seller's bank has recourse against the seller if the buyer's bank refuses to pay; if it is not irrevocable the buyer's bank may revoke the settlement without consent from the involved parties.

Payment against documents has a cost, reflected in the risk of the arrangement – less for CAD and higher for confirmed and irrevocable L/C.

Credit is normally given to business partners with whom the exporter has a long and trusted relationship, and who have a proven payment record. The credit line varies from case to case, and from industry to industry. In consumer goods transactions it may stretch to six months – varying from one country to the other – in which case the buyer may issue a cheque, which the seller can cash in at their bank. For capital goods (ships, large machinery plants, infrastructure, etc.), it may extend over 10–12 years or more. In this case, the seller needs to secure long-term finance for the operations. This may be provided by export finance institutions with a guarantee from a state-owned export credit agency, often offering a subsidised insurance premium. Most countries have this kind of agency.[14] The OECD has regulated this type of guarantee, called "The Arrangement on Export Credits", in order to provide a level playing field for the participant countries (minimum interest rates, risk fees and maximum repayment terms).[15]

Countertrade includes a wide range of payment arrangements involving barter trade – goods in payment for goods. This form of trade is as old as history, and has re-emerged as a response to market imperfections. It takes place for the most part where the importing country (or the importer) has limited financial capabilities. It is a dominant form of settlement within sectors such as infrastructure, military equipment and energy. There are several forms of countertrade:

–   *Counter-purchase* is an agreement whereby the exporter commits him- or herself to buy a product from the importing country at a value corresponding to that of the export contract. The deal is concluded in two separate but mutually-dependent contracts.
–   *Barter* is direct exchange of goods in the same contract.
    As an example, we mention the deal between India and Iraq in 2000: India and Iraq agreed on an "oil for wheat and rice" barter deal, subject to UN approval under article 50 of the UN Persian Gulf War sanctions, that would facilitate 300,000 barrels of oil being delivered daily to India at a price of $6.85 a barrel, at a time when Iraqi oil sales into Asia were valued at about $22 a barrel. In 2001, India agreed to swap 1.5 million tonnes of Iraqi crude oil under the oil-for-food programme.[16]
–   *Buy-back* occurs when the importer of a plant (refinery, chemical plant, aluminium plant, etc.) pays the proceeds (or part thereof) in the form of products provided by the plant.
–   *Switch trading* happens when, for instance, a buyer (Party A) is selling wheat to a third party as a payment for coal bought from Party B. The third party, known as the switch trader, then pays Party A for the wheat at a discount, enabling this party to pay Party B for the coal.

Countertrade is a response to a situation where the buyer lacks foreign currency, and offers the equivalent amount in goods instead. This form of settlement is linked with an extra commercial risk and with extra hassle for the seller that requires a premium for the seller.

The exporter's terms of payment depend on four factors: industry norms, risk (currency, credit), financial position and competition.

12.3.3 Risk reduction and risk coverage

We shall in this section discuss three types of risk in international markets:

1   *Commercial risks* are related to the customer's solvency. To what extent can we expect our invoices to be settled?
2   *Political risk* is about the economic and political regime in the import countries, both of which may influence the transfer of payment from the country in question. There are four indicators of political risk: internal instability, external conflicts, general political climate and economic balance (inflation, unemployment, GNP, foreign debt).[17]
3   *Economic risk* involves potential changes in economic factors determining the exporter's price calculations such as currency fluctuations or interest rate changes.

The exporter may alleviate such risks, either through their own strategic choices or by insuring against possible losses through insurance companies. We cover these two separately.

Internal risk alleviation

Risk is related to information. The better the information, the better the background to evaluate the risk, and the better able one is to take precautions to reduce the potential effects of the risk factor. The options available to the exporter are as follows:

Commercial risk can be reduced by spreading the sales around different customers or through several members of the distribution system – in other words: "avoid putting all one's eggs into one basket". Selling through a sole distributor is a case in point: if credit-worthy, the distributor represents limited risks, but at the same time constitutes a risk by the mere fact that sales are concentrated in one customer; selling through an agent who brokers the transaction to a number of different customers in the market then represents a distribution of risk. In both cases, whether they are distributors, dealers or end users, the exporter should ascertain its customers' credit-worthiness before granting credit. There are several sources providing this kind of information: own and/or third-party experience through trading with the customer; information through export promotion agencies; and bank or credit reports. The last often use special wording – diplomatic formulations describing the financial situation of a firm. The conclusions may take various forms such as "reasonable credit is recommended" (a positive statement) or "credit reliant on guarantees" (negative).

Also *economic risk* can be reduced by the exporter, both by spreading its sales to different markets and – in case of currency risk – by selling *and purchasing* using the same currency. Another option is to buy currency forward – i.e. to buy, for instance, Chinese Renminbi at today's exchange rate, for delivery at the day of settlement. This action carries a cost, depending on the volatility and the interest rate of the currency.

The firm does not have any internal levers to cope with *political risk* other than: 1) spreading its sales over different markets thus reducing its vulnerability, or 2) simply avoiding exporting to countries susceptible to political risk according to the indicators mentioned above. In this

Risk Category	Year Ago	Current 06/13	One Year Ahead		Five Years Ahead	
			Worst Case	Best Case	Worst Case	Best Case
Political Risk	53.5	55.5	52.5	60.0	51.0	65.5
Financial Risk	39.0	43.5	39.5	44.0	37.5	45.5
Economic Risk	34.0	37.0	35.5	41.0	27.0	42.5
Composite Risk	63.3	68.0	63.8	72.8	57.8	76.8
Risk Band	Mod.	Mod.	Mod.	Low	High	Low

Figure 12.2 Political and economic risk assessment of Paraguay.

case management needs to make its own assessment of the risks involved. The following anecdote is a telling story of how difficult this may be:

When the Sri Lankan government cancelled a contract for eight fish trawlers to be delivered from Norway in January 1978, it came as a result of a change in political regime the year before. The conservatives had just won the elections with promises of economic moderation in the wake of inflation and high foreign debt. The original order was actually confirmed by representatives of the new regime, and yet, half a year later, it was cancelled.

Many different internet-based services continually assess the economic and political risks in most countries of the world. Enter "political risk", and a plethora of offers will pop up. Figure 12.2 gives an example of one such assessment of Paraguay from PRS Group Inc.

External risk coverage

We have already mentioned state-sponsored/state-owned credit insurance agencies that offer different guarantees covering credits to foreign customers. Each country has specific regulations; the following are excerpts of the Norwegian GIEK (Garantiinstituttet for Eksportkreditt):

Contract guarantees cover risks that arise in the period between contract signing and delivery. These cover risks such as if a buyer becomes insolvent before delivery (commercial risk) or the government introduces currency restrictions holding back payments (political risk). This happened at the beginning of the 1980s in the wake of the Mexican financial crisis, when the monetary authorities stopped all payments in foreign currency.
Credit guarantees are used for sales of capital goods where the credit warranted by the exporter stretches over two years or more. The policy covers the commercial and political risk but with a maximum rate of 90% for commercial risk and up 100% for political risk. Bank guarantees are roughly the same, but given to the exporter's lenders (banks).
Contractor guarantees are relevant for large projects abroad – such as infrastructure and plants. Examples are:

- A Bid Bond (to guarantee that the exporter can deliver when bidding for the project).
- A Performance Bond (to guarantee that he can deliver when the contract has been awarded).
- An Advance Payment Bond (to guarantee to the buyer for advance payment).

Financial guarantees stand security for a bank for its financing of the exporter's production and stocking of products relating to long-term delivery contracts. It normally covers 50% of potential losses incurred by the bank. The same applies to credit given to cover costs relating to an exporter's sales campaign abroad, in the event of a failure. *Investment guarantees* cover political risk for investments in developing countries.

12.4 International pricing and profitability

Any firm needs to report profits in order to survive in the longer term. Profitability should therefore also be the guiding principle for marketing (and pricing) in international markets. Previously in this chapter we have briefly discussed cost and contribution methods of price calculations and also argued that the contribution method gives more leverage to the marketing manager. In this section, we shall analyse these two methods from a profit analysis perspective. We shall see that that depreciation and other fixed costs will play a decisive role in this analysis.

Let us take as a point of departure a medium-sized firm with the following cost structure:

Depreciation and fixed costs	11.0 million euros
Variable manufacturing costs	1.65 million euros
Total manufacturing costs	27.5 million euros
Total manufacturing volume (= sales volume)	11,000 units
Maximum domestic sales	10,000 units
Cost per unit (ex-works)	2,500 euros

If the firm has a marginal export activity, then the export pricing can be subsidised by a marginally higher domestic price level. Let us see what happens with an export of 100 units (9% of total sales).

Table 12.2 (contribution method) suggests that a small price rise in the domestic market from 2,500 to 2,600 euros per unit (4%) is enough to cover the marginal costs of exporting (variable costs) and to sell at (a minimum) 1,500 euros in the export market. The exporter is enabled, through this method, to sell cheaper abroad than at home, at prices that cover the variable costs (plus the additional costs of exporting). A nice word for this kind of pricing is price discrimination; a nastier word (at least as seen by the exporter) is dumping. We have already seen how dumping can trigger counteractions (anti-dumping measures) initiated by local competitors, directed against an exporter (Sections 2.2.1 and 2.4.1). In any event, for the purpose of this exercise, we notice that the firm – depending on its cost structure – can manoeuvre within a span of price alternatives.

Another possibility is to charge the fixed costs, making the domestic and export prices equal. This situation is shown in Table 12.2 (cost method). This way of calculating allows the firm to lower the domestic price to 2,500 euros.

Let us now assume that exports constitute 60% of the firm's output. This situation is described in Table 12.3.

In this case, taken to the extreme, the contribution method forces the exporter to charge a domestic price of 4,000 euros in order to keep the export price level at 1,500 euros. The conclusion is that a home-market-oriented firm can play with the contribution method, charge lower prices in export markets than at home and yet profitably run its operations. When exports begin to grow, the contribution method becomes increasingly untenable, and the export price should be charged with fixed costs. The validity of this line of reasoning is a function of the

Table 12.2 Contribution and cost methods in marginal exporting

	Contribution/market method		Cost plus method	
	Domestic	Exports	Domestic	Exports
Depreciation and fixed manufacturing costs (million euros)	11.0	–	10.0	1.0
Variable manufacturing costs (million euros)	15.0	1.5	15.0	1.5
Total manufacturing costs (million euros)	26.0	1.5	25.0	2.5
Sales volume	10,000	1,000	10,000	1,000
Unit cost (euros)	2,600	1,500	2,500	2,500

Table 12.3 Contribution and cost-based methods at different export ratios

	Contribution/market method		Cost plus method	
	Domestic	Exports	Domestic	Exports
Depreciation and fixed manufacturing costs (million euros)	11.0	–	4.4	6.6
Variable manufacturing costs (million euros)	6.6	9.9	6.6	9.9
Total manufacturing costs (million euros)	17.6	9.9	11.0	16.5
Sales volume	4,400	6,600	4,400	6,600
Cost per unit	4,000	1,500	2,500	2,500

cost structure within the firm. The higher the capital/fixed costs, the easier it is to carry out price discrimination at marginal export volumes. It also depends on the market position of the firm in its home market: a leading position at home opens up for price discrimination abroad. If it is weak, a lower price in (particularly) neighbouring markets will more easily ricochet back to the home market. There are however many variations between these two extreme situations, as described in Table 12.4.

We observe that, when fixed costs are distributed, the firm is losing money in France: 70,000 euros → sales of 5.88 million euros minus total costs – 5.95 million euros (total variable costs of 3.85 million euros and fixed costs of 2.1 million euros), whereas all the other markets have a net contribution representing more than their share of the fixed costs. This does not imply, however, that the firm should leave the French market for the benefit of other markets. This will most likely require reinforced sales promotion, possibly also including a lower base price or discounts, which will potentially lower the contribution rate in the markets concerned. We further notice in Table 12.4 that the lower contribution rate obtained in the French market "subsidises" a higher contribution in the other markets. At the same time, therefore, the French market gives a contribution that – taken together – allows a lower price level in all other markets. Without the involvement in France, the firm would need to raise its price level by 228.10 euros on average, or between 7% and 8% of the existing price level.[18]

If the firm wants to improve its sales returns in France (and in other countries), that is another matter. Critical issues here are, among others, how to compose the marketing mix, the market potential and the firm's ability to deliver. If they can manufacture another 200 units for the French market, but reduce the price by 20 euros on average for all products to France, the French case would be as shown in Table 12.5.

Table 12.4 International pricing

	Germany	France	Sweden	Denmark	UK	Total
Base price (euros)	2,900	2,800	2,850	3,000	2,900	2,881[a]
Sales volume (units)	4,400	2,100	2,000	1,000	1,500	11,000
Sales (million euros)	12.76	5.88	5.70	3.00	4.35	31.69
– variable manufacturing costs (million euros)	6.60	3.15	3.00	1.50	2.25	16.50
– marketing costs (million euros)	0.50	0.30	0.20	0.10	0.20	1.30
– freight/customs (million euros)	0.60	0.40	0.30	0.20	0.30	1.80
Contribution (million euros)	5.06	2.03	2.20	1.20	1.60	12.09
Fixed cost – evenly distributed (million euros)	4.40	2.10	2.00	1.00	1.50	11.00
Contribution rate (%)[b]	39.7	34.40	38.60	40.00	36.70	38.20

Notes: [a]Average base price; [b]Contribution rate = contribution/sales.

Table 12.5 Price recalculation in France

Base price	Euros	2,780
Sales volume	Units	2,300
Sales	Euros	6.325 million
Variable manufacturing costs	Euros	3.450 million[a]
Marketing costs	Euros	0.330 million[a]
Freight, customs	Euros	0.440 million[a]
Contribution	Euros	2.174 million

Note: [a]For simplicity, the manufacturing costs increase proportionally.

The total contribution will – with this – increase by 0.144 million euros: the new contribution in France (2.174 million euros) minus previous contribution in France (2.030 million euros), with the average total *contribution rate* increasing to 40.9%.

Instead of lowering the price in the French market, the firm has other ways of increasing the total profitability of its operations. Referring back to the product chapter (see Table 10.3) we can use the PM matrix to analyse how different qualities in the product range are distributed in different segments in France – market 2 in Table 10.3. Segment 2 in this market for product quality Bc is showing a loss. Instead of lowering the price for the whole French market by 50 euros, a closer look at the PM cell Bc/2.2 will probably give a more nuanced diagnosis, and the firm is enabled to direct its attention more selectively to the concrete market situation:

– What is needed to improve the performance in Bc/2.2?
– Should we retire entirely from this segment?

Possible actions are: increase prices in this particular segment, increase sales promotion, adapt the product. If the firm retires from Bc/2.2, the question will be whether other markets can offset the loss in France.

We conclude this section by asserting that active pricing in international markets involves detailed analysis of the firm's accounts, and that management needs to take a comprehensive approach to pricing in all its markets in order to find optimal solutions. Price differences in each market open up interesting opportunities to increase profits. The higher the fixed costs of operation the more flexibility management has to optimise its pricing in different markets.

Another – more indirect – inference is that the price manipulations as suggested above should be made in close collaboration with the local representative in the market, be it an agent, distributor or the exporter's own sales subsidiary. This statement is substantiated by research by Obadia (2013) and Obadia and Stöttinger (2015) who find that the role of close and proactive distributor relations is crucial for understanding the details of the local pricing context, and for giving the right kind of discounts and support to the distributor. It is worth noting that firms resorting to this kind of partner incentives reveal significantly higher performance in international markets than those that don't – even if this entails a lower price. The other end of the equation is partner support and higher sales.

12.5 International pricing and the firm's strategic position

So far in this chapter, we have taken for granted that prices can be set individually in each market, and that the price in one market will not influence the price level in another market.[19] This may be so in some cases, for example, with many agricultural products. The main reason for this is that governments in many countries have decided to protect farmers and the food industry from foreign competition. Also, in industry sectors where scale economies are relatively limited, the price will typically be calculated locally, based on domestic factors of production such as salary levels, competitive intensity or access to raw materials. These industries are normally dominated by small firms that create their own market niches (restaurants, hairdressers, handicrafts, etc.), and the price level here is not readily transferred to other markets.

Yet, in many markets, price levels are crossing borders. As we have seen, this is most conspicuously found in raw material markets. In industries with monopolistic competition – i.e. a situation where the individual player has developed certain features related to brand image, quality, distribution, etc. and thereby is able to differentiate from their closest competitors – the price levels will not necessarily be the same across markets, but they will indeed be influenced by each other. In monopolistic competition, with a few large players operating globally, the price transparency across markets is a typical hallmark. We conclude by asserting that the more global the industry, the more the price level in one market is influenced by that in another market, implying limited opportunities to differentiate between markets. On the other hand we assert that firms with high market share and superior international business competence – scoring high on the preparedness for internationalisation axis – are positioned to proactively make use of the price lever in their marketing. This section will therefore discuss how these two factors – using the logic of the Strategic Windows framework – fashion the development of international pricing policies in the firm. Figure 12.3 constitutes the basis for this discussion.

Local price follower

In this cell, firms have low preparedness for internationalisation and operate in multi-local markets. These are also less intertwined when it comes to price levels. Since the firms are generally small with low market shares and only have limited local market insight, they will have to accept the price level that they find in each market. The main challenge for firms in this position is their limited market insight, thereby limiting their understanding of the potential that might lie in the pricing, as described in the previous sections in this chapter.

Confronted with partners who are struggling to achieve sales, the temptation may become overwhelming to yield to price pressures. As discussed above, partners may have the upper hand

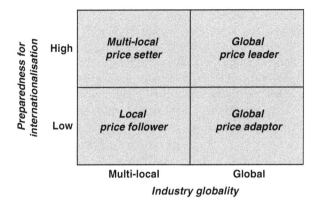

Figure 12.3 Pricing in different strategic positions.

Source: Solberg et al. (2006).

in discussions on strategic move, including pricing, and may persuade the exporter to lower the price because of what the partner calls "competitive pressures". The information asymmetry may lead to what we could term "defenceless acquiescence" with the partner's viewpoints (in the absence of complementary and balancing insight). The situation described here may also conceal the partner's own limitations in the local market: that they are not appropriately positioned, or do not sufficiently engage in local market activities to tap the price potential.

Furthermore, the exporter will experience different price levels in the different markets, thereby in principle enabling the firm to tap the potential (as described in Section 12.3) and actively exploit the local price mechanism. Developing a differentiated pricing strategy requires, however, a market insight not yet attained by this group of exporters. The latter, therefore, will often resort to cost-based pricing, providing better control, but at the same time involving a too low price in some markets (potentially resulting in higher than expected sales), or on the contrary too high a price in other markets (limiting sales). The result may therefore be different brand positions in different markets. In a multi-local market setting, this may not constitute a big problem, but is a potential challenge should the markets become more globalised.

Finny Sirevaag is a medium-sized exporter of peeled shrimps in southern Norway with sales of around 8 million euros. They are active in eight European countries and operate with different price levels in these markets. The reason for their price differentiation is that their customers are locally-oriented, and the market is divided into segments with relatively limited competition. Even though the firm is not an export newcomer, they still have some way to go to call themselves a well-seasoned exporter: they have limited insight into the local pricing situation, and little information about market shares, competitors' market activities, customer preferences, etc. The point of departure for their pricing is cost plus pricing, but the base price charged in each local market is based upon what they call "gut feeling" of what the customers can accept. If they do not get a minimum price, they turn down the deal. In markets where they are well-established, they strive to keep a fairly even price level, so as not to "meet their former selves", as their sales manager puts it.

Multi-local price setter

In this case, firms are still operating in a multi-local market setting, but their competence and resources are much stronger. They can therefore operate in a more proactive way than firms in the former cell. With different price mechanisms in each of the markets they are active in, and given the market insight they possess, they have a much richer repertoire to play with in their pricing.

> Jøtul, a leader in the wood stove market in Europe, with sales of about 100 million euros, is located in this cell. Two factors determine their pricing: 1) they seek to consciously price their products higher than those of their competitors in order to underline their allegedly superior quality; and 2) they seek to adapt their pricing to each individual market, where prices can vary by between 10% and 15%. Countries such as Poland, the Czech Republic and Latvia are examples of low-price countries. However, they are still the price leader in these markets.

As we have repeatedly emphasised, price differentiation may come in conflict with article 85.1 of the Treaty of Rome, in particular when coupled with sales through exclusive distributors.

Global price adaptors

Firms with low preparedness and operating in global markets with roughly the same price picture across countries are located here. These firms would typically be inclined to charge a standardised price in all countries because the markets have more or less the same price level. Given their marginal position in global markets, they have limited bargaining leverage and may be compelled to adopt the price level set by global market leaders. In this context, the local representatives may come in as an influencer and gatekeeper of relevant information (Myers 1997, Myers and Harvey 2001). Although at times these firms may be in a position to develop niches in which customers associate higher prices with better performance, they are typically under constant pressure from their more efficiently distributed and globally-branded counterparts to adjust their prices.

> AMV Koltek in Norway, providing access systems to buildings and installations, generating sales of around 2 million euros, is marketing its systems through local distributors to a wide range of countries. The main competition in international markets comes from five much larger suppliers from Finland, Belgium and Norway. The price level is more or less the same across countries, with little differentiation from one market to the other. Information on price and competition is obtained through their local partners; AMV Koltek does not have adequate resources to collect independent price information. For instance, they are unable to go all the way to the end customers to check the validity of the price information obtained from their partners – a situation that, at times, is perceived as problematic. They try to follow the price level of their main competitors – although occasionally bidding below in order to win reference projects.

Some of the firms in this cell fall into the Born Global group of firms, offering innovative products and solutions to the market. These are still confronted with the same resource handicaps as those described above, but – with new products/innovations – they are in a different competitive position, and thereby freer to determine the price level independent of any competition yet to be defined.

Global price leader

These firms have a leadership position in world markets, and are able to act as price leaders. This does not imply, however, that they are in a monopoly situation. On the contrary, competition in global markets is normally hard-hitting and firms need to defend themselves from attack from all corners of the world. This may be competitors located in low-cost countries; it may be an MNC seeking a better position in key markets, subsidising its price levels from profitable operations in other markets (Hamel and Prahalad 1985); or it may come as a "puff of wind" from a competitor that wants to get rid of commodities.

Before responding to such strikes from competitors, the firm should analyse the situation and understand the intentions of the assaulting competitor. In principle there are four ways to confront a price attack by a competitor:

1   Follow the attacker, and "hope for the best". This may be shrewd in situations where the competitor wants to get rid of some overcapacity, or where it does not have the clout to withstand a "counterattack". If the attack is a step in a long-term strategy to gradually build market shares, there is a risk of seeing their own market shares weaken. The firm may therefore want to follow the price challenger in order to make the competitor nervous.

> Large multinational companies, dominant in their market segment, resort to this kind of tactic. When confronted with a price war for a big project, they often underbid the competitor(s) in order to prevent them from getting a reference project to add to their "bragging list". The multinational would prefer to lose money on an isolated contract than allow the competitor the opportunity to secure such a project.

2   One can also give the aggressive competitor a taste of their own medicine in their main markets, usually their own home markets, where they are a dominant player. This may however be risky, particularly if the firm has not yet obtained a certain footprint in that market and is trying to break into existing relationships (see also Section 7.2.1). Hamel and Prahalad (1985) suggest that this was the case in the 1980s when Japanese firms managed to elbow their way into Western markets without credible threats of retaliation since Japan is such a difficult market to enter.
3   A more subtle way of meeting price competition is to exploit opportunities in a differentiated market. Kotler and Keller (2011) mention the classic example of what we may term proactive price differentiation, where price attacks are met with a price *increase* (often combined with an enhanced product). At the same time, they also introduce a new and less costly product at a price lower than that offered by the challenger. The challenger new to the market risks being squeezed by the market leader, between the enhanced brand and the low-cost brand. Figure 12.4 shows how a larger part of the price curve is exploited in this new situation.
4   Price collusion is one way of trying to reduce the effects of price competition. This is not uncommon in cases where dominant competitors meet each other with cut-throat, damaging price wars. This is however a risky business, of which the following two anecdotes are a testimony:

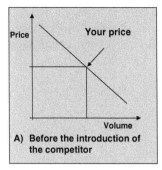
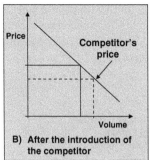
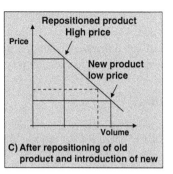

Figure 12.4 Meet price competition with price differentiation.

In 2007, British Airways was fined £270 million and Virgin Atlantic was caught price-fixing on long-haul flights and fined by the British Office of Fair Trade (121.5 million pounds) and the US Department of Justice (148 million pounds). The two companies met to agree and collude on the extra price of fuel surcharges in response to oil price rises.[20]

In another case, three of the largest chemical carriers in the world, Odfjell, Stolt Nielsen and Jo Tankers were indicted by the US Department of Justice in 2004 and were fined $62 million, $42.5 million and $19.5 million respectively for their participation in a price-fixing arrangement. And if that was not enough, managers from Odfjell and Jo Tankers had to go to jail in the US. Stolt Nielsen exchanged information on the other two in return for immunity from prosecution. In addition to the fine and jail sentences, they also met demands for refunds from their customers who had paid too much for the freight.[21]

12.6 Chapter summary

Pricing in international markets is, in principle, no different to pricing in general. In both cases, the firm needs to factor in the same elements, but in an international setting pricing offers both opportunities and challenges rarely experienced in domestic pricing. These may be price subsidisation in introductory phases in a new market, price differentiation based on divergent price mechanisms in different countries, or internal transfer pricing to optimise tax regulations (which is not legal, but still practised). Effective international pricing requires massive amounts of market information. Indeed, the study by Obadia (2013) indicates that information asymmetry reduces the effects of price adjustments, suggesting that close partner relationships between the exporter and its trading partners abroad are paramount. Obadia (2013, pp. 74–75) concludes that, "An adequate level of information about the importers' actions in favour of the brand and about their performance with the exporter's products is required to secure a good performance when offering discounts."

Firms without experience in international markets are disadvantaged in this regard as they will often have to take advice from their local partners at face value, without having the chance to check its validity in detail. The more seasoned the exporter, the more levers at hand. This is particularly true of firms operating in multi-local markets, where they can operate more freely, separate from global market forces, and take into account local context in each individual market. The task is more challenging for firms operating in a more "unprotected" world, where intertwined markets make pricing decisions more consequential for the whole operation (and not only isolated to each country market).

Notes

1 Hans Petter Evensen, marketing manager at Jordan.
2 Lars Tomasgård, general manager of Nordox.
3 Based on communications with industry sources.
4 *Chemical Business*, August 2011.
5 Hans Petter Evensen, marketing manager at Jordan, 2014.
6 C- and D-clauses are examples of Incoterms – see Section 12.3.1.
7 *Financial Times*, 28 January 1997, p. 10.
8 https://www.fxcm.com/insights/top-10-most-volatile-currencies-in-2014/
9 Ex-works means that the exporter quotes the price from the gate of the factory and does not take responsibility for freight or insurance of the products all the way to the customer. Ex-works is one of the E-clauses in Incoterms – see Section 12.3.1.
10 For more information see the WTO: https://www.wto.org/english/res_e/statis_e/statis_bis_e.htm? solution=WTO&path=/Dashboards/MAPS&file=Tariff.wcdf&bookmarkState={%22impl%22:% 22client%22,%22params%22:{%22langParam%22:%22en%22}}.
11 There is a lot of information about local taxes on the internet. I have used the following source in this paragraph: http://www.uscib.org/valueadded-taxes-vat-ud-1676/ and http://www.tax-rates.org/ taxtables/sales-tax-by-state.
12 Sources: http://www.bbc.com/news/business-22607349 and http://www.smh.com.au/business/the-economy/apples-85-million-tax-bill-is-a-fraction-of-its-almost-8-billion-revenue-20160126-gmej0z.html
13 The internet is full of articles and descriptions of Incoterms. ICC, World Bank, Wikipedia are among the most accessible ones.
14 For a list of credit insurance agencies see: https://en.wikipedia.org/wiki/Export_credit_agency#Export_ credit_agencies.
15 http://www.oecd.org/tad/xcred/arrangement.htm.
16 Boundless, "Countertrade." *Boundless Business*, 26 May 2016. Retrieved 1 February 2017 from https://www.boundless.com/business/textbooks/boundless-business-textbook/international-business-4/types-of-international-business-41/countertrade-217-1786/
17 Political risk has been considered by many. For a thorough discussion we refer to Howell (2013).
18 This is calculated as follows:

   Contribution in France (2.03 million euros) = basis for the average price increase divided on 8,900 units (Total sales volume 11,000 less sales volume in France 2,100) = 228.10 euros.

19 Parts of this section have been adapted from Solberg et al. (2006).
20 http://news.bbc.co.uk/2/hi/business/6925397.stm
21 Sources: *Dagens Næringsliv*, 30 September 2003; and http://offshore.no/sak/40415_judge_grants_ stolt-nielsen_anti-trust_immunity.

Part III

Planning and organising the international marketing effort

So far in this book, we have discussed the firm's international business environment, its strategic resources and marketing decisions in international markets. Now the time has come to discuss how to establish concrete marketing objectives, and develop a strong marketing plan. And how then should the plan be implemented? And by whom?

We have emphasised on several occasions throughout the book that strategy is not something that is decided based on rational grounds or by managers who have complete market information to develop and carry out the strategy. It normally evolves over time – "emergent strategies" as Mintzberg (1994) called it – and is formed in the intersection between different influences both within and outside the firm, and as a result of a gradually increasing recognition of the needs and demands of the market. Many firms are not able to rationally address all the challenges they are exposed to in international markets; for this, they lack both resources and managerial skills. More seasoned exporters are better off, but even *they* meet unexpected situations, such as a partner being acquired by competitors, political turbulence, currency instability, new trends and technologies that affect their strategic trajectory set out for the next couple of years.

"Common knowledge" suggests that planning is good for business. The planning process helps the firm structure and evaluate facts and in this way enhances management's consciousness of the opportunities and challenges that the firm faces – often by use of SWOT analyses (Strengths, Weaknesses, Opportunities and Threats). In the wake of SWOT, a number of different management buzz-words have appeared in the form of acronyms such as PEST, SLEPT, PESTEL, STEEPLED.[1] We regard these as mnemonics that help management to structure its presentation of strategic challenges. These are described in general marketing and strategic management texts.[2] Carrying out this kind of analysis is seen as an integral part of planning.

However, the performance effects of (formal) strategic planning have been disputed. Strategic planning – formal planning in particular – requires resources that many firms do not necessarily possess and often results in building bureaucratic structures and rigidity in organisations (Lorange 1980, Shrader et al. 1984). Some researchers (Mintzberg et al. 1998a) maintain that strategic planning is promoting short-sightedness and incremental change (as opposed to innovations). Planning also requires good "accurate forecast", which is a delusion according to Mintzberg et al. (1998b). Strategic planning requires "organisational redundancy", leaving this activity mostly to large firms (Nonaka 1994). A number of studies of the effects of planning on performance have been carried out over the years, but their results are either contradictory or inconclusive.[3] Solberg et al. (2014) conclude in their study of 133 Norwegian exporters that neither firm size nor formal planning has any impact on the international performance effects of factors such as positioning, network development, market insight or cost leadership. They conclude that:

> large firms as well as small firms may develop prosperous international marketing strategies; internationalisation is not the realm of large firms only. This is further supported by the number of start-ups that seem to prosper in international markets, despite their young age and – in many cases – lack of experience.
>
> Also, formal planning does not seem to make a significant difference. This does not imply that formal planning is not desirable altogether, but that for a good number of firms it does not seem to help. There are indications in our data that formal planning is negatively correlated with financial performance in the B2C sector. This sector [in Norway] consists to a large extent of fish exporters; to our knowledge this is a business characterised by strong network relations, substituting the need for planning and where any "attempt to force any plans on one's partners is seen as a nuisance". And as a matter of fact, networks are the single most important factor explaining financial performance in this sector (B2C).
>
> Furthermore in high growth industry sectors, planning seems to be counterproductive. Intuitively we believe that this is due to the complex and ever changing market environment featured by high growth markets, placing high demands on flexibility and adaptation, rendering plans redundant after a short time.
>
> Important elements of planning are nevertheless accounted for in the model and do play a crucial part. This is particularly true of the different information capture / market surveillance / market insight elements of the model, all [being] important constituents of the market orientation construct. Market insight is a prerequisite to develop viable strategies and much of the processes from market insight to concrete plans leading to such strategies are difficult to capture by a questionnaire.

Rather than planning as such, we would claim that the commitment and dedication mustered by members of the organisation determine its success in international markets (Aaby and Slater 1989). Then, building an organisation with such involvement becomes a key task for top management. When we discuss organisational solutions in Chapter 14, we claim that this point is rather more critical than the structure of the organisation as such. Perhaps the strategic planning process should be viewed in this perspective, namely as a means to mobilise the co-workers of the firm.

Having said this, Part III starts with the process of defining marketing objectives in international markets. Setting such objectives requires information, and such information is – as we have seen in Chapter 5 – often scant or inaccurate, or it is held by a third party, generally a partner, who may have his or her own agenda. We then go on to describe the planning process and present a sample plan. Organisation of the international marketing effort is then explored, before we conclude with a discussion of critical factors that determine success or failure in international marketing.

Notes

1 PEST = Political, Economic, Social, Technological; SLEPT = PEST + Legal; PESTEL = PEST + Environmental and Legal; STEEPLED = PESTEL + Ethics and Demographics.
2 See for example Cravens and Piercy (2009), Kotler and Keller (2011).
3 See for example Armstrong (1989), Falshaw et al. (2006), Ogunmokun and Tang (2012), Aldehayyat and Twaissi (2011), Solberg et al. (2014).

13 Planning the international marketing effort

13.1 Introduction

Setting up a marketing plan requires that objectives have been decided. They depend upon a wide range of factors. We have already seen in Chapter 3 how firms develop different trajectories in international markets – gradual vs. rapid international expansion, neighbouring countries vs. global presence. The objectives vary widely between these paths to international markets, and – more often than is recognised – firms have *not* gone through a deliberate process of goal-setting and activity planning; rather "the road is paved as you go". This chapter analyses how international marketing goals can be developed in the intersection between the firm and its environment, explores different approaches to planning using the Strategic Windows framework, and discusses the planning process. The backdrop of this discussion is the market insight possessed by managers. This insight has been formed through two main processes, described in Chapter 5: international market research and market experience through networks and operations.

13.2 Setting marketing objectives

What do we really want to achieve in international markets? How much can we expect to sell in this or that market? Well, the answers to these questions are never straightforward because they depend on innumerable factors, which can basically be summed up in Figure 13.1.

Let us imagine a Dutch firm that is considering exporting to either Germany or Scandinavia for the first time. At face value, Germany with 80 million people seems more interesting, based on the mere fact that it is far more populous than Scandinavia with just 20 million people. Yet, our newcomer may still choose to export to Scandinavia:

–   No one in the organisation speaks German, and Germany is not known for English language proficiency, whereas English is well-spoken in Scandinavia and could be used as a *lingua franca*.
–   Scandinavia is culturally much closer to the Netherlands than Germany (see Hofstede 1980).
–   The firms resources are insufficient to engage in markets as large as Germany.
–   The products are more adapted to the Scandinavian markets than to Germany.
–   Competition is much tougher in Germany.

So, in spite of the fact that Germany is both closer to the Netherlands and a larger market, the exporter may still go for Scandinavia. On the other hand, Scandinavia consists of three different countries, with three sets of market conditions. But do we – during the first couple of years – have

Figure 13.1 Factors determining marketing objectives.

the capacity to cover more than just one of the Scandinavian markets? We conclude that the market potential should take into consideration not only the size of the market as an objective number, but also the firm's resource base and its capabilities to service its potential customers. If management desires a broader market involvement, the organisation might need additional resources.

This description fits a small or medium-sized company that has limited manufacturing capacity, and it does not do anything more than give some initial indication of where to start. For an operational goal-setting, we need additional background information about the market. One way to get this is to define the customer base and identify the main customers in the area. Our Dutch company may be a manufacturer of equipment for the processors of vegetables. A check in the Kompass industry directory (kompass.com) would give a quick insight into the number and names of potential customers and, sometimes, also a brief description of their business. In this case, we find that there are 88 candidates (48 in Denmark, 23 in Norway and 17 in Sweden). It would therefore be a good start to take a closer look at Denmark with 48 potential customer at best; but bear in mind that some of the entries may not be relevant or may be wrongly registered in the directory. A realistic objective may be to sell to around 10% of these firms over the next couple of years, in other words – about five potential customers. Assuming – based on experience from the domestic market – that customers buy the equipment every second year at the cost of between 20,000 and 1 million euros (average 150,000 euros), we can calculate a very roughly estimated sales volume to Denmark during the first two years of operation to be in the area around 750,000 euros.

This little exercise demonstrates that setting concrete marketing objectives is relatively straightforward. However, it rests on assumptions that may not be valid in Denmark so, in order to get closer to a realistic sales figure, other information is needed: more detailed data about the 48 potential customers (size, technologies used, purchasing practices) and competitors.

If we now assume instead that our Dutch friends have a relatively large international operation, marketing to some 15 countries – 5 of which are outside Europe – the question of marketing objectives becomes a bit more complex. In order to get some structure to our discussion we suggest a hierarchy of goals, starting with the firm's purpose or mission and ending with operational goals that may take the form of activities more than goals as such. The latter might be setting up a website in the main languages of the customers, participation at the Anuga FoodTec trade fair in Cologne, or renegotiation of the agency contract with their Portuguese partner. Table 13.1 gives an overview of such a hierarchy.

We shall briefly make some comments about this table. First, we need to mention that it is of course not necessary for the international marketing plan to discuss the purpose of the company and its mission every year. On the other hand, with experience from different market contexts, it may be useful occasionally to review the firm's position in its product grid (see Figure 10.1), and to reassess its business model. For our Dutch equipment manufacturer, it may be relevant to ask if they should concentrate on the hardware only, or on the engineering of the plant, or if they should rather engage in turn-key delivery of the whole plant (hardware *and* engineering). Alternatively, they might also perhaps consider licensing or "Build-Operate-Transfer" (BOT)

Table 13.1 Goal hierarchy for international market planning

Level	Content	Comments
Purpose	The firm's field of business and business model	Don't be too concrete; start with customer needs and the firm's technological basis.
Economic goals	Long-term income objectives, for instance: return on sales or return on investments	Should be related to those of the industry.
	Short-term liquidity	The firm has to survive in the short-term! For instance: sales growth needs to be financed; so-called growth pains are often underestimated.
Strategic objectives	Role in the market	Determines the firm's relations to its customers. What are our main market segments, and how are we perceived? Are we the main supplier, or just a marginal one? Defines customer groups and position relative to that of competitors.
	Technology Competence level Growth	Determines quality and cost levels. Critical determinant for firm's survival. Growth is critical in order to maintain market shares, and to secure organisational dynamics.
Operational goals	Sales volume next year Participation at Anuga FoodTec New packaging for Europe Planning seminar with distributors and subsidiaries	Comments will be dealt with in the marketing plan section

in overseas markets. The answers to these questions depend on customer competencies and preferences in the different markets, on competition, and on the internal resources and competencies within the firm. The decisions will inexorably have ramifications for its operations (operation modes, partners, own competence): it is quite a different business to deliver equipment only and to engage in BOP or licensing.[1]

Second, management should distinguish between the operative goals (short-term – 1–2 years) and the strategic, long-term goals (5–10 years). Let us remind ourselves of the fact that "Things Take Time" (TTT), and that "In International Marketing, Things Take Extra Long Time" (IIMTTELT!). Breaking through into a new market may not come the same year or the year after a marketing campaign has been launched. In other words: the firm needs to factor in its financial and organisational staying power, in order to persevere in the face of lethargy and late responses from customers, or reactions from competitors.

Third, defining the firm's role in the market (strategic objective) should come as a result of an understanding of the needs in the market, how they are expressed in terms of products and services, and how competitors operate to satisfy those needs. The management has to identify in what ways the firm's products and services (quality, function, design) differ from those of competitors, and to explore customer groups that are responsive to what in particular the firm can offer. The technology and competencies of the firm are strongly linked to this role, and should therefore be nurtured to sustain and further develop its position in the market.

Spain's leading cava producer Freixenet's road to international markets is an interesting case of how this firm has evolved from being a modest exporter trailing far behind its French competitors in the international sparkling wine market to become a challenger or even a market leader (by volume) in some markets outside their home base. Their vision today is to be "*A reference company in the wine sector at a worldwide level*". To this end, they have gradually developed their strategy in a "traditional internationalisation process way à la Uppsala" (see Section 3.2.3) – through to exporting, strategic alliances and acquisitions of wineries and vineyards – to become an assertive market leader in many of its more than 100 markets. They make their products in 16 wine districts around the world, mainly in Rioja, California, Australia and Argentina. Their value proposition is "value for money", distinguishing them from the premium segment occupied by French wineries, and has in fact led them to be US market leaders in terms of volume. In Japan they are number two – just behind their French rival Moët & Chandon. In Germany, the world's largest market for sparkling wines – dominated by their domestic Sekt – Freixenet has reached a market share of 10%. The sparkling wines are the spearhead of the company's product range, but this range includes more than 30 different brands – including still wines. In order to reach this position, Freixenet has gradually asserted control over its marketing activities, operating mainly through its own marketing subsidiaries. It appears as though the company has indeed reached its goal.[2]

Fourth, the product-market matrix (see Table 13.2) may be an adequate model to use through the goal-setting process. For example, this matrix helps management to localise products/markets that have a precariously high share of the firm's sales (leading to vulnerability). It also facilitates spotting areas which warrant more attention (stagnating or falling sales); or to identify potential gains through better co-ordination; or simply to drop products or markets altogether that do not contribute to financial performance (see also discussions in Section 10.3.4 and Section 12.4).

The hierarchy of objectives discussed above gives a structural presentation of a process that in many firms is carried out every day. Through feedback from customers and dealers, through internal deliberations involving relevant departments, through testing out new ideas and through facing competitors' moves, the firm gradually builds experience that is embedded in the organisation and gives direction to strategic decisions and then to operational actions. Many

Table 13.2 Product market matrix

Product	Market							
	Denmark	*Sweden*	*Norway*	*Germany*	*France*	*Spain*	*Portugal*	*UK*
Alpha 11								
Alpha 12								
Alpha 21								
Beta 11								
Beta 12								
Beta 21								
Beta 22								
Gamma 11								
Gamma 12								

firms do this automatically, without having defined it as a structural process; it is just an innate feature of the organisational culture of the firm. Other firms have not built this culture, and need a template to follow in order to define their "role in the market", and subsequently, to lay out the detailed activities that naturally ensue.

13.3 Strategy dynamics

We have seen that the content of strategy varies significantly with the firm's position in the Strategic Windows framework. This model gives the management indications as to the firm's main strategic orientation. The fact that the firm's resources and the market development are constantly changing will inevitably affect the firm's objectives and strategy. A Polish firm with sporadic exports to Lithuania of their radio tracking devices needs to revise its strategy when it seeks a foothold in a broader set of export markets. Table 13.3 suggests the main elements of the two situations.

This table does not give a universal solution to either of the two marketing objectives described; other strategic approaches may be considered in both cases. The essence here is to illustrate how different objectives warrant different strategies. Sometimes a strong foothold (in the sense of building a local organisation) is necessary from day one, either because resources are needed to build market shares, or because the market demands extensive customer inter-action or local service.

We will now return to the strategic windows model, and analyse the firm's objectives and strategies in that context – see Figure 13.2.

13.3.1 The careful newcomer

The challenge for the careful newcomer is to be engaged in what we have termed the "beneficial export circle" (see Section 3.4.2). Its prime objective – in addition to achieving sales – should be to secure feedback from the market, to make sure that market information is not being held back by its local partner, to get in direct contact with the end customer and to build systems to make this happen. Detailed planning is normally difficult, partly because management have scant information and partly because of a lack of experience of "what works and what does not

Table 13.3 Different objectives – different strategies

Strategic element	Sporadic exports	Foothold in export markets
Market	Regular customers difficult to establish	Regular customers imperative
Operation mode	Direct distribution (no local partner) may be necessary to bring down costs	Distribution depends on market structure; normally a local partner is needed
Product	Adaptation too costly → ruins economies of scale	Adaptation may be imperative and depends on the market; but it may be justified by high sales volume
Price	Low price is necessary to trigger sales	High price should be possible because the firm has an entrenched position in the market.
Promotion	Limited promo; direct with occasional customers	Promo is necessary to build relations with customers
Organisation	No specific export organisation	A dedicated export organisation is required

Figure 13.2 Strategic archetypes.

work". The sales objectives should be discussed in depth with the local partner. This strategic approach is possible because the firm can treat each individual market as just that – individual markets – without influence from global markets or global competitors. With more experience, the firm should be capable of taking on more challenging steps into international markets. Yet, we observe many firms that have been exporting perhaps just 5–6% of their total sales for decades, without any further international growth. We claim that this is made possible only because globalisation drivers have not yet affected their industry.

13.3.2 Multinational player

The multinational players have many opportunities to expand internationally. The fact that they operate in a multi-local setting and that they have a good position in some key markets[3] gives them leverage to further strengthen their positions in these markets and seek stepwise expansion into new markets without fear of being challenged by global competitors. Centralised goal-setting and coordination of marketing are not advisable in this position, since markets by definition are quite different from one another. Rather, the multinational player should let each local sales subsidiary and partner come up with objectives and plans for their respective market without too much interference from the centre. We have previously (page 243) called this cell "Confer and monitor, but allow local implementation". Some participation and monitoring is definitely advisable: to give signals of the priorities of the centre; to learn from the market; and as a preparation for a potential future trend towards a more global industry and market situation. The challenge here is to find the right balance between tight monitoring and free rein. There may come a time when more co-ordinated planning is required (due to competition and/or pressure on costs) and when a reorganisation of the product and brand portfolio is needed. There will be a time during which mutual understanding of central versus local needs and challenges is crucial in order to implement imperative changes in the marketing mix across countries. If this is not achieved, the firm risks entering the "Civil war" cell (see Figure 8.1, page 232).

13.3.3 The bold newcomer

The bold newcomer is in a vulnerable situation – often akin to that of the Born Global. Developing an international marketing strategy and plan is a major challenge for small and resource-poor firms in the presence of large global companies eager to take over their idea or technology. A good start would be to register patents (if applicable) and trademarks. Whereas some firms need partnering with large multinationals to benefit from their marketing network, others may manage to rapidly conquer a large catchment area through the internet. Key words for firms in this strategic position are networking and niches: networking – to be connected with vital parts of the market; niches – to build entry barriers to potential competitors. We have seen that planning is counterproductive in high-growth industries (see Part III), a situation frequently met by firms in this cell. Their challenge is that a clear-cut definition of their market is often lacking, since the market for their product or service has not yet been fully developed and demarcated. Detailed market planning is therefore futile most of the time.

Huddly, a hi-tech start-up company in computational imaging based in Oslo, Norway, and Palo Alto, California, uses the internet extensively in their international marketing. They have in just half a year reached about 20,000 Facebook followers, and get requests from potential customers at an increasingly higher rate, even before the product is launched internationally. It is not straightforward to predict next year's sales.

13.3.4 The global market leader

The imperative of global market leaders is to secure and further develop their position. They are among the three or four largest players in their industry worldwide, and are challenged by both their main competitors and new entrants "at all times". This position, therefore, requires constant market surveillance and co-ordinated actions in order to fight off competitors. Interestingly, based on findings in Norway, this is the only cell in the Strategic Windows framework where market planning seemingly has any unambiguously substantial positive effect.[4] The reason, we believe, is that firms in this cell operate in an environment with few major competitors, where the market is like a "game of chess" in which all the pawns are mutually interdependent. In this setting, it is 1) easier to get an understanding of the general competitive picture (few major players) and 2) the firm – through its experience and resources – is better informed. Keep in mind that even medium-sized (and in specific cases: small) firms may find themselves in this cell. This is when they have managed to carve out a niche in global markets, protected from attacks from larger firms because of high entry barriers: specialist knowledge/technology and/or special relationships with a limited group of customers.

Swix is a good example of a global leader within its niche of ski wax. Swix is a market leader in major ski nations, with sales of only some 80 million euros in 2016. Ski wax is a specialist market: there are about 115 million skiers worldwide, mainly in Europe (60%), Japan (10%) and North America (15%),[5] and only a fraction of these are actively using ski wax.

We have so far discussed the situation of firms that are unambiguously located in one of the four cells in the windows framework. A large number of firms – particularly conglomerates – are present in different positions in this framework, a fact that may cause concern for management when assessing their strategies according to the model. Often the management culture is instilled on one main approach to planning and strategy development. This may be counterproductive as the challenges vary markedly between the four cells. On the other hand, if executives are aware of potential pitfalls of using a company-wide template for planning, it may also be able to adapt this template to those that are "outsiders".

13.4 International marketing plan

The marketing strategy, as discussed above, gives management direction in their international marketing endeavours. In the international marketing plan and the budget, management expresses the firm's operational goals.

There are, in principle, two approaches to planning and budgeting: top-down and bottom-up. In the former, top management allocates resources to activities to be carried out during the next budget period. Allowances are made per department and, for marketing, this means a certain amount that they can spend on their activities. This process gives top management good financial control. On the other hand, the international marketing department has to content itself with the allocation provided through the budget and has to tailor its activity level to the resources provided regardless of the requirements in the market place. There is therefore a risk that the international marketing staff – including its members abroad – can feel alienated, causing frustration and a feeling that top management does not understand what it takes to carry out a successful marketing campaign abroad. Top-down budgeting is probably most appropriate for firms that operate in stable environments.

The bottom-up approach gives the staff at lower levels the opportunity to come up with inputs to the budget, based on their activity plans and the resources they deem necessary to carry them out. For the international marketing department, this implies that they can promote their ideas for the marketing plan, and build a case to "spend more resources than last year" on specific activities in order to attain certain sales goals or other goals such as customer awareness, or dealer coverage in specific markets. The participation from the bottom up normally leads to a more collaborative culture within the firm, since it gives the bottom a say in the allocation of the firm's resources. However, it could also result in cost overruns, prompted by overeager and unrealistic sales and marketing staff, without the necessary input from in-depth market insight. On the other hand, bottom-up budgeting puts pressure on the lower levels to perform; in a way it constitutes a "contract" between the lower level (in our case: marketing department) and top management to achieve what the former claimed it could.

Both approaches have merits and disadvantages. In international marketing – and particularly in new markets – we deem the bottom-up method to be more appropriate. Each situation is new, with its own characteristics, such as market dynamics, competition, demand patterns, industry structures, regulations, etc. This calls for a fresh look at the promotional requirements, the price level and staffing needed to attain the sales objectives set for the market. Therefore, the bottom-up model is particularly appropriate in multi-local markets. Also, given uncertainties inherent in the international business environment (currency fluctuations, political decisions), flexibility is needed in this process.

In the following, we shall describe how the firm may approach the basic planning. The budgeting as such – in terms of euros, pounds, USD, kroner, forint, rial, yen or any other currency – is not subject to discussion here; rather we shall look at sales forecasts and the marketing programme.

13.4.1 Sales forecasts

Sales forecasts are the backbone of any budget. They provide the foundation for the activity level of the company and constitute the main premise for the whole budget. This section will not go deeply into all the conundrums of sales forecasting.[6] Instead, we shall describe the process of getting concrete "data" on customer purchases and their propensity to buy from the firm. Using quotes to express "data" refers to the often approximate information that is the basis for the forecasts, borrowed from Scott Edinger who also uses the term "wish-cast" to designate the often loosely founded sales estimates.[7]

Sales forecasts are a function of the sales potential in the market, the marketing strategy and activities carried out by the firm. Figure 13.3 indicates the causal relationships between the main factors affecting sales volume and profits, which should then be factored in when anticipating sales. Therefore, it is imperative to get a good understanding of customer behaviour, customers' relationships with competitors, trends in the market, etc. Acquiring this understanding is not straightforward for the newcomer, and not even for firms that have operated in the market for a while. Referring back to our Dutch manufacturer of machinery to the food processing industry (see Section 13.2), we clearly see that estimates are at best approximate. For the more experienced firm with a long history in diverse markets, knowing the dealer network, industry and competitors, it is tempting just to extrapolate a "line" based on this experience. The risk then is that unexpected events in the market will be disregarded.

In any event, applying the bottom-up method, the firm should involve its partners and local sales subsidiaries actively in the forecasting process. These are the ones best positioned to interpret the signals from the market, and they should report their viewpoints and estimates to headquarters. Not only do they know the market, but their input also constitutes some kind of commitment to perform accordingly. However, the realism of the forecast needs to be checked against the marketing activities that are planned. Participating at a trade fair, visiting

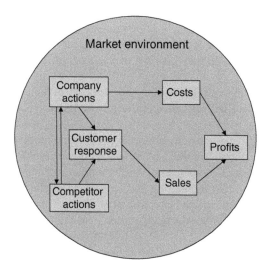

Figure 13.3 Factors affecting sales.

customers and dealers, setting up a bonus plan for the sales force, advertising, etc., all carry costs, and their effects on sales are uncertain! So, the local sales unit needs not only to substantiate its estimates, but also relate them to the long-term strategy in the market. We believe this is best done in a dialogue between the international sales and marketing staff and the local representative.

When all the local sales forecasts (including their planned marketing activities) have been submitted to the centre, the marketing manager should get an overview and consider whether the forecasts are too modest relative to their sales objectives, or perhaps too ambitious. In either case, one should reconsider the objectives, make priorities between markets, reassess the proposed activity plan, and go back to the local partner/subsidiary in order to redefine the forecast.

13.4.2 The marketing programme

The marketing programme is the lever that helps management to monitor its activities in each market. Table 13.4 gives an example of the marketing programme over a one-year period of a medium-sized firm selling safety systems to the hotel sector. The company is operating in 12 European countries, and is seeking expansion into Asia and Scandinavia.

The programme has six main features:

- The firm is planning to launch a new product, which occupies a good part of the organisation's attention. The launch will be executed in Germany, Austria and Switzerland first, and will be followed up in the rest of Europe after experience has been gained in the test countries and potential adaptations implemented.
- It will participate at the Fagfa Trade Fair in Innsbruck (Austria) in September. Here the marketing people will have the opportunity to present its new products to the market, including invited key customers. Note that the new product is concurrently launched in three countries.
- The annual sales seminar takes place in Spain this year. This is a regular event that takes place ahead of the planning process for the coming year. Top management discuss strategies and issues with its marketing partners and sales subsidiaries, present new products, and receive the input for the next budget year.
- The exploratory visit to Asia in February, to be followed up later in the year. This visit may lead to new market avenues for the firm and may give it a major boost in international markets.
- Market research in Scandinavia and Finland. This region, with some 25 million inhabitants, has constantly scored high on welfare and competitiveness rankings and should constitute an interesting new market.
- Other than these main activities, the firm plans to reinvigorate its presence in France, and to redefine its role in Italy. Other "daily chores" of the marketing department are not registered in the plan, as they are routine tasks. One such task is the *monthly report* sent by the subsidiaries and partners – see below under monitoring and control. In addition, many activities are not possible to plan, since unexpected circumstances "always" emerge and area managers and even top management have to be ready to step in at short notice.

Take a look at the distribution of responsibilities and execution. We observe that the marketing vice president (VPM) is responsible for most of the activities in the programme, but that the execution is the realm of the operative area managers and export manager. Note also that the

Table 13.4 Marketing programme – an example

Date	Activity	Market	Responsibility	Execution	Budget	Actual cost	Comments
Jan	Registration Fagfa Trade Fair Innsbruck (September)	Austria	Area manager	Secretary			Check with export promo agency: potential funding and activities
	Presentation to new customers in France	France	Area manager	Partner/area manager			Partner proposes the agenda
	Yearly reports from local partners/subsidiaries	All	VPM	Partners/subsidiaries			
	Preparation of sales campaign in Germany	Germany	Area manager	Partner			
Feb	Yearly reports follow-up	All	VPM, VPF	Area manager			
	Follow up in France	France	Area manager	Export manager Partner			Info to export promo agency and embassies
	Exploratory visit to Asia	Japan, PRC, S. Korea, Singapore	CEO Chairman	CEO, VPM, Export manager			Marketing strategy seminar for all markets
	Preparation for yearly "All Star" event in Barcelona	All	VPM, Export manager	Export manager Area managers			
Mar	Renegotiate contract with Italian agent	Italy	Area manager	Area manager			Brief lawyer
	Initiate market research in Scandinavia/Finland	Dk, N, S, SF	VPM, Export manager	Export manager			Select and brief market research institute
	Adapt website to local languages	Esp, France Germany, Poland	VPM, IT manager	Area managers, partners			

(Continued)

Table 13.4. (continued)

Date	Activity	Market	Responsibility	Execution	Budget	Actual cost	Comments
April	Follow up Asia visit	Asia	CEO	VPM			Inform export promo agency and embassy
	Prepare press visits "All Star" event	Europe All	VPM VPM	Secretary Export and area manager			Input to planning/ budgeting for next year Briefing for product launch
May	Follow up Barcelona "All Star" seminar	General	VPM	VPF/VPM, area managers			Budget/planning start-up
	Preparation for new product launch	Germany, Austria, Switzerland	VPM, Tech manager	Area managers, partners			Ad agency brief Check potential funding with export promotion agency
June	Press release related to new product launch	General	VPM, Tech manager	PR consultant			
	Product launch prep continued	Germany, Austria, Switzerland	VPM	Area managers, partners			Ad agency proposal
July	Product launch prep continued	Germany, Austria, Switzerland	VPM	Area managers, partners			Ad agency proposal Obs! Summer holidays in Scandinavia
August	Summer holidays Product launch final prep	Germany, Austria, Switzerland	VPM	VPM			Continental Europe Brief technical manager
	Prep for Fagfa Trade Fair	All/Austria	VPM	Area manager, partner			

Table 13.4. (continued)

Date	Activity	Market	Responsibility	Execution	Budget	Actual cost	Comments
Sept	Product launch	Germany, Austria, Switzerland	VPM	Area managers, partners			
	Fagfa Trade Fair, Innsbruck	All/Austria	VPM	Area managers, local partner			Invite key customers to seminar at Fagfa
Oct	Fagfa and product launch follow-up	All/Austria	VPM	Area managers, partners			Discuss entry mode and marketing mix
	Market research report	Scan DK,N, S, SF	VPM	Export manager			
	Follow up visit to Scandinavia/Finland		VPM	Export manager			
	Revisit Asia, follow up	Japan, PRC, S. Korea, Singapore	CEO	CEO?, VPM, tech manager			
Nov	Next year plan/budget preparation	All	VPM	VPM, Area managers, partners			Draft plan/budget for each market sent out for comments
	Follow up market research report	Denmark Norway Sweden Finland	VPM, Area manager	Area manager, partners			Market strategy for the region
Dec	Plan/budget review and	All	VPM, VPF	VPM, Area managers			Final decision
	Season greetings	All	CEO	VPM, Area managers			Send Xmas cards to partners and key customers

Note: Abbreviations: VPM=Vice President marketing; VPF=Vice president finance.

firm has – in addition to area managers – an export manager responsible for sales through independent partners.[8] It should further be noted that the chairperson is included in the delegation to visit Asia. This is in recognition of the importance placed on seniority in this part of the world, the firm then showing its commitment to the approach.

We may divide the programme into three groups:

1   Monitoring and control
2   Marketing and sales activities in established markets
3   Initiatives in new markets.

Monitoring and control is a major task for the marketing department. It should be carried out in collaboration with the finance and accounting departments. We have already, in Chapter 8, discussed different approaches to the monitoring of sales subsidiaries and partners (outcome, behaviour and clan controls). Also, in Chapter 5, we have explored a system for market intelligence that helps the firm structure the information capture and analyse the collected data. In the present context, we shall delve into the "technical parts" of this responsibility. There are in principle three such tasks: setting standards and routines, reporting the outcome and analysis of deviations, and discussions of appropriate corrections.

The standards involve what should be reported and how often. Below is an example of how this is done:

Gannet Guard Systems, selling radio tracking and GPS systems in Poland, reports the following data *weekly* to headquarters in Norway:

–   Sales last week for the different product groups – both new customers and renewals; including numbers from the past four years in the "same" week.
–   Rolling averages (four and eight weeks) to smooth unexplained abrupt deviations, and to detect possible trends.
–   Total sales during the year to date, compared with previous years.
–   Liquidity – both cash and goods in stock.

This information gives management at the centre a quick status of the development in the market, and the opportunity to react if something unexpected happens. It also constitutes the basis for a weekly discussion with local management. Note also that financial data is reported. In addition to the weekly reports, the subsidiary sends a monthly report summing up the results of the month, including an overview of the performance of each sales person (registered per sales region), sales per customer group and some general charts and statistics of the development in the market.

Weekly sales reports may seem overambitious, but this has two beneficial outcomes: it instils a sense of vigilance and attention to performance throughout the whole organisation, and it gives management an early warning if numbers deviate. It is also easily implemented using appropriate data programs. As discussed in Chapter 8, too much reporting and control may however be counterproductive. For instance, independent partners, and in particular distributors (taking title to the goods), are generally unwilling to report too much in detail, as such reporting intrudes on their independence. Also, whereas some subsidiaries may welcome tight controls and follow-up since this helps them in their own efforts to improve their performance, others may react negatively to such rigorous monitoring because it intrudes on their "way of doing things". Furthermore, being at different stages in the market presence of the firm warrants different aspects to be controlled. For instance, in the early stages of a market introduction one should allow for deviations to the sales forecasts, since the firm has no references from the market place. Later – with more experience – the firm also has a better background from which to make forecasts and to compare outcomes.

Another issue is that of the financial requirements in terms of market contributions to profits. In that context, we refer to our discussion in Chapter 12 (Pricing decisions) where we advocate a cautious stance to "jumping to conclusions". Rather than using a standard response to poor financial performance in one market, management should explore alternative routes to improve market contributions. This requires in-depth analysis of the market situation: customer behaviour, potential restructuring of local distribution, competitor reactions, sourcing, etc.

Marketing and sales activities are the realm of the local sales representative (partner or sales subsidiary). However, the centre has a different perspective on the market than each local subsidiary and partner. The yearly sales and marketing seminar is one lever for the firm to instil a sense of clan feeling in the whole organisation – including the independent partners. In the present context, two projects require a more global approach: the product launch and the participation at the Fagfa trade show in Innsbruck. In the former, management intends to build on experiences from the launch in Germany, Austria and Switzerland before introducing the new product to other countries. In the latter, potential customers from around the world are expected, and it may therefore be expedient to involve more area managers (than just the one responsible for Austria) in the event.

Initiatives in new markets are carried out in two distinct ways. In Asia, a high-level delegation from headquarters embarks on an exploratory fact-finding mission to investigate opportunities, to identify potential partners, and to tie in with relevant network relationships. Later in the same year, a new and a more operational delegation is sent to pick up the loose ends and – hopefully – initiate discussions with potential partners identified during the first trip. Involving officials (embassy, export promotion agency) in the planning and during the visit normally heightens the status of the project in the eyes of the hosts. In Scandinavia, with its low context (Hall 1959) and individualistic and low power distance culture (Hofstede 1980), a more analytical approach is used: market research, strategy discussion and then visit potential partners/customers.

13.5 Chapter summary

In spite of a certain scepticism expressed towards formal planning in the Introduction to Part III, we have spent three sections on setting objectives, strategic orientation and a sample plan, including sales forecasting and a concrete marketing programme. This is done in recognition that some structure is needed and that a plan may constitute some sort of "glue" in the organisation, a means to shape a common consciousness of the role of the firm in international markets. The level of detail of such a plan is another matter. In international markets, and in particular in multi-local markets, the marketing context is widely diverse, and there is a risk that detailed *central* planning becomes futile, and sometimes even counterproductive.

Yet, some processes should prove effective. Setting objectives is meaningful in this context, particularly at the higher levels of the goal hierarchy. Defining the role of the company in the market is possibly a good start. The operational goals and the marketing programme should find their inspiration here. The goals should however be realistic, and based on market insight, which is sometimes scarce in foreign markets – particularly for newcomers. In this case, reliance on information from partners becomes indispensable. Building and nurturing trusting relationships with partners is therefore critical. Also, developing internal mechanisms for organisational learning about market developments is a key to securing market insight in the longer run. It is about creating a culture of market orientation in the organisation. We shall discuss different organisational solutions in the next chapter.

Notes

1 For a review of different approaches to defining the product offering, see Section 10.2.
2 This anecdote is based on a case study by Joan Freixanet (a professor at University of St. Petersburg), "The sparkling internationalization of a global leader".
3 This is the definition of the firm's position on the y-axis, see Section 4.2.
4 This statement is based on unpublished research carried out by the author. In fact, in a sample of 130 Norwegian exporters, planning – defined as planning before market entry, importance of planning and coincidences (reversed) – is non-consequential in the other cells. In the Global leader cell, it is significantly and positively related to market performance. Note that this does not imply that planning is altogether redundant for the firms in the three other cells; statistically it suggests that some firms may benefit from planning, whereas for others, for reasons that have been discussed above, international market planning is in fact counterproductive. On average, however, planning has no consequence for performance.
5 Laurent Vanat, 2014. "2014 International Report on Snow and Mountain Tourism", Geneva, http://www.isiaski.org/download/20140517_ISIA_Vuokatti_1b_presentation_vanat.pdf
6 For an in-depth treatment of this area, we refer to Armstrong (2001).
7 http://www.forbes.com/sites/scottedinger/2013/06/03/four-principles-for-great-sales-forecasts/#120cbce7d8f5
8 We shall in the next chapter discuss different organisational solutions; the present firm has a regionalised structure.

14 Organising the international marketing effort

14.1 Introduction

We have seen how a newcomer to international markets seldom has sufficient resources to carry out exporting "according to the textbook". We have also seen that well-seasoned firms with a leadership position in international markets need to build substantial resources to take on planning, monitoring and control. In this chapter, we shall discuss different organisational solutions to address these tasks. Parts of this subject have been covered in other chapters (Chapter 7: Operation modes and Chapter 8: Monitoring the partner). Its main tasks should constitute the starting point for setting up the international marketing organisation:

- Information capture and analysis
- Defining goals and objectives in international markets
- Developing international marketing strategy
- Preparation and implementation of the international marketing plan
- Monitoring and control.

The firm needs an organisation to deal with all these tasks, either in-house or by outsourcing selected functions to a third party – such as an independent marketing partner, a logistics partner, a market research institute, a factoring company, legal advisor, etc. In Chapter 7, we discussed how different members of the distribution system contribute to the international marketing effort of the firm. For instance, the trading house takes over the responsibility for the international marketing before the product leaves the country, and the internal organisation may therefore be reduced to a part-time co-worker in the sales department. Exporting through a sales subsidiary places demands that are far more challenging on the organisation.

The international marketing organisation depends mainly on three factors: 1) the nature of the products; 2) the strategic position of the firm, its resources and its competitors; and 3) its marketing objectives and strategies.

Jordan's (oral hygiene) way of working with their foreign distributors illustrates the issues raised above. They are represented in some 80 countries around the globe and do not have enough resources to take care of the distribution of their products to all these markets. The product requires a great deal of follow-up in the retail store, demanding too many resources for the firm to tackle this task itself. In primary markets, Jordan has established regional sales managers at headquarters that maintain the relationships with its local exclusive distributors. In the overseas markets, they have invested in permanent local sales representatives to carry out this function, chiefly because of the geographic distance. The tasks of the centrally-placed regional sales managers and local sales representatives vary from one market to another.

In addition, everything that has to do with the product – design, colour, packaging, product range, product development – is taken care of by Jordan centrally. Development of marketing campaigns, advertising materials, etc. is split in different ways between Jordan and its distributors.

In many ways, we may claim that the internal international marketing organisation is the first member of the firm's distribution system. This chapter will discuss different organisational designs to tackle the firm's international market engagement, and relate them to the firm's strategic position in the Strategic Windows model. Before doing that, we shall briefly discuss the role of top management and potential internal organisational tensions inherent in the internationalisation of the firm.

14.2 Top management involvement and internal conflicts

14.2.1 Top management involvement

Chapter 13 discussed the planning and implementation process of the international marketing effort. We noticed in the proposed marketing programme (see pages 351–352) that the vice president for marketing (VPM) has a key role throughout the process, delegating tasks to area managers (or product managers – depending on the organisation) and seeking assistance from the top manager and even the chairperson of the board of directors. The decision to expand in international markets, to identify opportunities and allocate resources to developing them is, however, a top management responsibility. Senior managers should actively be involved in market selection, and in formulating the general guidelines for the international marketing strategy as it has been discussed throughout this book. This also implies that top management should be the main driver behind the internationalisation process of the firm. Without this, it is practically impossible to muster the necessary commitment from the rest of the organisation (see Chapter 3: the "Beneficial Export Circle").

Top management should also relate to the owners, primarily through the board of directors, and bring the internationalisation process to the agenda at board meetings. The directors have an unambiguous responsibility to give general guidelines to top management concerning major strategic moves such as international market involvement. Signals given by the board and by main shareholders of the company help management in their strategic deliberations.

An appropriate composition of the board of directors is therefore critical for the international market involvement of the firm. Describing the service role of the board, Van den Heuvel et al. (2006) distinguished between the *strategic role*, the *service role* and the *resource dependence role*. The strategic role includes the board's involvement in defining the firm's business concept, mission and selecting and implementing the company's strategy. The service role includes advising the CEO and top management, as well as initiating and formulating strategy. For instance, the directors can actively contribute to the successful operations by linking to relevant, previous network connections in international markets and legitimise the firm *vis-à-vis* its environment, such as government agencies, banks, suppliers or customers (Johannisson and Huse 2000). The resource dependence role concerns the acquisition of resources critical to the firm's success through networks to financial sources and/or markets.

In Chapter 3, Section 3.5.1, we noticed that one of the main differences between successful and unsuccessful exporters was the involvement of boards in strategic discussions. Uncertainty – and worse, incompetence – by members of the board of directors regarding what it takes to engage in international markets is possibly a major weakness in an era of increasing global competition. Sometimes board members have a different perspective to that of the top management and perhaps marketing managers in particular. The appreciation of the time and resources it takes to build a foreign market presence is not always a prevalent feature among the directors of internationalising firms. These are archetypally more concerned with financial numbers and when such numbers do not satisfy board members they may become impatient too early in the process, starting to ask critical questions of top management. These are, of course, normally justified, but should not translate into undue ambivalence and hesitation about the international involvement of the firm. In fact, one of the main reasons for failure in international markets is, according to Doole and Lowe (2004c), vacillating commitment by the firm, often stemming from disagreements within or equivocal signals from the board.

14.2.2 Cooperation with other functions

The international marketing function is naturally linked with other parts of the organisation, such as:

– Purchasing and manufacturing departments – reporting demand forecasts and controlling the quality of the purchased material and that of the finished products.
– Finance department – establishing the budget and controlling the costs.
– Logistics department – for the dispatch of the products.
– Research and development department – participating in the product development and product adaptation.
– Legal department – assisting in contracting, negotiations, patenting and trademark protection, and monitoring the development of the legal environment.

This cooperation does not always happen smoothly, the main reason being that in every company there are inherent conflicts of interest. These conflicts risk being exaggerated with the increasing international market involvement of the firm. Traditionally the marketing and sales department wants adaptation of products in order to appeal to the diversity of customer preferences, whereas the manufacturing department, supported by finance, wants long production runs in order to achieve simplification and scale economies. The finance department often expresses a "reserved enthusiasm" for the international ventures for other reasons.

– We have seen that terms of payment vary from one market to the other (Chapter 12, Section 12.2). The accounting manager, used to working on the basis of 30–45 days of credit, may not be happy if this is doubled in some markets.
– We have discussed the extra costs of international ventures (Chapter 12, Section 12.2), some of which may come as an unpleasant surprise to the unprepared and uninformed. The following exclamation was overheard in a company that had just started to explore the Russian market: "Is it really necessary to travel this much?" This revealed a total lack of understanding of the demands of initiating new relationships.

Also, the relations between domestic and foreign sales may become strained when the allocation of resources is determined.

> In the quest for new market opportunities, a company had employed an export manager who during her first year in the job had been successful in finding a large British customer. The "only" snag was that this customer was quite demanding and quite big, and requested special solutions including irregular deliveries. All this caused disturbances in the production runs and – as a result – deliveries were delayed, both in the home market and abroad. The export manager was quite frustrated because she did not feel appreciated by the rest of the organisation; the domestic sales manager was infuriated because his traditional customers did not get the service they were used to; the finance manager was worried because margins were down. And of course, the general manager – who at the outset had employed the new export manager as a result of an internal process with the board of directors – was upset because the outcome of the whole exercise was so disappointing, just the opposite of expectations. What went wrong?

In this case, the firm's ongoing domestic operations were apparently doing fine, and management considered exports to be an interesting extension of their domestic business. However, the new export manager was not duly involved in the strategic planning of the firm, coming in as some kind of stranger not yet fully acknowledging the conditions under which the firm was operating, hence pursuing the "wrong" kind of customers.

14.3 Organisation and different strategic positions

Organisation is about structuring the tasks of the firm in a meaningful way. It is about developing a culture that contributes to the achievement of the purpose of the company. It is about adapting to external and internal demands. It is about securing relevant information and establishing channels of communication between groups within the firm. And finally, it is about balancing the power between groups in the firm.

Traditionally, organisational design has been classified by

- Function
- Product
- Customer groups
- Geography
- Matrix.

We shall discuss these forms of organisation throughout this chapter. The leading principles should be simplicity, flexibility, reliability, economy and acceptance (Johnson et al. 1973). The firm's basic structure depends on a wide range of factors: resources and competencies within the firm, type and number of products, the nature and number of markets serviced, the nature of its customers, and competition. Attempting to make the discussion meaningful, we shall – by use of the Strategic Windows model – explore how the parameters of the model (globality of the industry and the firm's preparedness) may lead to different organisational solutions. The model takes account of several of the above-mentioned factors, for instance, industry globality factors in competition and the nature of markets and customers, whereas preparedness looks at internal resources and competencies of the firm. We do not claim that this perspective gives the full answer to the organisational challenges confronting international marketers, but – hopefully – it

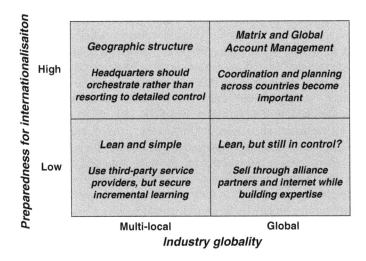

Figure 14.1 Organisational solutions and strategic position in international markets.

will give the manager ideas on how to structure the tasks between the members and groups of the organisation. The terminology used in Figure 14.1 gives some hints as to possible organisational solutions in the different windows.

14.3.1 *Lean and simple*

In this cell, there are few threats from global competitors, and the firm has limited resources and experience. By definition, the firm has limited market insight and usually needs assistance to carry out the export venture. In most cases, firms in this window operate in only a few markets and do not need any complex coordination. Normally, the firm already has an ongoing domestic operation. The main challenge is to find the "right" customers (through a partner) and to service those customers in a satisfactory way, without straining the organisation (see the case above). The logistics and accounting imperatives need to be established, either within the relevant departments inside the firm, or by outsourcing these tasks to third parties. Some firms have specialised in assisting exporters in the practicalities of implementing export operations with a wide range of services. Here is a short description of what Export Corporation Ltd, Michigan, USA, can offer its clients:

> Packaging and logistics company with services that include contract packaging, sub-components assembly, inspection, sorting, warehousing and distribution (with inbound and outbound management, consolidation and deconsolidation, overseas shipping and receiving, unit and bulk distribution, returns and restock management and program design). Packaging capabilities range from custom, export, private label and specialty to environmental, flexible, plastic and stretch wrap; includes ID marking, labelling and shipping. Services also include consulting and package design for products of all types. Industries served include automotive, military, aerospace and consumer. JIT delivery is also available.[1]

Depending on its international ambitions, the firm should consider how to secure feedback from its partner(s) and customers, so as to start building market insight. Particularly firms that outsource most of the practical parts of the venture (local distributor/trading house, logistics, factoring) should beware of the risk of not getting involved in the daily chores of exporting, hence not properly getting into the "Beneficial export circle" (Chapter 3, Section 3.5.2). An important issue in this context is the built-in conflict of interest between the exporter and its foreign partner. The former should preferably create systems to secure market information, build its experience and understanding of local market conditions, and in this way prepare itself for "the next step" in its internationalisation process. On the other hand, its partner – in fear of losing his representation contract – is essentially interested in giving only limited feedback, and in restricting the direct contact between the exporter and the final customers, thereby limiting the exporter's ability to deal directly with its customers. In anticipation of such potential conflicts, the exporter should ideally select a partner that understands these concerns and that therefore encourages such learning processes. Resources should be allocated to make visits to the market – together with the local partner.

In this phase of its internationalisation, the firm may not need to build up an export department or employ a person to be engaged in export activities full-time. Rather, it should consider appointing one or two among its current staff to take on the part-time task of exploring market opportunities abroad, and to ensure that relevant parts of the organisation are involved whenever they are needed. The advantages of this solution are that it is simple and flexible, but not costly. Another advantage is the staff members' knowledge about the firm, its products and its limitations concerning capacity to deliver. On the other hand, this "part-time export manager" risks getting stuck between his/her original function and the new demands of the export venture, and "no one is really happy".

Sometimes, two or more firms enter into some kind of collaboration in the export venture, in order to pool resources, limit the costs and to appear stronger when confronted by powerful foreign customers. This solution may take a number of different organisational forms: anything from a joint office set up locally in the market with one person employed who works on behalf of all the collaborating partners, to a full-fledged incorporated export company, with the participants as the main shareholders. The most conspicuous benefits of export cooperation are as follows (Welch and Joynt 1987):

- The total export costs per firm is lower.
- The total offer from the group is more powerful.
- The internal competition will be reduced.

However, there are also disadvantages of this kind of cooperation:

- The individual firm loses direct control and communication with the market.
- Conflicts may easily emerge, since each member of the group often has different objectives and strategies.
- Difficulties may arise since the products offered by the different members of the group will most likely be accepted in the market in differing degrees, which makes finding an equitable distribution of the costs of operation problematic.

Export cooperation – or export grouping schemes as they are sometimes called – is a demanding exercise for several reasons. Particularly for newcomers to international markets, the challenges of internationalisation are compounded with those of cooperation. The lack of experience generally leads to unrealistic expectations and therefore also provides fertile soil for misunderstandings. Often export groups are created on the instigation of, and/or with the assistance and part-funding of, export promotion agencies in an attempt to establish stronger clusters of related firms. The process concentrates on finding appropriate firms, coaxing them to join the group, and establishing the group before undertaking concrete international marketing research (finding specific market opportunities). The success rate of such schemes varies greatly, but depends on a number of factors, such as previous relationships between the participating firms (Welch et al. 1996), the commitment by each firm to the group and its commitment to exporting (Welch 1991), and the degree of competition between the firms. Concerning the last, Finnish government-supported export groups (called export circles) emphasise complementarity as a selection criterion for group membership (Luostarinen et al. 1994).

Perhaps the best results are achieved with projects that are narrowly defined, be it a joint participation at a trade fair or a marketing campaign in a specific country.

Austrade's[2] campaign, together with ten Australian exporters of oaten hay to Japan, is a case in point. Each exporter had established their own distribution system in the country – through a trading firm, a cooperative or directly to large farming operations. After years of operating as individual firms, the exporters had experienced stagnating sales and increased competition, not only from their main American competitors, but also between themselves. Quoting Welch et al. (1996): "At Austrade's instigation, a Joint Action Group of oaten hay processors was formed in October 1992 with the general purpose of developing a more coordinated and market-responsive approach to the Japanese market, particularly addressing the issues of quality and reliability of supply. Ten major processors – representing about 75% of Australian oaten hay exports to Japan – contributed financially to enable the JAG to operate through a company, Australian Hay Pty. Ltd. The JAG is somewhat unusual in that it comprises of direct competitors, who also jointly own a registered trademark: Australia Oat Hay, with a distinctive logo. The trademark arose out of initial activities aimed at addressing the quality issue. The JAG sought to develop an industry standard which would form a base-line that members would need to meet. In order to use the Australia Oat Hay brand on produce exported to Japan, processors now have to undergo quality assurance certification." Among the results noted were a more coordinated approach to the market, better market understanding, and mutual learning among the participating firms.

14.3.2 Geographic structure

As in the previous cell, the multi-local nature of the business environment suggests that market conditions vary greatly from one market to the other, implying that the firm should adopt country specific strategies in each market. Another implication is that coordinated marketing across countries is not warranted. On the other hand, the firm's resources and the market insight allow management to initiate major marketing campaigns inside individual countries, independent of the situation in other countries. In this cell, the firm normally needs to organise the international marketing effort in a separate department.

Its location in the hierarchy and its structure will vary depending on the size of the firm, type and number of products, and number of markets serviced. In its simplest form, an export

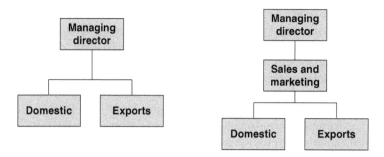

Figure 14.2 Separate export department.

Figure 14.3 Geographic structure.

department is subordinate to the managing director or the marketing department, as shown in Figure 14.2

The advantage of this structure is the attention each department gives specific markets, and the idiosyncratic market insight, know-how and network relations that develop over time. It will function well as long as the number of markets remains limited and exports do not surpass a threshold amount. With the increasing international involvement of the firm, the export manager will normally be replaced by area or country managers, some of whom may be located in the market (as was the case of Jordan, see page 353–354). Depending on the structure further down the distribution chain (for instance, sales through wholesalers or direct to customers), country managers will often develop into local sales subsidiaries, sometimes as a result of acquisition of the partner. Critical issues in the transition process have been described in Chapter 8, Section 8.6.

The structure of the marketing department may in this case be presented as in Figure 14.3. Note that other markets are "lumped into" one department, headed by a general export manager. These are secondary markets not warranting the focus or resources allocated to primary markets.

In large multinational enterprises, this structure is normally much more complex, with regional vice-presidents (such as Asia-Pacific, Europe, Middle East, Africa, Americas), or product groups or divisions, local sales subsidiaries and administrative staff functions. The structure and ensuing issues are however principally the same: different strategic foci, coordination, monitoring and control, lines of communication, and power balance.

Concerning power balance, it has been noted that the foreign subsidiary over time is appropriating more power at the expense of headquarters (Ghauri 1990, Prahalad and Doz 1981). This development has been described in three phases:

1   A newly established subsidiary is generally dependent on resources and expertise from the centre.
2   As the foreign subsidiary is maturing, it tends to develop its own local power bases. Local managers acquire market insight, and develop networks to local authorities and customers. In addition, the aspirations of local managers may exacerbate potential conflicts between the centre and the periphery.
3   As a final stage on this development ladder, the foreign subsidiary develops its own expansion strategies, more or less independent of the strategic intentions of the centre. This is what Forsgren (1990) has labelled "internationalisation of third degree", citing cases of expansion by Swedish multinationals into neighbouring countries out of hubs in Asia.

We have already seen how centre and periphery have different perspectives on the need for coordination, monitoring and control (Chapter 8, Section 8.6). We have seen how too much control can impair the relations between headquarters and subsidiary, and how the desire to seek standardised solutions to local markets may be counterproductive.

The extent to which area managers at HQ should actively participate in the detailed planning of local market campaigns depends on resources and competencies at the centre and the distribution of roles between the centre and the local sales subsidiary or the partner. Generally, we would advocate an "arms-length planning and control involvement", implying prototype advertising, giving general directions for use of logo, advertising themes and positioning (see Chapter 11, Section 11.6). The international marketing department should orchestrate a process with the periphery with the aim of identifying the least common denominators, possibly not for every individual market, but for regions (for instance, Nordic, British, German, Latin America, North America).

14.3.3 Lean but still in control?

Firms in this cell are vulnerable to globalisation drivers. They are small, often innovative and ambitious, but also resource-poor firms that need to reach out in order to position themselves in key markets. However, with a limited resource base and little experience in international markets, their position is constantly threatened by larger players in world markets – be it customers, distribution channels or competitors. Given the industry environment, marketing in this situation is often more a question of finding the right alliance partner(s) than developing a detailed marketing plan (for which they do not have the necessary market insight). There is a risk, however, that the partner will overrun the firm by its mere size and resources.

A newly established Norwegian firm specialising in high-end PA amplifiers had entered into an exclusive distribution contract with a large British dealer that covered most of the Western world. The British were to take care of the world market except for Scandinavia, whereas the Norwegian firm would service the Scandinavian market through a part-owned trading company. The problem was that the contract negotiations dawdled because some product details were not in place. At the time of the signature – a year later – the British firm had to file for bankruptcy and the Norwegian firm had not only lost a potential partner, but also time in the market place. Parallel to this development, the firm had worked to find dealers in the Nordic market, but, as we have seen TTT, and indeed IIMTTELT (see page 338 for an explanation).

This is perhaps an extreme case of bad luck. Or was it poor craftsmanship? They should have analysed the financial situation of the contract partner; they could also have sought more than just one major partner. One problem in this particular firm was the organisation of the marketing through the part-owned trading company. The firm wanted to concentrate on the things they thought were the most important (research and development and production), but did not have any direct control with the marketing and sales.

Many firms in this position do not have a marketing department as such. Rather they have tight relationships with their partners – a task that is possibly best handled by the top manager (or the founder – often the same person). The partners may be of "all kinds": dealers, licensing or franchising partners – depending on the nature of the product/service and on the resources of the firm.

ASK of Norway is a case in point.[3] They started their internationalisation through direct sales to dealers in Europe and Asia. In this endeavour, they employed citizens from their most important markets. The marketing channel was direct, non-exclusive contracts with local dealers.

14.3.4 Matrix organisation and global account management (GAM)

In this cell, the firm is one of just a few dominant players in world markets within its field of operation. By definition, it has a leadership role, but at the same time it is vulnerable to attacks from competitors at a global scale. It therefore needs to build an organisation that caters to its strategic thrust: "Strengthen your global position" (see Chapter 4, Section 4.3). The industry globality suggests that there are potential gains in both coordinating and standardising the marketing effort. For this to happen, some level of central control is necessary, and – as discussed in Chapter 8, Section 8.6 – the firm will do well by instilling a clan culture throughout the organisation in order to create a common sense of purpose. Implementation of global, standardised strategies across markets then becomes less strenuous and challenging. Yet, seeking uniform solutions to global marketing is not without problems. During the 1980s – when this approach was *en vogue* – several multinationals had to retreat, and leave more influence to their local subsidiaries. Kotabe and Helsen (2014) cite how Kraft General Foods Europe was forced to abandon their centralised marketing planning system in the face of opposition from local managers. We would add that Kraft was possibly not located in the upper-right corner of the matrix, and thus misinterpreted the "imperative" to standardise and centralise.

Another case is Parker Pen's failed standardisation strategy. They wanted to reduce the number of pen models from 500 to 100 in order to rationalise production. At the same time, they engaged Ogilvy and Mather, an advertising agency with an excellent reputation, to carry out a global marketing campaign in all markets. Parker's top management was well aware of the risks, and addressed them through internal processes in order to obtain acceptance of the new strategy. Still, the marketing campaign was a failure: the "Not invented here" syndrome appeared yet again. Top management was dismissed as a result (Lipman 1988).

The correct organisational "answer" to these challenges is not straightforward. Stopford and Wells (1972) suggested that, as international sales increase, firms tend to structure their organisation by geographic area, as discussed above. As the foreign product diversity of the firm builds up, either by organic growth, or (as in many cases) by acquisitions, a product-oriented organisation will emerge. When firms expand both internationally and by product, they typically develop a matrix organisation.

ABB's organisational development epitomises this point. The company was the result of a number of mergers and acquisitions throughout the 1980s and 90s in the wake of a shake up and restructuring of the electromechanical and engineering industry, and became one of the world leaders within its field of operation. It had until the 1990s been organised geographically. As a response to the increasing globalisation, and the need to control the profitability of product lines that had multiplied as a result of the mergers, they felt the need to introduce a new line of command: that of the chain of production. The product managers directly responding to ABB headquarters in Switzerland got a mandate to oversee the whole value chain in the product line, and not the individual daughter company, providing financial insight into the profitability of subunits in individual subsidiaries organised by country. This model instilled a financial responsibility and understanding throughout the whole organisation. It also allowed for flexibility in the sense that country managers prevailed when local adaptation was warranted, whereas product managers had the last word when coordination was required. The ultimate objective was to strengthen global product management (Christensen 2014). Bartlett and Ghoshal (1989) call this matrix organisation the transnational firm (with a combined emphasis on central coordination *and* local adaptation).[4]

There is, however, more to the organisation than mere structure; as we have pointed out earlier, the organisational culture plays an equally important role. We believe that *processes* within the firm and with its foreign marketing partners will play a critical part in this endeavour. For instance, the planning cycle described in Chapter 13 epitomises one such process. However, national cultural differences come into play when implementing such processes.

When Swix (winter sports gear) implemented their market planning system – with requests to "follow the timetable" and deliver market reports with concrete information about customers, competitors, trends and so forth – they found that their local subsidiaries and partners in countries such as the US, Germany and Japan willingly procured this information – in time. In Scandinavia, this procedure was met with scepticism. Possibly, this is a manifestation of Hofstede's (1980) power distance dimension (where Scandinavia rates lower than the three countries mentioned), which suggests that orders are more willingly accepted in countries scoring high on this dimension.[5]

Many industries are characterised by large multinational customers – be they retail chains or industrial buyers (manufacturers of cars, electronics, machinery, raw materials, etc.) with units across several countries. Many of these firms see potential gains in securing product supplies for their units in different countries from the same supplier, and will therefore try to standardise product specifications and service levels, and (lower) price levels in concerted negotiations, rather than letting each unit purchase them individually. In order to achieve such benefits, the buying firm needs to coordinate its purchasing function across units. As a response to this development, the selling firm needs to coordinate its international marketing effort in what has been termed Global Account Management (GAM). Such coordination is not without impediments: a survey among 165 large multinationals indicates that only one third of the companies were happy with their GAM programme, and "even for them the success came hard" (Yip and Bink 2007). On the other hand, the study showed that there is a lot to gain on introduction of GAM: 20% higher customer satisfaction and 15% increase in revenues and profits. Although these are evident gains from GAM, most literature on GAM suggests that its main benefits lie in enhanced relationships between the seller and the buyer.

Even if the strategic imperative suggests that GAM should be introduced, it constitutes an organisational overlay over national sales and marketing organisations and therefore invariably implies higher costs. In addition, firms find that they generally achieve lower prices with GAM, but this loss is hopefully compensated by higher sales and lower costs, or simply by retention of an important customer (Arnold et al. 2001). A number of conditions need therefore to be in place before considering GAM: the buyer is coordinating purchasing across countries, the

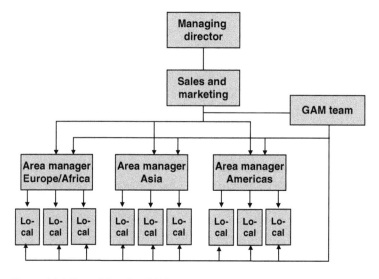

Figure 14.4 Organising the GAM.

buyer constitutes an important part of sales, or multinational customers in general make up a significant part of the business (Yip and Bink 2007).

Figure 14.4 suggests a GAM organisation. The main feature of GAM is that there are many communication lines between the different subsidiaries and departments and the GAM team, and there are potentially many areas of conflict between the different departments. Who has the final say concerning product adaptation or pricing – the national marketing manager or the GAM manager? There are no clear-cut answers to this question. Also, the GAM team may be dispersed in different countries. For example, if the GAM customer's head office is in country A and another one in country B, it is natural to place the corresponding GAM manager in those countries, rather than at headquarters, making a uniform approach to GAM a bit harder.

14.4 Chapter summary

This chapter has described the tasks of the international marketing organisation, and discussed potential areas of conflict between related departments of the firm. These conflicts emerge in the wake of different demands from customers in different countries and in the intersection of different demands within the firm: the more internationally involved the firm, the higher the demands for variety between markets and the more conspicuous the conflicts between the centre and the periphery. It is suggested that such conflicts are alleviated through implementation of a clan culture within the firm, with a common purpose and common sets of beliefs. It should be noted, however, that too much agreement within the organisation potentially represents a risk of being entrapped in a strategic impasse, where the beliefs become a "religion" that makes the firm immune to alternative thinking and solutions. This was the case of Kodak, which did not want to see the surge of digital photography and this eventually lead to its demise.[6]

The concrete structure of the organisation helps management distribute tasks among the different members and departments of the firm. This structure will partly depend upon the position of the firm in the Strategic Windows framework, varying from a lean export department with part-time export co-workers, to a complex matrix organisation with GAM. The suggested structures in each cell of the model are just that: suggested organisational solutions adapted to the strategic context of the firm. Other structures may serve the purpose.

Notes

1 http://www.exportcorporation.com
2 Australia's semi-public export promotion agency.
3 See also Chapter 4, Section 4.4.2.
4 The other organisational solutions suggested by Bartlett and Ghosal are "The global company" – focusing on global integration and coordination of activities; "The multinational organization" – focusing on local adaptation as a response to differentiated demand patterns in international markets; and "The international company" – where the majority of the value chain is maintained at HQ.
5 Interview with information manager at the holding company, Ferd.
6 See for instance: http://www.forbes.com/sites/chunkamui/2012/01/18/how-kodak-failed/3/#5eacb8df7603

15   Epilogue – concluding remarks

Globalisation has put an imprint on both business and academia over the past three to four decades; it has indeed influenced the content of this book. I think that globalisation, defined as a process towards an increasingly intertwined international market and competition dominated by few large players, poses tremendous challenges to *firms of all kinds* – large and small, high-tech and low-tech, B2B and B2C. Sometimes, the globalisation drivers are easy to detect: trade deals, entrance of large multinational players in the domestic market, instant access to information through the internet, application of (new) technologies creating new opportunities (examples of which are Spotify, Uber, Amazon and Kahoot!), though their implications are not obvious. At other times the trends are more subtle, and their consequences difficult to fathom: change in consumer patterns and buyer behaviour, restructuring of industries – partly as a consequence of the above drivers. Indeed, the trend may also go in the opposite direction – towards de-globalisation, as may be the result of international conflicts or more nationalistic currents in leading countries – be they Brexit, Trumpism or any other flavour of national centrism.

Some firms are greatly influenced by this process, whereas others are affected only to a limited extent. The strategic response is unique for each firm, and requires an understanding of the globalisation drivers that matter. The main thrust of this book has been to give the reader a set of tools to analyse a firm's strategic position, and as a consequence devise appropriate marketing strategies. The marketing toolbox is full of instruments, the mix and use of which vary greatly according to the strategic situation of the firm. This is where the Nine Strategic Windows model (and its four-window version) comes into the picture – as a method of identifying challenges and opportunities, and to attune the use of marketing tools accordingly. Models and management tools do not solve "all" problems of the manager. But they can give direction and ideas in the firm's strategic deliberations.

15.1 Science, art and attitudes

Marketing is being treated in academia as a science, and indeed scientific inquiry over more than fifty years has greatly helped us understand critical relationships between different marketing strategies and activities, and their outcomes both for firms (performance) and for customers (satisfaction). The scientific approach helps you analyse the market, its segments, customers, competitor behaviour, and the effects of marketing activities. Nevertheless, marketing is also an art, both in the creation of an advertisement, in the design of the product or the fine-tuning of the instruments used to find the "right" price. The art is manifest through a creative process that interprets and "translates" the (scientific) analysis into concrete marketing activities. It is, however, difficult to scientifically measure the beauty of an artwork; this beauty lies in the eyes of the beholder. This book has not delved into this part of marketing.

Marketing in the sense of planning, implementation and control involves collaboration between a host of players. Marketing is therefore also about relationships between partners; relationships based on trust. In international marketing the most important partner is the local representative in the market, be it a distributor, dealer, agent, licensee/franchisee, joint venture partner or the wholly-owned foreign subsidiary. Different cultures, different marketing contexts and different ideas on how to reach out to the final customer – in short, different perspectives – flavour these relationships. The international marketer needs to comprehend these matters and meet them with an open mind.

We live in a world driven by uncertainty, but also one that is full of opportunities. Thriving in this environment requires not only vigilance and a fundamental understanding of the challenges, but also the right set of attitudes. I would therefore claim that marketing is not only a science and an art, but it is also about attitudes. This is possibly best expressed through market orientation as a culture, consisting of a set of values and norms that in turn – through rituals, arrangements, language and stories – affect behaviours and eventually the development of marketing strategies (Homburg and Pflesser 2000). Market orientation was one of the "pet research topics" from 1990 and well into the 2000s. Even if research on market orientation has somewhat faded and ceded ground to other issues, its importance has not, and I would claim that it has not yet been fully explored. In an international marketing setting it becomes particularly critical in that the organisation needs to relate to a great number of different marketing contexts and try to bring together these contexts into a common denominator eventually defining what the company should be.

15.2 Five success factors

Performance in international markets has been the object of a great number of studies over the years. We have discussed this in Chapter 3, and we end the book with a brief presentation of findings from a research project in Norway (Solberg et al. 2015a,b). We developed a model of strategy development, attempting to capture critical elements of successful exporting.[1] To that end, we studied the export behaviour of 133 randomly sampled firms. We also explored in somewhat more detail issues of strategy development in six case companies. Our analysis highlights five essential drivers of export success (measured as market share in primary markets and financial performance): networks, market insight, positioning and cost leadership. It also identifies important factors that determine the path of these drivers. The fifth factor was brought to light through our case analyses: the importance of the owners' role. Each of these are briefly discussed below.

15.2.1 Networks

The importance of networks, and more specifically relationships with marketing partners, is underlined in both our survey and in our six case studies. Most conspicuously we notice the role of building an *esprit de corps* or a "clan culture", where the firm's subsidiaries and partners abroad share the values and norms of HQ and also take part in further developing them. This is particularly critical when building brand value across borders, as experienced by two of our cases, Swims (see Chapter 11, Section 11.3) and Helly Hansen (see Chapter 11, Section 11.5).

We conclude that network development is time-consuming and needs attention by management, but yields rewards. Typically we see that market information in some form is predominant and critical for networks to develop along with market visits, active information capture, market surveillance and participation in organised clusters.

15.2.2 Market insight

Market insight is the second driver identified in our survey, emphasising the importance of market orientation. Interestingly market insight is not directly coupled with information capture as such; rather it depends on the extent to which the firm analyses its markets through active market surveillance and, indirectly, through networks that purportedly have already interpreted and passed on pertinent market information. This is something we have found in other projects as well: market information gained through network partners seems to outdo (in terms of effect on performance) information gained through market research (Gripsrud et al. 2006). The reason – we believe – is that this information is more relevant, non-redundant and more directly related to the decisions to be taken. And it emphasises yet again the role of networks.

15.2.3 Positioning

Thirdly, positioning in specific market segments seems to be a key driver for achieving market shares in export markets. Positioning entails the ability of the exporter to be recognised as offering specific advantages to its customers abroad. This is not straightforward given the amount of information needed to understand local idiosyncrasies – both concerning the specific needs of customers, the position of competitors and local regulations. Therefore, market insight and also information capture emerge as key factors driving effective positioning strategies. We notice that Porter's differentiation strategy – in other words: the ability to "stand out from the crowd" – is also linked to positioning. For some reason the much-revered niche strategy concept does not crop up as a factor in this context. In our survey, we find that Norwegian exporters seem to cherish differentiation strategies (unique products, high value, different from competitors) much more than niche strategies (addressing special needs, small customer groups, barriers to entry in the niche).

Positioning also comes up as one of the critical issues in our case studies, from the perspective of branding. The case of Helly Hansen reveals how complex this topic is. They have struggled for decades to develop a brand that is internationally recognised with the values they want to communicate. This is not only a question of advertising strategies, but indeed a far more overarching issue of the "soul" of the company, and how this soul is being interpreted by all the parts of the company and its partners, and in particular its marketing branches.

15.2.4 Cost leadership

Cost leadership strategies are unsurprisingly a fundamental driver of Norwegian exporters' successful international expansion. Yet, in spite of Norway's high cost level, we find that one third of our sample indicate that they have cost levels in line with, and sometimes better than, their main competitors. A closer analysis reveals that these are predominantly in the non-financial service sector (for instance, engineering companies). Some of this may stem from the fact that wage levels do not represent an important part of their total costs – or that there is a relatively low wage level in high competency trades in Norway. Some of these firms may have developed business models that make them less vulnerable to Norway's high cost levels. Nevertheless, two thirds of our survey companies report problems in keeping pace with foreign competitors' cost levels.

Just a few factors seem to have an impact here. Product standardisation is the most evident one, and it is fair to say that the two (standardisation and cost leadership) mutually enhance each other. We also find that network relations are strongly linked to cost leadership, possibly because outsourcing and subcontracting with specialised firms in world markets are key elements of a winning strategy.

15.2.5 The role of ownership

Our case studies highlighted three areas of importance: the role of brand value, of relationships and of ownership. The two former having been discussed above, we will briefly deal with the role of owners and boards of directors in the development of firms in international markets. This element of market strategy is often underestimated in the literature, yet it is – we would maintain – of primary importance for any company, a fact that is underscored by our case studies. In more general terms, the literature suggests that owner structure and board membership structures matter: fewer, larger and more direct owners are linked to better performance. This pattern is supported in our study.

15.3 Conclusion

There is of course no final conclusion to this book. For that, the issues are too complex and the situations and solutions are too varied. However, international marketing is a field that will be increasingly relevant to a great number of firms from virtually all countries. Understanding the challenges and fathoming the opportunities in the global market place is therefore critical, both for firms and for governments. There is no recipe for managers to find the road to success. We have found some elements that are critical, where market orientation, market insight and networks are possibly the three most important factors that determine the fate of most international marketing ventures. It is about a mind-set, knowledge and connecting to the right people – and treating them well. Then, above all, it is about the will to carry it out – which in our terminology is called commitment.

Note

1 These are discussed in more detail in a report to Innovation Norway: Carl Arthur Solberg, Geir Gripsrud, and Auke Hunneman. 2014. *Mapping and Analysing Norway's Export Patterns and Strategies of Norwegian Exporters.* BI Norwegian School of Management, Oslo, Norway.

Bibliography

Aaby, N.E. and S.F. Slater. 1989. "Management influences on export performance: a review of the empirical literature 1978–1988." *International Marketing Review*, 6(4).

Aaker, Jennifer L. 1997. "Dimensions of brand personality." *Journal of Marketing Research*, 34(3): 347–356.

Adams, Christopher P. and Van V. Brantner. 2016. "Estimating the cost of new drug development: is it really $802 million?" *Health Affairs*, 25(2): 420–428.

Aharoni, Y. 1966. *The Foreign Investment Decision Process*, Boston, Division of Research, Graduate School of Business Administration, Harvard University.

Aldehayyat, Jehad and Naseem Twaissi. 2011. "Strategic planning and corporate performance relationship in small business firms: evidence from a Middle East country context." *International Journal of Business and Management*, 6(8): 255–263.

Anderson, E. and H. Gatignon. 1986. "Modes of foreign entry: a transaction cost analysis and propositions." *Journal of International Business Studies*, 17(3): 1–26.

Andersen, Otto. 1993. "On the internationalization of firms: a critical analysis." *Journal of International Business Studies*, 24(2): 209–231.

Anonymous. 2006. "Logitech: from a born global to a mature global." Term paper in Masters Programme in International Marketing, Autumn 2006, BI Norwegian Business School.

Ansoff, I. 1957. "Strategies for diversification." *Harvard Business Review*, September–October 1957.

Armstrong, J. Scott. 1989. "Combining forecasts: the end of the beginning or the beginning of the end?" *International Journal of Forecasting*, 5(4): 585–588.

Armstrong, J. Scott (ed.) 2001. *Principles of Forecasting: A Handbook for Researchers and Practitioners*, Norwell, MA, Kluwer Academic Publishers.

Arnold, David, Julian Birkinshaw, and Omar Toulan. 2001. "Can selling be globalized? The pitfalls of global account management." *California Management Review*, 44(1): 8–20.

Askegaard, Søren and Tage Koed Madsen. 1998. "The local and the global: exploring the traits of homogeneity and heterogeneity of European food culture." *International Business Review*, 7(6): 549–568

Aspelund, A., Madsen, T.K. and Moen, Ø. 2007. "A review of the foundation, international marketing strategies, and performance of international new ventures." *European Journal of Marketing*, 41(11–12): 1423–1448.

Aulakh, Preet, Masaaki Kotabe, and Arvind Sahay. 1996. "Trust and performance in cross-border marketing partnerships: a behavioural approach." *Journal of International Business Studies*, 27(5): 1005–1032.

Aulakh, Preet S. and Esra Gençtürk. 2008. "Contract formalization and governance of exporter–importer relationships." *Journal of Management Studies*, 45(3): 457–479.

Axelsson, B. and Jan Erik Johanson. 1992. "Social ties and foreign market entry," in Axelsson B. and Easton G. (eds), *Industrial Networks: A New View of the Reality*, London, Routledge.

Bakka, B. 1973. "Internasjonaliseringsprosessen i norsk industri." Paper Presented at the Yearly Business Seminar at the Norwegian School of Economics and Business Administration, Bergen.

Barney, J. 1991. "Firm resources and sustained competitive advantage." *Journal of Management*, 17(1): 99–120.

Barney, J. 2002. *Gaining and Sustaining Competitive Advantage: Concepts and Cases*, Upper Saddle River, NJ, Pearson Education.

Barney, Jay B. and Mark H. Hansen. 1994. "Trustworthiness as a source of competitive advantage." *Strategic Management Journal*, 15(4): 175–190.

Bartlett, C.A. 1986. "Building and managing the transnational: the new organization challenge," in Porter M.E. (ed.), *Competition in Global Industries*, Boston, Harvard Business Press.

Bartlett, C.A. and S. Ghoshal. 1989. *Managing Across Borders: The Transnational Solution*, Boston, Harvard Business Press.

Bello, D.C. and D. Gilliland. 1997. "The effect of output controls, process controls, and flexibility on export channel performance." *Journal of Marketing*, 61(1): 22–38.

Bello, D.C. and R. Lohtia. 1995. "Export channel design: the use of foreign distributors and agents." *Journal of the Academy of Marketing Science*, 23(2): 83–93.

Bello, D.C., C. Chelariu, and L. Li. 2003. "The antecedents and performance consequences of relationalism in export distribution channels." *Journal of Business Research*, 56(1): 1–16.

Benito, G. and G. Gripsrud. 1992. "The expansion of foreign direct investments: discrete rational location choice or a cultural learning process?" *Journal of International Business Studies*, 23(3): 461–476.

Benito, G.R.G., H. Biong, I.D. Berg, and P.J. Thorenfeldt. 1991. *Norske bedrifters erfaringer fra handel med Øst-Europa*, Sandvika, NIM.

Benito, G.R.G., C.A. Solberg, and L.S. Welch. 1993. "Exploration of information behaviour of Norwegian exporters." *International Journal of Information Management*, 13(4): 274–286.

Benito, G.R.G., T. Pedersen, and B. Petersen. 1999. "Foreign operation methods and switching costs: conceptual issues and possible effects." *Scandinavian Journal of Management*, 15: 213–229.

Bergen, M., S. Dutta, and O.C. Walker Jr. 1992. "Agency relationships in marketing: a review of the implications and applications of agency and related theories." *Journal of Marketing*, 56(3): 1.

Berger, D. 1986. "Theory into practice: the FCB grid." *European Research*, 14(1): 35–46.

Bilkey, W.J. and E. Nes. 1982. "Country of origin effects on product evaluation." *Journal of International Business Studies*, 8(1): 88–99.

Bilkey, W.J. and G. Tesar. 1977. "The export behavior of smaller-sized Wisconsin based manufacturing firms." *Journal of International Business Studies*, 8(1): 93–98.

Birkinshaw, Julian. 1996. "How multinational subsidiary mandates are gained and lost." *Journal of International Business Studies*, 27(3): 467–495.

Birkinshaw, J. and N. Hood (eds). 1998. *Multinational Corporate Evolution and Subsidiary Development*, London, Macmillan.

Blas, Javier. 2015. "The rise of the national trading house." *Bloomberg Businessweek*, 6 August, pp. 48–49.

Bleeke, J.A. and L.L. Bryan. 1988. "Globalization of financial markets." *McKinsey Quarterly*, Winter: 17–38.

Blomstermo, Anders and D. Deo Sharma. 2003. "Three decades of research on the internationalisation process of firms," in Blomstermo A. and Deo Sharma D. (eds), *Learning in the Internationalisation Process of Firms*, Cheltenham, Edward Elgar, 16–35.

Boddewyn, J.J., R. Soehl, and J. Picard. 1986a. "Standardization in international marketing: is Ted Levitt in fact right?" *Business Horizon*, 29(6): 69–75.

Boddewyn, J.J., M.B. Halbrich, and A.C. Perry. 1986b. "Service multinationals: conceptualization, measurement and theory." *Journal of International Business Studies*, 16: 41–57.

Borsheim, J.H. and C.A. Solberg. 2002. "The internationalization of born global internet firms." Cahiers de Recherche, Bordeaux École de Management, Talence, France.

Brøgger, Jan. 1993. *Kulturforståelse*, Oslo, Cappelen Damm.

Brouthers, L.E. and G. Nakos. 2005. "The role of systematic international market selection on small firms' export performance." *Journal of Small Business Management*, 43(4): 363–381.

Buckley, P.J. and M.C. Casson. 1976. *The Future of Multinational Enterprise*, London, Macmillan.

Buckley, P.J. and M.C. Casson. 1985. *The Economic Theory of the Multinational Enterprise: Selected Papers*, London, Macmillan.

Buckley, P.J. and M.C. Casson. 1998. "Models of the multinational enterprise." *Journal of International Business Studies*, 29(1): 21–44.

Burmo, Alexander and Maja Heedman. Masters thesis, BI Norwegian Business School, Oslo 2014.

Burt, Ronald S. 1992. "The network structure of management roles in a large matrix firm." *Evaluation and Program Planning*, 15: 303–326.

Buzzell, R.D. and Bradley T. Gale. 1987. *The PIMS Principles: Linking Strategy to Performance*, New York, The Free Press.

Buzzell, R.D. and J.A. Quelch. 1988. *Multinational Marketing Management: Cases and Readings*, Reading, MA, Addison-Wesley Publishing Company.

Cadogan, J.W., Kuivalainen O. and Sundqvist S. 2009. "Export market-oriented behavior and export performance: quadratic and moderating effects under differing degrees of market dynamism and internationalization." *Journal of International Marketing*, 17(4): 71–89.

Calof, J.L. 1993. "The mode choice and change decision process and its impact on international performance." *International Business Review*, 2(1): 97–120.

Calof, J.L. and P.W. Beamish. 1995. "Adapting to foreign markets; explaining internationalization." *International Business Review*, 4(2): 115–131.

Campbell, D. and L. Lafili (eds). 1990. *Distributorship, Agency and Franchising in an International Arena: Europe, the United States, Japan and Latin America*, Deventer, Kluwer Law and Taxation Publishers.

Cantwell, J. and R. Harding. 1997. "The internationalization of German companies' R&D." Discussion Paper in *International Investment and Management, No. 233*. University of Reading.

Casson, M.C. 1985. "The theory of foreign direct investment," in Buckley P.J. and Casson M.C. (eds), *The Economic Theory of the Multinational Enterprise*, London, Macmillan.

Casson, M.C. 1987. *The Firm and the Market: Studies on Multinational Enterprise and the Scope of the Firm*, Oxford, Blackwell.

Casson, M.C. and M. Chukujama. 1991. "Countertrade; theory and evidence," in Buckley P. and Clegg J. (eds), *Multinational Enterprise in Less Developed Countries*, London, Macmillan.

Caves, R.E. 1982. *Multinational Enterprise and Economic Analysis*, Cambridge, Cambridge University Press (reprint 1990).

Caves, Richard E. and Michael E. Porter. 1977. "From entry barriers to mobility barriers: conjectural decisions and contrived deterrence to new competition." *The Quarterly Journal of Economics*, 91(2): 241–261.

Cavusgil, S.T. 1980. "On the internationalization process of firms." *European Research*, 273–281.

Cavusgil, S.T. 1983. "Success factors, in export marketing." *Journal of International Marketing and Marketing Research*, 8(2).

Cavusgil, S.T. 1984. "Differences among exporting firms based on their degree of internationalization." *Journal of Business Research*, 12(2): 195–208.

Cavusgil, S.T. and S. Zou. 1994. "Marketing strategy–performance relationship: an investigation of the empirical link in export market ventures." *Journal of Marketing*, 58(1): 1–21.

Cavusgil, S.T., Gary Knight and John Riesenberger. 2017. *International Business – The New Realities*, 4th ed., Pearson.

Chandy, Rajesh K. and Gerard J. Tellis. 2000. "The incumbent's curse? Incumbency, size, and radical product innovation." *The Journal of Marketing*, 64(3): 1–17.

Chaney, Thomas. 2013. "The gravity equation in international trade: an explanation." *Working Paper 19285*, Cambridge, National Bureau of Economic Research.

Chase-Dunn, Christopher, Yukio Kawano, and Benjamin D. Brewers. 2000. "Trade globalization since 1795: waves of integration in the world-system. *American Sociological Review*, 65(1): 77–95.

Christensen, Sverre. 2014. "Globaliseringens fortellinger; ABB Norges konsernansvar for olje- og gassvirksomheten," in Ekberg, Lönnborg and Myrvang, *Næringslliv og historie*, Oslo Norway, Pax Forlag, pp. 61–92.

Chwastyk, Piotr and Mariusz Kołosowski. 2014. "Estimating the cost of the new product in development process." *Procedia Engineering*, 69: 351–360.

Colley, R.H. 1961. *Defining Advertising Goals for Measured Advertising Results*, New York, Association of National Advertisers.

Coleman, J.S. 1988. "Organizations and institutions: sociological and economic approaches to the analysis of social structure." *The American Journal of Sociology*, 94: S95–S120.

Conway, Ed. 2017. "Great trading nation? That's just a delusion." *The Times*, 7 April, p. 26.

Cooper, P. and A. Branthwaite. 1977. "Qualitative technology: new perspectives on measurement and meaning through qualitative research." *MRS Conference Proceedings*, Brighton.

Cornell, B. 1977. "Spot rates, forward rates, and exchange market efficiency." *Journal of Financial Economics*, 5(1): 55–65.

Coviello, N. and Munro H. 1997. "Network relationships and the internationalisation process of small software firms." *International Business Review – August*, 6(4): 361–387.

Craig, Samuel and Susan Douglas. 2009. *International Marketing Research*, 3rd ed., Chichester, Wiley and Sons.

Cravens, David W. and Nigel F. Piercy. 2009. *Strategic Marketing*, 9th ed., Boston, McGraw-Hill.

Crossman, S. and C. Jarret. 1984. *The Change from National to International Research–A Turbulent Journey into a Challenging European Business and Economics Environment–A Case Study*, Amsterdam, ESOMAR.

Cullen, Brenda and Alan Whelan. 1997. "Concentration of the retail sector and trapped brands." *Long Range Planning*, 30(6): 906–916.

Cunningham, M.T. and R.I. Spigel. 1971. "A study in successful exporting." *British Journal of Marketing*, 5(1): 1–12.

Cunningham, R. and Y.K. Sarayrah. 1993. *Wasta: The Hidden Force in Middle Eastern Society.* New York, Praeger.

Czinkota, M. and W.J. Johnston. 1983. "Exporting: does sales volume make a difference?" *Journal of International Business Studies*, 14(1): 147–153.

Dahl, Ø. and K. Habert. 1986. *Møte Mellom Kulturer*, Oslo, Universitetsforlaget.

Dalgic, Tevfik and Maarten Leeuw. 1994. "Niche marketing revisited: concept, applications and some European cases." *European Journal of Marketing*, 28(4): 39–55.

D'Angelo, Alfredo, Antonio Majocchi, Antonella Zucchella, and Trevor Buck. 2013. "Geographical pathways for SME internationalization: insights from an Italian sample." *International Marketing Review*, 30(2): 80–105.

Davies, N. 1996. *A History of Europe*, London, BCA/Oxford University Press.

de Bortoli, Mario and Jesús Maroto. 2001. "Translating colours in web site localisation." *Proceedings of the European Languages and the Implementation of Communication and Information Technologies (Elicit) Conference*, Paisley, University of Paisley.

Deligonul, Seyda and S. Tamer Cavusgil. 2006. "Legal versus relational ordering in channel governance: the case of the manufacturer and its foreign distributor," in Solberg C.A. (ed.), *Relationship between Exporters and Their Foreign Sales and Marketing Intermediaries, Advances in International Marketing*, Vol. 16, pp. 49–80.

de Mooij, Marieke. 2013. *Global Marketing and Advertising: Understanding Cultural Paradoxes*, 4th ed., Thousand Oaks, CA, Sage Publications.

de Mortanges, Charles Pahud, and Joost Vossen. 1999. "Mechanisms to control the marketing activities of foreign distributors." *International Business Review*, 8: 75–97.

Dess, Gregory G. and Peter S. Davis. 1984. "Porter's (1980) generic strategies as determinants of strategic group membership and organizational performance." *Academy of Management Journal*, 27(3): 467–488.

Dholakia, N. and Firat, F.A. 1988. "Development in the era of globalizing markets and consumption patterns, research in marketing," in Kuman I.E. and Firat F.A. (eds), *Marketing and Development: Toward Broader Dimensions*, Greenwich, CT, JAI Press, 79–101.

Diamantopoulos, A. and A. Souchon. 1999. "Measuring export information use: scale development and validation." *Journal of Business Research*, 46: 1–14.

Diamantopoulos, A., B.B. Schlegelmilch, and C. Allpress. 1990. "Export marketing research in practice: a comparison of users and non-users." *Journal of Marketing Management*, 6(3): 257–273.

Diuba, Iuliia. 2011. *Standardisation and Adaptation in International Marketing and Management – A Bibliometric Study*, Oslo, Norway, BI Norwegian Business School.

Doole, I. and R. Lowe. 2004. *International Marketing Strategy*, 4th ed., London, Thompson.

Douglas, S. and R. Schoemacher. 1981. "Item non-response in cross-national surveys." *European Marketing Research*, October: 9.

Douglas, S.P. and Y. Wind. 1987. "The myth of globalization." *Columbia Journal of World Business*, 22(4): 19–29.

Dow, Douglas. 2000. "A note on psychological distance and export market selection." *Journal of International Marketing*, 8(1): 51–64.

Doz, Y. 1986. *Strategic Management in Multinational Companies*, Oxford, Pergamon Press.

Doz, Y., C.K. Prahalad, and G. Hamel. 1990. "Control, change and flexibility: the dilemma of transnational collaboration," in Bartlett D. and Hedlund G. (eds), *Managing the Global Firm*, London, Routledge.

Dunning, J.H. 1977. "Trade, location of economic activity and the multinational enterprise: the search for an eclectic approach," in Ohlin B., Hessleborn P.O., and Wijkman P.M. (eds), *The International Location of Economic Activity*, London, Macmillan.

Dunning, J.H. 1987. "Cross-border corporation integration and regional integration." *University of Reading, Discussion Papers, in International and Business Studies, No. 105*.

Dunning, J.H. 1988. "The eclectic paradigm of international production: a restatement and some possible extensions." *Journal of International Business Studies*, 19(1): 1–31.

Dunning, J.H. 1998. "Location and the multinational enterprise: a neglected factor?" *Journal of International Business Studies*, 29(1): 45–66.

Dziubla, Robert. 1982. "International trading companies: building on the Japanese model." *Northwestern Journal of International Law & Business*, 4(2).

Eckstein, H. 1988. "A culturalist theory of political change." *American Political Science Review*, 82: 789–804.

Eisenhardt, K. 1989. "Agency theory: an assessment and review." *Academy of Management Review*, 14(1): 57–74.

Eliot, T.S. 1948. *Notes Towards the Definition of Culture*, London, Faber and Faber.

Enderwick, P. (ed.). 1989. *Multinational Service Firms*, London, Routledge.

Engelhardt, W.H., M. Kleinaltenkamp, and M. Reckenfelderbäumer. 1993. "Leistungsbündel als Absatzobjekte." *Zeitschrift für betriebswirtschaftliche Forschung*, 45(5): 395–426.

Engwall, L. and M. Wallenstål. 1988. "Tit for tat in small steps: the internationalization of Swedish banks." *Scandinavia Journal of Management*, 4(3/4): 147–155.

Evans, J. and K. Bridson. 2005. "Explaining retail offer adaptation through psychic distance." *International Journal of Retail & Distribution Management*, 33(1): 69–78.

Falshaw, J. Richard, Keith W. Glaister, and Ekrem Tatoglu. 2006. "Evidence on formal strategic planning and company performance." *Management Decision*, 44(1): 9–30.

Fama, E. and M. Jensen. 1983. "Separation of ownership and control." *Journal of Law and Economics*, 26: 301–325.

Fannin, R. 1984. "What agencies really think about global theory." *Marketing and Media Decisions*, 19(15): 74–82.

Ferraro, G.P. 1990. *The Cultural Dimension of International Business*, Englewood Cliffs, NJ, Prentice-Hall.

Fisher, R., W. Ury, and B. Patton. 2011. *Getting to Yes. Negotiating Agreements Without Giving In*, 3rd ed., New York, Penguin Books.

Forsgren, M. 1990. *Managing the Internationalization Process: The Swedish Case*, London, Routledge.

Forsgren, M. and U. Holm. 1990. "Internationalization of management: dominance and distance." *AIB Conference*, Glasgow.

French, John R.P. and Bertram Raven. 1959. "The bases of social power," in Dorwin Cartwright I. (ed.), *Studies in Social Power*, Ann Arbor, University of Michigan Press, pp. 150–167.

Frishammar, J. and S. Andersson. 2009. "The overestimated role of strategic orientations for international performance in smaller firms." *Journal of International Entrepreneurship*, 7: 57–77.

Gabrielsson, M. and M.V.H. Kirpalani. 2004. "Born globals; how to reach new business space rapidly." *International Business Review*, 13: 555–571.

Gabrielsson, M., V.H.M. Kirpalani, P. Dimitratos, C.A. Solberg, and A. Zucchella. 2008. "Born globals: propositions to help advance theory." *International Business Review*, 17(4): 385–401.

Gerard, Prendergast and Leyland Pitt. 1996. "Packaging, marketing, logistics and the environment: are there trade-offs?" *International Journal of Physical Distribution & Logistics Management*, 26(6): 60–72.

Ghauri, Pervez, Fatima Wang, Ulf Elg, and Veronica Rosendo-Ríos. 2016. "Market driving strategies: beyond localization." *Journal of Business Research*, 69(12): 5682–5693.

Ghauri, P.N. 1990. "Emergence of new structures in Swedish multinationals," in Farmer R.S. (ed.), *Advances, in International Comparative Management*, Greenwich, CT, JAI Press.

Ghemawat, Pankaj. 2012. *World 3.0: Global Prosperity and How to Achieve It*, Boston, Harvard Business Review Press.

Ghemawat, Pankaj and Fariborz Ghadar. 2006. "Global integration ≠ global concentration." *Industrial and Corporate Change*, 15(4): 595–623.

Ghobadian, Abby, Nicholas O'Regan, Howard Thomas, and Jonathan Liu. 2008. "Formal strategic planning, operating environment, size, sector and performance: evidence from the UK's manufacturing SMEs." *Journal of General Management*, 34(2): 1–20.

Ghoshal, S. and P. Moran. 1996. "Bad for practice: a critique of the transaction cost theory." *Academy of Management Review*, 21(1): 13–47.

Gibbon, P. 2014. "Trading houses during and since the great commodity boom." *Working Paper*, Danish Institute for International Studies, WP 2014:12.

Gilbert, K. 2001. "In search of Russian culture: the interplay of organizational, environmental and cultural factors in Russian–Western partnerships." *Working Papers*, Management Research Center, University of Wolverhampton. Available from: <http://www.wlv.ac.uk/PDF/uwbs_WP003_01_Gilbert.pdf> [Accessed in Dec 2008].

Golden, Brian R. 1992. "Research notes. The past is the past–or is it? The use of retrospective accounts as indicators of past strategy." *Academy of Management Journal*, 35(4): 848–860.

Gomes-Casseres, B. 1987. "Joint venture instability: is it a problem?" *Columbia Journal of World Business*, 22: 97–102.

Gottschalk Sveaas and Thorstensen 2013. "Formal and informal contractual mechanisms: Norwegian companies in China." BI Norwegian Business School, p. 55.

Granovetter, M. 1985. "Economic action and social structure: the problem of embeddedness." *American Journal of Sociology*, 91(3): 481–510.

Granovetter, Mark S. 1973. "The strength of weak ties." *American Journal of Sociology*, 78(6): 1360–1380.

Gripsrud, G. and U.H. Olsson. 2000. *Markedsanalyse*, Kristiansand, Høyskoleforlaget.

Gripsrud, G., C.A. Solberg and A.M. Ulvnes. 1999. "Exporter's information collection behavior: An exploratory study." *Proceedings from the Annual IMP Conference*, Dublin.

Gripsrud, G., C.A. Solberg, and A.M. Ulvnes. 2006. "The effect of information collection behavior on market performance: the role of partner relationships," in Solberg I. (ed.), *Advances in International Marketing*, Vol. 16, pp. 135–155.

Gripsrud, Geir, Auke Hunneman, and Carl Arthur Solberg. 2015. "Comparing 'born globals' and other exporting firms: a longitudinal study." *Proceedings ANZIBA Conference*, Melbourne.

Gripsrud, Geir, Auke Hunneman, and Carl Arthur Solberg. 2017. "Survival of new ventures in exporting." *CIMaR Conference, Local–Global Connections in International Marketing*, Florence, Italy.

Grubel, H. 1989. "Multinational banking," in Enderwick P. (ed.), *Multinational Service Firms*, London, Routledge.

Grubel, H.G. and P.J. Lloyd. 1975. *Intra-Industry Trade: The Theory and Measurement of International Trade in Differentiated Products*, London, Macmillan.

Hagedoorn, J. and J. Schakenraad. 1990. "Leading companies and the structure of strategic alliances in core technologies," Paper Presented at Workshop on Europe and Globalization, EIASM, May.

Håkansson, Håkan and Ivan Snehota. 1995. *Developing Relationships, in Business Networks*, London, Cengage Learning.

Hall, E.T. 1959. *The Silent Language*, Garden City, NY, Anchor Press/Doubleday.

Hall, E.T. and M.R. Hall. 1990. *Understanding Cultural Differences*, Yarmouth, MA, Intercultural Press.

Hambrick, Donald C. 1983. "High profit strategies in mature capital goods industries: a contingency approach." *Academy of Management Journal*, 26(4): 687–707.

Hamel, Gary. 1996. "Strategy as revolution." *Harvard Business Review*, 96: 69–82.

Hamel, G. and C.K. Prahalad. 1985. "Do you really have a global strategy?" *Harvard Business Review*, 27(3): 13–14.

Hamill, J. and S. El-Hajjar. 1990. "Strategic alliances–way forward for Europe," Paper Presented at Academy of International Business, Glasgow, April.

Hamill, James, Stephen Young, Colin Wheeler, and J. Richard Davis. 1989. *International Market Entry and Development*, Hemel Hempstead, Harvester Wheatsheaf.

Hampden-Turner, C. and F. Trompenaars. 1993. *The Seven Cultures of Capitalism*, New York, Doubleday, Currency.

Hampden-Turner, C. and F. Trompenaars. 2000. *Building Cross-Cultural Competence. How to Create Wealth from Conflicting Values*, New Haven, Yale University Press.

Harris, G. 1984. "The globalization of advertising." *International Journal of Advertising*, 3(3): 223–235.

Heckscher, E. 1919. "The effect of foreign trade on the distribution of income," *Ekonomisk Tidskrift*, 21, reprinted in Flam H. and Flanders M.J. (eds), *Heckscher–Ohlin Trade Theory*, Cambridge, MA, Harvard University Press, pp. 43–69.

Hedlund, G. 1986. "The hypermodern MNC–a heterarchy?" *Human Resource Management*, 25(1): 9–35.

Hedlund, G. and D. Rolander. 1990. "Action, in heterarchies–new approaches to managing MNCs," in Bartlett, Doz and Hedlund G. (eds), *Managing the Global Firm*, London, Routledge.

Heide, Jan B. 1994. "Interorganizational governance in marketing channels." *Journal of Marketing*, 58(1): 71–86.

Heide, Jan B. and Kenneth H. Wathne. 2006. "Friends, business people and relationship roles: a conceptual framework and a research agenda." *Journal of Marketing*, 70: 90–103.

Helgesen, T. 1992. "The rationality of advertising decisions: conceptual issues." *Journal of Advertising Research*, 32(6).

Helgesen, T. and M. Micalsen. 1998. "STAS–new empirical evidence from Norway," The 1998 European Advertising Effectiveness Symposium, Advertising Seminars International, Hamburg.

Hill, Charles W. and Thomas M. Hult. 2017. *International Business – Competing in the Global Marketplace*, 11th ed., New York, McGraw-Hill.

Hill, K. 1997. "Electronic marketing, the Dell computer experience," in Peterson R.A. (ed.), *Electronic Marketing and the Consumer*, Thousand Oaks, CA, Sage Publications.

Hofstede, G. 1980. *Culture Consequences: International Differences in Work Related Values*, Beverly Hills, Sage Publications.

Hofstede, G. 1993. "Cultural constructs in management theories." *Academy of Management Executive*, 7(1).

Hofstede, G. and M. Bond. 1988. "The Confucius connection: from cultural roots to economic growth." *Organizational Dynamics*, 16(4): 4–21.

Homburg, Christian and Christian Pflesser. 2000. "A multi-layer model of market oriented organizational culture: measurement issues and performance outcomes." *Journal of Marketing Research*. 37: 449–462.

Howell, Llewellyn D. 2013. *The Handbook of Country and Political Risk Analysis*, 5th ed., PRS Group.

Hveem, H. 1989. "Countertrade: the global perspective: the growth and proliferation of bilateral contracting and its political implications," *PUFO, Oslo Countertrade Project Report No. 1*, Oslo.

Inglehart, R. and W.E. Baker. 2000. "Modernization, cultural change and the persistence of traditional values." *American Sociological Review*, 65(1): 19–51.

Isdell-Carpenter, P. 1986. "Global marketing." *The First European Advertising and Media Conference*, Brussels.

Ivens, Björn Sven. 2006. "Identifying differences in foreign customers' relational behavior: an exploratory study using multidimensional scaling," in Solberg Carl Arthur (ed.), *Relationships Between Exporters and Their Foreign Sales and Marketing Intermediaries. Advances in International Marketing*, Vol. 16, pp. 245–266.

Jensen, M. and W. Meckling 1976. "Theory of the firm: managerial behavior, agency cost and ownership structure." *Journal of Financial Economics*, 3: 305–360.

Jensson, M. and T.-B. Lintho. 1994. *Norske Bedrifters Internasjonale Markedskommunikasjon. Diplomoppgave*, Sandvika, Handelshøyskolen BI.

Johannisson, B. and M. Huse. 2000. "Recruiting outside board members in the small family business: an ideological challenge." *Entrepreneurship & Regional Development*, 12: 353–378.

Johanson, J. and L.G. Mattson. 1986. "International marketing and internationalisation processes–a network approach," in Turnbull P.W. and Paliwoda S.J. (eds), *Research in International Marketing*, London, Croom Helm.

Johanson, J. and J.E. Vahlne. 1977. "The internationalization process of the firm–a model of knowledge development and increasing foreign commitments." *Journal of International Business Studies*, 8(1): 23–32.

Johanson, J. and J.E. Vahlne. 1990. "The mechanisms of internationalization." *International Marketing Review*, 7: 11–23.

Johanson, Jan and Jan-Erik Vahlne. 2009. "The Uppsala internationalization process model revisited: from liability of foreignness to liability of outsidership." *Journal of International Business Studies*, 40(9): 1411–1431.

Johanson, J. and F. Wiedersheim-Paul. 1975. "Internationalization of the firm; four Swedish case studies." *The Journal of Management Studies*, 12(3): 305–323.

Johanson, J.K. and I. Nonaka. 1987. "Market research the Japanese way." *Harvard Business Review* 65(3): 16–22.

Johnson, Richard A., Fremont E. Kast, and James E. Rosenzweig. 1973. *The Theory and Management of Systems*, 3rd ed., New York, McGraw-Hill, pp. 144–146.

Jones, Gareth R. and John E. Butler. 1988. "Costs, revenue, and business-level strategy." *Academy of Management Review*, 13(2): 202–213

Kale, H. 1995. "Grouping euroconsumers: a culture-based clustering approach." *Journal of International Marketing*, 3(3): 35–48.

Kamath, S., P.J. Rosson, D. Patton, and M. Brooks. 1987. "Research on success in exporting: past, present and future," in Rosson P.J. and Reid S.L. (eds), *Managing Export Entry and Expansion*, New York, Praeger.

Keegan, W.J. 1984. *Multinational Marketing Management*, Englewood Cliffs, NJ, Prentice-Hall International.

Kennedy, P. 1988. *The Rise and Fall of Great Powers*, New York, Random House.

Keohane, R.O. 1980. *After Hegemony: Cooperation and Discord in the World Political Economy*, Princeton, Princeton University Press.

Kern, H., H.C. Wagner, and R. Hassis. 1990. "European aspects of a global brand: the BMW case." *Marketing and Research Today*, 18: 47–58.

Kernan J.B. and T.J. Domzal. 1993. "International advertising–to globalize, vizualise." *Journal of International Consumer Marketing*, 5(4): 51–72.

Khadra, B. 1990. "The prophetic-caliphal model of leadership: an empirical study." *International Studies of Management and Organization*, 20: 37–51.

Kharbanda O.D. and E.A. Stallworthy. 1983. *How to Learn from Project Disasters*, Aldershot, Gower Publishing Co.

Kidwell, Roland, Arne Nygaard, and Ragnhild Silkoset. 2007. "Antecedents and effects of free riding in the franchisor franchisee relationship." *Journal of Business Venturing*, 22(4): 522–544.

Kirca, Ahmet H., Satish Jayachandran and William O. Bearden. 2005. "Market orientation: a meta-analytic review and assessment of its antecedents and impact on performance." *Journal of Marketing*, 69(2): 24–41.

Kindleberger, C.P. 1973. *The World in Depression, 1929–1939*, Harmondsworth, Allen Lane, The Penguin Press.

Kitching, J. 1973. "Acquisitions in Europe: causes of corporate success and failures," *Business International European Research Report*. Geneva.

Knight, G. and S.T. Cavusgil. 1996. "Born globals." *Working Paper*. University of Michigan Press.

Kohli, A.K. and B.J. Jaworski. 1990. "Market orientation: the construct, research propositions, and managerial implications." *Journal of Marketing*, 54: 1–18.

Konig, Gabor. 2009. *The Impact Of Investment And Concentration Among Food Suppliers And Retailers In Various OECD Countries*, Hungarian Ministry of Agriculture – Agricultural Economics Research Institute (AKI).

Korhonen, Heli, Reijo Luostarinen, and Lawrence Welch. 1996. "Internationalization of SMEs: inward-outward patterns and government policy." *Management International Review*, 36(4): 315–329.

Korneliussen, Tor and Inger Øwre. 1998. Hvilke eksportbarrierer møter norske eksportbedrifter? *Magma*, 4.

Korten, D. 1995. *When Corporations Rule the World*, West Hartford, CT, Kumarian Press.

Kotabe, Masaaki and Kristiaan Helsen. 2014. *Global Marketing Management*, 7th ed., Chichester, Wiley & Sons.

Kotkin, J. 1992. *Tribes. How Race, Religion and Identity Determine Success in the New Global Economy*, New York, Random House.

Kotler, P. 1986. "Global standardization–courting danger." *Journal of Consumer Marketing*, 3(2): 13–15.

Kotler, P. 1994. *Marketing Management*, Englewood Cliffs, NJ, Prentice Hall.

Kotler, Philip and Kelvin Keller. 2011. *Marketing Management*, 14th ed., Englewood Cliffs, NJ, Prentice-Hall.

Kroeber, A.L. and C. Kluckhorn. 1952. *Culture: A Critical Review of Concepts and Definitions*. Anthropological Papers, No. 4, New Haven, Yale, Peabody Museum.

Kublin, M. 1990. "A guide to export pricing." *Industrial Management*, 32(3): 29–32.

Kuhri, Fuad. 1968. "The etiquette of bargaining in the Middle East." *American Anthropologist*, 70(4): 698–706.

Kverneland, Å. 1988. "Japan's industry structure-barriers to global competitions," in Hood N. and Vahlne J.E. (eds), *Strategies in Global Competition*, Stockholm, School of Economics.

LaBahn, D.W. and K.R. Harich. 1997. "Sensitivity to national business culture: effects on US–Mexican channel relationship performance." *Journal of International Marketing*, 5(4): 29–51.

Lages, Luis Filipe, G. Silva and C. Styles. 2009. "Relationship capabilities, quality, and innovation as determinants of export performance." *Journal of International Marketing*, 17(4): 47–70.

Lasserre, P. and H. Schütte. 1999. *Strategy and Management in Asia Pacific*, London, McGraw-Hill Publishing Company.

Lee, W.-Y. and J.J. Brasch. 1978. "The adoption of exports as an innovative strategy." *Journal of International Business Studies*, 9.

Leonidou, Leonidas C. 1989. "The exporter–importer dyad–an investigation." *Journal of Managerial Psychology*, 4(2): 17–28.

Leontiades, F. 1984. "Market share and corporate strategy in international industries." *Journal of Business Strategy*, 5(1): 30–37.

Leontiades, M. 1990. "Flaws in Porter's competitive diamond." *Planning Review*, 18(5): 28–33.

Leontief, H. 1953. "Domestic production and foreign trade: the American capital position re-examined," *Proceedings of the American Philosophical Society*, 97(4).

Levitt, T. 1960. "Marketing myopia," *Harvard Business Review*, July/August.

Levitt, T. 1983. "The globalization of markets." *Harvard Business Review*, May.

Lewicki, R.J., B. Barry, and D.M. Saunders. 2015. *Negotiation*, 7th ed., Singapore, McGraw-Hill.

Linder, S.B. 1961. *An Essay on Trade and Transformation*, New York, Wiley & Sons.

Lindgren, U. "Foreign Acquisitions. Management of the Integration Process." PhD dissertation, Institute of International Business, Stockholm 1982.

Lipman, J. 1988. "Marketers turn sour on global sales pitch guru makes." *Wall Street Journal*, 12.

Lorange, Peter. 1980. *Corporate Planning: An Executive Viewpoint.* Englewood Cliffs, NJ, Prentice-Hall.

Loukakou, Maria Doriza and Nampungwe Beatrice Membe. 2012. "Product standardization and adaptation in International Marketing: A case of McDonald's," MSc thesis, West University, Sweden (http://hv.diva-portal.org/smash/get/diva2:543563/FULLTEXT01.pdf).

Lunnan, R. and S. Haugland. 2008. "Predicting and measuring alliance performance: a multidimensional analysis." *Strategic Management Journal*, 29(5): 545–556.

Luostarinen, R. 1980a. "Internationalization of the Firm: An Empirical Study of the Internationalization of Firms with Small and Open Domestic Markets, with Special Emphasis on Lateral Rigidity as a Behavioural Characteristic in Strategic Decision Making." PhD dissertation, The Helsinki School of Economics, Helsinki.

Luostarinen, R. 1980b. *Foreign Business Operations*, Helsinki, Helsinki School of Economics.

Luostarinen, R. and L. Welch. 1990. *International Business Operations*, KY Bookstore, Helsinki School of Economics.

Luostarinen, R., H. Korhonen, J. Jokinen and T. Pelkonen. 1994. 'Globalisation and SME: globalization of economic activities and small and medium-sized enterprises (SMEs) development.' *Study and Report* 59. Helsinki, Ministry of Trade and Industry.

Lyons, B. 1980. "A new measure and minimum efficient plant size in UK manufacturing industry." *Economica*, 47(185): 19–34.

Macho-Stadler, Inés and Pérez-Castrillo, David. 2010. "Incentives in university technology transfers." *International Journal of Industrial Organization*, 28(4): 362–367.

Madsen, T. and Servais, P. 1997. "The internationalization of born globals – an evolutionary process." *International Business Review*, 6(6): 1–14.

Malhotra, Naresh K. 2010. *Marketing Research: An Applied Orientation*, 6th ed., Pearson.

Marchi, Gianluca, Marina Vignola, Gisela Facchinetti, and Giovanno Mastroleo. 2014. "International market selection for small firms: a fuzzy-based decision process." *European Journal of Marketing*, 48(11/12): 2198–2212.

Mårtenson, R. 1987. "Is standardization of marketing feasible in culture-bound industries? A European case study." *International Marketing Review*, 4(3): 7–17.

Matthyssens, Paul and Wouter Faes. 2006. "Managing channel relations in China: an exploratory study," in Solberg C.A. (ed.), *Relationships Between Exporters and their Foreign Sales and Marketing Intermediaries. Advances in International Marketing*, Vol. 16, pp. 187–212.

McAlister, D.J. 1995. "Affect and cognition based trust as foundations for interpersonal cooperation in organizations." *Academy of Management Journal*, 38: 24–59.

McDougall, Patricia Phillips, and Benjamin M. Oviatt. 1996. "New venture internationalization, strategic change, and performance: a follow-up study." *Journal of Business Venturing*, 11(1): 34–40.

Meffert, H. and J. Althans. 1986. "Global advertising: multi-national vs. international pros and cons." *International Adviser*, 13(4): 34.

Messelin, Patrick. 2013. "The Mercosur–EU preferential trade agreement." *CEPS Working Paper No. 377*, Brussels, Belgium.

Meyer, J.P. and N.J. Allen. 1991. "A three-component conceptualization of organizational commitment." *Human Resource Management Review*, 1(1): 61–89.

Miles, Robert E. and Charles C. Snow. 1978. *Organizational Strategy, Structure, and Process*, New York, McGraw-Hill.

Mintzberg, Henry. 1994. "The fall and rise of strategic planning." *Harvard Business Review*, 72(1): 107–114.

Mintzberg, Henry, Bruce. W. Ahlstrand, and Joseph Lampel. 1998a. *Strategy Safari: The Complete Guide Through the Wilds of Strategic Management*, New York: The Free Press.

Mintzberg, Henry, James B. Quinn, and Sumantra Ghoshal. 1998b. *The Strategy Process*, London, Prentice-Hall.

Miranda, J., R.A. Torres, and M. Ruis. 1998. "The international use of anti-dumping: 1987–1997." *Journal of World Trade*, 32(5): 5–71.

Mitchell, R. 1965. "Survey materials collected in development countries: sampling measurement and interviewing. Obstacles to intra- and international comparisons." *International Social Science Journal*, 17.

Mooi, Erik A. and Ghosh, Mrinal. 2010. "Contract specificity and its performance implications." *Journal of Marketing*, 74(2): 105–120.

Mole, J. 1992. *Mind Your Manners*, London, Nicholas Brealey Publishing.

Morgan, R.M. and S.D. Hunt. 1994. "The commitment-trust theory of relationship marketing." *Journal of Marketing*, 58: 20–38.

Moore, Fredrick T. 1959. "Economies of scale: some statistical evidence." *Quarterly Journal of Economics*, 73(2): 232–245.

Mueller, B. 1992. "Standardization vs. specialization: an examination of Westernization in Japanese advertising." *Journal of Advertising Research*, 32(1).

Mühlbacher, H., L. Dahringer, and H. Leihs. 1999. *International Marketing–A Global Perspective*. London, Thomson Business Press.

Muna, F.A. 1980. *Arab Executive*, New York, St. Martin's Press.

Myers, M.B. 1997. "The pricing of export products: why aren't managers satisfied with the results?" *Journal of World Business*, 32(3): 277–289.

Myers, M.B. and M. Harvey. 2001. "The value of pricing control in export channels: a governance perspective." *Journal of International Marketing*, 9(4): 1–29.

Mytelka, L.K. (ed.). 1991. *Strategic Partnerships and the World Economy*, London, Pinter Publishers.

Nadolska, A.M. and Barkema, H.G. 2007. "Learning to internationalize: the pace and success of foreign acquisitions." *Journal of International Business Studies*, 38(7): 1170–1186.

Narver, J.C. and S.F. Slater. 1990. "The effects of a market orientation on business profitability." *Journal of Marketing*, 54: 20–35.

Nes, Erik B. 2014. "Antecedents and consequences of replacing international independent intermediaries." *European Business Review*, 26: 218–236.

Nes, Erik and Geir Gripsrud. 2014. "When does it pay off to link a brand name to a country?" *Journal of Euromarketing*, 23(1): 22–36.

Nes, Erik B., Carl Arthur Solberg, and Ragnhild Silkoset. 2007. "The impact of national culture on exporter–distributor relations." *International Business Review*, 16: 405–424.

Nes, Erik B., Rama Yelkur, and Ragnhild Silkoset. 2012. "Exploring the animosity domain and the role of affect in a cross-national context." *International Business Review*, 21(5): 751–765.

Nes, Erik B., Rama Yelkur, and Ragnhild Silkoset. 2014. "Consumer affinity for foreign countries: construct development, buying behavior consequences and animosity contrasts." *International Business Review*, 23(4): 774–784.

Newbould, G.D., P.J. Buckley, and J. Thurwell. 1978. *Going International–The Experience of Smaller Companies Overseas*, London, Associated Business Press.

Nielsen, B.B. 2007. "Determining international strategic alliance performance: a multi-dimensional approach." *International Business Review*, 16: 337–361.

Nonaka, Ikujiro. 1994. "A dynamic theory of organizational knowledge creation." *Organization Science*, 5(1): 14–37.

Nordström, K. 1990. "The Internationalisation of the Firm in a New Perspective." PhD Dissertation, Institute of International Business, Stockholm.

Norman, V.D. 1998. "Forskningshotell?" *Dagens Næringsliv*, 13 June.

Obadia, Claude. 2013. "Competitive export pricing: the influence of the information context." *Journal of International Marketing*, 21(2): 62–78.

Obadia, Claude and Barbara Stöttinger. 2015. "Pricing to manage export channel relationships." *International Business Review*, 24(2), 311–318.

Ogunmokun, Gabriel O. and Elaine Chen Hsin Tang. 2012. "The effect of strategic marketing planning behaviour on the performance of small to medium-sized firms." *International Journal of Management*, 29(1): 159–170.

Ohlin, B. 1935. *Inter-Regional and International Trade*, Boston, Harvard University Press.

Ohmae, K. 1990. *The Borderless World: Power and Strategy in the Interlinked Economy*, London, Collins.

Ohmae, K. 1985. *Triad Power: The Coming Shape of Global Competition*, New York, The Free Press.

Okpara, J.O. and J.D. Kabongo. 2009. "Entrepreneurial export orientation, strategy, and performance of SMEs in an emergent African economy." *African Journal of Business & Economic Research*, 4(2/3): 34–54.

Olson, Eric M., Stanley F. Slater, and Tomas M. Hult. 2005. "The performance implication of fit among business strategy, marketing organization structure and strategic behavior." *Journal of Marketing*, 69: 49–65.

Olson, L.B. 1997. "The impact of the culture's platform religion on consumer behavior in the global market place," *Presentation at the Academy of International Business*, Monterrey, Mexico.

Østerud, Ø. 1999. *Globaliseringen and Nasjonalstaten*, Oslo, AdNotam Gyldendal.

Ouchi, William G. 1977. "The relationship between organizational structure and organizational control." *Administrative Science Quarterly*, 22(1): 95–113.

Outters-Jaeger, I. 1979. *The Development Impact of Barter in Developing Countries*. Paris, OECD.

Oviatt, Benjamin M. and Patricia Phillips McDougall. 1994. "Toward a theory of international new ventures." *Journal of International Business Studies*, 25(1): 45–64.

Ozsomer A., M. Bodur, and S.T. Cavusgil. 1991. "Market standardization by multinationals in an emerging market." *European Journal of Marketing*, 25(12): 50–61.

Panagiotou, George. 2006. "The impact of managerial cognitions on the structure-conduct-performance (SCP) paradigm: a strategic group perspective." *Management Decision*, 44(3): 423–441.

Panagiotou, George. 2007. "Reference theory: strategic groups and competitive benchmarking." *Management Decision*, 45(10): 1595–1621.

Papadopoulos, Nicolas and Louise Heslop. 1993. *Product-Country Images: Impact and Role in International Marketing*, New York, International Business Press.

Parnell, John A. and Peter Wright. 1993. "Generic strategy and performance: an empirical test of the Miles and Snow typology." *British Journal of Management*, 4(1): 29–36.

Pedersen, Inger Beate and Aksel Rokkan. 2006. "Buyer tolerance of conflict in cross national business relationships: an empirical study," in Solberg C.A. (ed.), *Relationship Between Exporters and Their Foreign Sales and Marketing Intermediaries, Advances in International Marketing*, Vol. 16, Elsevier Science.

Pedersen, T., B. Petersen, and G.R.G. Benito. 1997. *Change of Foreign Operation Method: Impetus to Change and Switching Costs. Proceedings of the University of Vaasa*, Reports 24, pp. 32–58.

Peebles, D.M. and J.K. Ryans Jr. 1984. *Management of International Advertising: A Marketing Approach*, Boston, Allyn and Bacon Inc.

Penrose, E.T. 1959. *The Theory of the Growth of the Firm*, 2nd ed, Oxford, Basil Blackwell.

Perlmutter, H.V. and D.A. Heenan. 1986. "Cooperate to compete globally." *Harvard Business Review*, 136–152.

Peters, T.J. and R.H. Waterman Jr. 1982. *Search of Excellence: Lessons from Americas Best-Run Companies*, New York, Harper & Row Publishers.

Petersen, B., D. Welch, and L.S. Welch. 2000. "Creating meaningful switching options in international operations." *Long Range Planning*, 33(5): 688–705.

Petersen, Bent, Torben Pedersen, and Gabriel R.G. Benito. 2006. "The termination dilemma of foreign intermediaries: performance, anti-shirking measures and hold-up safeguards," in Solberg C.A. (ed.), *Relationship Between Exporters and Their Foreign Sales and Marketing Intermediaries, Advances in International Marketing*, Vol. 16, Elsevier Science, pp. 317–337.

Pfeffer, J. and G.R. Salincik. 1978. *The External Control of Organizations–A Resource Dependence Perspective*, New York, Harper and Row Publishers.

Phromket, C. and P. Ussahawanitchakit. 2009. "Effects of organizational learning effectiveness on innovation outcomes and export performance of garments business in Thailand." *International Journal of Business Research*, 9(7): 6–31.

Piercy, N. 1981. "Company internationalization." *European Journal of Marketing*, 15: 3.

Pinder, J. 1991. *The European Community and Eastern Europe*, London, Royal Institute of International Affairs.

Porter, M. (ed.). 1986. *Competition in Global Industries*, Boston, Harvard Business School Press.

Porter, M. 1990. *The Competitive Advantage of Nations*, London, Macmillan.

Porter, M.E. 1980. *Competitive Strategy*, New York, The Free Press.

Porter, M.E. and H. Takeuch. 1986. Three roles of marketing in global strategy," in Porter M.E. (ed.), *Competition in Global Industries*, Boston, Harvard Business School Press, pp. 111–146.

Poynter, T.A. and A.M. Rugman. 1982. "World product mandates: how will multinationals respond?" *Business Quarterly*, 47(3): 54–61.

Poynter, T.A. and R.E. White. 1984/1985. "The strategies of foreign subsidiaries: responses to organizational slack." *International Studies of Management & Organization*, 14(4): 91–106.

Prahalad, C.K. and Y.L. Doz. 1981. "An approach to strategic control in MNCs." *Sloan Management Review*, 22(4): 5–13.

Purdy, L. and A. Carl-Zepp. 1988. "International advertising tracking–some lessons learned in the UK and Germany." *ESOMAR Conference*, UK, November.

Quelch, J.A. and E.J. Hoff. 1986. "Customizing global marketing." *Harvard Business Review*, 59–67.

Quelch, J.A., R.D. Buzzell, and E.R. Salama. 1990. *The Marketing Challenge of 1992*, Reading, MA, Addison-Wesley Publishing Company.

Rachman, G. 2016. *Easternisation: War and Peace in the Asian Century*, London, Bodley Head.

Rangan, S. 1998. *The Problem of Search and Deliberation in International Exchange: Exploring Multinationals' Network Advantages*, Fontainebleau, Insead.

Rappaport, A. 1979. "Strategic analyses for more profitable acquisitions." *Harvard Business Review*, July: 99–110.

Rauch, A., J. Wiklund, G.T. Lumpkin and M. Frese. 2009. "Entrepreneurial orientation and business performance: An assessment of past research and suggestions for the future." *Entrepreneurship Theory and Practice*, 33: 761–787.

Reich, R.B. 1991. *The Work of Nations: Preparing Ourselves for the 21 Century Capitalism*, New York, Alfred Knopf.

Reid, S.D. 1983. "Firm internationalization, transaction costs and strategic choice." *International Market Review*, 1(2): 44–56.

Rialp, A., J. Rialp, and G.A. Knight. 2005. "The phenomenon of early internationalizing firms: What do we know after a decade (1993–2003) of scientific inquiry?" *International Business Review*, 14(2): 147–166.

Ricardo, D. 1981. *Principles of Political Economy and Taxation*, 1st ed., Cambridge, Cambridge University Press.

Ricks, D.A. 1983. *Big Blunders in International Business*, Homewood, IL, Dow-Jones Irwin.

Ricks, David. 2006. *Blunders in International Business*, 4th ed., Wiley.

Rigault, Didier. 2011. *International Business Agreements*, Oslo, Dege Brækhus.

Robinson, Richard B. and John A. Pearce. 1984. "Research thrusts in small firm strategic planning." *Academy of Management Review*, 9(1): 128–137.

Robock, S.H. and K. Simmonds. 1974. *International Business and Multinational Enterprise*, Homewood, IL, Irwin.

Rodinson, M. 1974. *Islam and Capitalism*, Harmondsworth, Penguin.

Rosen, B.N., J.J. Boddewyn, and E.A. Louis. 1989. "US brands abroad: an empirical study of global branding." *International Marketing Review*, 6(1).

Rosenbaum, Stephen Mark, and Tage Koed Madsen. 2012. "Modes of foreign entry for professional service firms in multi-partner projects." *Service Industries Journal*, 32(10): 1653–1666.

Rosson, P.J. 1987. "The overseas distributor method: performance and change, in harsh environment," in Reid S. and Rosson P.J. (eds), *Managing Export Entry and Expansion*, New York, Praeger.

Roth, M.S. 1992. "Depth versus breadth strategies for global brand image management." *Journal of Advertising*, 21(2): 25–36.

Roth, M.S. 1995. "Effects of global market conditions on brand image customisation and brand performance." *Journal of Advertising*, 24(4): 55–75.

Ruedi, A. and P.R. Lawrence. 1970. "Organizations in two cultures," in Lorsch J.W. and Lawrence J. (eds), *Studies in Organizational Design*, Homewook, IL, Irwin, 54–83.

Salacuse, Jeswald W. 2004. "Negotiating: the top ten ways that culture can affect your negotiation." *Ivey Business Journal*, Sept/Oct: 1–7.

Samiee, S. and K. Roth. 1992. "The influence of global marketing standardization on performance," *Journal of Marketing*, 56(2): 1–17.

Sampson, P. (ed.). 1997. *Qualitative Research: The New, the Old and a Question Mark*. ESOMAR Marketing Research Monograph Series, Vol. 2, Amsterdam, ESOMAR.

Sampson, P. and M. Bhadur. 1985. "Qualitative techniques in the context of different time frames." *Technical Paper*, Burke Marketing Research.

Saprykin, V.A. 2005. *Russian Culture: Concept, Genesis, Originality*, Tutorial, Moscow, MIEM (МИЭМ).

Scherer, F.M. 1990. *Industrial Market Structure and Economic Performance*, 2nd ed., Boston, Houghton Mifflin Company.

Schilke, O., M. Reimann, and J.S. Thomas. 2009. "When does international marketing standardization matter to firm performance?" *Journal of International Marketing*, 17(4): 24–46.

Schlegelmilch, B.B., A. Diamantopoulos, and K. Tse. 1993. "Determinants of export marketing usage: testing some hypotheses on UK exporters," in Baker M.J. (ed.), *Perspectives on Marketing Management III*, New York, Wiley and Sons.

Schmid, Stefan and Thomas Kotulla. 2011. "50 years of research on international standardization and adaptation–from a systematic literature analysis to a theoretical framework." *International Business Review*, 20(5): 491–507.

Schwenk, Charles R. and Charles B. Shrader. 1993. "Effects of formal strategic planning on financial performance in small firms: a meta-analysis." *Entrepreneurship Theory and Practice*, 17(3): 53–53.

Selnes, F., J. Henriksen, and E. Olsen. 1993. "Eksportsuksess: en analyse av et utvalg TBL-bedrifter som deltar i TOPP-programmet," Norsk Institutt for Markedsforskning, NiM Rapport 15.

Setreng, S.K. 1998. *Naturens Nei: om EU, frihandeland økologisk kaos*. Norsk bonde and småbrukarlag.

Shapiro, J.M., J. L. Ozanne, and B. Saatcioglu. 2008. "An interpretive examination of the development of cultural sensitivity in international business." *Journal of International Business Studies*, 39(1): 71–87.

Shenkar, Oded. 2001. "Cultural distance revisited: towards a more rigorous conceptualization and measurement of cultural differences." *Journal of International Business Studies*, 32(3): 519–535.

Sheth, J.N. and A. Eshghi. 1985. "The globalization of consumption patterns: an empirical investigation," in Erdener K. (ed.), *Global Perspectives in Marketing*, New York, Praeger, pp. 133–148.

Shimp, T.A. and S. Sharma. 1987. "Consumer ethnocentrism: construction and validation of the CETSCALE." *Journal of Marketing Research*, 24: 280–289.

Shrader, C., L. Taylor, and D. Dalton. 1984. "Strategic planning and organizational performance: a critical appraisal." *Journal of Management*, 10: 149–171.

Sinkovics, R. and N. Pezderka. 2010. "Do born-global SMEs reap more benefits from ICT use than other internationalizing small firms?," in Solberg C.A. (ed.), CIMaR 2010 Conference Proceedings, Oslo, Norway, May 26–28.

Skarmeas, D., C.S. Katsikeas, and B.B. Schlegelmilch. 2002. "Drivers of commitment and its impact on performance in cross-cultural buyer-seller relationships: the importer's perspective." *Journal of International Business Studies*, 33(4): 757–783.

Slangen, Arjen H.L., Sjoerd, Beugelsdijk, and Jean-Francois Hennart. 2011. "The impact of cultural distance on bilateral arm's length exports." *Management International Review*, 51(6): 875–896.

Smith, Adam. 1776. *An Inquiry into the Nature and Causes of the Wealth of Nations*, London, Strahan/Cadell.

Solberg, C.A. 1986. *Internasjonal markedsføring*, Oslo, Universitetsforlaget.

Solberg, C.A. 1987. "Export strategy and pricing policies in Norwegian export companies." *Monterey Review*, Fall: 20–27

Solberg, C.A. 1988. "Successful and unsuccessful exporters: an empirical study of 114 Norwegian exporters." *Working Paper*, Handelshøyskolen BI.

Solberg, C.A. 1989. "Adaptation and standardisation in international marketing; more than just economies of scale and market homogeneity," in Luostarinen R. (ed.), *Dynamics of International Business–EIBA-Conference Proceedings*, Helsinki, pp. 829–849.

Solberg, C.A. 1997. "A framework for analysis of strategy development in globalizing markets." *Journal of International Marketing*, 5(1): 9–30.

Solberg, C.A. 2000. "Standardization or adaptation: the role of the local subsidiary/representative." *Journal of International Marketing*, 8(1): 78–98.

Solberg, C.A. 2002a. "Culture and industrial buyer behaviour: The Arab experience." *IMP Conference*, Dijon, France.

Solberg, C.A. 2002b. "The perennial issue of adaptation or standardization of international marketing communication: organizational contingencies and performance." *Journal of International Marketing*, 10(3): 1–21.

Solberg, C.A. 2006a. "Introduction," in Solberg, C.A. (ed.), *Advances in International Marketing*, 16: 1–10.

Solberg, C.A. 2006b. "Relational drivers, controls and relationship quality in exporter-foreign middle-man relations," *Advances of International Marketing*, 6(16): 81–104.

Solberg, C.A. 2006c. "Market research and information through networks in international markets," in Asche F. (ed.), *Primary Industries Facing Global Markets*, Oslo, Universitetsforlaget, pp. 21–43.

Solberg, C.A. 2006d. "Exporter governance of marketing channel members in international markets: moderating effects of stage of relationships and operation mode," in Solberg, C.A. (ed.), *Advances in International marketing*, 16: 351–369.

Solberg, C.A. 2007. "Product complexity and cultural distance effects on managing international distributor relationships: a contingency approach." *Journal of International Marketing*, 16(3): 57–83.

Solberg, C.A. 2010. "Switching export operation modes: partner dynamics as inter- and intra-mode switch motivator," CIMaR 2010 conference, Oslo.

Solberg, Carl Arthur. 2012. "The born global dilemma: trade-off between rapid growth and control," in Gabrielsson M. and Manek Kirpilani V.H. (eds), *Handbook on Research on Born Globals*, Cheltenham, Edward Elgar.

Solberg, Carl-Arthur. 2014. "International branding: a framework for classification and analysis." *Journal of Euromarketing*, 23: 5–21.

Solberg, C.A. and B.H. Andersen. 1991. "Informasjonsadferd i norske eksportbedrifter." Research note, Handelshøyskolen BI.

Solberg, Carl Arthur and Vidar Askeland. 2006. "The relevance of internationalisation theories: a contingency framework approach," in Fai F. and Morgan E. (eds), *Managerial Issues in IB*, London, Palgrave.

Solberg, Carl Arthur and Trine Bretteville. 2012. "Inside the boardroom of born globals." *International Journal of Entrepreneurship and Small Business*, 15(2): 154–170.

Solberg, C.A. and F. Durrieu. 2006. "Access to networks and commitment to internationalisation as precursors to marketing strategies in international markets." *Management International Review*, 56(1): 57–83.

Solberg, Carl Arthur and F. Durrieu. 2008. "Strategy development in international markets: a two tier approach." *International Marketing Review*, 25(5): 520–543.

Solberg, C.A. and F. Durrieu. 2011. "Exploring the role of nationality in strategy formulation in international markets: a study of German, Norwegian and Singaporean firms." *Proceedings CIMaR Conference*, Atlanta, April.

Solberg, Carl Arthur and F. Durrieu. 2015a. "The impact of globalization drivers on strategy performance relationships in international markets," in Julian C. (ed.), *Research Handbook on International Marketing*, Cheltenham, Edward Elgar.

Solberg, Carl Arthur and F. Durrieu. 2015b. "Internationalisation strategies and industry structure," *Advances in International Marketing*, 26: 33–59.

Solberg, C.A. and E.B. Nes. 2002. "Exporter trust, commitment and marketing control in integrated and independent export channels." *International Business Review*, 11: 385–405.

Solberg, C.A. and U.H. Olsson. 2011. "Management orientation and export performance." *Baltic Journal of Management*, 5(1): 28–50.

Solberg, C.A. and L.S. Welch. 1995. "Strategic alliances–a way for SME internationalization?" *Conference Proceedings, Nordic Conference on Small Business Development*, Vol. 2, Lillehammer.

Solberg, C.A., Birgitte Kristiansen, and Liv Karin Slåttebrekk. 2002. "Internationalisation strategies and globalisation: a test of the Nine Strategic Windows framework among Norwegian exporting firms." *Proceedings EIBA Conference*, Athens, Greece, December.

Solberg Carl Arthur, Geir Gripsrud, and Auke Hunneman. 2014. *Mapping and Analysing Norway's Export Patterns and Strategies of Norwegian Exporters.* BI Norwegian School of Management, Oslo, Norway.

Solberg, Carl Arthur, Barbara Stöttinger, and Attila Yaprak. 2006. "A taxonomy of the pricing practices of exporting firms: evidence from Austria, Norway and the United States." *Journal of International Marketing*, 14(1): 23–48.

Solberg, Carl Arthur, Marit Owe Tryggeset, and Even Johan Lanseng. 2013. "Challenging the market orientation construct: the role of data processing and market insight." *Johan Arndt Conference*, Oslo.

Solberg, Carl Arthur, Geir Gripsrud, and Auke Hunneman. 2014. *Kartlegging og analyse av eksportmønsreand–strategier, Forskningsrapport*, Handelshøyskolen BI, Oslo.

Solberg, Carl Arthur and Anzhelika Osmanova. 2017. "Opening the black box of Russian B2B relationships," in Marin Marinov (ed.), *Research Handbook on Marketing in Emerging Economies*, Cheltenham, Edward Elgar Publishing, pp. 197–221.

Solli-Sæther, Hans and Petter Gottschalk. 2008. "Myter og realiteter om outsourcing," *Magma*, 5.

Song, Michael, Subin Im, Hans van der Bijand, and Lisa Song. 2011. "Does strategic planning enhance or impede innovation and firm performance?" *Product Development and Management Association*, 28: 503–520.

Sorenson, R.Z. and U.E. Wiechmann. 1975. "How multinationals view marketing standardization." *Harvard Business Review*, 53(May/June).

Sousa, Carlos M.P. and Frank Bradley. 2008. "Antecedents of international pricing adaptation and export performance." *Journal of World Business*, 43(3): 307–320.

Stevenson, Thomas H. and David W. Cabell. 2002. "Integrating transfer pricing policy and activity-based costing." *Journal of International Marketing*, 10(4): 77–88.

Stopford, J. and L. Wells. 1972. *Managing the Multinational Enterprise*, New York, Basic Books.

Stopford, Martin. 1997. *Maritime Economics*, London, Routledge.

Stump, R., S. King, and C. Oh. 2002. "Relative influence in marketing channels: an empirical test of the influence of distributor specialized investments in an Eastern versus Western culture," in Bigné E., Hassan S.S., and (Vic) Johar J.S. (eds), *Proceedings from AMS "Multicultural Marketing Conference,"* Vol. IV, Valencia, Spain, pp. 1096–1113.

Sveaas, Gottschalk and Nina Frederikke Thorstensen. 2013. *Formal and Informal Contractual Mechanisms: Norwegian companies in China*, Oslo, Norway, BI Norwegian Business School, p. 55.

Sui, Sui and Matthias Baum. 2014. "Internationalization strategy, firm resources and the survival of SMEs in the export market." *Journal of International Business Studies*, 45: 821–841.

Szymanski, David, Sundar G. Bharadwaj, and P. Rajan Varadarajan. 1993. "Standardization versus adaptation of international marketing strategy: an empirical investigation." *Journal of Marketing*, 57(3): 1–18.

Takeuchi, H. and M.E. Porter. 1986. "Three roles of marketing in global strategy," in Porter M.E. (ed.), *Competition in Global Industries*, Boston, Harvard Business School Press, pp. 111–146.

Tantong, P., K. Karande, A. Nair and A. Singhapakdi. 2010. "The effect of product adaptation and market orientation on export performance: a survey of Thai managers." *Journal of Marketing Theory & Practice*, Spring, 18(2): 155–169.

Taylor, F. 1929. *The Principles of Scientific Management*, New York, Harper.

Terpstra, V. and C.M. Wu. 1988. "Determinants of foreign investments of US advertising agencies." *Journal of International Business Studies*, 19(1): 33–46.

Theodosiou M. and L.C. Leonidou. 2003. "Standardization versus adaptation of international marketing strategy: an integrative assessment of the empirical research." *International Business Review*, 12: 141–171.

Thjømøe, H.M. Eksponeringseffekt og merkepreferanse. PhD Dissertation. Københavns Universitet/ Handelshøyskolen BI, Copenhagen 1996.

Timlen, Thomas. 2000. "Troubled waters." *American Shipper*, October, p. 26.

Tinbergen, Jan. 1962. *Shaping the World Economy; Suggestions for an International Economic Policy*, New York, Twentieth Century Fund.

Turnbull, P.W. 1987. "A challenge to the stages theory of the internationalization process," in Reid S. and Rosson P.J. (eds), *Managing Export Entry and Expansion*, New York, Praeger.

UNCTAD. 1997. *World Investment Report 1997: Transnational Corporations, Market Structure and Competition Policy*, Geneva, UN.

UNCTAD. 2013. *World Investment Report*, Geneva, UN.

United Nations (UN). 1988. *Report by the United Nations Conference on Trade and Development*, New York, UN.

Usunier, J.C. 1990. "The European consumer, globalizer or globalized?" Paper Presented at Work Shop on Globalization and Europe, Brussels, EIASM.

Usunier, J.C. 1996. *Marketing Across Cultures*, London, Prentice-Hall Europe.

Uzzi, Brian. 1997. "Social structure and competition in interfirm networks: the paradox of embeddedness." *Administrative Science Quarterly*, 42(1): 35–67.

Van den Heuvel, Jeroen, Anita Van Gils, and Wim Voordeckers. 2006. "Board roles in small and medium-sized family businesses: performance and importance." *Corporate Governance*, 14(5): 467–485.

van Raaij, W.F. 1997. "Globalization of marketing communication?" *Journal of Economic Psychology*, 18(2): 259–270.

Vardar, N. 1993. *Global Advertising–Rhyme or Reason?* London, Paul Chapman Publishing.

Verlegh, P.W.J. and J.E.M. Steenkamp. 1999. "A review and meta-analysis of country-of-origin research." *Journal of Economic Psychology*, 20(5): 521–546.

Vernon, R. 1966. "International investment and international trade in the product cycle." *Quarterly Journal of Economics*, 80.

Waage, P.N. 1989. *Når kulturer kolliderer: et essay om Islam og Europa*, Oslo, Aventura Forlag.

Ward, Peter T., Deborah J. Bickford, and G. Keong Leong. 1996. "Configurations of manufacturing strategy, business strategy, environment and structure." *Journal of Management*, 22(4): 597–626.

Waheeduzzaman, A.N.M. and L.F. Dube. 2004. "Trends and development in standardization adaptation research." *Journal of Global Marketing*, 17(4): 23–52.

Walliser, Bjorn and Jean Claude Usunier. 1998. "The standardization of advertising execution: a review of empirical literature," *EMAC Conference*, Stockholm, May.

Walters, P.G.P. 1986. "International marketing policy: a discussion of the standardization construct and its relevance for corporate policy." *Journal of International Business Studies*, 17(2): 55–69.

Wathne, Kenneth H. and Jan B. Heide. 2000. "Opportunism in interfirm relationships: forms, outcomes, and solutions." *Journal of Marketing*, 64: 36–51.

Webster, F. 1992. "The changing role of marketing." *Journal of Marketing*, 56(4): 1–17.

Weiss, L. 1997. "Globalization and the myth of the powerless state." *New Left Review*, 225.

Welch, Lawrence S. 1991. *The Use of Alliances by Small Firms in Achieving Internationalisation*, Melbourne, Monash University.

Welch, Lawrence S. and Pat Joynt. 1987. "Grouping for export: an effective solution?" in Rosson Philip J. and Reid Stan T. (eds), *Managing Export Entry and Expansion*, New York, Praeger.

Welch, L.S. and F. Wiedersheim-Paul. 1978. "Initial exports, a marketing failure?" *Journal of Management Studies*, 17(4).

Welch, Lawrence S., Gabriel R.G. Benito, and Bent Petersen. 2007. *Foreign Operation Methods: Theory, Analysis, Strategy*, Cheltenham, Edward Elgar Publishing.

Welch, Denice, Lawrence Welch, Ian Wilkinson, and Louise Young. 1996. "A network analysis of new export grouping scheme: the role of economic and non-economic relations." *International Journal of Research in Marketing*, 13: 463–477.

Wiedersheim-Paul, F. and H.C. Olson. 1978. "Factors affecting pre export behaviour in non exporting firms," in Chertmanand M. and Leontiades J. (ed.), *European Research International Business*, New York, Elsevier, pp. 283–285.

Williams, J. 1991. "Constant questions or constant meanings? Assessing intercultural motivations in alcoholic drinks," *Esomar Proceedings, International Marketing Research: New Tasks, New Methods, New Scenarios*, Ljubliana, pp. 159–177.

Williamson, O.E. 1975. *Markets and Hierarchies: Analysis and Antitrust Implications*, New York, The Free Press.

Williamson, O.E. 1985. *The Economic Institutions of Capitalism*, New York, The Free Press.

Williamson, O.E. 1996. *The Mechanisms of Governance*, Oxford, Oxford University Press.

Willoughby, David. 1983. "A marketing fable for our times." *Journal of the ACCJ*, June.

Wills, J.R. and J.K. Ryans. 1977. "An analysis of headquarters executive involvement in international advertising." *European Journal of Marketing*, 11(8): 577–584.

Xu, Shichun, S. Tamer Cavusgil, and J. Chris White. 2006. "The impact of strategic fit among strategy, structure, and processes on multinational corporation performance: a multimethod assessment." *Journal of International Marketing*, 14(2): 1–31.

Yip, George S. and Audrey J.M. Bink. 2007. "Managing global accounts," Harvard Business Review, Sept. https://hbr.org/2007/09/managing-global-accounts (retrieved April 1st, 2017).

Yoshino, M.Y. and U.S. Rangan. 1995. *Strategic Alliances: An Entrepreneurial Approach to Globalization*, Boston, Harvard Business School Press.

Zaichowsky, J.L. and J.H. Sood. 1988. "A global look at consumer involvement and use of products." *International Marketing Review*, 6(1): 20–33.

Zandpour, F., C. Changand, and J. Catalano. 1992. "Stories, symbols and straight talk: a comparative analysis of French, Taiwanese and US TV commercials." *Journal of Advertising Research*, 3: 25–38.

Zhang, Chun, S. Tamer Cavusgil, and Anthony S. Roath. 2003. "Manufacturer governance of foreign distributor relationships: do relational norms enhance competitiveness in the export market?" *Journal of International Business Studies*, 34(6): 550–566.

Zimmerman, A.S. and M. Szenberg. 1996. "Uses of primary research around the world." Advertising Research Foundation Global Research Workshop Proceedings, New York, 9–10 October.

Zou, S. and S.T. Cavusgil. 2002. "The GMS: a broad conceptualization of global marketing strategy and its effect on firm performance." *Journal of Marketing*, 66: 40–56.

Zou S., D.M. Andrus, and D.W. Norvell. 1997. "Standardization of international marketing strategy by firms from a developing country." *International Marketing Review*, 14(2): 107–123.

Zuchella, Antonella, D. Palamaraand, and S. Denicolai. 2007. "The drivers of early internationalization of the firm." *Journal of World Business*, 42(3): 268–280.

Zucker, Lynn G. 1986. "Production of trust: institutional sources of economic structure 1840–1920," in Staw B.M. and Cummings L.L. (eds), *Research in Organizational Behavior*, Vol. 8, Greenwich, JAI Press, pp. 53–111.

Index

CPSIA information can be obtained
at www.ICGtesting.com
Printed in the USA
LVHW05s2009190718
584342LV00017B/130/P

9 781138 738058